The Economist

ATLAS OF THE NEW
EUROPE

The Economist

ATLAS OF THE NEW EUROPE

A Henry Holt Reference Book
HENRY HOLT AND COMPANY
NEW YORK

Managing Editor Nicholas Bevan
Art Editor Nigel O'Gorman
Deputy-Editor Vivianne Croot
Section Editors Susan Berry, Trevor Morris, Nigel Richardson, Sarah Temple-Smith
Text Editors John Browning, Ian Carson, Sarah Child, Janet Dignan, Marsha Dunstan, Caroline Smith
Editorial Coordinator Caroline Sutcliffe
Editorial Assistant Eleanor Martlew

Map Editor Zoë Goodwin
Picture Research Jan Croot
Research Consultant Peter Holden
Researchers Victor Earl, Simon Hix, Jennifer Mussett, Maurice Noë, Tina Norris, Bettina Wassener
Designers Chuck Goodwin, Stephen Moore, Keith Savage, Jason Vrakas
DTP Manager Jonathan Harley
Production Assistant Christine Campbell
Indexer Hilary Bird

Editorial Director Stephen Brough
Art Director Douglas Wilson
Production Manager Charles James

CONTRIBUTORS
History Vivianne Croot, Professor Felipe Fernandez-Armesto
Communications Paul Betts, Dr F.G.T. Bridgham, Herbert Fromme, Roger Hailey, Daniel John, John Williamson
Business Robin Anson, Martin Barrow, Kevin Eason, Martin Giles, John Heilemann, Graham Lewis,
Wolfgang Münchau, Kate Prescott, Angela Smith, John Strak
Finance Mary Brasier, John Coombe-Tennant, Dr Richard Flavell, Francis Matthew, Jonathan Prynn,
Sonia Purnell, Brook Unger
Politics Dr Howard Machin, Professor Gordon Smith
International Relations John Andrews, David Bradshaw, Dr Jacqueline Fear-Segal, Professor Lawrence Freedman,
Nicholas Harman, Dr Michael Hodges
War and Defence Dr Michael Orr
Environment Paul K. Hatchwell, Professor Timothy O'Riordan
People and Culture Helen Garlick, Ruth Gledhill, Frances Kennett, Rita Laven, Karen MacGregor, Dr Martin McKee,
Richard Madden, Pat Mayhew, Bob Moore, Professor Charles Normand, Joshua Rozenberg, Diane Spencer
Country by Country Peter Holden
Chronology Pru Davies, Dr Jacqueline Fear-Segal, Caroline Smith

Maps and charts by Lovell Johns

A Henry Holt Reference Book
First published in the United States in 1992 by
Henry Holt and Company, Inc., 115 West 18th Street,
New York, New York 10011.

Originally published in Great Britain in 1992 by
Century Business, an imprint of Random House UK Limited.

Library of Congress Cataloging-in-Publication Data

The Economist Atlas of the New Europe. – 1st American ed.
p. cm. – (A Henry Holt reference book)
Includes index, gazeteer, and glossary.
1. Europe–Maps. 2. Human geography–Europe–Maps.
3. Europe–economic conditions–Maps. I. Title: Atlas of New Europe.
II. Series.   92-10565
G1797.2.E2 1992 <G&M>   CIP
ISBN 0-8050-1982-0   MAP

Henry Holt Reference Books are available at special discounts for bulk purchases for sales promotions, premiums,
fundraising, or educational use. Special editions or book excerpts can also be created to specification.

For details contact: Special Sales Director,
Henry Holt and Company, Inc., 115 West 18th Street,
New York, New York 10011.

First American Edition–1992

Printed in the United Kingdom
1 3 5 7 9 10 8 6 4 2

CONTENTS

INTRODUCTION

Europe in the 1990s is exciting because it is in flux. Maps, charts and statistics illustrate a continent-in-motion, not a still-life. Will the momentum of change settle down? Not in a hurry, if history is any guide. The end of the Soviet empire was such an earthquake that the aftershocks will last for years. The 1945–89 cold war froze Europe into a degree of stability that was quite unnatural. Now the continent has reverted to type: it is once again seething with conflict, full of uncertainty, but also full of fresh opportunity. With the demise of communism, the big ideological argument has given way to a host of familiar ethnic and territorial conflicts. From the Balkans to the TransCaucasus, war – "the usual condition of Europe", as Peter Kropotkin wrote a century ago – has returned to old trouble-spots. Refugees stream across the continent. Yet the descent into local chaos is not the whole story. At the same time, the pressure on European nations to cooperate – and their willingness to do so – is greater than ever before. Ranged against the powerful forces pulling Europe apart are formidable forces pulling it together. The future will be determined by whichever proves the stronger.

The rebirth of the East has already played havoc with Europe's frontiers and created a clutch of new countries and currencies. The Soviet Union has chosen to dismantle and Yugoslavia has fallen to pieces. Czechoslovakia has decided to split into two. Yet in the West the members of the European Community are meanwhile trying to build an "ever closer union", complete with a single currency, and a lengthening queue of countries want to join them. Rich neighbours (Austria, Sweden, Switzerland, Norway and Finland) hope to be in the EC club by the mid-1990s, poorer ones (Hungary and Poland) aim for membership around the turn of the century. But the process of European integration is driven by far more than mere politicians. German unification and economic interdependence are powerful motors. In particular, the Community's push to create a single market – the biggest in the world – has generated a momentum that will be hard if not impossible to stop.

The federation of Yugoslavia, created after the second world war, began to break up in 1991. Slovenia and Croatia were the first republics to be recognised as independent states, though not by the Serbian-dominated government in Yugoslavia's capital, Belgrade. Bosnia was next to declare independence and in 1992 the region saw the start of a fierce war between Serbia and local forces.

Velvet divorce…in Czechoslovakia the president resigned in July 1992 and the two parliaments agreed that future cooperation will only come about after the establishment of two independent states.

Population

- ■ More than 1,000,000
- ● 500,000 - 1,000,000
- ● 250,000 - 499,999
- • Less than 250,000

◉ ▣ Capital city

— International boundary
--- Undefined/disputed boundary

BARENTS
SEA

Murmansk

FINLAND

Gulf of Bothnia

WEDEN

Tampere

Turku

Vasteras
Uppsala
Stockholm
Vänern
Linköping
Vättern
Gotland

Aland

Helsinki

Tallinn

ESTONIA

Tartu

BALTIC SEA

Bornholm

Liepaja

LATVIA

Riga

Daugavpils

LITHUANIA

Kaunas
Vilnius

Kaliningrad

Gdynia
Gdansk
Szczecin

Bydgoszcz
Poznan

rlin

Vistula

Białystok

Warsaw

POLAND

Łódź

Radom

Lublin

Wrocław

Walbrzych
Czestochowa
Katowice

Oder

Kraków

rague

CZECH LANDS

Brno

ECHOSLOVAKIA

SLOVAKIA

Kosice

ienna

Bratislava

Miskolc
Debrecen

Budapest

HUNGARY

Pécs

VENIA

Zagreb

CROATIA

Novi
Sad
VOJVODINA

Belgrade

BOSNIA &
HERCEGOVINA
Sarajevo
YUGOSLAVIA

SERBIA

MONTE
NEGRO

KOSOVO

az

Oradea

Cluj-Napoca

Arad

Timişoara

ROMANIA

Braşov

Ploieşti

Craiova

Bucharest

Danube

Ruse

Nis

Skopje

MACEDONIA

Tiranë

ALBANIA

Sofia

Plovdiv

Rhodope Mts

BULGARIA

Burgas

Varna

Constanţa

Galaţi

Iaşi

MOLDOVA

Kishinev

Odessa

CARPATHIAN MOUNTAINS

Dneister

Chernovtsy

Vinnitsa

Balkan Mountains

ADRIATIC SEA

Split

Bari

Taranto

rno

Reggio di Calabria

Messina

ania

Etna

Sicily

ratah

Benghazi

IONIAN
SEA

Pindhos Mts

Ionian Is.

GREECE

AEGEAN
SEA

Thessaloniki

Patrai

Athens

Iráklion

Crete

Rhodes

MEDITERRANEAN SEA

Alexandria

Dumyât

Port Said

EGYPT

Cairo

Suez

L.Onega

Petrozavodsk

L.Ladoga

Vyborg

St. Petersburg

Novgorod

Pskov

Vitebsk

Minsk

Mogilev

BELARUS

Bobruysk

Gomel

Dnieper

Chernigov

Sumy

Kiev

Zhitomir

UKRAINE

Cherkassy

Kirovograd

Krivoy
Rog

Nikolayev

Kherson

Simferopol
Sevastopol

Arkhangelsk

Kotlas

Vologda

Cherepovets

Andropov

Yaroslavl

RUSSIA

Kostroma

Kineshma

Ivanovo

Dzerzhinsk

Nizhny
Novgorod

Kalinin

Vladimir

Moscow

Kolomna

Ryazan

Kaluga

Smolensk

Tula

Novomoskovsk

Bryansk

Orel

Tambov

Lipetsk

Kursk

Belgorod

Poltava

Kharkov

Kremenchug

Dneprodzerzhinsk

Dnepropetrovsk

Donetsk

Zaporozhye

Don

Gorlovka

Makeyevka

Shakhty

Voroshilovgrad

Tagonrog

Mariupol

Rostov-na-Donau

Sea
of Azov

Novorossiysk

Sochi

Krasnodar

Armavir

Maykop

Stavropol

BLACK SEA

Samsun

Istanbul

Bursa

Eskisehir

Ankara

TURKEY

Izmir

Konya

Antalya

Kizil Irmak

Sivas

Kayseri

Taurus Mts

Adana

Mersin

Aleppo

Hama

Homs

CYPRUS

Nicosia

Tripoli

Beirut

LEBANON

Damascus

SYRIA

Haifa

Tel Aviv

Jerusalem

Gaza

ISRAEL

Az Zarqa

Amman

JORDAN

Beersheva

Syrian Desert

SAUDI ARABIA

Ukhta

Syktyvkar

URAL
MOUNTAINS

Serov

Berezniki

Tyumen

Nizhny
Tagil

Ob

Perm

Sverdlovsk

Kurgan

Kirov

Izhevsk

Zlatoust

Chelyabinsk

Miass

Kazan

Brezhnev

Ufa

Cheboksary

Kustanay

Magnitogorsk

Ulyanovsk

Sterlitamak

Saransk

Togliatti

Kuybyshev

Syzran

Orenburg

Orsk

Penza

Saratov

Volga

Aktyubinsk

Uralsk

KAZAKHSTAN

Volgograd

Guryev

Ural

Astrakhan

UZBEKISTAN

CASPIAN
SEA

Elbrus
5642

CAUCASUS

Kutaisi

Batumi

GEORGIA

Tbilisi

Leninakan

Kirovabad

AZERBAIJAN

Baku

ARMENIA

Yerevan

Ararat
5165

AZERBAIJAN

Groznyy

Ordzhonikidze

Makhachkala

TURKMENISTAN

Tabriz

Rasht

ELBURZ MTS

Damavand
5601

Tehran

Qom

Orumiyeh

Hamadan

Erzurum

Diyarbakir

Malatya

Mosul

Irbil

Kirkuk

Gaziantep

IRAQ

IRAN

Bakhtaran

Esfahan

Baghdad

Karbala

Al Hillah

An Najaf

Tigris

Euphrates

Dizful

Khorramshahr

Al Basrah

Abadan

Kuwait

KUWAIT

THE GULF

Irbid

HOW THE BOOK WORKS

The European Community has been a powerful unifying force. This book looks at the future shape of Europe: closer integration or, following Yugoslavia, the Soviet Union and Czechoslovakia, further disintegration.

This thematic atlas presents a picture of the new Europe. It takes nine subject areas and looks at how Europe has evolved, where it is now, and the problems and prospects that lie ahead. Europe is treated broadly as stretching from Reykjavik to Istanbul, and from the Rock of Gibraltar to the Urals. Inevitably some parts are covered in more detail than others; there is a lot more hard and reliable information about western Europe than there is about the former communist bloc of eastern European states.

Each section (chapter) is divided into discrete themes covering a separate topic. Most topics are examined on a single two-page spread, though some are given additional space.

Main section contents

Each two- or four-page section is designed to be accessible and easy to dip into, and is made up of a variety of the following ingredients

- **An overview**   The main text. For longer sections, a ▷ indicates that it continues over the page

- **Features**   These are sometimes text only, but most are related to a map or a chart or a table.

- **Maps**   The maps are drawn with reference to the subject being covered. So some show the Soviet Union as a single country and some show Germany as two countries. This is because either that reflects the situation at the time the accompanying feature relates to

or it reflects the latest available statistics at the time the book was researched. On the opposite page are a few examples of the map styles illustrated.

- **Charts and tables**   These follow a range of standard styles adopted for the book. As with the maps, they reflect the latest available statistics at the time the book was researched.

Connections and cross-references

The references at the bottom of left-hand pages highlight sections that include material on a connected topic or even the same one from a different perspective. For precise cross-referencing, refer to the detailed index.

Other sections

In addition to the nine chapters on different themes, the book contains two other sections

- **Country analysis**   This contains basic facts about all the countries of Europe. Not all data is equally available for all countries. The section is organised country by country in a schematic geographical order; refer either to the contents list at the front of the book, or the one on page 251 at the beginning of the section.

- **The postwar years**   This chronology covers the period from 1945 to the end of the century. Its focus is Europe but within the context of major events throughout the world. For a view of events in Europe over the past 2,000–3,000 years, refer to pages 12–15.

NOTES

Statistics

The statistics used in the book are the latest available at the time the book was researched during 1991 and 1992. Two things need to be borne in mind: the extent and quality of statistical data varies from country to country; the statistics available do not fully reflect the changes that have taken place in Czechoslovakia, Germany, Yugoslavia and the former Soviet Union.

Currencies

For the most part, and for ease of comparison, monetary amounts are presented in US dollars or in ecus (European Currency Units). Where necessary, the dollar or ecu amount has been calculated using the exchange rate applying at the relevant time. Because exchange rates are not fixed this means that the monetary amounts in the book are useful guides to the scale of income, expenditure, etc, but they should not be used to calculate the exact amount in the local currency.

Abbreviations

m = million (also metres when clearly referring to height or distance)
bn = billion (1,000,000,000)

Acronyms

Most acronyms are explained in the book. Some of them are not.
BIS   The Bank for International Settlements is the central bankers' bank, based in Basel.
CIS   The Commonwealth of Independent States was founded in December 1991 by the former Soviet

Socialist Republics with the exception of Georgia. It has 11 members: Armenia, Azerbaijan, Belarus, Kazakhstan, Kyrghystan, Moldova, Russia, Tadzhikistan, Turkmenistan, Ukraine, Uzbekistan.
GDP   Gross domestic product is the best measure of a country's level of economic activity. It is the total value of a country's annual output of goods and services, discounted for depreciation. It is normally valued at market prices but can be valued at factor cost, by subtracting indirect taxes and adding subsidies. To eliminate the effects of inflation, GDP growth is usually expressed in constant prices.
GNP   Gross national product is a country's GDP plus residents' income from investments abroad minus income accruing to non-residents from investments in the country.
NMP   Net material product was the measure for economic performance used by communist countries in the eastern bloc. GMP (gross material product) differs from GDP by excluding services. NMP also discounts for depreciation.
OECD   The Organisation for Economic Cooperation and Development is the rich developed nations club. It has 24 members: Australia, Austria, Belgium, Canada, Denmark, Finland, France, Germany, Greece, Iceland, Ireland, Italy, Japan, Luxembourg, Netherlands, New Zealand, Norway, Portugal, Spain, Sweden, Switzerland, Turkey, United Kingdom, United States of America. The former Yugoslavia had a special status, halfway between observer and participant.
OPEC   The Organisation of Petroleum Exporting Countries has 13 members: Algeria, Ecuador, Gabon, Indonesia, Iran, Iraq, Kuwait, Libya, Nigeria, Qatar, Saudi Arabia, UAE, Venezuela.

BORDERS AND FRONTIERS

Postwar western Europe has not been the subject of border disputes. However, once the iron curtain was raised central and eastern Europe and the former Soviet Union in many cases quickly reverted to conflict over frontiers. The Balkans have descended in a violent struggle as have parts of the former Soviet Union. Germany unified and Czechoslovakia chose to divide, both without an armed insurrection. The maps used in the book reflect these changes – sometimes it is necessary to revert to "old" Europe but throughout we are looking forward to the "new" Europe.

The political map

In the example right, Europe is presented as a standard map projection where the relevant countries are colour coded to represent, for example, a political persuasion or membership of an organisation. The omission of a colour for a country generally indicates that reliable, comparable data is unavailable, or that the country plays an unquantifiable part in the discussion.

A single country

From time to time the book uses a single European country as a "case history" to emphasise a point. In this case, France has been taken and its relationship with the rest of Europe is represented using boxes containing comparable data. The relationship between countries is quantified by numbers and qualified with colour within the box.

Beyond Europe

On many occasions figures are given to show the contrast between Europe and countries in other parts of the world, notably the USA and Japan.

The world

There are times when Europe's actions can be considered only in the context of the whole world. When this is the case the map used is a world projection with Europe at the centre.

The economic map

A stylised version of Europe overlaid with data presented in a graphic form – such as the columns on this map – is used to give an easy-to-read visual guide to the similarities and differences between countries. This allows immediate access to who's worth what across Europe, for example. Again reference may be made to a non-European country.

Europe eludes easy definition. Its geographical limits are uncertain along the eastern edge where it meets the landmass of Asia; it expands and contracts with the acquisition of new regions and the loss of old ones; and the boundaries within countries change and shift with regularity.

Despite this, the concept of European-ness, the idea of Europe, is very strong and has been since the name was first coined in the 5th century BC. In the continual conflict between the urge to unity and the tendency to fragment that has characterised European history, unity is the overall winner on points. How did this come about?

This chapter studies the ties that bind Europe together: how it gradually took shape, when and where its outlines were mapped out; how wars and conquest, religion, trade networks and the impact of technological innovation shaped the continent; how the rise and fall of empires, the imperial longings of individual men, the dynastic momentum built up over centuries and the threat of the barbarians at (or even inside) the gate changed the internal geography by welding hostile nations together in unlikely alliances or dividing long-time friends. It traces how Christianity developed from a local Palestinian cult into a sophisticated pan-European religion with enormous political and sociological power. It shows how monasticism and medieval scholarship kept together a continent crumbling in the dark ages; how shared cultural assumptions based on the classical premise of Greece and Rome united an educated elite from St Petersburg to Oporto; how the superstructure of Europe is supported by an armature of interlocking trade routes and systems so interdependent that a Florentine banker could be ruined by a tight-fisted English king. In conclusion, the chapter analyses how unity is still the desired goal in spite of the breaking up of great empires and long-term associations.

EUROPE TAKES SHAPE

A 15th-century wooden carving from the choir stall at Ulm cathedral shows Claudius Ptolemy, the first-century astronomer, cartographer and mathematician. A tireless chronicler and improver of the works of previous scholars, he was greatly valued by the Renaissance humanists as the main conduit for the transmission of ancient knowledge to modern times.

Repeatedly shaken like the contents of a kaleidoscope into different shapes and patterns, Europe has always projected a bewildering variety of images, sometimes threatening to dissolve into nothingness under critical scrutiny. Yet the idea of Europe – the sense of a European identity and location – is tenacious, however uneasily concept and reality fit together.

As a term, Europe has been current for at least 2,500 years. The name "Europe" first occurs before 600BC, in a hymn to the god Pythian Apollo. It refers, in poetic but imprecise terms, to a region of Greece somewhere between "the rich Peloponnesus" and the "wave-washed isles". Throughout the 6th century BC, its usage expanded to cover Greece's vast hinterland. During the 5th century BC, the poet Pindar fixed the western limits beyond Cadiz and the historian Herodotus lined up the eastern frontier with the lower Danube. By the beginning of the Christian era, Europe's northern boundary was drawn at the Don and the Sea of Azov.

Europe's geographical validity has been questioned for almost as long as the idea has existed. Its frontiers and boundaries, unrestricted by any objective correlative, such as an embracing coastline, have drifted and flowed with the political tide. Other continents are more obviously discrete, but no clear barrier separates Europe from Asia; indeed, it could easily be described as nothing more than a ragged outcrop of Asia with an additional scattering of islands around its edge. In the absence of a satisfactory geographical definition, its limits have been expanded and contracted to suit the perspectives and prejudices of the beholder.

In about 500BC, the Tyrant of Miletus, anxious to enlist Spartan aid for a projected invasion of the Persian Empire, showed the king of Sparta a map which presented the known world divided roughly in half, with Europe sprawling and distended at the top and Africa and Asia crammed together in the lower half. The Tyrant's object was to make Asia look like easy pickings; ever since, the meaning of Europe has been adapted to the convenience of the moment. Cartographers' projections were devised to reinforce their masters' cultural assumptions or justify short-term policies.

Europe's self-perception was never so modest as in the period between the rise of Islam in the 8th century and the Renaissance, when the ruling convention placed Jerusalem at the centre of the world, preventing the development of a literally Euro-centric image.

Other cultures, understandably, had other ideas of Europe: the Persian geographer al-Ishtaqri arranged his own world map with his homeland in the centre and Europe crammed into a tiny corner; medieval Chinese cartographers identified several European lands but had no conception of a continent. In 1610, the Jesuit missionary Matteo Ricci drew his Great Map of Ten Thousand Countries and scandalised his Chinese hosts by giving Europe the central position. By the end of that century, projects for mapping the planet more exactly than ever before were being masterminded from the meridians at Paris and Greenwich.

A clearer outline

The most familiar map of the world is still the one devised by the Flemish cartographer Mercator (Gerhard Kremer, 1512–1594). The globe of the earth is shown as projected on a cylinder, with the true area of countries becoming increasingly distorted the farther north and south they are from the equator. However, the projection introduced in 1973 by the German historian Arno Peters is becoming increasingly popular not only as a more accurate representation in terms of size but also as more politically correct in shifting attention away from the old world. This displacement from the centre stage may have shrunk Europe's share of the map but has not diminished its sense of identity and cultural cohesion.

Until the 16th century, Europe saw itself reflected in the maps based on those drawn up by the enigmatic Ptolemy. His eight-volume Geographica listed latitudes and longitudes, gave brief descriptions of many places in Europe, Asia and Africa, and provided 26 colour maps and a map of the world. There were a few mistakes – the equator was too far north, the size of what is now known as the Atlantic was underestimated, and explorers spent fruitless years searching for the mystery continent Ptolemy indicated to the south of the Indian Ocean – but it inspired Columbus to search for the westward route to Asia, and was the basis of the modern cartography founded by Mercator.

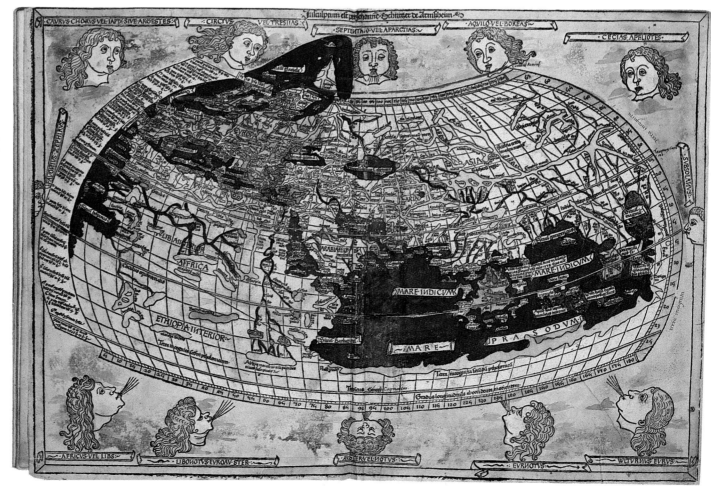

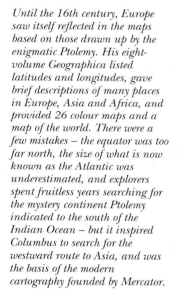

Connections: Patterns of empire 16–17 Religion 228–229 Who are the Europeans? 224–227

A BRIEF HISTORY

This time chart plots some of the events and personalities that have helped to shape Europe over the last two and a half thousand years, from just before the Iron Age in the 8th century BC until 1945. Echoes of the Minoan culture on Crete (1700–1500 BC) and the Mycenean culture (1400–1200 BC) filter down to Europe via the Greek civilisation, but little is left of the Etruscan culture (fl. 500–300 BC) so methodically obliterated by the Romans. While the power and the influence of Rome moulded and shaped European culture, the common background to Europe is probably the La Tène culture, which expanded from La Tène in Switzerland from about 450 BC: the establishment of family groups and village settlements, the cultivation and storage of cereals, and the domestication of cattle and horses shaped the pattern of living that would predominate over the next millennia. Against this broad outline, the rise and fall of empires and dynasties, the opening of trading routes, discoveries in technology and science, and the influence of religions have drawn their individual flourishes.

How the chart works

The time chart (below) runs from just over 1000 years before the birth of Christ until the end of the second world war, covering a selection of the major events that have helped to shape Europe: wars and conquests, political machinations, economic developments and trading patterns, religious doctrines and their far-reaching influence, scientific breakthroughs and technological advances. The chronological listing makes plain the reciprocal effects of war and pestilence on trade and technology, and the interplay between religion and politics and brings out some startling juxtapositions: for example, while Napoleon fought on the battlefield of Jena in 1806, the lights were going on all over Europe.

BEFORE CHRIST

c 1100 BC Iron ploughshares in Mesopotamia

c 1000 BC City monarchies established in Athens, Thebes and Sparta (city states)

900 BC Iron mines in Italy

814 BC Carthage (North Africa) founded by Phoenicians

c 759 BC Greek cities founded colonies in Sicily and southern Italy

753 BC Rome founded as a centre of Etruscan power

700 BC Owl-stamped silver coins in use in Greece; coins also in use in Lydia, Asia Minor

630 BC Rise of Sparta as a power

594 BC Solon of Athens abolished mortgages on small landowners and slavery as a punishment for debt

c 560 BC Founding of Peloponnesian League, based on Spartan military strength and education

510–509 BC Rome expelled Etruscan kings and became a republic

508 BC Cleisthenes established democratic principle in Athens

c 500 BC Second Iron Age; spread of La Tène (Switzerland) celtic farming culture began

492–479 BC Persian wars (against Greece)

490 BC Battle of Marathon (Greece); Greeks halt Persian invasion

480 BC Battle of Salamis (Greece); Persian fleet led by Xerxes (519–465) outwitted by Greeks

478 BC Founding of the Delian League (alliance of Greek city states against Persia); the rise of Athenian power

445 BC Expansion of Rome into Italy; constitutional rights for plebeians

431–405 BC Peloponnesian wars between Athens and Sparta; naval defeat for Athens

404 BC Athenian power collapsed

c 400 BC La Tène culture spread to France; hill fort communities

371 BC Battle of Leuctra (Greece); Athens allied with Thebes to defeat Sparta; Sparta's power faded

350 BC Druidic religion established

333 BC Alexander the Great (356–323 BC) defeated Persians and crossed the Indus to establish his empire

287–212 BC Archimedes of Syracuse invented Archimedes' screw to move water, thereby improving irrigation

264–241 BC First Punic war between Rome and Carthage (North Africa); Rome gained Sicily

218–201 BC Second Punic war; Hannibal of Carthage invaded Italy; Carthaginians routed at the battle of Metaurus (Italy)

200 BC Water wheel in use in Mediterranean countries

168–165 BC Jews won religious freedom in Roman empire

149–146 BC Third Punic war; Rome destroyed Carthage and Africa

147 BC Rome annexed Greece

112 BC Gaius Gracchus (157–86 BC) reformed land use and introduced relief plans for unemployment and poverty in Roman empire; state control of grain supply

100 or 102–44 BC Julius Caesar

75 BC Mithraism, the worship of the ancient Persian god Mithras (the heavenly light) introduced into Roman world via Asia Minor

49 BC Julius Caesar conquered Gaul

27 BC Roman republic transformed into an Empire with Augustus (63 BC–AD 14) as emperor

3 or 4 BC (according to St Matthew) Birth of Jesus Christ

THE FIRST MILLENIUM

AD 6 Judea became a Roman province

AD 20–60 Civil engineering reached its height in the Roman empire

AD 30 Jesus Christ crucified

AD 43 Roman conquest of Britain

AD 45–62 Journeys of St Paul took Christianity into Europe

AD 64 St Paul and St Peter executed in Rome

AD 66–70 Jewish revolt defeated by Romans

AD 100 Water mills in use in Roman empire

AD 115 Trajan (53–117) took Roman empire to its greatest extent

AD 132 Jewish rebellion led to dissolution of Jewish state and diaspora of the Jews in AD 135

AD 150 Claudius Ptolemy preserved and passed on knowledge from ancient Greece and Rome

AD 166–7 Plague depopulated Roman empire

AD 212 Caracalla (176–217) granted citizenship to most free inhabitants of Roman empire

c AD 236 Manicheanism founded by Mani (c 216–76); combined teachings of Jesus, Buddha and Zoroaster; popular all over Europe

AD 257 Goths took Dacia

AD 285 Diocletian (245–313) divided Roman empire into east and west halves with two emperors and two capitals: Milan and Byzantium

AD 300 Heavy taxation from Rome crippled Mediterranean economy

c AD 300 Foot stirrup invented in Asia

AD 305 St Antony (251–356) established first Coptic Christian monasteries, in Egypt

AD 313 Constantine the Great (c 274–337) converted to Christianity; all religions tolerated, but Christianity became the official religion of the Roman empire

AD 314 Council at Arles recognised Rome's primacy

AD 330 Constantine the Great established Constantinople (previously Byzantium)

AD 367 Visigoths crossed the Danube and allied with Theodosius the Great (r 379–95) to confront Rome

AD 383 Rome withdrew from Britain

AD 402 Western capital of Roman empire moved from Milan to Ravenna

AD 406 Franks and Burgundians occupied Flanders and the Rhineland

AD 410 Visigoths under Alaric I (c 370–410) invaded Italy, sacked Rome and overcame Spain

AD 432 St Patrick (c 385–c 461) sent to Ireland to convert the inhabitants

AD 476 Rome fell to Barbarians under Odoacer (d 419)

AD 486 Frankish kingdom and Merovingian dynasty founded by Clovis 1 (465–511)

AD 449–547 Saxons, Angles and Jutes invaded Britain

AD 529 Benedict (480–547) founded first Benedictine monastery at Monte Cassino (Italy)

AD 534–554 Western and eastern parts of Roman empire briefly united by Emperor Justinian (c 482–565)

AD 563 Monastery founded on the Scottish island of Iona by St Columba

AD 570 Muhammed born in Mecca

c AD 600 St Augustine (d 604) undertook mission to England

AD 600 Irish missionaries in Scotland and Germany

AD 600 Invention of Greek fire (saltpetre and sulphur) in Byzantine empire

AD 610 Muhammed began mission

AD 651–2 Koran reached final form

AD 670–700 Lindisfarne Gospels produced in Northumbria

AD 700s Catalan forge (for iron) developed in Spain

AD 711 Muslim invasion of Spain

AD 732 Battle of Poitiers (France); Charles Martel (688–741), leader of the Franks, halted Arab expansion in western Europe

AD 757–96 Offa (d 796) king of Mercia (England) created a unified currency minted in different towns

AD 774 Charlemagne conquered northern Italy

AD 793 Viking raids all over Europe

AD 800 Charlemagne (742–814), king of the Franks, crowned Holy Roman emperor at Aachen, Germany

AD 850 Scandinavian trade with Byzantium

AD 900 Windmills introduced into Spain from Persia

AD 910 Abbey of Cluny (France) founded

AD 911 Rollo (c 860–932) leader of the Norse Vikings made a treaty with Charles the Simple (879–929) of France and settled in Normandy

AD 955 Otto 1 (936–73), king of the Germans and Holy Roman emperor, stopped Magyar invasion of Germany at the battle of Lechfeld (Bavaria)

AD 960 Polish state founded by Duke Miezsko I (fl. 956–966)

AD 972 Hungarian state founded under Duke Geisa

AD 990 Arabic numerals introduced into Europe via Cordoba (Spain)

AD 992 Commercial treaty between Venice and Byzantium

THE 11TH CENTURY

1000 Rise of trade fair towns along trade routes between Italy, France and Flanders

1000 Viking invasions of Europe

1014–1035 Cnut (Canute) (994–1035) built up Danish empire (Denmark, Norway, southern Sweden, England)

1054 Schism between papacy and Greek Orthodox church

1055 Portugal reclaimed from Muslim rule by Ferdinand of Castile (1035–65)

1060–91 Norman Conquest of Muslim Sicily by Roger I (1031–1101) and his brother Robert Guiscard (1015–85)

1066 Norman conquest of Britain by William of Normandy; feudal system introduced to England

1084 Foundation of Carthusian order by St Bruno (c 1030–1101) at Grande-Chartreuse near Grenoble (France)

1085 Domesday Book recorded land use and tenure for taxation purposes

1096–1270 The Crusades; Christianity clashed with Islam over the possession of Jerusalem

Roman engineering in Segovia, Spain; the granite block aqueduct, built in the 1st century AD, is over 6,000m long and still in use.

The Lindisfarne Gospels, created at the end of the 7th century by the monks of St Aidan's monastery on Holy Island.

Charlemagne (742–814), king of the Franks and real life hero of medieval legend and romance, was crowned Holy Roman emperor in 800 in the Royal Chapel at Aachen. He held together a vast empire that stretched from Saxony to Spain.

The Black Death, a form of bubonic plague, devastated Europe during the 14th century; one important side effect was the collapse of the feudal system and the subsequent reorganisation of the agricultural workforce.

Frederick II the Great of Prussia (1712–86) the military genius and architect of Prussia's might; the country doubled in size during his reign.

On March 1st 1815, Napoleon Bonaparte (1769–1821) returned from well-appointed exile in Elba, to make his last and unsuccessful attempt to become emperor of all Europe.

THE 12TH CENTURY

1120–50 Trades guilds established to preserve balance of power between merchants and craftspeople

1150 Coal used for iron smelting at Liège (Belgium)

1176 Frederick Barbarossa (1152–90), Holy Roman emperor, invaded Italy but was defeated by the league of Lombard towns

1184 Spanish Inquisition set up

1189–91 The Third Crusade took back Jerusalem from the Muslim leader Saladin (1169–93) who won it in 1187

THE 13TH CENTURY

1204 Capture of Constantinople allowed Genoa to establish Black Sea trading posts

1207–30 Franciscan and Dominican orders founded

1209 Jews expelled from England

1215 Magna Carta; King John of England (1199–1216) forced to sign to agree that the monarchy would be subject to the law

1232 Inquisition conducted by Dominican friars

1237 St Gotthard Pass opened; trade between southern Germany and northern Europe made easier

1252 Gold and bimetallic currencies reintroduced after some centuries of absence; Emperor Frederick II issued the *augustale*; Genoa issued the *genovino*, Florence minted the *florin*

1263 Louis IX (1215–70) French king minted the *ecu*

1264–5 Simon de Montfort (c 1208–65) founded the Model Parliament, a precursor to the modern parliamentary system in England

1273 Rudolf of Habsburg (Rudolf I of Austria) (1218–91) elected king of Germany; Habsburg empire established

1276 Paper made at Fabriano in Italy

1284 Venice produced own currency, the ducat

1291 Beginnings of Swiss confederation (cantons united to form independent force); confederation formally recognised in 1356

THE 14TH CENTURY

1306 Jews expelled from France

1309 The papacy moved to Avignon until 1379

1337 100 Years war between France and England began, caused by rival claims from Edward III (1327–77) of England and Philip of Valois (1293–1350) for the French throne

1337–45 Weavers in Ghent strike for shorter working week

1340 Development of the blast furnace in Belgium and Prussia; higher temperatures made cast iron manufacturing possible

1340 Beginning of the Golden age of the Hanseatic League

1343–6 Failures of Florentine bankers Bardi and Peruzzi after popes and king of England refuse to pay back their debts

1348–1352 Black Death almost halved population of Europe and signalled the end of the feudal system

1358 Peasant uprising in northern France suppressed; 20,000 insurgents massacred

1376 John Wycliffe (1328–84) foreshadowed Reformation with proposals

for a church without property and direct communication between God and man

1378 Populist revolt in Florence put down

1380–1417 The Great Schism split the papacy between the Pope Clement V (r. 1305–14), in Avignon and Pope Urban VI (r. 1318–89), in Rome

1381 Peasants' Revolt in England put down

1385 Portugal defeated Castile at Aljubarota and gained independence

1389 Battle of Kossovo (Serbia); Ottoman empire gained control of Balkans

1397 Union of Kalmar (Scandinavian alliance between Sweden, Denmark and Norway, including Iceland)

THE 15TH CENTURY

1405 Florence's purchase of Pisa gave it sea access for trade purposes

1406 Bartholomew Diaz (1450–1500) rounded the Cape of Good Hope

1415 Battle of Agincourt; Henry V of England (1387–1422) took Normandy

1445 First book in the west printed from movable type, probably by Johannes Gutenberg (c 1400–68)

1449–92 Lorenzo de Medici ruled Florence and oversaw the flowering of the arts in Florence

1450 Florence, Naples and Milan alliance ensured balance of power in northern Italy

1453 Fall of Constantinople to Ottoman Turks; end of Byzantine empire

1455–85 Wars of the Roses; battle for the throne between Lancaster and York

1462 Louis XI issued protectionist edict to boost Lyon fairs

1479 Ferdinand II of Aragon (1452–1516) married Isabella of Castile (1452–1504)

1482 Spanish church and Inquisition came under royal control

1484–1531 Huldreich Zwingli, Swiss preacher who expressed Lutheran ideals even before Luther

1487 Rise of the Fuggers banking dynasty, based in Augsburg

1488 Antwerp superseded Bruges commercially

1492 Columbus (1451–1506) funded by Genoa discovered the Americas; trade patterns changed irrevocably

1492 Jews expelled from Spain

1492 Fall of Granada to the Christians; end of Muslim rule in Spain

1495 Charles VIII of France (1470–98) invaded Italy; beginning of the Italian wars (ended 1559) between the Habsburgs and the Valois (the house of French kings)

1496 Jews expelled from Portugal

THE 16TH CENTURY

1503 Casa de Contratacion (Chamber of Commerce) founded in Seville

1516 Charles V (1500–58) inherited Spanish crown; proclaimed Holy Roman emperor in 1519

1517 Martin Luther (1483–1546) nailed 95 Theses to the door of Wittenberg Castle church

1519 Fuggers backed the election of Holy Roman emperor Charles V

1520 Luther excommunicated

1521 Diet of Worms (Germany); the Reformation begun by Luther swept over Europe, finding most favour in northern countries

1525 Bible translated into vernacular by Luther

1526 Genoese Bank established

1527 Medicis expelled from Florence

1531 Stock Exchange established at Antwerp (Belgium)

1534 Henry VIII broke with Rome and assumed authority of English church; monasteries dissolved in England

1540 Jesuits (Catholic intellectual order) founded by Ignatius Loyola (1491–1556) in Spain

1540 Bank interest legalised in Netherlands by Charles V

1540 American silver flooded into Spain, causing unprecedented inflation

1541 John Calvin (1509–64) founded reform church at Geneva (Switzerland)

1543 Nicholas Copernicus (1473–1543) published *De Revolutionibus* which proved mathematically that the Earth goes round the Sun; the church taught that all heavenly bodies revolve round the Earth

1545 Council of Trent (Austria); beginning of Counter Reformation

1549 Church of England's Book of Common Prayer issued by Thomas Cranmer (1489–1556)

1555 Peace of Augsburg (Germany); Lutheranism acknowledged

1553 Mary I (1516–68) restored Catholicism in England

1558 Elizabeth I reinstated Protestantism in England

1560 Protestantism became national faith of Scotland under John Knox (1513–72); Presbyterianism, a Protestant sect, established

1560 Death of Anton Fugger and decline of Fuggers bank

1562–98 Wars of religion (between Catholics and Huguenots) in France

1563 39 articles adopted; Church of England established

1566 Synod of Antwerp established Calvinist church in Netherlands

1577–80 Francis Drake (1540–96) circumnavigated the globe

1580 Portugal and Spain united on the death of Philip I of Portugal

1587 England declared war on Spain; Spanish Armada sunk in 1588

1598 Edict of Nantes (France) granted freedom of worship to Huguenots

THE 17TH CENTURY

1600 British East India Company founded

1602 Amsterdam Bourse (stock exchange) opened

1602 Dutch East India Company founded

1609 Bank of Amsterdam established

1609 Telescope invented by Hans Lippershey (1570–1619) in Holland

1610 Galileo Galilei (1564–1620) studied stars through the telescope; confirmed Copernicus's theory

1618 Outbreak of 30 Years war in Bohemia

1619 Bank of Hamburg established

1620 First weekly papers in Europe (Amsterdam)

1632 Invention of the slide rule in England by William Oughtred (1595–1660)

1632 Blaise Pascal invented the adding machine in France

1642–46 English Civil war; Oliver Cromwell (1599–1658) became Lord Protector of England; King Charles I executed 1649

1648 Peace of Westphalia ended the wars of religion caused by the Reformation and the Thirty Years war

1648–53 The Fronde peasant and noble uprisings in France put down

1649 Oliver Cromwell (1599–1658) established the Commonwealth in England; lasted 11 years

1650 The rise of paper money, originally goldsmiths' receipts for the hard currency stored in their vaults

1652 Quakers founded in England by George Fox (1624–91)

1652–73 Anglo-Dutch wars

1654–7 Russia won the Ukraine from Poland

1656 Bank of Sweden founded; first bank notes printed in Sweden

1660 Monarchy restored in England; Charles II crowned

1665–7 Anglo-Dutch trade war; inconclusive

1670 Two party parliamentary system emerged in England

1673 Test Act passed; aimed to prevent Catholics taking any political office in England

1685 Edict of Nantes revoked; Huguenots fled from France

1688 James II of England (1633–1701) expelled for trying to restore Catholicism as official religion

1689 The Bill of Rights confirmed constitutional monarchy in England

1694 Bank of England founded

1698 London Stock Exchange established

THE 18TH CENTURY

1701 Seed-drill invented in England by Jethro Tull (1674–1741)

1702–13 Wars of the Spanish Succession, caused by the death of Charles II of Spain in 1700, leaving Philip of Anjou as his heir

1703 England exchanged trading rights with Portugal in return for possession of Gibraltar

1707 Unification of Scotland and England

1709 Abraham Darby (1677–1717) developed iron smelting process using coke in England

1709 Battle of Pultowa; Peter the Great of Russia (1672–1725) defeated Sweden, took Baltic provinces and part of Finland

1713 Treaty of Utrecht ended the War of the Spanish Succession; France and Spain never to be united under one ruler

1727–8 Anglo-Spanish war; England affirmed possession of Gibraltar finally (in 1729)

1731 Treaty of Vienna; Oostend East India Company dissolved

1738 John Wesley (1703–91) founded Methodism

1740–8 War of the Austrian Succession; Austria defeated at battle of Fontenoy (1745) by alliance of France and Prussia

1756–63 Seven Years war between Prussia and Austria; Prussia victorious under Frederick II the Great (1712–86)

1764 Spinning Jenny invented in England by James Hargreaves, revolutionising textile industry

1769 James Watt (1736–1819) discovered the principle of the steam engine in Scotland

1776 Adam Smith (1723–90) wrote *An Enquiry into the Nature and Causes of the Wealth of Nations*

1778 Joseph Bramah (1748–1814) invented the water closet in England

1779 Spinning mule invented in England by Samuel Crompton (1753–1827); spinning multiple threads made possible

1780 Beginning of Industrial Revolution in England

1780 Cheap soap made available by chemist Nicholas Leblanc (1742–1806) in France

1788 Threshing machine invented by an anonymous Scottish inventor

1789 The French Revolution

1791 Thomas Paine (1737–1809) wrote *The Rights of Man* in England

1792 Coal gas first produced by William Murdock (1754–1839) in Britain

1795 Metric system introduced in France

1795 Methodism breaks from the Church of England

1796 Edward Jenner (1749–1823) developed smallpox vaccine in England

1797 Treaty of Campo Formio; Austria ceded Belgium to France

1799 Income tax introduced to England by William Pitt to pay for Napoleonic wars

1799 Combination Acts curbed trade union activity in England

1792 France declared a republic

1793 Louis XVI (b 1754) executed

THE 19TH CENTURY

1800 Battery invented by Count Volta (1745–1827) in Italy

1800–1 Napoleon established the Prefecture

1803 *Traite d'Economie Politique* by Jean-Baptiste Say (1786–1832) described the laws of market forces

1801 Britain and Ireland linked constitutionally

1803 Start of Napoleonic wars; Britain, Russia, Austria and Sweden allied to fight France

1804 Napoleon crowned emperor

1805 Battle of Austerlitz (Bohemia, modern Czechoslovakia); Russia defeated by Napoleon

1805 Battle of Trafalgar; Napoleon defeated

1805 Napoleon crowned king of Italy

1806 End of Holy Roman empire; Francis II (1732–1835) the last emperor

1806 Napoleon introduced the Continental System which raised food prices and destabilised the textile industry

1806 Napoleon defeated Prussia at battle of Jena-Auerstadt

1806 Gas lighting in European cities

1812 Napoleon took Moscow, but forced to retreat

1814–24 French monarchy restored under Louis XVIII (1755–1824)

1814–5 Congress of Vienna restored thrones of Austria and Prussia and founded the kingdom of the Netherlands

1815 Napoleon defeated at Waterloo by new alliance of Austria, Prussia, Russia and Britain

1816 Beginning of photography; pioneered by Nicéphore Nièpce (1765–1833) in France

1817 *Principles of Political Economy and Taxation* became a text book for the new study of economics

1819 *New Principles of Political Economy* by Jean Charles Sismondi, 1773–1842) discussed the problems of unregulated market forces

1821 Revolt in Naples crushed by Ferdinand I (1751–1825); liberal regime established

1821–32 Greek war of Independence (from Ottoman empire); Greek kingdom established 1832

1823 Liberal revolt in Spain crushed

1825 First passenger steam railway Stockton to Darlington, England; made by engineer George Stephenson (1781–1848)

1827 Charles Babbage (1792–1871), English mathematician, built the difference engine, a primitive form of computer

1829 Turkey recognised Greek independence

1830 Belgium gained independence from Netherlands

1830 Charles X (1757–1836) of France expelled; Louis-Philippe (1773–1850) put on throne

1831 Giuseppe Mazzini (1805–72) founded Young Italy Group to unite Italy

1831 Michael Faraday (1791–1867) developed electromagnetic induction, paving the way for generation of electricity

1832 First steam railway in France

1834 Tolpuddle Martyrs transported from England to Australia for trade union activity

1834–9 Carlist wars in Spain between liberal regime and stricter regions

1835 *England, Ireland and America,* a pamphlet advocating free trade published by Richard Cobden in England (1804–65)

1837–40 Chartism developed in England (radical working class movement)

1837 Railways built in Russia

1837 Electric telegraph patented by William F Cooke (1806–79) and Charles Wheatstone (1802–75) in England

1842 Treaty of Nanking; Chinese ports opened to British trade

1844 Bank of England given monopoly to print money

1846–8 Potato famine in Ireland led to mass immigration to USA

1846 Corn Laws repealed in England

1848 Louis-Philippe expelled from France; republic established

1848 Hungary declared independence

1849 Reinforced concrete invented in France by Joseph Monier (1823–1906)

1850 Telegraph cable laid across the channel from England to France

1852 Napoleon III (1808–73) restored French empire

1854–6 The Crimean war; Russian expansionism into eastern Europe checked by alliance of France, Turkey and Britain

1855 Celluloid invented by Alexander Parkes (1813–90) in England

1856 Steel making process introduced by Henry Bessemer (1813–98); this made cheap steel possible

1861 Louis Pasteur (1822–95) expounded his germ theory of disease in France

1861 Giuseppe Garibaldi (1807–82) united Italy

1861 Serfs emancipated in Russia by Alexander II (1855–81)

1861 German empire proclaimed by Wilhelm I (1861–88)

1863 First underground railway built in London, England

1864 First International in London presided over by Karl Marx (1818–83); Communist Manifesto issued

1865 Salvation Army founded by William Booth (1829–1912)

1866 North German confederation established by Otto von Bismarck (1815–98)

1866 Dynamite invented by Swedish scientist Alfred Nobel (1833–96)

1867 Dual monarchy of Austria-Hungary established

1868 Trades Union Congress founded in England

1876 Telephone patented in the USA by Scottish born inventor Alexander Graham Bell (1847–1922)

1870 Declaration of Papal Infallibility

1870–1 Revolutionary Commune in France suppressed

1870 Franco-Prussian war; subsequent treaty of Frankfurt (1891) ceded Alsace Lorraine to Prussia

1874 Third Republic set up in France

1875–98 Growth of labour/socialist parties in Europe: Germany 1875, Belgium 1885, Holland 1877, Britain 1893, Russia 1898

1876–7 *The Frigorifique* sailed from South America to Rouen (France) carrying the first consignment of deep frozen meat

1878 Congress of Berlin decided a future of Balkans

1879 Dual Alliance formed between Germany and Austria-Hungary

1879–80 Light bulb invented by Thomas Edison (1847–1931) and Joseph Swan (1828–1914)

1881 Electric trams in Berlin

1885 Motorcar pioneered in Germany by Gottleib Daimler (1834–1900) and Karl Benz (1844–1929)

1885 Safety bicycle produced commercially

1888 Pneumatic tyre invented by Scotsman John Dunlop (1840–1932) in Northern Ireland

1890 Social Democratic Party declared legal in Germany

1893 Independent Labour Party established in England

1895 Cinefilm invented by the brothers Lumière

1895 X-rays discovered by Wilhelm Röntgen (1845–1923), in Germany

1896 Rudolf Diesel (1858–1913) invented diesel engine in Germany

THE 20TH CENTURY

1901 Gugliemo Marconi (1874–1939) sent radio signals across the Atlantic by wireless telegraph

1903–4 Entente Cordiale between France and Britain

1905–6 Rebellion in Russia; Tsarist concessions granted

1908 Bosnia Herzogovina annexed by Austria

1908 Establishment of the Vienna Psychoanalytical Society by Sigmund Freud (1856–1939)

1909 Nationalist unrest in Catalonia

1909 Louis Bleriot (1872–1936) flew the channel (France to England)

1910 Experimental broadcasting of radio services in US

1912–13 Balkan Wars; Serbia emerged as the most powerful military force in the Balkans

1914 Stainless steel invented in Germany

1914 Archduke Franz-Ferdinand of Austria (b. 1863) assassinated in Sarajevo

1914–18 World War I

1916 Easter Rebellion in Ireland boosted Irish Republican Cause

1917 Russian revolution; Lenin (1870–1924) came to power

1919 Treaty of Versailles settled Europe after World War I

1919 League of Nations founded

1919 Regular commercial flight service established between London and Paris

1920 Home Rule Act partitioned Ireland

1922 Treaty of Rapallo: Germany and Russia became allies

1922 Fascism established in Italy by Benito Mussolini (1843–1945)

1922 Formation of Union of Soviet Socialist Republics

1923–5 Massive inflation in Germany

1924 The Dawes plan made German war reparation payments easier

1926 Germany joined League of Nations

1926 General strike in England

1927 Establishment of the British Broadcasting Company, London

1928 Josef Stalin (1879–1953) forced industrialisation on Russia

1928 John Logie Baird (1888–1946) invented mechanical scanner, the basis for television

1929 Wall Street Crash; repercussions throughout Europe

1930 *Treatise on Money* by John Maynard Keynes (1883–1946) and *The General Theory* (1936); Keynesian economics dominated western policy until the 1970s

1931 Republic established in Spain

1933 Adolf Hitler (1889–1945) made chancellor of Germany; established Nazi dictatorship

1935 Stalinist purges began

1935 Mussolini invaded Abyssinia

1936–9 Spanish Civil war; victorious General Francisco Franco (1892–1975) became dictator

1936 Television service established in Britain

1938 Germany annexed Austria

1939 Hitler took Prague and threatened to annex Poland

1939–45 Second world war

1945 Conference at Yalta (Russia) decided Soviet and Western spheres of influence; the "Iron Curtain" rung down

1945 Founding of the United Nations

Allons enfants… swingeing taxes united landowners, the bourgeoisie and peasants to revolt against the monarchy that had imposed them; the storming of the Bastille on July 14th 1789 was the trigger for action.

The Iron Chancellor, Otto von Bismarck (1815–1898), broke the alliance between Prussia and Austria in 1866 and reorganised Germany, putting Prussia at its helm.

Josef Stalin(1879–1953) imposed his dictatorship on the USSR after the death of V. I. Lenin in 1924 and held the Soviet empire together for 45 years.

PATTERNS OF EMPIRE

Justinian (c482–565AD) was the son of a Slavonic peasant. He was proclaimed consul in 521 and six years later became the most glittering of the late Roman emperors, uniting the ageing empire and restoring it, for a short but glorious period, to its ancient limits.

E uropean history is characterised by intense struggle for imperial supremacy, the political shape of the continent changing with the rise and fall of various factions. The nature of empires has had an almost infinite variety. Some, like the Roman empire, consolidated and lasted for centuries; others, like the short-lived Ostrogothic empire of Theodoric the Great, began to fade almost before the last outpost had been settled; some depended on the vision, energy and charisma of a great leader – Alexander the Great, the Emperor Constantine, Charlemagne, Napoleon Bonaparte; others, such as the French Capetian or the Angevin Plantagenet, put their faith in the power of dynasty.

The Roman empire, a model for successful hegemony, lasted for almost a thousand years. After Rome fell in 476AD, Europe was buffeted by waves of barbarians crashing in from all sides to fill the power vacuum. In the late 4th century, Huns had swept into northern Europe, dislodging the Germanic peoples living north of the imperial frontier; consequently Visigoths, Alans, Vandals, Sueves, Alemanni, Franks and Ostrogoths poured into the European heartland where they tussled with each other over territories. Meanwhile, the Slavs, forced southwards, were taking the western shore of the Black Sea and effectively cutting off Constantinople's land bridge to the west. Hardly had Europe drawn breath when it was beset by Saracens from the south, Magyars from the Hungarian plain, and Vikings from Norway and Denmark via Russia. During these turbulent centuries, only the Franks and the Ostrogoths made any lasting impact; other invaders were fast in the saddle but lacked the political coherence and institutions necessary to build robust empires.

Medieval empire-builders

The Ostrogoths under Theodoric (455–526) established themselves first in Macedonia and then in Italy, where Theodoric's reign was characterised by prosperity, stability, freedom of worship and civil rights. Charlemagne (742–814), king of the Franks, was probably the most powerful empire-builder of medieval Europe; subduing the Saxons to the east and blocking the Moorish invasion from the south, Charlemagne allied with the papal states of Italy, creating the conditions for the birth of the Holy Roman empire.

Roman empire

The Roman empire started as a confederation of Latin settlements around the Etruscan-ruled city of Rome in the 6th century BC. Two centuries later it was powerful enough to challenge Carthage, the commercial power of the western Mediterranean. Victory in the Punic wars (264–146BC) delivered a ready-made empire – Sicily, Spain, Corsica, Sardinia and North Africa; the annexation of the Hellenistic kingdoms of Macedon, Syria and Egypt in 146BC and western Turkey in 133BC spread the Roman influence still further. In the first century BC, Julius Caesar (c100–44BC) conquered Gaul and Britain, while Pompey (106–48BC) secured the parts of Asia not yet under Roman rule. In 31BC the first Roman emperor was crowned, Octavianus Augustus (63BC–14AD), who presided over almost half a century of prosperity and stability; but the empire reached its greatest size under Trajan (53--117AD), who conquered Dacia. Decline set in soon after and Rome itself finally fell to the barbarians in 476AD.

Byzantine empire

The unwieldy sprawl of the Roman empire eventually proved its undoing. In 264AD, Diocletian split it into four, sharing the burden of power with Maximian, Constantius Chlorus and Galerius. In 303, Diocletian abdicated, taking Maximian with him; after much imperial scuffling, Constantine the Great, son of Constantius, became sole emperor in 323, establishing his capital in Byzantium (modestly renamed Constantinople). The power base of the Roman empire moved inexorably eastwards as the western capital sank into decline and the empire split in two. Justinian briefly reclaimed the old imperial frontiers, but although Heraclius repelled the Persians (c628), the empire steadily withdrew from its ancient borders, pinched between Islam and the Slavs. In the 11th century, the Seljuk Turks in the east, the Normans in the west and the Venetians pressed hard on the imperial frontiers; when the Ottoman Turks rose, the Byzantine empire sank; Constantinople fell in 1453.

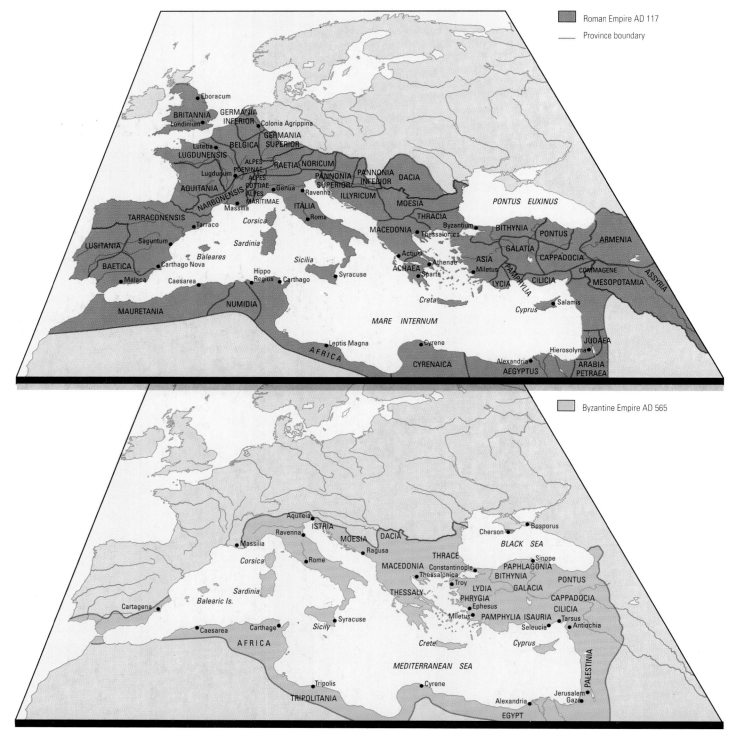

It was not until the 11th century that a precarious equilibrium was restored. The Crusades kept Islam at bay; and the Germanic kingdoms on the eastern side of the Frankish empire developed a strong imperial grip. Otto I, king of Saxony and Franconia, began to shape the beginnings of a German identity. Inheriting the Carolingian mantle, he was crowned Holy Roman emperor in 962, and cemented an alliance with the powerful papal states. Then in 1273, Rudolf I, Duke of Habsburg was crowned Holy Roman emperor, the first of many Habsburgs to rule over both empires simultaneously. For the next six centuries, Habsburgs occupied most of the thrones of Europe, until the first world war made abdication inevitable.

Napoleon's legacy

Long before that, the Habsburg imperial monopoly had been successfully challenged by Napoleon Bonaparte (1769–1821), the spiritual (if not actual) heir to Charlemagne, who crowned himself emperor of France in 1804, abolished the Holy Roman empire in 1806, and by 1812 held all of western Europe and parts of Spain and Russia in his hand. Although his supremacy was short-lived, defeated by atrocious weather in Russia in 1812 and the Duke of Wellington at Waterloo in 1815, Napoleon's ambitions and achievements reformed and rationalised the shape of Europe, drawing the outline of the pattern familiar today.

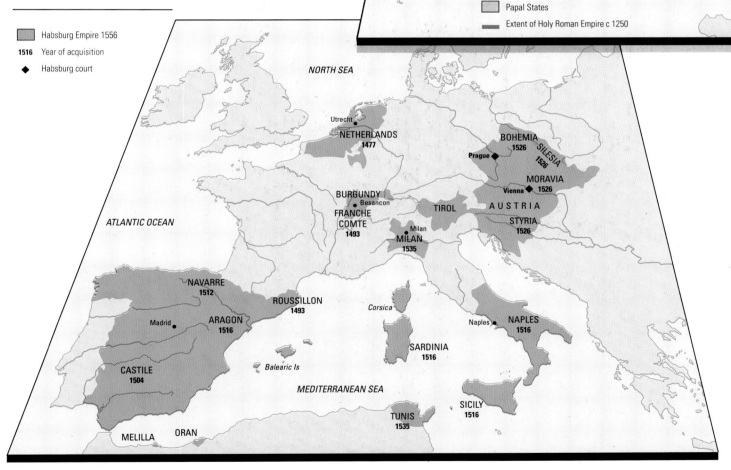

Holy Roman empire

The Holy Roman empire was the result of an uneasy but mutually beneficial alliance between the papal states under Pope Leo II (c750–816) and Charlemagne (742–814), the emperor of the Franks. This was the Germanic tribe which emerged victorious and powerful from the territorial struggles that raged over western Europe after the fall of Rome in 476. Frankish muscle backed up the temporal power of the popes and papal supremacy conferred authority on the newly established Frankish kingdom. Charlemagne was crowned emperor in 800; at that time the empire stretched from the Ebro to the Elbe and from the Baltic to the Mediterranean. Under Otto I (912–973), crowned in 962, the empire grew, reaching its height under the Hohenstaufen family: Frederick Barbarossa (1123–1190), who married his son to Constance of Sicily, and his grandson Frederick II (1194–1250), king of Sicily and Holy Roman emperor from 1215. After his reign, the empire began to fragment, being partly subsumed by the Habsburg empire; even so, it lasted until 1806 when it was abolished by Napoleon Bonaparte.

Habsburg empire

The Habsburg empire started out modestly as a small dukedom of the Habichtsburg (hawk's castle) at Aargau in what is now Switzerland. The first notable Habsburg was Rudolf I, elected Holy Roman emperor in1273; defeating Ottakar of Bohemia in 1278, he acquired Austria and Bohemia; after that the empire grew by astute alliances, advantageous treaties and political marriages rather than conquest.

Frederick III (1415–93) allowed much of the power to seep away – the Swiss gained independence, Milan, Bohemia and Hungary were claimed by others – but he secured the future by marrying his son Maximilian to Mary, daughter of Charles the Bold, thereby gaining Burgundy and Flanders. The Tirol was gained peacefully and Maximilian's subsequent marriage to the daughter of the Duke of Milan brought Milan and Verona into the Habsburg orbit. But the masterstroke was the marriage of Maximilian's son Philip to Joanna the

Infanta of Spain in 1496, bringing Spain, Naples and Spanish America to the Habsburgs. Their son became Charles I of Spain (1516) and Holy Roman emperor (as Charles V) in 1519, and his brother Ferdinand's marriage brought back Bohemia and Hungary. Charles split the empire in two, leaving Spain and her possessions to his son Philip (husband of Mary Tudor of England) and the Austrian possessions to his brother Ferdinand.

The last Habsburg king of Spain, Charles II, died childless in 1700,

precipitating the wars of the Spanish succession (1702–13). Austria gained Belgium and Spain's Italian possessions; and the French prince, Philip of Anjou (1683–1746), became the first Bourbon king of Spain. However, the wars seriously weakened the Habsburg grip on Europe and their power base shifted back to Austria. The last imperial Habsburg was Charles, emperor of Austria and king of Hungary; his reign, and the Habsburg empire, ceased abruptly as a result of the outcome of the first world war.

THE CLASSICAL LEGACY

The idea of a common European culture was well expressed by Edward Gibbon (1737–94) in The Decline and Fall of the Roman Empire: *"a philosopher may be permitted to enlarge his views [beyond patriotic duty] and to consider Europe as one great republic whose various inhabitants have attained almost the same level of politeness and cultivation".*

The Baroque style popularised in 18th-century France spread quickly to Russia, being particularly well received in St Petersburg. Peter the Great built his summer palace Petrodvorets as a Baltic homage to Versailles.

Although Europe remains an intricate mosaic of distinctive microcultures, which are firmly rooted in long-established national heartlands, it has an undeniable sense of overall cultural unity. Edward Gibbon was among those who subscribed to the idea of a common culture, or at least a common framework of reference shared by educated Europeans. Gibbon was writing at the end of the 18th century when the uniformity of enlightened classical taste, humanist values and an education in Greek and Roman letters made it possible for the elite of Europe to glide between widely separated frontiers with little more cultural dislocation than a modern traveller feels in a succession of airport lounges.

The philosophy, science, aesthetic and literature of the Graeco-Roman empire proved remarkably robust, transmitting itself with ease through subsequent ages: thus, in 16th-century Italy, Andrea Palladio was inspired by Vitruvius, whose work *De Architectura* appeared before 27AD, and Palladio himself inspired his 18th-century successors in England, Inigo Jones and Christopher Wren; Petrarch, writing in the 14th century, professed and admired Greek and Roman humanistic ideals; in 18th-century France, Racine and Molière wrote tragedies and comedies following the dramatic unities laid down by Aristotle. In revolutionary France, Jean-Louis David, the father of neoclassical painting, celebrated the Roman virtues of heroism and republicanism.

Doing as the Romans did

Within the frontier of the empire, romanisation was an astonishingly potent and pervasive force, even in remote areas where colonisation was slight. On the Iberian peninsula, the villas at Conimbriga, built to metropolitan standards of craftsmanship, defied the Atlantic; in Switzerland,

St Gall housed classical manuscripts to fuel a future renaissance; and in Jarrow, in England, writing 300 years after the Romans had left, Bede dreamed of Rome and doodled in Greek. Romance speech stamps Dacia today, even though the region was only a briefly occupied part of the empire. The Franks invaded Gaul long after the Romans left but they succumbed to Latin speech.

Beyond the extremities of the Roman empire a sense of continuity with classical civilisation has always been sought with extra eagerness and every renaissance and classical revival has extended the frontiers of classicising culture. The earliest of the renaissances conventionally said to have dappled the European Middle Ages were centred on Northumbria and Aachen; the next came in 10th-century Saxony; although Rome never reached there, the Benedictine nun, Hroswitha of Gandersheim, wrote Latin poetry and comedies in the style of Terence. In later revivals, Prague became the capital of "Roman" emperors, notably Rudolf II, Tycho Brahe's patron; Moscow was called the "Third Rome" and Edinburgh became the "Athens of the north".

Even so, the culture of the Graeco-Roman empire might have perished had it not been for Christianity. As the official religion of the empire it was a source of patronage and inspired a wealth of great art and architecture; a rich established church could afford lengthy and expensive works such as cathedrals. Wherever Christianity reached, the aesthetic canons established in the imperial heyday continued long after the empire itself had dissolved. When the reformation transformed the church in northern Europe, the role of patron fell to merchants and princes. They continued to uphold established classical principles in secular art and architecture of royal palaces and temples to commerce.

Connections: Europe takes shape 12–51 Christian hegemony 20–21 Speaking a language 44–45 Religion 228–229 Education 230–233

Ideas on the move

The map shows the establishment and spread of universities which took place as monasticism underwent reform in the 10th and 11th centuries. Italy led the way; and the 14th and 15th centuries saw the full bloom of the university system.

Universities grew out of the monastery and cathedral schools. Teachers and students banded together in corporations (*universitas magistrium et scholatrium*) and were granted administrative and judicial autonomy. Bologna (specialising in law) and Salerno (medicine) were the first to be established.

A century later, a university was founded in Paris, to study theology and the arts, a pattern followed by most universities. Oxford, founded in 1170, was modelled on Paris. Most of the Spanish universities were incorporated in the 13th century, the remaining French ones in the 14th century and the German in the 15th century.

Universities gradually emerged from the skirts of the church, but their common language of Latin still enabled students and teachers to study anywhere, regardless of their native tongues. The resulting cross-fertilisation of ideas created a vigorous intellectual climate and a common culture gradually spread across Europe.

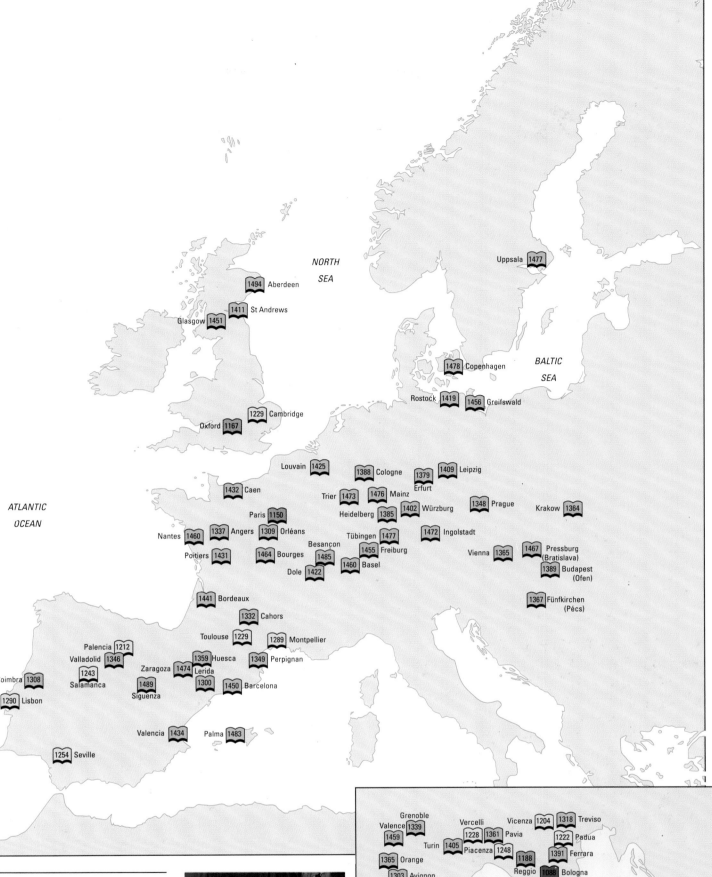

Universities founded before
1100
1200
1300
1400
1500

A NEW CHAPTER

Copying books was one of the main tasks of monasteries until the invention of moveable type in the 15th century. Itinerant German printers took their art around Europe and by 1476 presses were established in Mainz, Bamberg, Cologne, Augsburg, Venice, Rome, Paris, Basel, Strasbourg, Seville and London. During the 16th century the printing industry was concentrated in the university towns and trading centres where the demand for books was generated by commerce and learning. By the end of the century more than 200 towns and cities could boast their own printing shops.

Production in Paris doubled between 1500 and 1550. Venice dominated the south, publishing the views of catholic authority; Antwerp, Lyon and Frankfurt (where the first book fair was held in 1564) rose in powerful counterpoint, publishing theses and theories of humanism and the reformation.

A 15th-century woodcut shows clerks copying manuscripts at the university of Perugia, Italy, established in 1276.

CHRISTIAN HEGEMONY

St Bernard (1090–1153) was the first abbot of Clairvaux in France, one of the foundation abbeys of the Cistercian order. This was founded in 1098 at Cîteaux in Burgundy by a group of monks who were disillusioned by the pomp and hierarchies of the Cluniac order and who wanted to return to the austere egalitarian ideals of St Benedict. Renouncing luxury and elaborate ritual, they embraced the simple, selfless life in remote abbeys dedicated to St Mary the Virgin. St Bernard is pictured here healing two blind sisters in a 16th-century panel in the church of St Mary at Shrewsbury, England.

Until the European expansion of the 16th century, the terms Europe and Christendom were almost interchangeable. Medieval writers rarely mentioned "Europe" except in a strictly geographical context, while "Christianitas" could have a geographical as well as cultural meaning; and in 1458, when Pope Pius II lamented the fate of "Europe", he was referring to the threat to Christendom from the power of the Ottoman Turks. Christianity has now been carried beyond the frontiers of Europe, but the centuries when the faith was confined to and defined the continent have stamped Europe with a common experience and a distinct character.

Christianity came to Europe borne on the powerful shoulders of the Emperor Constantine I. Converted to the faith in 312AD, Constantine had emerged triumphant from the undignified scramble of six emperors vying for power. In 313, the edict of Milan granted toleration and civil rights to Christians and by 324, Christianity was the official religion of the Roman empire. It radiated from the twin imperial hubs of Rome and Constantinople to the far edges of the empire, touching every town, city and garrison. What was once a local near-eastern religious cult was transformed into the most potent shaping force of European politics and culture.

Once adopted by the Roman empire, Christianity fast became institutionalised and by the time of Pope Leo I (440–461), the church was a highly organised hierarchy of bishoprics and dioceses, based in Rome and inextricably enmeshed in politics. Evangelisation consequently became both a political act and the first source of European cultural unity. Even so, it was no smooth process. Vast territories were lost at intervals to pagan or Muslim invaders; missions from Rome had to pursue backsliders, notably Lombardy and England in the 6th century. Some eastern frontier areas were not permanently incorporated into Christendom until the 9th or 10th centuries; Sicily had to be clawed back in the 11th and Islamic Spain held out until 13th. The northernmost parts of Europe were slowest to succumb: St Olaf's conversion in 1013 brought Scandinavia into the fold .

Even so, there was a European tendency to fragmentation. The fall of Rome in 476 left the western side of the empire open to barbarian invasions and, from the end of the 8th century, disputes over rites, languages and disciplines exacerbated the doctrinal differences between the sees of Rome and Constantinople until the schism of 1054 became inevitable. Conversion to Christianity divided rather than united people, with western Christians becoming Catholic and eastern Christians belonging to the Orthodox Church.

The challenge of Islam

It took the threat of the Seljuk Turks in the 11th century to reunite Christendom, albeit temporarily. Seven Crusades were mounted, with princes, kings and emperors from every country in Europe eager to reclaim the Holy Land. Jerusalem was won and lost again and again over the 200 years from 1096. However, the grand unifying idea of the Crusades had no match in reality and the factions who came together against Islam wasted their energies jostling for power. The lasting impact of the Crusades was on trade and culture.

Despite the divergent Roman Catholic and Orthodox traditions, the medieval formation of Christendom gave Europeans something in common which distinguished them from the rest of the world. This balance lasted until the reformation in the 16th century, which resulted in the geographical pattern of faith familiar today.

The pilgrim way

The map shows the distribution of the major abbeys belonging to the four main monastic orders. Pilgrimage sites developed at several of the abbeys.

Monasticism began in the 4th century with St Anthony of Egypt (251–356), who founded a monastic community in Memphis. St Benedict of Nursia (c480–547) set up the Benedictine order at Monte Cassino in 529 and laid the foundations of western monasticism. A wave of reform in the 10th and 11th centuries lead to the foundation of the Cluniac, Cistercian, and Carthusian orders which established monasteries across Europe. These also functioned as mission centres, from where monks undertook long missionary journeys to convert heathens or re-evangelise backsliders.

In the 14th century when pilgrimages became popular, monasteries offered shelter along the pilgrim routes and were, in the cases like Santiago de Compostela and Canterbury, themselves destinations of pilgrimages.

✻ Pilgrimage Centre
🏠 Monastery
🏛 Foundation Abbey
— Monastic Mission
▨ Catholic Rite
▢ Orthodox Rite

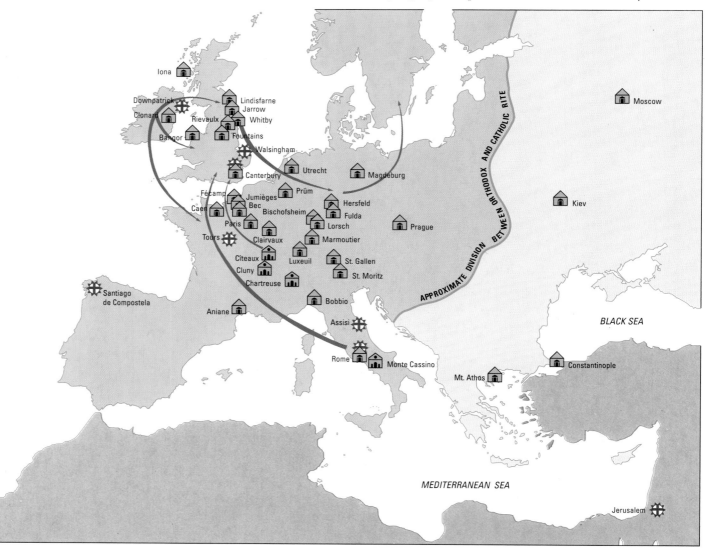

Connections: Europe takes shape 12–15   The classical legacy 18–19   Trading networks 22–23   Who are the Europeans? 224–227   Relgion 228–229

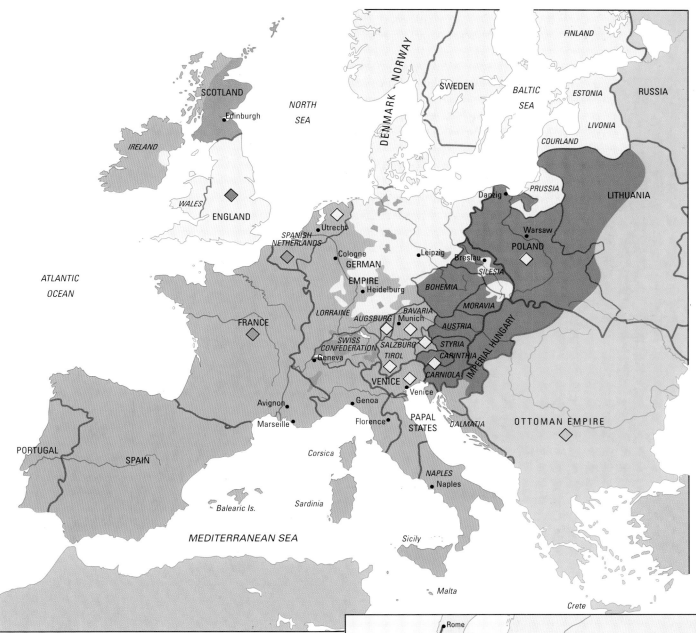

Divided by faith

The reformation redefined Europe in political as well as religious terms. In 1517 Martin Luther (1483–1546) led the protest against papal power and began a struggle between Catholics and reforming Protestants that lasted until the Peace of Westphalia in 1648 imposed a compromise solution. Henry VIII of England (1491–1547) dissolved the monasteries and declared himself head of the Church of England leaving a minority of Catholics in the north-west; except for the six counties of the Pale, Ireland remained Catholic as did north-west Scotland; Calvinism claimed the rest of the country. France, Spain and Italy remained largely Catholic, with scattered Calvinist minorities. Most of northern Europe went with Luther, Switzerland with its own Protestant leader Zwingli, with eastern Europe subscribing to a rainbow alliance of catholicism, Lutheranism and Calvinism; Bohemia and Moravia contained followers of John Huss (c1369–1415), a forerunner of reformation theories. Catholicism itself was split, as a result of the schism of 1054 when the eastern half of southern Europe followed the Orthodox rule.

Religious situation c1560

- Anglican
- Calvinist
- Catholic
- Lutheran
- Orthodox
- Mixture of Calvinist, Catholic and Lutheran
- Muslim
- ◇ Significant minority

LUTHER AND THE REFORMATION

The reformation was the work of three men: Martin Luther (1483–1546) from Saxony, John Calvin (1509–64) from Picardy, and the Swiss Huldreich Zwingli (1484–31). Calvin began to preach the doctrine in the late 1520s and in 1536 he went to Geneva, where the Reformation had just been embraced as policy. There he established a theocracy that dominated every aspect of the Genevan citizen's life.

Rather more open-minded, Zwingli was preaching reformist ideas a year before Luther's famous declaration. As preacher in the minster of Zurich, his rejection of all sacraments inspired the catholic forest cantons of Switzerland to declare war on Zurich, and Zwingli died defending his minster.

However, it was Martin Luther whose passionate commitment elevated protestantism from a sectarian dispute to a world religion. He produced 95 theses supporting his belief which he famously nailed to the church door at Wittenberg on October 31st 1517. Luther, an Augustinian monk who was increasingly alienated by the greed and power of the catholic bishops and princes and the sale of indulgences, looked for a different interpretation of the Christian message.

His search led him to conclude that grace and the forgiveness of sin is a direct gift from God to humanity and needs no intercession from the pope, considered by Roman Catholics to be God's earthly representative; the entire papal edifice was, he maintained, irrelevant. Luther's beliefs led to his excommunication in 1521; there followed more than a century of riots, wars, religious persecution and the foundation in 1534 of the Jesuits, the formidable Roman Catholic order which was specifically charged with refuting Luther's claims.

Lighting the darkness... The menorah is the Jews' seven-branched candlestick and the portable focus for religious ceremony, first used in the makeshift temples built when Moses led the Jews out of Egypt and into desert exile. After the dissolution of the Jewish state in 135AD, the Jews spread throughout Europe in a diaspora that lasted until 1948, when Israel was re-established. They took their skills and learning with them, becoming an important vector in the transmission of knowledge. At best tolerated and at worst vilified and persecuted, Jews remained a strong community wherever they were, sustained by their religious beliefs. This giant menorah stands· outside the Knesset in Jerusalem.

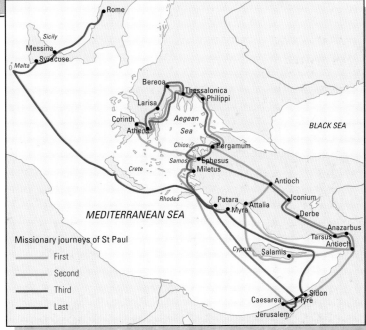

Missionary journeys of St Paul

- First
- Second
- Third
- Last

THE JOURNEYS OF ST PAUL

After his dramatic conversion on the road to Damascus, St Paul the Apostle started the first of his three missionary journeys (above) around the north-east Mediterranean in 47AD. The founding of the church at Philippi on the Greek mainland marked the advent of Christianity in Europe and Paul's indefatigable preaching and letter-writing made many converts. Paul's return to Jerusalem sparked riots by Jewish opponents and he was sent to Rome, mainly for his own safety, where he was placed under house arrest. He was executed by the emperor Nero some time between 64 and 67AD. However, by then Christianity was firmly established within the Roman empire.

TRADING NETWORKS

Venice minted its own coinage for hundreds of years. This silver lira from the mint of Andrea Gritti dates from the mid-16th century. Founded in 452, Venice established a network of links along the Adriatic and with Constantinople. As a powerful and independent city-state it peaked in the 15th century, when its empire included the area bordered by Austria and Yugoslavia to the north and east and the river Adige to the west, as well as part of the Dalmatian coast, Crete, Cyprus and the Ionian islands. After trade moved to the Americas, Venice declined, losing its empire to the Turks. In 1797 Napoleon Bonaparte annexed it to Austria; in 1866 it became part of the kingdom of Italy.

For Amsterdam, "het goldene eeuw" (the golden century) was the 17th, when it dominated European trade and banking. The city's harbour (below), regularly depicted by Old Masters, was always crammed with commerce.

Trade forges strong, comprehensible bonds; there is nothing mysterious about the unified network of economies – a "European economy" – that has lasted for 500 years. It has had a patchy history, and staggered more than once, but it is a solid and remarkable achievement, made against difficult geographical odds.

Between Europe's three great routes of long-range exchange – the Mediterranean, the Atlantic and the Volga – communications are hard and distances daunting. A mountain watershed screens the Mediterranean lands from the vast area of north-west Europe. From the Castilian plateau in Spain and the Cantabrian mountains along the Pyrenees and the Alps, only the Toulouse gap and the Rhône-Saône corridor provide routes of mutual access for carriage in bulk. The only maritime link is between the Pillars of Hercules, either side of the Strait of Gibraltar, which links the rough Atlantic with the calmer Mediterranean. Markedly different sailing conditions along the two seaboards have been a deterrent to shipping for most of history. The Bay of Biscay has always been treacherous to seaborne traffic.

Hansa and the Levant

It is not only geography that dictates trade routes; political stability is also a prerequisite. Trade flourished when the Roman empire held Europe together and slumped with its decline in the 5th century. Five hundred years later, when the post-imperial dust had settled, conditions were ideal for the establishment of two independent yet interlocking trading systems which were to prosper and flourish until the 15th century, when the westward search for a quicker route to Asia came by accident upon the Americas and changed the pattern of European (and world) trade for ever.

In the south, the Levantine trade focused on the rival ports of Genoa and Venice, both enriched by carrier trade generated by the Crusades. Both traded with the East, bringing in silks, porcelain, spices, perfumes and dyes. In the north, the Hanseatic League, based in Lübeck, dominated trade all over the Baltic and northern Europe, linking up overland with Kiev to the east and Venice and Genoa in the south.

Another unexpected economic side effect of the Crusades was the rise of currency rather than cumbersome barter for trading purposes. With currency came capitalism; the profit motive became the engine that drove the trading system and the competition to monopolise a particular product or trade was cut-throat. Entrepreneurs, merchant bankers and entrepôts evolved. Entrepreneurs shipped in raw materials, put them out for manufacture, sold the products and pocketed the difference; merchants dealing in specialist bulk trade became rich enough to bankroll their customers: the Italian merchants who shipped Mediterranean alum to England and English wool to Italy became bankers to an English king. Currency encouraged centralisation: Bruges, where raw materials for the Flemish cloth industry were brought in from Phocaea, Burgos and the Lincolnshire wolds became an entrepôt "where all the nations of the world meet". As Christianity forbade usury (without which capitalism cannot function), Jewish bankers financed most trade. However, in the 14th and 15th centuries they presented too much of a commercial threat to the rising merchant bankers of Italy and Germany, and were expelled from many countries.

Even when a European-wide network of exchange was complete and functioning, imperialism and mercantilism kept Europe's national economies divided from one another by protective barriers and by competition from colonial markets. But the formation of a European economy gave Europe enough experience of long-distance trade and geographic specialisation to create a basis for early industrialisation, which in turn has given it a distinct economic character.

THE GOLDEN AGE OF AMSTERDAM

From a fishing village built in 1275 below sea-level on the boggy ground where the river Amstel flows into the waters of the Ij, Amsterdam rapidly grew into a gracious and wealthy city. By the 17th century it had become the largest port in Holland, the central entrepôt of European trade and banker to the world, its population exploding from 30,000 in 1567 to 200,000 in 1675. Such spectacular success was a direct result of the fall of Antwerp to the Spanish in 1585 during the religious wars of the counter-Reformation.

During the 16th and 17th centuries, banking and trade power shifted from the south of Europe to the north and throughout the 1500s Antwerp had been the focus of financial activity. With Antwerp's commercial elimination, Amsterdam flourished. The Wisselbank, founded in 1609, was Europe's first public bank; the Stock Exchange opened two years later.

Even before the fall of Antwerp, Amsterdam had grown rich on brewing and trade with the Baltic ports (although it was never a member of the Hanseatic League) for timber, wax, turpentine, flax, iron and grain; its Spanish connections brought in leather, wool, steel weapons and salt. With the founding of the Dutch East India Company in 1602, Amsterdam's warehouses bulged with spices, precious stones, porcelain and sugar. The transshipment of these goods was monopolised by the Dutch merchant fleet; no wonder the great harbour on the Ij, shown here in a painting by Ludolf Backhuysen (1631–1798), was filled with vessels of all sizes but most flying the one flag.

Connections: Patterns of empire 16–17   History of European finance 88–89

THE HANSEATIC LEAGUE

Founded in 1259 with the union of Lübeck, Hamburg, Rostock and Wismar, the Hanseatic League (from the German *Hansa* group) developed into a powerful mercantile confederation of north German and Baltic cities which dominated fur, fish and wool trade throughout northern Europe until the 15th century. There were over 200 cities in the league; offices were set up in Bergen, Novgorod and London, and strong links established with Venice and Genoa. League members decided trade policy at council meetings and used monopoly and boycott to keep each other in line. In the 15th and 16th century, the league declined as trade with the new world destabilised the trading centres of Europe; but it left a legacy of business methods and a system of commercial and maritime laws still used today.

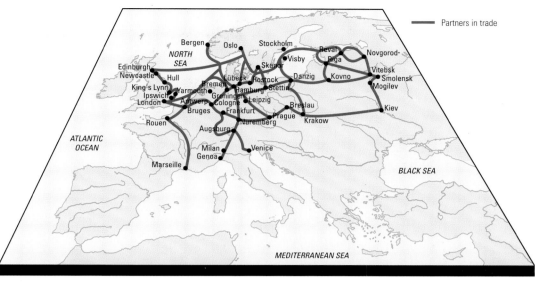

VENICE AND GENOA

From the 11th century on, Mediterranean trade was dominated by the rival city republics of Venice and Genoa. Both grew rich on the carrier trade created by the Crusades. Genoa, Pisa and Naples took the western side of the Mediterranean and Venice and Sicily looked east, bringing silks, spices, dyes, ivory, porcelain, medicine, precious stones and perfumes, either via the Arab-controlled Silk Road or by sea from the Indian Ocean. The establishment of the Holy Roman empire and the alliance between what is now Germany and northern Italy kept trade routes open, and goods from the East could be exchanged with northern European merchandise at the great trade fairs of France, Germany and Flanders. Merchant fleets from Genoa and Venice also braved the Bay of Biscay to trade directly with the Hanseatic ports.

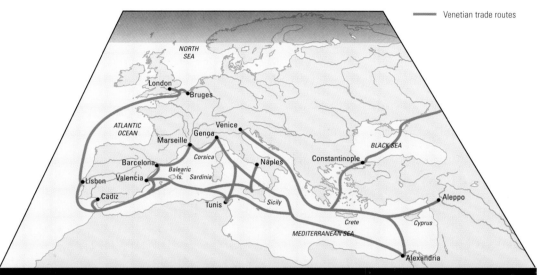

THE MEDICIS

During the 14th century barter trade gave way to a money-based economy. Merchant bankers, who traded in goods and also manufactured their own products, were able to extend credit to their trading partners. Banks were opened, originating in Italy and southern Germany. One of the richest and most influential was the company set up by Giovanni de Medici (1360–1492) in Florence, which was financed by successful oriental trade and a monopoly of alum (used in the dyeing of textiles). The Medicis owned more than 300 factories manufacturing textiles. They also invested heavily in ship building and the pioneering of trade routes, and established trading stations abroad. Their commercial power lasted until the 16th century when unwise speculation and too enthusiastic patronage of the arts finally ruined them.

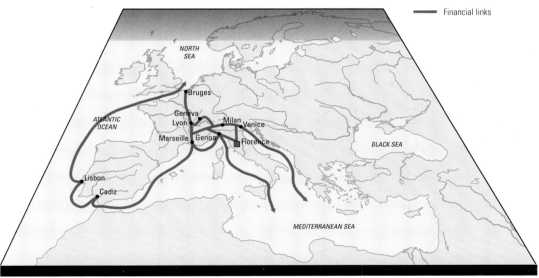

THE FUGGERS BANK

Between them, the Medicis and the Fuggers bankrolled the whole of Europe, dividing up the territory neatly. The Fuggers' financial dynasty was founded in Augsburg in southern Germany. Johannes Fugger (1348–1409) was originally a weaver; his sons and grandsons went on to deal successfully in money and trade, and the Fuggers eventually became bankers to the popes and to the Habsburg empire. The family also controlled the production of lead, copper and silver in Europe and held the monopoly on mercury. Enriched and ennobled by Habsburg kings to the ranks of counts and princes, the Fuggers also became prominent patrons of the arts and sciences. Their slow decline and family squabbles in the 16th century were linked to that of their patrons and the fragmentation of the Habsburg empire.

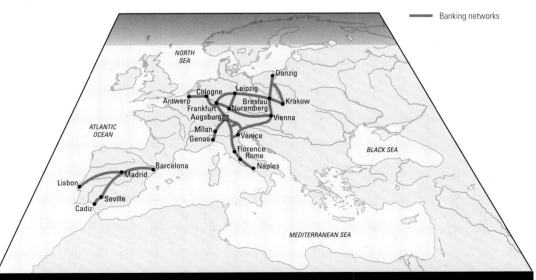

TOWARDS UNITY

Sign of changing times… A winery in Alsace Lorraine, the French-German province that has shuttled between its parent countries for centuries, blending languages and blurring cultural edges. Wine and food help to maintain the bonds; a clue to the origins of the region's cuisine and viniculture is signalled by the tiny star of David in the sign above. In the 15th century, Jews fleeing persecution found a reasonably congenial home here, partly because the Alsace dialect with its roots in 8th-century German, is very like Yiddish. They brought with them chocolate, foie gras, spices and fine wines.

Europe today is being ground between the millstones of two vast, slow and apparently contradictory changes: a fragmentary process, which threatens empires and federations with break-up and other states with erosion by devolution; and an integrative process, which is extending the limits of Europe and the reach of European institutions. Integration is essential if Europe is to compete with the rest of the world economically; but diversity is and always has been the dominant trait of the European "personality".

Viewed from a distance – or even from the height of some seats of European government – the nation-state is still the cultural unit of which Europe is composed. Yet most so-called national frontiers enclose a variety of highly self-aware historic communities. Europe is scored by long and deep cultural trenches which divide speakers of Romance, Germanic and Slavonic languages, and members of Roman Catholic, Protestant and Orthodox communions. Historic experiences, sometimes centuries-old, have erected barriers of hostility or national boundaries between neighbours of otherwise similar culture – Portugal and Galicia, for example, or Norway and Sweden, Londonderry and Donegal.

Today, within the shell of European integration and homogenisation, the old historical communities are reviving. Nation states, provinces, cities and a variety of ethnic groups have rediscovered or are reasserting ancient identities; some have attained devolution or autonomy; others are clamouring for it. All include even smaller local and regional variations in culture and historic experience. From Brandenburg to Saxony the houses are built on a different plan; the citizens of Regensburg speak a different dialect from the Bayrisch

of the south and the *Hoch-deutsch* of the north; the people of s'Hertogenbosch are of a different religion to their neighbours for reasons derived from the fortunes of a 16th-century war; differences in language barely detectable to a visitor's ear are badges of identity to native speakers from Barcelona to Valencia. Even France – the most successful unitary state ever created in the western world – is now seen by its own historians as a mixture of immutable provincial and civic identities. The break-up of the Soviet Union and the Yugoslav Federation into their constituent parts is only the most violent and conspicuous example of a pan-European phenomenon of self-discovery (or rediscovery) by historic communities.

The forces for unity

European homogenisation and the convergence of European institutions has come not from within nor as a result of the efforts of the EC, but on the back of two waves of political and economic realignment; first in southern Europe from 1974 to 1978, when Greece, Portugal and Spain all abandoned authoritarian systems; and again in 1989–92, when most of eastern Europe followed suit. These changes have recreated Europe by bringing the historical experience of European peoples again into alignment.

Common historical experience remains at the core of the unity or potential unity of Europe. Its ingredients include the shared legacy or influence of the Graeco-Roman civilisation; a Christianity wary of pagan and Islamic worlds beyond; industrialisation; democratisation. It is this shared past that has made Europe what it is and differentiates European peoples from others.

In Poland, folk dancing is not the arcane "heritage" activity that it is in other European countries. Industrialisation came late to Poland; until the first world war, agriculture was the biggest industry. Today, even in towns, rituals, rites of passage and parties are still celebrated unselfconsciously in the rural manner, with traditional costume dancing and singing.

POLAND: PARADIGM AND PIONEER

The history of Poland could easily be read as a history of Europe in miniature: a long rise from nothing to imperial status, a speedy decline brought on by weak monarchy, ruinous wars, greedy neighbours and the ambition of ruthless individuals, an ignominious fall and a cautious renaissance.

Positioned in the middle of Europe, Poland has always been in the thick of things, and its development has been characterised by the dramatic. Its empire, at its height in the 16th century, once stretched from Breslau (now Germany) to the eastern rim of the Ukraine. When the empire dwindled Poland did not merely decline, it actually disappeared from the world map, twice. Once in 1795, when it was ruthlessly partitioned and carved up between Austria, Prussia and Russia, and again from 1939 to 1945, when it was annexed by Germany until 1944 then overrun by Russia. Poland's friends and foes were also in the major league. It made a powerful ally in Napoleon, who clawed back Prussian Poland and created the Duchy of Warsaw; but it had a powerful enemy in Adolf Hitler whose lust for the possession of Poland triggered the second world war.

It is not surprising, therefore, that it was Poland out of all the eastern bloc countries, which first began to shrug off the decaying bonds of communism. Poland was the battleground on which Marxism was finally anaesthetised by "the opium of the people". Catholicism, which had proved the one bond strong enough to hold Poland together culturally if not geographically since 966, allied itself with the rebellious shipworkers of Gdansk and was midwife to the birth of Solidarity, the rebel trade union which later transformed itself into a political party.

FRANCE: EMPERORS AND GENERALS

Many men have dreamed of imposing their will on Europe, but few succeeded so well as the French. Charlemagne and Napoleon Bonaparte both transcended their origins to become European emperors; both used military and intellectual might, subduing by conquest when necessary and treaty when possible; both endeavoured to hold their empires together by introducing legislation designed to civilise, unify and harmonise: codes of law, systems of measurement, standardised coinage, the promotion of literacy; both very nearly succeeded in forging a unified Europe. Charlemagne at least handed on his empire intact to his son; in the 19th century, it was the British naval strength that prevented Napoleon from realising his imperial dream; and in the 20th century, it was another powerful Frenchman who retaliated by opposing British intentions.

General Charles de Gaulle (1890–1970), architect and first president of France's Fifth Republic, successfully frustrated all efforts in the 1960s to press towards a "United States of Europe"; driven by strongly nationalistic feelings, de Gaulle feared that national sovereignty would be undermined and division between western and eastern Europe perpetuated if the Euro-enthusiasts succeeded. Above all, he wanted to see France once more a world power in its own right. Despite American pressure, de Gaulle insisted that France maintain its own independent nuclear deterrent, and pulled it out of NATO in 1966. The 1963 treaty with West Germany provided for political, scientific, cultural and military cooperation, efficiently hog-tying a recent powerful enemy; and the blocking of Britain's entry into the EC in 1962–63 and again in 1967 effectively stonewalled any attempts by France's traditional "old enemy" to interfere with the progress of *La Gloire*.

Connections: Speaking a language 44–45   Rebuilding democracies 120–121   The future shape 142–143   The birth of nations 176–177   Who are the Europeans? 224–227

THE BIRTH OF THE EC

European institutions were unnecessary while Europe's elites enjoyed the comfort of a common culture, colonial supremacy and industrial lead. After the "civil wars" of 1917–1945, Europe was left divided between armed camps. At the same time, Europe's world hegemony was in a state of collapse: the Dutch, French and British empires had been irremediably damaged; colonial nationalisms throve under the impact of war, breeding tough liberation movements. It took this crisis to give Europe's sagging identity some institutional backbone. The first step in creating supranational structures is usually credited to Jean Monnet, a former Cognac salesman who had worked wonders in coordinating Anglo-French supply policy during the second world war. He proposed a high authority for coal and steel to overtrump Franco-German rivalry and on April 18th 1951, the European Coal and Steel Community was formed, with six countries participating. This was one of the planks of the EC, together with the European Economic Community (EEC) and the European Atomic Energy Community (EURATOM).

In its first years, this European initiative developed all the promise and the limitations that continue to characterise it, with member states adamantly refusing to surrender "one iota of sovereignty". The realisation of the ideals of the Messina Declaration of 1955 (the fusion of economies, common institutions, common market, harmonisation of social policies) was postponed indefinitely by the 1957 Treaty of Rome.

However, the treaty did achieve some of its aims, mostly bureaucratic. Ten years after it was signed, the members established the four main institutions of the present-day Community: the Commission, the Council of Ministers, the European Parliament and the European Court of Justice, which protects the tenets of the Treaties of Rome.

GERMANY: A SINGLE NATION ONCE MORE

The Berlin wall was torn down in 1989, but it was not until October 3rd 1990 that East and West were officially reunited as the Federal Republic of Germany. This reborn nation of 78m people forms 21% of western Europe's population and is exerting an ever-increasing influence on its neighbours.

Although governed by two very different ideologies, the 40 years' separation of East and West did nothing to dim their fierce sense of being a single people. Even after the euphoria wore off and the costs were counted, no one doubted the permanency of reunification.

The cost to the former West Germans of taking in this poor relation was high. Economic growth slowed and there was a large negative shift in the balance of payments. Fear of recession was fuelled by doubts about West Germany's ability to compete in world markets with businesses facing high wage claims, high interest rates, a comparatively short working year, high taxes and stringent environmental controls on industry. Initially unemployment rose to 40% in the former East Germany and the Treuhand agency was put in charge of privatising more than 8,000 state-run businesses.

Unified Germany has proved itself a potent force in the European Community and has called loudly and repeatedly for a single European currency based on the Deutschemark and even a "United States of Europe". Even after paying the price of reunification, Germany avoided the worst ravages of the recession of the early 1990s.

Politicians and commentators in other European states have expressed concern about this new era of German power, claiming to detect undertones of an unhealthy nationalism; their opponents deride this as envy.

Send in the clowns… In spring carnival comes to the southern Belgian town of Binche. On Shrove Tuesday, les Gilles (left), parade through the town, dressed in masks and ostrich feathers, distributing oranges to the crowd. Pre- and post-Lenten celebrations with parades and masks, fancy dress and feasting are an annual feature of the southern edges of the Lowlands in marked contrast to their northern Calvinist neighbours. This is a cultural legacy from the 16th century, when the Netherlands belonged to Catholic Spain.

Have passport, will travel… young East Germans poured into Vienna, having crossed the border in 1989.

Communication is about the exchange of information and ideas, and the free movement of goods and people; it is essential to the growth of trade and the binding together of society. As a small, densely populated continent containing over 50 different nationalities speaking some 120 different languages, Europe faces a communications challenge.

This chapter reviews Europe's transport infrastructure – road, rail and air. It looks at what is being done to get round (or under) physical barriers and bottlenecks that cause congestion; how far along the line (32,000km in 1992) is Europe towards compatible rail systems so that the single European can travel in one movement from Malmö to Murcia; how journey times are being slashed by the development of a high-speed rail network; what plans are underway to expand airport capacity; how different countries solve the problem of urban transport. It takes in freight as well as passenger traffic: how the impact of the barrier-free single market will be absorbed by the freight industry; how close Europe's roads are to gridlock and what the state of play is in the battle for supremacy (and investment) between road and rail; how the inland waterway system could help to open up eastern Europe to the West. After transport, telecommunications are examined: how countries are updating their networks and how far we are away from efficient pan-European telecommunications. This is followed by a final section on the most fundamental method of communication, language: how linguistically diverse Europe is and to what extent Europeans are learning each other's language.

ROAD TRANSPORT

La Périphérique, the peripheral boulevard which encircles Paris, was first planned in 1940 but did not reach completion until April 1973, at a final cost of $3.7bn. An urban thoroughfare built to motorway specifications, it carries a million vehicles a day and, in theory, Parisian drivers can circumnavigate their city in only 25 minutes.

By the year 2000 cross-border goods traffic between the present member states of the European Community plus Austria, Switzerland, Sweden and Norway will be at least 25% up on the current volumes. Most of the growth will be in road traffic.

The opening of eastern Europe is increasing further the amount of road transport, though estimates of the additional traffic vary widely. Conservative estimates that it would increase more than tenfold by the end of the decade are likely to be beaten.

Demand for road freight services is fuelled by a number of factors, not least the growth of economic activity. As transport services become cheaper, division of labour is emerging between the different European regions. Manufacturers are reducing "production depth" by buying in components they used to produce themselves. Stocks of goods and parts are being kept to a minimum, in order not to tie up capital. European companies are adopting the Japanese concept of "just-in-time" – goods are delivered just when they are needed.

In addition to freight, people are on the move, on business, on holiday, or simply enjoying their newly-found freedom to travel. The traffic of private cars and buses between east and west alone is expected to increase 18-fold by the year 2000. The citizens of western Europe, too, will travel more, although their additional mileage in cars and buses will increase by a much lower margin.

But the enlarged Europe of nearly 692m inhabitants, including most of the former USSR and eastern Europe, already has enormous problems with a system of roads that is insufficient to cope with such demand.

Europe's road infrastructure consists of badly linked and inadequately maintained national networks. According to the EC's Council of Ministers, investment in transport systems dropped from 1.5% of gross national products in 1975 to 0.9% in 1984, while traffic increased by 2.5% annually in the same period. Germany has the largest motorway network, but also the highest degree of motorisation coupled with the heaviest transit load. Due to its central position, it is experiencing traffic jams of unheard of length and duration.

Major growth zones

The economic geography of Europe makes it unlikely that the flow of goods and passengers will ever be distributed evenly between regions. Instead, a concentration on three major growth zones can be expected. The leading transport axis stretches from Scotland, via the Benelux countries, western Germany, and Switzerland to northern Italy. The second axis covers the centre of France, from the country's north coast, via the Paris region, to Marseille. The third includes northern and eastern Germany, and parts of Czechoslovakia and Austria.

Congestion is already having an adverse impact both on "just-in-time" concepts and on plans to centralise production or warehousing on a European level. This is partly due to natural barriers such as the Channel and the Alps. The Channel tunnel is designed to overcome one of them; Switzerland and Austria are making late efforts to ease Alpine transit, for example by building new tunnels. But for many years, these barriers will create bottlenecks which will make close cooperation between the different modes of transport, especially road and rail, all the more necessary.

In the fast lane

Although a tiny country built largely on land reclaimed from the sea, the Netherlands has the highest motorway density in Europe. This is a result of its critical position as a port of entry into Europe for international freight which is then distributed by road.

MOTORWAY DENSITY

	Density: km per 1,000 km²	Total km

COUNTRY		
NETHERLANDS	56.05	2,074
BELGIUM	48.27	1,593
SWITZERLAND	36.46	1,495
GERMANY W.	35.02	8,721
ITALY	20.69	6,083
AUSTRIA	16.75	1,407
DENMARK	13.98	601
UK	12.27	2,993
FRANCE	12.71	6,950
CZECHOSLOVAKIA	4.11	527
YUGOSLAVIA	3.85	871
SPAIN	3.69	1,863
HUNGARY	3.34	311
PORTUGAL	2.78	256
BULGARIA	2.40	266
SWEDEN	1.84	830
POLAND	0.78	243
FINLAND	0.64	215
ROMANIA	0.48	113
IRELAND	0.12	8

MOTORWAYS AND TRAFFIC

Not only is eastern Europe badly in need of new motorways to connect its economies with those of the West; there are wide gaps in the networks in parts of the European Community, especially in the southern member states. Spain's second national road plan calls for spending of $14.3bn up to the year 2000, adding about 4,000km of motorway.

Almost everywhere, traffic growth has been underestimated and in most countries roads are crumbling much faster than they can be repaired. This means that funds for road building in the major industrialised countries are almost exclusively used for repairs and upgrading. In 1977, the motorway network was 6,700km long, on which 69.1bn kilometres were travelled. In 1987, the length of the network was 8,600km – an increase of 28%. Traffic increased in the same period by 60% to 110.8bn kilometres per year. The massive $20.7bn road building programme undertaken by the UK government will lead to an expansion of just 2% of total road capacity up to the year 2000. For the same period, forecasts for traffic increases, calculated in vehicle kilometres, range from 83% to 142%.

Road building programmes for this additional traffic cannot be financed by governments alone. Those in eastern Europe are under even tighter financial constraints. Toll roads, or privately financed motorways leased by governments, could provide an alternative as they do in France, Italy and Spain. But, as the Czechoslovak government experienced when it attempted to introduce tolls on the existing motorway between Prague and the Austrian border, this is hugely unpopular. The Germans also abandoned plans to introduce a motorway fee. However, in Switzerland local cars carry a sticker to allow them to travel on motorways; foreign cars pay for them at the border.

SAFETY AND NUMBERS

Safety has become a major selling point for car manufacturers – small wonder when although accident figures have been going down for some time, a country like Germany still suffered 7,906 road deaths and 448,158 injured in 1990 alone. What is surprising is that it is not the countries with the most motorways which show the highest accident figures, but those with poor road systems and a stock of old and badly maintained cars, such as Turkey and Poland. The figures indicated in the chart below show the notified accidents per vehicle/km for 1988.

Strangely, in Britain and several other European countries, pedestrian deaths caused by cars have actually risen as car-passenger deaths continue to drop after the introduction of seatbelt laws.

ROAD ACCIDENTS , PER 100 VEHICLE/KM, 1988

COUNTRY	KILLED	INJURED	ACCIDENTS
TURKEY	29	329	–
POLAND	7.0	66	56
SPAIN	6.8	178	115
BELGIUM	3.9	165	120
LUXEMBOURG	2.8	63	42
IRELAND	2.7	50	33
FRANCE	2.5	57	41
ITALY	2.2	69	50
DENMARK	2.0	43	28
GERMANY W.	1.9	107	80
FINLAND	1.9	30	24
UK	1.7	109	84
NETHERLANDS	1.5	53	47
USA	1.4	109	72

Connections: **The future shape** 142–143   **Air pollution** 202–203   **Economic impacts** 212–213   **Institutional responses** 218–219

Road blocks

The map shows the density of road networks and indicates the "black spots" where congestion presents special problems. Natural barriers, such as mountains and bodies of water, produce their own bottlenecks, but many traffic problems are the result of insufficient capacity for the increased volume. Congestion is particularly bad in the area of northern Europe shown in the inset, where investment in infrastructure is failing to keep pace with demand, in spite of a pro-road policy professed by the governments of the countries in question. The cities marked have particularly recalcitrant congestion problems. In the south, Athens is enveloped in the poisonous *nefos*, an almost permanent cloud of exhaust gases.

The map (right) indicates the level of road density, calculated by the km of road per sq km of country. Figures are from 1989.

2.0
1.5
1.0
0.5
No available data
Road bottlenecks
Air traffic problem frontiers
Natural boundaries
● City regions of congestion

Pay as you drive

The chart below shows the overall tax burden borne by the vehicle owner in one year, combining purchase, road and fuel taxes in 1989.

Larger vehicles, which have higher fuel consumption and do more damage to roads, are in most countries taxed far more heavily than smaller models.

Many governments reward efforts to reduce vehicular pollution (such as changing to unleaded petrol and the installation of catalytic converters) with lower levels of taxation.

CAR OWNERS AND TAXATION

1,500cc car, travelling 15,000km and consuming 1,500l petrol every year

4,500cc car, travelling 15,000km and consuming 2,700l petrol every year

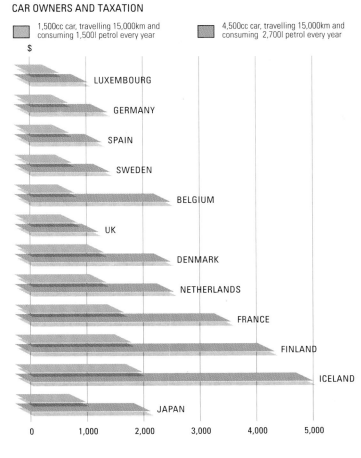

$

LUXEMBOURG
GERMANY
SPAIN
SWEDEN
BELGIUM
UK
DENMARK
NETHERLANDS
FRANCE
FINLAND
ICELAND
JAPAN

0   1,000   2,000   3,000   4,000   5,000

THE COST OF CONGESTION

The road systems of European centres have long passed saturation point, but growth forecasts for car ownership continue to point strongly upwards. According to an estimate by the Confederation of British Industry, congestion is already costing the United Kingdom's economy $25.9bn a year. It is no longer possible to solve the occasional traffic jam by building a new road. Such solutions are either unaffordable or politically unenforceable; protests against noise and pollution have stopped more than one road building scheme.

One option is "smart" road pricing, not to be confused with flat road-user fees or with normal tolls, which are difficult and expensive to collect. Road pricing systems can charge different fees, according to the area and/or the time of the day. Technical systems already available include the post-pay method, where each vehicle is identified by either infra-red or microwave transmitters. Their signals are reflected by an "electronic number plate" on the car. The user is then either billed, or the amount deducted from his or her account.

The alternative "pre-pay" system works with chip cards, which the driver has to purchase in order to "load" a device in the car. Each time the car passes a toll station, a certain sum is deducted. Costs for such a device are still comparatively small and would not exceed $75.

Higher taxes on cars and petrol, tolls and road pricing systems have been proposed to discourage the use of motorcars. Measures to combat illegal parking include wheel clamping and towing away. Although unpopular, there is no evidence that they are very effective deterrents – for every victim who learns his lesson, there is another motorist willing to take the risk of being caught.

Driving forces

Car ownership has increased by almost 25% over the past decade; at the last count, Germans were top of the table with 486 vehicles for every thousand people. Western society is prepared to pay a high price for the personal mobility offered by the motorcar, but if current trends are allowed to continue unchecked, roads will be clogged to gridlock, and this highly-prized mobility will cease to exist.

Japan has a significantly higher standard of living than Germany but an average of 42 people per car, compared with 2.2 in Germany.

The chart below indicates the sharp increase in car ownership over the last decade.

GROWTH IN PASSENGER CARS
Ownership per million

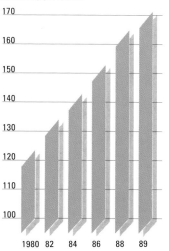

170
160
150
140
130
120
110
100

1980 82 84 86 88 89

RAILWAYS

A century of dominance followed by half a century of decline; and now an opportunity to expand again. Will it really happen? Or are Europe's railways so hobbled by nationalist structures they cannot rise again?

In the 1960s and 1970s, railways were widely seen in the western world as technically obsolete and doomed to decline. Governments struggled to control huge deficits as overstaffed and overcomplex rail networks built in the age of the horse and cart failed to adapt quickly enough to a situation in which road was faster and cheaper. The airlines added competition for passenger services, where even the railways' traditional attractions of comfort and service ceased to be enough to keep their markets. Thousands of kilometres of track were torn up, with more than half the British railway network gone by 1975, for example; other countries, such as Switzerland, kept their rail networks almost intact. Even so, they were heavily subsidised and devoured large chunks of state money.

Market share shrank dramatically. From a near monopoly in the 1920s, the proportion of all travel undertaken by rail has dwindled in western Europe to around 10%. The position for freight is somewhat better, perhaps 20% overall, but much of this tonnage is low-value bulk commodities carried at low rates. In revenue terms, Europe's railways probably collect less than 10% of total spending on consumer transport.

Pressures for change have built up in recent years because of serious congestion in road and air corridors, which has been exacerbated by resistance to the creation of enough motorways and airports to meet the huge growth in traffic forecast. A balance in pricing is gradually being struck as the true costs of road transport in environmental and economic terms begin to emerge. Measures to ease congestion and reduce pollution will inevitably increase the cost of truck and car traffic, which means the railways will be able to compete on a more equal footing.

Prospects for expansion exist in three distinct areas: high speed intercity services, urban railways and intermodal freight over long distances.

High speed sans frontières?

The most visible and exciting manifestation of the new railway age is the high speed train, running on dedicated track. Credit for this concept goes to the Japanese, who in 1964 introduced the first trains in the world to travel at more than 160kph. The French have long since outpaced Japan. The first TGV began running in 1981 at 256kph

Rail network 2010

The map shows the railmap of Europe, indicating existing lines, upgraded lines, link lines and proposed new connections. The blueprint for Europe's high speed rail network was published in 1989 by the Community of European Railways, representing the EC, Austria and Switzerland. Starting with existing high speed lines and upgrading proposals, the CER report added plans for new lines to form a coherent network which would feature France, Britain, Italy, Spain, Germany, Denmark and Sweden. However, the long term ideal is for this to extend in a series of web-like structures across the continent. In 1990, the European Council of Transport Ministers approved a similar plan involving the construction of 8,960km of new lines and the upgrading of a further 14,880km of existing lines to be able to take trains travelling at over 200kph.

— New lines >250km/h
— Lines upgraded +/-200km/h
— Link lines
- - - New lines or upgraded lines (undetermined routing)

Connections: Road transport 28–29 Airline travel 34–35 Freight systems 36–39 Single market 96–97

between Paris and Lyon; 296kph TGVs speed west and south from Paris now. In May 1991, the French government approved a master plan to build a national network of TGV lines totalling almost 4,800 kilometres by 2025 at a cost of $37.17bn, while development of trains capable of 320kph is going ahead. The first 320kph line will run between Paris, Lille and the Channel tunnel.

Apart from the French, only the Germans have devised a dedicated track system, the Inter City Express (ICE) which is slower than the TGV and too heavy to run on TGV tracks. Britain's flawed attempt at an Advanced Passenger Train (APT), designed to run on existing tracks, was abandoned in 1981. The Italians are now developing the Pendolino, another APT-type system which does not require dedicated track. Only the Spanish are helping to standardise Europe's disparate rail systems. They have bought the French TGV, and the first route being planned runs from Madrid to Seville.

Differing technical standards adopted by Europe's railways are still a problem. While the distance between the rails is the same, except in Iberia, the system of electric traction changes at most frontiers along with the signalling. Worse, each government-owned railway buys unique rolling stock from national suppliers, which ▷

Picking up speed

Speed is essential in international rail travel if the dream of a pan-European network is to be realised. So far most of the journey times predicted below are still the stuff of timetablers' dreams, scheduled for achievement at the end of the century.

Journey times will decrease significantly over the next decade. The diagrams show the time that will be saved on journeys originating in Paris

and Frankfurt. For example, a trip from Paris to Barcelona will take less than half the time in the year 2000 than it did in 1983, and the journey time between Frankfurt and London will be cut by about two-thirds.

The final forging of the cross-channel link and the closer ties between EC members will help the expansion of cross-border services. Cities with good international rail connections will inevitably rise in prestige.

JOURNEY TIMES

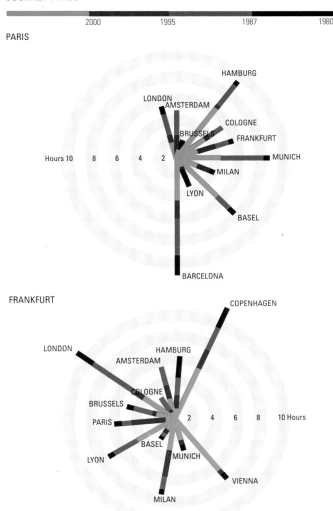

Government subsidies

Railways are not cheap; routine maintenance and technological development require regular investment. In most European countries, state support is considered essential if both network and trains are to survive in competition with road and air services, and most governments accept the need for subsidy, however reluctantly.

The graph below indicates the level of subsidy per km the main countries of

western Europe are prepared to invest in railway infrastructure. There is remarkable similarity in spending on rail systems. Sweden's modest input reflects the 1988 separation of infrastructure (state-owned and maintained) and passenger routes (some of which have been sold off to private profit-making companies). Italy's staggering subsidy reflects its railways' huge overstaffing, union and corruption problems.

SUBSIDY, $ per km

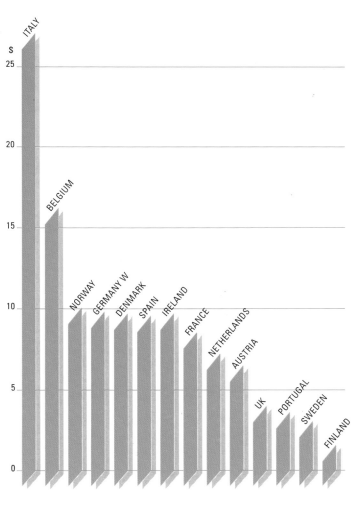

When it was launched in 1981, the Train à Grande Vitesse *(TGV) captured 90% of the Paris-Lyon air traffic.* TGVs *now streak south and west of Paris to Grenoble, Geneva and Marseille.* TGV Atlantique *serves Le Mans, Brest, Nantes and Bordeaux, while* TGV Nord *will take international Channel tunnel trains to Britain.*

On the right track

Geography, population density and wealth are three factors affecting the extent of the rail network in each country (below). Two out of the top three countries in this table are in the old eastern bloc where railways, however antiquated, never went out of fashion as they did in Britain, for instance.

Few of the systems here are truly compatible and a European-wide network would depend on agreement about international guidelines for gauge, speed and specifications for rolling stock.

DENSITY OF RAIL NETWORKS

COUNTRY	per 1,000km²
BELGIUM	108
HUNGARY	82
POLAND	77
SWITZERLAND	73
NETHERLANDS	76
UK	68
AUSTRIA	68
FRANCE	63
DENMARK	58
ITALY	54
YUGOSLAVIA	41
PORTUGAL	39
SPAIN	25
SWEDEN	25
GREECE	19
NORWAY	11
TURKEY	11

drives up costs and slows technical progress.

Under the single market programme the barriers are already coming down, mainly because mergers have created big international suppliers such as ABB (Asea Brown Boveri) and GEC Alsthom. The Channel tunnel has been the catalyst for the first really international order for high-speed trains to link London with Paris and Brussels. Spain has bought the French TGV, but there is no sign yet that Germany or Italy are going to do a deal with the French to develop a standard high-speed train for Europe.

As high-speed rail travel improves, attention will focus on two other connected issues: domestic networks and how they will link with the high-speed international routes, and services connecting countries in eastern Europe. Local and regional services will need to improve both their infrastructure (track and signals) and rolling stock. All of Europe's services are heavily subsidised and investment in regional services is a low priority. Sweden was first to find a solution. Infrastructure is largely separate from the running of services and is state-funded. Lines that had previously been unprofitable were put out to tender and so far the company that has taken over three of them, BK Train, has halved fares and increased passenger traffic by 40%.

While high-speed trains steal the limelight, an equally important development is taking place out of the public eye. This is the creation of some 30 key international freight routes which will be improved to a common standard, for instance clearance heights for bridges and tunnels. The aim is to triple within a decade the tonnage of intermodal or combined transport, which can take various forms: mostly containers and swapbodies (which are dual-purpose rail and road vehicle bodies) are carried, but in some cases complete lorries are carried with their drivers. Many experiments are taking place with bi-modal vehicles that look like normal trailers on the road, but can be coupled to trains.

Open access across Europe

The failure of national railways to compete with road for international freight is largely caused by the lack of a unified management system for the whole transit. As a result, the EC Transport Commission proposes that private transport companies should have the right to run their own trains anywhere in Europe. This novel idea has met stiff resistance from some railway managements, but the idea of open access is being embraced by several European governments and has been adopted as policy by the British. If it comes about, it will mark a major revolution in the way railways are managed, since open access was tried and then abandoned as unworkable with the opening in England of the Liverpool and Manchester Railway in 1830. However, the immense advances in communications technology since then could well make the concept viable.

Watching these developments with a mixture of envy and apprehension are the railways of eastern Europe. They face real difficulties. Technically, their situation is not too bad because they got a lion's share of what transport investment was available; but in commercial and operational terms, they are 30 years behind western railways. Until the fall of the iron curtain in 1989, about two-thirds of all freight and at least one-third of passenger movement took place by rail. This cannot last, and cutbacks are inevitable, but the railways of the east neverthe-

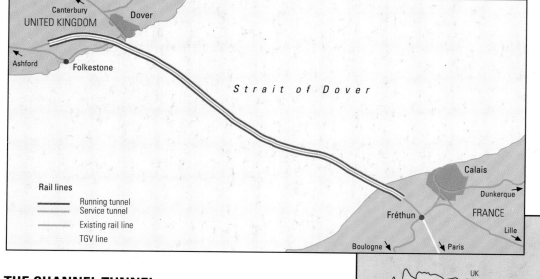

Rail lines

— Running tunnel
---- Service tunnel
····· Existing rail line
— TGV line

THE CHANNEL TUNNEL

After a false start in the 1970s, the Channel tunnel project began in earnest in 1985, when the French and English governments signed an accord which declared a commitment to dig, with an end date of sometime in 1993. The immense cost of the project – almost double its original $7.87bn estimate – is being borne largely by the private sector. Eurotunnel, the owner and operator, raised finance from all over the world. On present statistics, early next century the Channel line will be the busiest railway in the world, carrying more than the gross tonnage of any track which exists today. A train will pass through every four minutes on average in each direction.

About a third of these trains will carry passengers and freight between the national rail networks. Two-thirds will consist of giant wagons shuttling cars, coaches and trucks between two terminals close to Calais and Folkestone. This shuttle service will have a capacity equal to a four-lane motorway.

The tunnel will link three major cities – Paris, London and Brussels – with a high-speed rail system. On the French side, TGV Nord will take passengers to Paris and beyond at speeds of

almost 320kph. The lines are due to be completed shortly after the tunnel. In Britain, the proposed high-speed link to London will not open until at least 1998, delayed by political, environmental and financial considerations.

Problems are arising on the English side mostly because the Channel tunnel rail link is not eligible for government subsidies so needs to catch a large Kent commuter market to make it profitable. Trains emerging from the French side will have to slow down to 96kph on the congested domestic line. In 1991, Belgium agreed routes for links with Germany and France costing $2.3bn. The 90km link from Brussels to the French TGV Nord track will not be finished until 1996.

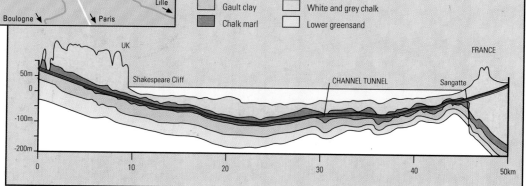

☐ Gault clay		☐ White and grey chalk	
■ Chalk marl		☐ Lower greensand	

Under the channel

The tunnel complex runs for 48km, 40km of which lie under open sea, the longest distance any tunnel has been driven without access to the surface. There are three parallel tunnels, two single rail tracks and a central service and escape tunnel.

ELEMENT.

less expect eventually to link up with the high speed and intermodal networks in the west. Such integration is bound to come as the economies of East and West level up, but the transition will not be painless.

Meanwhile, railways in the West will also be facing the pains of adjusting to the spread of deregulation and the need to operate in a more competitive market.

Overall, the outlook for Europe's railways is brighter today than at any time in the past 60 years, mainly because governments now see rail as a key part of the solution to the congestion problem, rather than an isolated financial problem solved only by cutting back.

Undeterred by snow, a passenger train crosses the Langwies Viaduct on Switzerland's Rhadetin railway as it travels from Chur to Arosa.

ALPINE CORRIDORS

Routes across the Alps are congested by road freight traffic. The Swiss wish to maintain their traditional role as the transport hub of Europe while protecting the environment and believe rail tunnels to be the solution. First to be built will be the 48km Gotthard base tunnel and the complementary 12.8km tunnel under Mount Ceneri. Together with the present route, freight capacity will be increased from 12–15m tonnes to 50m tonnes. A 27km Lötschberg base tunnel is then planned to feed into the existing Simplon tunnel. These two schemes will cost $9.24bn and will take 20 years to complete. Meanwhile, the Bern-Lötschberg-Simplon extension to a double track was finished in 1991 and extended piggyback services by 1994–95 will ease congestion, as freight traffic is shifted from road to rail to cross Switzerland. To the east, Austria and Italy are planning a 53km tunnel under the Brenner Pass as part of a major upgrading of the Munich-Verona corridor.

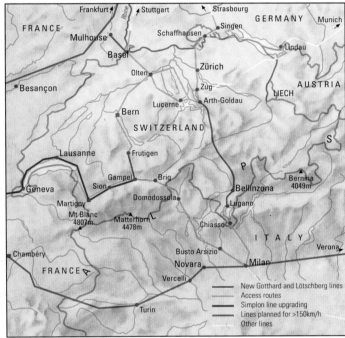

Making tracks

The map shows Denmark's main rail system and how planned fixed link crossings between the islands that make up Denmark and between Denmark and Sweden will fit into existing networks. Denmark, the only Scandinavian EC country to date, plans to capitalise on its direct land connection with mainland Europe by building fixed links to join up its islands. This will make rail freight movement within Denmark easier and quicker; the projected southern link between Denmark and Sweden will offer all traffic a competitive second option to the longer Frederikshavn–Göteborg crossing in the north.

Planned fixed link
Major train ferry
Existing line

SCANDINAVIAN LINKS

Despite many rail and road ferries, Norway and Sweden are cut off from continental Europe, while Denmark's capital, Copenhagen, lies on a large island. An ambitious bridge and tunnel network aims to end this isolation. Non-EC Scandinavia is worried about being commercially sidelined by the single market. Transport links are being developed to promote trade.

Three major rail and road crossings over the sea are planned, at a cost of around $10bn, partly financed by tolls. The first, 17.6km long across the Great Belt between the islands of Fyn and Sjaelland, is already under construction. The rail connection, half bridge and half tunnel, is expected to open in 1994, if tunnelling difficulties can be overcome. The road, requiring two massive bridges, follows three years later.

Another 17km road and rail link across the Oresund between Copenhagen in Denmark and Malmö in Sweden has been approved and construction may start in 1992. It will consist of a 4.2km tunnel under a shipping channel, a 10km viaduct and a 5.6km, high-level bridge allowing ships to pass beneath.

Another link, across the 20km wide Fehmarnbaelt, is still at the planning stage with no decision on the form it will take. Although there will be a continuous rail route between Sweden and Germany after the other two are completed, the link is much more direct, and could well carry a Copenhagen-Hamburg high speed line.

AIRLINE TRAVEL

Jumbos at rest at Heathrow, London. This is Europe's busiest airport, where more than 40% of passengers make connecting flights.

The development of the jet aircraft during the 1960s introduced an era of fast, safe and relatively cheap air travel in Europe. Demand for both business and leisure travel has also been stimulated by rising national wealth in Europe during the past three decades.

The airline industry is a highly cyclical one, yet passenger air travel grew in Europe by an annual average of 5.7% during the 1980s. In 1990–91, however, European airlines faced their worst downturn since the second world war as economic recession was compounded by the slump in air travel caused by the Gulf crisis. Even so, demand is expected to show average annual growth of around 4.9% during the 1990s and 4.7% over the following decade.

Business or pleasure?

The balance between leisure and business travel is expected to swing heavily towards the leisure market over the next 20 years. The deregulated low discount charter airline market already accounts for nearly 70% of international air travel in the EC, while about 40% of scheduled traffic currently consists of leisure travellers. Airbus, the European aircraft consortium, confidently expects about 80% of all air travel to involve non-business trips by early next century.

However, while leisure will dominate the air travel market, airlines continue to develop new business services because these have traditionally been a source of high margin. Freight is also expected to continue expanding faster than passenger traffic.

The European Commission's efforts to complete its gradual process of air transport liberalisation in the 1990s is expected to stimulate further air travel in Europe. The EC has already introduced three separate packages of liberalisation measures which have given airlines greater freedom to decide their own fares and greater flexibility on air routes throughout Europe.

Liberalisation has created greater choice and increased services for travellers and in many cases held down and even cut fare prices, especially in the leisure market. The overall network of air routes expanded significantly from 1985 to 1990 both at big hub airports (37%) and commuter services between regional airports (119%). London, Europe's leading international hub, is facing growing competition from Paris, Amsterdam and Frankfurt which are all seeking to expand as international gateways as well as European hubs. To maintain its position, there are plans to build an express rail link between Heathrow and central London, a fifth terminal

Sky-high demands

European airlines flew into the 1990s carrying about 400m passengers a year, compared with only 40m in 1970. By the end of the century, about 80% of all passengers will be travelling for leisure, not business purposes.

Number of passengers using routes

— over 1 million
— 800,000-1 million
— 600,000-800,000
— 400,000-600,000
······ upper air space divisions

GROWTH IN AIR TRAFFIC DEMAND

Billion revenue passenger miles RPM

Average annual RPM growth %

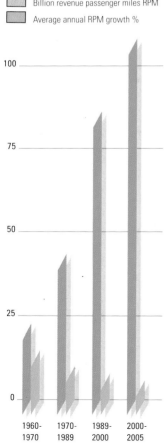

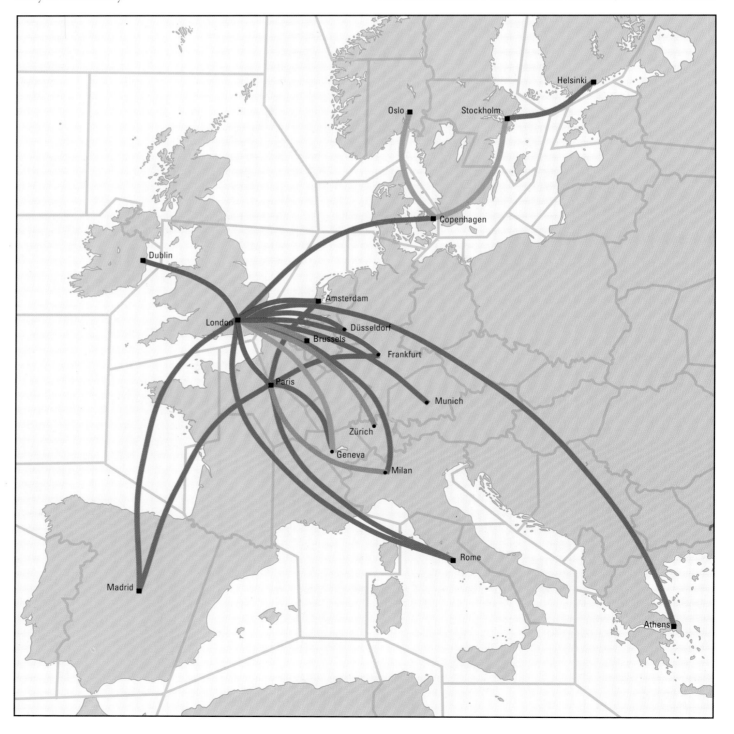

at Heathrow and eventually a new runway.

The ultimate aim of liberalisation is to create in Europe a total "open skies" environment driven by market forces. But this is likely to be a slow process with some governments reluctant to give up their sovereign rights and keen to protect their national flag carriers.

Competition in European air travel also risks being undermined by the growing trend of concentration, with the larger carriers forging alliances, mergers and partnerships building up to a "critical mass" to compete in an increasingly global market against the so-called "megacarriers" of the USA and Asia. This concentration is threatening to squeeze smaller airlines out of the market.

Air travel is also facing competition from the renaissance of railways in Europe. High-speed train networks are already competing against air travel in some European markets, especially in France. These new generation train services could also complement air travel in certain short-haul markets, easing the congestion at busy airports by helping to release valuable take-off and landing slots so they can be used more efficiently for medium and long distance air services.

Overcrowding on the ground

While air transport remains the safest form of travel and air safety standards continue to be tightened, inadequate ground and air infrastructure could clip the wings of future growth in Europe. As a result of congestion, one out of every four flights in Europe is delayed by more than 15 minutes. The cost of delays is put at more than $5bn a year while lack of slots at congested airports is frustrating efforts of new entrants into the market.

Although there are plans to integrate Europe's different air traffic control systems into one single system, political differences have hampered the progress of harmonisation. Similarly, ambitious plans to develop

more airport capacity are held up because of environmental objections and planning consent.

IATA (International Air Transport Association) believes congestion is the "single biggest barrier to growth" for air transport in Europe, where capacity is likely to come under even greater pressure as a result of the opening of eastern Europe. The USSR, even before *glasnost*, accounted for 13% of world passenger traffic on scheduled flights, and despite the uncertain economic future of the former eastern bloc, the region is expected in time to show above-average growth.

Umbrella pines shade the elegant liveries of Italy's national carrier at Rome's Fiumicino airport, more artistically known as Leonardo da Vinci.

Airport expansion

Most airports are handling as many passengers as the amenities can cope with. Seven major airports reached their frequency limits (maximum aircraft movements) before 1990 (see map). In response, airports throughout Europe are investing in expansion projects.

Athens A new runway and terminal are due for completion in 2005.

Amsterdam Schiphol international airport continues its $2bn investment to expand capacity to 30m by 2003.

Barcelona A new international terminal with 24 gates and 12m capacity is part of the $200m redevelopment for the 1992 Olympic games.

Berlin With demand intensifying, Shönefeld and Tegel, presently handling 8.7m passengers per year, are both being expanded to take 20m. There are plans to build a new airport, Berlin international, by the turn of the century. Together the projects will cost $4.8bn.

Frankfurt Europe's largest airport expansion is the $5bn Ausbau 2000 project at Frankfurt, where international traffic will be doubled by the year 2000.

Hamburg A new terminal complex at Hamburg-Fuhlbüttel, costing $480m, is due to be finished by 1993.

Istanbul A new terminal, costing $200m, is to be operative by 1992.

London London is the busiest air centre of Europe, with 65.5m passengers passing through in 1990. Both Heathrow and Gatwick are nearing capacity; Stansted Airport's new $250m terminal (with a capacity of 8m) opened in 1991.

Madrid Barajas airport, presently handling only 16.7m passengers, is to be expanded to provide for 80m passengers.

Munich The huge $2.9bn Franz Josef Strauss airport will open in spring 1992, providing for 14m passengers, which is to be extended to 28m.

Oslo With Fornebu airport's noise restraints, capacity limitations and a short-falling runway, a new $1.8bn airport is in the planning stages, for possible completion in 1997--98.

Paris Charles de Gaulle is Europe's largest capacity airport with four runways and six terminals providing for 80m passengers every year and the capacity to extend to 100m.

Frequency - Limited airport

● Capacity reached 1990

Capacity forecast 1995

● Capacity forecast 2000

Warsaw The $200m new terminal and cargo centre will be at the centre of eastern Europe's new air travel market. It is due to be completed by 1992.

Taking off

The chart below lists airports in terms of how many passengers pass through them.

AIRPORT	PASSENGERS
HEATHROW	42,647,000
FRANKFURT	28,862,000
CHARLES DE GAULLE	22,506,000
ORLY	24,330,000
GATWICK	21,047,000
ROME AIRPORTS	17,916,000
AMSTERDAM	16,178,000
MADRID	15,869,000
STOCKHOLM	14,947,000
COPENHAGEN	12,768,000
ZURICH	12,695,000
DUSSELDORF	11,935,000
MUNICH	11,424,000
MILAN AIRPORTS	11,388,000
PALMA	11,319,000
MANCHESTER	10,154,000
ATHENS	10,077,000
BARCELONA	9,041,000
BRUSSELS	8,025,000
HELSINKI	8,008,000

TOKYO	21,600,000
NY KENNEDY	29,700,000

FREIGHT SYSTEMS

Europe's freight distribution map has been re-drawn in the early 1990s. The opening up of eastern Europe means that previously incompatible systems have to adjust and mesh; and the prospects of the single market and the removal of customs barriers has transformed transport operations in road, rail, sea and air.

About 80% of European-based manufacturing companies have reassessed their transport needs for the 1990s to capitalise on the removal of customs borders. Instead of a thinly spread network of factories in Europe, they can concentrate on a few core manufacturing centres. Such a business philosophy relies on just-in-time delivery of inventory to keep expensive stock levels at a minimum. More than 30% of German goods transported are just-in-time and this is expected to rise to more than 55% by the mid-1990s.

European freight distribution is increasingly dominated by environmental issues, as politicians demand greener transport. The EC has given priority to the intermodal revolution, in which more cargo is transferred from trucks to the cleaner and cheaper railways for longer freight hauls.

Such road/rail "swapbody" traffic will use the railways for long cross-border freight routes, while local collection and delivery will still be by truck.

A directive from the EC issued in 1990 promoted the use of railways as part of intermodal operation; and the directive of 1993 will make it possible for railways to sell off or rent out stretches of track to customers who want to put their own rolling stock on it. This will allow road hauliers or freight forwarders to move whole trainloads

RUNNING COSTS

The romance of the road is costing the earth. As the chart below indicates, it is the noisiest, most polluting, most expensive, greediest in energy terms and most dangerous method of transport. Cars clog transport arteries, outnumbering lorries by three to one, but one juggernaut produces as much wear and tear on the road as 10,000 cars. The addition of an extra axle on lorries over 24 tonnes would reduce such damage by one-third but there are no plans to introduce pan-European legislation. Despite the green lobby, road transport will still be the prime means of moving goods.

Levels of environmental consciousness vary across Europe. Countries with a presentable green record include Switzerland with a road-rail freight transport split of 52%:47% (1% goes by water); Sweden with a 55.2%: 44.8% split; and the Netherlands, which moves over half (57.2%) of its freight by water. The road hog is Greece scoring 95.9%, followed by Spain, at 91.7% and Ireland, 90.1%.

% OF ENVIRONMENTAL DAMAGE DONE BY TRANSPORT METHODS

SOCIAL COSTS	AIR	RAIL	WATER	ROAD
AIR POLLUTION	2	4	3	91
NOISE POLLUTION	26	10	0	64
LAND COVERAGE	1	7	1	91
CONSTRUCTION/ MAINTENANCE	2	37	5	56
ACCIDENTS/ CASUALTIES	1	1	0	98
ENERGY CONSUMPTION	11	3	2	84

The semi-trailer freight system operates by physically lifting loaded trailers, complete with wheels, on to flatbed rail trucks (above). Over the past decade, the semi-trailer share of the market has declined to only 20% in favour of the swapbody system which uses transferable container units. A common European standard for the size and height of freight units is needed if swapbodys are to supersede semi-trailers completely.

of goods using their own timetable. This is already in limited action, but for bulk aggregate goods (sand, gravel, etc) rather than containerised freight.

British Rail, through its Railfreight Distribution subsidiary, will have an initial 27 freight trains a day through the Channel tunnel, feeding into nine intermodal cargo terminals, or freight villages, strategically located in the UK to maximise road/rail business. British Rail will no longer be confined within the relatively short, and therefore less economic, UK rail freight routes. Instead, working in partnership with road hauliers for swapbody traffic, it will be able to link into the 240,000km of track in continental Europe. ▷

THE INTERMODAL REVOLUTION

Intermodal transport, the combined use of road and rail for a single freight movement, is set to expand in the 1990s. The cross-border rail trunking of freight over long distances in Europe, with pick-up and delivery at either end by truck, has the potential to triple to 43.2m tonnes a year by 2005. Such rapid growth depends on free access to rail track and traction for private sector freight operators.

One group able to take advantage of such access is the UIRR (International Union of Combined Road–Rail Transport Companies), a Brussels-based group of companies which in 1990 carried 14.4m tonnes in 550,000 consignments.

The railways will concentrate on key freight traffic routes, including Europe's major ports which will act as leading intermodal hubs. The Channel tunnel will be a link in the intermodal chain with up to 30 UK-based road hauliers taking shares in the newly formed Combined Transport Limited (CTL).

Austria and Switzerland are keen intermodalists. Both countries move about half of their freight by rail, in marked contrast to the rest of western Europe. Their bottleneck mountain passes strangle road traffic and their crossroads position in the new Europe means that they will have to deal with an increased rate of through traffic. They are therefore keen to get as much freight as possible off the backs of lorries and on to the rail system for border-to-border transhipment. To encourage such a shift, Austria has already banned weekend road freight and, along with Switzerland, has imposed a weight limit of 28 tonnes, ignoring EC pressure for a 40-tonne limit.

One factor that could stunt the expected growth in road/rail traffic is a lack of technical standards in the equipment necessary for intermodal transport. Swapbodies, developed in the USA, are freight units that can be carried by lorry or rail. They already account for 80% of present road/rail traffic.

Connections: Railways 30–33 Environmental stress 208–211 Institutional response 218–219

Trade flows

The map shows how the principal inland waterways link up with the main navigable rivers. Unified Germany boasts the longest canal system in Europe; plans to link up with eastern Europe depend on funding. Other proposals include linking the Rhône with the Rhine and the North Sea with the Mediterranean.

——— Principal canals

——— Principal inland waterways

COUNTRY	LENGTH km
GERMANY	6,684
FRANCE	6,384
FINLAND	6,239
NETHERLANDS	5,016
POLAND	3,805
UK	2,351
YUGOSLAVIA	2,001
ROMANIA	1,628
BELGIUM	1,514
HUNGARY	1,373
ITALY	1,366
CZECH	483
BULGARIA	470
SWEDEN	439
AUSTRIA	358
PORTUGAL	124
LUXEMBOURG	37
SWITZERLAND	21

INLAND WATERWAYS

Inland waterways in Europe are expected to handle 117bn tonne-kilometres of freight in the year 2000, one-tenth the figure for road and half that of rail. The system is underused and is likely to stay so until well into the next century.

Bucking the trend, barge traffic on the Rhine is experiencing healthy growth and the new Rhine-Main-Danube link canal is scheduled to open in 1992. Stretching between Bamberg on the Main and Kelheim on the German Danube, the link canal will open up a 3,500km waterway skirting nine countries between Rotterdam and the Black Sea.

The cost involved means that it could be years before the entire Danube is navigable in all seasons. At present, only 10% capacity is being used, although it has potential to become a major artery for bulk cargo. Investment is needed to bring eastern European canal systems up to western standards.

Barges crammed into Rotterdam, the busiest port in Europe. Every year 32,000 sea-going vessels visit the port where some of their load continues its journey on the 180,000 barges which depart upstream along the rivers Rhine, Waal and Maas each year to the cities of inland Europe.

Patterns of growth

The graph plots projected growth of three transport modalities (road, rail, water) to the year 2010 . Figures are given in billion tonnes per km. Rail freight's share is likely to shrink, waterborne freight will remain more or less the same, but the road freight share will expand hugely, almost tripling its 1970 figure. Intermodal transport, using combined road and rail routes, offers better value for money than road alone. Improving the infrastructure to support intermodal activity throughout EC countries is estimated at $2.2bn, enough to build just 325km of motorway.

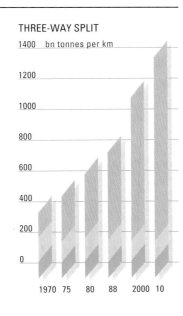

Road
Rail
Water

On the road

The dominance of road freight is reflected in the distance/market share ratio. The shorter the distance, the less likely it is that goods go by rail. Whatever the journey, freight will always finish its journey by road as rail cannot service specific delivery targets; even so, rail does not begin to take a significant share of the market until distances reach 500km. Figures are given in percentage of market share and kilometres, and refer to EC countries only. The opening up of eastern Europe will mean even more road traffic. A north-south express motorway linking the Baltic with the Black Sea is in the early stages of construction.

Freight by road
Freight by rail

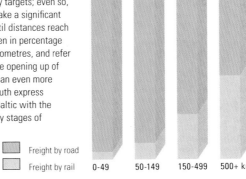

The EC is funding the creation of intermodal freight corridors in order to avoid constructing more motorways to carry trucks. However, as railways only carry about 4% of unitised international cargoes, the volume of intermodal traffic will have to increase dramatically to have any real impact on congestion.

The dominance of the road

Despite the political impetus behind such intermodal distribution, road haulage will remain the dominant transport mode across Europe mainly because rail only becomes price-efficient against trucking for journeys over 400km, leaving a vast delivery territory available to the truck. The 19 ECMT (European Conference of Ministers of Transport) countries predict that by the year 2010, road haulage will account for 79% of freight transport at 1,442bn tonne-kilometres. By the same year, rail will carry around 14% of freight traffic.

Europe's road haulage industry will also be fully deregulated by the mid-1990s, as truckers from the EC will be able to offer a domestic pick-up/delivery in another member state. This will alter the economics of road haulage, with intense competition likely to push down tariffs and so encourage greater road usage.

Sea and air

Western Europe's ports and airports face increased freight traffic, both from international and eastern European trade. Although accounting for just 5% of seaborne container trade in the early 1990s, eastern European box traffic is expected to increase gradually in the next decade.

Most of that extra traffic will transit via Europe's northern container ports at Le Havre, Rotterdam, Antwerp and Hamburg. Those four ports are expected to maintain their 45% market share of deep sea trade, although the competition between them will intensify. Rotterdam, home of Europe Container Terminus, Europe's largest container terminal, is currently the busiest, shifting more than 300m metric tonnes a year.

Ports in southern Europe, particularly Barcelona, will increase their box throughput, by taking up traffic from the Mediterranean and sending it overland by rail to the consumer heartlands of northern Europe.

The Channel tunnel and the new megabridges planned to link the islands of Denmark will not eliminate ferries as an important element in freight movement. Hazardous cargoes, for instance, will not be permitted through the Channel tunnel and ferries are the only answer. Some of the freight routes, such as Ireland–UK and Netherlands–UK, are economically best served by ferries and ro-ro (roll on, roll off) ferries sail to and from Rotterdam, Le Havre, Göteborg, Dover, Rostock and elsewhere. P&O, a big ferry operator, is planning superferries at a cost of $4.3m each.

Europe's neglected inland waterways, used mainly for bulk cargoes such as chemicals, will want a larger slice of available containerised trade. Cheaper and more ecologically sound, the canal/river system will exploit the move towards combined transport as an alternative to congested motorways. The opening of the Rhine-Main-Danube link will accelerate the growth in waterborne traffic, although massive investment will be needed if this mode of transport is to carry more than its predicted 7% of total trade.

New directions

The biggest change in the European freight scene in the mid-1990s will be the emergence of the express parcel carriers, the so called "integrators", led initially by American and Australian-based companies like DHL, Federal Express, United Parcel Service and TNT. These document and small-parcel carriers have a closed loop distribution system where every link of the collection and delivery chain is performed by their own staff on board their own aircraft, lorries or vans; hence, the universally accepted term, "integrator".

Companies such as DHL led the door-to-door document revolution in the early 1980s. They are now poised to move into the 48-hour market, traditionally dominated by national post offices; and it will not be long before the business base is broadened to make larger shipments in bigger trucks.

With the liberating of eastern Europe and the deregulation of transport services bringing intense competition on all fronts, perhaps truck wars are a real possibility in the near future.

The map shows the busiest ports in Europe. Most are concentrated in the north, but Barcelona is gearing up for a challenge.

EUROPE'S BUSIEST PORTS

Million shipping tonnage a year

- over 200
- 100-200
- 50-100
- 30-50
- 20-30

NORTH SEA

Turku
Helsinki
Oslo
Stockholm
Göteborg
Helsingborg
Tees & Hartlepool
Copenhagen
Malmö
Liverpool
Lübeck
Bremen
Rostock
Felixstowe
Vlissingen
Ports
Hamburg
Milford Haven
Amsterdam
London
Rotterdam
Dunkirk
Antwerp
Zeebrugge
Ghent
Le Havre

ATLANTIC OCEAN

Bilbao
Venice
Genoa
Marseille
Livorno
Tarragona
Barcelona
Lisbon
Valencia
Naples
Algeciras
MEDITERRANEAN SEA
Piraeus

A CHALLENGE FROM THE SOUTH

Container ports in the Le Havre-Antwerp-Rotterdam-Hamburg range currently handle around 44% of European box traffic. Containerised trade through Europe's busy ports is expected to grow from 22.7m boxes in 1990 to around 38m by the year 2000, boosted by the single market and the emergence of the eastern European countries, whose trade accounted for a meagre 5% of the total at the start of the decade.

Europe's northern ports will also face a challenge from those in the south, led by Barcelona, which has ambitions to become the main transshipment hub for freight between south-western Europe and the Far East. Part of the Llobregat river is being shifted 2km to accommodate a logistics centre in the port area. Road links are planned and the first European-gauge railway in Spain is being built between Barcelona and the French border.

The first container ship to dock in Europe arrived from Japan in 1972. Since then containerisation has revolutionised the freight market and given rise to the giant vessels now familiar worldwide.

TAKING WING

Air-carried freight has doubled over the past decade and IATA predicts an annual growth rate of 6% between 1991 and 1995. Germany, France and the UK dominate European airfreight business. London Heathrow, a "feeder" airport, distributes freight to 150 destinations; Cologne, the home base for the German national carrier Lufthansa, is also one of the hubs for integrator traffic; Frankfurt has more international connections, particularly with eastern Europe. The biggest national carrier is Lufthansa which achieved over 4,000m freight-tonne km in 1990, beaten only by the integrator service Federal Express. Air France, which together with its subsidiary UTA, owns ten freight-dedicated wide-bodied jets, came second of the nationals.

GROWTH IN AIR CARGO FREIGHTS

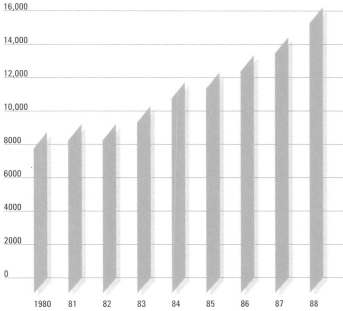

million tonne-km

Shipping forecast

This chart shows the forecast container port throughput until the end of the decade expressed in '000 TEUS. (A TEU is a "20-foot equivalent unit", the basic international unit of measurement for deep-sea container shipping.) Growth of each category is predicted in favourable (a) and unfavourable (b) circumstances. In both cases growth will occur.

WESTERN EUROPE			EASTERN EUROPE		
CATEGORY	1990	1995	1995	2000	2000
INTER-EUROPE	6.33	8.14	8.76	11.28	13.64
FEEDER	2.79	3.72	3.5	4.44	4.01
DEEPSEA	13.6	17.96	17.28	22.53	19.85
TOTAL	22.72	29.83	19.45	38.25	37.5

☐ Actual   ☐ Favourable   ☐ Unfavourable

The road east

Eastern and western Europe are almost mirror images; in the east, almost three quarters of goods travel by rail, while in the west the same amount goes by road. However, this pattern is already shifting and the biggest road haulage contractor in Europe is currently Hungary-based Hungaria Camion.

Now that Hungary is positioned at the centre of Europe's redrawn map, its tourist trade and road infrastructure is suffering as heavy trucks rumble westward past Lake Balaton. The Hungarian government has invited tenders for the construction of toll motorways to divert traffic away from residential and tourist areas.

EAST-WEST TRANSPORT PATTERNS

% of total ton per km

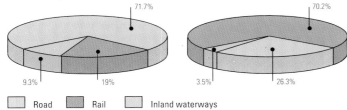

☐ Road   ☐ Rail   ☐ Inland waterways

THE INTEGRATION EXPRESS

Europe's fastest growing freight business is the door-to-door delivery of documents and parcels, a market dominated by non-Europeans. Federal Express, United Parcel Service, DHL and TNT are all billion-dollar companies whose arrival on the European scene in the 1980s caused a major shake-up of traditional home-grown freight movers: freight forwarders and the national state-owned post offices.

These express carriers have poured millions of dollars into Europe, setting up air and ground delivery networks based on the hub-and-spoke principle with Cologne and Brussels airports as the hubs. Their huge investment anticipates the long-planned liberalisation of European postal services. After US deregulation, over a decade ago, growth boomed by 46%.

However, the two EC directives on the subject are in discord. In spite of powerful representations by the European Express Organisation (EEO), an association of European private courier services, the telecommunications directive of 1991 is not in favour of wholesale deregulation as this will penalise rural and remote areas. On the other hand, the competition directive (1991) is all for smashing monopolies. Private companies complain that state post offices can cross-subsidise their services so undercutting the competition. A compromise seems likely with the EC proposing and the private couriers agreeing that letter and printed-paper services remain state-owned while value-added services are opened to tender.

Such measures have put state post offices on their mettle. Already the UK's Royal Mail and the Netherlands' PTT are restructuring their services to compete with the integrators.

Sailing through the air... A Russian Airfoyle Antonov freighter loading up. The huge land mass of the former Soviet Union makes air freighting economically viable. In 1990 the Russian national carrier Aeroflot moved 2.8m freight tonnes, more than twice as much as the private courier Federal Express.

URBAN LINKS

Although the age of uncritical support for the car as the major means of urban transport is long over, few European public transport systems so far have provided an adequate alternative.

In the early 1970s, many cities began to close their centres to cars, among them Göteborg (Sweden), Bremen (Germany), Groningen (Netherlands) and Nottingham (England). Since the late 1980s, more severe measures for larger areas have been taken, for example by Bologna (Italy) and Lübeck (Germany) at weekends; others such as Bergen and Oslo in Norway introduced road pricing schemes. Amsterdam may be the first capital city to close its centre to cars altogether.

Parking in inner cities has become prohibitively expensive, although no one in Europe has yet proposed – as has been suggested in Japan – to send parking offenders to jail. An increasing number of urban commuters, motivated by environmental as well as financial considerations, are travelling by bicycle. Some countries encourage cyclists by building dedicated cycle lanes into their traffic systems. The Netherlands has a countrywide network of cycle paths of over 9,000km, which is the model for cycling programmes being introduced in towns and cities across Europe.

However, the number of cyclists has not reduced the demand for inner city public transport. Millions of commuters still need to use their cars every day. This is only partly the result of changed transport habits and wealthier societies with more car owners: it reflects changing economic circumstances and employment trends. Commuting has become the rule, rather than the exception. Public transport systems taking account of these developments have to offer speed, coupled with a high penetration, which makes them expensive. Costs for the proposed 7.5km Crossrail underground project in London will run to $2.4bn or $327.6m per kilometre.

Although futuristic projects such as magnetically elevated trains have been in trial phases (for example in Berlin), many European cities are now returning to the tram systems. These went out of fashion (and were often scrapped altogether) in the 1960s and 1970s – to make way for urban thoroughfares for cars, which proved in many cities to be inadequate and are seriously congested. In Berlin, the tramway is making an important contribution to join the two halves that grew apart over more than 40 years. Over the next decade, the city will spend $363m on new track alone, plus $6.1m on new rolling stock.

This is much cheaper than underground lines; even so fare income alone is only sufficient to cover costs of public transport systems in exceptional cases. Huge additional funds are needed. Advocates of public transport argue that these are not subsidies, but reflect the savings society as a whole is achieving when public transport is used instead of private cars. Such calculations take into account savings made in fuel costs, environmental expense, road building and maintenance, and accident prevention. For Bremen, for example, a model calculation was made for the year 1986: it indicated that public transport saved $16m with regard to the environment, and $11.5m in terms of energy. All told, economies of $67.8m were calculated, compared with $29.7m of public money spent on the city's tramway and bus system.

Experts no longer believe that there is a single answer to urban traffic problems; even the motor industry is funding public transport research projects. A sensible combination of modes of transport is needed to prevent millions of cars from clogging city streets. Such an ideal system would enable commuters from outlying suburbs or villages to reach their jobs on time and in safety and comfort. Whatever the solution, transport costs are expected to rise throughout Europe.

Electric trams like this one in Austria, have long been a feature of European city life. Clean, reliable and environmentally sound, they are making a comeback in the UK where they went out of fashion in the 1960s. Manchester opened a new tramway system in 1992.

MUNICH BY TRAIN

Munich is one of the most attractive German cities to visit, partly due to its excellent underground and S-Bahn system. The S-Bahn is a fast urban train built for when Munich hosted the 1972 Olympic games. Since then, the city has spent billions of dollars expanding and maintaining the system. In 1990, $125.2m was spent on the underground alone, which in 1991 had a track length of 57km, with a further 15.2km under construction and 17.6km in the planning stages. Another $58.1m was used for the S-Bahn, operated by the state railways. Together, underground and S-Bahn moved 507m passengers in 1990, compared with 358m in 1973.

Time and motion

The target diagram indicates the distance that can be travelled over a certain time by car, train, bus or on foot. Travellers setting out from central London will still go farthest in an hour by car. However, due to the congestion caused by private vehicle transport, those passengers travelling by bus will only get a bare 2km farther than pedestrians.

DISTANCE TRAVELLED IN 1 HOUR

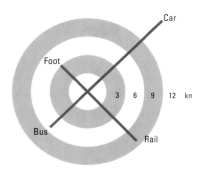

Connections: Air pollution 202–203 Environmental stress 208–211

VENICE BY WATER

Public transport in the old centre of Venice is largely waterborne; cars are banned. Water buses serve 12 regular lines all year round and four tourist lines, open only in the main season. Most lines operate between 5am and 10.45pm. Frequency varies between every ten minutes and every hour, depending on the route. *Vaporetti*, the slower boats, provide a more leisurely trip, but native Venetians scud to and from work in the faster and more hectic expresses, the *motoscafi*. The Linea Mista is a mixed ship and bus service, connecting the inner city with the Lido. There are also water taxis and, of course, 400 very expensive gondolas for hire.

ROAD TOLLS IN NORWAY

In January 1986, Bergen introduced a road pricing system, the first European city to do so, charging a toll of 77 cents for each motorist entering the city. Six toll stations were sufficient due to the city's position between fjord and mountains. The capital Oslo introduced a similar system in 1990 and access to the city was limited to 18 points with toll stations. Around 5% of the 240,000 cars passing through the toll stations (which have through lanes) are filmed by video cameras and their number plates automatically compared with those of season ticket holders. The fine for drivers without a ticket is higher than the cost of a monthly ticket.

Water works: the canals of Venice are much more than a glorious tourist attraction, they are the city's commercial arteries. All goods have to be transported by water and hundreds of small motor boats make their water-gate to water-gate deliveries daily. This extra transport cost contributes to Venice's high prices.

Taken for a ride

All capital cities and most big towns with a regular supply of fare-paying passengers (business or tourist class) support a fleet of licensed taxicabs. Competition is often good news for the passenger, but prices are not going down overall.

The chart (right) shows the initial meter charge ($) in 1985 and 1991. The figure at the top of each column is the cost ($) of each kilometre travelled. With the exception of Frankfurt, Berlin and Warsaw, the price of going by taxi has escalated alarmingly. Only in Athens and Budapest is it actually cheaper. London, Rome and Stockholm are the most expensive places to call a cab.

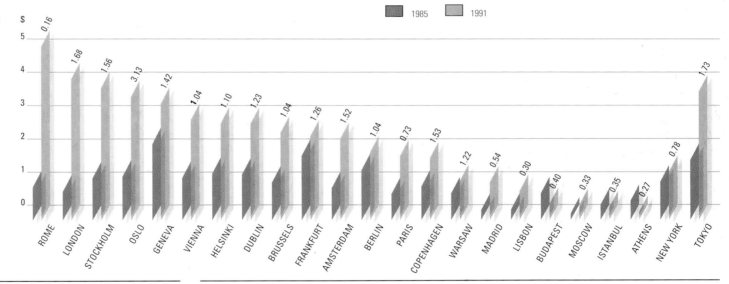

PRAGUE BY TRAM

The tramway is set to continue its important role in Prague's public transport. The system carried 417m passengers in 1990, compared with 428m using buses and 472m on the underground. The network for the 34 tram lines covers 130km (the underground covers 38km, bus routes 685km). The municipality is expanding the network further, although the increased use of the car has led to a minor drop in passenger figures. A new line in the southern part of the city is scheduled for completion in 1992. During peak hours, 699 tramcars run every 4–12 minutes.

NEW PASSENGERS: CITY POPULATION GROWTH (MILLION INHABITANTS)

CITY	1950	1960	1970	1980	1990	2000
ISTANBUL	1.1	1.7	2.8	4.4	6.7	9.5
MOSCOW	4.8	6.3	7.1	8.2	8.8	9.0
PARIS	5.4	7.2	8.3	8.5	8.5	8.6
LONDON	8.7	9.1	8.6	7.7	7.4	7.5
MADRID	1.6	2.2	3.4	4.3	5.2	5.9
MILAN	3.6	4.5	5.5	5.4	5.3	5.4

BARCELONA BY ROAD

Barcelona, the city of the 1992 Olympic Games, proves that roads built in the right places can still make a major contribution towards reducing pollution and inner-city congestion. The two new ringroads and a new high-speed thoroughfare under construction will transform the face of the inner city. There will be three new parks and improvements to streets were budgeted at Ptas95bn. Altogether Ptas399bn have been allocated to new buildings, communications and infrastructure.

After years of neglect, the Olympic games have done for Barcelona what the 1972 Olympics did for Munich – provided it with a good urban transport system and much improved roads. Barcelona is squeezed between mountains and the sea. Its main Olympic sites have been placed on the Montjuic mountain south of the city. The Olympic village on the other hand has been built in the old dock area to the north of the city, once an obsolete industrial wasteland. Public transport and new road links connect the two sites, with a coastal expressway as well as the two ringroads.

METRO LINES IN MAJOR CITIES

CITY	LENGTH km
LONDON	398
PARIS	192
COPENHAGEN	145
BERLIN	106
STOCKHOLM	103
MADRID	100
BIRMINGHAM	70
BARCELONA	59
NEWCASTLE	56
MILAN	49
OSLO	40
DUBLIN	37
ROTTERDAM	35
ATHENS	26
BRUSSELS	26
ROME	25
AMSTERDAM	23
LISBON	12

TELECOMMUNICATIONS

The development of an efficient network is now accepted as essential to economic growth. By the early 1990s more than six European jobs out of ten depended on information and communication technology. According to some estimates, by the year 2000 telecommunications alone will generate up to 7% of regional gross domestic product.

With this in mind, the EC telecommunications policy since the late 1980s has had three goals: the promotion of an advanced European telecommunications infrastructure, the stimulation of a homogeneous regionwide market for services and equipment, and the encouragement of greater competitiveness on the part of European industry and service providers. More recently, the EC has also become involved in efforts to expand telecommunications in eastern Europe, starting with a plan to establish local telephone companies in Poland.

Pursuing these aims has not been easy. Europe is a highly fragmented market with different, often incompatible, national regulations governing equipment standards and suppliers of services.

Despite the obstacles, however, progress has been made. The regional terminal equipment market – worth over $3.5bn annually – has been liberalised, and a start has been made on freeing the $94bn services market. A European telecommunications standards body has been established, and a number of regional research programmes set up, including the $64m RACE (Research and Development in Advanced Communication Technologies in Europe) project investigating ultra-high speed communication. Although somewhat delayed at the start, the GSM digital cellular telephone system, named after the committee which sponsored its standardisation, is becoming more wide-spread. With many countries licensing second operators, GSM has been a major factor in opening up national markets to competition; it has also been exported to Australia, China, Hong Kong and various countries in the Middle East.

The full benefits of the EC reforms will not be felt until the mid-1990s. In the meantime, the Community is casting its net wider, with future liberalisation of the satellite and mobile sectors, and a review of telephone tariffs, high on its agenda. Pricing is clearly an area suitable for reform since the cost of intra-European calls is much higher than national calls over longer distances, and charges for calls from the USA to Europe are a fraction of those in the opposite direction.

Geosynchronous satellites are essentially radio repeaters orbiting 36,000km above the earth in the equatorial plane. In 1965, the first commercial geosynchronous communications satellite weighed 38kg and provided 240 telephone channels. Five spacecraft generations later, Intelsat VI weighed nearly three tonnes and carried 120,000 telephone and three TV channels.

THE RISE OF THE SUPER-CARRIER

Until the early 1980s, telecommunication services and equipment in most European countries were provided on a monopoly basis, often by state-owned enterprises called Public Telecommunications Operators (PTOS). Since then, the sector has been opened up to competing companies.

This deregulation of government monopolies was partly prompted by the belief that consumers would get a better deal. It gathered impetus with the recognition that access to modern telecommunication facilities, such as ultra-high speed data links, videotelephony, digital voice and two-second facsimile transmission, was becoming critical in the quest for corporate competitiveness. "Communications-intensive" businesses (such as financial services and information technology) can, and do, relocate to countries with the most liberal telecommunications regulatory regimes.

Advances in digital technology and software created opportunities for service providers and made possible privately-operated voice and data networks. As competition has begun to eat into their highly profitable corporate customer business, the PTOS have responded with the launch of new services. One is ISDN (Integrated Services Digital Network) which provides subscribers with integrated high speed voice, text, data and video facilities. Others derive from the "intelligent network" concept in which public circuits are shared among many users but give the facilities associated with exclusiveness. One of these is the US-developed Centrex, in which parts of a local exchange are dedicated to act as office switchboards for nominated users. Centrex is designed to provide the benefits of a private network without the expense.

Another response to competition is for the PTOS to run private networks for their clients. For example, French Telecom runs the data network for London Regional Transport via its subsidiary Transpac Network Services (TNS). The forging of such "super-carrier" alliances to extend the geographic reach of such services, and provide one point of contact instead of many for the users of international networks, is a logical one. Companies in the super-carrier league include British Telecom, AT&T, France Telecom, Deutsche Telecom and NTT.

MOBILE COMMUNICATIONS

In 1995, the European cellular telephone market will reach an estimated $10.1bn; the three market leaders will be Germany with 20%, France 16% and the UK 19%. By the year 2000, 50% of all phones will be mobile.

MOBILES PER '000 SUBSCRIBERS, 1991

COUNTRY	RADIO-PAGER	CELLULAR PHONE
AUSTRIA	10.72	12.16
BELGIUM	12.05	4.56
DENMARK	9.4	31.48
FINLAND	8.16	52.73
FRANCE	4.58	5.9
GERMANY	3.91	4.74
HUNGARY	–	1.31
ICELAND	6.48	21.79
IRELAND	3.5	7.64
ITALY	1.69	7.53
LUXEMBOURG	8.18	7.53
NORWAY	19.43	52.09
NETHERLANDS	19.66	6.76
PORTUGAL	1.05	0.93
SPAIN	2.04	2.0
SWEDEN	15.15	64.08
SWITZERLAND	5.95	22.84
UK	11.69	20.87

JAPAN	6.33	7.0
USA	2.79	21.0

Although private mobile radio (PMR) will continue to satisfy many European business users, the big expansion of the mobile voice medium in the 1990s is expected to come from new technologies aimed at the public: Digital European Cordless Telecommunications system (DECT), the new digital cellular telephone system known as GSM and Personal Communication Networks (PCNS). DECT, which can accommodate high user numbers, is aimed at the office environment which generates most telephone call revenues.

GSM is a regional cellular system which allows the same mobile telephone to be used in all EC countries, and some farther afield. GSM is designed to have sound quality comparable to that of a compact disc system.

PCN is derived from GSM but uses much smaller radio cells. Handsets will be smaller, subscriber populations larger. It will be possible to tailor coverage areas to individual requirements and lower subscription charges.

Mobile technology is vital for telecommunications development in eastern Europe. New analogue cellular systems, which re-use scarce radio frequencies, are being developed in the Baltic states, Hungary, Poland and Russia. In eastern Germany, mobile technology is being used instead of cables to provide rapid connections.

MANAGED NETWORK SERVICES, 1990

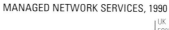
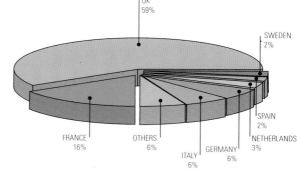

UK 59%
SWEDEN 2%
FRANCE 16%
OTHERS 6%
ITALY 6%
GERMANY 6%
SPAIN 2%
NETHERLANDS 3%

Connections: Computers and electronics 64–65 Labour and immigration 138–139 Education 230–231

Telephone numbers

The map gives an idea of the ratio of telephone lines to population across Europe.

Main telephone lines per 100 people (1990)

- 55
- 40-55
- 25-40
- under 25
- No available data

Connections

Numbers do not tell the whole story; each country has different priorities and their services have evolved to meet different needs.

Austria The PTT is the country's biggest employer.

Belgium Although it has a modest domestic telephone density, Belgium is rapidly expanding its international business, particularly in the USA and eastern Europe.

Bulgaria Telecommunications spending is set to grow from $190m in 1990 to $539m by 2000.

CIS The former USSR was estimated to have the world's third largest telephone system and the third fastest growing. Each republic can now run its own telecommunications system. Russia is investing $500m in a high-capacity fibre-optic cable system which will link the Baltic states to the Crimea in the south and Nakhodka on the Sea of Japan coast.

Czechoslovakia A contributory factor to low telecommunications density in eastern Europe was unrealistic service tariffs: in Czechoslovakia in 1991 a local telephone call cost 3 US cents.

Denmark The five Danish telephone companies merged into one in 1990.

Finland Finland has 50 local telephone companies as well as a national carrier.

Baltic states Link-ups with the Scandinavian countries is accelerating local telecommunications development. Sweden has taken control of Estonia's national and international systems.

France France is a pioneer of ISDN (a commercial service started in Brittany in 1987) and Minitel, the mass videotext system: the terminal population reached 5.6 million in 1990.

Germany The Telecom 2000 programme to upgrade telecommunications in the east of the country plans to spend $33.3bn to install 7.2m new telephone connections, 68,000 payphones, 360,000 fax connections, 50,000 packet data connections, 5m cable TV connections and 300,000 mobile connections.

Greece In the early 1990s 13 types of analogue system were in use in the public network and 10-year waiting lists for phones were reported in some areas.

Hungary The first cellular telephone service in eastern Europe began in Budapest in October 1990.

Iceland The national cellular system is heavily used by fishing boats at distances up to 100km offshore.

Ireland By 1991 Ireland had spent some $3.5bn digitising its network.

Italy Cellular telephone subscribers increased by some 300% in 1989/90.

Netherlands Dutch subscribers make eight international calls every second.

Norway Norwegian and other Scandinavian manufacturers dominate the market for intercom equipment.

Poland In 1991, Poland set up experimental local telephone companies in an effort to expand the telecommunications infrastructure in rural areas.

Portugal Telephone numbers in Lisbon and Oporto are predicted to increase by over 50% in the period to 1993.

Romania Around 800,000 people were waiting for telephones in 1991 and the potential demand was put as high as 5m.

Sweden The first European country to license three cellular phone operators.

Switzerland With more than seven machines per 1,000 inhabitants, Switzerland was top of the European fax league in the early 1990s.

UK At the forefront of research and commercialisation of mobile technologies such as cellular, telepoint, paging and Personal Communications Network.

Yugoslavia A contract for first public videotex service signed in early 1990.

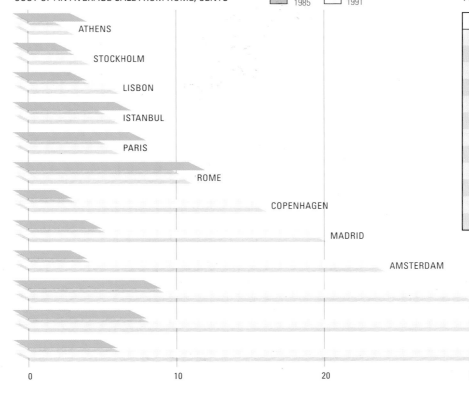

Dialling for dollars

Switzerland led in investment in telecommunications and even so earned more than twice its outlay. Throughout most of Europe, however, revenue was between three and five times investment.

INVESTMENT AND REVENUE IN $ PER HEAD

COUNTRY	REVENUE	INVESTMENT
AUSTRIA	273.9	111.7
BELGIUM	199.19	50.0
DENMARK	340.63	88.3
FINLAND	297.4	97.7
FRANCE	313.12	86.3
GERMANY	336.66	114.1
GREECE	89.87	18.3
ICELAND	350.01	50.1
IRELAND	228.42	54.6
ITALY	206.34	49.9
NORWAY	513.58	129.3
NETHERLANDS	243.76	49.5
PORTUGAL	81.81	25.9
SPAIN	112.73	36.5
SWEDEN	381.1	122.7
SWITZERLAND	568.8	208.7
TURKEY	20.93	16.5
UK	270.48	54.0

JAPAN	318.81	80.3
USA	468.84	87.2

Phoning from home

The cost of local calls in most of Europe has gone up on average by 250%. In many cases this reflects the growing popularity of mobile telephones which are more expensive to use than fixed instruments. Deregulated phone companies have to juggle customers' interests with shareholders' expectations and the need to invest in new equipment and technology.

COST OF AN AVERAGE CALL FROM HOME, CENTS □ 1985 □ 1991

ATHENS
STOCKHOLM
LISBON
ISTANBUL
PARIS
ROME
COPENHAGEN
MADRID
AMSTERDAM
LONDON
VIENNA
HELSINKI

0   10   20   30

Small change

As mobile phones and radio waves supersede cables and fixed phones, the number of public phones being installed each year has dwindled. Although only ranking number eight in the table below, Spain had some 42,000 pay phones in operation by the end of 1990.

PAYPHONES PER '000 PEOPLE

COUNTRY	TELEPHONES
BELGIUM	1.51
DENMARK	1.17
FRANCE	3.4
GERMANY	2.25
GREECE	0.6
ITALY	1.81
IRELAND	3.67
LUXEMBOURG	0.81
NETHERLANDS	0.47
PORTUGAL	0.67
SPAIN	1.08
UK	1.58

SPEAKING A LANGUAGE

Europeans speak some 120 different languages. Within the European Community alone, bilingual interpreters working in the nine main languages must cover 36 permutations; if Turkey, Norway or Sweden become members, that number rises to 66, and it will continue to rise as Europe expands eastward. In the 1980s, the EC more than doubled its expenditure on interpreting services for its administration.

For small, linguistically isolated countries, knowledge of foreign languages is essential to economic survival and anyone who wants to do business with America must speak English. At present, English and French are the official languages of the EC, and the addition of German is long overdue; but is a single lingua franca likely to emerge from these three? And what of Russian, said to be spoken as a second language by some 125 million people in the former Soviet Union and its satellites?

Linguistic imperialism

For 2,000 years Latin was the language of European civilisation, and for 200 it was French. The British empire spread English worldwide, but if Germany in this century had been content to fight European rather than world wars, the language of Mitteleuropa might well now be spoken from Antwerp to Baghdad. Instead, the vacuum at the heart of Europe in 1945 was "Coca-Colonised" by America. Besides being the language of the world's most powerful nation, English has the advantage that it lacks genders and complex inflections, and so in its basic form is relatively easy to learn.

The other allies were less successful in a linguistic respect. Since Napoleon, the French have defended their language at home and imposed it abroad with considerable panache, but after 1918 English joined French as a formal diplomatic language, and even de Gaulle could not halt infiltration by English and American culture. The 33 French-speaking countries of Africa, which account for most of the world's 190 million French speakers, use francophone summit conferences mainly to solicit French economic aid which might otherwise be diverted to eastern Europe. In Europe itself, especially the newly westernised Poland and Romania, the French language is fighting a prolonged and determined rearguard action against the advance of English.

Russian has fared worse than French: the more oppressive the Russification of eastern Europe, after 1956 and 1968, the more Hungarians and Czechs, Poles and Romanians resisted the language of a country which exported only its ideology. Passive knowledge of Russian, undoubtedly extensive, will perhaps find another outlet as trade with the new *sodruzhestvo* (friendship association or commonwealth) replaces the *soyuz* (union) and extinguishes unhappy memories of the cold war, and the Soviet vocabulary is purged of words with unpleasant associations in the same way that Nazi terms disappeared from German after 1945. Russian will continue to be spoken at the United Nations, and will remain the lingua franca for much of central Asia.

At the other end of Europe, increased trade with Latin America is likely to be accompanied by a growth of the number of Spanish and Portuguese speakers, already some 400 million worldwide – slightly more than speak English. Italian is useful in North Africa and of course in *trattorias* and opera houses everywhere. Within Europe itself, however, only German, with over 90 million native speakers (and 120 million worldwide who use it as first or second language), challenges the role of English.

The German influence

From the Baltic states through Germany and Austria to Slovenia and Croatia, the German language exerts an influence commensurate with German economic might. German was the language of the Austro-Hungarian empire – which lasted from 1697 until 1918, a longer and deeper contact than eastern Europe experienced under Soviet domination – and its enhanced significance today is the one context in which it is really possible to speak of an expansionist Greater Germany.

It is not just native-born Europeans who are learning German. A mobile and international labour force, willing to migrate to where the work is, means that many people no longer share a mother tongue with their country of residence. Germany, which has a very large Turkish and Moroccan *Gastarbeiter* population, tops this league.

However, throughout Europe, it is English as a Foreign Language that people are learning at every level, serviced by a flourishing EFL industry. It is the language of science and computing, and the anglophone culture of Hollywood, pop music and fast food retains its grip, especially on European youth. EC polls show the number of young people between 15 and 24 who speak English rose from 34% in 1987 to 42% in 1990, and that figure looks set to rise even higher.

¿Podría alguien decirme dónde está mi Guinness?

GUINNESS
La otra cerveza

Pure genius in any language: the distinctive logo, typography and colour makes this Spanish advertisement for Guinness instantly recognisable.

TALKING BUSINESS

The role of English as the language of computer hardware and software has reinforced its already wide acceptance as the leading international business and banking language. Japanese businessmen in Düsseldorf or Paris probably know English before they learn German or French, but English-speaking firms which rely too strongly on this, and on local agents/interpreters, lose goodwill and export opportunities to those who can approach trading partners directly in their own language. Increasingly, companies are buying in foreign language teaching, tailored to their export markets. French is slipping in importance, German and Spanish rising. Fluent German is an invaluable asset to anyone trading in eastern Europe.

Connections: The classical legacy 18–19 Towards unity 24–25 Media 82–83

Second languages

This map shows the proficiency of populations in major European languages other than their particular mother tongues.

- English: strong/weak
- French: strong/weak
- German: strong/weak
- Russian
- No available data

A word in your ear...

Education, inclination, geography and commercial need all play a part in forming the pattern of languages spoken across Europe.

Belgium Split between French-speaking Walloonia, Flemish/Dutch-speaking Flanders and German-speakers along its eastern border; they are often better linguists than the diplomats in Brussels.

Czechoslovakia The political tension reflected linguistically: Czechs natural German speakers, Slovaks less so.

Denmark With Norway and Sweden, one linguistic area with variations, also close affinities with German.

Finland Besides excellent English and German, Swedish and Russian extensively spoken.

France Some two million German-speakers, of which three-quarters are in Alsace and eastern Lorraine. Among French 15- to 24-year-olds, more than half allegedly speak English.

Germany Appreciate foreigners' attempts at speaking their language, but equally want to impress with their own grasp of other languages, particularly English; 62% of young Germans speak English. French speakers mainly in Saarland. Inhabitants of the erstwhile GDR were obliged to learn Russian.

Greece Tourist menus written in English and German. Greek *Gastarbeiter* in Germany are also spreading the language southward.

Hungary Budapest–Prague–Vienna: *Hier spricht man deutsch*. Burgeoning trade links with the West through Austria mean Hungarians use German (though still with the not so *léger accent hongrois* of the mustachioed, flamboyantly uniformed Hungarian officers in Viennese operetta). English on the increase here too – the Hungarians are good linguists.

Italy In south Tirol more German than Italian is spoken but outside the northern industrial belt patchy knowledge of language of main trading partner. The Italian language which imposed a sense of national identity after unification again locally challenged by Fruilano, Slovene, Ladino, Occitano, Provencal, Sard, Albanian, Catalan, Greek, etc. English overshadows French and German in tourism.

Netherlands First prize for languages. Excellent English and good French, also 7–9 million German speakers. In industry, Spanish is increasingly in demand.

Poland The French connection weakening as trade with the West through Germany grows. Not thought of as particularly gifted linguists, but increased use of German inevitable.

Portugal Spanish naturally (if somewhat reluctantly) first foreign language, but surprisingly good French, and keen students of English.

Romania Native German-speakers in Transylvania; most French-orientated of East European countries, but English now overtaking French among the young.

Switzerland The German-speakers look down on the French, the French on the Italians, and all of them on outsiders, especially from the south. Money understood everywhere.

Turkey Fast catching up with Greeks' proficiency in English as tourism expands and the Common Market beckons. In addition, now some one and a half million Turkish *Gastarbeiter* in Germany (compared with half a million Italians, half a million Yugoslavs, a quarter of a million Greeks – all of whose children are increasingly bilingual). German railway stations at weekends provide evidence that Turkey itself must now have many more German-speakers than the 100,000 of a decade ago (when the German government estimated there were perhaps three times that number in Yugoslavia, and six times as many in Italy and Greece).

Yugoslavia English and German the main tourist languages, Slovenia and Croatia also close linguistic links with Mitteleuropa (and best integrated *Gastarbeiter*).

UK Must try harder. Signs in language labs, though not in government, that the message is being learnt; even so, only one in three 15- to 24-year-olds claim to speak French and only 8% of young Britons speak any German.

SPREADING THE WORD

In spite of the purists of the Académie Française, for whom *un pipeline* is *un oléoduc*, the language of American culture – from nylons and Walt Disney to Levi jeans and McDonalds – has permeated France as thoroughly as the rest of Europe. Word exportation has its more confusing side, however. Hesitate before ordering a round of *Drinks* (cocktails) in a German *Bar* or a French *pub*, or trying to feed the kids in a café. German logic has produced a *Pullunder* as the short-sleeved version of a pullover; French basketball players wear *baskets* on their feet, babies wear a *brassière* to keep them warm, men wear a *veste* over their *chemise*, and only monks wear *frocs*.

What Proust observed of the French – that they call everything vaguely British by a name that it does not have in England – is also true of most of their neighbours. *Chips* are not chips but crisps, though the Belgians are Europe's real *hommes frites*. In some recent *joint ventures*, the east Germans have been providing the unfortunate pig for *Ham'n eggs*. Keep your *gusto* for the food and drink – at a *Kostprobe*, perhaps, or a *dégustation* or *Degustation* – but don't drink any *Gift* (poison). And why is a *Schellfisch* a haddock and *Krabben* prawns? Or an *Engländer* a monkey wrench? Or a rare steak *englisch*? Europeans can make up their own Esperanto in infinite individual permutations.

On film

Cinéastes may prefer French films, but it is the Hollywood product – such as the *Indiana Jones* trilogy (left) – that dominates popular cineculture. Almost 60% of western European imported films come from the USA.

% OF FILMS IMPORTED FROM USA

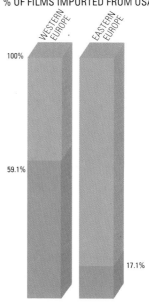

WESTERN EUROPE — 100% — 59.1%
EASTERN EUROPE — 17.1%

SECTION 3

BUSINESS

Business and trade are the life-blood of any modern economy. Europe is the world's biggest trading bloc. The countries of the European Community alone account for more than 40% of world trade, and the single market programme has proved a remarkable success story even though the EC is still quite some way from achieving a barrier-free Europe. So successful has the project been that members of both the European Free Trade Association (EFTA) and the former Comecon eastern bloc trading association want to be part of it. In 1991, EFTA and the EC agreed to create a free-trade zone of 380m people to be known as the European Economic Area, and in the same year three eastern European countries – Czechoslovakia, Hungary and Poland – signed association agreements with the EC.

This chapter begins with an overview of the fundamentals of business in Europe. It looks at how much Europe trades with the rest of the world and how European countries are increasingly trading with each other. It examines industrial competitiveness and the new enthusiasm for privatisation. The effects of the single market are covered in detail with particular emphasis on how cross-border mergers and acquisitions and foreign investment are changing the face of European business. Which countries are being most open? Where are the Japanese investing in order to get a foothold in what some outsiders fear may become "fortress Europe"? Eastern Europe's problems are reviewed: how the former communist countries are going about transforming their business environment and the countries that are investing in this huge potential market.

After the overview sections, the focus moves to individual sectors from cars to chemicals and computers, revealing how Europe is good at some business but not others.

TRADE

Europe is one of the world's leading trading regions, occupying a key position in the global economy alongside America and East Asia. The European Community's trading relationship with America is still its most important, with bilateral trade flows totalling $195.5bn in 1990. Although the EC's bilateral trade with Japan grew considerably throughout the 1980s, it is still less than half that between the EC and the United States.

Another way of measuring the Community's trading muscle is to compare the size of its total exports and how much it earns from them. In 1990, EC exports to third countries accounted for about one-fifth of total world exports, compared with 15% for America and just 9% for Japan. And in 1990, the EC earned $535bn from its overall exports, compared with $393bn for America and $287bn for Japan. Such a performance is explained by the fact the Community includes Germany, the world's biggest exporter, and countries like Britain and Holland which have been involved in international trade for centuries.

The members of EFTA also form an important trading group. Nations like Switzerland and Sweden have long been major exporters, partly because they have very small domestic markets. Sweden boasts international manufacturing firms like the car and truck maker Volvo, and consumer goods company Electrolux, while Switzerland has chemicals and pharmaceuticals giants like Ciba-Geigy and Sandoz. In a classic example of EFTA cooperation, Asea Brown Boveri, a Swedish-Swiss group, has become a powerful player in Europe's engineering industry.

The world's largest trading club

Agreements negotiated by the EC and EFTA are set to create the world's biggest free-trade grouping known as the European Economic Area, or EEA. This area, including some 380m consumers, will account for nearly half of total world trade. Eastern European countries like Hungary, Czechoslovakia and Poland hope they will eventually be able to join this trading club, too. For now, though, they must be content with agreements with the EC which create a free-trade zone for industrial goods and

Six years after joining the EC, Spain celebrated its emergence as one of the Community's most dynamic economies by hosting the 1992 Expo in Seville (below) as well as the Olympic Games in Barcelona. The EC now accounts for about 70% of Spain's exports and 60% of its imports.

Japanese sales drive

While the EC's trade balance with America went from deficit to surplus and then back to deficit again in the 1980s, its balance with Japan stayed firmly in the red. This deficit with Japan grew substantially after 1985 as the Community began to open up its markets to foreign competition. This led, in turn, to a big increase in EC imports of video recorders and hi-fis, two products in which Japanese manufacturers excel.

It also led to a big increase in imports of Japanese cars. So to give European car makers a chance to adapt, the EC has struck a deal with the Japanese limiting imports to the Community between 1993 and 1999. After this period all restrictions on Japanese cars will be lifted. Even if this gentlemen's agreement holds, and even though Japan is easing the barriers that in practice limit entry to its market, the EC's trade deficit with Japan is likely to get worse before it gets better.

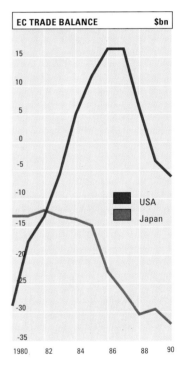

EC TRADE BALANCE $bn

USA
Japan

1980 82 84 86 88 90

Trade flow

The map shows the value in $bn of the goods Japan, America and the European Community exported to each other in 1990. The figures reveal how exports between the USA and the EC almost net off, and how formidable a trade competitor Japan is, exporting nearly twice as much as it imports from both the EC and the USA.

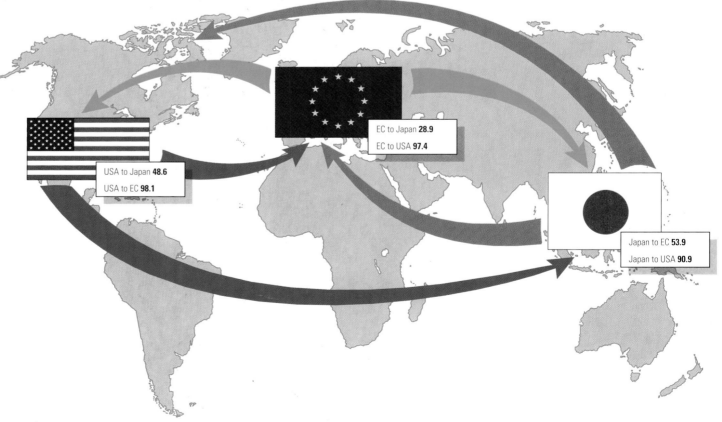

USA to Japan **48.6**
USA to EC **98.1**

EC to Japan **28.9**
EC to USA **97.4**

Japan to EC **53.9**
Japan to USA **90.9**

Connections: Competition in industry 50–51   A wider Europe 52–53   The European effect 146–147   Europe and America 148–151   Europe and Asia 160–165

envisage a substantial liberalisation of agricultural trade between western and eastern Europe.

Thanks to such agreements, the EC could soon be at the core of one of the most dynamic areas of the world economy. But that does not necessarily mean Europe's trade performance will improve dramatically. The problem is that while the region is still strong in sectors like chemicals, pharmaceuticals and mechanical engineering, it is falling behind in fast-growing, high-technology industries like computing. This is reflected in the Community's trade balance. After showing a surplus in 1986, it has deteriorated rapidly, registering a deficit of 34.5bn ecus in 1990. Even the EC's long-standing surplus in services has declined.

The trade deficit has grown partly because of increased demand for imports created by deregulation in Europe. But the productivity gap between European companies on the one hand, and Japanese and American ones on the other, is also to blame. Though corporate profits soared in the late 1980s, European companies had to concede big wage increases. Rising costs, and the difficulties of operating in a market with 12 sets of national regulations, have handicapped European industry.

However, rather than accepting that they are inefficient, some European businesses blame their problems on unfair foreign competition – especially from Japan. They note that, while the EC's trade with America is now roughly balanced, the value of EC imports from Japan is still more than twice that of its exports to the Japanese. To balance this, they want the Community to force Japan to open its domestic market to EC imports, and to restrict the flow of Japanese cars and electronic goods to the Community. This will lead to further trade friction.

The liberalisation of economies in eastern Europe could also cause problems. As members of Comecon, an eastern bloc trading system, eastern states used to sell industrial and agricultural products to the former Soviet Union in return for oil products and raw materials. But since Comecon began to crumble, then finally collapsed in 1991, eastern states have been looking elsewhere for markets. Hence their exports to major western industrialised countries increased by almost a third in 1989–91. These will grow even faster throughout the 1990s.

The West's new competitors

Much has been made of the threat that these eastern European exports pose to western European companies in, say, the steel or textile industries. The Polish government, for example, has estimated its association deal with the EC will lead to a 15–20% increase in its exports of industrial goods to the Community. Yet though some western firms will suffer as competition from low-cost eastern European producers increases, the threat should not be exaggerated. In 1990, about 1% of EC imports came from Czechoslovakia, Hungary and Poland. Their share in sensitive sectors such as steel was even smaller.

A more optimistic view suggests that eastern Europe offers western European firms vast opportunities. The same companies that moan about price-cutting imports from the East could themselves benefit in the 1990s from a new supply of cheap labour, and from a market containing 115m frustrated consumers. But before they go East, these and other firms will want to finish the restructuring they have started at home. For only by redrawing the industrial map of western Europe in the 1990s can European companies close the gap that still exists between them and more efficient American and Asian rivals.

THE COMMUNITY EFFECT

EC states are trading more, especially with each other as a consequence of the single market which has made it easier to sell across their national borders. An average of 61% of the trade of EC member states was with other EC countries in 1985–89, compared with an average of 51% in 1960–67. In comparison, intra-regional trade accounted for about a third of the total trade of East Asia and North America respectively in 1985–89. And in 1990, trade between EFTA countries accounted for just 13% of that group's total trade.

Not surprisingly, the intra-European trade shares of the EC's original six members (Belgium, France, Italy, Luxembourg, the Netherlands and West Germany) are higher than those of latecomers but the gap has narrowed since the early 1970s. While intra-EC trade grows, trade between countries in eastern Europe and the former Soviet Union is shrinking, especially since the Soviets moved transactions with their former partners in Comecon on to hard-currency terms. They are also trading less with one another and exporting more to western countries.

IMPORTS PLUS EXPORTS AS % GDP, 1960–67

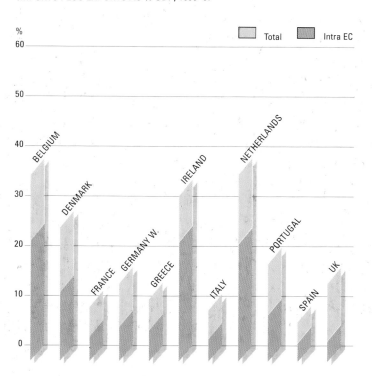

IMPORTS PLUS EXPORTS AS % GDP, 1985–89

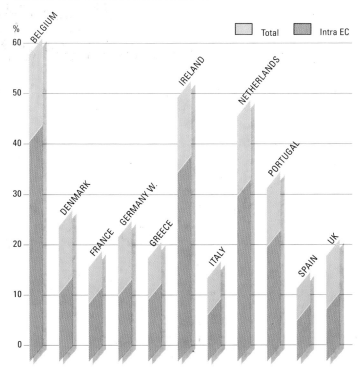

Cultivating services

The growing importance of service industries such as transport, travel, banking and insurance to many European economies is clear from this chart. Indeed, until 1989, France was the world's biggest exporter of services, though America has since overtaken it. While industry still accounts for a large proportion of European countries' national income, the agricultural sector has declined in importance. Only Greece still depends on agriculture for more than one-tenth of its GDP.

The structure of eastern European economies had been dictated by the Comecon system which had revolved around the exchange of oil products and raw materials from the former Soviet Union for industrial, agricultural and consumer goods from satellite states. Of the three biggest satellites, Czechoslovakia is more dependent on industry than Hungary and Poland, which both have large agricultural sectors.

CONTRIBUTION TO GDP, %

COUNTRY		1989
AUSTRIA	60.2	3.1
BELGIUM	67.2[1]	2.0
DENMARK	71.9	4.1
FINLAND	63.2	5.6
FRANCE	67.4	3.5
GERMANY W.	58.9	1.6
GREECE	60.6	15.2
ICELAND	65.2[1]	9.9
IRELAND	58.0	9.7
ITALY	63.0	3.5
LUXEMBOURG	61.0	2.1
NETHERLANDS	64.7	4.4
NORWAY	61.2	2.8
PORTUGAL	54.7[2]	7.4
SPAIN	55.6[1]	5.3[1]
SWEDEN	66.7	2.9
SWITZERLAND	60.9[3]	3.6[3]
UK	69.4	1.3

☐ Services ☐ Agriculture

1 1988 2 1986 3 1985

Exporting to the world

The Community's share of world exports accounts for about two-fifths of the total. That puts it ahead of both America and Japan. It also explains why Europe stands to lose most if the world divides up into protectionist trading regions.

EC SHARE OF WORLD EXPORTS

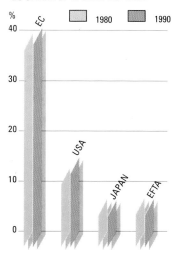

COMPETITION IN INDUSTRY

Japan's dominance in robotics was swift and complete. By 1986 more robots had been installed in Japan than in all other countries combined. Europe has frequently failed to compete effectively in high-technology.

In the first industrial revolution more than 150 years ago, Europe started early and came out ahead. But in the second half of this century, it has grown used to following the pack. The biggest gap between the European firms and their more efficient American and Japanese rivals is in fast-growing, high-technology sectors.

A divided European market is partly to blame. This has prevented European companies from spreading their spending on research and development, and has forced them to spend a fortune tailoring their products to meet different national standards. Take the telecommunications industry. To meet various national norms for a given product, European telecoms manufacturers have been producing on average three times more variants than their American rivals, and four times more than Japanese ones.

In American footsteps

American and Japanese companies have been quicker to develop strategies to overcome these problems than European ones. Ford is a good example. It has adopted a pan-European approach to car-making since 1968, when Henry Ford II established Ford of Europe to coordinate sales and manufacturing. This has allowed it to benefit from decentralisation while at the same time reaping the rewards of European integration. IBM and other American companies were also quick to adopt pan-European strategies, and Japanese firms like Sony and Nissan have subsequently copied them .

European companies, on the other hand, found it hard to think of Europe as one. Governments are partly to blame. By nurturing nationalised companies, they damaged Europe's competitiveness. The principal objective of these firms, which were often monopolies, was not to make a profit but to keep domestic unemployment low. Government subsidies also helped keep inefficient firms in business. EFTA countries were better in this respect than EC ones. Their subsidies to manufacturing average only 2% of manufacturing output compared with 6% in the Community.

Convinced state firms were too small to compete in key sectors like electronics and aerospace, politicians merged them together in the 1970s to create "national champions". Partly because of this merger activity, the number of EC firms in the list of the world's top 100 companies ranked by turnover rose from 31 in 1983 to 37 in 1989. Over the same period, the number of Japanese companies in the list rose from 9 to 17, while the number of American ones fell from 46 to 35. The biggest firms of the Community are concentrated in Britain, Germany and France.

Size, however, has not helped Europe to turn the competitive tide. Exactly the opposite. Huge and hugely inefficient European firms have steadily lost ground to Japanese and American competitors in businesses like cars, computing, consumer electronics and semiconductors. The only industries in which European companies are still clearly world leaders are those like chemicals and pharmaceuticals which have long been open to international competition.

The future viewed from East and West

Western Europe's decline is not irreversible. The region's steelmakers, who looked doomed in the 1970s, turned themselves around once, if currently relapsing. And European companies have been winning business from their competitors in the food, paper and packaging industries. The region has also become a major exporter of financial, software and other services. But much more remains to be done if European firms are to catch up with their competitors in leading-edge businesses.

If the situation in western Europe looks bad, the one in eastern Europe is infinitely worse. Many firms there are "value subtractors" – that is, at world prices the value of the resources they consume is worth more than what they produce. Though a few companies in the East have been making what they claim is a profit, that is partly because they are selling inventories hoarded while under communist rule.

In eastern Europe, only a handful of the existing companies will have a long-term future. Those in Poland, Hungary and Czechoslovakia have the best prospects. So far, Hungary has been the quickest of this trio to privatise firms, and to attract foreign investment. However, Poland and Czechoslovakia are likely to catch up fast. Their brightest prospects are in labour-intensive industries like textiles where their low wage costs are a big competitive advantage.

BIG BUSINESS

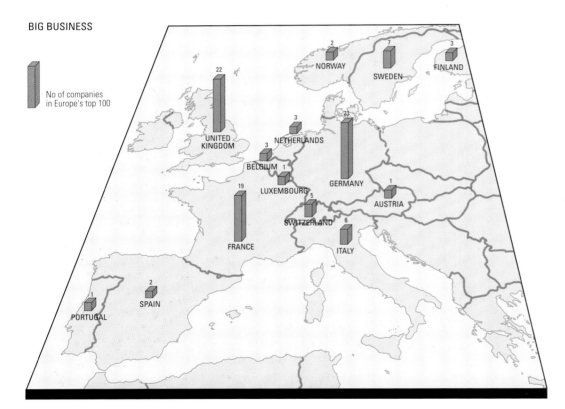

No of companies in Europe's top 100

NORWAY 2
SWEDEN 7
FINLAND 3
UNITED KINGDOM 22
NETHERLANDS 3
BELGIUM 3
GERMANY 23
LUXEMBOURG 1
AUSTRIA 1
FRANCE 19
SWITZERLAND 5
ITALY 6
PORTUGAL 1
SPAIN 2

NEW RIVALS IN OLD MARKETS

Which European industries are likely to be leaders in the 1990s, and which will be laggards? Among the leaders will be those industries like telecommunications which already have a foothold in fast-growing Asian economies, and which will benefit from the deregulation of the European Community's public procurement markets. Providing it makes the transition from communism to capitalism successfully, eastern Europe could also give a boost to capital-goods producers and high-technology industries.

At the other end of the scale, EC companies in the minerals and metals industry, as well as those in textiles and clothing, face a difficult decade. Not only will they have to contend with growing competition from Asian rivals, but they will face a new threat from eastern European firms moving gradually up market to produce high-quality goods and services. Despite sharp increases in productivity, western European producers will be unable to match their rivals' low prices.

FEWER JOB PROSPECTS

Although the total number of jobs in the European Community increased by more than 1% per year between 1985 and 1989, the number of redundancies in Europe has risen sharply since then. This is partly the result of slower economic growth worldwide. But it is also due to corporate restructuring in Europe in preparation for when the single market comes into effect .

A number of EC industries cut jobs in the late 1980s. Among them were the railway equipment and shipbuilding industries, which both lost business to low-cost Asian competitors. Thousands of jobs have been axed in the car and electronics industries too. However, the Community is betting that fast-growing service industries such as tourism and finance will absorb many of the workers laid off in sluggish sectors. It estimated that the level of increase in overall employment in the EC should be just under 1% in 1992, compared with an average annual rate of 1.7% since 1988.

So far, Europe's unions have provided little opposition to restructuring, largely because high unemployment and falling membership has sapped their strength. Even in western Germany, where powerful trade unions have long protected their members' interests, employers in the car, steel and chemicals industries are planning big job cuts.

The only countries where unions may block change are Scandinavian ones where some 90% of the non-agricultural workforce is unionised. That may make it harder for Swedish, Norwegian and Danish companies to adjust to the rigours of a single market.

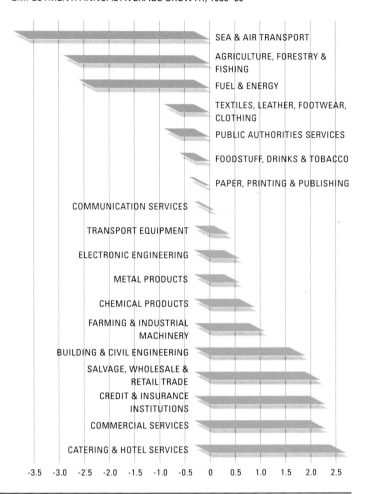

EMPLOYMENT: ANNUAL AVERAGE GROWTH, 1985–89

As the chart shows, air and sea transport is the sector which had the highest negative growth rate in employment in the EC over the second half of the 1980s. The biggest growth was in service industries such as finance, hotels and catering.

THE CURE FOR EUROSCLEROSIS

For most of the 1980s, levels of industrial investment in Europe were below those in Japan and America. At the same time, the labour costs of European companies rose faster than those of Japanese and American rivals. These were the symptoms of ``Eurosclerosis'', a nasty disease which sapped Europe's competitiveness in fast-growing industries such as electronics and computing.

Investment levels have risen in most of Europe since 1985 when the EC launched its single market programme, though the recession which began in 1989–90 has dragged them down again. The capital investment figures for southern European countries such as Spain show that they made a big effort to modernise their industry by investing heavily in new plant and

industrial machinery anticipating an increase in demand.

On the other hand, the south has in general found it hard to control rising unit labour costs. In part, this reflects a catch-up phase as wages in southern European countries move closer towards the European average – a problem that Germany experienced after reunification with workers in the eastern half of the country. But it is also a sign that high unemployment has yet to tame exorbitant wage claims.

Most other European countries also have a long way to go to match Japanese and American performance. Getting there will require some unpopular changes in working practices. After all, European workers are the ones who, on average, still work the least hours, have the longest holidays and get the biggest perks from their employers.

Patent advantage

Although the number of patent applications in Europe and America has hardly risen since the 1970s, those in Japan have tripled. Moreover, whereas 90% of applications in Japan are made by Japanese companies, in most European countries foreign firms account for most patent requests. Within Europe, there is a clear north-south technological divide. Spain, Portugal and Greece had a total of 30 patent applications per 100,000 inhabitants between them in 1988, compared with 296 for Sweden and 172 for Denmark. Switzerland clocked up an impressive 486 patents, outshining even Japan, but over 90% of these were from inventive foreigners.

GROWTH OF PRIVATE NON-RESIDENTIAL CAPITAL %

COUNTRY	1985	1986	1987	1988	1989	1990
AUSTRIA	8.6	3.7	5.7	7.3	7.9	5.8
BELGIUM	2.4	6.5	7.1	14.9	17.3	9.8
DENMARK	18.9	18.8	-5.5	-7.6	2.7	2.7
FINLAND	5.7	2.9	6.6	11.0	15.5	-6.8
FRANCE	4.4	6.6	6.0	10.2	8.1	5.0
GERMANY	5.5	4.6	4.0	5.9	8.5	10.5
GREECE	7.2	-11.4	-4.1	12.4	13.6	6.4
IRELAND	-12.4	-2.3	-0.6	14.7	20.2	10.4
ITALY	2.3	3.2	10.3	11.6	5.0	3.7
NETHERLANDS	13.0	11.8	1.4	7.4	6.7	8.7
NORWAY	-19.4	29.5	-5.4	1.9	-2.5	-31.7
SPAIN	0.5	14.2	21.0	14.1	15.6	3.9
SWEDEN	12.3	2.5	7.4	4.1	12.4	-3.3
SWITZERLAND	9.0	12.8	10.4	8.2	6.3	2.7
UK	12.0	0.9	16.9	17.7	8.1	-0.7

JAPAN	12.1	4.4	6.7	14.8	15.6	13.9
USA	6.7	-3.3	2.6	8.3	3.9	1.8

CHANGE IN UNIT LABOUR COSTS %

COUNTRY	1988	1989	1990	1991	1992	1993
AUSTRIA	-0.9	1.5	2.1	6.8	3.8	3.0
BELGIUM	-1.4	1.9	2.9	3.2	2.7	2.3
DENMARK	0.2	-0.2	-0.2	0.1	0.6	1.0
FINLAND	3.8	5.1	9.3	5.3	-6.8	-1.3
FRANCE	0.9	2.0	3.2	3.4	1.8	1.6
GERMANY	0.1	0.4	2.3	4.3	4.8	3.5
GREECE	17.7	12.3	21.3	13.6	11.2	8.3
IRELAND	2.9	-1.8	2.8	3.7	2.5	2.0
ITALY	4.2	5.8	7.6	8.3	5.8	4.9
NETHERLANDS	0.5	-2.0	2.7	3.6	2.2	3.2
PORTUGAL	7.1	8.9	12.2	16.0	12.1	10.9
SPAIN	3.1	4.6	6.2	5.7	4.9	4.0
SWEDEN	7.1	9.6	10.8	6.8	2.9	2.7
SWITZERLAND	2.6	2.8	7.2	7.3	4.0	2.5
UK	7.4	9.6	11.1	7.1	2.2	2.5

JAPAN	-1.3	1.0	0.5	1.1	2.4	0.9
USA	3.5	2.9	4.2	3.8	3.1	2.6

PATENT APPLICATIONS PER 100,000

COUNTRY		PATENTS
AUSTRIA	133	95.3
BELGIUM	69	97.5
DENMARK	172	89.2
FINLAND	176	75.2
FRANCE	118	81.2
GERMANY	261	63.6
GREECE	16	97.3
IRELAND	47	81.4
NETHERLANDS	156	93.6
PORTUGAL	2	97.8
SPAIN	12	93.0
SWEDEN	296	93.2
SWITZERLAND	486	92.3
UK	133	75.2

JAPAN	334	10.6
USA	112	48.8

Total		% from abroad

A WIDER EUROPE

Wool, paper and related products account for around 40% of Finland's export earnings. As trade with the former Soviet Union has declined steadily since 1985, some two-thirds of Finland's trade is now with EC and EFTA countries.

In the 1990s, the frontier-free trading zone under construction in the European Community is likely to expand both to the north and to the east. The members of the European Free Trade Association (EFTA) – Austria, Finland, Iceland, Norway, Sweden, Switzerland and tiny Liechtenstein – have already agreed to set up a European Economic Area (EEA) together with the 12 members of the EC. Once it is established, the EEA will be the biggest free-trade area in the world, stretching from the Arctic in the north to the Mediterranean in the south and containing 380m consumers.

The existing links between the two regions of Europe are already very close. They are big trading partners, and many EFTA companies have invested heavily in the EC. In the past few years as much as two-thirds of EFTA's foreign direct investment has gone into the Community, and EFTA companies now employ some 700,000 workers there.

The EEA will give an added boost to these firms by allowing them to compete on equal terms with EC firms for major public-sector contracts, which are being opened to competition. This is particularly important for companies such as Ericsson, the Swedish telecoms giant, and Asea Brown Boveri, a Swedish-Swiss electrical-engineering group, which sell a big slice of their output to public utilities.

EFTA countries are not the only ones lining up to join the EC's club. Poland, Hungary and Czechoslovakia have all signed association accords with the Community. These should eventually lead to freer trade between themselves and western Europe. Under the terms of the agreements, the EC will slowly reduce barriers to imports from eastern Europe of steel, textiles and chemicals over the next ten years. Critics of the deal point out that these are the industries in which the three countries are most competitive, and call for the barriers to be lifted faster. But western European producers say they need time to adjust to a flood of imports from the East.

If western Europe does not provide new markets quickly for eastern European exporters, the former communist countries' economic problems could get worse. On some estimates, output in most eastern European states dropped by 10–20% in 1991, largely because of the collapse of the Comecon trading system. Bulgaria, which relied on the Comecon for over 80% of its trade, has been hardest hit. In spite of these problems, western European businessmen see plenty of eastern promise. After all, the big gap between living standards in the East and those in the West suggests that there is a vast potential market for consumer and other goods in the former communist states.

Some western European companies have already taken the plunge, western car makers have been leading

Eastern promise

The map gives an indication of living standards and the degree of economic sophistication across Europe by showing, where figures are available, the level of car and telephone ownership. It reveals a big potential market in eastern Europe.

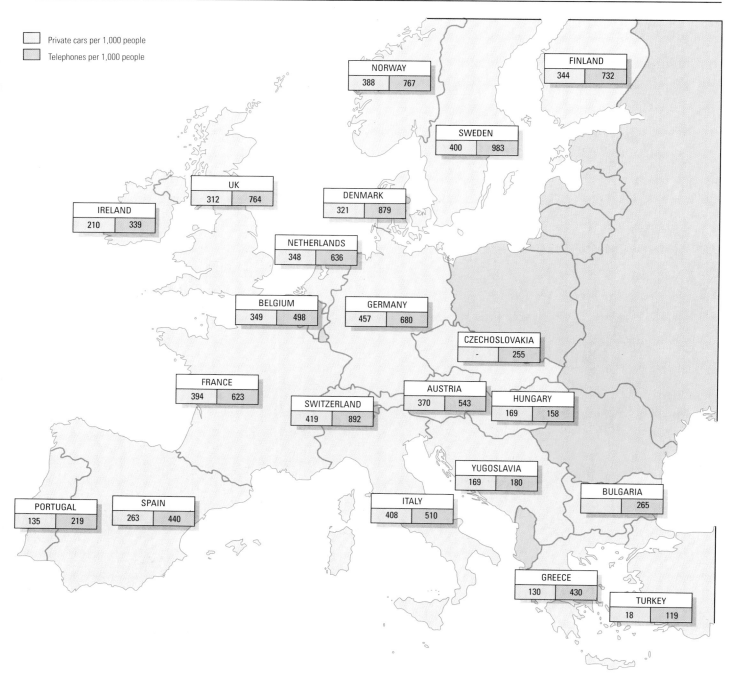

Private cars per 1,000 people
Telephones per 1,000 people

	Cars	Telephones
NORWAY	388	767
FINLAND	344	732
SWEDEN	400	983
UK	312	764
DENMARK	321	879
IRELAND	210	339
NETHERLANDS	348	636
BELGIUM	349	498
GERMANY	457	680
CZECHOSLOVAKIA	-	255
FRANCE	394	623
SWITZERLAND	419	892
AUSTRIA	370	543
HUNGARY	169	158
YUGOSLAVIA	169	180
ITALY	408	510
BULGARIA		265
PORTUGAL	135	219
SPAIN	263	440
GREECE	130	430
TURKEY	18	119

Connections: Trade 48–49   Single market 56–59, 96–97   Rebuilding democracies 120–121

the way. Germany's Volkswagen has taken a 70% stake in Skoda, a Czech car company, and Italy's Fiat has invested heavily in Poland, where it has taken a majority stake in FSM. Engineering companies have also been looking for partners. Germany's Siemens has signed a wide-ranging cooperation agreement with Skoda Pilsen, Czechoslovakia's nuclear and conventional engineering outfit, and America's General Electric has bought Tungsram, a Hungarian lighting company.

In spite of this, foreign direct investment in eastern Europe totalled just $3bn in 1991, a tiny amount in comparison with the region's needs. About half of this went to Hungary, which has been the quickest country to privatise state assets and dismantle price controls. Poland and Czechoslovakia have also been learning the rules of capitalism fast, and could soon catch up.

Businessmen will continue to be drawn to these countries, even though they have far to go before the recognisable structure of a market economy is in place. On present trends, the private sector (including the black, or unofficial, economy) could account for half of Hungary's and Czechoslovakia's GNP by the end of 1992, compared with less than one-fifth in 1989. Bulgaria and Romania, on the other hand, still have much to do to create the critical mass of infrastructure, incentive and entrepreneurial .spirit necessary for a market economy.

EC EXPORTS TO EASTERN EUROPE

Germany has traditionally held a dominant position among western European countries in regard to trade with eastern Europe. As well as buying up a large number of eastern German companies, western German business leaders have also been on a shopping spree in Czechoslovakia. However, a united Germany still has plenty of scope to expand its trade with the East. Before the depression of the 1930s, 17% of Germany's exports went to eastern Europe and the Soviet Union; in 1989, it was no more than 4%.

Other western European countries should benefit from the collapse of communism in the East too. The chart below shows that France and Belgium are well placed to export chemicals to to eastern Europe, while Britain should do well exporting consumer goods. As for Italian firms, they should benefit from rising demand in the East for capital goods. Italian businessmen, who are used to dealing with a corrupt and bureaucratic regime at home, have long been adept at dealing with eastern European companies.

EC COUNTRIES' SPECIALISATION IN EXPORTING TO EASTERN EUROPE*, 1989

Note: for each product group the share of the EC as a whole is represnted by 100. Hence energy sources' share in Denmark's exports is 5.22 times its share in total EC exports to Eastern Europe.

* Excluding Eastern Germany

	BELGIUM¹	DENMARK	FRANCE	GERMANY	ITALY	NETHERLANDS	UK	REST
FOODSTUFFS	43	250	175	77	21	296	98	229
DRINK & TOBACCO	44	241	177	66	58	108	208	223
RAW MATERIALS	176	58	160	49	81	226	131	425
ENERGY SOURCES	314	522	110	44	60	247	53	344
VEGETABLE OILS & FATS	413	9	76	57	83	323	39	259
CHEMICALS	153	29	178	83	79	127	117	76
OTHER PRE-PRODUCTS	175	32	76	109	114	38	65	126
INVESTMENT GOODS	49	128	55	115	130	55	100	50
CONSUMER GOODS	72	116	85	103	97	81	148	92
OTHER	61	59	19	71	39	548	288	316
1 Including Luxembourg								

JOINT VENTURES

For western businessmen who are reluctant to go it alone in eastern Europe, a joint venture might be the best solution. Hungarian companies seem to be the most willing partners. According to PlanEcon, a Washington-based research outfit, there were 4,400 joint ventures established in Hungary in 1990, compared with nearly 2,800 in Poland, and about 1,500 each in Czechoslovakia and Romania. However, many of these are tiny, or exist only on paper. Bulgaria is still a wallflower. It reported just 140 joint ventures in the same year.

The snag is that East European countries are still far from being functioning market economies. Property rights in many states remain unclear as émigrés return to stake their claims, making investment decisions risky. Moreover, few companies in the East have reliable accounting systems, which makes it difficult to value their assets. Poor infrastructure, lack of housing for employees and restricted access to credit from banking systems can all cause problems for western companies setting up in eastern Europe.

That is not all. Unless they are careful, western buyers may find themselves liable for environmental damage wrought by East European companies. And they may also find that rapidly changing rules and regulations in many areas may affect the value of the firms they have bought. No wonder, then, that the motto in the East is *caveat emptor* – buyer beware.

Eastern European exports to western Europe, 1989

Exports to western Europe now equal 5–10% of most eastern European states' GDP. In 1990, there was even a mini export boom as firms sold off the inventories hoarded under communism. This will not last. Output in eastern Europe fell an estimated 10% a year over 1990 and 1991, and with energy prices rising firms will have to charge market rates. In labour-intensive industries, however, eastern European producers can still compete.

PRIMARY PRODUCTS

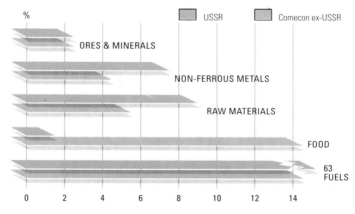

MANUFACTURERS

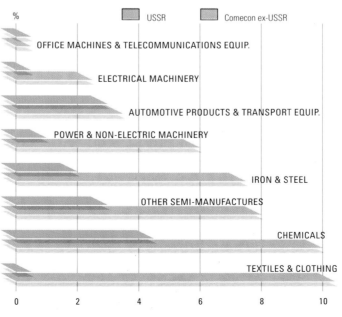

Inter-club trade

EFTA is a tiddler compared with its next-door neighbour: Its population is only one-tenth of the EC's and its total GDP is only half that of Germany. Yet as a block, it is the Community's largest trading partner ahead of both America and Japan. The EC is even more important to EFTA , taking more than half of its exports.

Many EFTA countries see the EEA as a first step towards full membership of the EC. Austria and Sweden have already applied to join. Finland intends to soon. But does the Community offer such big economic rewards? A crude comparison of the two trading blocs shows that the six EFTA economies outperformed those of the EC in the 1980s. From 1981to 1990, the EFTA countries had an average unemployment rate of 2.4%; the EC's was 10%. EFTA's inflation rate averaged 5.7%; the Community's was 7.4%. Economic growth in both blocs was roughly the same, but in 1990 EFTA's average income per head was 15% higher than the EC's.

So why are the EFTA nations so keen to join the Community? Gains to EFTA's industries from taking part in the single market could be two to three times bigger than the corresponding gains for a typical EC company. EFTA countries' domestic markets are small and tend (despite low protective barriers) to have a higher degree of market concentration than in EC countries. This offers bigger potential gains in efficiency.

TRADE BETWEEN EC AND EFTA 1990

COUNTRY		$bn
AUSTRIA	34.5	26.7
FINLAND	11.7	12.5
ICELAND	0.8	1.1
NORWAY	11.8	22.0
SWEDEN	30.2	31.2
SWITZERLAND	52.3	36.9
▢ EC exports to		
▢ Exports to EC		

PRIVATISATION

State ownership of industry is widespread in Europe. Many firms were nationalised after the second world war as countries struggled to rebuild their economies. Later, more were taken over as governments in Europe sought to promote and protect "strategic" industries such as information technology and defence. Nationalisation was also used to rescue bankrupt firms whose failure would have caused major social unrest.

A number of European countries, like France, have a tradition of state ownership. As a result, the state's share of final consumption is relatively high. But to help balance their budgets and to prepare industry for the new Europe, many governments are now selling off their industrial holdings.

Britain has led the way. Under a right-wing government headed by Margaret Thatcher, it sold off some £29bn-worth of nationalised companies between 1979 and the end of 1990, roughly halving the size of its state sector. Spain and Portugal have followed suit. Even étatiste France has joined in, although it still wants to retain majority control of its nationalised companies.

The privatised path to recovery

The European Commission has encouraged privatisation by making it harder for governments to pay illegal aid to state-owned companies. Though the Treaty of Rome, the EC's founding charter, does not discriminate between private and public ownership, it makes clear that state firms should not benefit from any state aid which distorts competition. The Commission has already taken companies to court to force them to repay unauthorised subsidies.

While some western European governments are still reluctant to privatise, eastern European ones cannot wait to sell off their industries. First, though, they must create the conditions for fledgling private sector companies to flourish. Most countries now have some form of company law and a growing number of incorporated firms (ie, companies that have been granted a legal identity which is distinct from their owners). At the end of 1991, Czechoslovakia had 5,000 such firms, Hungary 30,000 and Poland 40,000. There are many times this number of unincorporated businesses in all three countries.

Yet privatisation is still a massive task. In the mid-1980s, state-owned firms in eastern Europe accounted for over 80% of total value added, a measure of an economy's wealth creation, compared with 17% or less in Europe and America. The growth of an official and unofficial private sector in eastern Europe may have reduced this figure, but it is still high.

On some estimates, private companies may now account for almost a third of Hungary's economy and up to two-fifths of Poland's. But even if these estimates are correct, a lively private sector may be suffocated by state firms unwilling to supply it or give it access to distribution systems. Hungary alone has 2,300 state firms, Poland 8,000, Czechoslovakia 4,800, Bulgaria 5,000 and Romania 40,000.

The first three countries hope to privatise about one-half of their state-owned assets by 1994. That is optimistic. According to the World Bank, fewer than 1,000 compa-

State consumption

In nearly all the countries of western Europe the state's share of total spending on capital goods is a little over 20%. Spain is the lowest at 19%. The Scandinavian countries have recently made considerable efforts to reduce their significantly higher proportion, but as the map shows Denmark is still a very high 32.1%.

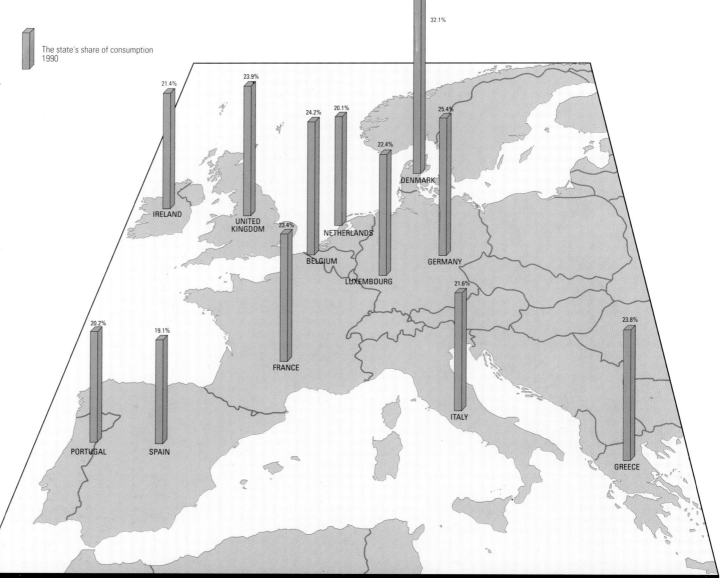

The state's share of consumption 1990

nies were privatised worldwide between 1980 and 1987, when privatisation peaked. By July 1991, Poland had sold only 16 of the 8,000 companies it had listed for sale.

Maintaining support for mass privatisation may prove difficult. In Bulgaria and Hungary there have been cases of "spontaneous" privatisation where companies have been bought in dubious circumstances. Such deals, and mass lay-offs of workers by newly privatised companies, have increased public resistance to the sale of state firms.

Consequences of foreign investment

Vague property rights are delaying the privatisation process in eastern Europe. So too, is the task of valuing companies. Accounting standards and systems are still being developed and tax systems in most countries are temporary ones. Also many eastern European citizens do not have sufficient savings to invest in privatisations. That raises the risk that former state firms will be owned mainly by a wealthy (and often foreign) elite.

Even so, Hungary is pressing ahead with privatisation. Burdened with a $20bn foreign debt, it cannot afford to wait. Foreign investors have been quick to buy companies put up for sale. As a result, some $3bn has been invested in Hungary since 1988, and most of the car, paper, cement and sugar industries are now in foreign hands.

However, in Czechoslovakia, which is also privatising rapidly, there has been a backlash against foreign investment. Most of the resistance is aimed at German companies, which account for about 80% of the foreign investment in Czechoslovakia.

DIFFERENT ROUTES TO THE SAME GOAL

Eastern Europe is taking privatisation into uncharted territory. Both Hungary and Poland have said that they want to privatise half of their state assets by 1994, an enormous task given that they jointly have more than 10,000 state firms. Foreign companies have already snapped up some former state firms (the table below covers the period from market liberalisation to mid-1991), but traditional methods of privatisation could take decades. And real change will not take place until private owners take responsibility for inefficient state firms. So eastern European governments are turning to mass privatisation.

As well as selling state firms to foreigners, the Polish government hopes to distribute shares in 200 companies to the population via a voucher system. The shares will be placed in large mutual funds for several years before being traded openly, creating the type of institutional investor common in western economies. Czechoslovakia also has a programme of privatisation by voucher involving over 1,000 companies.

Hungary relies on conventional channels for privatisation, a policy helped by the gradual introduction of market forces to its economy over the past few decades. Some of its companies are now being traded on the Budapest stock exchange.

BIG INVESTORS IN EASTERN EUROPE

COUNTRY	CZECH	HUNGARY	POLAND	ROMANIA	TOTAL $m
GERMANY	6,751	0	0	35	6,786
FRANCE	175	80	0	0	255
AUSTRIA	0	93	0	0	93
ITALY	0	25	0	0	25
SWEDEN	0	83	0	0	83
SWITZERLAND	0	0	50	0	50
UK	0	7	140	0	147

JAPAN	0	110	0	0	110
USA	80	560	0	0	640

THE SECOND-HAND COMPANY BUSINESS

The Treuhandanstalt, which has inherited former East Germany's state-owned firms, is the world's largest holding company. Since it was set up in 1990, it has sold off some 5,000 of its 11,000 or so businesses, usually by tender offer. However, the highest bidder may not necessarily win. In keeping with Germany's "social market" tradition, the agency may favour cheap offers which promise new investment in existing plants and retraining for workers. Critics charge that the Treuhand may be slowing down the process of change in eastern Germany by refusing to liquidate companies which clearly have no future. Although it is supposed to be a temporary agency, the Treuhand may well end up keeping those companies it cannot sell.

The privatisation and market liberalisation programmes in eastern Europe have thrown up all kinds of problems. At the beginning of 1990 some 96% of agricultural land in Czechoslovakia was run by state or cooperative farms. When prices were liberalised in 1991 food sales plummeted. In May 1991 a law was passed giving land back to its pre-1948 owners, but few are interested in farming.

Who gets what

The chart shows subsidies by sector as a percentage of the value added in the sector. The figures come from a European Commission survey of the state aid given to EC industry between 1986 and 1988; the commission noted that the average level of subsidies had fallen in the 1980s — but not by much.

EFTA countries are less generous supporters of industry than their EC counterparts. Their subsidies to manufacturers average only 2% of manufacturing output, compared with 6% in the Community. Southern European governments are the most generous in this field. In spite of an enormous budget deficit, the Italian government still spent an average of 9.6bn ecus a year on industrial aid in 1986–88, more than any other EC state. This is an average subsidy per employee of 3,136 ecus, second only to Greece's 3,545 ecus.

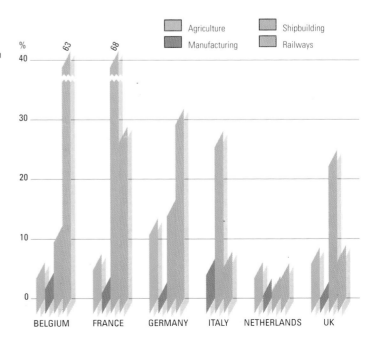

THE SINGLE MARKET

The single market programme aims to remove all EC internal border controls so that goods and people can travel freely between member countries. Poland, Hungary and Czechoslovakia were the first eastern European countries to sign association agreements with the EC in the hope in time of becoming full members of the Community and its single market.

In June 1985, the European Commission published a list of 282 measures designed to abolish restrictive practices and lift non-tariff barriers in Europe by the end of 1992. In the same year, European governments approved the Single European Act, which introduced majority voting for all single market matters except taxation, the movement of people and employment conditions. It also introduced the principle of "mutual recognition" which obliges one EC country to accept another's commercial rules providing they meet minimum European standards.

Armed with these powers, the Commission has been sweeping away physical barriers to cross-border business. The number of customs documents required at frontier posts has been greatly reduced and restrictions on cabotage – the right of truck drivers to pick up and deliver goods within another state's borders – are gradually being phased out.

Technical barriers to trade, such as product standards, are also disappearing. Given that Germany has some 20,000 product standards and Britain around 12,000, the task of harmonising them would be enormous. Instead, the EC is replacing national norms with European ones only in cases such as toys and gas cookers where existing standards are so diverse that mutual recognition is quite impossible.

Shared standards like these should make it easier for foreign companies to prise open national procurement markets in Europe, both in the field of public works (construction) and in public supplies (investment goods and equipment). Together, these are estimated to be worth some 15% of the European Community's combined GDP:

4.7 trillion ecus in 1990. New rules on public procurement now require that tenders are open to bidders from all member states of the Community.

Europe is dismantling financial barriers too. Exchange controls have all but vanished from most European countries, and the planned introduction of a single European currency by the end of the century should help European companies save some 13bn ecus a year in currency conversion costs. Though some progress has been made on tax harmonisation, fiscal hurdles to trade could prove harder to abolish.

That is one reason why the work of building a single market will continue long after January 1st 1993. Another is that some countries like Italy are painfully slow at translating EC directives into law. Finally, some European governments worried about the growth of drug-dealing, terrorism and illegal immigration must still be persuaded to drop all national border controls.

Business requirements

If these delaying tactics alarm businessmen, so does Europe's Social Charter. Endorsed in 1991 by every EC state except Britain, the charter outlines basic rights for European workers. Company managements believe these rules will give too much power to unions. Businessmen also complain about Europe's inefficient and expensive transport infrastructure and that Europe's educational systems are still not producing enough skilled labour for fast-growing, high-technology industries.

The single market alone will not cure these handicaps, but it will make it easier for companies to overhaul operations in a bid to improve their performance. Many are ▷

Euro-standards

Talking about a single market is one thing, getting governments to implement it is another. Of the 282 directives specified for implementation when Project 1992 was launched, 198 had been accepted by the members at the end of June 1991. But states have not been equally good at implementing them. Britain, which is typically viewed as a reluctant European, had one of the best records for implementing EC directives, and sluggish Italy the worst.

◼ Implemented

▨ Not implemented

Excuse me

Not all the single market directives apply to all members and several countries are seeking derogation (exemption) from particular edicts which they consider irrelevant. The table below shows the number of directives that are either inapplicable or which countries are seeking exemption from. Greece and the other two most recent members of the Community head the list of derogation-seekers.

DIRECTIVE EXCEPTIONS

COUNTRY		
BELGIUM	0	5
DENMARK	1	5
FRANCE	0	4
GERMANY	1	5
GREECE	8	4
IRELAND	2	6
ITALY	0	4
LUXEMBOURG	0	7
NETHERLANDS	0	5
PORTUGAL	6	2
SPAIN	6	2
UK	1	5

☐ Derogation sought

▨ Inapplicable

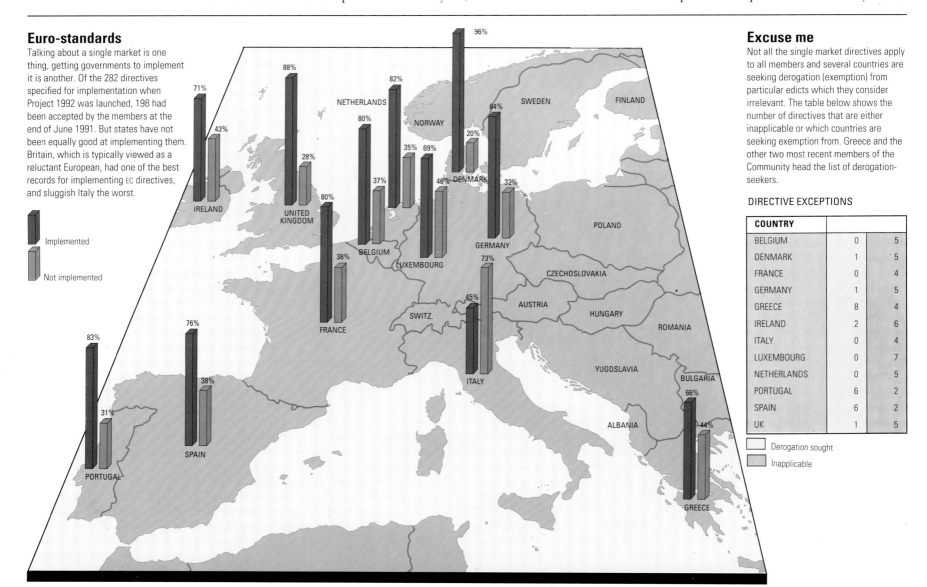

CUSTOMS AND PRACTICES

For businessmen in the European Community, customs formalities and other types of administrative barriers are the biggest hurdle to intra-EC trade. Border delays are particularly costly for companies in traditional manufacturing industries like chemicals and steel, while different technical standards may be an even bigger barrier to trade in complex manufacturing fields.

According to a report for the European Commission published in 1988, intra-EC customs procedures cost firms around 8bn ecus a year, roughly equal to 2% of their cross-border sales. The report reckoned that scrapping border controls would not only save companies a fortune, but would also generate up to 15bn ecus-worth of new business.

The European Commission could save EC industry billions more by sweeping away different national product standards and replacing them with a set of Euro-norms. But harmonising every standard in the Community would take for ever. That is why the Commission is using the principle of "mutual recognition" instead. According to this, a product standard in one EC country must be accepted in another providing it meets basic requirements in matters such as health and safety. EC standards will only be required in those cases where national standards are so diverse that mutual recognition is impossible.

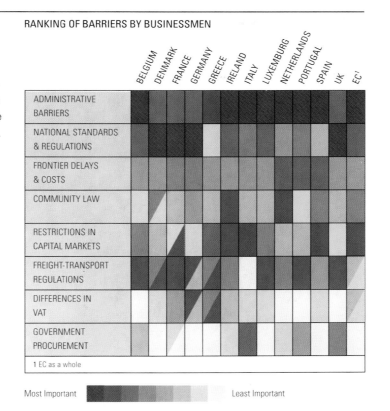

RANKING OF BARRIERS BY BUSINESSMEN

1 EC as a whole

Most Important — Least Important

MERGERS AND ACQUISITIONS

The industries most likely to be affected by the single market are those where trade barriers have led to big differences in price for the same product across the European Community. Among the sectors that fit this bill are energy and railway equipment businesses. Intra-EC trade in these industries is low (8% compared with an average of 18%), while price differences are high (a spread of 25% across the Community compared with an average of 15%).

So, while engineering businesses combined come close to the top of the EC mergers and acquisitions league, with 71 intra-EC acquisitions and 358 in total over the period covered by the chart, takeover activity is still greater (172 intra-EC acquisitions and 373 in total) in the chemicals industry. This is also partly due to chemicals firms already operating in a global market with few trade barriers.

EC food companies are also takeover targets. Thanks to strict national standards for foodstuffs and other barriers to entry, many relatively small food firms have long been able to occupy leading positions in their home markets. But they are now on the shopping lists of big food groups like Switzerland's Nestlé and Unilever, an Anglo-Dutch food group, which want to expand their European operations.

The lifting of trade barriers during the 1990s will create enormous opportunities for those who are prepared for the rough and tumble of an unprotected marketplace.

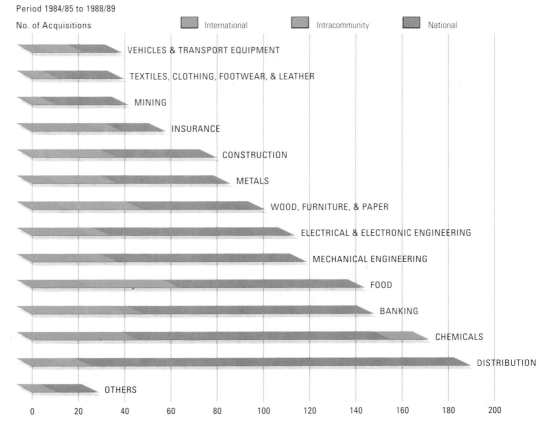

MERGERS AND MAJORITY ACQUISITIONS INVOLVING EC COMPANIES

Period 1984/85 to 1988/89

No. of Acquisitions   ■ International   ■ Intracommunity   ■ National

VEHICLES & TRANSPORT EQUIPMENT
TEXTILES, CLOTHING, FOOTWEAR, & LEATHER
MINING
INSURANCE
CONSTRUCTION
METALS
WOOD, FURNITURE, & PAPER
ELECTRICAL & ELECTRONIC ENGINEERING
MECHANICAL ENGINEERING
FOOD
BANKING
CHEMICALS
DISTRIBUTION
OTHERS

0   20   40   60   80   100   120   140   160   180   200

Why merge?

Trying to identify a single reason for a takeover or merger is hard because such deals are struck for many different reasons. Nevertheless, according to the European Commission, the desire to strengthen market position and develop commercial activities is the main motive behind EC takeovers. That is a sign that firms in the Community are preparing for a more competitive decade. Yet, despite businessmen's claims to the contrary, there is little conclusive evidence to show that synergy – mutual benefits for shared research and technology – really is a natural result of takeovers and mergers.

MAIN MOTIVES FOR MERGERS
Within EC

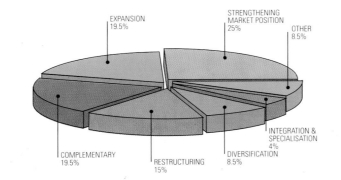

1987–88

EXPANSION 19.5%
STRENGTHENING MARKET POSITION 25%
OTHER 8.5%
INTEGRATION & SPECIALISATION 4%
DIVERSIFICATION 8.5%
RESTRUCTURING 15%
COMPLEMENTARY 19.5%

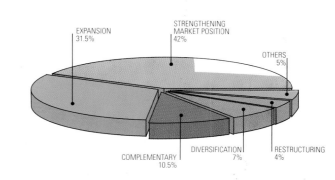

1988–89

EXPANSION 31.5%
STRENGTHENING MARKET POSITION 42%
OTHERS 5%
RESTRUCTURING 4%
DIVERSIFICATION 7%
COMPLEMENTARY 10.5%

already doing so, and many are becoming much more international in the process.

Changing the rules by which Europe does business has led to a wave of restructuring. According to the European Commission, the number of mergers and acquisitions made by the EC's 1,000 leading companies leapt from 303 in 1986–87 to 622 in 1989–90. Significantly, cross-border deals outnumbered national ones for the first time in 1989–90.

In the merger and acquisitions stakes, French and Swedish companies have established a reputation as some of the most acquisitive in Europe. The most popular targets were British companies, mainly because Britain has Europe's most open market for corporate control. Plans to harmonise takeover regimes in Europe, and to strengthen the rights of minority shareholders, would eventually make takeovers easier in traditionally closed markets such as Germany. Some defence mechanisms, such as limitations on the voting rights of shares, are already under attack. As these other barriers to takeover are dismantled, Europe's mergers and acquisitions market will become the most active in the world.

As well as takeovers, looser cross-border European alliances, such as the one between France's Renault and Sweden's Volvo, have also become popular. The number of joint ventures involving companies from two different EC states rose from just 16 in 1986–87 to 55 in 1989–90. These have the advantage of allowing both partners to keep their independence, but without a united management team they can be difficult to steer.

Faced with the prospect of a barrier-free Europe, companies have used mergers and acquisitions to enter new markets or to reap cross-border economies of scale. Banks like France's Crédit Lyonnais have bought up branch networks in several different EC states. And a group of European retailers, including France's Casino and Britain's Argyll, has set up a pan-European alliance whose purpose is to buy goods in bulk.

Takeovers and mergers are not only becoming more common in the EC, they are also getting bigger. Given that many EC industries are still fragmented in comparison with, say, American ones, such merger activity is hardly surprising. But big may not necessarily be best if the result is reduced competition in European markets.

That is why the European Commission is strictly enforcing the EC's merger regulations. Since September 1990, it has had the power to vet mergers involving firms with a joint turnover of over 5bn ecus – providing that at least 250m ecus-worth of these sales are in the Community. In its first year of operation, the EC's merger watchdog was notified of 54 deals and made 48 final decisions.

Of five not approved within a month of notification, one was cleared without change; three were approved after modification; and one, the plan by France's Aerospatiale and Italy's Alenia, two state-owned aerospace companies, to share in the acquisition of De Havilland, a Canadian aircraft maker, was blocked on the grounds that the new company would have had a dominant share of the EC market for commuter aircraft. This led to a row between the companies and the European Commission. As cross-border activity grows, the EC is likely to face even more controversial competition issues.

Cross-border deals

The map shows the value of cross-border mergers and acquisitions during the first six months of 1991. The value of companies sold reflects the fact that Britain is the most open market in Europe for mergers and acquisitions. The value of companies bought shows how acquisitive French companies (often state-owned) have been, giving rise to fears that French state firms have effectively been nationalising companies in other countries. The figures also show that, although down on the same period for 1990, the EC mergers and acquisitions market was still bubbling at a time when activity in North America and the rest of the world slumped.

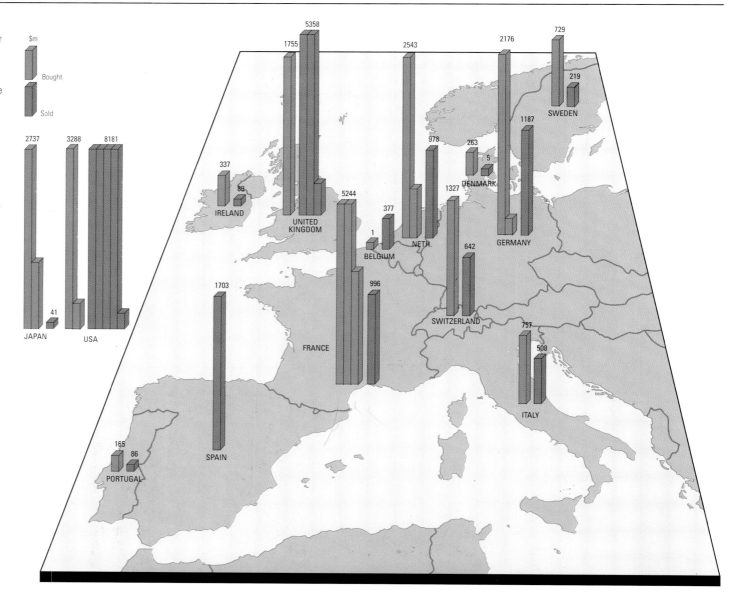

"... Dommage de quitter si vite ce magnifique pays et son chocolat Frigor..."

Robert et Edith – St Moritz–Dorf, le 14 juillet 1935

SIZING UP

Big is not necessarily beautiful in business, but many EC industries like paper and packaging, banking and food retailing are more fragmented than their American equivalents. That may leave the Europeans at a disadvantage because they cannot reap economies of scale in research and development, manufacturing and distribution. To make up for this, some European governments have been encouraging mergers which create big, national champions in industries like air travel and electronics. The biggest European companies still tend to be concentrated in the chemical, car and food sectors. And they are usually British, French or German. Two Anglo-Dutch giants, Unilever and Royal Dutch Shell, also appear in the rankings.

EC COMPANIES AMONG THE WORLD'S BIGGEST COMPANIES

COUNTRY	1-100	101-200	201-300	301-400	401-500	TOTAL
BELGIUM	1	1	1	1	0	4
FRANCE	10	2	7	6	5	30
GERMANY	12	9	2	5	2	30
ITALY	4	2	0	1	0	7
LUXEMBOURG	0	0	1	0	0	1
NETHERLANDS	1	1	1	2	2	7
PORTUGAL	0	0	1	0	0	1
SPAIN	2	0	0	1	1	4
UK	6	8	11	7	11	43
UK/NETHERLANDS	2	0	0	0	0	2
EC	38	23	24	23	21	129

	1-100	101-200	201-300	301-400	401-500	TOTAL
JAPAN	16	24	22	24	25	111
USA	33	35	35	31	30	164

L'INOUBLIABLE CHOCOLAT SUISSE AU FONDANT D'AMANDES.

Nestlé c'est fort en chocolat!

Chocolate wars... Switzerland's Nestlé's takeover of Rowntree, a big British confectionery maker, was an example of a non-EC based company's forthright response to the challenge of the single market.

A growing trend

In 1986–87, there were 89 national, intra-EC and international deals involving EC firms which produced new companies with a turnover of more than 5bn ecus; in 1989–90 there were 257. The number of deals creating companies with a turnover of more than 10bn ecus nearly trebled over the same period, reaching 157 in 1989–90.

Most of the deals recorded by the European Commission have been purely national ones. This reflects the fact that many continental European companies have a panoply of anti-takeover defences to protect them from foreign bidders. But the Commission has plans to weaken some of these.

HOLDINGS ANALYSIS

TURNOVER $m	NATIONAL			EC			INTERNATIONAL		
1-2	144	170	211	57	108	163	19	64	75
2-5	94	110	155	46	80	123	11	50	72
5-10	55	61	74	27	44	79	7	35	46
OVER 10	24	30	30	14	26	55	3	17	28

☐ 1986-87   ☐ 1987-88   ☐ 1988-89

SECTORAL DIFFERENCES

European industry is once again being transformed by a wave of mergers and acquisitions similar to that which occurred in the 1970s. But at that time, change was driven by the two oil crises and mainly affected heavy industries like steel, shipbuilding and textiles. This time round, the single market programme has led to a restructuring of almost all areas of European business.

In the first six months of 1991 over $26bn was spent on takeovers in the EC; the chart gives a breakdown by sector. The chemical and pharmaceutical industry, which is already operating on a global scale, has always been an active M&A market. But in service industries like banking and retailing, big takeover deals have been rare. The single market has changed all that. With companies looking for quick ways to enter new markets, acquisitions look more tempting.

As Europe liberalises, expect big takeovers in other industries too. America's experience with airline deregulation gives a foretaste of things to come. After the American market was flung open to competition in the 1970s, some 200 new companies took to the sky. Of these, less than a third are still flying. Airlines that were already operating before deregulation suffered too. Less than half of them survived the following decade. The rest either failed or were taken over.

PURCHASES AND SALES, BY EC COMPANIES

◨ Electrical & Electronics   ◨ Chemical & Pharmaceutical
◨ Oil & Gas   ◨ Paper & Board
◨ Retailing   ◨ Printing & Publishing
◨ Banking & Finance   ◨ Engineered products

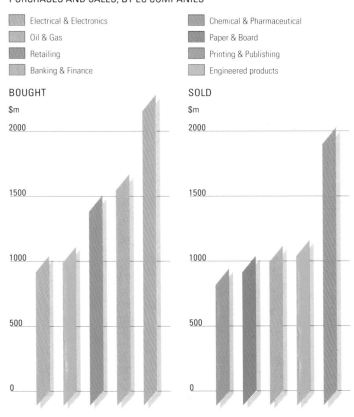

BOUGHT
$m

SOLD
$m

FOREIGN INVESTMENT

Spain has attracted considerable foreign investment with several car companies setting up manufacturing plants.

Foreign direct investment started with manufacturers anxious to get round trade barriers by producing within the local market. Local production often also helps market penetration. But now such investment is part of a much wider trend, extending also into service sectors. As companies increasingly operate on a global scale, their investment pattern also reflects the search for the cheapest available source of acceptable labour.

The pattern now is largely determined by the world's three great trading blocs: North America, Europe and Japan. They dominate both the outward and the inward flows – as they invest largely in each other's areas. The total world stock of foreign direct investment is reckoned to be around $1,000bn. The United States has about $326bn, but four European countries (Britain, Germany, the Netherlands and France – in that order) among them have more than that – $400bn. Japan has $100bn, but is catching up fast.

During the 1980s the flow of inward investment into Europe slowed down. This was the period when the Japanese were buying American assets and creating their large investments there in consumer goods and motor cars; Europe was less important to them. Meanwhile, Europeans were also investing heavily in the United States, as British, French, Dutch and German companies saw how they could acquire instant market share by taking over existing American businesses in areas like chemicals, building materials and consumer products.

Europe gets interesting

Towards the end of the 1980s, however,there were new reasons for inward investment coming to Europe, or at least the EC. The progress being made towards the creation of a single market underlined to outsiders, like the Americans and the Japanese, the need to get inside this rapidly forming trading bloc. The Americans in particular have been very active in acquiring European companies. This has the twin advantages of instant acquisition of skilled personnel on the spot and a ready-made market share with established products or services which can subsequently be developed. There is no need to build up sales and distribution networks from scratch.

Beyond the single market, another impetus was the creation of the European Economic Area (EEA). This was part of the process of the EC and the countries of EFTA (the European Free Trade Area) drawing closer together. One effect on inward investment will be to increase the attractiveness of the Nordic countries to non-Europeans. Until the creation of the EEA they suffered from being physically on the edge of the European market and from being excluded from the trading bloc. Hence the inward investment they attracted was very small, and aimed only at servicing the local market.

The latest growth in inward investment is most evident in central and eastern Europe, as countries there develop capitalist economies. The attractions are twofold: these countries will become bigger markets as they grow richer, and they will become efficient, low-cost sources of production – for instance, of basic-model motor cars for the west. There are already notable examples of western European companies tapping the potential of their eastern neighbours.

Fiat is expanding its traditional links with Russian and Polish car firms. Volkswagen's purchase of a stake in Czechoslovakia's Skoda cars is the most striking example, but there are others in Hungary where the Japanese and Americans are investing in the consumer goods and pharmaceutical industries. To begin with, most of the western investments started as joint ventures, but this is expected to change as eastern Europe's economies adapt to capitalism and the idea of straightforward takeovers of local companies.

Inward investment is not without pain. The leading French car companies, Peugeot and Renault, along with Fiat in Italy, howled at perhaps the most spectacular inward investment Europe saw in the 1980s: the arrival in Britain of three big Japanese car makers, Nissan, Toyota and Honda. By the end of the 1990s these firms will be making one million cars a year – all aimed at the European market. Inevitably, this risks driving out less efficient production by the traditional car firms in Europe (among them the American twins Ford and GM, in Europe so long people forget they are American based). But that's really the whole point: to allocate capital to where it can best be employed.

Direct investment flows

The map shows net investment flows into EC countries during 1990. While Germany (the figures are for western Germany for the first six months, the whole country thereafter), France and the Netherlands saw their net outward investment increase throughout the 1980s, recession and high interest rates caused the UK to switch from being a big net outward investor to a net inward one at the end of the decade.

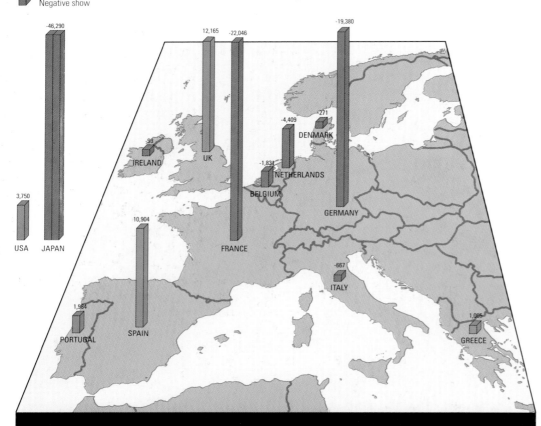

Positive show

Negative show

-46,290

3,750

USA JAPAN

12,165 -22,046

-99
IRELAND

UK

-4,409

-271
DENMARK

-1,831
NETHERLANDS

BELGIUM

10,904

FRANCE

GERMANY

-19,380

1,984
PORTUGAL

SPAIN

-667
ITALY

1,005
GREECE

INWARD FOREIGN INVESTMENT IN EUROPE

The four European leaders in both inward and outward investment had a net outflow of capital investment in the 1980s. By 1988, Britain's external assets were $184bn, Germany's $97bn, the Netherlands' $70bn, and France's $58bn.

The southern European countries – Spain, Portugal and Greece – saw a marked rise in their inward investment as they moved into the EC. EFTA countries, notably Sweden, have disproportionately large outward flows because their small local markets and high labour costs force companies outward to expand their sales.

Connections: Single market 56–59   Rebuilding democracies 120–121   The European effect 146–147   Europe and America 148–151   Europe and Asia 160–165

WHO'S INVESTING WHERE

Intra-EC investment has accounted for more than half of the annual value since the mid-1980s. Indigenous companies have taken steps to strengthen their pan-European coverage. The annual inward flows from America have slowed somewhat, but the stock of American inward investment remains dominant, with well-established networks (for example, Ford and GM) for production and distribution.

The Japanese, often assumed to be major European investors, are relative newcomers, reflecting their need to overcome trade barriers since the late 1970s. The outward investment pattern reflects the difficulty of gaining reciprocal access to the Japanese market and the significance of the United States as an attraction for British, German, Dutch and (latterly) French companies. That such investment exceeds intra-EC investment indicates the drive for global reach.

INWARD DIRECT INVESTMENT, 1985

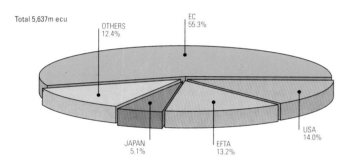

Total 5,637m ecu

OTHERS 12.4%
EC 55.3%
JAPAN 5.1%
EFTA 13.2%
USA 14.0%

INWARD DIRECT INVESTMENT, 1988

Total 14,278m ecu

OTHERS 9.6%
EC 57.2%
USA 1.8%
JAPAN 4.4%
EFTA 27.0%

OUTWARD DIRECT INVESTMENT, 1985

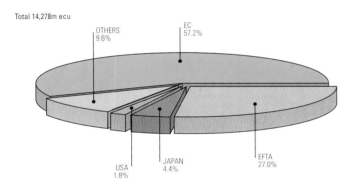

Total -15,349m ecu

USA 65.6%
EFTA 4.9%
JAPAN 0.2%
OTHERS 29.3%

OUTWARD DIRECT INVESTMENT, 1988

Total -30,711m ecu

USA 65.3%
EFTA 7.5%
JAPAN 0.06%
OTHERS 27.14%

Upping their stakes

Since the single market programme got under way, fears of a fortress Europe with trade barriers to keep non-members out of its market has raised Japanese and American interest in EC investment since the mid-1980s.

While the Americans have vociferously complained about policies which compel them to invest, they have considerably increased their position in Europe's "big four" – France, Germany, Italy and the UK. They have also raised their stake in the Netherlands which, close to Europe's economic core, is a strong base from which to serve the single market.

Japan's share of outward direct investment going to Europe has also risen dramatically. This is particularly evident in the UK.

JAPAN'S OUTWARD INVESTMENT

Total $12,200m, 1985

EUROPE 5.8%
NORTH AMERICA 45.0%
UK 3.1%
OTHER AREAS 39.2%

Total $67,500m, 1989

EUROPE 21.9%
NORTH AMERICA 50.2%
UK 7.8%
OTHER AREAS 27.9%

INVESTMENT SECTORS

Two major themes emerge from the sectoral data covering direct investment in the European Community by non-EC countries: the decline in investment in agriculture, minerals and mining and more internationalisation in services. European countries are as anxious as others to keep primary sectors to themselves and this has discouraged inward investment in industries such as energy. But the growing trend towards global manufacture and marketing will break down that traditional resistance as more liberal economic and trade policies are applied in the 1990s. In consequence, companies will seek foreign partners rather than hide behind protective barriers. The car industry is just one example where American and Japanese firms already have a big European presence through investment and alliances.

Inward investment in services is nearly double that in other industries. The nature of service industries – consumption at the point of production (for instance, fast-food outlets) means that companies have to be in the market. Likewise, financial services need local presence to deliver the product.

The huge Canary Wharf development in London's docklands was the brainchild of the Canadian Reichmann brothers, owners of property giant Olympia & York. They envisaged it taking over from the City of London as Europe's financial centre. But events conspired against them. A shortage of office space in the City became a glut after the City changed its planning rules to combat the threat of Canary Wharf. And boom turned to recession, bringing slump to the property market. In 1992 Olympia & York went into administration. One of the most grandiose foreign investments ever in London had gone spectacularly wrong.

CARS AND MOTOR PARTS

Not since the first cars rolled off primitive assembly lines a century ago has the motor industry faced such radical and widespread change. The structure under which the American and European car makers built their huge empires has been shaken first by increasing competition from Japan and its satellite factories, and now by the new challenges resulting from changes in eastern Europe.

The shift in the former eastern bloc countries to more market-based economies has presented the European car industry with the opportunity to expand: to set up new manufacturing plants and develop sales networks which can cash in on any rise in prosperity among a population eager for modern cars. But the most pressing challenge has been to increase efficiency and develop new products rapidly enough to be able to fend off the entry of rival models from Japanese manufacturers based in Europe, particularly in Britain. Japanese "transplants", as the UK factories have become known, will remain the single most contentious issue within the European motor business throughout the decade.

The Japanese tide

Although agreement was reached effectively to limit imports until the end of the century and restrict the increase in transplant output, the early signs are that the new Japanese-owned factories will grow very quickly. By the mid-1990s, it is estimated that as many as 500,000 cars with Japanese badges will be rolling off assembly lines in the UK alone. The European Community might then start to reflect upon the experience of the market in the USA, where Japanese models now account for one-third of all new car sales and the top-selling car is a Japanese brand made in America.

The repercussions of the Japanese entry will be felt by Europe's "big six" car makers – Ford, General Motors, the PSA group (Peugeot-Citroën), the Volkswagen group,

Renault and Fiat – which expect Japanese marques to have at least one-fifth of the western European market by the year 2000 and to be moving rapidly towards a market share of 30%.

The trend of acquisitions and mergers of the late 1980s, which started with Ford and General Motors buying Jaguar and Lotus respectively in the United Kingdom, and Volkswagen acquiring Seat in Spain and Skoda in Czechoslovakia, was seen as only a start of bigger things to come during the 1990s. A new series of mergers, which could see the traditional big six manufacturers contract to five or even as few as three, could happen before the end of the decade.

Fiat and Peugeot have both been seen as the most vulnerable because of two key factors: their heavy dependence on domestic sales, particularly the lack of outlets in the United States, and their lack of links with Japanese manufacturers. Their main competitors, on the other hand, all have a broad sales base, straddling much of the globe with varying degrees of success.

By the early 1990s, contraction was already the biggest single item on the agenda of motor manufacturers. Ford, for example, has restructured by reducing its European workforce from 150,000 to 100,000 while raising output by 400,000 vehicles – about 30% more vehicles produced by 33% fewer employees with the aim of achieving a market share of one-third. The pace of restructuring was being accelerated, with even the strongest of the German manufacturers, Mercedes-Benz, planning a major reduction of up to 20,000 staff.

The quest for greater productivity has been forced by the rapid return on Japanese investment of almost $2bn in UK manufacturing plants by Nissan, Toyota and Honda. Nissan's bold strategy of being the first – opening its plant at Washington, Tyne & Wear, in 1986 – put the company on course to be Britain's third largest car producer by mid-decade.

A brake on new cars

The expansion of new car registrations in western Europe was halted by recession at the start of the 1990s. Manufacturers enjoyed rapid growth throughout the 1980s as major economies boomed; however, only the strength of the German market, driven by the reunification of East and West, pushed registrations to a record 13.5m in 1991. Other key markets suffered badly in the recession, particularly the UK where sales plummeted by 20.7% in 1991, France where registrations fell by 12% and Spain, also down by 9.8%. Registrations were widely expected to remain level before rising again towards mid-decade as major economies revived.

WESTERN EUROPEAN CAR
REGISTRATIONS
million units

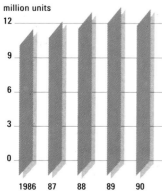

THE EUROPEAN DILEMMA

Component manufacturers throughout the EC are benefiting from the spin-off from Nissan's policy of sourcing heavily from European-based suppliers. The company's spending on components in 1992 was scheduled to reach $850m while another $700m a year was planned by Toyota plus $300m by Honda.

That level of spending would guarantee that the UK-produced cars carrying Japanese marques would have the 80% European content demanded by the EC. Nations like France and Italy, which have traditionally shunned Japanese products, will see the market share of Japanese badges grow rapidly from less than 4% at the start of the decade. That means that the impact of that new Japanese production could be severe without substantial market growth in both western and eastern Europe.

Car makers have been presented with new openings in eastern European countries as they move to market-orientated economies. Investment by western companies in new assembly facilities and joint ventures with established eastern European manufacturers has led to the prospect that current production capacity will be raised from 2.5m cars annually to about 4.75m, effectively supplying the bulk of the pent-up demand in former under-supplied communist countries.

But if the economic transformation of eastern Europe runs into trouble, growth in car sales could be far slower than anticipated, intensifying the battle for survival.

WESTERN EUROPEAN SALES, 1990

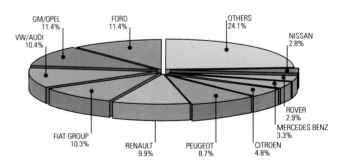

WESTERN EUROPEAN CAR REGISTRATIONS, 1990

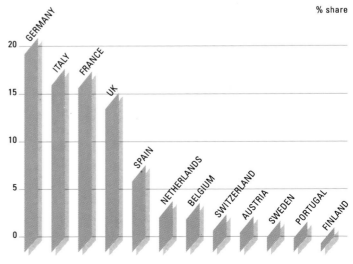

Connections: Trade 48–49   Competition in industry 50–51   Single market 56–59   Eastern Europe 110–111   Europe and Asia 160–165

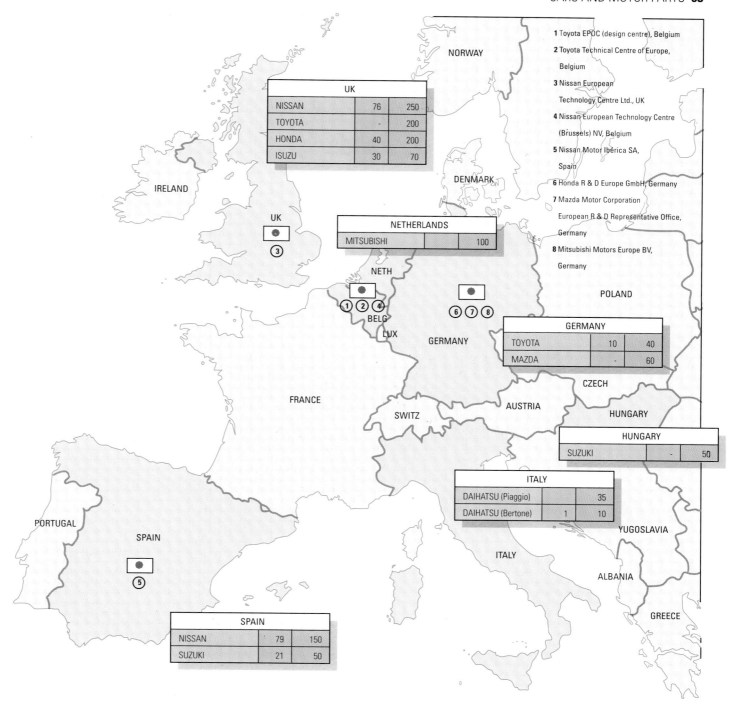

Western promise for Japan

The impact in Europe of Japanese car manufacturers will be felt most over the next ten years as their production plants in the UK reach full output. Nissan, the first to set up in Britain, has expanded rapidly, extending investment to more than $13m, the biggest inward investment in the European Community. By mid-decade, Nissan is expected to be making 250,000 cars a year in Britain. Not far behind will be Toyota, making 200,000, and Honda, 100,000. The scale of that output will present the EC's established manufacturers with their biggest challenge and could propel Britain towards becoming the Community's third largest car maker after France and Germany. However, the influence of the Japanese has been felt more widely with Nissan, Toyota and Honda recruiting heavily among EC-based component manufacturers.

1 Toyota EPOC (design centre), Belgium

2 Toyota Technical Centre of Europe, Belgium

3 Nissan European Technology Centre Ltd., UK

4 Nissan European Technology Centre (Brussels) NV, Belgium

5 Nissan Motor Ibérica SA, Spain

6 Honda R & D Europe GmbH, Germany

7 Mazda Motor Corporation European R & D Representative Office, Germany

8 Mitsubishi Motors Europe BV, Germany

UK		
NISSAN	76	250
TOYOTA	-	200
HONDA	40	200
ISUZU	30	70

NETHERLANDS		
MITSUBISHI		100

GERMANY		
TOYOTA	10	40
MAZDA	-	60

HUNGARY		
SUZUKI	-	50

ITALY		
DAIHATSU (Piaggio)		35
DAIHATSU (Bertone)	1	10

SPAIN		
NISSAN	79	150
SUZUKI	21	50

PROJECTED JAPANESE VEHICLE PRODUCTION IN EUROPE

'000 units

- 1990
- 1995
- ○ Major vehicle production centres
- ⊙ R & D and design facilities

EASTERN EUROPE BECKONS

Western European motor manufacturers are facing a period of the most rapid change ever experienced because of the removal of barriers between East and West. The former Comecon nations offer the prospect of a huge new market. Establishing sales networks and new service and maintenance facilities, however, require substantial new investment.

For those motor manufacturers seeking lower production costs, eastern Europe also presents an opportunity to invest in new assembly lines operated by workforces keen to secure their livelihoods at a time of turmoil in the emerging economies.

Companies such as Fiat, Volkswagen and General Motors have invested heavily in new facilities in eastern Europe. Fiat's plant at Togliatti in Russia started production in 1966 and is the longest running. Output of the Fiat Cinquecento at the Bielko-Biala factory in Poland is rising rapidly from 180,000 units per year in 1991 to a projected 240,000 units per year, following an $841m investment. More modest is the British company Rover's project for the production of 50,000 Maestros a year by 1994 in Tolbulhin, Bulgaria.

This trend is likely to be followed by other western European and American manufacturers who want assembly plants which offer a buffer against rising costs, particularly from higher wage demands, in their established factories in the EC. Companies which were attracted by countries such as Spain may now focus on eastern Europe.

THE PRODUCTIVITY QUESTION

Rapidly rising costs and the prospect of competition from new and efficient Japanese factories working from greenfield sites in the UK is forcing established manufacturers in the European Community into a further round of cost-cutting.

Evidence provided by analysts showed that companies such as Nissan, using young, eager workforces and methods developed in Japan, would be able to achieve remarkable productivity levels during the 1990s. Older companies, particularly Ford in the UK, face a difficult shakeout of manpower and changes in working practices in order to compete with emerging rivals.

According to Nikko Securities in London, Ford's British operation achieved only eight cars per man per year compared with 75 expected at Nissan in Britain during 1992. The decision by Mercedes-Benz and BMW, two German luxury car makers, to cut their workforces also showed that they too were not immune to the difficulties of rising wage costs and less than ideal efficiency levels. If workers in established European factories hope that the vast new market of eastern Europe will provide enough demand to keep cars rolling out of plants in western Europe, there could be disappointment.

Joining the Japanese are cars from the United States (albeit mainly from Japanese manufacturers as well as models from Chrysler and others), marques from Korea and Malaysia which are not controlled by quotas, and new factories tooling up in eastern Europe itself.

Sales strategy

The strategy of the major Japanese manufacturers in western Europe is to establish fully integrated regional operations from manufacturing to wholly owned importer/distributors. This is illustrated by Nissan's struggle to take full control of these operations in the UK, as well as the company's acquisition of its French distributor, and Toyota's establishment of a wholly owned importer/distributor in Italy.

The number of Japanese cars registered in Europe has risen steadily from an overall 10.8m in 1985 to a projected 14.4m in 1993. Nissan leads the pack with almost one in four registrations, reaping the rewards of its early establishment of transplant production in Britain in 1986.

JAPANESE CAR REGISTRATIONS

COMPANY		1990
NISSAN	377,274	24.5
TOYOTA	353,825	23.0
MAZDA	276,368	17.9
MITSUBISHI	172,385	11.2
HONDA	159,649	10.4
SUZUKI	97,222	8.3
SUBARU	50,716	3.3
DAIHATSU	39,976	2.6
IZUZU	13,104	0.9

■ Total   ■ % share

COMPUTERS AND ELECTRONICS

Since the start of the 1990s, the European electronics and computer industries have been in steep decline. Once they were going to be the industries of the future in which Europe would shine. But for the main European contenders, profits have turned to losses, while a wave of closures and job losses reflects retrenchment all round.

There is little argument over what went wrong. While increased international competition was driving down prices, European companies over-expanded their production without investing enough in new products or technology; they fell farther behind as the cost of R&D favoured bigger producers. But there is no agreement about what, if anything, the European industry should do to get out of the mess.

Europe is the world's largest market for electronics, yet its own electronics industry is falling farther behind

private money is topped up by EC contributions. The idea is that companies should proceed to develop competing products out of the technology jointly developed.

The Netherlands' Philips and France's Thomson, Europe's two largest consumer electronics companies, have been trying to solve their own problems. In response to mounting losses, which reached $2.3bn in 1990, Philips started a radical slimming-down. It cut its activities in some areas, such as domestic appliances, and streamlined production in other sectors to become competitive. This rationalisation is eliminating one in six jobs which comes to 50,000.

While Philips gets smaller to survive, the state-owned Thomson group is growing bigger. In late 1991, the French government merged it with the nuclear power side of the Commissariat à l'Energie Atomique to form a new behemoth, Thomson CEA Industries. Quite how this was supposed to solve Thomson's problems was unclear.

The computer industry has been slower to face up to its plight. There are three European-owned companies making large computers: Siemens-Nixdorf Informationssyteme (SNI), which is a subsidiary of Germany's Siemens electrical and electronics group, France's Groupe Bull and Italy's Olivetti; all three made huge losses in 1991. In addition, there is ICL in Britain, since 1990, four-fifths owned by Fujitsu of Japan – and profitable.

Risc-taking alliance

The most severe problem for the computer companies has been the dramatic fall in prices, particularly in 1991, as more powerful chips mean smaller, cheaper computers can tackle more processing that used to require big mainframe machines. The cost of developing computer technology, basically new microchips and the software to drive them, has risen. The reason is the industry is on the verge of what it calls a new generation, after a period of refining existing technology and products. The French government, the main shareholder in Bull, has rather surprisingly encouraged the company to form a strategic alliance with IBM to keep up with these new developments. This will probably be the most important development in the European industry in recent years. It amounts to an admission by Europe's leading economic nationalists, the French, that there is no purely European solution to the industry's problems.

This alliance will give Bull access to IBM's new computer chips, known as Risc chips. (Risc means reduced instruction set computing: an elegant compromise solution to overcrowded micro circuits that improves computer performance). Risc chips will be the basis of the computer industry for a decade, and there is a furious battle over whose version of Risc technology will dominate. IBM is trying to set the standard as it did with personal computers in the 1980s. Bull's decision to rally to IBM so soon is an indication that Europe's computer companies are second rate, fit only to adapt foreign technology to the European market. Olivetti and SNI have yet to enter such alliances, but that is only a matter of time. Olivetti had to undergo a phase of drastic slimming at the start of the 1990s, reminiscent of what it went through a decade earlier to emerge as an effective competitor in the 1980s. But all the European companies will have to become global businesses like the Americans and Japanese, buying their components from wherever they are cheapest. Like ICL, to survive they must become less European.

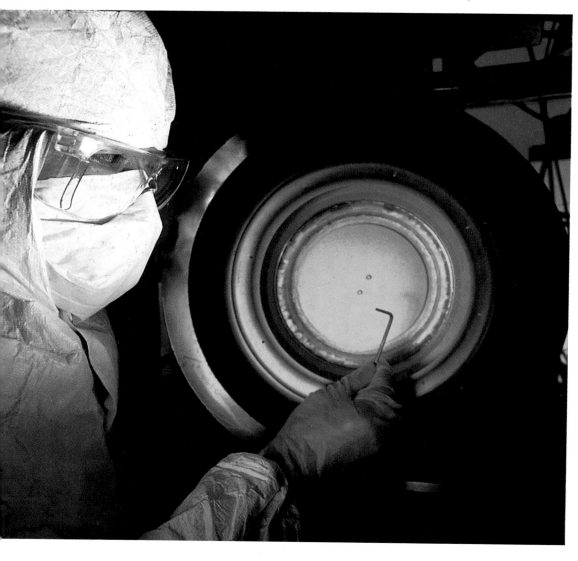

Making semiconductors. This technician is inspecting a gold sputtering target chamber used for depositing thin films onto semiconductor wafers. The individual circuits (chips) of an integrated circuit are built up on wafers based on silicon or gallium arsenide.

Japan and the United States. Japan's market share rose from 20% in 1984 to 26% in 1990, while the European share fell from 22% to 21%. That may not seem much, but these statistics count Japanese plants in Europe as European. Based on ownership, Europe would have a share of only 19%, while Japan's would rise to 28%.

Rather than rejoice that Europe manages to attract so much Japanese production, the European Commission, pressed by France, thought something should be done to stop the rot. The most notable attempt has been the microchip research programme, known as Jessi, which has a budget of $5bn. There are other, more modest projects: the aim is to promote cooperative research efforts in new technology areas. This is not as crude as pure industrial policy subsidies. It works by companies being drawn together to produce a research programme, with some advice and other help from the Commission. The

Connections: Trade 48–49 Competition in industry 50–51 Europe and Asia 160–165

A SEMICONDUCTED TOUR OF INDUSTRY

The gap between Europe and Japan is widest in the semiconductor industry. While European investments in this industry have risen gradually to just under $10bn since 1980, Japanese semiconductor producers made investments of $35bn, and spent another $35bn on research and development (see graph, right). This amounts to more than the entire value of the world semiconductor market in 1990 and represents about 35–40% of the annual revenues of the companies concerned. US semiconductor producers have fared better than their European counterparts, but have little chance to recapture the market leadership which they lost to Japan in the mid-1980s. As result Japan's market share is growing at the expense of Europe and the USA (see graph, far right). This trend is expected to continue through the 1990s.

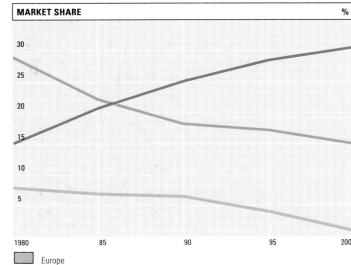

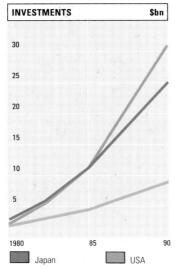

JAPAN TAKES THE LEAD

In 1990, Philips was the ninth largest semiconductor maker in the world, the only European company among the world's top ten, after having declined from third position in 1980 and sixth in 1985. Japanese companies account for six of the world's top ten semiconductor producers, including the top three: NEC, Toshiba and Hitachi. In 1990 Japanese companies accounted for 50% of the world market, compared with 30% in 1980.

SGS-Thomson, the Franco-Italian chip maker, has calculated that strict extrapolation of the respective positions of semiconductor companies in the world league table would give European companies a negligible share of only 5% of the world market by the year 2000. If this is the case, they will have trouble staying in the business.

REVENUE OF LEADING COMPUTER COMPANIES, 1990

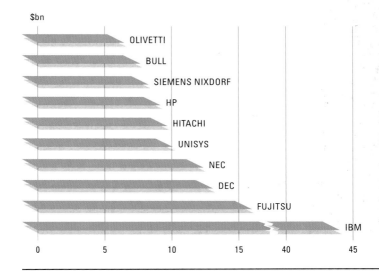

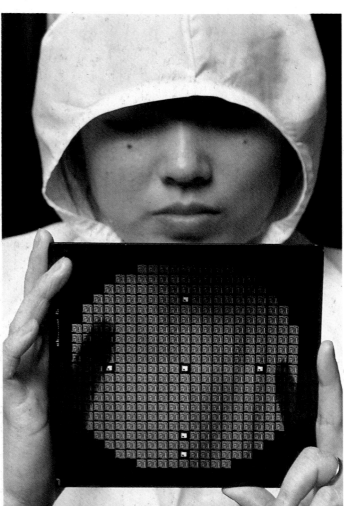

A photomask used in the manufacture of a very large scale integration (VLSI) semiconductor wafer. Each small rectangle corresponds to individual integrated circuits, which are later separated out.

TV'S NEW GENERATION GAME

High Definition Television (HDTV) will not arrive in Europe until after the year 2000 although it is already in Japan. In Europe, Philips and Thomson Consumer Electronics have invested over $1bn each in the development of a European HDTV standard, known as HDMac. HDMac will not be compatible with Europe's PAL system. It requires the introduction of an intermediate step, known as D2Mac. Like PAL, D2Mac is a low resolution standard, but unlike PAL, it features a wide-screen panoramic-view TV screen.

D2Mac requires new television sets, which will be capable of receiving D2Mac as well as the old PAL signals. Meanwhile, the European Commission has been trying to force television companies into broadcasting in the existing PAL as well as the new D2Mac standards simultaneously.

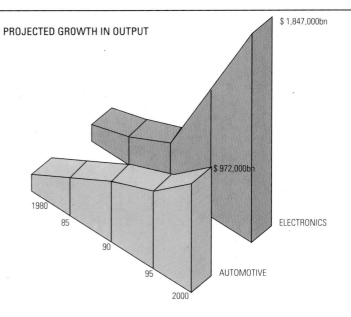

PROJECTED GROWTH IN OUTPUT

The electronic age

Whereas the automobile industry was the mainspring of the vast growth in the industrialised world's output during the period 1950–1980, that role is being taken over by electronics in the 1990s. Electronics is set to take the lead by the mid-1990s, as it more than doubles in value, while automobiles continue to rise moderately.

As the chart (left) shows, by the year 2000, the electronics industry will be twice as big as the traditional lead industry. This is also happening while the cost of much electronic equipment is falling in real terms. But the opportunities for applying electronics multiply, and produce growth.

TEXTILES AND CLOTHING

Despite a drift to the Far East over the last two decades, Europe remains a major force in world textiles and clothing. The textile and clothing industries in the European Community had a combined output in 1990 of 132bn ecus; 70% of that was accounted for by textiles, which employed 1.5m people. To produce the remaining 30%, clothing employed a further 1m – together equal to 7% of the industrial workforce. In eastern Europe, employment in 1989 was more than double the EC total at around 6m with 4m in the former Soviet Union alone.

Asia dominates the world spinning and weaving market, and supplies nearly 30% of western Europe's clothing imports.

The markets in western and eastern Europe are evenly matched in volume terms at 6.4m tons and 6.3m tons respectively. However, western European production was able to supply only 75% of this total with the balance met by imports. Eastern Europe, on the other hand, had a small production surplus of 100,000 tons in 1990.

Eastern Europe's policy of regional self-sufficiency isolated it from world markets and left it in poor shape to compete internationally. Despite low labour costs, its share of western markets has been marginalised by faster import growth from the Far East. The textile industry is relatively poorly equipped and overmanned, with an output per employee of only 2 tons compared with 3 tons in western Europe. Moreover, its products are of low added-value and outdated design, geared mainly to the markets of the former Comecon countries.

In the West, several years of restructuring have put the industry – written off in the 1970s as "sunset" – in a more favourable position. Continuing import growth, despite quota protection under the Multi-Fibre Arrangement (MFA), has forced moves to shed labour, invest in the latest technology and focus on higher value products. Over 40 of the world's top 100 textile enterprises are based in western Europe.

The EC has managed to retain a surplus in the value of its textile trade (1.4bn ecus in 1990). However, it runs a deficit in volume terms (812,000 tons), reflecting the higher value of EC exports compared with its imports. And in clothing, it has long suffered from a trade deficit in both value (8.8bn ecus) and volume (805,000 tons). Textile production rose by almost 3% during 1985–90 but clothing output was down by a tenth. The industry faces the prospect of rising imports in a market which is growing only slowly.

A major concern of many western companies is the intended phasing out of quota protection over the rest of the century. Import penetration is certain to accelerate and western firms will be forced to find new markets. Eastern Europe is one source of new opportunities as markets open. Perhaps the best prospects, however, are in the fast growing economies of the Far East although access will depend on these countries lowering their barriers in return for western Europe agreeing to a liberalisation of the MFA.

INTERNATIONAL CLOTHING PRODUCTION COST COMPARISON

DM/standard minute[1]

1 Includes transport cost to Germany
2 Disparity between north & south Italy is statistically significant

☐ 1990   ☐ 1985

0.6
0.5
0.4
0.3
0.2
0.1
0.0

ITALY (N)[2] GERMANY W. ITALY (S)[2] FRANCE IRELAND UK USA SPAIN GREECE HONG KONG PORTUGAL TURKEY MOROCCO INDIA TUNISIA

INTERNATIONAL CLOTHING COSTS

At its most basic, a textile or clothing industry is simple and cheap to create. The output serves a basic need. So the sector is a natural priority for poor countries wishing to industrialise. Moreover, there are export opportunities because intense competition in rich markets forces retailers to look for the cheapest sources of merchandise from countries able to meet their standards for quality and reliable supplies. In 1990 hourly labour costs in textiles were only 25 cents in Indonesia but as high as $16.46 in western Germany. In India they were only 72 cents against Italy's $16.13. Yet western Germany and Italy were the world's two leading exporters of textiles, and Italy the second biggest exporter of clothing.

Low productivity in developing countries, however, erodes their labour cost advantage. The graph shows that the true production cost gap in clothing is narrower than the wage differential. Also, as fashion cycles get shorter, quick response is starting to favour local suppliers. Shorter fashion cycles mean retailers are prepared to pay a premium if they can delay ordering until the season is under way – or if they can obtain variations (like colours) in mid-season. However, many western European clothing firms can compete only by subcontracting labour-intensive operations to eastern European countries. The cost gap is much smaller in textiles where automation has almost eliminated labour in some mills.

Connections: Eastern Europe 110–111   Europe and Asia 160–165

WORLD SPINNING AND WEAVING CAPACITY

Asia dominates textile producing capacity, with about half the world's total against western Europe's 9%. But the west is more productive, helped by re-equipment with more advanced open-end technology in spinning and shuttleless looms in weaving. Surprisingly, eastern Europe has been the biggest investor in these machines. In 1990, it had 18% of world spinning capacity but 61% of all open-end spinning machines (a Czech invention). In weaving, its share was 21% overall, but 38% in shuttleless looms.

However, both regions are seeing their shares decline as Asia's grows. During 1981–90 western Europe took only 9% of new spinning capacity against Asia's 36%. And while eastern Europe's share over the ten years was 34%, almost matching Asia's, by 1990 it was only 19%. In Asia's favour is the fact that, whereas shuttleless looms are undisputed as the superior technology, the conventional ring spinning machines preferred by Asian countries are proving to be more versatile and often produce better quality. Asia's dominant position in both spinning and weaving looks secure.

SHARES OF WORLD SPINNING CAPACITY, 1990

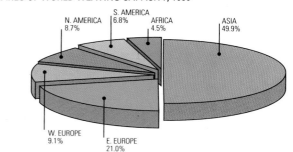

SHARES OF WORLD WEAVING CAPACITY, 1990

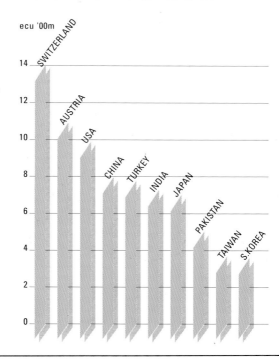

Trade

The charts show western and eastern Europe's share of world textile and clothing imports and exports in 1989.

IMPORTS $182bn

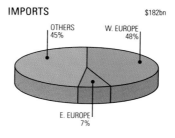

EXPORTS $182bn

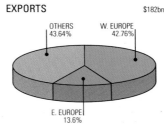

THE EC'S SUPPLIERS

Of the ten main textile exporters to the European Community, the top three, Switzerland, Austria and the USA, are high cost countries, demonstrating that it is still possible to manufacture textiles competitively in industrialised countries. Switzerland's and Austria's shares of EC textile imports rose during the 1980s, but the USA's fell to only 9% in 1990 compared with 12% ten years earlier. Turkey, however, more than doubled its share from 3% to 7%, while China's rose by almost as much, from 4% to 7%.

Austria is the only developed country among the top ten clothing suppliers. Clothing imports from Yugoslavia, Morocco and Tunisia reflect the extent of subcontracting in those countries on behalf of EC clothing firms. Hong Kong's long established lead is being challenged by Turkey, whose share multiplied tenfold during the 1980s to 11%. China's increased more than sixfold, reaching 10%.

The driving force behind the growth in suppliers' market shares will be the way the internal trade of multinational textile companies develops. Ultimately, they want the cheapest, reliable source of supply.

THE EC'S LEADING TEXTILE SUPPLIERS, 1990

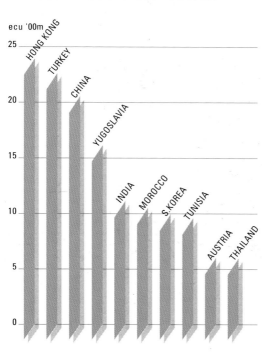

THE EC'S LEADING CLOTHING SUPPLIERS, 1990

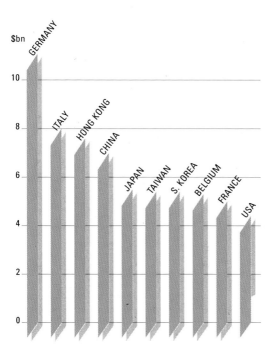

THE BIG EXPORTERS

The leading ten exporters of textiles account for two-thirds of world trade. Six of them are developed countries and all the rest, except China, are newly industrialising countries (nics). Germany leads by a large margin, but Italy is barely ahead of Hong Kong and China. Some 70% of Hong Kong's trade consists of re-exports, much of which originates in China. Hong Kong textile exports showed rapid growth in the late 1980s, as did those from Taiwan.

Even in clothing, five EC countries are among the world's ten biggest exporters. Hong Kong retains its commanding lead, but South Korea is fast catching up with Italy. The fastest growth in the late 1980s came from China and Turkey. Clothing exports are even more concentrated than textiles with the top ten countries accounting for 80% of world trade.

Western Europe still accounts for 43% of world textile and clothing exports (46% in textiles, 36% in clothing). However, about four-fifths of this is intra-regional trade. Only 5% of west European textile exports go to North America (7% in clothing) while Asia takes 6% (5% in clothing).

WORLD CLOTHING EXPORTERS, 1989

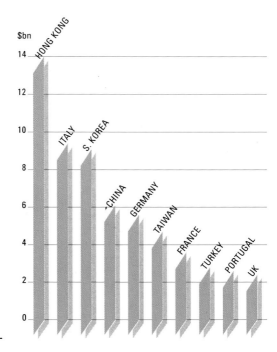

WORLD TEXTILE EXPORTERS, 1989

STEEL

Within the space of a few weeks at the end of 1991, Europe's largest steel maker, Usinor Sacilor, announced a plan to cut 8,000 jobs; the last steel plant in Scotland, Ravenscraig, was closed; and two stalwarts of Germany's heartland in the Ruhr, Krupp and Hoesch, started merging, threatening thousands more jobs.

If ever there was evidence that the steel industry was back in crisis, this was it. By the middle of 1992, there was a uniform picture of falling profits or dramatic losses at the steel companies. Back in the mid-1970s, the arrival of good, cheap Japanese steel from modern, efficient mills first exposed the weaknesses of Europe's aged installations. A decade of closures, cut-backs and modernisation (helped by a bit of EC protectionism) made European steel healthier; state subsidies fell; profits began to resurface and optimism revived in booming markets.

Then suddenly it all fell apart; steel was back in crisis. And not just in some of the more backward corners, but in the Ruhr, where companies like Krupp had held their heads high in earlier crises. Once again two critical factors were over-capacity and falling prices. If steel was a normal industry, the solution would be painfully simple: capacity would fall to a sustainable level, at which the survivors could make acceptable profits. But steel is not like that. Always regarded as a strategic sector, in much of Europe it is owned by governments, either from conviction or from bailing out broke companies long ago. So there are subsidies to cover losses and a reluctance to close surplus mills that sustain thousands of voters.

Behind the early 1990s crisis was a slide in prices of around one third, which began at the turn of the decade. It had nothing to do with recession or a specific decline in steel demand, which remained steady at around 110m tonnes in the European Community. Political upheavals in China and economic troubles in the Soviet Union in 1990 increased the supply of footloose Far East steel that drifted into the EC market, while local producers had high stocks. Anxious not to lose market share to imports, they released stocks at lower prices, and the downward spiral started. This process goes on until stocks are low enough for prices to become firm again.

But the important point was that the turn of the cycle revealed enduring weaknesses and instability in an industry many thought had solved all its horrendous problems. Such cycles are bound to be exaggerated in a sector where there is over-capacity. Despite the removal of about 40m tonnes of steelmaking in the 1980s, with the loss of about a quarter of a million jobs, Europe still had more steel mills than it needed. As each plant improves efficiency it inevitably increases throughput capacity. For this reason the best way to get cuts will be to reduce the number of players in the game: previous restructuring has been internal to companies, in the rest of the 1990s it will have to be about takeovers, mergers and alliances.

Steeling industry for the future

Steel has an odd structure compared with some of the sectors to which it sells its product. Compare the 15 big steel companies in Europe with only six car makers. The industry has resisted the trend towards globalisation; it is as if, preserved in the aspic of state ownership, the latter half of the century has passed it by. Yet British Steel went private and rose from bottom to top of Europe's efficiency league; now Italy is anxious to bring private capital and commercial nous into its nationalised Ilva.

But cutting down over-capacity in European steel will face political obstacles. The EC did an effective job in cutting outright subsidies, but nationalised firms get cheaper capital. When that happens, inefficient state firms' capacity drives out private production. The challenge is to make sure that it does not happen, while encouraging cross-border mergers to rationalise the industry.

There will also be changes brought about by the race to apply emerging new technologies in bulk steelmaking. Perhaps the most significant of these is what is called thin-slab casting. This means going direct from scrap metal melted in an electric-arc furnace to steel slabs cast thinner than the industry norm. This saves energy, because it takes less re-rolling to turn the slabs into finished steel products. The technical theory was developed by several European companies, but was first applied successfully by new, small independent American companies like Nucor and Chapparal. Whichever European companies team up with them will reap the early benefits of this significant new development in bulk steelmaking.

Steel and engineering have traditionally been the most important industries in eastern Europe, and their recent decline amounted to a crucial factor in the recession during the early years of the economic reform process. Between 1987 and 1991, the production of crude steel in eastern Europe fell by 50% on average, while specialist products also declined, but at a lower rate.

REVERSING THE TREND

European steel companies are fighting hard to reverse the trend towards ever lower prices. From a peak in 1989 the price for hot-rolled wire coil has come down by 28% to about DM500 per tonne. Much of the decline in prices occurred between the spring and the autumn of 1991. Prices for galvanised steel fell further, by 32.5% from its peak level in 1989. In an industry where costs have risen by 10% over the same period, the squeeze on margins is only too clear.

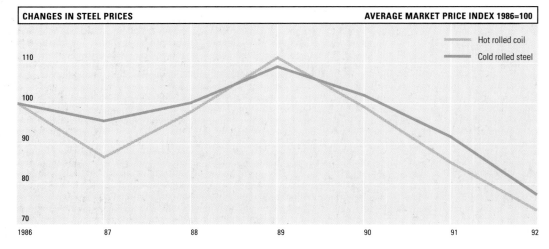

CHANGES IN STEEL PRICES	AVERAGE MARKET PRICE INDEX 1986=100
	Hot rolled coil
	Cold rolled steel

110
100
90
80
70

1986   87   88   89   90   91   92

Connections: Trade 48–49   Competition in industry 50–51

GLOBAL STEEL

EC output of crude steel is estimated to have declined from 136.2m tonnes to about 132.1m in 1991, but the pattern within the EC is uneven. The post-unification boom in Germany has led to a rise in western German steel production by 1m tonnes to 39.3m, while British steel output went down from 18m to 16.1m tonnes because of the recession. Crude steel production in the EC excluding Germany was about 5% lower in the first three quarters of 1991, compared with the same period a year before.

Also affected by the world recession were US steel producers, who suffered a heavy fall in crude steel output from 88.8m tonnes in 1990 to an estimated 78m in 1991. The prospects for 1992 are thought to be slightly better. Japan, too, has been suffering from overcapacity, with crude steel output in the fourth quarter of 1991 estimated to have been 3% below 1990 levels, with further falls expected for 1992.

STEEL PRODUCTION, '000 TONNES

COUNTRY	1990	1991
GERMANY W.	38,339	39,294
FRANCE	18,792	18,144
ITALY	25,439	24,184
BENELUX	20,389	19,405
UK	17,942	16,090
SPAIN	12,631	12,460
OTHER EC	2,667	2,565
AUSTRIA	4,293	4,243
SWEDEN	4,455	4,198
TURKEY	9,288	9,361
YUGOSLAVIA	3,611	2,248
OTHER W. EUROPE	4,185	4,007

USA	88,816	78,357
JAPAN	110,316	111,753

A STAINLESS POLICY?

Between 1980 and 1988, the EC paid subsidies to the European steel industry of about $31.9bn. Since 1988, the subsidies have gone down and are now limited to only a few specialist areas, such as research and development, and environmental programmes. Exemptions exist for Portugal, Greece and eastern Germany. The steel industry is also increasingly affected by EC competition policy.

In 1990, a number of European producers of stainless steel have been fined for engaging in a cartel, and in 1991 the European Commission raided a number of companies, including British Steel and Usinor Sacilor of France, to investigate price-fixing.

Such cartels are endemic in capital-intensive process industries such as steel. It took a long time for the EC to start mending its ways, but the European market is still distorted by practices in eastern Europe.

GERMAN STEEL

Germany is western Europe's largest steel producer, and its output of crude steel is more than half the level of American production. The largest European steel makers are Usinor Sacilor of France and British Steel. The German steel industry is much less concentrated, and includes a number of well-established firms like Thyssen, Krupp, Hoesch and Klöckner.

But pressure towards greater concentration has been building up in Germany. Thyssen is streamlining its operations, while the Essen-based Krupp is forging ahead with plans to merge with Hoesch of Dortmund, in a deal aimed at reducing capacity. Separately, Klöckner has forged an alliance with C.Itoh, the Japanese trading house, and Rautaruukki, a Finnish steel maker, to build a joint plant in Bremen.

The outlook for the German steel industry is uncertain, especially after the steel employers agreed in 1991 a controversial 6.4% wage settlement with the IG Metall, the steel and metalworkers union. The settlement was criticised for adding to the industry's already formidable problems. Germany's fractious 1992 wage round gave more cause for concern.

LEADING PRODUCERS, 1990

COUNTRY	COMPANY	RANK	TONNES m
GERMANY	THYSSEN	4	11.27
	KRUPP STAHL	7	4.4
	PREUSSAG	8	4.3
	HOESCH	9	4.2
FRANCE	USINOR SACILOR	1	14.02
	ILVA	3	11.6
UK	BRITISH STEEL	2	23.6
BELGIUM	COCKERILL SAMBRE	6	4.4
NETHERLANDS	HOOGOVENS	5	5.3
AUSTRIA	VOEST ALPINE	10	4.2

Hot work, hard times. The early 1990s saw the European steel industry in crisis again.

BRITISH STEEL

British Steel is Europe's second largest and the world's fourth largest steel company. Formerly known as British Steel Corporation (BSC), the company underwent a transformation during the 1980s. In 1980, BSC made losses of £1.8bn, but from this low point onwards the company staged a spectacular recovery. Privatised in late 1988, British Steel subsequently became Europe's most efficient steel maker, and in the financial year to March 1991 it reported profits of £471m on turnover of £5.04bn.

From then on the situation worsened. The company was hit by a combination of factors: recession in Britain, overcapacity in the European steel industry and the ensuing collapse in steel prices. Pre-tax profits for the first half year to end-September 1991 collapsed from £307m to just £19m.

In January 1992, British Steel aroused political controversy when it announced that the Ravenscraig steel plant, the last remaining steel mill in Scotland, was to close by the autumn of 1992, two years earlier than expected, with the loss of over 1,200 jobs. British Steel's workforce, which was once over 250,000, has declined to under 47,000. But the company is expected to lead the way in cross-border mergers, which may be its salvation.

CHEMICALS AND PHARMACEUTICALS

Bust follows boom in the petrochemical industry with depressing regularity. Just as the late 1980s were a time of boom, so are the early 1990s a time of bust – with profit margins squeezed throughout the industry. The only small consolation for companies in chemicals and pharmaceuticals is that the bust is so far not as bad as that of 1980–84, when the industries were swamped by heavy losses. But with more petrochemicals capacity coming on-stream in Asia and elsewhere, the good times are not expected to return until at least 1995. Or later: in ethylene, for example, worldwide demand is expected over the next five years to grow at 2.5–5% a year, but worldwide capacity is expected to grow at an even more robust 6% a year.

Perhaps the greatest frustration for executives is that the bust-beating strategies so carefully conceived in the 1980s have failed to bear fruit. Then, the prevailing wisdom among large producers of commodity chemicals was

that diversification into speciality chemicals – which sell into niche markets at high prices – could protect their profits from the chill winds of recession. They diversified, but were disappointed. For several reasons. One is simply that everybody diversified in the same direction, which pushed up the prices paid in the spate of acquisitions of speciality chemical producers in the middle and late 1980s. Another reason is that speciality chemicals themselves turned out to be more cyclical than commodity-chemical producers had first thought. Last, and probably most important, speciality chemicals is a different sort of business, requiring a different mix of skills to compete profitably.

Not only do speciality chemicals require more research and development, they also require marketing organisations that can form relationships with customers. Speciality marketeers must understand both their products and the customers' businesses well enough to anticipate why such-and-such an innovation, just emerging from the lab, might provide some advantage to a particular customer. Similarly, they must communicate customer's frustrations back to their own research departments, in order to focus the search for solutions. Traditional commodity-chemical producers, by contrast, sell largely on price. To achieve low prices, they concentrate not on relationships but on achieving economies of scale in production – and staying a step ahead of the competition on the learning curve for the production of each new product.

The pharmaceuticals industry increasingly finds itself caught between a need to stay nimble enough to keep pushing ahead the pace of technological change and the need to be big enough to support the ever-increasing cost of creating and marketing new drugs. Two related factors bear heavily on drug economics: the decreasing product life cycle of each drug due to the longer periods required for clinical trials and testing; and the lengthy and complex authorisation procedures needed to satisfy regulatory authorities. Over the past decade, the pharmaceuticals industry has undergone a dramatic consolidation – even though growth rates for pharmaceuti-

Pain-relievers are bread and butter business for drug companies. Aspirin was first produced in 1899 and is produced in huge quantities today.

Market shares
With total sales estimated at $413bn in 1990, the West European chemical industry is the world's largest chemical producer, accounting for almost 34% of estimated world production. In terms of the value of its production, it is Europe's second-biggest industry, after the food and drink industry. Although still growing faster than average western European GNP, European chemical output is now slowing. Until at least the end of the 1990s, the Asia-Pacific region will be the world's fastest-growing chemical producer. Traditionally a big exporter, western Europe's chemical industry exported 13% of its turnover in 1990. Europe's exports totalled over $50bn in 1990, compared to exports of about $25bn from the USA and $12bn from Japan. But Europe's trade surplus is shrinking – with imports now growing faster than exports.

EUROPEAN CHEMICAL SALES, 1990

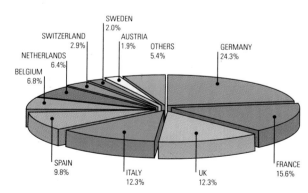

SWEDEN 2.0%
SWITZERLAND 2.9%
AUSTRIA 1.9%
NETHERLANDS 6.4%
OTHERS 5.4%
GERMANY 24.3%
BELGIUM 6.8%
SPAIN 9.8%
ITALY 12.3%
UK 12.3%
FRANCE 15.6%

WORLD CHEMICAL SALES, 1990

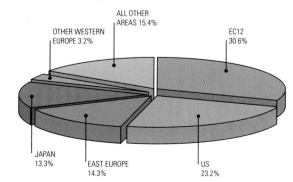

ALL OTHER AREAS 15.4%
OTHER WESTERN EUROPE 3.2%
EC12 30.6%
JAPAN 13.3%
EAST EUROPE 14.3%
US 23.2%

Sectors
The chemical industry is its own biggest customer. More basic chemicals are sold to other chemical companies for conversion into more sophisticated products than are sold to firms in other industries. Many chemicals are used in the production of consumer products such as detergents, paints, pharmaceuticals and cosmetics, while others are used as auxiliaries in the manufacture of other products. According to Cefic (the European Confederation of Chemical Associations), the final markets for chemicals are varied. About 38% of chemical production is eventually sold to other manufacturing industries, 27% goes directly into private consumption, 19% goes to the services industry, 10% to agriculture and 6% to construction. Performance and outlook for the various sectors differ markedly: pharmaceuticals remains strong, although the profitability growth is declining, while sectors such as fertilisers, fibres and inorganics remain weak.

WESTERN EUROPEAN CHEMICAL INDUSTRY

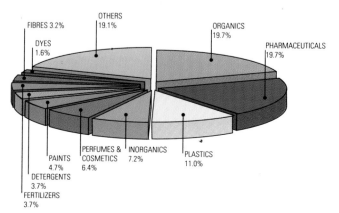

OTHERS 19.1%
FIBRES 3.2%
DYES 1.6%
ORGANICS 19.7%
PHARMACEUTICALS 19.7%
PAINTS 4.7%
DETERGENTS 3.7%
FERTILIZERS 3.7%
PERFUMES & COSMETICS 6.4%
INORGANICS 7.2%
PLASTICS 11.0%

Connections: Competition in industry 50–51   Single market 56–59   Energy 72–73   Waste 206–207   Health 242–245

cals have far outstripped those for other sectors of the chemicals industry.

That growth, however, has brought a backlash as governments are now trying to cap the rapidly rising price of drugs. In Japan and many western European countries – where governments pay the bills for most drugs through national health schemes – governments are experimenting with direct price controls on drugs, forbidding doctors to prescribe some very expensive drugs, and, in Britain, profit controls on drug companies. Given that the price of a given drug can vary by as much 100% between one western European country and another, there may yet be room for further experimentation ahead.

Increasingly stringent environmental legislation has pushed up costs for chemical companies everywhere. New environmental requirements costs can make the capital costs of a petrochemical plant more than 15%

higher than they were at the beginning of the 1980s. Led often by moves in America, western European companies are making strenuous efforts to improve their poor environmental image. In Germany, Bayer has spent over $1bn over the past four years to make its plants cleaner – and it expects to spend at least $500m more by the end of the decade. In many cases companies strive for standards beyond the basic regulations, adopting voluntary codes of practice.

Efforts to cut energy consumption go hand in hand with efforts to create cleaner chemical plants. For some basic chemicals, energy costs account for over two-thirds of total production costs. Over the 1980s, energy consumption by the western European chemicals industry fell by 30%. The need to diversify energy sources away from petroleum, which is plagued by unstable crude oil prices and supply, was amply demonstrated once again during the Iraqi invasion of Kuwait.

All drugs have to be tested. The "working heart" is one alternative method to experiments on animals. It doesn't cut out testing on animals but it reduces the number used in tests.

Going green

Spending by the western European chemical industry on environmental protection has been increasing dramatically for several years, driven by legislation and public pressure. Germany's Bayer, for example, will invest some DM3bn in 1987–95 on environmental protection and safety measures. Not coincidentally, operating costs for the company almost trebled between 1980 and 1990. Environmental investment is moving gradually away from end-of-pipe measures, such as incineration and landfill, to preventive measures, such as utilising low-waste technologies and reusing or recycling byproducts. Companies are also increasingly subject to national or EC-wide environmental taxes and levies.

BAYER AG INCREASE IN COSTS

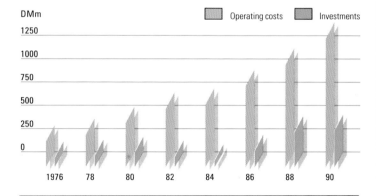

DMm

| Operating costs | Investments |

1250 1000 750 500 250 0

1976 78 80 82 84 86 88 90

JOINING FORCES

The most dramatic consolidation in the chemical industry has occurred in the pharmaceutical sector, where skyrocketing R&D costs and the need for a global marketing force has pushed companies into mergers, marketing or licensing arrangements. A single pharmaceutical now costs over $230m to develop. Two of the industry's biggest mergers have married European firms with American partners: SmithKline Beckman got together with Britain's Beecham, and France's Rhône-Poulenc joined up with Rorer. As the cost of developing drugs mounts and the period between regulatory approval and the expiration of patents shortens, "ethical" pharmaceuticals face increasing competition from generic products. Not surprisingly, the terms of that competition have become the subject of intense lobbying and political debate. European companies are particularly concerned about losing competitiveness against US and Japanese rivals, and so are encouraging the EC to draft directives giving them greater patent protection, and their competitors less freedom to advertise, license and market their drugs. Meanwhile governments, which buy most drugs in western Europe, are becoming increasingly unhappy with the high prices which pharmaceutical companies say they must charge to turn a profit on innovative pharmaceuticals.

Drug companies' spending on R&D

Investing in R&D is essential for drug companies. The costs are high but so are the rewards; revenues from Zantac, an ulcer treatment which became the world's best-selling drug completely transformed the fortunes of Glaxo. The figures in the table relate to pharmaceuticals only.

COUNTRY	COMPANY	RANK	$m		%
USA	BRISTOL-MYERS SQUIBB	1	657.0	4,442.0	14.8
	JOHNSON & JOHNSON	7	419.0	2,652.0	15.8
	MARION NERRELL DOW	10	329.0	2,211.0	14.9
GERMANY	HOECHST	3	613.3	4,410.6	13.9
	BAYER	5	487.2	4,237.8	11.5
	BOEHRINGER INGELHEIM	8	367.0	1,914.4	19.2
UK	GLAXO	2	654.2	4,679.5	14.0
SWITZERLAND	SANDOZ	6	484.1	3,464.1	14.0
FRANCE	RHÔNE-POULENC	9	350.9	2,784.6	12.6
USA/UK	SMITHKLINE BEECHAM	4	552.5	3,668.8	15.81

| | R&D $m | | Sales $m | | R&D as % of sales |

Chemical leaders

The three German majors, BASF, Hoechst and Bayer, lead both the European and the international league table of chemical companies in terms of sales. Eight European companies now number among the top ten worldwide – the two others being the American Du Pont and Dow Chemical; and 19 European companies appear on the list of the world's 30 biggest chemical firms – compared to 10 American firms and only one Japanese.

SALES

COMPANY	TURNOVER $m
BASF	31,195
HOECHST	30,017
BAYER	27,863
ICI	24,909
RHÔNE-POULENC	15,483
CIBA-GEIBY	15,459
ELF AQUITAINE[1]	14,323
ENICHEM	13,363
ROYAL DUTCH/SHELL[1]	12,703
AKZO	10,229

1 Chemicals/Petrochemicals only

ENERGY

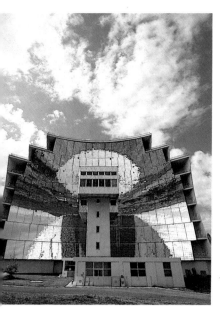

Two issues will determine European energy policy for the foreseeable future: the environment and the incorporation of former Soviet bloc states into the open market for energy. The two are related because it is inconceivable that the European Commission can pursue its goal of cleaning up smoke-stack industries and restraining carbon emissions through higher taxes in western Europe, while eastern neighbours continue to pollute on a grand scale.

The United Nations estimates that upgrading the energy infrastructure of central and eastern Europe could cost $120bn by 2010. Its Economic Commission for Europe (ECE) has tabled proposals to reduce the gap in energy efficiency between East and West by half, saving 450m tonnes of oil equivalent (MTOE) by the year 2000 and 600 MTOE by 2010 – nine-tenths of it fossil fuels.

The ECE believes its programme can be financed through foreign investment, sustained growth and a reduction in the difference between local and international energy price levels.

Alternative energy sources, such as solar power from this French station, are being encouraged but still account for a very small proportion of energy produced.

An improved infrastructure will mean cleaner, more efficient power stations and factories, reducing drastically the environmental pollution in eastern Europe. Until that becomes a reality, the EC's proposed carbon tax, which could put $10 on the cost of a barrel of oil by the turn of the century, will receive a cool reception from western industry.

The investment in big rigs to get oil out of the North Sea was immense. The oil came on stream in 1975. Production peaked in 1985 but will continue well into the next century.

The EC hopes that dearer oil will encourage the development of alternative fuels. That strategy was undermined by the weakness of oil prices as OPEC failed to control production after the Gulf war. But, as the effects of the war faded, OPEC gradually tightened up.

Grid ambitions

The map and the charts below it show the energy consumption of the different regions of the world. The high per capita consumption levels for economically backward eastern Europe illustrate just how inefficiently those countries have used energy.

It is against this background that an ambitious plan has been conceived to make optimal use of Europe's indigenous energy capacity through an ambitious energy network.

A vast Euro-energy grid is the eventual aim of the European Energy Charter. National gas piped from the Russian Federation or electricity generated by power stations in the Ukraine could be used to heat and light buildings in Britain and Germany and, in theory at least, the removal of barriers to competition would benefit consumers.

The proposals are among the most far-reaching to emerge from the European Commission. Electricity and pipeline interconnections are planned between signatory nations. Not only would these make possible the flow of supplies; modern facilities could also stem huge losses from leaky eastern European pipelines and cables.

The charter, conceived by Ruud Lubbers, the Dutch prime minister, could unlock the vast resources of the former Soviet Union, where up to 40% of the world's gas and half of its coal and oil reserves are located. Gas could be piped from Russia to France or Spain, for example, without third-party countries charging prohibitive tariffs.

Western countries would be able to repatriate cash and to employ western labour in return for agreeing to train local workers. Different charges for local and foreign companies would be outlawed.

Implementation of the energy charter should ensure continuity of supplies of oil, gas and electricity throughout Europe at competitive prices. It will also provide the basis for future cooperation between East and West in other matters not

ENERGY CONSUMPTION PER HEAD PER YEAR, TONNES OF COAL EQUIVALENT

- 5.0
- 2.5
- 1.0
- 0.5
- 0.25

☐ no reliable data

related to energy.

Supporters of the charter envisage a number of benefits. It should bring closer to reality an internal energy market within the European Community itself

REAL MARKET PRICES

As the eastern bloc crumbled, former Soviet satellites discovered the cost of real market prices for their oil and gas. Before the removal of subsidies, members of Comecon paid little over $7 a barrel for oil produced in the Soviet Union. They have had to come to terms with a near-trebling of energy costs as they purchase crude in the open market. By the same token Russia and other oil-producing countries seeking to consolidate their independence find that they no longer have a guaranteed market for their oil.

Although there are huge oil and gas reserves in the former Soviet Union, it will require enormous foreign investment and expertise for them to be exploited effectively and that cannot happen until the newly independent states have energy policies. Even then, the nature and remote location of much of these reserves mean that they will need the latest technology to extract it and a strong oil price to make it worthwhile.

Meanwhile, higher oil prices sparked by the Gulf war cost eastern Europe $7bn in 1990. At subsidised prices of $7 a barrel, oil imports consumed about 28% of Bulgaria's hard currency revenues, but just 3% in oil-rich Romania. A $25 barrel of oil would wipe out hard currency earnings in Bulgaria, while Czechoslovakia would have to devote 76% of its export revenues to paying for oil at market prices.

Connections: Single market 56–59 Europe and Russia 154–159 Operations after 1945 182–183 Air pollution 202–203

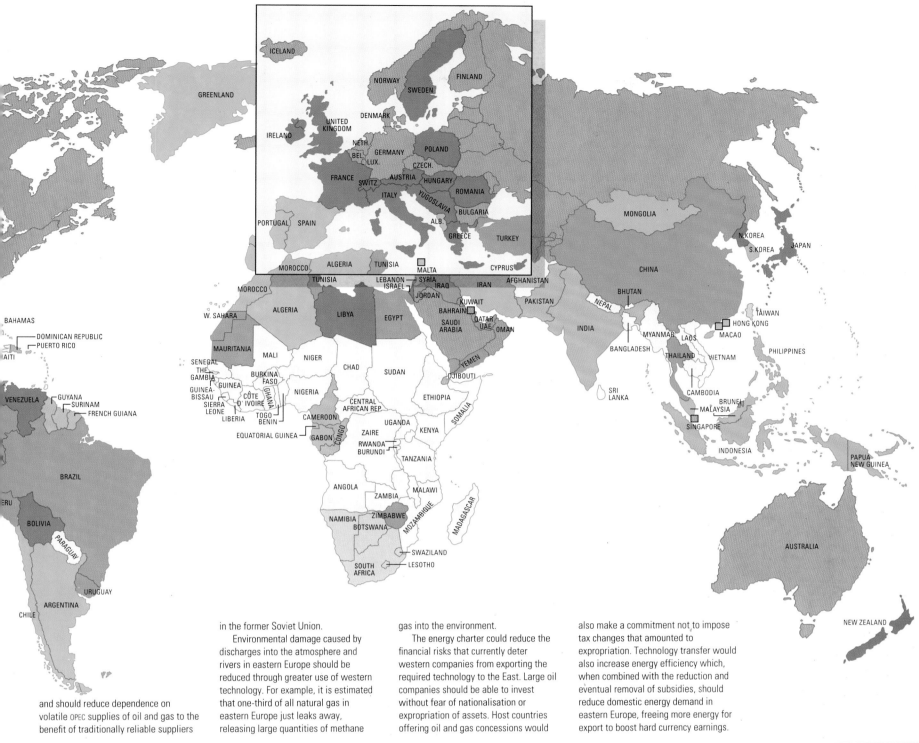

in the former Soviet Union.

Environmental damage caused by discharges into the atmosphere and rivers in eastern Europe should be reduced through greater use of western technology. For example, it is estimated that one-third of all natural gas in eastern Europe just leaks away, releasing large quantities of methane gas into the environment.

The energy charter could reduce the financial risks that currently deter western companies from exporting the required technology to the East. Large oil companies should be able to invest without fear of nationalisation or expropriation of assets. Host countries offering oil and gas concessions would also make a commitment not to impose tax changes that amounted to expropriation. Technology transfer would also increase energy efficiency which, when combined with the reduction and eventual removal of subsidies, should reduce domestic energy demand in eastern Europe, freeing more energy for export to boost hard currency earnings.

and should reduce dependence on volatile OPEC supplies of oil and gas to the benefit of traditionally reliable suppliers

Taxing matters

Europe is determined to show America and Japan that it is serious about environmental matters, and the European Commission is in the process of quantifying the potential economic impact of a new carbon tax .

European energy and environmental ministers have given agreement in principle to the tax which, it is estimated, could put $3 on the price of a barrel of oil by 1993. Consumers would immediately feel the impact of this measure, which in Britain would add about 12p (20 cents) to a gallon of four-star petrol.

The tax is intended to cut carbon dioxide emissions and combat global warming by acting as an incentive to find alternative less polluting energy sources. Taxation would increase annually, adding about $10 to the price of a barrel of oil by the year 2000.

According to proposals that have yet to be endorsed by all EC members, the new tax would be split into two equal levies; one on all non-renewable fuels according to energy value, the other targeted on fossil fuels graded according to the content of carbon.

COAL

PRODUCTION

3,189.4 million tonnes coal equivalent

CONSUMPTION

3,188.5 million tonnes coal equivalent

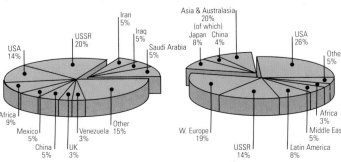

OIL

PRODUCTION

4,415.3 million tonnes coal equivalent

CONSUMPTION

4,426.8 million tonnes coal equivalent

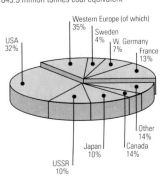

NATURAL GAS

PRODUCTION

2,458.7 million tonnes coal equivalent

CONSUMPTION

2,439.9 million tonnes coal equivalent

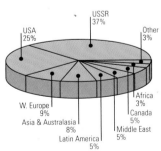

NUCLEAR POWER

CONSUMPTION

643.9 million tonnes coal equivalent

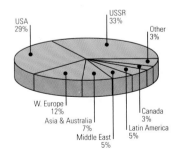

HYDROELECTRICITY

CONSUMPTION

751.9 million tonnes coal equivalent

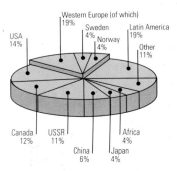

DEFENCE AND AEROSPACE

The periodic historic problem of defence industries has been the switch from swords into ploughshares. This is hard enough when defence spending falls at the end of a war; how much more difficult in the early 1990s for Europe's defence and aerospace industry that the end of the cold war coincided with recession. And the fall-out from a local war in the Gulf triggered a slump in civil aircraft without itself stimulating much military demand. Never before has the aerospace business suffered a simultaneous slump in its military and civil wings.

For some of the big groups there was worse. British Aerospace had diversified into cars and property only to find both these dropping by about 30% just as the aircraft businesses were hit. The mighty Daimler-Benz found itself facing unprecedented competition from new luxury Japanese motor cars just as it was having to adjust to the military and civil aircraft market problems.

The long-term prospect is at least clear. Defence spending in the West is heading for an unprecedented

A Milan2 antitank missile used by both Iraqi and allied forces in the Gulf war. It was their superior technology in the air war, however, that enabled the allies to crush the Iraqis.

decline with the collapse of the former Soviet Union. The precise trend will remain obscure until military strategists get the measure of what kinds of forces and weaponry will be needed to deal with the ever-present danger of local conflagrations. Large world stocks of nuclear and other weapons mean that any local war could become a wider conflict. But inevitably the trend is downwards.

Worldwide military spending was about $950bn in 1990, but the cuts are obvious already. The USA aims to cut $50bn over five years, while the British government is aiming to save about $3bn over four years. In the international arms market trade was down 35% in 1990 to $22bn. The Americans still held the market lead with 40% of sales, followed by Europe with 21%. What happens to this market in the 1990s depends on the politics and the economics of key regions like the Middle East, which have always felt the greatest need (and enjoyed the resources) to build up their military forces. Western governments will have to make delicate judgements on what is required for diplomatic aims, as opposed to the needs of their domestic defence companies to win sales that might only increase the military risks in dangerous parts of the world.

One thing that makes governments nervous about defence cuts, particularly when economic growth is low, is the concentration of production in specific towns. In Britain, where over 500,000 jobs in defence are at risk, there are towns such as Barrow-in-Furness which depend entirely on defence work.

Does Europe need its fighter?

At a European level, the fate of the European Fighter Aircraft has been bedevilled by worries about whether it would really be needed in the original volumes now that the Soviet threat has disappeared. Development went ahead of the aircraft designed to replace the ageing Tornados, but with no confidence for the manufacturers that the final production volumes would meet the levels they need to recoup sufficient profits. What may save the project is that Europe needs to maintain its technological ability to develop and manufacture advanced military aircraft in an uncertain world, where American commitment to Europe might wane with the decline in the traditional Soviet threat. But, with Germany now unwilling to participate further in the grand design, the project will struggle to remain viable on a reduced scale with fewer participants.

On the civil aerospace side, the trend is clearer, and in the longer term more hopeful. The fright the Gulf war gave travellers cost the airlines $4bn in lost revenues. That fed back through to the aerospace companies with a drop in the take-up rate of spares as airlines flew fewer miles. It is in spares rather than aircraft that the industry makes its real profit. The difficulties in raising capital by the Irish-based GPA in 1992 illustrated the effects of recession on the industry, but no one is gainsaying the longer-term trend for real volume growth in travel, which inevitably means airline travel.

In the years to 2005, Boeing forecasts healthy demand for civil aircraft, based on airline travel volumes increasing by at least 5% a year. The American company, which dominates the civil aircraft business, foresees a need for 8,850 aircraft worth some $617bn to meet that growth and replace ageing fleets with more fuel-efficient models. With the rival European Airbus in surplus for the first time, holding one-fifth of the market, the companies buried the hatchet on their long-running feud over subsidies.

REDEPLOYING SOVIET RESOURCES

In the years before *glasnost* and *perestroika*, priority in the allocation of raw materials, manpower and technology ensured that defence was by far and away the most effective and dynamic sector of the Soviet economy, as well as the biggest.

Today, an important plank of the republics' economic modernisation programme is to shift resources away from defence to other sectors, notably consumer goods.

Peace dividend

After Britain has completed the planned 6% reduction in defence spending by 1995, the proportion of Britain's gross national product taken up by defence will have dropped from its 1991 level of 4% to about 3%, the lowest since the mid-1930s. Britain's expenditure on defence relative to GNP is greater than that of any other western European country, though the French spend more on a per capita basis.

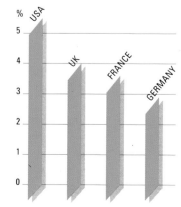

DEFENCE SPENDING AS % OF GNP

DEFENCE ON A BUDGET

The two western countries most affected by the combination of the end of the cold war and the recession are Britain and the USA. In his 1992 State of the Union address, America's president, George Bush, announced a $50bn cut in defence spending over five years. This will reduce costs by 17.2% from their 1992 level, in what amounts to the most drastic example of defence spending cuts in history. The president's plan includes the reduction in the number of active army divisions by half from 24 to 12, and of air force tactical fighter wings from 24 to 15.

Britain is also clipping the wings of its armed forces. The size of the British army is to be cut by one-quarter in four years, as part of a programme to save £1.2bn, or 6% of the defence budget. Other European countries are pursuing similar measures. Germany is to cut the size of the Bundeswehr, the federal army, from over 400,000 to under 300,000 as part of an agreement reached in the early 1990s with the former Allied Powers.

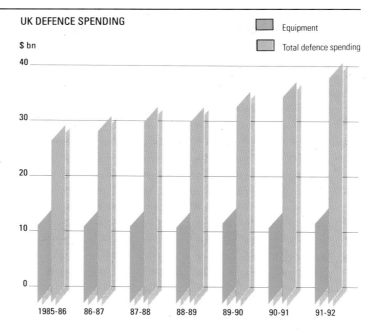

UK DEFENCE SPENDING

$ bn

Equipment
Total defence spending

40
30
20
10
0

1985-86 86-87 87-88 88-89 89-90 90-91 91-92

Airbus in the making – the Europlane to take on Boeing. It is being made by a consortium of Germany's DASA, British Aerospace, Spain's CASA and France's Aerospatiale.

THE AIRBUS CONSORTIUM

Airbus Industries, the four-nation European aircraft consortium, has been the centre of a transatlantic row over hidden subsidies ever since its birth just over 20 years ago. But finally Airbus achieved a small operating profit in 1990 and in 1991, although officially the figures were never disclosed. The recession in the aircraft business did not have an immediate effect on sales and profits, since today's profits are the result of yesteryear's sales. However, pessimists ponder the difficult state of the airline business and suggest that cancellations of orders could threaten the honeymoon.

MANUFACTURERS OF AIRBUS

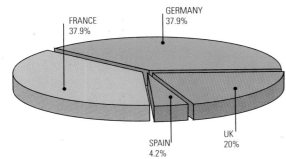

FRANCE
37.9%

GERMANY
37.9%

SPAIN
4.2%

UK
20%

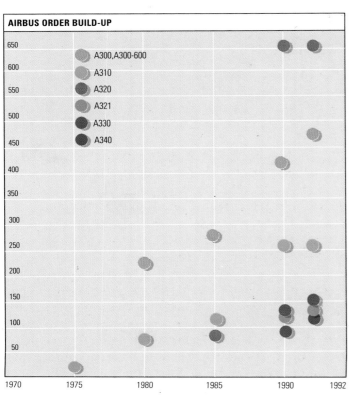

AIRBUS ORDER BUILD-UP

650
600
550
500
450
400
350
300
250
200
150
100
50

A300, A300-600
A310
A320
A321
A330
A340

1970   1975   1980   1985   1990   1992

EUROPE'S DEFENCE GIANTS

British Aerospace is Britain's largest defence company, with a turnover in 1990 of £10.5bn. Defence accounted for over 75% of the company's turnover in 1986, but it is now about 40%.

The steep relative fall in defence expenditure came mainly because of diversification into other business areas, most notably BAe's acquisition of the Rover car company in 1988. But the company's fortunes turned in 1991, because of the recession and the fall in defence expenditure. This led it to an ever-increasing dependence on one single contract with Saudi Arabia.

Daimler-Benz, most noted for its Mercedes-Benz car business, diversified into the defence sector through a series of acquisitions, which were later combined into DASA, Germany's largest defence company. DASA's defence-related business accounts for around half of its turnover, which includes MBB, the defence contractor, and Telefunken Systemtechnik, a defence electronics producer. The remaining businesses consist of Dornier, the light aircraft manufacturer, and the MTU engine maker. DASA hopes to cut the proportion of defence-related activities to about 25% of sales.

BAE'S PRE-TAX PROFITS

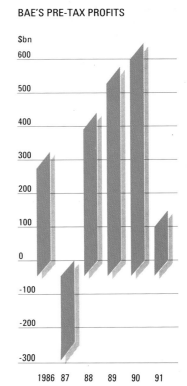

$bn

600
500
400
300
200
100
0
-100
-200
-300

1986 87 88 89 90 91

FOOD AND FARMING

The Italian agricultural labour force shrank by half in the 1980s and the country has a big deficit in food and agricultural products.

The dominant themes of farming and agricultural policy in the 1990s are reforming the hugely inefficient subsidy system of the Common Agricultural Policy (CAP) and making farming methods more environmentally friendly. Progress on both fronts is bound to be slow, but at last the tide has turned from endless increases in subsidies and expansion of environmentally damaging monoculture farms.

In the years since 1984, when the EC first took fright at its farm subsidies getting out of control, product prices have at last started to turn down – by 30% in real terms by the early 1990s. The EC is determined to press on with cutting price support, by 40% in cereals and by 15% in beef. The basic problem is that the CAP, framed for a postwar world more interested in agricultural autarchy, is still causing Europe's farmers to produce 15% more than they can sell at home, or abroad, without the benefit of price supports. The cost of this by the early 1990s was

running at about $50bn a year to Europeans as taxpayers, and another $85bn as consumers deprived of cheaper food at world prices.

It was the Uruguay round of talks of the General Agreement on Tariffs and Trade (GATT) that increased the pressure on the EC's farmers to accept reform, with the USA taking a particularly hard line against the CAP. For some time, the EC's timidity in reforming the system to let in more imports and to stop subsidising uneconomic exports brought the trade talks to a halt. Although the United States spends as much as the EC on subsidising farming, the form this takes means the cost to American consumers is much less. Reform has been held up by the special pleading of small farmers who find it most difficult to survive. But under the Irish farm commissioner, Ray MacSharry, it at last became accepted that the main function of the CAP was to slow the rate of departure of small farmers from the land, and the support system is being gradually transformed into the social transfer required with less disruption to market forces. The price-support system in any case always benefited the big farms, with four-fifths of aid going to one-fifth of farmers.

The development of programmes to pay farmers for looking after the countryside – planting copses, maintaining hedges, and so on – neatly dovetails with mounting environmental concerns. Mass production of single crops can be bad for the environment: it encourages ever-more intensive working of land, leaving no respite for natural features as bogs and bits of heathland go under the plough. Monoculture also encourages soil erosion and unbalanced specialisation, such as in the Netherlands, which by the mid-1980s was being submerged not by the old enemy, the sea, but by manure from huge pig farms.

In eastern Europe, the main obstacle to farming development has been the slow growth in private farms, caused by lack of capital. The growth of export opportunities to the West will help, particularly in Hungary, Poland, Romania and Bulgaria.

Putting on corporate weight

Europe's largest food companies grew even larger by mergers in the 1980s, but overall the industry is still extremely fragmented given its total size in the European economy. The drive for size is because the rewards from being biggest are seen as unassailable profits, while the numbers two and three in a sector are struggling.

But even huge food companies in Europe and the United States tend to be peculiarly specialised organisations. Swiss-based Nestlé may be omnipresent in marketing and production round the world, but its products are nearly all related to only two commodities, milk and coffee. Likewise, the fortunes of the food side of Unilever, an Anglo-Dutch multinational, revolve around edible fats, ice-cream and tea.

This, says Unilever, gives it the size and muscle to lead research in areas such as polyunsaturates, which is a critical factor in maintaining market leadership. And some other heavyweights have a narrow base: half of BSN's sales are in France, a further quarter in Italy alone, while Britain's Northern Foods earns its title as Europe's biggest chilled foods supplier largely from its predominance in its home market. Nor is there any great sign that the single market from 1993 is changing the structure. Even such a strong brand as Mars incorporates differences from one country to another, and supermarket chains seem unable to leap borders or form the pan-European buying chains the food companies fear.

THE IMPORTANCE OF FARMING

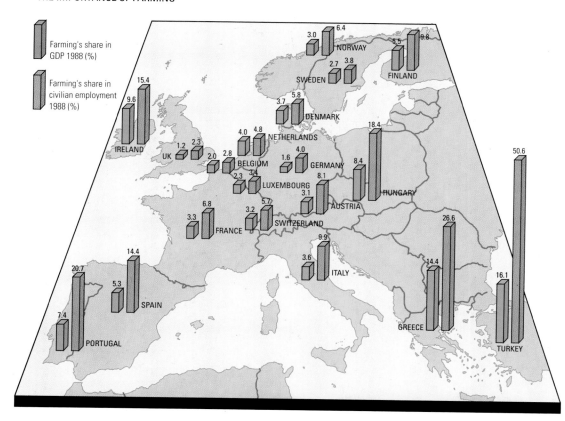

Farming's share in GDP 1988 (%)

Farming's share in civilian employment 1988 (%)

GROWING CONCERNS

The structure of agriculture and its importance to the general economy varies widely across Europe. There are large-scale, low-cost grain growing areas in the UK, France and Hungary, for example. But there are many smaller-scale, labour-intensive farming systems, especially in the Mediterranean countries.

The importance of agriculture to the national economies of Europe is not simply a matter of how many people are directly employed on the land. In many cases a smaller labour force is counterbalanced by a larger, more capital-intensive agricultural system, and the trend over time has been for labour to move out of agriculture and for the land to be more intensively cultivated using machinery, fertiliser and pesticides. The UK is the most obvious example of this process and is held up as the example of how the agricultural labour force can be absorbed into alternative occupations. However, this redeployment in the UK occurred against a background of industrial growth and prosperity that provided a strong demand for redundant farm labour. It is difficult to see how the rest of Europe can follow the same model with the same success.

GROWTH INDUSTRIES

Europe's cereal and meat production is comparable in size with that of North America. Europe's cereal production is soft wheat and barley while in North America maize and the hard wheats used in bread production predominate. Parts of Europe are competitive with North America in cereal production, but there are many thousands of smaller farms with less favourable climates where production can only continue with subsidies.

Europe's sheep population is much larger than that of North America. The countries of the former eastern bloc have potential in both meat and cereals. When Europe is defined to include the Ukraine, it is clear that European grain production will threaten North American producers.

As a result of the way the EC's Common Agricultural Policy guarantees farmers minimum prices, Europe has produced huge mountains of surplus food which either have to be stored or got rid of, both of which options are expensive. Since spring 1988 surpluses have been shrinking but overproduction remains a problem.

CEREAL AND MEAT PRODUCTION

m tonnes · Cereals · Meat

COUNTRY	1989		1990	
W EUROPE	178.8	29.8	176.2	30.2
E EUROPE[1]	94.2	9.8	92.7	9.9[3]
N AMERICA[2]	331.6	30.8	370.3	30.9
REST OF WORLD	1279.4	98.4[3]	1316.7	101.3[3]

1.Poland, Czech, Hungary, Romania, Yugo, Bulgaria 2.USA & Canada 3.Estimate

STAPLE DIETS

The overall picture is one of a Europe that can more than provide for itself in cereals, sugar and beef. The potential for an exportable surplus in these commodities is supported by the large growth in cereals exports from the European Community throughout the 1980s. These exports have reduced the market share of traditional exporters such as the USA and Australia. The EC is now the second largest producer of wheat in the world behind China and ahead of the USA. It is the second largest wheat exporter, behind the United States.

The export market for cereals has generally been a weak one and, increasingly, the Community's exports have only been obtained at the cost of large government subsidies. Beef surpluses in the EC have periodically been exported to the Soviet Union and, although sugar production is controlled in the Community by a quota system, there is still a significant exportable surplus. But that is bound to fall as GATT pressure and EC reforms bring a freer market. Significant lowering of barriers for eastern Europe is under way.

SELF-SUFFICIENCY RATES %

COUNTRY	Cereals 1981-83	1987	1988	Sugar 1981-83	1987	1988	Beef 1981-83	1987	1988
BENELUX	51	50	55	263	202	225	109	136	148
DENMARK	108	120	136	208	189	261	412	295	253
FRANCE	177	220	223	225	–	–	115	125	121
GERMANY W.	91	93	106	140	122	132	112	121	114
GREECE	105	102	108	110	76	64	53	26	41
IRELAND	87	96	–	145	180	–	507	692	754
ITALY	81	80	77	99	112	97	60	55	54
NETHERLANDS	29	27	–	174	176	–	113	133	118
PORTUGAL	25	52	45	0	0	0	97	83	85
SPAIN	62	99	113	106	101	–	92	98	97
UK	108	104	107	55	59	57	84	83	75
AUSTRIA	112	123	126	133	106	91	117	142	134
FINLAND	103	78	95	59	36	68	113	119	108
NORWAY	65	70	61	0	0	0	108	100	95
SWEDEN	119	118	119	98	88	86	113	105	97
SWITZERLAND	39	46	55	42	39	45	89	93	86
TURKEY	103	103	103	134	106	92	105	94	97

OUTPUT, EMPLOYMENT AND TRADE

The European Community has a strong record of production and trade in food and drink. Food sector production represents about 8% of total manufacturing production by value. Much of the growth in recent years is due to the Mediterranean countries: Italy, Spain, Portugal and Greece. It is likely that growth in the future will come from the emerging capitalist economies of eastern Europe.

Employment in the European Community's food sector was around 1.7% of total EC employment in the late 1980s and has been decreasing at around 1% per year. It has fallen from 2.5m employees at the beginning of the 1980s to 2.3m at the end of the decade. As the chart (right) shows, there is a positive net trade balance in food and drink, with the export/import ratio improving from 1:15 in 1986 to 1:23 in 1989.

Food companies such as Nestlé, Grand Metropolitan and Unilever are international giants on any scale, with worldwide production and marketing. And Guinness, which bought Distillers in a notorious takeover battle in the 1980s, has emerged as a global drinks leader from its European base.

PRODUCTION OF FOOD AND DRINK

COUNTRY bn ecu	1981	1985	1988
EC	203.7	272.5	331.3
JAPAN	98.4	152.9	182.6
USA	242.1	392.8	421.95

THE EC'S BALANCE OF TRADE IN FOOD AND DRINK

Imports · Exports · '000m ecu

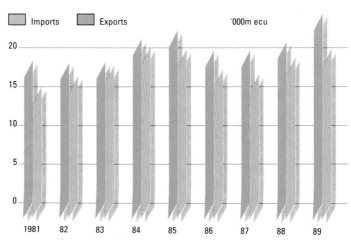

Businesses with bite

Of the top 30 multinational food firms in the world in 1989, half came from the USA. Nine came from Europe, accounting for about 30% of the sales of the top 30.

FOOD TURNOVER BY REGION

'000m ecu

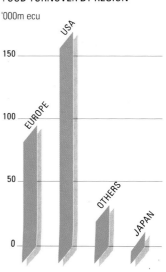

RETAILING AND DISTRIBUTION

As barriers to free trade within Europe tumble, the region's retailing and distribution industries struggle to find a balance between newly unleashed market forces – which push for consolidation of the industry – and the vast traditional differences in the tastes and shopping habits of the region's consumers – which thwart consolidation. For now, the forces of consolidation are winning. The retail industry is concentrating itself into fewer, larger and more powerful groups of stores. Stores themselves are also getting bigger. Ties between big retailers and big distributors are getting closer. How far the trend to consolidation will continue, however, is anybody's guess.

The ultimate fate of Europe's retailers and distributors depends in part on the intelligent use of information technology. The technology underlies many of the economies of scale accruing to big retailers and distributors. It also promises to allow big firms to cope with the complexity of customising their service to the differing needs and tastes of Europe's consumers. Another key factor will obviously be the extent to which the members of the European Community make good their bold pledge to remove barriers to the movement of goods between member countries. Last but also probably most important, the pace and extent of consolidation depends crucially on the homogenisation of taste and buying habits within Europe. Italians today buy different sorts of fabric softener, in different-sized packages, from different sorts of shops from the British. Such difference, repeated across thousands of products, can nip economies of scale in the bud.

So far, investment in superstores and hypermarkets has been greatest in France, Germany and the UK. Small shops have been systematically shut down. About a third of all retail trade and more than 80% of the packaged grocery business in France is now handled by hypermarkets (outlets with a sales area of more than 2,500 sq m) and supermarkets (more than 400 sq m). By comparison in the EC as a whole – excluding Italy, Spain, Portugal and Greece, for which accurate statistics are not available – over half of grocery sales go through such stores.

Out-of-town shopping centres – or malls as they are known in America – are spreading across Europe. Their attractions usually include one or more superstores, shops of various sizes offering a wide choice of products and price ranges, covered walkways, restaurants, entertainment and ample parking space. The growth of malls, in turn, has hastened the decay of city centre shopping streets. Small convenience stores are now prominent in the town centre grocery trade in some countries. What they offer against the attraction of the out-of-town malls are long hours and seven-days-a-week opening.

Mail order retailing, or "home shopping", has a long history in Europe, but new systems of communication and payment are speeding up its growth and changing some of its features. Germany is Europe's leader in mail-order, with 4–5% of all retail sales made by mail order. The big German mail order operators have large subsidiaries in several other countries and they have been among the first retailers to invest in eastern Europe. In France, the Minitel (a small computer screen linked to the telephone) installed in 5m homes is used to place about 10% of orders in the mail order business.

Hardly any annual report of a major company in the distributive trades is without mention of investment in advanced data processing equipment and its contribution – existing or expected – to profitability, efficiency and competitive strength. In eastern Europe for many years to come the priority spheres for investment and improved technology will be handling, transport and storage from point of production or import to point of sale. In the West, investment in better logistics and data processing equipment will continue. In its most advanced forms this investment will offer possibilities for many further changes in the distribution of consumer products. Increasingly, consumers in western Europe will come to know and, possibly, love: bar code readers in the home to transmit orders by telephone line to a shop or warehouse; direct funds transfer from the home; the "smart" or "intelligent" shop where standard products are ordered at a single point by the reading of bar codes and where the socio-economic profiles and buying habits of individual customers are recorded. The chief constraint – and it is a big one – will be the readiness of the customers to use the new electronic equipment and forgo what is for many the pleasure of shopping in traditional ways.

Department stores like the huge Galleries Lafayette in Paris (below) are increasingly renting out their sales area and becoming a collection of shops within a shop.

A key sector

The distributive trades – retailing, wholesaling, hotels and catering, repair and recovery services – account for 15–17% of GDP and of employment in western Europe; in eastern Europe their share is much lower, though reliable figures are not available for comparison. In most western countries, these sectors, particularly those parts linked to leisure and transport, have grown faster than manufacturing industries. In the command economies of eastern Europe, distribution and retailing were looked on as adjuncts to production and, like consumers, had very little influence on the volume, quality, characteristics or prices of products supplied. In the West, however, power has moved decisively from producers to retailers and consumers. This means that retailers often impose precise requirements for every aspect of the products they buy. Their technology and marketing expertise give them a greater knowledge of

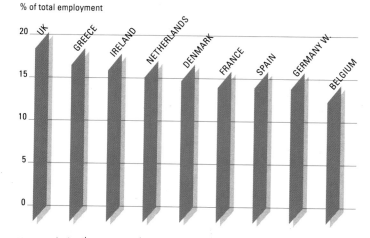

DISTRIBUTIVE TRADES
% of total employment

consumer tastes than many producers. Often this knowledge gives an influence over product design equal to or greater than the influence of producers themselves.

CONCENTRATING ON IT

At least 20m people are employed in the distributive trades in the European Economic Area – though the figure may be considerably higher because there are many small family enterprises, especially in southern Europe, where employment is unrecorded. In the former eastern bloc states employment is much lower: about 11.5m are employed in retailing which, like other service trades, is comparatively underdeveloped.

In the West, a process of concentration has proceeded without interruption for over 40 years, the small independent retailers in all trades giving way to multiples of various types or surviving by uniting in voluntary chains and buying groups. The charts (right and bottom right) shows the level of concentration in 1990–91. Paradoxically, privatisation in the East may transform monolithic state-owned companies into distributive trades composed of many small independents.

GROCER POWER

The largest European retailers, all of whom are primarily in the grocery trade, are varied in character. Several operate a few different store types or formats, often using different names – one for large supermarkets, another for small neighbourhood stores, another for discount stores, and so on. The hope is to create different stores for different customer groups. The family-owned German company, Tengelmann, is unusual among big grocery firms in that over half its total sales are made outside its home country; its biggest foreign operation is the A&P chain in the USA. Some of the other big German and French firms also have important foreign investments: Metro has cash-and-carry wholesale businesses in many countries; Aldi, the leading discount retailer, is developing chains in several countries in Europe; Carrefour with its Pryca subsidiary is the biggest hypermarket operator in Spain and it has businesses in the USA, South America and Asia. But large British grocery retailers have not as yet set up in continental Europe; the grocery trade is a difficult sector of retailing for foreign investment. Moreover, average net profit margins are considerably higher in Britain than elsewhere. By contrast British retailers in other sectors – notably clothing, footwear, household goods and mail order – have successfully invested in foreign countries. All the leading German companies have rapidly established themselves in the former East Germany and foreign investment in eastern Europe has been growing, though much of it appears to be on a pilot basis.

OVERALL CONCENTRATION

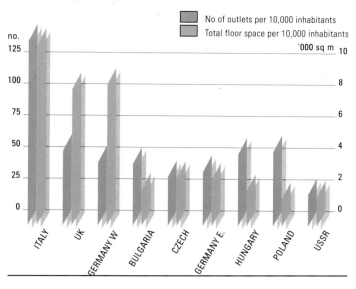

- No of outlets per 10,000 inhabitants
- Total floor space per 10,000 inhabitants

The irresistible rise of the bar code

The chart shows the remarkable increase in the percentage of turnover handled by scanners. The bar code has been around a long time, but it is only in recent years that businesses in Europe have invested in the technology to make full use of the bar code system. The benefits are considerable: much better stock control and much better pricing control.

Britain, a nation of shopkeepers with a high level of concentration among big multiples, has been one of the first to follow the US retail trade by investing heavily in scanners. But in France, where hypermarkets and supermarkets account for a large proportion of retail trade, the percentage of sales handled by scanners is much the same as in the UK. Of the five major European countries, it is perhaps surprising that Germany is the one that has shown least enthusiasm for the scanner.

Reeling in the business...French design flair at the checkout.

SCANNER USAGE

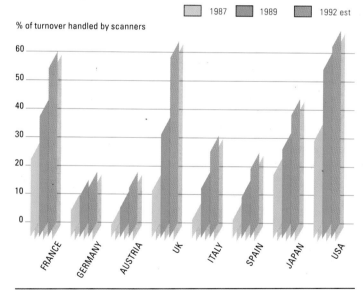

% of turnover handled by scanners

- 1987
- 1989
- 1992 est

Leading retailers

The table (below) shows the biggest European retailers by sales in 1990. It also reveals exactly how dependent most of them are on their domestic markets.

COUNTRY	COMPANY	RANK	SALES ECU bn	
GERMANY	TENGELMANN	1	8.3	20.6
	REWE	2	15.6	15.6
	METRO	5	5.1	12.3
	ALDI	6	8.9	12.2
	EDEKA	7	11.6	11.6
FRANCE	LEELERC	3	14.5	14.5
	INTERMARCHÉ	4	13.9	13.9
	CARREFOUR	9	7.5	10.9
ITALY	COOP ITALIA	8	11.0	11.0
UK	SAINSBURY	10	9.6	10.9

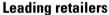
- Domestic
- Total

Eastern promise

After years of putting up with dreary shops with a poor selection of poor quality goods, eastern Europeans are now embarking on a consumer revolution. It will be slow and the initial stages after price controls are removed have already shown themselves to be quite painful. But in time the state-owned shops will disappear, cooperatives will become more responsive to consumer needs, and a new generation of shopkeepers will emerge, only now they will own the shop, not just keep it.

The chart (right) shows the trend in Hungary, which has led the way in eastern Europe in privatisation.

HUNGARY: RETAIL OUTLETS

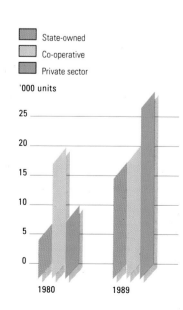

- State-owned
- Co-operative
- Private sector

'000 units

FOOD SHOPS CONCENTRATION

COUNTRY		
AUSTRIA	9,989	13
BELGIUM	14,399	15
DENMARK	4,823	9
FRANCE	46,221	8
GERMANY W	69,000	11
GREECE	26,044	26
IRELAND	7,808	22
ITALY	141,500	25
NETHERLANDS	16,976	11
NORWAY	6,712	16
PORTUGAL	39,358	37
SPAIN	101,968	26
SWEDEN	7,730	9
SWITZERLAND	7,400	11
UK	87,758	15

- Total number
- Per 10,000 inhabitants

ADVERTISING

Finland is one of Europe's highest spenders per head on advertising but is way behind the United States, which spends getting on for twice as much per head.

The 1980s were a time of growth and change for Europe's advertising industry. Local advertising agencies used to serve each country's advertisers and advertising spending in one country had little effect on advertising spending in others. This made sense. Consumer taste varies considerably between, say, Norway and Spain. In the former, people want anti-perspirants to keep them from sweating; in the latter, people are resigned to sweating but want deodorants to keep them from smelling. Brands, too, were local. Few Italians ever heard of a British brand of meatballs called "Faggots".

But in the past ten years, big consumer-goods companies such as Procter & Gamble and Unilever began to think of gaining economies of scale by marketing "pan-European" products. These would be produced, packaged and – crucially – advertised uniformly. These firms had always operated throughout Europe; many of their advertising agencies had followed them wherever they did business. But the attraction of pan-European marketing, spurred by the approach of a single market after 1992, provided additional impetus for ad agency net-

works to expand all over Europe. Just as many of the biggest and most aggressive consumer-goods companies are American (Philip Morris, Kellogg, General Foods), so too are many of the ad agencies that have flung themselves across the continent (McCann-Erickson, Grey, BBDO). America has since been matched by Britain, from whence four of the biggest global advertising networks have emerged due to the nearly limitless international ambitions of Martin Sorrell (of WPP) and the brothers Saatchi.

For much of the 1980s those ambitions seemed justified. Advertising spending in Europe grew at a unprecedented pace. But as recession hit many economies in Europe and, crucially, in North America (where so many big consumer-goods companies are headquartered), ad spending began to sag toward the end of the decade. Indeed, the slump in spending in some places, notably Britain, was deeper than any seen for at least 20 years, with the result that both Saatchi & Saatchi and WPP found themselves almost crushed by debt.

The 1990s promise better – though a return to boom

Advertising spending

After a dismal start, European ad spending soared in the middle of the decade, then collapsed again at its conclusion. It seems likely to improve, but so far there are no miracles on the horizon. The only certainty is that ad spending on television will remain robust as Europe's broadcast media sector benefits from the sweeping deregulation of the 1980s.

The rise and fall of advertising spending in the mid- and late-1980s can be seen in countries throughout Europe. In 1985, virtually all markets were thriving. By 1991, nearly all experienced a severe slump. Of the four biggest markets, Britain and France have been devastated; Germany and Spain have done better. Indeed, Spain is the only major market that has kept up an impressive pace – though one that pales beside its phenomenal growth in 1986–88. The German market's growth in the middle of the decade was less spectacular, but its downturn has been less crippling. With the addition of the East to its total, a unified Germany should be Europe's top market well into the future.

MEDIA BREAKDOWN

$ '000m at current prices

- ■ Newspapers
- ■ Magazines
- ■ TV
- ■ Other

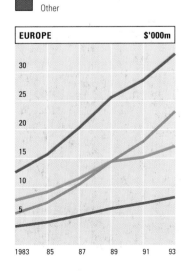
EUROPE $'000m

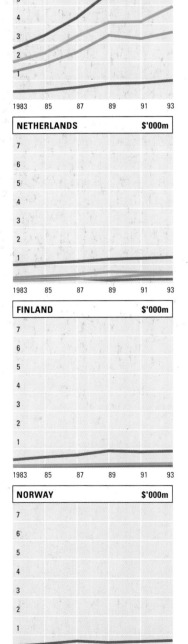

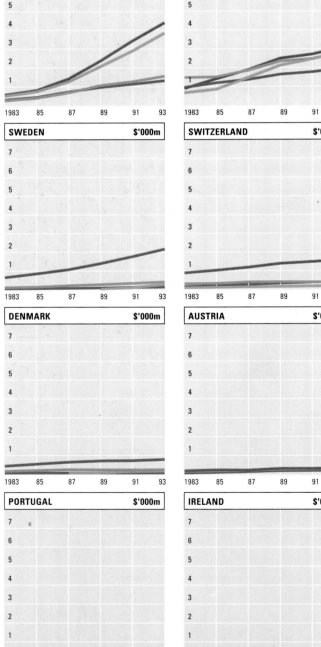

Connections: Rebuilding democracies 120–121 Leisure 234–235 Consumerism 236–237

years like the mid-1980s seems unlikely. More daunting to those agencies placing great hopes on pan-European advertising, the onset of the single market seems to be having a negligible effect on erasing local differences among consumers. To prosper, even big agencies need to continue to reap most of their profits from clients advertising within a single country.

With the collapse of communism in eastern Europe, many big agencies are setting up shop in places like Poland in anticipation of rising consumerism. It would seem an easy sell: millions of customers fresh to the suasive charms of Madison Avenue and Charlotte Street. But so far, ad agencies have proved far too optimistic in gauging the opportunities for new business there. Consumer-goods companies are keen on exploiting new markets in eastern Europe, but are stymied by lack of infrastructure and chaotic economies. Until those conditions improve, their marketing efforts will remain limited. Worse for the ad agencies, survey research is finding that eastern European consumers regard western ads with the same scepticism they formerly reserved for the men who used to run their governments.

Advertising is about building distinct images for companies and products. No European company has caused more of a storm than Italian clothing firm Benetton. After its successful mid-1980s "United colors of Benetton", which helped turn the firm into a powerful global brand, it embarked on a series of posters designed to shock: a black woman breast feeding a white baby, a blood-smeared newly delivered baby, a nun and priest kissing, a man dying from AIDS. None of the ads had anything to do with clothing but the outraged reaction they produced guaranteed large amounts of publicity for the company.

LEADING AGENCIES

COUNTRY	AGENCY	RANK	BILLINGS $m
FRANCE	PUBLICIS CONSEIL	1	1173.03
	RSCG	2	1165.66
	BDDP	3	920.26
	HDM	4	865.92
	BELIER WCRS	5	846.64
	YOUNG & RUBICAM	7	642.99
	DDB NEEDHAM	12	455.22
	LINTAS	17	401.96
UK	SAATCHI & SAATCHI	6	674.62
	J. WALTER THOMPSON	8	606.8
	BSB DORLAND	9	544.08
	McCANN-ERICKSON	10	490.79
	YOUNG & RUBICAM	11	476.51
	GREY	13	451.53
	D'ARCY MASIUS BENTON & BOWLES	14	431.01
	BMP DDB NEEDHAM	18	394.42
GERMANY	LINTAS	15	426.52
	TEAM/BBDO	16	407.21

Anglo-French dominance

Looking at the 1990 list of Europe's leading advertising agencies (left), one might logically conclude that only France and Britain have adverts. The highest non-Anglo or French agency in terms of billings is Lintas in Germany, which is number 15. The dominance of French advertising agencies is explained by three things: France's large market for ad spending; relatively few big agencies competing with one another; and a strong, historic advertising culture. Britain also has a large market, though it is dominated by American-based agencies in London (all the top ones save Saatchi & Saatchi). By contrast, other countries with big markets, such as Germany, Spain and Italy, have lots of medium-sized agencies, few of which are large enough individually to make the list. That may soon change in Germany.

Madison Avenue accounts for seven of the top ten pan-European networks but France has two of the top three: Euro RSCG and Publicis.

UNITED COLORS OF BENETTON.

Going for brokerage

The deregulation of media, especially television, in many European countries in the 1980s gave birth to a number of powerful media conglomerates. These groups, some with holdings in both print and television and across national borders, presented a challenge to the fractured European advertising industry and its clients. Few advertisers have enough clout individually to negotiate discount deals with media companies. But with their ad budgets lumped together, they could get such deals. To help them do it, specialist "media-buyers" sprouted. They would buy time in bulk and sell it back to the advertisers. These companies were a threat to traditional ad agencies, who normally are responsible for buying airtime and ▷

GROWTH IN MEDIA-BUYING CLUBS

1980   1990

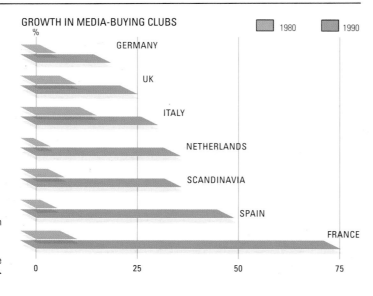

GERMANY
UK
ITALY
NETHERLANDS
SCANDINAVIA
SPAIN
FRANCE

0   25   50   75

print space, and who receive their commissions based on the amount they buy. In response, several big agency networks banded together to form joint "buying clubs" to perform the same function. Together, as the chart (right) shows, buying clubs and specialist buyers made great gains in the 1980s, and their market share increased nearly four fold from 11% to 42%.

As the chart (left) shows, France was, by far, the market in which media-buying was most widespread. Rules there governing "time brokerage", as the practice is called in its most extreme form, are considerably more lax than elsewhere. The biggest media-buying company in Europe is Carat, which is based in France but has gradually expanded into other countries.

MARKET SHARE

Advertising agencies
Media specialists

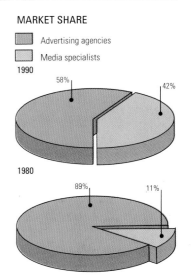

1990
58%   42%

1980
89%   11%

MEDIA

Rupert Murdoch built a globe-spanning media company virtually from scratch. He started with newspapers and expanded into TV, most recently invading British broadcasting with satellite television.

The 1980s were a decade in which the European media landscape shifted more dramatically, and more fundamentally, than at any time since the advent of television. Sweeping political and regulatory changes throughout western Europe, coupled with innovations in communications technology, created vast new opportunities for media companies. As a result, few sectors in European business have grown as fast recently as media. That trend will undoubtedly continue in the 1990s.

The driving force behind the growth of media – especially the broadcast side – has been deregulation. At the start of the 1980s, media operations in many West European countries were tightly regulated, in terms of their programming, operations and potential growth (vis a vis takeovers, expansion across borders and across media). Television was affected in a particularly dramatic way: in many countries, state-owned channels often held a monopoly or duopoly over the market. That is, to some extent, still the case. But after the 1980s' wave of deregulation introduced a degree of competition into virtually every media market in western Europe, the long-held dominance of state-controlled media is gradually being cut away.

This process is being sped along by, on one hand, technological advances, and on the other, the coming of the single European market after 1992. For their part, satellite and cable technologies have made it possible for broadcasters to take advantage of the opportunities afforded by deregulation. These alternative delivery mechanisms have paved the way for new entrants into previously closed markets. In particular, they have allowed some of the biggest and most ambitious European media groups – France's Canal Plus, Italy's Fininvest, Luxembourg's CLT – to begin expanding across national frontiers. Indeed, the approach of the single market has also spurred print press giants, such as Germany's Bertelsmann and France's Hachette, to develop magazines targeted towards readers in more than one country. Media reaching such "pan-European" audiences will be increasingly attractive to big consumer-goods companies seeking economies of scale by selling (and advertising) standard products throughout Europe.

Eastern gap

The exception to the widespread growth of media in Europe has been, of course, eastern Europe. In the former communist countries state control of the media has only recently been cast off. While the appetite for uncensored information is considerable, the infrastructures needed to produce it have been severely retarded. In some places, such as the former East Germany, newspaper publishers are pouring into the capitalise on new markets. But despite these and other groundbreaking ventures – America's music-video television channel, MTV, is one – it will take years for a thriving media industry to establish itself in most of the countries that made up the eastern bloc.

LEADING PRESS AND TV OWNERS

Given the sizes of the German, British, French and Italian advertising markets – the top four in Europe, in that order – it is no surprise that companies from these countries take up virtually all of the spots on the lists of the top press and television owners. In 1990 the top three press companies by revenue were Britain's Reed International, Germany's Bertelsmann and France's Hachette; the top three television companies were Italy's Fininvest, Spain's RTVE and Germany's ARD.

Dominant forces

Despite the proliferation of media companies throughout western Europe, many national markets in television and the press are still dominated by one or two big companies in each. State-controlled television channels remain powerful, often leading their competitors in audience share by a healthy margin. As many of these state-run channels shift away from licence fees and instead are funded by advertising revenue, the increasing reliance of advertisers on television will work to their advantage. Forecasters reckon that by 2000, the amount of money spent on television advertising across Europe will have doubled from its 1990 level of $15bn.

As elsewhere, big is best in European media. The most successful and aggressive media groups are generally those with strong positions in large domestic markets. Thus are Britain, France, Germany and Italy home to most of Europe's important media players.

Media might

The map shows the number of media companies in different countries that are in the European top fifty, together with their combined revenue.

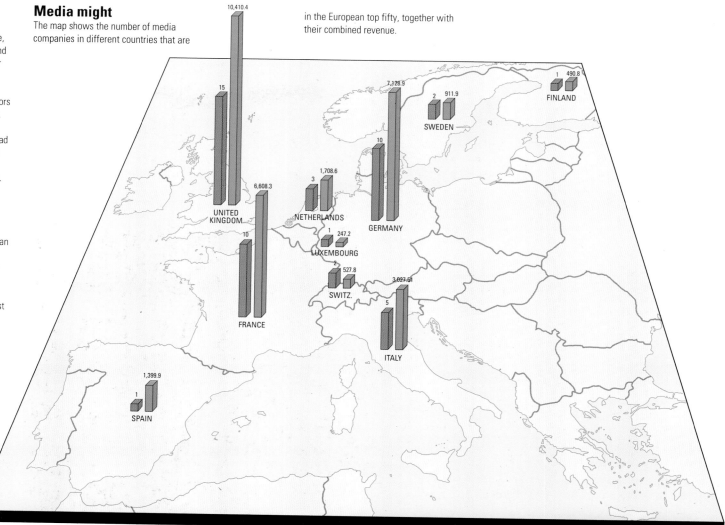

No. of media owners in European Top 50

Combined media revenue ($m)

Connections: Single market 56–59 Advertising 80–81

EUROPE AND HOLLYWOOD

Hollywood and the European film industries have never had much use for one another. For decades Hollywood, its movies hugely popular in Europe, has been content to ignore Euro-critics and make sacks of cash. European film-makers were content to gobble up government subsidies and make movies that only locals (and few of them) wanted to see. At any given time Hollywood films flicker on 85% of Europe's television screens and account for a similar share of Europe's box-office receipts. But as the European media scene has grown and become more competitive, its big players are looking increasingly to Hollywood as a source of expertise – and money. Companies such as Canal Plus and Berlusconi's Penta Films are setting up their own studios and pan-European distribution networks, while at the same time investing in Hollywood and teaming up with studios there on "co-productions".

For the Europeans, such alliances guarantee access to American movies and television programmes. This is crucial. The European television boom will send total number of hours of air-time soaring, from 125,000 a year in 1990 to 300,000 a year in 1995. There is no way the European film industry can

American films still dominate the European market and bidding for the TV rights to films has become extremely competitive in recent years.

CABLE AND SATELLITE GROWTH

The chart (near right) shows the growth in penetration of cable and satellite television. Much of the growth of television across Europe in the 1990s will come on the back of new delivery systems. At the end of 1990, a fifth of western European households could receive multi-channel television – an array of satellite channels via cable or miniature direct-to-home satellite dishes. Both systems will grow rapidly in the next decade, but cable will be the far more significant, with penetration more than doubling by the year 2000. By then, three quarters of all homes in seven European countries will receive their television signal by cable. Belgium, for example, will be about 95% cabled; Germany will account for fully 30% of the total of Europe's cable households. Where direct-to-home dishes are concerned, Britain and France will lead the way. After an extremely expensive start, which led to the two competing companies merging, satellite television in Britain is now in sight of making money, aided by some surprising programming alliances with the state-owned BBC. The spread of these delivery systems, and the proliferation of channels that will accompany it, has important implications for advertisers. By the turn of the century, analysts reckon that satellite television will eat up nearly 20% of all European advertising spending.

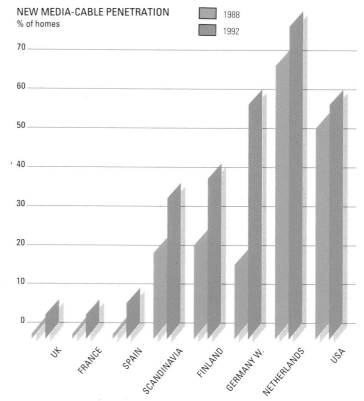

NEW MEDIA-CABLE PENETRATION
% of homes

■ 1988
■ 1992

70
60
50
40
30
20
10
0

UK · FRANCE · SPAIN · SCANDINAVIA · FINLAND · GERMANY W. · NETHERLANDS · USA

Channel growth

The chart shows the growth in the number of channels European countries have on average.

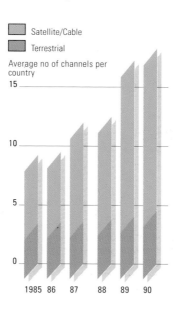

■ Satellite/Cable
■ Terrestrial

Average no of channels per country

15
10
5
0

1985 86 87 88 89 90

Canal Plus on air. This Paris based TV company broadcasts in France, Belgium, Germany and Spain, giving it a 0.8% share of European TV audiences. Its 1990 revenue was $840m and sure to rise as cable channels become increasingly available.

GROWTH OF TV

Between 1960 and 1985, European television regulators were engaged in the (somewhat grudging) process of giving private commercial broadcasters limited and tightly regulated access to the radio spectrum. The gradual introduction of terrestrial channels increased average viewing choice from under two channels to just over three. Then, from 1985, the amount of choice exploded due to cable and satellite systems. That expansion will continue, both with new terrestrial channels (Britain's Channel 5) and cable/satellite ones (most dramatically in Scandinavia, but elsewhere as well). Much of this is the work of advertisers who have lobbied tirelessly for the allocation of spare radio frequencies and the loosening of any rules – regarding takeovers, ownership restrictions, etc – that inhibit growth of the medium on which they spend an increasing proportion of their marketing budgets.

While business is the motor of a modern economy, finance is the oil upon which it runs. Furthermore, as manufacturing declines and service industries become more important, the financial sector has a crucial part to play in a country's economy.

It was in Europe that many of today's financial institutions developed, and until America and then Japan took the lead in banking and the stock markets, Europe dominated the financial world. One hoped-for result of the European Community's single market programme and the proposed economic and monetary union is for Europe to become the world's most important financial bloc.

This chapter reviews the history of finance in Europe and how finance works across the continent today. It examines the different cultures: how British business uses the equity markets for raising capital, while German firms prefer to get their funds from banks; how British consumers in their millions now pay their bills with plastic, while possession of credit cards is extremely low in almost every other European country. The difficulties facing eastern Europe are outlined in a special section and the key role that Germany plays throughout Europe is highlighted: currency anchor in western Europe; chief investor in eastern Europe. The all important issue of economic and monetary union is analysed in detail, as is the effect of the single market on, for example, capital movement (considerable) and life insurance (not much, yet). Other sections look at banking, the securities markets and the insurance and pension business. How pan-European are they and who are the dominant players?

THE FINANCIAL MARKET PLACE

Europe's financial future depends on the success of the European Community in establishing monetary union, a common currency and the various central financial institutions necessary to support them. This will also influence the ultimate likely size of the EC, since it would be hard for any European country to remain outside a genuinely unified European financial bloc.

Europe is already one of the world's three leading economic regions, but it is not yet a single or homogeneous market in the way that both Japan and the United States are. A foreign investor wishing to place capital in the European stock market, for example, is faced with a choice of 20 or 30 stock exchanges, employing different trading systems, different currencies, different languages and different settlement periods.

The change that will result from harmonisation of laws, market practices and trading systems in the financial sector will be huge, presenting the potential for growth levels way beyond those expected in the USA or Japan. It might offer the possibility, in the next ten years or so, of a yen-ecu-dollar world, in which the ecu bloc would be both the largest and the most lightly regulated.

The EC's GDP is already almost as big as that of the USA and will surpass it when new members join, for instance from the EFTA bloc and eastern Europe. Some potential members are sophisticated western-style economies (Switzerland and Sweden, for example); others (like Turkey and Poland) are not, by the standards of most current EC member states .

Regardless of its precise make-up, the EC has the advantage of an express commitment in the Treaty of Rome (its founding document) to inter-state free-market competition. It could also be the beneficiary of capital flight from the dollar into ecus (European currency unit). This would be bound to happen if Europe became the world's dominant economic power; but it would also happen if the ecu offered a clear alternative to the dollar

The steady growth in cross-border equity investment worldwide is already increasing the amount of foreign capital flowing into the EC's stock markets, despite their fragmented nature. London is the largest market in the European time zone and is one of the three key prongs – along with New York and Tokyo – of the global stock market. The other major European markets are Frankfurt and Paris, both snapping at London's heels for a dominant market position, at least in some areas. Frankfurt may well have a claim in the bond market; and France's financial futures market, the Matif, juggles for first position in competition with London's LIFFE. Amsterdam, too, has aspirations, particularly in the options market, but London remains able to offer the most in terms of accessibility and liquidity. And, in the negotiations that have taken place so far, it has shown itself more concerned to retain this dominance as a financial centre than to achieve an integrated European, or EC, stock market.

One Community, one market?

Nevertheless, there is increasing pressure to unify all types of financial and commercial markets within the EC, and the financial services industry is no exception. EC financial institutions – principally banks and insurance companies – are being rationalised into much larger groupings than before. And non-EC institutions based in Europe and beyond are seeking to make commercial relationships with organisations within the EC in order to establish a foothold there. Generally, Europe is likely to see more and more concentration in the financial sector, leading eventually to the emergence of three or four globally significant banks, operating at the same level as a total of around ten such organisations worldwide.

LIFFE (London International Financial Futures Exchange) was set up in 1982 following the success of the financial futures markets in Chicago and Sydney. The exchange is supervised by the Bank of England.

STOCK MARKETS: CAPITALS AND CAPITAL

The ratio of stock market capitalisation to GDP in continental Europe is much lower than in Japan or the USA. This suggests significant potential for growth in the European stock markets, which they hope to realise through attracting more listings from both domestic and foreign companies. The major reason for this low market capitalisation is that on the continent companies rely more on bank lending and other debt instruments for their funding than on the equity markets.

The UK's stock market capitalisation is already about the same size in relation to GDP as the USA's. The London stock market is far more liquid than its continental counterparts – one reason why some major non-UK European companies find a significant proportion of trading in their shares has moved from their local exchanges to London. Japan's high market capitalisation reflects high price/earnings ratios.

Capitalisation vs GDP

This chart illustrates the significant difference in relative size between the stock markets and economies in the USA, Japan, the UK and the rest of Europe.

It does this by taking the total market capitalisation of the stock markets in the four regions, and then expressing each region's market capitalisation as a percentage of the total; and similarly, by expressing each region's GDP as a percentage of the total of all four regions' GDPs. The chart should not be used for its absolute figures, but to compare the different ratios of stock market size (expressed by market capitalisation) to the size of the economy (expressed by GDP).

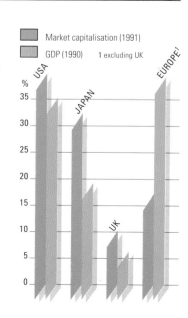

Market capitalisation (1991)
GDP (1990)   1 excluding UK

Connections: Foreign investment 60–61   Economic and monetary union 92–93   Single market 96–97   Securities 102–105

Europe's bankers

The map shows the relative sizes of Europe's national banking industry, expressed as assets of Bank for International Settlements (BIS) reporting banks, in $m during 1990. The UK's banking industry is easily the largest in the EC, almost double that of any other country's. This reinforces London's financial sector strength, particularly as the EC markets move closer together and the relative size of the UK industry begins to tell. France is the next largest, while Germany is only third-equal with Italy and Belgium–Luxembourg.

Germany's low ranking shows the lack of depth in its financial sector, despite its strong economy; and it represents a major obstacle to Frankfurt's desire to become the financial centre of Europe, since it would have difficulty meeting the operational requirement. Another contender, Zurich, with its legendary banking prowess, is ruled out by Switzerland having remained outside the EC.

The clash between Germany's economic power and the UK's financial services strength means that no natural EC financial centre has yet emerged. Industry commentators do not see London's pre-eminence being challenged in the short term, but London's stand-offishness in negotiations on integration of markets, together with the UK's hesitation about monetary union, count against London being chosen as the base for the European central bank.

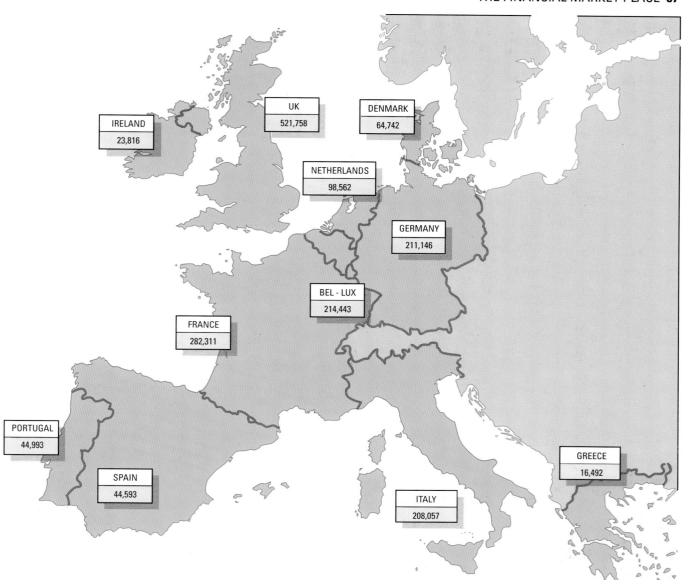

IRELAND
23,816

UK
521,758

DENMARK
64,742

NETHERLANDS
98,562

GERMANY
211,146

BEL - LUX
214,443

FRANCE
282,311

PORTUGAL
44,993

SPAIN
44,593

GREECE
16,492

ITALY
208,057

OPENING THE DOORS TO FOREIGN INVESTMENT

The major European stock markets are becoming more international, reflecting a worldwide trend. Indeed, foreign equity holdings are set to double their share from 7.7% to over 15% of all equity holdings by the year 2000. In gross value terms that means an increase from $830bn to almost $1,000bn.

The limit for this expected growth is calculated by Salomon Brothers on the basis that the proportion of international stocks held by investors of a given country should roughly equal the proportion of imports of that country. So in the USA, where imports are 10% of total sales, the proportion of non-US stocks should rise to around 10%. In the UK, the figure for imports is 34%, allowing considerably more room for growth in international stock holdings in UK funds.

This will link the world's economies more closely, and will have a profound effect on equity markets, balance of payments and all financial services. In theory, the EC's plans for open markets with transparent competitive rules should mean that EC stock markets will be able to take advantage of this. In practice, much of the investment into continental Europe, if not the UK, is still done outside the EC stock markets because of persistent problems with liquidity, transparency and settlement. This will remain the case until trading systems and standards on the continental exchanges are brought up to the highest international levels, and these issues are currently being addressed by the EC.

Outside the EC, countries as dissimilar as Turkey and Finland, Hungary and Sweden, have been trying to attract foreign investment to their domestic stock exchanges. Most eastern European countries are striving to develop modern exchanges, with varying success, in their efforts to convert their economies from being command-based to market-based; and Sweden and Finland both removed legal restrictions on foreign ownership of their domestic companies in the early 1990s.

FOREIGN ASSETS AS A PERCENTAGE OF TOTAL ASSETS, 1989

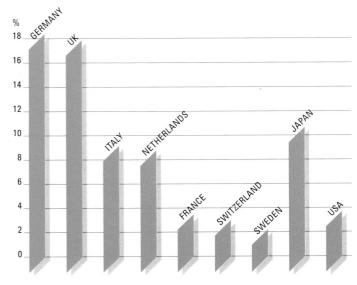

America's stockmarket, led by the New York exchange (above), and Japan's accounted for more than half the world's market capitalisation in the early 1990s. The UK stockmarket accounted for about a tenth, roughly the same as the combined stockmarkets of France, Germany, Italy and Spain.

Outward investment

This chart shows the amount of foreign assets which are owned in each country as a percentage of the total assets of that country's investors.

It illustrates how international investors are in the countries i.e. not very in the USA and most of Europe; very in the UK and Germany. Japan also has widely spread investments.

HISTORY OF EUROPEAN FINANCE

Grandson of Giovanni, the founder of the great Medici fortune, Lorenzo the Magnificent (1449–92) was a banker, businessman, poet and generous patron of the arts.

Europe's international political clout, from the 15th century until the second world war, gave it unrivalled financial strength. Its trade networks required sophisticated and flexible financial systems and structures to deal with the myriad small medieval and renaissance states which comprised Europe, and which forced its early financiers to develop effective techniques for operating across borders and in different financial regimes. These skills came to later fruition as European countries became world powers with international empires, and the bankers had to follow to provide financial services.

Modern European banking has its roots in the medieval trade fairs, the leading one of which, during the 12th and 13th centuries, was at Champagne in France which handled trade from all over Europe. However, it was supplanted in the 14th century, first by Geneva, then by Genoa.

Genoa's pre-eminence as a trading centre came at a time of great financial innovation in northern Italy, as financial activity moved away from the fairs to become a business in its own right. Banks sprang up in Florence, Sienna and Lucca, and later in Venice and Genoa.

The city states recognised the value of financial business, each moving to support it with political stability and with regulation. In one lasting innovation, they began to require banks to keep records of their business.

During the 14th century the dominant banking families were the Bardi and Peruzzi of Florence, who maintained correspondents at Avignon, Barcelona, Bruges, the Champagne fairs, and later at Lyon, Antwerp,

Amsterdam and London. However, by the 15th century, the Medicis dominated Florentine banking.

But Italy slowly receded as the financial centre in the early 16th century, when the French launched a series of devastating wars on the region, affecting Florence in particular. Genoa briefly became the main centre, but soon gave way to Amsterdam.

By the mid-16th century the massive flow of gold and silver from the Americas to Europe had increased the extent to which the European markets were now using currency. The Italians again had been the innovators and were the first to give state banks the power to regulate currency. It was for this purpose that Genoa launched the first state deposit bank in 1407 and that the state took over the Bank of Venice in 1587.

A new role for Europe

After the zenith of European imperialism in the late 19th century, and the devastation of two world wars, by the 1950s the financial industry in the European states was looking weak. Increased competition, initially from the USA, later from the resurgent Japan, was taking its toll. The European nations recognised the implications, not just for the financial sector, but in wider economic, commercial and social terms as well. They addressed the problem in part by establishing the European Community. Today, the Community has far wider ambitions, aimed at securing a dominant role in global finance, to be achieved through the powerful weapons of a single market and monetary union.

Steps forward

The chart shows the broad progress of financial development in Europe. In the early medieval and renaissance periods, financiers began to develop institutions, still recognisable today. Next came the changes brought by imperialism, as the major powers acquired large overseas possessions.

Financial turning points included a gambling and investment boom based on tulip bulbs which led to a massive financial crash in the UK and the Netherlands, and an investment stampede into a company which failed.

Then, after the second world war, the European financial industries had to struggle to find a role, which they saw in a united Europe that would allow them to regain their former global status.

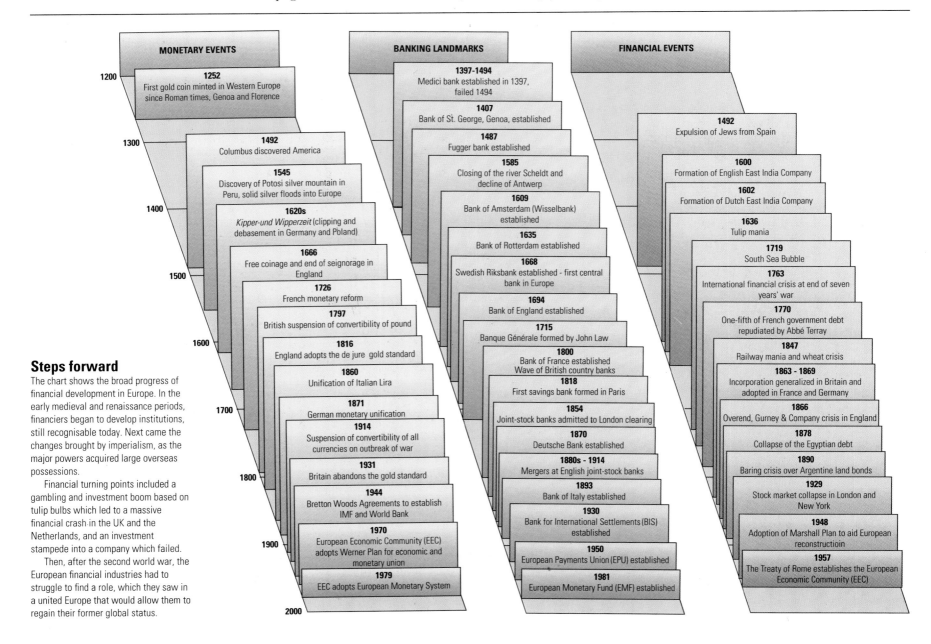

MONETARY EVENTS

- 1200
- **1252** First gold coin minted in Western Europe since Roman times, Genoa and Florence
- 1300
- **1492** Columbus discovered America
- **1545** Discovery of Potosi silver mountain in Peru, solid silver floods into Europe
- 1400
- **1620s** *Kipper-und Wipperzeit* (clipping and debasement in Germany and Pbland)
- **1666** Free coinage and end of seignorage in England
- 1500
- **1726** French monetary reform
- **1797** British suspension of convertibility of pound
- 1600
- **1816** England adopts the de jure gold standard
- **1860** Unification of Italian Lira
- **1871** German monetary unification
- 1700
- **1914** Suspension of convertibility of all currencies on outbreak of war
- **1931** Britain abandons the gold standard
- 1800
- **1944** Bretton Woods Agreements to establish IMF and World Bank
- **1970** European Economic Community (EEC) adopts Werner Plan for economic and monetary union
- 1900
- **1979** EEC adopts European Monetary System
- 2000

BANKING LANDMARKS

- **1397-1494** Medici bank established in 1397, failed 1494
- **1407** Bank of St. George, Genoa, established
- **1487** Fugger bank established
- **1585** Closing of the river Scheldt and decline of Antwerp
- **1609** Bank of Amsterdam (Wisselbank) established
- **1635** Bank of Rotterdam established
- **1668** Swedish Riksbank established - first central bank in Europe
- **1694** Bank of England established
- **1715** Banque Générale formed by John Law
- **1800** Bank of France established Wave of British country banks
- **1818** First savings bank formed in Paris
- **1854** Joint-stock banks admitted to London clearing
- **1870** Deutsche Bank established
- **1880s - 1914** Mergers at English joint-stock banks
- **1893** Bank of Italy established
- **1930** Bank for International Settlements (BIS) established
- **1950** European Payments Union (EPU) established
- **1981** European Monetary Fund (EMF) established

FINANCIAL EVENTS

- **1492** Expulsion of Jews from Spain
- **1600** Formation of English East India Company
- **1602** Formation of Dutch East India Company
- **1636** Tulip mania
- **1719** South Sea Bubble
- **1763** International financial crisis at end of seven years' war
- **1770** One-fifth of French government debt repudiated by Abbé Terray
- **1847** Railway mania and wheat crisis
- **1863 - 1869** Incorporation generalized in Britain and adopted in France and Germany
- **1866** Overend, Gurney & Company crisis in England
- **1878** Collapse of the Egyptian debt
- **1890** Baring crisis over Argentine land bonds
- **1929** Stock market collapse in London and New York
- **1948** Adoption of Marshall Plan to aid European reconstructioin
- **1957** The Treaty of Rome establishes the European Economic Community (EEC)

Connections: Europe takes shape 12–15   Securities 102–105   The European Community 130–131

Charles VII of France (1403–61) was crowned in Reims in 1429 as a result of Joan of Arc raising the siege of Orleans. He is pictured above handing down the "Royal Regulations on the Use of Money". His administrative skills were considerable and he organised the country's first standing army which by 1453 had expelled the English from all France except Calais.

FAIR TRADING IN THE LOW COUNTRIES

A fair flourished in the 15th century at Bruges, and later Antwerp, where trade went on all year. The bourse, built in 1531, was a model for London's Elizabethan Royal Exchange.

Antwerp fell victim to a series of wars in the 16th century and was shunned by foreign merchants, who quickly moved to Amsterdam, which became the centre of European trade and payments systems for 150 years, before London took over.

The Dutch developed the role of the central bank, launching the Bank of Amsterdam in 1609. Its success inspired imitations in Middleburg, Delft and Rotterdam, but all of these failed, owing to the third Anglo-Dutch war.

Amsterdam's trading and financial power was evident in the 17th century when it had a flourishing business in minting silver coins for export. The raw material came from Mexico via Seville, and the coins went to the Baltic states, Poland, the Levant, Asia Minor and the Far East.

LONDON SLIPS

In 1700 London was the world's largest city (population: 600,000), attracting the lion's share of world trade. London had also introduced certain critical financial innovations, including the Lloyd's insurance market, the Stock Exchange and a developed inter-bank money market.

London's political stability after the Napoleonic wars boosted its position and, during the late 18th and early 19th centuries, it acquired unrivalled command of trade and the finance which followed it. This made London the world's prime provider of capital for most of the 19th century.

During the late 19th century, sterling's position as the reserve currency of the world was unassailable. However, the first world war saw the disappearance of the trade surplus; and the US dollar became dominant. London remains Europe's major financial centre, but the UK has lost its dominant position in the financial world to the USA and Japan.

THE RISE OF THE EUROMARKETS

The Euromarkets were effectively created in the 1950s by a piece of US legislation, Regulation Q, which meant Americans wanting to lend dollars to foreigners had to move them offshore. Meanwhile, European countries were struggling to prop up their currencies in the wake of the second world war. The tight controls of the 1950s and 1960s on their home currencies encouraged European banks to look to the dollar for new opportunities.

But the Euromarkets really took off after the oil shock of 1973, when their growth was facilitated by improved communication and information systems. There followed an explosion in the foreign currency activities of the European banks, particularly those based in London, but also those in Zurich, and later Paris and Frankfurt.

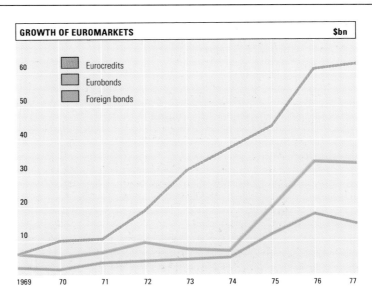

GROWTH OF EUROMARKETS $bn

- Eurocredits
- Eurobonds
- Foreign bonds

60
50
40
30
20
10

1969 70 71 72 73 74 75 76 77

Eurobonds, Eurocredits

In the chart, Eurobonds are bonds sold internationally outside any single national authority's jurisdiction; foreign bonds are bonds issued on behalf of non-resident borrowers; Euro credits are medium term foreign currency credits by international syndicates of banks.

POLITICS OF MONEY

In Spain, as in most of the EC, the sale of lottery tickets is a familiar sight. The UK has now decided to introduce a national lottery, too.

Until the 1980s, most European countries pursued currency management policies aimed at ensuring competitive pricing in the international market, or at paying off government debt. This involved manipulating the exchange rate and turning the occasional blind eye to inflation, which in the end just postponed the problems of under-productive industry and profligate government.

However, in the 1980s most western European, and all EC, governments – inspired by the economic success of Switzerland and Germany – accepted that low inflation was a prerequisite for a stable currency environment, and that both were essential if business and government were to be able to build for the future.

Added impetus came from the EC's move towards the so-called single market programme, launched in 1985, and later expanded to include the EFTA economies with those of the EC, through the planned 19-nation European Economic Area. Until 1991, the European Commission concentrated on removing barriers to trade and business, but it then switched its attention to monetary union.

Stage one of this is based on the exchange rate stabilisation programme of the European Monetary System (EMS) and its Exchange Rate Mechanism (ERM), which links EC currencies within fixed bands. The details of the ultimate monetary union were provisionally agreed, albeit with an opt-out clause for the UK, at the Maastricht summit of December 1991.

A dream or an illusion

Under the Maastricht agreement, the preliminary deadline for achieving a single currency was set at 1997, with a final deadline of 1999. The agreement also set various convergence criteria for member states to meet, which many observers thought posed considerable problems for several countries.

Italy, one of the four major EC economies, remains stubbornly inflationary, and the government has run a large deficit for many years which it has managed by encouraging moderate inflation. These factors, as well as Italy's overall failure to exercise monetary discipline, may mean it will be excluded from full monetary union. Real problems are likely to emerge by the end of the 1990s unless the Italian government proves able to exercise a degree of economic and fiscal control which it has been unable to achieve in the last 50 years.

The convergence criteria will also be difficult for Spain, Portugal, Greece and Ireland. However, they used the Maastricht summit to get a deal to double the EC's structural funds in return for agreeing to EMU. The funds are largely to be spent in these four countries, to mitigate the impact of the single market and monetary union.

One of their major problems in achieving convergence will be conquering inflation, not least because of the political cost of doing so. But this is even more difficult for many of the potential future EC members. The EFTA countries in line for membership will not have much trouble, but the countries from eastern Europe face a much more daunting task.

Taxing matters

Taxation is one of the biggest political problems of the single market programme. Governments and Treasury departments vigorously guard their right to decide taxation levels. The proposals for increasing harmonisation of tax rates across the EC will mean a fundamental shift of political powers from individual nations to the European centre.

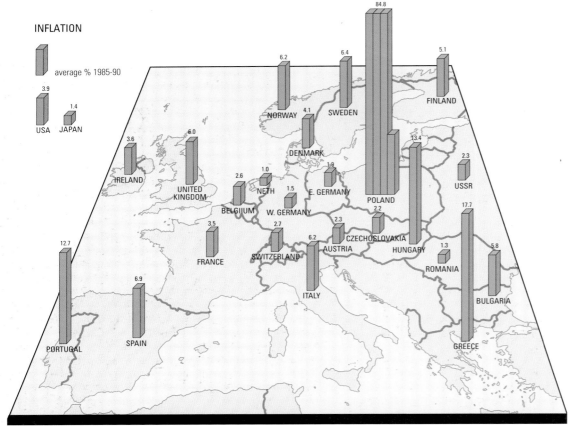

INFLATION

average % 1985-90

3.9 USA
1.4 JAPAN
3.6 IRELAND
6.0 UNITED KINGDOM
2.6 NETH
1.0 (NETH)
6.2 NORWAY
4.1 DENMARK
6.4 SWEDEN
5.1 FINLAND
1.5 E. GERMANY
1.9 (E. GERMANY)
2.7 W. GERMANY
84.8 POLAND
2.2 POLAND
13.4 HUNGARY
2.3 USSR
17.7 ROMANIA
1.3 ROMANIA
5.8 BULGARIA
6.2 AUSTRIA
2.3 CZECHOSLOVAKIA
3.5 SWITZERLAND
12.7 PORTUGAL
6.9 SPAIN
ITALY
GREECE
FRANCE
BELGIUM

Highs and lows

This map shows average inflation rates between 1985 and 1990 in the different European states. Three significant features stand out:
1. The group of countries in the centre of Europe with low inflation, based on Germany and France.
2. The higher inflation of the more peripheral, or less efficient, EC economies, like Italy and the UK, although they both performed far better than Spain, Portugal and Greece.
3. The high inflation in the eastern bloc, although that region was going through such massive political change at the time that the statistics should be treated with caution, and taken as a general illustration rather than accurate absolute figures.

INFLATION: WHAT GOES UP...

During the 1980s, the governments and central banks controlling European currencies changed their policies to make low inflation a main economic target, because they saw hard money (non-inflationary) as fundamental to long-term growth.

Germany's Bundesbank had always worked for low inflation, and the success of the German economy was crucial in the mid-1980s in persuading the rest of Europe to accept that low inflation should be a primary goal. This was boosted in 1984 when France, a member of the ERM since 1979, changed its policies to support low inflation; and when the UK, as it recovered from the credit boom of 1987 and 1988, raised interest rates in an attempt to squeeze inflation out of its economy.

This meant the three leading European economies were now striving for low inflation, backed by countries like the Netherlands and Belgium, whose currencies had already been shadowing the Deutschemark for some time. The result was a consensus in favour of institutionalising low inflation policies, reflected by the EC member states in their Maastricht summit of December 1991.

Nevertheless, Italy's inflation remains worryingly high, with little evidence that it will be able to fall during the mid-1990s. Among the fringe members, Greece and Portugal have exceptionally high inflation, although they will still be absorbed into the EC's single market; and Spain's problems seem to be coming under control.

Outside the EC, low inflation policies pose no real problems for the EFTA countries; and Switzerland has had low inflation for years. However, in the former communist bloc, countries like Hungary, Poland and Czechoslovakia face an uphill struggle, in both political and economic terms, if they are to meet the criteria of the EC, which they hope eventually to join as full members.

Connections: Single market 50–59, 96–97   Economic and monetary union 92–93   Securities 102–105   Eastern Europe 110–111   The future shape 142–143

MONEY AGGREGATES

Money supply affects inflation: high growth in the supply of new money makes inflation more likely. The success of the German economy has been due in part to the Bundesbank's strict control of the money supply, which has helped keep inflation low. Unification has made this policy more difficult to pursue – not least because of the political decision to allow eastern Germans to convert their Ostmarks into Deutschemarks on a one-to-one basis.

France came into line in the mid-1980s, with policies emphasising budgetary and monetary discipline. The budget deficit has steadily decreased since then, except in the recessionary year of 1991.

In the UK, the latter half of the 1980s saw a loosening of control over the money supply, largely as a result of over-reaction to the October 1987 stock market crash and associated domestic economic policies. The resulting credit boom contributed to a surge in inflation, which the government then brought down through a policy of high interest rates.

Italy, the fourth major EC economy, has high but not uncomfortable money supply growth; while the EFTA countries (except Iceland) are mostly well in line with the EC.

CAPITAL CONTROLS

The confidence of EC countries in their currencies grew during the 1980s and they all accepted a 1990-deadline to remove all capital and currency controls, although some failed to meet the deadline. In large part, their confidence was a product of the successful stage one of monetary union, the EMS and its exchange rate mechanism (ERM), which could never have worked without relaxation of controls.

The UK abolished all exchange controls unilaterally in 1979, thus matching Germany whose financial freedom had been instilled by the Americans after the second world war, although Britain remained outside the ERM until 1989. By 1990, only the UK, Germany, France and the Netherlands had succeeded in abolishing controls totally, but Belgium and Luxembourg had very few left by then. Denmark still had some restrictions in 1991; Italy, Spain, Ireland, Greece and Portugal all had more.

Outside the Community, many EFTA countries retained some controls for fear of capital flight from their currencies into the EC. But several of these, including Sweden, Norway and Finland, dealt with this by linking their currencies to the ecu, so pre-empting their formal membership of the EC and building international confidence in their currencies.

CURRENCY LINKAGE

The chart shows the strong effect the ERM had on international exchange markets. It shows how the French franc after President Mitterrand's U-turn early in the 1980s formed part of the "Deutschemark block" within the ERM, whereby several governments aligned their currencies with the Deutschemark by shadowing the Bundesbank's currency policy.

Sterling was not in the ERM at the start of this period, and both it and the yen show the effect of the late 1980s boom as the currencies strengthened against the dollar, falling during 1988 as the boom dissolved into recession. During 1990 sterling joined the ERM and moved in line with its member currencies, while the yen continued on its own way, substantially down from the 1987 high.

The Italian lira remained the weakest currency of those shown. The Spanish peseta went high, benefiting from the effects of Spain's economic boom.

GROWTH IN MONEY SUPPLY

COUNTRY	1974-79	1980-85	1986-90
AUSTRIA	15.9	11.0	7.0
BELGIUM	11.2	5.8	9.5
DENMARK	11.8	15.8	3.7
FINLAND	15.2	15.2	11.5
FRANCE	13.2[1]	10.8	8.8
GERMANY	7.3	6.0	8.5
GREECE	23.4	27.3	20.9
ICELAND	42.6	54.4	27.1
IRELAND	19.7	10.0	7.2
ITALY	20.6	12.8	10.1
NETHERLANDS	10.2	7.6	8.1
NORWAY	14.0	12.9	8.1
PORTUGAL	32.6[1]	33.1	14.4
SPAIN	19.0	15.5	9.6
SWEDEN	10.5	8.5	7.9
SWITZERLAND	7.3	6.3	6.8
UK	13.4	15.5	16.0
JAPAN	11.9	8.5	10.0
USA	10.7	10.0	5.1

1 1978 & 1979 only

Deutsche Bank is Germany's leading commercial bank. It wields substantial business power through its large holdings in German companies.

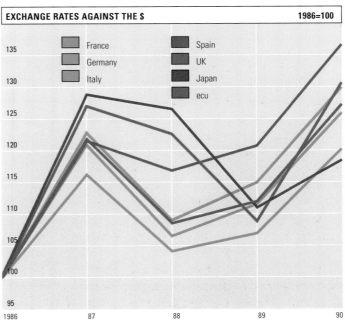
EXCHANGE RATES AGAINST THE $ — 1986=100 (France, Germany, Italy, Spain, UK, Japan, ecu; 1986–90)

The French franc has been part of the European Monetary System since its inception in 1977, and within the Exchange Rate Mechanism of the EMS, the French franc -Deutschemark relationship is a key one. During the 1980s, pressure on the franc led to five downward adjustments of its value against the Deutschemark.

ECONOMIC AND MONETARY UNION

This 25-ecu piece is a commemorative coin. The European Community does its accounts in ecus, and the financial markets deal in ecu bond issues, but the ecu is not yet able to be used by the man in the street, except in some European Commission bookshops and a few stores in Brussels.

A single currency is a logical development for a single market. In America, businesses can trade with businesses in other states with the certainty that a dollar is a dollar. In Europe, companies that import and export as most significant firms do have had to involve themselves in all kinds of currency-hedging activities. These are fun for those involved and can provide windfall profits, but they can equally result in big losses, as many companies have found to their cost. More important, currency fluctuations distort the aimed-for level playing field of the single market.

Merging the different currencies of the European Community member states has been the aim of the EC for many years. Jacques Delors thought it would "put a second tiger in Europe's tank" (the first being the single market programme). Margaret Thatcher described economic and monetary union (EMU) as involving "the biggest transfer of sovereignty we have ever known". Just over a year after she was replaced in power, the agreement on a timetable for EMU at the EC summit at Maastricht in December 1991 marked the latest in a long line of earlier attempts to move towards a single currency.

First steps

A significant early move towards Economic and Monetary Union (EMU) came in the report by the Werner Committee of 1969, which laid the ground work for the "Snake", a system for interlinking the exchange rates of EC countries, as well as those of some outsiders, such as Sweden. The Snake lasted from 1971 to 1979.

The next step was the European Monetary System (EMS), membership of which involved some general obligations to support fellow members' currencies and to coordinate policy by regular meetings of the governors of the central banks. The second phase, however, which involved joining the Exchange Rate Mechanism (ERM), was a much more binding commitment to maintain the value of member states' currencies, within either a 6% or a 2.25% band of each other. The aim was to narrow the bands progressively, leading eventually to fixed exchange rates and, eventually, monetary union.

The EMS and the ERM, limited to EC members, proved much more effective than the Snake. But they made little headway until the 1985 Single European Act and the associated single market programme gave a new momentum, leading to the development of the concept of full monetary union, and not just a situation where a "hard ecu" could exist in parallel to national currencies.

The Maastricht summit of 1991 identified two factors on which the EC's ability to move beyond the EMS and ERM towards this would depend.

A timetable is agreed

First, all member states had to agree to accept the same basic monetary policies. By then, all the EC countries had accepted the fundamental principle of putting low inflation ahead of economic recovery, making it a condition for recovery rather than a consequence of it, despite any short-term pain this might cause.

Second, the Maastricht agreement at the end of 1991 listed four main conditions for monetary union which constitute the convergence criteria to be met by each of the member states if they are to participate. Inflation should be within 1.5% of the average of the EC's three lowest rates; the interest rate within 2% of the lowest three; annual government deficits should be under 3% of GDP; and the public debt should be less than 60% of GDP.

At Maastricht, Britain secured the option to opt out of the single currency; then in 1992 the Danes threw the whole agreement into doubt by voting against it in a referendum. Political manoeuvring among members will continue until the final establishment of EMU. If and when it happens, the prospect of being a geographical member of Europe while staying outside the EC, and therefore EMU, will become increasingly untenable. This is already indicated by the unilateral moves on the part of the three governments of the EFTA states of Sweden, Finland and Norway which have all linked their currencies to the ecu.

AGENDA FOR A SINGLE CURRENCY

December 1991 Maastricht summit set provisional timetable.
1993 Applications for EC membership due from Sweden, Austria and Finland; possibly also from Norway and Switzerland.
January 1994 Second stage of EMU starts when member states will try to meet the convergence standards (covering inflation, interest rates, government deficit and public debt) for the introduction of fixed exchange rates and a single currency.
1995 End of transition period for Sweden, Austria and Finland, plus any others which apply for membership in 1993. All new members to join the EMS and the ERM.
End of 1996 European Commission to analyse progress on convergence and to fix a date for stage three (monetary union).
January 1997 Earliest date by which stage three may start, provided a majority of EC member states support it.
1997 The earliest new members can join stage three, assuming it's going ahead by now, since this is only open to countries which have been members of the ERM for at least two years.
January 1999 The third stage of EMU will start automatically, if it has not already done so, allowing for the introduction of a single currency and a European central bank.

Laughing all the way home from the bank...Karl Otto Pöhl stepped down as chairman of the Bundesbank in 1991. He had not seen eye-to-eye with Chancellor Kohl's rush towards reunification and had clashed with him over the generosity of terms for East Germany. Pöhl was concerned about the extra financial burden on West Germans. He was succeeded by Helmut Schlesinger.

THE GERMAN ANCHOR

At the start of the ERM in 1979, members were following two divergent monetary policies: Germany, backed by the Netherlands, was pursuing low inflation; France and the others were not. After 1985 and the French U-turn on inflation, most member currencies ceased to drop against the Deutschemark.

However, the Deutschemark remained the undisputed benchmark currency. At any change in Bundesbank interest rates, for example, other central banks were obliged to follow suit. This remained the case until the early 1990s, when re-unification brought inflationary pressures to the German economy and, in consequence, a less marked divergence between its economy and those of the other member states.

YEAR	no of issues	ecu m	% change
1981	8	235	–
1982	18	715	204
1983	42	1,832	156
1984	51	2,751	50
1985	114	7,609	117
1986	66	5,336	-30
1987	62	6,051	13
1988	89	9,058	50
1989	110	12,238	35
1990	72	16,263	33
1991	85	24,628	51

□ no of issues □ ecu m
□ % change

Ecu bond issues

The ecu is not a hard currency, for general use in shops, for example, but it is increasingly used in other ways. The European Commission's accounts are all in ecus, for instance, which means many member states have to use it to account for EC-related expenditure. And more and more companies are using ecus for billings in their pan-European operations, to reduce much of the exchange rate risk. But for many years the ecu's most widespread application has been in the bond markets, where its use has been substantial (see chart) and is expected to grow rapidly as full EMU approaches.

Connections: A wider Europe 52–53 Politics of money 90–91 The European Community 130–131 The future shape 142–143

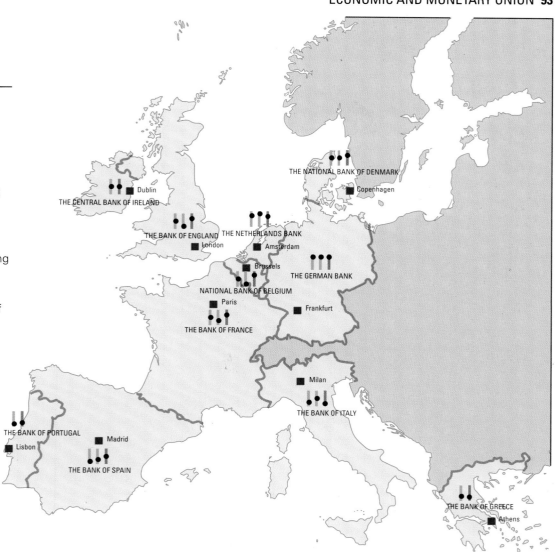

A MODEL OF INDEPENDENCE

The major institutional question still remaining about EMU is what form the future European central bank should take, and how independent it should be from the politicians.

The Germans have a very powerful 50-year tradition of a central bank – the Bundesbank – which is largely independent of the government of the day, so removing the option of altering monetary policy to suit the politics of the time. The Bundesbank's marked success in keeping inflation under control has been a key reason for the independent model being accepted as the basis for the European central bank.

Other EC member states' central banks operate with a variety of levels of independence. The freedom of the Bank of England to operate at will, for instance, is restricted by its relationship with the Treasury, and therefore the political and other motives of the Chancellor of the Exchequer of the day. And in France the central bank – Banque de France – has relatively little control over the operation of monetary policy, which is kept firmly in the hands of the French Treasury.

■ City where Central Bank is based

Central Bank independence
| most | least

Political independence
| most | least

Economic independence
| most | least

HAPPILY EVER AFTER?

The Exchange Rate Mechanism, started in 1979, did not initially succeed in promoting currency stability. That needed political and economic consensus among ERM members.

The chart shows how all ERM currencies fell against the Deutschemark, except for the Dutch guilder, from 1981 to 1983. In France, Mitterrand was following expansionist and inflationary policies, but between 1983 and 1985 he began to implement a U-turn in policy.

The franc, along with the smaller countries which were members of the ERM, then adapted to keeping their currencies in the narrow band of the ERM and, therefore, maintaining their value against the Deutschemark. However, in Italy, the lire continued to slide because successive Italian governments failed to take anti-inflationary steps.

The Netherlands fared best, having linked the guilder very closely to the Deutschemark from the outset.

The significance of this chart is: first, it shows how crucial consensus is for successful currency union; and second, it makes clear how far currency union had gone in Europe, even before the detailed discussions on full currency union.

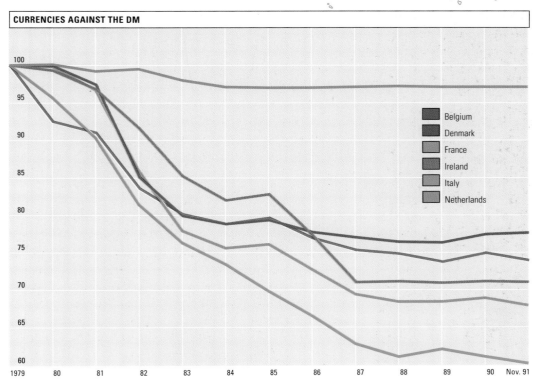

CURRENCIES AGAINST THE DM

Belgium
Denmark
France
Ireland
Italy
Netherlands

ANATOMY OF AN ECU

The pie chart shows the composition of the ecu, as agreed by EC finance ministers in June 1989. The weighting of each currency within the basket changes in line with exchange rates. The altered composition for October 1990 is shown in brackets.

The effect of this definition of the ecu is that it floats in the markets, in proportion to its constituent parts. It is not yet a stand-alone currency with a value of its own. The debate on how to proceed towards full monetary union is largely about whether the ecu should gradually subsume the independent currencies into itself (as is now planned) or whether it should be launched as a separate 13th European currency on to which all the others can be latched.

WHAT IS IN AN ECU?

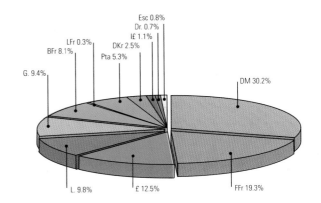

Esc 0.8%
Dr. 0.7%
IE 1.1%
DKr 2.5%
Pta 5.3%
LFr 0.3%
BFr 8.1%
G. 9.4%
DM 30.2%
L 9.8%
£ 12.5%
FFr 19.3%

ECU EXCHANGE RATES, 1992

COUNTRY		RATES
BELGIUM	BFr	42.4032
DENMARK	DKr	7.84195
FRANCE	FFr	6.89509
GERMANY	DM	2.05586
GREECE	Dr	205.311
IRELAND	I£	0.767417
ITALY	L	1538.24
LUXEMBOURG	LFr	42.4032
NETHERLANDS	G	2.31643
PORTUGAL	Esc	178.735
SPAIN	Pta	133.631
UK	£	0.696904

THE BUSINESS OF MONEY

Despite the increase in electronic systems of payment, cash plays a particularly important role in countries such as Italy with a large black economy.

Europe, eastern or western, is far from having a unified business culture. Each country retains its individuality and the path to harmonisation is fraught with conflict. Most companies have strong national identities and genuinely pan-European boards of directors are rare.

In Italy, for example, the rich north has made more effort than most regions to become part of central Europe, in preference to focusing purely on its domestic market. This, in turn, has led to the widening of the gulf between the north and south of the country, which has yet to resolve the problem of organised crime.

Organisations like the right-wing Lega Lombarda thrive on the growing desire for a divorce between the rich north and the poor south. And certain companies, such as Fiat, the car manufacturer, which is based in Turin, will lay off workers in the north while expanding their workforce in the lower wage economy of the south.

As in many other European countries, Italy's business community is dominated by a relatively small number of institutions: the huge state holding companies (undergoing a partial privatisation programme with qualified success); the ubiquitous and influential merchant bank, Mediobanca, which is at the centre of Italy's inner circle of finance; and a handful of business dynasties led by industrial patriarchs, such as Agnelli, Gardini and De Benedetti, who run a very complex network of cross-shareholdings in each others' companies and who sit on Mediobanca's board.

Italy is not the only country with a web of political and business power which seems impenetrable to outsiders. France has certainly made efforts to make its business world less opaque, although foreigners still complain (even those whose home patch is protected by their own government) of excessive interference from the state. The official policy of the socialist government in the late 1980s and early 1990s was one of "neither nationalisation, nor privatisation". But this did not prevent the partial sale of several state enterprises, and a relaxation of restrictions on their ownership.

Old Spanish practices

In Spain, the economy has energetically thrown off the shackles of the Franco era and the period since it joined the EC has been characterised by impressive growth. However, the business community remains preoccupied with a desire to avoid paying taxes, which is a reason why

Equity culture

As the table below shows, German stock market capitalisation ($360bn at the end of 1991) remains tiny by comparison with the UK ($1,021bn), where the equity culture is far more developed. This reflects the close relationship between German companies and their banks, which own large slices of German companies and take the lead in funding them, obviating the need to go to outside shareholders to raise cash. Further, listing on the stock market requires a degree of corporate disclosure which the typical medium-sized German company often finds unacceptable. But the tight hold over industry by the powerful German banks has led to companies riding rough-shod over minority shareholders, who are starting to revolt in support of their rights.

More progress has been made in France, where the stock market has seen significant regulatory changes and dramatic growth in capitalisation to $384bn. A tussle between some of Europe's most powerful businessmen over control of Perrier forced authorities to introduce radical takeover rules early in 1992, including greater recognition of minority shareholders' rights.

VALUE OF DOMESTIC COMPANIES

COUNTRY	1985	1991
AUSTRIA	5	29
BELGIUM	21	72
DENMARK	15	45
FINLAND	6	25
FRANCE	87	384
GERMANY	178	360
IRELAND	3	12
ITALY	58	152
LUXEMBOURG	3	10
NETHERLANDS	59	176
NORWAY	10	226
SPAIN	20	123
SWEDEN	38	102
SWITZERLAND	84	200
UK	398	1021

PERSONAL SHARE OWNERSHIP

% households where someone owns stocks/shares

NORWAY 22
SWEDEN 46
FINLAND 38
DENMARK 40
UNITED KINGDOM 22
NETHERLANDS 22
DENMARK 12
GERMANY 10
BELGIUM 23
LUXEMBOURG 9
AUSTRIA 7
FRANCE 26
ITALY 5
PORTUGAL 4
SPAIN 6
GREECE 2

RETAIL INVESTMENT

London boasts the most international, liquid and active stock market in Europe by far; and its international market attracts an increasing share of the trades of leading continental and other foreign stocks. But as the market becomes more sophisticated, it increasingly alienates retail investors, whose savings are more likely to reach the stock market via collective investment funds than through direct holdings. Even the trumpeted privatisation programme made little impact on this.

Elsewhere in Europe, bonds often hold more appeal for private investors, particularly in traditionally low-inflation economies. Many argue that this reflects not only a more risk-averse culture, but also a healthier, longer-term approach by industry and investors alike.

Connections: Banking 98–101   The financial market place 86–87   Economic and monetary union 92–93   Consumerism 236–237

many of its corporate sectors are so under-represented on its stock exchanges. In 1991, for instance, there were no companies quoted on the stock market from its fragmented and largely family-owned retail industry.

German reunification and the cost of upgrading industry in the old East Germany is undoubtedly unsettling for the country's otherwise robust economy. But Germany's geographical position and economic might are still the envy of the rest of Europe. Its companies have been well ahead of most others in Europe in terms of expansion into eastern Europe (and not just in the former East Germany). Across the German border, Poland will struggle for years to overcome the legacy of communism. Its burgeoning business community is still out of step with its government, but it shares a desire to sort out local problems locally, rather than handing them over to westerners, of whom there is still deep-rooted suspicion.

In the UK, business and corporate culture continues to have more in common with the USA than the rest of Europe. Its company laws and approach to company accounting, for instance, emphasise transparency so the corporate attitude to outsiders seeking information is more open than elsewhere in Europe except for Scandinavian companies which are refreshingly open.

The language of money … this Dutch bank advertises its investment services in Asia in English.

DEALING OUT THE CARDS

The British are readier users of credit and charge cards than any other nation in Europe, with the possible exception of Iceland. About a third of the population has a credit card compared with just over a tenth in France.

However, according to Visa International, French credit card holders spend more with their cards. The British buy an average $156-worth of goods a month, on 2.2 purchases. The French use their 9m Visa cards on seven transactions a month, worth an average total of $566; while in Iceland, Visa cardholders spend an average $596 a month on more than ten transactions.

Germany appears to disdain credit cards and is the home of the Eurocheque. This can be used for payments outside the home country drawn from the purchaser's current account. This may not be merely puritanism, however, since the Germans enjoy relatively flexible overdraft arrangements.

Whatever the reasons, only 1% of Germans hold credit cards, placing them on a par with the Italians and the Dutch (see chart). The keenest credit card users are in Japan, where 63% of the adult population carry plastic payment cards. Interestingly, Japan also has three times more cash machines per 10,000 people than Italy, the Netherlands or Germany. Belgium has just one cash machine per 10,000 people.

Credit card ownership is almost as popular in the USA as it is in Japan, with 60% of American adults having a credit or charge card.

The tables are turned, however, at least where the Americans are concerned, when it comes to ordinary bank accounts. All but 3% of Swiss adults have bank accounts; and the proportion is almost as high throughout Europe. Italy is the exception, with only 59% of its people trusting their money to banks. But Americans are almost as sceptical, with well over a third keeping their money out of bankers' hands.

Although most of Europe has been slow to catch on to credit cards, the growth of credit and charge card use in Britain over the last two decades has been phenomenal. Today many UK retailers make a significant proportion of their profits through store charge cards or other means of credit.

MEETING THE MAASTRICHT GOALS

The chart shows the government debt of European Community countries as a percentage of GDP in 1990. The 1991 Maastricht summit spotlighted those countries with government debt problems, notably Belgium and Italy. In Belgium, two decades of spending on infrastructure improvements have left enviable roads and metro systems, but a public debt mountain equivalent to 128% of GDP and an annual deficit running at over 6%.

These figures are well outside the Maastricht convergence criteria, which set a total government debt target of no more than 60% of GDP; and an annual deficit target of less than 3%. The problem is the cost of the interest payments on these debts, without which Belgium would be running a budget surplus of 4% of GDP.

Italy, whose budget deficit is 10% of GDP a year, also faces huge interest payments, despite making inroads into its primary debt. In the mid-1980s, the deficit ran at just over 5% of GDP, but by 1991 this had been reduced to 0.4%. Nevertheless, government debt was more than 103% of GDP.

In the 1980s Britain actually found itself in the unusual position of paying off some of its debt but towards the end of

GOVERNMENT DEBT, 1990

% of GDP

BELGIUM 125
ITALY
IRELAND 100
GREECE
NETHERLANDS 75
PORTUGAL
DENMARK
GERMANY 50
SPAIN
UK
FRANCE 25
0

the decade the government was back to running a budget deficit, which rose in the early 1990s. Only two countries met the Maastricht goals, which also covered inflation, at the time of the summit. They were France and Denmark.

THE SINGLE MARKET

Freedom of capital movement and an increase in consumer choice over buying insurance or investing are two guiding principles behind the initiatives to create a single market in financial services.

In macro-economic terms, the removal of barriers between financial markets in Europe has led to changes ranging from the abolition of exchange controls to initiatives among securities and commodity markets to work more closely together to compete with rival American and Japanese exchanges.

At the consumer level, the changes have been most widespread and significant in banking and insurance, since these directly affect the access of customers, both individuals and companies, to goods and services across the Community.

The direct effect of EC directives in this area has been the establishment of a number of cross-border joint ventures and mergers by financial institutions. The removal of barriers in financial services as well as moves to establish the ecu as a single currency have encouraged acquisitions by commercial banks, insurance companies and building societies. Smaller banks have set up alliances and improved access for their customers to branches of banks in other member states.

Similarly, the major stockbroking and investment banking firms have now established pan-European networks to facilitate cross-border trading and to allow them to service corporate customers more effectively. So, for instance, a French stockbroker might have offices in a number of EC member states through which it will be researching and trading equities and other securities in the local markets. And a merchant bank from one country will have either its own, or joint venture, offices in other countries so that it can help corporate clients looking to make acquisitions in other parts of the Community.

The underlying principle of both banking and insurance legislation has been to give companies the right to operate with a single licence in any member state while establishing common rules and financial standards to ensure customer protection. The aim is to allow individuals, such as stockbrokers and insurance sales people, to operate anywhere in the EC with a professional European passport.

Selling to the whole Community

In the investment field, one of the earliest examples of this kind of change came in the late 1980s with the directive on collective investment undertakings. This made it possible for institutions like banks, insurance companies and stockbrokers to market their collective investment products (investment trusts, unit trusts and other pooled investment products) to individuals anywhere in the Community. In practice, selling such investments directly to non-domestic consumers has proved difficult. But a similar result has been achieved in a slightly different way. Recognising the difficulty of a UK stockbroker, for example, selling a UK unit trust direct to German individuals, that broker has instead typically opted to establish an alliance with a German firm, which then sells the UK investment vehicle to its own customers. At the same time, the UK broker will sell a similar fund, invested in German stocks by the German firm, to its UK customers.

On the regulatory side, the EC aims to increase the level of transparency in financial dealings within the single market. Institutions will be regulated primarily by organisations in their home country, but the regulators will have improved access to records and information in other member states to ensure financial standards are maintained. Proposals are also being outlined for a uniform consumer protection scheme.

Exchange mechanism… automatic money changing machines like the one above change banknotes into other currencies and have replaced bureaux de change in many places such as airports.

POLICIES ON INSURANCE

The EC's proposals for a single market in non-life insurance allow companies to operate anywhere in the European Community, provided they have a licence from their home country. The legislation is contained in three directives of 1973 and 1990 for non-life insurance, and three further directives, which culminated in 1991 legislation, for life insurance companies.

Individual policyholders can buy insurance from anywhere within the EC, but their rights are protected by their own national law. Insurance companies have to maintain common financial standards; national regulators can intervene to stop abuses but cannot set premium rates.

Proposals for an Insurance Accounts directive are aimed at standardising the financial bases of insurance companies by setting standards on reporting of reserves, provisions, solvency margins and investment policies.

LEADING EUROPEAN INSURANCE COMPANIES

COUNTRY	COMPANY	RANK	$ bn
UK	PRUDENTIAL	2	62
	LEGAL & GENERAL	6	28
	ROYAL	10	22
GERMANY	ALLIANZ	1	71
	ALLIANZ LEBENSVERSIOCHERUNG	5	40
NETHERLANDS	NATIONALE NEDERLANDE	3	48
	AEGON	9	23
FRANCE	UNION DE ASSURANOCES DE PARIS	4	46
	AGF	8	25
SWITZERLAND	SWISS RE	7	27

STOCK EXCHANGES AND OPINIONS

Harmonisation of Europe's stock exchanges has proved elusive so far, with exchange bureaucrats more concerned to protect their own markets than to build an integrated exchange. London remains the leading European exchange for equities, despite advances by France and Germany, but in futures and options trading the situation is less clear cut. The Paris Matif and London's LIFFE battle for pole position in futures trading; and Amsterdam has a key role in options.

Proposals for market players include an Investment Services directive and regulations on minimum capital requirements for non-bank stockbrokers, and a European passport to allow brokers to operate throughout the EC. For companies, the EC wants standard disclosure requirements and a standard public offer prospectus.

STOCKMARKET VALUE $m

EXCHANGE	1986	1987	1988	1989	1990
AMSTERDAM	178,456	214,659	229,056	293,633	306,200
ATHENS	4,320	10,729	16,455	—	40,431
BARCELONA	87,049	125,705	146,486	175,182	162,330
BRUSSELS	114,202	148,202	158,349	180,885	193,051
GERMANY	263,627	218,423	252,076	367,551	443.,811
HELSINKI	19,553	33,068	30,552	—	—
LONDON	710,535	1,024,081	1,057,861	1,125,760	1,227,936
MADRID	85,806	131,769	158,534	192,865	179,897
MILAN	416,515	513,081	—	670,097	—
PARIS	463,888	534,929	586,403	772,794	794,598
VIENNA	49,781	68,561	70,279	89,739	106,358
ZURICH	193,415	210,009	214,780	242,676	253,383

THE ECU

The European currency unit, or ecu, is a basket currency made up of the prevailing values of EC member currencies, with the Deutschemark making up the largest share.

The ecu is the world's second largest currency after the dollar. It was created in 1979 as a unit of account for the European Monetary System, with the intention that it should become the single European currency once the target of full monetary union was eventually attained. Since then, it has established a leading role in the financial markets and there are now effectively two ecus: the official ecu and the private ecu. The former is used by EC institutions for paying grants, duties, levies, and so on, as well as for credits and debits between central banks and for settlement between these institutions. This official ecu cannot be reconverted into the individual currencies which make up its value. The private ecu is different. It is a product of the official ecu, but it is not officially legal tender and has no lender of last resort.

The commercial use of the ecu is now widespread. It has been quoted on exchanges around the world for some time, and derivative instruments have been created on the ecu, ecu bonds and ecu interest rates. Governments, supranational bodies and companies all raise debt in ecu-denominated bond issues, and it is also used by many companies for invoicing and accounting purposes, as a way of minimising foreign exchange risk. In practice, banks deal between themselves in ecus, as if it were a hard currency; and they have established a private clearing system for it.

In the absence of a firm single currency, the stability of the ecu is its main attraction since fluctuations are restricted by the rules of the EMS, which fixes limits on the movements of member state currencies within fixed bands (either 2.25% or 6%, depending on the currency).

STOCK MARKET GROWTH

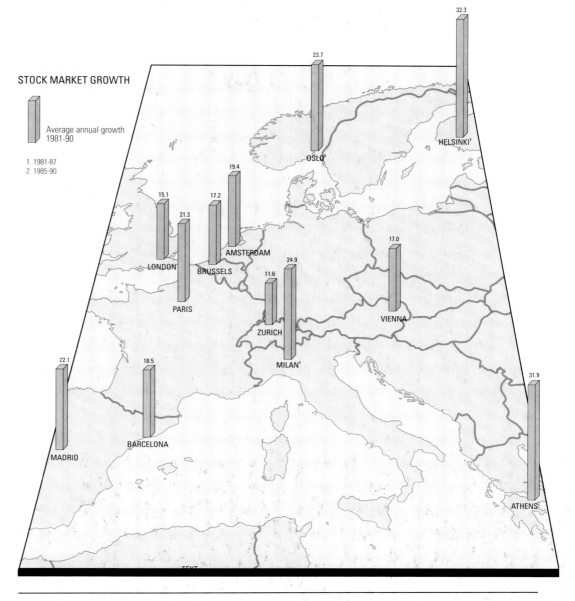

Average annual growth 1981-90

1. 1981-87
2. 1985-90

ECU BOND MARKET

ecu '000m   [Share issues]

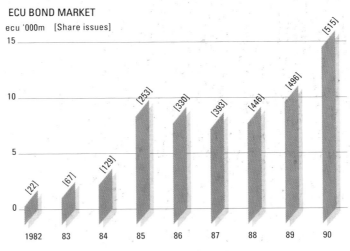

	1982	83	84	85	86	87	88	89	90
	[22]	[67]	[129]	[253]	[330]	[393]	[446]	[496]	[515]

LEADING EUROBANKS

COUNTRY	COMPANY	RANK	$ bn
FRANCE	CREDIT AGRICOLE	1	268.6
	BANQUE NATIONALE DE PARIS	2	256.1
	CREDIT LYONNAIS	5	233.3
	SOCIETE GENERALE	8	194.5
GERMANY	DEUTSCHE BANK	3	247.2
	DRESDNER	9	174.9
UK	BARCLAYS	4	240.6
	NATIONAL WESTMINSTER	6	216.1
NETHERLANDS	ABN AMRO	7	215.2
SWITZERLAND	UNION BANK OF SWITZERLAND	10	169

Borrowing in ecus

The very first ecu-denominated bond was issued in 1981 by SOFTE, the Italian state telecommunications agency. Since then, its use in the bond market has grown dramatically. Ecu borrowers from within Europe include European supranational institutions, such as the EC itself, the EIB and the ECSC, and European governments (Denmark, Ireland and Portugal) and their agencies. Outside Europe, a wide range of borrowers have tapped the ecu bond market. They include the World Bank, sovereign governments (Iceland and New Zealand), government agencies, commercial banks and private sector companies.

Banking directives

The Second Banking directive of 1989, covering deposit taking, lending, investment banking and fund management, allowed banks to operate in all member states with a single licence. A bank's home state is the main regulatory authority, but the directive also encourages greater access to information in other member states and increased co-operation between regulators. The aims of the legislation are to encourage greater capital flows and to remove the need for expensive and slow national clearing systems.

Another key directive for the banking sector is the Capital Adequacy directive. Banks are already subject to a directive on solvency, but this one aims, amongst other things, to create a level playing field between banks and securities houses when both are operating in the investment field.

BANKING

Bank on wheels ... the Banc' Eireann provides a travelling bank service for its far-flung customers in rural southern Ireland. Bank mergers such as the rejected one proposed by Lloyds of its UK "big four" competitor Midland would reduce the number of banking outlets.

The here are nearly 10,000 banks within Europe, although the definition and scope of the term varies considerably. Generally, though, it includes all organisations permitted to carry out deposit and credit activities and to offer investment and other financial services. However, the UK has a narrower definition of a bank, which excludes unincorporated deposit-taking organisations, like the building societies and the representative offices of overseas banks. In France, on the other hand, the 1984 banking law covers over 2,000 institutions providing credit, regardless of their legal form, the nature of their shareholding or their range of activities.

The scale of banking operations within countries varies enormously, too. Germany has more than 4,200 banks, ranging from Deutsche Bank with consolidated assets of $204bn at the end of 1989, to a vast number of small local urban and agricultural cooperative banks.

Banks can operate in foreign countries in various ways: they can incorporate a new bank; open a branch or a representative office; or just provide a limited range of securities services. The extent of foreign operations in European financial centres varies markedly from one country to another. Extreme examples are the UK, with well over 300 foreign banks represented at the end of 1989, and Switzerland with 135.

Luxembourg and Switzerland stand out in European banking by virtue of their special role as offshore banking centres. A ranking of countries' banking strength by reference to the amount of all activity undertaken by banks located within their borders, irrespective of their country of incorporation or legal ownership, would place countries with strong international banking sectors – Luxembourg, Switzerland and the UK – at the top.

Banks are becoming increasingly subject to regulation on minimum capital to asset ratios. The overall average Tier One capital requirement for the major banks, at 4.28%, is probably too low for comfort since, although the assets are not risk-weighted, off-balance sheet activities are excluded. However, some countries have considerably lower averages than this; and of course, some of the individual banks within them are operating on ratios well below the national average. The ratio requirements are starting to have a serious impact on the range of banking activities, especially after the 1990–91 recession. The Scandinavian banks have been particularly badly affected, but banks with strong capital bases – including Deutsche Bank, Crédit Suisse, Union Bank of Switzerland and Swiss Bank Corporation – are likely to be able to expand and should see increasingly profitable business. For lesser banks, the problems remain. ▷

Numbers and size

The map opposite gives one measure of banking strength: the total asset values of banks incorporated in the various European countries. The table below gives another measure: the number of banks in each country, divided into domestic, foreign and savings banks.

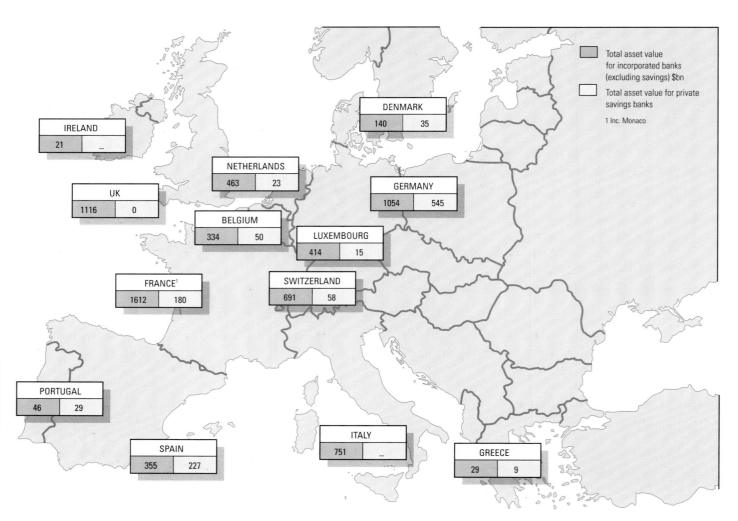

Total asset value for incorporated banks (excluding savings) $bn

Total asset value for private savings banks

1 Inc. Monaco

DENMARK | 140 | 35
IRELAND | 21 | –
NETHERLANDS | 463 | 23
GERMANY | 1054 | 545
UK | 1116 | 0
BELGIUM | 334 | 50
LUXEMBOURG | 414 | 15
FRANCE¹ | 1612 | 180
SWITZERLAND | 691 | 58
PORTUGAL | 46 | 29
SPAIN | 355 | 227
ITALY | 751 | –
GREECE | 29 | 9

BANKING NUMBERS

COUNTRY			
BELGIUM	53	32	29
DENMARK	71	6	122
FRANCE¹	523	71	224
GERMANY W.	3,497	60	602
GREECE	16	18	3
IRELAND	26	6	3
ITALY	1,035	38	7
LUXEMBOURG²	144	30	3
NETHERLANDS	933	50	53
PORTUGAL	220	10	14
SPAIN	88	58	78
SWITZERLAND	149	135	210
UK	204	326	0

1 Inc. Monaco   2 Figs. from 30 Nov 1990

☐ no of incorporated banks

☐ no of non-incorporated foreign banks

☐ savings banks

BANKING SERVICES

Banking culture varies across Europe. Cheques are popular in France and the UK; cash is still preferred in Germany and Italy. Automated Teller Machine figures reveal differences, too, with over 200 per million people in France and the UK; only 60–80 per million in Belgium, Germany, Italy and Ireland. Electronic funds transfer at point of sale (EFTPOS) usage is growing, with Switch card facilities available at over 50% of retail outlets.

Home banking – the ability to check statements and pay bills through a TV or telephone link – is growing. And the electronic linking of a bank computer to a business customer computer, to allow transfers, records and reports without re-entry, is becoming widely available. Since 1991 electronic data interchange (EDI) has been available for larger corporates in the UK, allowing for electronic placing of orders for goods as well as electronic payment.

Connections: Foreign investment 60–61   The business of money 94–95   Single market 96–97

RELATIVE STRENGTH

The table opposite attempts to show comparable numbers of banks in the various countries of Europe, excluding specialist financial organisations. However, the straight numbers for each country shed little light on the overall level of banking activity, since they mask differences in the sizes of the individual banks.

Another way of assessing the depth of a nation's banking industry is to measure the total asset value of the sector. The table does this by giving the asset value of all banks incorporated in each country, regardless of the domicile of their parent companies. It also shows the aggregate equity value of incorporated banks in each country.

One important point is that the nature and relative size of the savings bank sector varies considerably (see map), reflecting structural differences in the finance sector. Savings banks cannot generally undertake a full range of banking activities, although in Italy they may now operate as full banks. In Germany, the savings banks lend predominantly to the private consumer, mostly for mortgages; but the larger ones have assumed traditional banking functions, and the savings banks as a group now increasingly serve local industry and trading companies, eroding the distinction between savings and commercial banks. In France, the savings banks are officially non-profit-making and pay neither dividends nor taxes.

CAPITAL REQUIREMENTS

The capital requirements imposed on international banks in 1988 by the Bank for International Settlement were as follows.
1. Half of a bank's total capital (defined as mainly equity, reserves and subordinated debt) must comprise Tier One capital (shares and disclosed reserves).
2. Each bank activity, on or off-balance sheet, was allocated a risk weighting of between zero and 100. The total risk assets were the sum of the individual assets, each multiplied by its relevant weighting.
3. The ratio of capital to risk assets had to be 8% or higher.

Central banks were given discretion over the deadline for meeting these requirements, provided all were met by the end of 1992. Their effect is to limit the amount of new business banks may undertake, forcing them to concentrate on the impact of each activity on the capital requirement.

BANKING COMPARISONS

COUNTRY	BANKS	ASSET VALUE ($bn)	EQUITY VALUE
AUSTRIA	19	235	4.4
BELGIUM	11	380	2.3
DENMARK	13	189	5.7
FINLAND	11	168	5.9
FRANCE	26	1,907	3.7
GERMANY	89	2,435	3.1
GREECE	9	77	2.0
HUNGARY	5	20	6.0
IRELAND	2	51	4.9
ITALY	103	1,481	4.9
LIECHTENSTEIN	3	13	6.9
LUXEMBOURG	4	62	2.6
NETHERLANDS	15	498	4.5
NORWAY	5	80	2.9
POLAND	4	18	6.1
PORTUGAL	13	90	5.7
SPAIN	50	631	5.7
SWEDEN	16	350	4.2
SWITZERLAND	37	691	6.0
TURKEY	13	45	9.8
UK	35	1,083	5.1
YUGOSLAVIA	7	43	–

The days of banks hoping to contain the risk of robbery by building ever stronger bank vaults may be numbered. Sophisticated thieves have no need of drills, guns or face masks. They opt instead for computer theft, hacking their way into banks' computers and issuing instructions to them to transfer sums to bank accounts of their choice. More demanding on the intellect, this approach is also more difficult for the banks to prevent and often takes them time even to detect that the crime has taken place. Major banks now have anti-fraud departments, whose job is to stay a jump ahead of the computer whizz kids who, on the one hand, are finding ways to extract small sums from automatic teller machines (ATMs); on the other, are threatening the security of their mainframe computer systems.

BIGGEST BANKS

Another way of looking at the banking sector of a country is to consider its relative strength within that country. The banks included in the *Financial Times*'s Top European 500 companies, as measured by share capital and combined asset value, probably reflect the domestic banking scene more accurately, since only national banks – rather than subsidiaries of foreign ones – are likely to be big enough to qualify for inclusion. However, the FT's list only includes publicly-owned companies, so private or nationalised companies are left out.

The January 1992 edition of the Top European 500 companies included 68 banks in all, a net increase of five over 1991. However, 42 of the banks included in both years had moved down the rankings, underlining the difficulties being faced by banks in the early 1990s. Indeed, four banks appear in a separate list of the 25 companies showing the biggest profit decreases over the year (Den Danske Bank and Unidanmark, both Danish; CS Holding, of Switzerland; and Banco de Santander, of Spain).

The turnover and profits figures included in the FT 500 show that Europe's stronger banks tend to be in Germany,

Switzerland and Spain, where domestic markets have been relatively closed to outside competition; economies have remained reasonably buoyant; and bankers have pursued traditionally conservative lending policies. But even banks in these areas generally saw profits decline. Deutsche Bank, for example, made disclosed profits of $1390.2m in 1991, against $2047.5m in 1990. Nevertheless, Deutsche Bank is still easily the biggest European bank and is also the 12th largest European company overall. Barclays comes second, ranked 21st overall; followed by Union Bank of Switzerland (30th); National Westminster (35th) and Lloyds (44th).

At the other end of the scale, the problems suffered by the Scandinavian banks saw representatives from this region fall sharply. There is not a single Norwegian bank in the FT 500, partly because of the high level of state ownership in Norway, but also because of the recession and property slump there in the late 1980s and early 1990s, which prompted the government's rescue operation for the entire banking system. Swedish and Finnish banks also plummeted down the rankings as a result of severe losses on loans to the finance and property sectors.

EUROPE'S LEADING BANKS

COUNTRY		
UK	12	180.5
GERMANY	9	64
FRANCE	8	67.5
ITALY	8	33
SPAIN	8	31
SWITZERLAND	5	25.5
BELGIUM	4	16.5
SWEDEN	3	29.5
DENMARK	2	12
AUSTRIA	2	4
FINLAND	2	5
IRELAND	2	4
NETHERLANDS	1	17.5
LUXEMBOURG	1	3
PORTUGAL	1	1
NORWAY	0	6
TOTAL	68	500

☐ Banks in FT-500
☐ All companies in FT-500

The European Community published its agreed timetable for the completion of the single market in financial services in 1975, setting a deadline of 31st December 1992. Two years later, in 1977, the First Banking directive allowed banks to open branches or subsidiaries in any member state, provided they observed the host country's rules.

The Second Banking directive, adopted in 1990, introduced the concept of a single banking licence based on the principle of home country control. As a result of this, it should be possible by 1993 for any EC bank to set up a branch in another member state without the need for host country authorisation. The home country's supervisory authority will have sole responsibility for prudential control. The Second Directive defines permissible banking activities widely, blurring the boundaries between bank and non-bank financial institutions.

The future picture of banking within the EC is unclear, but it is bound to have a significant impact on banks' activities. For example, the legalisation of money market funds in Germany in 1993 could, if they sell as well as in France, reduce that country's annual banking profits from $3bn to $1.8bn. The payment of interest on current accounts in the UK could reduce profitability by as much as 10–15%.

Banks are pursuing various internal and external strategies in anticipation of the changes. Some are building a new branch network. Barclays, for example, is doing this in France and Spain, with a view to selling its credit card system; and Citicorp has a 700 branch network throughout Europe. The difficulty with this strategy is that it is both slow and expensive.

Others are acquiring a branch network. Crédit Lyonnais, for example, has bought Banque de Commerce in Belgium, Kredietbank in the Netherlands and 49% of Credito Bergamasco in Italy. Deutsche Bank has bought Banca d'America e d'Italia, one of Italy's largest private banks, Banco Comercial Transatlantico in Spain, Antoni Hacker in Austria, and Morgan Grenfell in the UK. National Westminster has been trying to create a network of private banks, building on its long-standing ownership of Coutts, a leading UK private bank.

More common within the smaller countries whose banks are looking increasingly vulnerable is the approach of merging with other banks. The Netherlands, for example, had five big banks at the beginning of 1989, but has

Cross-border banking

The map shows the number of banks per country in the European top 500 and their combined asset value. The tables below the map give an indication of the general level of cross-border activity by the world's top 150 banks between January 1989 and April 1991. Europe – east and west – saw most of the activity.

Further, despite the perceived need for size in international banking, and despite the impetus for acquisitions and mergers provided by the single European market programme, there have been no major mergers of banks across borders of EC member states. Bankers do see the chance to make incremental profits by selling their services throughout the Community – and beyond – but most of the acquisitions to date have been relatively small. Barclays, for instance, the biggest bank in the UK, bought the Paris-based private bank, Européene de Banque in 1991.

There has, in fact, been much more publicity about banks taking cross shareholdings in each other. However, despite their perceived benefits, fewer than 3% of the arrangements made so far have been of this type.

One reason for the relatively low level of activity in the years leading up to the completion of the single market is that this period coincided with a worldwide recession. Having been hit hard by their imprudent lending to third world countries, bankers throughout Europe were now preoccupied with preventing the economic slowdown prompting unsustainable loan losses. They haven't been that successful. In the UK, for example, banks have been making record provisions against possible credit losses, amounting to around 2% of their domestic loan portfolios. French banks, too, expanded their loan book by about 20% a year in the late 1980s, exposing themselves both to the ailing British and American property sectors and to big, highly-geared international companies. As a result, the biggest deal was not intra-European at all, but involved the takeover of UK clearing bank, Midland, by the Hongkong and Shanghai Bank.

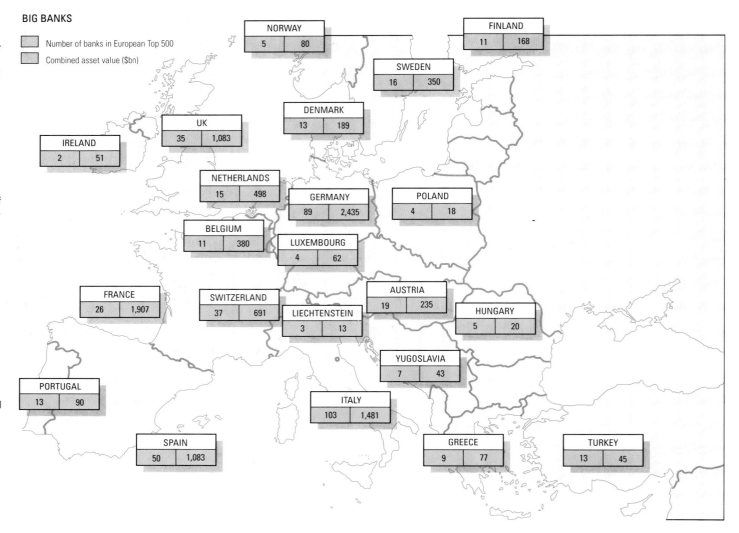

BIG BANKS

Number of banks in European Top 500

Combined asset value ($bn)

NORWAY	5	80
FINLAND	11	168
SWEDEN	16	350
DENMARK	13	189
UK	35	1,083
IRELAND	2	51
NETHERLANDS	15	498
GERMANY	89	2,435
POLAND	4	18
BELGIUM	11	380
LUXEMBOURG	4	62
FRANCE	26	1,907
SWITZERLAND	37	691
LIECHTENSTEIN	3	13
AUSTRIA	19	235
HUNGARY	5	20
YUGOSLAVIA	7	43
PORTUGAL	13	90
ITALY	103	1,481
SPAIN	50	1,083
GREECE	9	77
TURKEY	13	45

BANKING ACTIVITY BY TYPE

ACTIVITY	NUMBERS
OPENING OF NEW BRANCHES OR SUBSIDIARIES	99
ACQUISITION OF CONTROLLING INTEREST	87
ACQUISITION OF MINORITY INTEREST	63
RECIPROCAL EQUITY SHAREHOLDINGS	12
JOINT VENTURES	61
CO-OPERATION AGREEMENTS	42
NEW FOREIGN NON-BANK SHAREHOLDERS	25
DISPOSALS OR CLOSURES OF OVERSEAS OPERATIONS	49

LENDING ACTIVITY BY SECTOR

BUSINESS AREA	CONTROLLING[1]	MINORITY[1]	MINORITY[2]	OPENINGS
COMMERCIAL BANKING	47	26	16	53
INVESTMENT BANKING	16	12	12	32
LEASING	10	–	–	2
INSURANCE	–	3	2	2
FUND MANAGEMENT	5	–	–	5
OTHER	9	22	10	5
TOTAL	87	63	40	99

1 Acquisitions   2 Acquisitions > 10%

seen two major mergers since then: NMB and Postbank; and ABN and Amro in 1990. Unibank in Denmark was formed by the merger of three banks (Privatbanken, Andelsbanken and Sparekassen SDS) in 1990, as was Den Danske Bank. There is concern in Ireland about the survival of its two main banks, but awareness that their merger would create an undesirable monopoly.

Another tactic among several big banks has been to establish inter-bank alliances and cross-share-holdings. Commerzbank and Crédit Lyonnais held protracted negotiations over a share swap, which eventually failed. BNP and Dresdner Bank are also negotiating, and have taken 10% stakes in each other. Such alliances and partnerships have generally failed to achieve widespread success.

One-shop finance

One aspect of continuing deregulation of the financial services market has been the liberalisation of the insurance sector. Lending money has little in common with selling insurance policies, so banks and insurance companies have traditionally operated in separate markets. But with increased competition and falling profits, banks have started looking at the insurance sector with interest. One factor in this is demographic. Governments worried about ageing populations have started to offer tax incentives to encourage people to take out their own insurance and pension policies. As a result, banks have seen money on deposit diverted into insurance products.

One impact of this change has been a series of deals and alliances among bankers and insurers. These have become common enough for new terms to be coined to describe the phenomenon: *Allfinanz* in Germany; *bancassurance* in France. Companies have pursued a variety of strategies, but one company worthy of particular note in this context is Allianz, Germany's biggest insurer. Its recent moves have included buying 24% of Bayerische Hypotheken-und-Wechselbank, 10% of Bayerische Vereinsbank and 25% of Münchener Rückversicherung, the world's largest reinsurer. It also bought Cornhill Insurance in the UK and Rhin et Moselle, a French insurance company; and it took majority stakes in both Ercos, the Spanish insurer, and Adriatica di Sicurita, the second largest reinsurance company in Italy. Finally, it has established joint ventures with both Banco Popular Español and with Dresdner Bank, in which it also took a stake.

OFFSHORE CENTRES

There are numerous offshore financial centres, or tax havens, all over the world. They offer to the wealthy the desirable combination of a favourable tax environment, anonymity and, typically, a reluctance to collaborate with foreign tax authorities. The proposed harmonisation of financial services within the European Community has created an opportunity for many of Europe's offshore financial centres to offer tax-efficient services. Such centres are offshore in the sense that they are outside the regulatory control of the EC.

Many investors, inside and outside Europe, benefit from being able to place funds through an offshore centre for subsequent investment within the EC without becoming subject to tax at the rates applying on the mainland. Luxembourg presents a special case as the Community's "onshore" offshore centre, although there is some doubt about its future status. Both Gibraltar and the International Financial Services Centre in Dublin are at least temporarily exempt from EC tax harmonisation.

BANK-INSURERS

"Allfinanz" or "bancassurance" strategies already adopted by Europe's bankers and insurers have included the following.
Start an insurance company. TSB, Crédit Agricole and Deutsche Bank have all gone this route. Mapfre, a large Spanish insurer, responded by starting its own bank.
Acquisition. Lloyds bought a controlling stake in Abbey Life; Compagnie Financière de Suez bought French (Groupe Victoire) and German (Colonia) insurers. Insurance companies have responded by buying banks.
Mergers or equity swaps, usually within one country. The formation in the Netherlands of Internationale Nederlanden group, through the merging of insurer Nationale Nederlanden and savings banks NMB Postbank is probably the most spectacular example of this.
Joint ventures. These have been particularly successful, and mostly cross-border, although the UK's National Westminster linked with Clerical Medical in November 1991.
Marketing agreements. This has been the most common route. In the UK for example, there are very few significant banks or building societies that have remained entirely independent of insurance companies.

Bankers to the rescue ... Jacques Attali, long-time confidant of François Mitterrand, was appointed president of the London-based European Bank for Reconstruction and Development which hopes to guide and help the emerging democracies of eastern Europe. One of its aims is to help these countries establish western-style financial and banking infrastructures (see "Supra-national banking", below).

President of the European Bank

Supranational banking

In 1944 the International Bank for Reconstruction and Development (the IBRD, or World Bank) was established with the aim of financing the rebuilding of postwar European economies. Overshadowed in this by the Marshall plan, however, the bank soon turned its attention to the Third World.

In 1958 the European Investment Bank (EIB) was founded to finance development on a non-profit-making basis within the EC. Today it also provides funds further afield, particularly in the Mediterranean rim, former or existing colonies of EC states, EFTA countries and, more recently, in eastern Europe. Outstanding loans of $75bn at the end of 1990 (55bn ecus) were forecast to reach $95bn by the end of 1991, compared with a June-1991-figure of just $91bn for the much higher profile World Bank.

The general spread of the EIB's activities is shown in the accompanying table. It favours the funding of small and medium-sized enterprises (SMES), not

least because more than two thirds of employees within the productive sectors of Europe work for firms with fewer than 500 staff. A significant proportion of EIB money also goes into attempts to even out imbalances across the Community.

In March 1991 OECD governments set up the European Bank for Reconstruction

and Development (EBRD), whose role seems to be to support development projects in, and the restructuring of, eastern European economies. It is currently working to develop banking systems in central and eastern Europe, with a view to getting private sector banks established there.

AREAS OF EIB LENDING

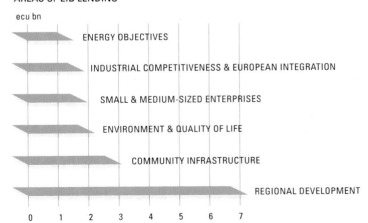

ecu bn

ENERGY OBJECTIVES

INDUSTRIAL COMPETITIVENESS & EUROPEAN INTEGRATION

SMALL & MEDIUM-SIZED ENTERPRISES

ENVIRONMENT & QUALITY OF LIFE

COMMUNITY INFRASTRUCTURE

REGIONAL DEVELOPMENT

0   1   2   3   4   5   6   7

SECURITIES

The Irish GPA aircraft leasing firm was a stockmarket success story of the 1980s. The pulling of its massive share offer in 1992 was an example of how market fortunes can go down as well as up. Some of the planes in this Mojave desert graveyard have never been up.

There are few more potent images from the 1980s than the young securities dealer standing at his desk shouting instructions down a telephone tucked under one ear in response to movements in figures flashing up on a bank of electronic screens. Although normally associated with the major financial markets of London, New York and Tokyo, an almost identical scene can be witnessed on the stock markets of almost every capital in the developed western world, and increasingly in the emerging and post-communist world, too. Even the dealers at the embryonic Budapest exchange wear the same red braces sported by their western counterparts.

Modern markets never sleep

The dealer, the foot soldier in the constant battle being played out on the international stock market, is the creation of two immensely powerful forces – deregulation, and information and communications technology. These have allowed vast flows of capital to slosh from country to country and from continent to continent as 24-hour dealing has become a reality. Ten years ago, cross-border transactions represented one share trade in 16. In the

early 1990s, the figure is nearer one in seven, and in Europe, foreigners account for one deal in three.

Europe's front-runner in both technological development and deregulation has been London, and the City remains the leading financial centre in Europe. Big Bang, the 1986 package of reforms of the London stock market, introduced American-style market practices and screen-based trading to Europe. The competitive advantage that Big Bang gave London, despite the devastation wreaked on many of the City's long-established players, forced most other European stock exchanges to modernise and deregulate as well.

The days when the Madrid and Milan stock exchanges were essentially social venues, where business was occasionally transacted during the markets' few brief opening hours, are long gone. Even so, the introduction of electronic trading to Milan, the leading securities market in Europe's fourth largest economy, remains problematic and has at times led to brokers going on strike and the exchange being closed altogether.

London's strong base, its head start on deregulation and the development of its Stock Exchange Automated

Sizing up stock markets

The map below shows stock market capitalisation and trading volume figures. The figures given for the five years from 1986 to 1991 disguise a period of unprecedented change between those two dates. Most markets, for instance, reached a peak in both turnover and capitalisation during 1989, before falling sharply back in 1990. Most also saw increased turnover at the time of the stock market crash of October 1987, as dealers desperately sold unwanted stock. But because prices fell so dramatically, 1987 also witnessed a trough in market capitalisation levels.

The Tokyo Stock Exchange followed a strong and consistent growth path from 1985 to 1989, and it was much less affected by the 1987 crash. The prices of stocks fell, but Tokyo did not experience the level of panic-selling seen in other financial centres. Conversely, the general decline in 1991 figures was far more marked in Tokyo: market capitalisation fell by 37% from the end of 1989 to the end of 1990; and turnover dropped by 44% in 1990, and a further 40% in 1991.

Company count

The table below shows the number of companies listed on leading stock exchanges worldwide. In these terms, New York is easily the world leader, although its 6,342 companies are in fact traded on more than one exchange. Tokyo is the runner-up, but can boast only a third of the Big Apple's number of corporate stocks.

London has the third longest list, with a similar count to Tokyo's. But within the European time zone, London's domination is clear cut. The aggregate number of company listings in France and Germany, each with economies significantly bigger than the UK's, is still only three-quarters of the total traded in London. This underscores the fact that equity remains relatively unimportant in continental Europe.

CAPITALISATION AND TURNOVER

- Capitalisation
  - $m 1991
  - % change since 1986
- Turnover
  - $m 1991
  - % change since 1986

NEW YORK

3,712,835	68.8
1,525,000	25.9

TOKYO

2,805,466	65.6
823,231	-13.8

COPENHAGEN

49,532	214.4
9,289	-31.4

LONDON

938,136	125.7
637,869	171.6

DUBLIN

4,958	67.6
2,142	78.5

AMSTERDAM

154,888	-1.3
77,685	23.8

BRUSSELS

65,319	93.5
8,492	28.2

GERMANY

393,470	147.3
895,976	227.2

LUXEMBOURG

190,842	693.4
1,020	82.1

PARIS

353,237	121.6
117,687	94.0

MILAN

143,002	11.9
25,007	-44.1

LISBON

8,665	1,085.4
1,120	2,566.7

ATHENS

12,921	1,054.5
2,400	7,400

MADRID

137,638	197.6
35,526	183.1

LISTED COMPANIES

COUNTRY	No.	1985
AMSTERDAM	260	12.1
ATHENS	145	27.2
BRUSSELS	182	-5.2
COPENHAGEN	258	6.2
DUBLIN	71	—
GERMANY	649	37.5
LISBON	181	654.2
LONDON	2,006	-5.2
LUXEMBOURG	54	69.1
MADRID	427	27.8
MILAN	334	127.2
PARIS	873	78.5

NEW YORK	6,342	-20.9
TOKYO	2,071	13.2

- Companies
- % change

Connections: Telecommunications 42–43   Trade 48–49   The financial market place 86–87   Economic and monetary union 92–93   Single market 96–97

Quotation System (SEAQ), an international screen-based market for foreign stocks, mean that the City still accounts for a staggering 95% of all cross-border share trading in Europe. The leading financial market in the European time-zone, it is still the only one worthy of comparison with Tokyo and New York. In 1991, the London stock market's total turnover of $322bn dwarfed the $255m achieved by its nearest competitor, the German Federation of Stock Exchanges. Technology may now have made it possible for a Dutch investor to buy a share in an Italian company through an American broker, but the deal is still most likely to be struck in London.

Nevertheless, London's position as the leading European financial market is under potential threat. Paris, Amsterdam and, most dangerously, Frankfurt all have ambitions to seize London's mantle in the 1990s.

Paris, traditionally Europe's second international financial centre, is currently suffering a crisis of confidence as it watches business steadily dribble away to its British and German competitors. Recent reforms to its bourse to encourage large-scale share trading may help, but failure to complete the process of deregulation, ▷

The principal stock exchange in France is the Paris Bourse which operates a partially automated screen trading system. The building itself was designed by Brongniart and finished in 1827.

Planting for futures… a cocoa nursery in Cameroon. The Coffee, Sugar and Cocoa Exchange Inc. of New York was first established to deal in coffee in 1882; cocoa was added in 1925. London is the other major centre of the world cocoa market and it is the most important centre in Europe for commodity trading in general.

EUROBONDED

The offshore Eurobond market, for which London has been the epicentre since its inception in the 1960s, took off during the free-wheeling 1980s, with bond issuance growing from $26bn in 1980 to $224bn in 1989. Originally a pure dollar market, Eurobonds are now issued in 21 currencies. Continental European currencies have enjoyed particular popularity in recent years as new currency sectors (the French franc, the Italian lira and the Swedish krona, for example) have come on tap but, with European monetary integration gathering pace, the ecu itself has become the Eurobond currency of the 1990s.

America is now progressively withdrawing from the market, as it endeavours to make its own domestic bond market more issuer friendly. US borrowers' share of the market fell during the 1980s from a peak of 27.4% in 1985 to 9.3% in 1990. Their place has been taken by the Japanese, who flooded the market with equity-related issues in the late 1980s.

After two decades of minimal regulation, the Eurobond market is now fighting attempts to draw it into a pan-European network of more closely controlled domestic capital markets. The market, needless to say, sees this as a threat to its fundamental competitive advantage: low-cost capital raising. Nevertheless, the days when the market could claim to be the world's most flexible and exciting source of large-scale funding, a genuine street market for capital, may be numbered.

Bond trading

The chart shows the growth in secondary market trading on the Euromarkets from 1985–90, a period of steady expansion.

Liquidity in this market is provided principally by the market makers, but also by brokers acting between market makers and end-investors. Institutional investors account for 75% of the market, and their average transaction size grew from $50,000–$100,000 in the early 1960s to $500,000–$5m in 1990. An increasing variety of instruments is now available, allowing investors to hedge against currency and other risks, and thereby adding depth to the underlying market. The Euromarkets have contributed to this diversification of instruments, introducing such derivative products as currency and interest rate swaps, and futures and options.

EUROMARKET TRADING

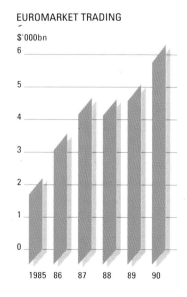

$'000bn

1985 86 87 88 89 90

Who borrows?

Traditionally the major market users, American companies and institutions were responsible for nearly a fifth of all issues in 1980, a proportion which peaked in 1984–5 at well over a quarter. But the balance began to change after the mid-1980s, as Japan moved into the dominant role. By the end of the decade, it was borrowing 22% of the total (1989 = 36%), with countries like the UK and France now level-pegging with the USA.

Other
Japan
International Institutions
UK
USA
France
W. Germany

BORROWING BY NATIONALITY %

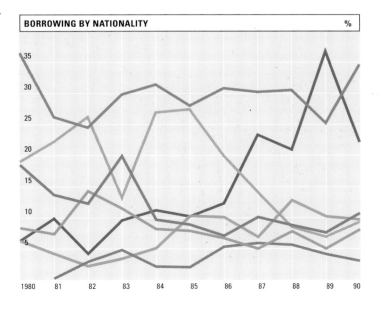

1980 81 82 83 84 85 86 87 88 89 90

initiated in 1988, will continue to deter foreign firms.

Frankfurt has the advantage of being the financial centre for the economic powerhouse of Europe, but Germany has an underdeveloped securities market, a relatively weak financial infrastructure and a historical bias against trading in equities. It also suffers from Germany's decentralised stock exchange system, with its eight bourses likely to be supplemented by yet more to be opened in the East. Frankfurt is also behind London on technology, only moving to an electronic system in 1991.

London still has much to offer, and is attempting to seize another initiative by establishing itself as the leading financial centre for the ecu. The Square Mile also has the advantage of being the long standing centre for Euromarket dealing. The Euromarket is primarily a bond market, but has seen increased diversification into bank loans and equities. For nearly three decades it has remained outside the reach of regulators, as an essentially offshore market, and, in general, has provided

Ahead or behind the game...Europe sits in the middle of the financial market clock. Broadly speaking, European stock markets open when Tokyo's (above) closes, and close when New York's opens. So when Wall Street dives marketmakers in Europe can see how the Japanese and other Far East markets react to the news before having to deal themselves.

INTERNATIONAL EQUITIES

Prior to 1984 companies and stockbrokers had little success in marketing equities Europe-wide, owing to a combination of regulatory barriers and thin markets. In addition, companies marketing their stocks on non-domestic exchanges often suffered from "flowback", where foreign purchasers sell their stock back to the companies' home markets.

However, the privatisation of state assets, primarily in the UK – where the government marketed huge public offerings of shares in British Telecom, British Gas and many other nationalised utilities – stimulated far greater cross-border activity. About 20% of the stock issued in UK privatisation sales was placed abroad; and today institutional placings of equity across borders has become relatively common.

By October 1987, initial public offerings of shares and other equity-like instruments placed internationally had swelled to around $15.5bn, but the world stock market crash set international equity activity back. In 1990, the overall volume of placements amounted to just under $7.3bn, compared with $7.7bn the year before. And issues of Euroequities proper shrank from $5.3 bn in 1989 to only $3.2bn in 1990.

THE BROKER'S GLOBAL VILLAGE

Observers could be forgiven for thinking that European brokers spend their mornings reacting to news from Tokyo and their afternoons watching events in New York. Domestic events still do influence stock exchanges, but global securities trading has made them far more interdependent. News from the major economies of Japan and America is bound to affect companies around the world, but markets are inclined to overreact. In October 1989, for instance, the failure of an attempted buy-out of an American airline triggered a 5–10% fall on European markets. Yet even in New York, the fall was only 3.8%.

During the October 1987 crash, the downward pressure on markets was exaggerated by computer-programmed selling, and this "contagion" effect has been fuelled by today's instant news dissemination and the global upheaval of the post cold-war era. The coup in Russia towards the end of the Gorbachev era, for example, caused markets to dive everywhere, although it was hard to see its immediate impact on western economies.

Market vulnerability

The crash in October 1987 – only in Japan was it below 20% – shocked youthful dealers everywhere, as they contemplated their ignorance of bear market trading. The ensuing panic has not been repeated since. However, recent shocks suggest that Japan may now have lost its ability to stand aloof.

- 1987 Crash
- October 1989 mini-crash
- Gulf crisis
- Soviet coup

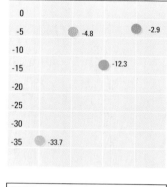

UK

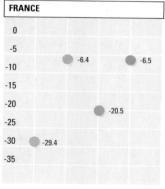

FRANCE

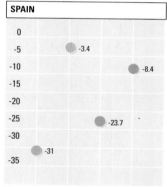

SPAIN

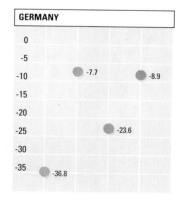

GERMANY

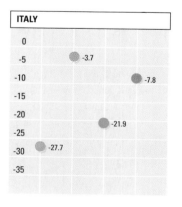

ITALY

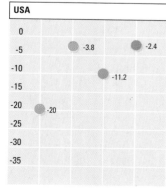

USA

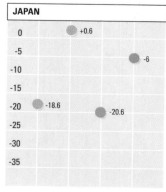

JAPAN

effective self-regulation. But although London may be the geographical focus for the Euromarkets, Britain is not the dominant force. More than 75% of the London-based players in the Euromarkets are, in fact, foreign.

Recent rapid growth in international securities dealing has been accompanied by the development of ever more complicated securities products, from Euroconvertible bonds to derivative products like equity options and index futures. In most main centres these products, which provide liquidity to the underlying "cash" markets, now have exchanges of their own, including the financial futures markets in London (LIFFE) and Paris (Matif).

One of the great questions facing the securities industry in the EC in the coming decade is whether it is serious about integration. The European Commission wants to see EC securities firms able to provide services throughout the stock exchanges of the Community. However, by 1992, widespread restrictive practices remained and in some cases seemed to be getting worse. This was particularly true of the so-called Club Med group of southern European countries, where the relatively underdeveloped local markets fear they will be swamped by Germany and the UK. Italy, for example, passed controversial legislation in early 1992 making it virtually impossible for foreign companies to trade on its stock exchanges.

The death of Euroquote

It was protectionism, too, that was largely responsible for killing off Euroquote, a proposed joint-venture trading system to be run by the EC's stock exchanges in preparation for an eventual integrated European stock exchange. Euroquote, in the planning stages for two years, was finally abandoned in 1991 when it became clear that the heads of the individual exchanges were unwilling to place their desire for a European exchange ahead of their domestic market concerns.

As the EC members negotiate over the future of their securities industries, the emerging democracies of eastern Europe are struggling to develop their own. Budapest is probably the most advanced, but there are plans for securities markets in other eastern European capitals, including Moscow and even war-torn Yugoslavia.

One day, but probably not this century, those infant markets may be sufficiently advanced to provide liquid, accessible sources of capital for commercial organisations in the former eastern bloc. By then, the securities industry in the western half of the continent is likely to be very different from today's.

The growth in international trade and capital movements make current attempts by some stock exchanges to seal themselves off from outside competition look retrogressive and probably doomed. Smaller European stock markets will probably be swallowed up by one of the four or five major players, three of which are bound to be London, Frankfurt and Paris. There might also be a sophisticated, competitive exchange representing southern Europe, with Milan likely to prove the strongest candidate. And there are bound to be further competitors for international securities trading from organisations without any clear geographical base, as screen-based trading systems offer an increasingly viable alternative to national or even multinational stock markets.

MARKETS AT THE CROSSROADS

The performance of the main European stock markets varied considerably during the late 1980s and early 1990s, as the accompanying chart shows on the right. In France and Italy, for example, the divergence in stock market performance in 1991 was almost 30 percentage points. But that was before Maastricht, and the formal agreement between 11 of the 12 member states on progress towards a single currency.

The jury is still out on whether European stock markets will follow the path of convergence being pursued by the currency and bond markets. Evidence in favour of convergence includes the Benelux countries' experience, where gradual merging of the economies in the 1980s significantly reduced the difference in stock market dividend yields and price/earnings ratios on the Brussels and Amsterdam stock exchanges.

However, according to Yamaichi International, the Japanese investment house, history suggests that exchange rate stability is generally won at the cost of interest rate volatility, which in turn brings volatility to the equity markets. Convergence also seems unlikely with the current diversity of dividend policies and accounting practices around the community.

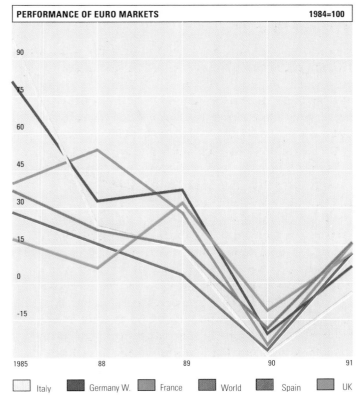

PERFORMANCE OF EURO MARKETS   1984=100

90
75
60
45
30
15
0
-15

1985   88   89   90   91

▢ Italy   ▇ Germany W.   ▢ France   ▇ World   ▇ Spain   ▢ UK

Hung up on the news... when modern information technology brought this London broker news of the attempted coup against Mikhail Gorbachev, the Soviet leader, in 1991, it took some time for the markets to work out what it meant to western economies. In the meantime, dealers went into overdrive.

INSURANCE

Lloyd's of London's tradition of unlimited liability buckled under the strain of huge reported losses for the late 1980s, when many of its members or "names" faced financial ruin.

I nsurance ranks alongside agriculture and textiles as one of the most protected industries in the world. The insurance industry makes up more than 8% of the European Community's aggregate GNP, and is twice the size of its agricultural sector. There are more than 1,000bn ecus in pension funds in the Community.

However, throughout the EC the insurance and pensions market remains immature. With a population of around 320m the EC generates premium income of around \$186bn. Eastern Europe, including the former USSR, generates about \$39.2bn.

Across the Atlantic, the USA, with its population of 240m, generates \$367bn in premiums. Indeed, the USA has the biggest insurance business in the world, running up against the problems of a mature market long before the European insurers had even contemplated them. America will probably continue to set the pattern for the industry in future; and the US dollar will probably remain the critical currency in the insurance business.

Japan boasts the world's second largest insurance industry, after the USA. But the Japanese, like the Americans, are tending to depress worldwide growth in

tal growth of financial services firms, leading to cross-border *bancassurance* and *allfinanz* concerns.

In October 1991 the European Commission approved the proposal for a Pension Fund Directive. This legislation does not impinge upon existing statutory social security schemes, nor does it seek to harmonise the level of provision across markets. But it does require member states to ensure that within the Community there is freedom of choice of investment assets, investment managers and country of investment.

The market for private pensions is proportionately far bigger in the UK than in most of continental Europe, where private schemes remain relatively rare. However, analysts expect a marked increase in the take-up of these schemes throughout the EC over the next 5–10 years.

In terms of the sale of straight life policies, UK penetration of European markets has been limited, particularly compared with the levels achieved in non-European markets. In 1986, British life assurers derived less than 6% of their premium income from other EC countries. Non-life insurers obtained only 9% of their premium income from the EC, against 40% from other foreign countries.

UK insurance policies appear cheaper than those generally available in continental Europe. This price advantage may not reflect the efficiency of the UK market so much as the divergent continental experience in claims frequency and policy breadth. Different taxation treatment and investment constraints on the management of premium income probably also play a part. Lloyd's of London is currently working with a management consultant on improving cost controls in its business.

The UK suffers from taxation penalties, in particular in the tax treatment of reserves, where the Inland Revenue attempts to maximise profit imputed on insurers. On the other hand, the UK suffers few restrictions on the investment of these funds.

TOTAL PREMIUM REVENUE, 1989

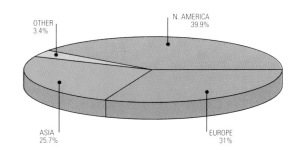

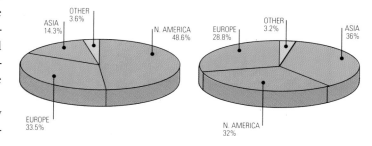

Titanic losses… a spate of mega-disasters, such as Hurricane Hugo and the Piper Alpha oil rig blow-out, was given as one reason why the British Lloyd's insurance market found itself in deep water in the early 1990s. A 1992 report blamed "seriously flawed" judgment on the part of underwriters as another.

this sector. If current developments in these more mature markets are anything to go by, the Europeans should tread warily. The USA is suffering from a government-induced squeeze on non-life profits and from crippling litigation arising from long-dated claims and consumer pressure groups.

For European insurance companies from EC member states the Second Non-Life directive allows non-life insurers, provided they are authorised by their domestic regulators, to sell all their products covering large risks throughout the European Community. And they will be able to do so on a services basis. This means they can market policies from their home bases without having a local office or agent. However, analysts expect that agency systems will continue to be the cornerstone of insurance marketing in Europe for the foreseeable future.

The Community's regulatory system is based heavily on the concept of "universality", and has fed the horizon-

LIFE AND NON-LIFE

In spite of efforts to open up insurance markets within Europe, life insurance in particular has remained bound within national barriers. Large complicated risks, which can generate the most profitable business for insurers, are tricky to standardise, and establishing cross-border insurance in Europe has proved more difficult than expected.

NON-LIFE PREMIUM REVENUE, 1989   LIFE PREMIUM REVENUE, 1989

INSURANCE CULTURES

The average premium volume per head of population indicates the spread of insurance in a given market, as well as the potential and the willingness of the population to take up private provision. An important element is the amount of disposable income in a country, although political and historical influences play an important part and should not be underestimated. The cautious Swiss, for example, tend to be big spenders on insurance and the market in that country – at least for existing products – is probably not far off saturation point. In southern Mediterranean countries and eastern Europe, however, the insurance culture has yet to establish itself and the market is less developed.

The traditionally high insurance spend in Switzerland places its nationals at the top of the league of premium payers. The Swiss consistently invest more money in insurance per head of population than any other nationality. In 1989, the average Swiss spent $2,376 apiece on insurance, not far off double that of the Finns, the next biggest spender per head in Europe. The chart below shows how much most of Europe is behind the Japanese and American in terms of average annual personal

expenditure on insurance.

In western Europe, the Greeks spend less on insurance cover than anyone else, paying in 1989 a mere $78 per head for premiums. They are followed by the Spanish, who spend $337 each; and the Italians, at $406. In eastern Europe expenditure on insurance is much lower – $101 a head in Czechoslovakia, under $3 a head in Poland.

In 1989 non-life insurance made up about 53% of Europe's total insurance premium income. In most countries non-life expenditure was higher than life, but in Switzerland, Finland, Sweden, the UK, France and Ireland, expenditure on life insurance was higher than on non-life insurance. In Finland it was close to double, in Britain the ratio was slightly lower. But no one spends more on life insurance than the Japanese – three times as much as non-life expenditure.

The market for insurance products across Europe as a whole is immature. Historical differences in the provision of insurance mean there is considerable scope for increased sales of both life and non-life cover. However, there are significant marketing barriers to be overcome and fierce competitive pressures will keep returns down, at least in the early stages.

The increase in the number of people undertaking dangerous activities has provided an area of growth for insurance companies.

PREMIUM BUSINESS, 1989

 Premiums per head   Premiums as a % of GDP

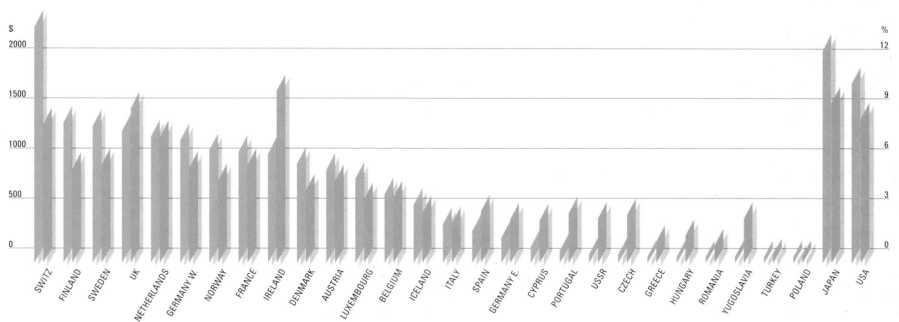

EASTERN EUROPE

The population of eastern Europe, excluding the former Soviet republics, is about 112.8m. In 1988 the insurance sector in eastern Europe generated $9.4bn in revenues. The premium per head was about $100 on average (if you include the former Soviet Union, $90 if you don't), as against $820 in the EC and $1,750 in the USA.

The 1988 figures for eastern Europe showed little change

PREMIUM DETAILS

COUNTRY	volume $m 1988	world share % 1988	Life/GDP % 1988
BULGARIA	–	–	–
CZECHOSLOVAKIA	3,827	0.33	0.74
GERMANY E.	4,010	0.34	1.71
HUNGARY	465	0.04	0.45
POLAND	623	0.05	0.19
ROMANIA	501	0.04	0.25
USSR	29,804	2.55	1.50

EC	266,674	22.77	2.70
USA	431,399	36.84	3.65

from 1987. In local currency Poland's premium volume increased by almost one-third, but in dollar terms dropped by a tenth. For nearly all other countries premium volume increased in both national currency and dollar terms. World share hovered at just over 3% but was only around 1% when the Soviet Union was excluded. As a percentage of GDP, premium volume was roughly half the rate for the EC and roughly a third of that for the USA.

As these figures make clear, the insurance market in eastern Europe is a long way behind that in western Europe, with the exception of countries such as Greece and Portugal. But the potential for growth is enormous. As standards of living rise, non-life insurance needs increase. All those people in the former eastern bloc hoping to become car owners will need car insurance once they achieve their aspiration (though there will be problems in setting insurance at affordable levels and policing it). Likewise, life-insurance habits should develop in eastern Europe as they have in the West. Furthermore, governments will want to offload some of their pension-type obligations to the private sector.

PENSIONS

The management of Europe's independent pension fund assets – worth about 700bn ecus – is concentrated in a handful of financial centres. The UK manages about 62%; the Netherlands 24%; and the rest is managed in Germany, Denmark, Ireland and Belgium.

The EC's Pension Fund directive aims to make supplementary pension insurance available in every EC country to compensate for dwindling social provisions. Nevertheless, self-administered and managed pension funds of the sort available in the UK and the Netherlands have yet to make inroads elsewhere.

France, Germany and Italy have high levels of state benefits. France has a pay-as-you-go (or repartition) system which requires compulsory membership of all company employees. Contributions are generally based on the amount required to meet current outgoings, which means that employees could forfeit their benefits if their employer were to go bankrupt. Funds paid are effectively invested for a year, then paid out in benefits, making the system extremely sensitive to demographic change and to the trend towards earlier retirement. In practice, however, most French pay-as-you-go systems have substantial accumulated reserves.

Such a system is prevalent in countries which lack pension legislation protecting employee rights and defining the taxation positions. The German system, which involves pensions being paid out of companies' book reserves, is beyond the scope of the EC's directive on Investment Services because these reserves do not represent separate assets. Allocations to internal financial reserves for pension schemes are tax deductible for the company. The charge goes through the profit-and-loss account and is transferred to the balance-sheet of the company each year.

A SINGLE EC PENSIONS MARKET

The single market concept will have a slower impact in the pension fund industry than in most other areas. The Pension Fund directive, being adopted by member states in late 1992, will not be implemented into many of their national legal systems until the mid-1990s. It will free pension funds to choose an investment manager anywhere in the Community; and allow those managers to invest their money where and how they wish, without any geographical restrictions. However, many multinational companies complain that the directive omits a key freedom, which would allow them to organise their employee pension arrangements more efficiently, specifically through cross-border membership of funds. The Commission says it has not abandoned the principle of this, but that trying to include such provisions in the directive would result in the slowing of down its implementation, mainly because of tax complications.

Differences will remain in the Community's pension market, anyway, until the current cultural divisions break down. Most of continental Europe remains suspicious of equity investment; and, except in the Netherlands, the private pension market remains in its infancy on the continent. Industry forecasts predict a doubling of continental pension fund assets between 1990 and 1995, however, which, if correct, would force continental managers to look much more seriously beyond traditional boundaries.

The EC has involved itself more and more with workers' rights and has produced a raft of proposals on everything from safety to hours of work. It has also passed a directive laying down the principal of equal pensionable age for men and women. Germany, Spain, Ireland and the Netherlands have a single retirement age of 65, Denmark one of 67 and France 60. Other members of the EC have a lower retirement age for women; mostly 60 as against 65 for men, though in Italy women retire at 55 and men at 60.

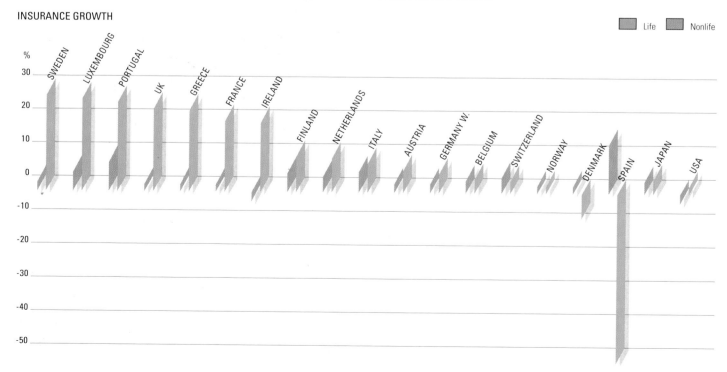

INSURANCE GROWTH

■ Life   ■ Nonlife

PREMIUM INCOME BY CONTINENT

The USA and Japan account for 59.4% of the world market, so poor performance in these markets severely limits overall growth. Europe accounts for 31%, and Asia for 25.7%. The shares of Oceania, Africa and Latin America range between 0.6% and 1.7%. West Germany has the greatest European share, followed by the UK and France.

Total worldwide premium income in 1989 was $1,210bn, up 3.9% on 1988. This was a slowdown in the rate of growth (8.0% in 1987) but it still exceeded by more than half a percentage point world GNP growth of 3.2%.

In real terms, Europe grew fastest in 1989 but Asia recorded the best growth in 1987 and 1988, and is likely to regain the lead. North and South America had hardly any real growth in 1989, while markets in Denmark, New Zealand and Spain all receded. The emerging markets of Thailand, Brazil, Zimbabwe, Chile and South Korea grew by more than 20% in 1989 and these countries all offer long-term promise.

Although Germany achieved only slow growth in 1989 (less than 5% according to Sigma), premiums will soar by about 13% to $92bn in 1991 and Germany's 440 primary insurers will enjoy an increase of about 12.5% in 1991 to $86bn. Reunification has added 16m new insurance customers and the next five years will see Germany's insurance industry starting to reap the benefits. Life insurance will remain the largest sector, with premium income of some $33.5bn, followed by the motor ($18.5bn) and private health ($11.2bn) sectors. New life insurance sums assured are expected to rise by 28% to around $202.2bn and total premium revenues in Germany will probably surpass $167.6bn before the year 2000.

AGEING POPULATIONS

Demographic experts predict that by the early part of the 21st century 20% of the population of OECD nations will be over 65 years old. Worse, in the major European markets the number of retired workers will exceed the number of people in work. This will happen in France first, probably in the year 2005. The ageing of populations in developed countries has caused a shift in savings patterns and stimulated equity investment as a means of matching inflation over time. Insurance business has grown strongly in Europe as well, reflecting increasing wealth across the continent.

Ageing populations will place a heavy burden on pension providers in all countries, but the prospect is particularly alarming in those countries where generous state benefits are the norm. Countries like Germany and Switzerland will have to move away from their reliance on company pension plans funded on a pay-as-you-go basis. And governments in France and Italy are already trying to stimulate private provision and directly funded pensions by offering generous tax concessions on savings put aside now.

In the meantime, the UK's independent pensions industry remains far more sophisticated than elsewhere in Europe. EC directives of 1990 and 1991 should free the banks to engage in pension fund management activities, but they may also make life more difficult for non-bank providers of pension management by imposing new restrictions.

In general, little real progress has been made in establishing a common European approach to pension provision. However, there has been a rise in the proportion of funds managed by independent professional institutions, and this is expected to continue. Hitherto, most continental companies with employee pension schemes have tended to manage these in-house, rather than through professional external institutions, as is common in the UK. These institutions tend to be more active in international markets and to invest more heavily in equities (rather than fixed income assets), since these offer a better match for future pension liabilities.

POPULATION OVER 65, %

COUNTRY	1950	1980	1990 est	2000 est	2010 est	2020 est
FRANCE	11.3	14.0	13.8	15.3	16.3	19.5
GERMANY W.	9.3	15.7	15.5	17.1	20.3	21.7
ITALY	8.0	13.5	13.8	15.3	17.3	19.4
NETHERLANDS	7.7	11.5	12.7	13.5	15.1	18.9
SWITZERLAND	9.6	13.9	14.8	16.8	20.4	24.5
UK	10.7	14.9	15.1	14.5	14.6	16.3

JAPAN	5.2	7.8	11.4	15.2	18.6	20.9
USA	8.2	11.3	12.2	12.1	12.8	16.2

Governments are faced with the increased pension burden of an ageing society, but others are delighted to discover the affluent "grey" consumer with money to spare on financial services, consumer goods and particularly leisure. Even "oldies" skydive these days.

One suggested Japanese solution to having too many old people was to buy big apartment complexes in Spain in order to create communities for Japanese senior citizens. Other senior citizens have already discovered the attractions of moving countries. In the last two decades many British pensioners have moved en masse to Spanish hotels for the winter because it was warmer and their pension money went further.

EASTERN EUROPE

Follow the leaders… the western dealer's uniform of red braces is worn with pride by dealers at the embryonic Budapest stock exchange. The exchange opened with the flotation of travel agency, Ibusz, in 1990. It now has seven fully listed companies and is open for an hour and a half daily.

Street fare… although prices soared in the former Soviet republics after controls were removed, individual traders like this Ukrainian woman are now encouraged where once they were banned.

Since autumn 1989 eastern Europe has swept away the outdated economic structures which had been in place for more than 40 years. Hard on the heels of the political revolutions which removed its communist governments, the region embarked on ambitious reforms, aimed at putting its crumbling economies onto a par with the West.

For countries like Czechoslovakia and Hungary, which became Soviet satellites after 1945, industrial economies and financial markets had existed in the past. So for them, the reform process has largely been a question of rebuilding a private sector and breaking artificial trading links within Comecon. For others, particularly in the old Soviet Union, the task of creating a modern economy has meant starting from scratch, trying to develop efficient businesses to replace cumbersome and corrupt bureaucracies.

The key to the change is privatisation, the transfer of property and businesses to private hands. This began in Hungary even before the revolutions of 1989 and 1990; and the Soviet Union started by encouraging cooperatives in 1987. In central Europe, most small businesses, shops and restaurants were transferred to private hands by auction in the first two years of the reform programme. Now mass privatisation programmes are being used to try to sell minority stakes in local firms to eastern Europe's new shareholder democracies, at attractive rates. Some showcase industries have also been sold to foreign investors.

Since 1990, the region as a whole has seen a wave of macro-economic reforms, involving liberalisation of prices and withdrawal of state support for industry. Monetary and fiscal policies have been tightened to fight inflation and the rouble-based Comecon trading system has been scrapped. In short, the old planned economies are rapidly giving way to systems based on market forces and the private sector.

The result of all this was that many of the region's economies plummeted, struggling from a combination of internal reforms and external pressures. The move to world prices meant a collapse in the region's traditional trade at home; and war in the Gulf caused a sudden jump in world oil prices, sending the new market economies into secondary shock. A lack of statistics or accurate accounting methods during 1945–1989, coupled with problematic property claims in countries where land had been expropriated after the war, contributed further to the economic turbulence.

The task of rebuilding economies and releasing market forces has fallen to a younger generation, often academics brought out of semi-exile with only text book knowledge of how business and finance work. Foreign advisers, spotting an opportunity, have flooded into the region, with accountants, lawyers and venture capitalists, amongst others, setting up operations in key centres. But even with western expertise, numerous problems remain. Citizens of the former communist countries had high hopes for their newly established democratic governments, assuming that living standards would rise while shortages and hardships eased. Instead, of course, the opposite has more often been the case.

Nevertheless, a number of successful joint ventures are being formed by western companies with local cooperatives or other groupings within the countries concerned. The country most active in this area, unsurprisingly, is Germany. German manufacturing companies have bought existing businesses in the eastern part of Germany, often very cheaply, through the offices of the Treuhand, the Berlin-based agency charged with selling off the old state-run enterprises. But many of Germany's industrial giants are expanding into other former soviet satellites as well, seeing the political turnaround as a chance to establish a manufacturing and sales presence in what could well become lucrative markets of the future.

CURRENCIES

One of the key challenges in eastern Europe has been to establish currencies which are both internally and externally convertible. If this is to be achieved, an essential requirement is the liberalisation of prices and the control of inflation by restricting the money supply. The main impediment so far has been a lack of hard currency reserves, which has also restricted the extent to which domestic businesses have been able to buy in expertise and equipment from abroad.

The former Soviet republics have faced the problem of trying to create currencies with separate identities from that of the old rouble. These include the Estonian and the Latvian lek, for example. The Ukraine began by introducing coupons.

National banks have seen their old departments split away to form new commercial banks which the state will eventually privatise. Their remaining role ranges from regulation of the financial system to hard currency auctions, and their political independence varies greatly. Czechoslovakia has one of the most independent central banks.

Connections: Competition in industry 50–51 A wider Europe 52–53 Privatisation 54–55 Foreign investment 60–61 Rebuilding democracies 120–121

REFORM AGENCIES

The collapse of communism has given rise to a new bureaucracy of organisations set up to deal with the transition to a market economy. The agencies responsible range from the Treuhand in eastern Germany to the State Property Agency in Hungary; from the Ministry for Ownership Change in Poland to the National Privatisation Agency in Romania.

But a new important reform agency with a brief that covers all eastern Europe is the European Bank for Reconstruction and Development. This was established in April 1991, with 42 nations as founder members and subscribers. The bank's headquarters are in London and its president is the controversial figure of Jacques Attali, a former French presidential adviser. The USA is the largest shareholder, with a 10% stake in the bank which began life with capital amounting to $10bn. The EBRD's brief is to make 60% of its funds available for private sector projects to encourage development of free enterprise democracies in the East. One area it is likely to stress is private sector banking; by 1992, its Financial Institutions Group was aiming to establish corporate finance advisory brokerages aimed at helping to select and identify new projects. The Bank may lend 40% of its resources for public infrastructure projects and it must give a high priority to environmental schemes.

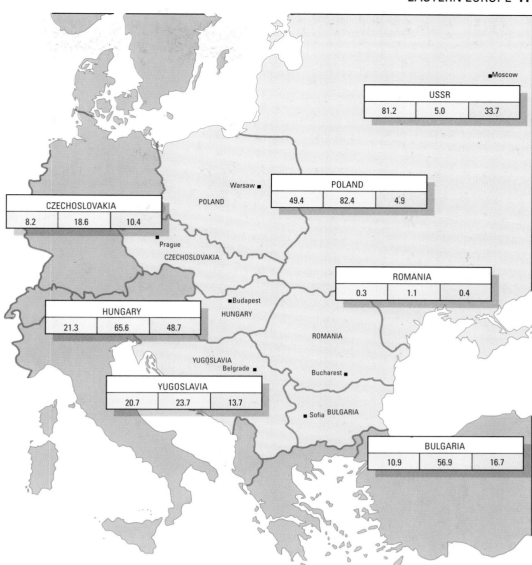

FOREIGN DEBT

	Foreign debt ($bn)
	Debt as % of GNP
	Debt-service ratio

REFORM MECHANISMS

Eastern Europe has borrowed heavily from western models and expertise to create new financial institutions capable of handling modern payment systems, foreign trade and, above all, the transfer of economic assets into private hands. These include private banks, fund management companies and financial markets. Western accountants, too, have been taken on as consultants to governments in eastern Europe to help them establish effective accounting systems, in order, for instance, that businesses can be valued more accurately before their sale to either domestic or foreign investors.

Stock exchanges are being developed in Budapest, Warsaw, Sofia and several Russian cities, despite an initial lack of either quoted stocks or investors. Most countries have relied mainly on banks to match buyers and sellers of shares and bonds, and none of the exchanges yet conducts significant business by western standards. They are open for only a day or so a week and trading volumes are very light. Budapest became the first, in 1992, to order a computerised trading system.

In Poland, the Warsaw exchange re-opened in April 1991 after a gap of 50 years. The Polish authorities modelled their exchange on the Lyon Bourse, using an order-matching system, and officials from the French Société des Bourses had provided advice on the setting up and running of the new exchange. It opened for business with trading in five privatised companies, all of which were brought to the public via a UK-style privatisation programme.

Countries have used different kinds of mass privatisation programmes for dispersing shares to the public. Czechoslovakia has used a voucher system, for instance. Others have offered shares in ownership funds which bring western fund management expertise into the process. Others have used electoral registers, utility companies and even police lists to access potential purchasers.

Carriage trade… this is one of the Hungarian train-building factories which have contributed to making this one of the country's most successful industries.

BANKING

Until 1990, eastern Europe's central banks had combined responsibility for control of the money supply, foreign trade relations and export finance. They still have responsibility for monetary policy, but their individual departments have now been turned into commercial banks.

Czechoslovakia's Banking Reform Act of January 1990 allowed investment banks to play a greater role in financing infrastructure and housing. Foreign banks may operate in the country. Hungary's Banking Act provides for foreign ownership of banks but permission is required for stakes over 10%. Only the government and other commercial banks can hold more than 25%. Commercial banks require minimum capital of 2bn forints; investment banks 500m forints; and savings banks 100m forints. Under Poland's 1989 banking law, nine commercial banks were created from the National Bank of Poland. They will be privatised and twinned with western banks. New legislation will cover the appointment of a central bank president, and licensing requirements for foreign banks.

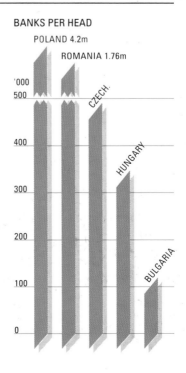

BANKS PER HEAD

POLAND 4.2m

ROMANIA 1.76m

POLITICS

The patchwork politics of Europe strive for an identity that reflects the nation state and a European identity for its neighbours. This led the governments of western Europe to band together into European alliances, the strongest of which is the European Community. As a result Europe has a democratic and wealthy core which attracts the new democracies of eastern Europe and on which Europe now bases its future.

The conundrum of European politics in the 1990s is aptly illustrated by events in central Europe where western Germany has achieved its postwar dream of reunification with eastern Germany, while the federation of Yugoslavia created after the second world war has been torn apart by civil war. This is also the first post-communist decade for eastern Europe in which democracy is being tested, and political divorce is reshaping the region with Czechoslovakia following the former Soviet Union in splitting up.

This chapter examines the ideals of nation states and trading organisations, reviews parliamentary democracies, stable and unstable, and the use of referenda. It tackles the consequences of federalism within the European Community, looks at re-establishing a political status quo and democratisation in eastern Europe. It explains how Europe has reacted and adapted to the fundamental shocks and upheaval that form the basis of most political change, how Christian Democratic parties were formed in response to postwar anti-fascism, and where the rot set in that led to the collapse of communism. Then comes the European Community: its institutions, the way it works and what it spends. Other sections look at the rise of the new right, the widespread shift towards reducing the role of the state and future scenarios for the political shape of Europe. Will it become a fortress, a cooperative, a superstate or just a muddle?

POLITICAL SYSTEMS

The nation state, as we know it in Europe today, was largely a product of the late l9th century, with German unification and Italian risorgimento as leading examples. The process of state creation continued after the first world war, when new states replaced the Austro-Hungarian and Turkish empires, influenced by the principle of self-determination. The equation of state and nation is essentially a phenomenon of the modern world, and the concept of the nation state implies that it is only nations that create states. But it is also true that states create nations, or at least seek to do so. If they fail, then behind the façade of the unified state, sub-state minorities with national identities will await the chance for independence. Europe today is a patchwork of nation states, some achieving an identity of state and nation, others uneasily combining a number of sub-state minorities. War has been both the means of securing the unification of some nation states and the way of destroying or subjugating others, but the two major European wars have shown

May 1940, Belgium...Adolf Hitler's Germany invaded the Low Countries, the phoney war ceased and the war that eventually spread throughout all of Europe began. It took a further 50 years before the political frontiers were reinstated.

the futility of nation-state aggrandisement.

A new era began after the second world war: the decline of the old nation state. But its dismantling took two different forms in Europe – The Soviet Union used a model of imposed supranationalism, a much more radical development than the label of the Soviet empire suggests. In western Europe, by contrast, what emerged was a cooperative version of supranationalism based on the principles of voluntarism and partnership. Different as they were, both shared the same three motivations – economic, political and strategic. Western European supranationalism is succeeding in eroding the loyalties to the old nation state. But in the wake of the collapse of the Soviet Union and Yugoslavia, and now the break up of Czechoslovakia, nationalism has become a rampant force in eastern Europe and is fuelling the bitter hostility between re-emergent nations wanting states of their own.

Eastern European supranationalism

The ideological basis for Soviet domination – the rationalisation of its power – was the underlying principle of socialist internationalism. In practice, this was a euphemism for the leading role of the Communist party in creating a socialist society in the USSR, and the imposition of socialism by the USSR in its eastern European satellite states. The

chief threat to achieving these goals lay in existing nation-state identities, along with the capitalist enemy. Despite all efforts to subjugate, if not eradicate, them, they proved far more resistant than was generally supposed. Indeed, just because they were the final bulwark, national identities were strengthened as a direct reaction to the attempt to suppress them. At the first chance, the eastern European countries lost no time in breaking the shackles binding them to the Warsaw pact and to Comecon. What resulted from the unravelling of the Soviet Union was not just the reappearance of national identities, but much more – a veritable Russian doll of minority demands for recognition as states.

Western-style supranationalism

In western Europe, the fact that no country was very much more powerful than any other facilitated cooperative ventures. Although the United States provided a protective strategic umbrella through NATO, it was neither in a position to impose its will on western Europe, nor minded to do so. American governments did, however, provide strong encouragement for economic and political cooperation, and a very real incentive in the form of the Marshall Plan.

The evolution of cooperative supranationalism was at first characterised by four features: the various supranational initiatives had no necessary linkages between them; within each supranational organisation, agreements were based at a level which represented a consensus; the supranational bodies avoided positing a final goal; their strength lay in their pragmatism and the ability to surmount crises as they arose.

On the road to a new kind of state?

A host of cooperative bodies emerged in the postwar era – the Organisation for European Economic Cooperation, Nordic Council, Council of Europe, European Free Trade Association, West European Union, European Coal and Steel Community, European Economic Community and European Atomic Energy Community. However, the three Community organisations, with common membership and overlapping institutions, quickly developed a powerful and different dynamic – one that explicitly allows for a pooling of national sovereignties over a wide area of policies. The Single European Act, in effect from l986, acknowledged their fusion as the European Community with a goal of a single market economy, a single currency and political union. The question now raised by the current events in Europe is whether Europe is now laying the foundations of a new type of cooperative superstate.

THE CONFERENCE ON SECURITY AND COOPERATION IN EUROPE (CSCE)

This was founded in 1975 as a result of the Helsinki summit of NATO, Warsaw pact and non-aligned countries. The Helsinki summit laid down ten principles concerning human rights, self-determination and inter-relations between states. The Helsinki process continued during a number of summit meetings, culminating in the 1990 Paris summit. The Paris charter institutionalised the CSCE structures, setting up a secretariat in Prague, a conflict-prevention centre in Vienna and an election observation office in Warsaw. It also agreed an Assembly of Europe, composed of national parliamentarians, meeting once a year in Strasbourg, and regular meetings of foreign ministers and heads of state or government.

Connections: **Patterns of empire 16–17** **Towards unity 24–25** EC: institutions 132–133 The future shape 142–143 The cold war balance 184–185

POSTWAR ORGANISATIONS IN WESTERN AND EASTERN EUROPE

- ▨ NATO (1947)
  Later members:Greece (52); Turkey (52);
  W. Germany (55); Spain (82)
- ▨ Marshall Aid (1947)/OECD
  Later recipients: Spain (58); Finland (69);
  Yugoslavia (observer only 55)
- ▨ Warsaw pact (1955)
- ▨ Comecon (1949)

NATO

In the Brussels Treaty of 1947, five European states pledged themselves to come to each other's aid in the event of armed aggression. In April 1948, the Canadian secretary of state put forward the idea of a single mutual defence system involving North America as well as the Europeans, which led, via the Vandenberg Resolution in 1948, to the creation of the North Atlantic Treaty Organisation (NATO).

The structure of NATO comprises the North Atlantic Council, shown above, which is composed of representatives of the 16 member states and the Defence Planning Committee, which are the main decision-making bodies. Both are chaired by the secretary-general, and serve as a forum for confidential intergovernmental consultation. (Ambassadors meet once a week, foreign ministers twice a year.) There is also a Nuclear Planning Group, meeting in the same way as those mentioned above.

The organisation also has a permanent secretariat of international staff.

Economic aid

The European Recovery Programme – the plan for the postwar economic reconstruction of Europe (commonly known as Marshall Aid), was proposed by General George C. Marshall, the secretary of state for the United States at a speech at Harvard on June 5th 1947. In 1948 the Organisation for European Economic Cooperation (OEEC) was launched to administer the aid. Between 1948 and 1952 the United States provided some $17,000m, most of which went to western Europe as the

Soviet Union had rejected the plan outright.

Although Marshall Aid ceased in 1952, the OEEC continued to function until it was replaced by the Organisation for Economic Cooperation and Development (OECD) in 1960. Although Switzerland is an

OECD member, it did not receive Marshall Aid. With the accession of the USA and Canada as full members, the OECD ceased to be a purely European body, but added development aid to the list of its activities. Its objectives today are to promote economic and social welfare throughout the OECD area.

Warsaw pact

This defence alliance was founded in May 1955 when the USSR and its eastern European satellites signed a two-year treaty of friendship and collaboration in Warsaw. The pact's Political Consultative Committee met annually in each of the member countries in turn, and established a Committee of Defence Ministers, a Technical Committee and a Committee of seven ministers. In February 1991, the members agreed to dismantle all military organs, institutions and activities by March of that year.

Comecon

The Council for Mutual Economic Assistance, or Comecon as it was popularly known, was founded in January 1949 in Romania to promote the development of the national economies of the member states, and the development of socialist economic integration through the cooperation of members in the most rational use of resources and the acceleration of economic and technical progress, industrialisation and productivity. In 1991 the members decided to abolish Comecon, replacing it with the Organisation for International Economic Cooperation.

WESTERN EUROPEAN ORGANISATIONS

- ▨ Council of Europe (1949)
  Later members: Turkey (49); Greece (49;
  withdrew 69; rejoined 74); Iceland (50);
  Germany (51); Austria (56); Cyprus (61);
  Switzerland (63); Malta (65); Portugal (76);
  Spain (77); Liechtenstein (78); San Marino (88);
  Finland (89); Hungary (90); Czechoslovakia (91)
  Special guest status to Poland, USSR and
  Yugoslavia in 1989
- ▨ Western European Union (1954)
  Later members: Spain (90); Portugal (90)
- ▨ European Community (1957)
  Later members: UK (73); Denmark (73);
  Ireland (73); Greece (81); Spain (86); Portugal (86)
- ▨ European Free Trade Association (1960)
  Later members: Finland (ass mem 1961-85);
  Iceland (70); Liechtenstein (91)
- ▨ Nordic Council (1952)
  Later members: Finland (55); Faeroes (70);
  Aland Islands (70); Greenland (84)

Council of Europe

Founded in London in 1949, but based in Strasbourg, the Council of Europe aims to "achieve a greater unity between its members for the purpose of safeguarding and realising the ideals and principles which are their common heritage, and facilitating their economic and social progress by discussion of questions of common concern and by agreements and common action… (which excludes) matters relating to national defence". The members agree European conventions (137 in total) and make recommendations to national governments.

The most important of the conventions is the European Convention of Human Rights, signed in 1950 and recognised now by 23 member states. It

▨ MALTA

provides for the European Commission and Court of Human Rights, which was established in 1959 in Strasbourg.

At the head of the structure of the Council of Europe is a Committee of Ministers, composed of foreign ministers, who meet twice yearly. Member states all have permanent representatives in Strasbourg who meet monthly, and there is also a Parliamentary Assembly with three week-long sessions a year.

The European Community

Founded in 1957 by the Treaties of Rome and effective from January 1958, the European Community subsumed the European Coal and Steel Community (created in 1951 by the Treaty of Paris). Article 2 of the Treaty of Rome declares that the Community shall have as its task

the job of promoting a harmonious development of economic activities, a continuous and balanced expansion, an increase in stability, an accelerated raising of the standard of living and closer relations between the states belonging to it.

European Free Trade Association (EFTA)

Founded in 1960 in Stockholm, EFTA had three main objectives: to achieve free trade in industrial products; to assist in the creation of a single market throughout western Europe and to contribute to the expansion of world trade. In 1991 EFTA and the EC reached agreement on the creation of a single market, to be known as the European Economic Area or EEA.

The Nordic Council

Founded in 1952, the organisation is now governed by the 1962 Helsinki Treaty. It is a vehicle for cooperation between the Nordic countries, especially in economic, political, social and cultural affairs. The Council itself consists of 87 members, in part elected by national parliaments and in part as delegates from governments. It meets once a year for a one-week session, and makes recommendations to the Council of Ministers and to member state governments. Ministers from each member state form the Council of Ministers.

Western European Union (WEU)

Founded in 1954, and based on the 1948 Brussels Treaty Organisation, the WEU aims to create a firm basis for economic recovery; to assist member states in resisting aggression, to promote unity and to encourage European integration. Its structure includes a council of foreign and defence ministers of member states, meeting twice a year, and a permanent Council of Ambassadors meeting regularly in London. Proposals have been made to enhance the role of the WEU to make it an effective European pillar of NATO, and to link it with the EC, by moving its headquarters to Brussels.

PARLIAMENTARY SYSTEMS

Switzerland has a long tradition of democracy and its open air parliaments date back to the 13th century. In the Lansgermeide or "folkmeet" every man had the same right to vote, to promote, to elect and to be elected.

West European democracies are described as liberal democracies, but the term liberal in this connection is often misunderstood. In fact, it is a restriction on democracy – effectively a check on majority rule. Liberal democracy in Europe was not a sudden acquisition, but an end-point of a long process. The European states generally became liberal first and democratic only later. Early on, the liberal struggle was against an arbitrary power of absolute rule: a challenge to despotism and the divine right of kings. By winning security and freedom for individuals – for instance, a 'bill of rights' – governments were brought under constitutional control. Later, when the mass of the people won the right to vote and to choose, and change governments, the liberal constitutional order was already in place.

At first the restrictions on the will of the democratic majority were seen as impediments by radicals, but they are now regarded as the major strength of western political systems. Liberal democratic institutions – constitutional checks and balances, the protection of minority rights and civil liberties, and the supremacy of the rule of law – can easily be set down on paper. However, combining these satisfactorily with the practice of democracy tends to lead to a continual process of instituting adjustment and conflict.

Stable and unstable democracies

West European democracies have a reputation for political stability, but that has not always been the case, and in the context of European history the present era is exceptional. Some, like the Scandinavian countries, Switzerland and the United Kingdom, have enjoyed a relatively trouble-free evolution. Others proved to be more fragile and, especially during the interwar years, succumbed to dictatorship. After 1945, the process of rebuilding democracy began (and that applied also to countries taken over by Nazi Germany). For some – the Netherlands and Norway, for instance – there were few problems in reinstating their democratic systems, while others – France and Greece – had prolonged problems. Spain and Portugal were the last to shed their dictatorships, but from the early 1980s onwards, western Europe as a whole has presented a uniform picture of democratic political stability. That does not necessarily mean that the governments are stable too, and that they have majority support – Denmark is a good example of minority government being a normal occurrence. But a succession of short-lived governments will almost certainly bring about a crisis for the regime.

How the Westminster model works – sometimes

The British system of parliamentary government is quite exceptional in western Europe because it is based on two dualities. First, it requires a two-party system (small parties are irrelevant). Second, it is based on a bipolarity of Government and Opposition – the major opposition party is the alternative government. The two parties alternate in government, aided by the first-past-the-post electoral system; a small shift in votes leads to a larger shift in party representation. The Westminster model usually guarantees stable, majority government. But there are several drawbacks: there is no certainty that alternation will take place at regular intervals, so that one party can be excluded from government for many years; the voting system distorts public wishes; more fundamentally, it depends on a high degree of consensus between the parties. If that is absent, the two-party system deepens divisions in society.

The consensual alternative

Unlike Britain, most European countries experienced a greater degree of social fragmentation in modern times with the result that they have entrenched multiparty systems which are nurtured by proportional representation – smaller parties are not squeezed out of parliament. Majority party government is the exception (although Portugal is a current example). Coalitions have to be formed, sometimes with five or six parties participating (such as in Belgium and Finland). Coalitions require the parties to compromise if they are to be accepted into government, and it is argued that parties are inclined to become more moderate in their outlook as a result. Furthermore, changes in government policy tend to be gradual, since usually one or more of the parties in the previous government will be in the next elected government.

The consensual model of government does not assume a consensus at the outset – far from it – but is a way of working towards one. All kinds of methods and constitutional arrangements may be used as well, such as the separation of executive, legislative and judicial powers, and federalism, in order to ensure that minorities are properly represented and protected.

POLITICAL SYSTEMS IN WESTERN EUROPE

- Continuous regime and stable government
- Continuous regime and unstable government
- Discontinuous regime and stable government
- Discontinuous regime and unstable government

NORWAY · FINLAND · SWEDEN · ESTONIA · IRELAND · UNITED KINGDOM · DENMARK · LATVIA · LITHUANIA · NETHERLANDS · BELGIUM · GERMANY · POLAND · LUX · CZECHOSLOVAKIA · FRANCE · SWITZ · AUSTRIA · HUNGARY · ROMANIA · PORTUGAL · SPAIN · ITALY · YUGOSLAVIA · BULGARIA · ALBANIA · GREECE · TURKEY

Four ways to rule

The map above shows the four main forms of government that have ruled Europe from 1945. The governments of France and Greece were both unstable at particular times; France during the Fourth Republic (up to 1958) and Greece under the monarchy (until 1967).

WESTMINSTER VERSUS CONSENSUAL MODEL

Some of the major distinguishing differences of the two systems are as follows: the Westminster model is based on one-party, bare-majority cabinets, fusion of powers and cabinet dominance, a two-party system, plurality system of elections, and an unwritten constitution, whereas the consensual model features executive coalition, separation of powers, a multiparty system, proportional representation and a written constitution.

Connections: Ideologies and parties 122–125 New movements 126–127

WHO VOTES FOR PR?

The map indicates the kind of voting systems in use and shows the level of proportionality at the most recent elections. The numbers show how many seats in a parliament bear a directly proportional relationship to the votes received. Representative government is party government and parties seek to maximise their representation in parliament. Most countries use a system of proportional representation, or PR as it is commonly known (in which the number of seats in the assembly is in proportion to a party's share of the vote).

Five ways to vote

First past the post   There are single-member or multi-member constituencies; candidate(s) with the highest number of votes are elected.
Second ballot   There are single-member constituencies; two rounds of voting; the candidate with a majority can be elected on first ballot. Otherwise, a limited number of candidates stand in the second ballot, on the first-past-the-post system.
List system   This has multi-member constituencies; the elector votes for a party list. Seats are either distributed according to the proportion of votes or seats are allocated to individuals according to their position on the party list.
Additional member   This is a mix of first past the post and a list system. Approximately half the seats are allocated from single-member constituencies on a first-past-the-post basis. Additional members are allocated proportionally on the basis of votes cast.
Single-transferable vote   This has multi-member constituencies; voters list preferences of candidates in order; candidates must reach a quota to be elected. Second preferences in excess of the quota and eliminated candidates are redistributed until a set number are elected.

ELECTORAL PROPORTIONALITY

- Proportional representation
- Single transferable vote
- Second ballot
- First past the post
- 95 Proportionality

  1. Additional member

NORWAY 91 · FINLAND 95 · SWEDEN 98 · ESTONIA · LATVIA · LITHUANIA · DENMARK 97 · IRELAND 96 · UNITED KINGDOM 85 · NETHERLANDS 96 · BELGIUM 91 · GERMANY 98 · POLAND · CZECHOSLOVAKIA · FRANCE 79 · SWITZ 96 · AUSTRIA 99 · HUNGARY · ROMANIA · ITALY 95 · YUGOSLAVIA · BULGARIA · PORTUGAL 94 · SPAIN 83 · ALBANIA · GREECE 88

Referenda in Europe

The chart indicates how many referenda are held in a sample of European countries and what importance is attached to them. Apart from in Switzerland, the use of the referendum is sporadic and used mainly to decide leading constitutional issues (for example, entry to the EC). One reason for this is its misuse in the past by dictators and others. Another is that it might undermine the authority of political parties. As a result, they usually hold a referendum only if there is no other way, although issues that cut across party lines can safely be left to the people to decide. Referenda are a valuable form of political education as the issues cut across party loyalties. However, they can undermine the principle of representative democracy.

USE OF REFERENDA

COUNTRY		
AUSTRIA	1	×
BELGIUM	1	×
DENMARK	8	××
FRANCE	10	×××
GREECE	4	××
IRELAND	8	××
ITALY	6	×××
NORWAY	1	×
SPAIN	5	××
SWEDEN	3	××
SWITZERLAND	>250	××××
UK	2	×

□ Referenda   Least important ×
□ Importance   Most important ××××

Realpolitik…Not quite. The waxworks of the leaders of Britain's three major parties prior to the 1992 election – Paddy Ashdown (Liberal Democrat), John Major (Conservative) and Neil Kinnock (Labour) – may look happy enough to share the same platform. But in the real world, British politics are adversarial rather than consensual because of the first-past-the-post electoral system. Coalition governments have only been formed during periods of crisis such as war.

AVOIDING UNSTABLE GOVERNMENT: GERMANY

In Germany, there are several articles in the constitution that help to prevent unstable government. Article 67 – the constructive vote of no-confidence – lays down that a vote of no-confidence in the chancellor can only be passed by the Bundestag electing a successor by an absolute majority, making it difficult for the chancellor to be challenged between elections (which are held after four years). Articles 63 and 68 – the dissolution of the Bundestag – dictate that the Bundestag can be dissolved only if the government is defeated on its own motion of no-confidence and with the assent of the president. In addition, the electoral system in Germany lays down that for a party to be represented in the Bundestag, it must receive at least 5% of the votes in the whole territory of the Federal Republic. This makes it very difficult for small and extremist parties to be elected to the Bundestag. A one-off exception was made to the 5% rule for representation in Parliament, with representation granted if a 5% share was reached in the territories of either of the former West Germany or the former East Germany. This enabled the Greens who lost seats in the former West Germany to win in the East.

ITALIAN DEMOCRACY – DOES IT WORK?

On the face of it, Italy is an excellent example of a liberal democratic constitution. Its economic performance, moreover, during the postwar period has been impressive. But the operation of its political system is widely regarded, particularly by the Italians themselves, as a national disaster.

The Italian constitution, laid down in 1948, provides for parliamentary government with two houses elected by proportional representation, a constitutional court, regional governments, the use of referenda and extensive civil rights. Unfortunately, a multiplicity of parties (up to ten different ones in any one parliament) has resulted in government instability, with 49 governments since 1945 of an average duration of less than 12 months.

The numerous proposals to improve government stability and public policy performance by reforming the constitution have proved fruitless. Instead of reform from within, many Italian politicians now look to the EC as the only body that is likely to be able to impose the policies that the domestic political system has failed to initiate, and has left a question yet to be answered concerning the value of democracy.

REGIONALISM AND FEDERALISM

The Italian elections in April 1992 had a record number of candidates but a singularly disenchanted electorate – Italy uses the regional list system of PR.

Europe's nation states vary in their patterns of distributing power between central and sub-state levels of government. These differences of territorial power-sharing reflect both distinct historic developments and the existence of more or less important groups and areas with strong identities as regions, or even as nations.

Some European states have attempted to overcome such internal diversity by centralisation, with all key political, economic, financial and legal decisions taken by central government. Effective centralisation dates back to Napoleon who redrafted the politico-administrative map, cutting old feudal provinces into equal-sized units, *départements*, and replaced local government by local administration under a central government overlord, the *préfet*. Italy, after reunification, followed the same pattern. Centralisation came to Spain and Germany, too, especially with the dictatorships of the 1930s. In all the mentioned cases political power was concentrated at the centre and attempts were made to impose a single national identity.

federal expansionism.

Such constitutional arrangements to protect federal provisions for extensive power-sharing between central and sub-state governments were adopted in Germany after 1945. Here the aim was to establish constitutional checks against the rise of a strong central power which might again threaten the peace of Europe. But there is no inevitable link between a large territory and federalism, as the political organisation of Austria, Switzerland and Belgium shows.

Some form of recognition for, and power-sharing with, hitherto repressed national groups may be essential for the maintenance of unity in states emerging from dictatorship. In Spain and Italy, governments opted for regionalisation, but while regions are recognised in their constitutions and given specific responsibilities, they remain subordinate to the centre, especially in terms of fiscal resources.

The resurgence of sub-state nationalism or regionalism has been triggered off by changing economic circum-

REGIONAL OR FEDERAL?

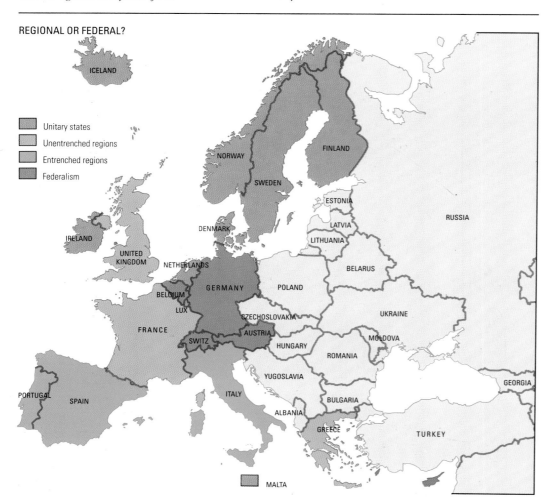

- Unitary states
- Unentrenched regions
- Entrenched regions
- Federalism

ICELAND, IRELAND, UNITED KINGDOM, NETHERLANDS, BELGIUM, LUX, FRANCE, SWITZ, PORTUGAL, SPAIN, NORWAY, SWEDEN, DENMARK, GERMANY, AUSTRIA, ITALY, FINLAND, ESTONIA, LATVIA, LITHUANIA, POLAND, CZECHOSLOVAKIA, HUNGARY, YUGOSLAVIA, ALBANIA, GREECE, RUSSIA, BELARUS, UKRAINE, MOLDOVA, ROMANIA, BULGARIA, TURKEY, GEORGIA, MALTA

BELGIUM AND THE LANGUAGE PROBLEM

Belgian society has been, and still is, divided by ethnicity and language. Today the group strengths are: Flemish 59%, Walloon 40% and German 1%. Deep-seated conflicts developed between these groups, especially in the 1970s and 1980s, with intense arguments about Brussels, a mainly French enclave in Flanders.

The constant debate about territorial organisation has been very divisive. There has been a territorial effect on the party system, splitting political parties (Liberal, Christian-Social and Socialist). National government is usually by grand coalition, with major regional parties represented.

In 1831, the new state adopted a constitution, with a unitary

THE LANGUAGE DIVISIONS

WEST-VLAANDEREN, OOST-VLAANDEREN, ANTWERP, LIMBURG, LIMBURG, HAINAUT, Brussels, BRABANT, LIEGE, HAINAUT, NAMUR, LUXEMBOURG, LUXEMBOURG

- Dutch-speaking (Flanders)
- French-speaking (Wallonia)
- German-speaking
- Bilingual area

The divisions of authority

The categories on the map above reflect the distribution of political authority.

Unitary states There is no division of political authority.

Unentrenched regions A limited amount of political authority is vested at the regional level, but the regions, and their powers, have no constitutional recognition.

Entrenched regions There is a clear constitutional vertical division of political authority between the centre and the regions, without the formal structures of a federal state.

Federalism There is a clear constitutional specification of federal and state powers, with significant powers held at the state level. State governments have their own sphere of policy competence.

Other states followed other paths. The United Kingdom combined four separate nations until the Irish opted-for independence. Britain retained distinct laws, administrations and legal systems for Scotland and Northern Ireland, and some separate laws for Wales, although all legislation is made by one Parliament at Westminster. The Netherlands, formed from the United Provinces, had both a strong national identity and a tradition of powerful local government. Switzerland, however, was established by the federation of its cantons, which, despite differences of language and religion, sought to defend their strong local control over policies by working together against take-over attempts from their neighbours. The constitution defined separate responsibilities for the federal and canton governments and provided means for the cantons to protect themselves against

state structure. In 1980 constitutional amendments introduced the first federalist features, and in 1989 amendments provided for territorial autonomy for the regions. In the last amendment in 1990 the provocative word "federal" was inserted in the constitution.

The constitution defines three language communities: Dutch, French and German; and four linguistic regions: Flanders, Wallonia, Brussels and German. The central government retains tight control over taxation. Both houses of parliament are elected by proportional representation; there is no separate representation for the regions. The four regional councils are elected and their areas of influence and control include: urban planning, the environment, energy, housing, local administration, industry, employment and social and cultural affairs.

Connections: Trading networks 22–23 Parliamentary systems 116–117 The birth of nations 176–177 The cold war balance 184–188 A sustainable future? 220–221

stances and anxieties over the declining use of some languages. It has also been encouraged by the fashionability of regional cultures, regional planning and regional funds from the EC. Even traditionally centralised states like France have adopted regions as an upper tier in their local government structures, admittedly with limited tasks and powers.

All regionalists now?

Regionalism and sub-state nationalism, however, reflect strong community identities either linked to large territorial areas with clear recognised boundaries or created by cultural, economic and traditional distinctions from other parts of the nation states of which they form part, or both. In Spain the extent of the Basque countries and the size of the Basque population are small, but the cultural distinctiveness is great. The populations of the large Mediterranean islands – Sardinia, Sicily and Corsica – all have clear identities and cultures. There is no single solution to the problem of regionalism and sub-state nationalism.

Spanish-French agreements allow for the expulsion of Spanish-born Basque separatists living in France under refugee status. This photograph captures the moment that separatists in Saint Jean de Luz chose to protest about the expulsion of José Varona Lopez, known as "Txema".

THE SPANISH EXAMPLE

After General Franco's death in 1975, the 1978 constitution provided for the reduction of centralisation. Between 1979 and 1983 each region negotiated its own solution. Four regions have constitutionally guaranteed status: Catalonia, Basque, Galicia and Andalucia. Thirteen other autonomous regions have statutory status only. Each region has an elected parliament and regional government, with significant rights of self-government, including fiscal control.

However, there is no formal or informal representation of the regions in national government or in parliament. Central government has control over autonomous regions by virtue of its control of the constitutionality of the regions and by its powers to act by default if autonomous regions fail to perform their duties. The constitutional court reinforces central authority.

Regions in Spain

The map shows the seventeen regions of Spain, some of which are divided into provinces, such as Andalucia with eight. The country has two contentious running battles. One is with the Basque separatists and their fight for independence; the other concerns their claim that Navarra should be included in the region. Many regions are very distinct with a unique dialect or even their own language.

FEDERALISM – THE GERMAN VARIANT

The present federal system in Germany was strongly influenced by the USA as an occupying power, and most of the Länder are artificial creations, with component parts put together from the three occupation zones in 1949. In the original plan, only 11 Länder were established; unification brought in a further five. The institutions are:

Upper House of Parliament (Bundesrat)
Representatives of the Länder governments, with weighted representation. The Upper House has equal powers on some issues affecting the Länder.

Länder
Each has its own constitution, court and civil service. Each Länder government is accountable to an elected legislature.

Federal Constitutional Court (Bundesverfassungsgericht)
Rules on disputes between Länder and Bund. Very important in protecting Länder from federal party-political conflict.

Financial equalisation and competences
Article 107 of the Basic Law provides for financial redistribution between the richer and poorer Länder (especially important after German reunification). A vast majority of competences are shared, the Länder are responsible for the implementation of federal laws, the Länder courts are responsible for most of the administration of justice. "Subsidiarity", embodied in Article 30 of the Basic Law, requires that nothing should be implemented at a higher level of government if it can be done at a lower one.

Länder

Four types of constitutional powers are defined in the Basic Law constitution, drafted in 1948–49 by Allied military governors and German provincial leaders: exclusive federal powers such as foreign affairs and defence; exclusive Länder powers such as education and health; framework powers – federal powers set conditions for Länder laws; concurrent powers so that the Länder can legislate if the federation has not.

The map, left, shows the 16 Länder, or regions, in Germany, established by the German constitution.

REBUILDING DEMOCRACIES

The countries of eastern Europe are now all strung out somewhere on the road to liberal democracy. A few, such as Hungary, seem to be well advanced. Others, such as Albania, have barely started. Yet they all have to be counted as being in a stage of transition, and it will be several years, maybe even decades, before it is certain that their democracies have been consolidated. What is remarkable is how the people of these countries have given such an unreserved welcome to western-style democracy and how quickly basic democratic reforms have been instituted.

One immediate effect of democratisation was the rise of a multiplicity of parties. Yet the new parties are for the most part quite different in character from those found in western Europe. Some are reformed communists under a new label, others try to latch on to political traditions that were strong in the past – a distant one – of a

The Bulgarian Socialist party maintained its grip on power in the 1990 elections, when its deputies won an absolute majority in parliament, taking 211 of the 400 seats. The union of Democratic Forces obtained 144 seats.

BANKING ON DEVELOPMENT

The European Bank for Reconstruction and Development (EBRD) was inaugurated in London on 15 April 1991. The political mandate of the bank is "to foster the transition towards open-market-orientated economies and to promote private and entrepreneurial initiative". The priorities of the bank are listed as primarily technical assistance and training, followed by the establishment of the framework of a market economy, public infrastructures, restructuring and privatisation, small and medium-sized enterprises, and regional projects and the environment. The bank has 42 shareholders, who supply the 10bn-ecu capital. On its establishment the bank was owned by 51% EC and member states, 12% eastern Europe, 12% EFTA, 10% USA, 8.5% each from Italy, Germany, France and Japan, and 6% the former Soviet Union.

previous era of democracy. For the most part, however, they are new formations, either taking the form of a popular rally – as Solidarity has in Poland – or of promoting moral values. To understand the problems of politics in the new democracies, and the difficulties parties are having in building substantial and reliable support, the lack of a firm connection between political forms and social realities has to be taken into account.

The aim of communist rule was to produce a homogenous classless society. The result was the eradication of cohesive social groups and their replacement by a largely proletarianised society, with a top-dressing of managerial and party elites – more generally, the intelligentsia. The collapse of communism left in its wake an atomised society. Concepts of left and right do not have the same meaning as in western Europe because the necessary social bases and interests are lacking, and the parties have to rely heavily on the stature of particular leaders or the credibility of the party message. However, there is one social force that can be harnessed securely to the new parties – nationalism. In this context, it is the demands of national minorities, or the solidarity of national majorities, that form the strongest party affiliations. They are also the most intractable in situations which threaten their own position: the collapse of Yugoslavia is a copybook example.

The Presidential option

A telling example of how an unstructured electorate reflects on the parties is provided by the 1991 parliamentary election in Poland. No fewer than 29 parties won representation, the largest party taking just 14% of the vote, and the party of the prime minister obtaining just 5%; only 40% of the electorate took the trouble to vote. Such an outcome raises the question as to the suitability of parliamentary government for any country in the early stages of transition. The democratic alternative is presidential government and, in the Polish case, effective power is in the hands of the president, so that the extent of parliamentary fragmentation is contained.

The recommendation of presidential rule is that it overcomes the weakness of the party system and acts as a unifying force for the whole country. However, it can lead to an undesirable personalisation of political power and a reversion to an authoritarian type of government; in the end, transition may be made more difficult.

Transitions: fast- and slow-track

It is clear that some eastern European countries will move more quickly into the pattern of western European democracies than others. The closest so far are Czechoslovakia, Hungary and Poland. To some extent, the reason is to be found in the level of economic development. Some countries also saw social and economic change before the end of communism. An approximate parallel can be drawn between the new democracies and the two dictatorships in western Europe – Portugal and Spain. They very rapidly became stable democracies because socio-economic change had continued unimpeded, and the subsequent political transition took place on that secure base. For eastern Europe, this socio-economic modernisation has been missing, except where, for instance, pluralist structures could develop. Much, therefore, depends on how rapidly the state/private balance can be altered, but the switch also invites political turmoil and hardship.

Connections: Eastern Europe 110–111   Political systems 114–115   Ideologies and parties 122–125

TROUBLE IN THE BALKANS

The federation of Yugoslavia was composed of the six constituent republics and two autonomous provinces, created by the April 1963 constitution, shown in the map below. There are substantial economic differences between the poor south and the richer north, and the intermix of nationalities is such that the borders cannot coincide with any national or linguistic or religious divisions. The official languages are Slovene, Macedonian and Serbo-Croat. Albanian and Hungarian are also spoken by minorities. There are also at least three religions: Orthodoxy, Roman Catholicism and Islam.

Under the 1963 constitution, socialist self-government was exercised by the representative bodies of communes, districts, autonomous republics, republics and the Federation. A new constitution, proclaimed in February 1974, directly transferred economic decision-making to the working people through the assembly system and, in January 1990, the government

announced an eight-point plan to rewrite the constitution, abolish the Communist party's monopoly of power, set up an independent judiciary, guarantee freedom of political association and institute economic reforms. Opposition parties were legalised in July 1990.

Dissensions between Albanians and Serbs in Kosovo, and between Croats and Serbs in parts of Croatia brought inter-ethnic tensions into violent conflict since 1988. After the elections of national governments in all six republics in 1990, the republics came increasingly into conflict with the federal government. At the end of 1991, both Croatia and Serbia proclaimed their secession from federal Yugoslavia, and fighting between the Serbian-dominated federal government and Croatia began. In 1992 Bosnia also seceded.

MODEL DEMOCRACY IN HUNGARY

The process towards democratisation in Hungary could be said to have started in 1956 when de-Stalinisation in the Soviet Union, following Khrushchev's speech in October of that year, prompted demonstrations about working conditions and repression. The old leadership in Hungary was thrown out, and the new leadership announced its intention of neutrality only to be met with repression, as the Soviet troops rolled in. Janos Kadar, the leader after the 1956 revolution, promoted economic development and made the raising of the standard of living a priority. He introduced a number of reforms in democratisation, agriculture, price reform and trade with the West. Since then, Hungary has always been seen as being one step ahead of reforms made elsewhere in eastern Europe.

Alexander Dubcek (the former reformist first secretary under the Communist regime) and Vaclav Havel, now the leader of the Czech Civic Forum and a former dissident playwright, making their first public speech together in November 1989 at the start of the democratisation of Czechoslovakia. Havel was elected president in December 1989, and Dubcek was elected speaker of parliament. In 1992, Czechoslovakia decided to split into two regions. Havel was strongly against such a move and resigned.

HUNGARIAN PR
How the parties fared in 1990 elections

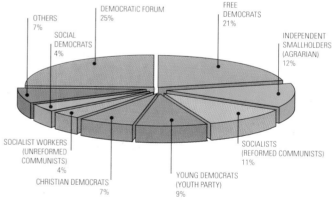

Ethnic minorities

The charts, right, indicate those eastern European countries with ethnic minorities comprising over 5% of the total population. In addition, most of these countries have sizable gypsy populations, the largest percentage of the population being in Hungary and Bulgaria. The gypsies are, in fact, the fastest-growing group in the continent, despite repression under the communist governments. There are six million in all in Europe, with 850,000 in Yugoslavia, 760,000 in Romania and 560,000 in Hungary.

Yugoslavia's much sliced pie underlines the problems with warring minorities that erupted in 1992. This created an enormous refugee problem, as millions tried to escape the fighting.

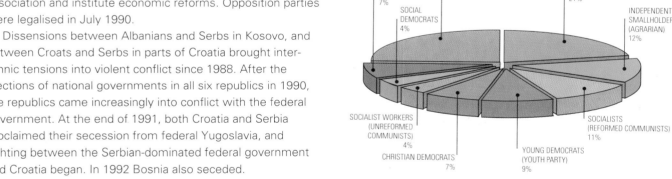

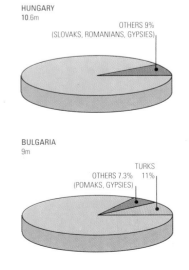

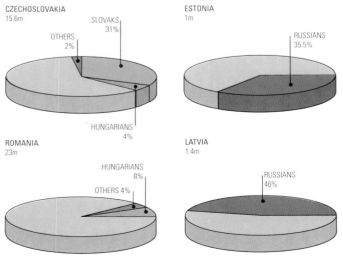

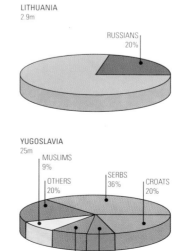

IDEOLOGIES AND PARTIES

Political development in Europe relates to a common history of social shocks: the rise of Protestantism, revolution and nationalism, the industrial revolution and the Communist movement.

The cumulative effect of these upheavals varied from one country to another. In some instances, the crises, or shocks, were bunched together; in others they were encountered one at a time. As a result, the pattern and intensity of social divisions varied from one country to another. Where the social rifts were strong, they were buttressed by equally powerful ideologies. Essentially these ideologies served two purposes. One was a justification – or rationalisation – of the demands made by a particular social group, and it expressed a view on how society as a whole should be ordered. The other purpose was to act as a rallying call for that section and to give it a greater cohesion.

By their nature, ideologies tend to be mutually exclusive. As a consequence, they reinforce the existing social divisions, or even make them sharper. In the past, Europe has been riven by wars of ideology – the politicisation of religious beliefs, nationalism and Marxism, for example. But even the more moderate ideological forces – conservatism and socialism – have produced bitter conflicts.

The freezing of party systems

The democratic revolution – the mass entry of the people into politics in the late 19th century – brought with it the rise of the modern mass parties. These formed around the existing social divisions – religious, social and national – and acted as a focus of loyalty for particular groups within society. Individual party systems varied in complexity in relation to the social structures beneath. The British system was exceptional in having only two major parties; others had a dozen or more, often leading to bitter conflicts and periods of unstable government. However, they shared one common characteristic: once developed, the party systems froze, and the evidence indicated that the essential structure of party systems (in place at the latest by the early 1920s) persisted well into the 1960s. This freezing effect was peculiar: the intensity of the original divisions lost most of their force, and yet the parties that represented them appeared to lose nothing of their dominance over politics or their hold on voters.

By the 1960s there were several signs of change. The basic factor was the increasing prosperity in western Europe once the postwar recovery had been established.

A referendum in June 1991 in Italy asked voters to approve reforms of the electoral system, which had been increasingly corrupted by both dishonest party officials and the Mafia.

CHANGING STRENGTH OF SOCIALISM – 1945–49 ELECTIONS

45% plus
35%-45%
25%-35%
15%-25%
under 15%
No entries for Portugal and Spain – dictatorships

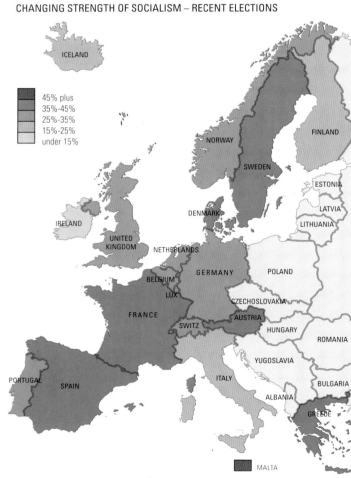

CHANGING STRENGTH OF SOCIALISM – RECENT ELECTIONS

45% plus
35%-45%
25%-35%
15%-25%
under 15%

SOCIAL DEMOCRACY AND SOCIALISM

Social democracy was founded as a movement with the almost exclusive aim of emancipating the working classes. This required the use of collective organisation through trade unions. Political democracy was a secondary consideration, or at least was instrumental only in achieving economic aims. For instance, the syndicalist movement rejected completely the political organisation of the state in favour of direct trade union power. Social democracy has always expressed this dualism, and for some time the revolutionary option looked attractive. The maps, above, illustrate the changes in allegiance over the last 40 years.

Yet this course was not taken for two reasons. First, trade unions saw advantages in winning improvement through using their bargaining power: strikes were used to gain specific advantages, not destroy the system. Second, as social democratic parties achieved greater strength in parliaments and participated in government, they could use political power to implement socialism. But they came to value parliamentary democracy in its own right. Despite the contradictory elements in the evolution of social democracy – or perhaps precisely because the outcome was a pragmatic tradition – it has proved to be the dominant force on the left, particularly after the collapse of international communism.

Connections: Europe takes shape 12–15   Parliamentary systems 116–117   Rebuilding democracies 120–121   The birth of nations 176–177

Seismic changes

Political change in Europe has come about as a result of four major upheavals in western society. The first of these was the impact of the Reformation with resulting religious conflicts. The second was the experience of the various national revolutions with all the attendant problems of nation- and state-building. The third was the coming of the Industrial Revolution: it resulted in class cleavages – a dominant bourgeoisie facing the growing industrial proletariat. These class cleavages were further intensified more recently by a fourth shock – the arrival of international communism. In recent decades the differences between parties of the left and right have been eroded, as the left gradually came to accept the flaws of state control and at least some of the virtues of the market – something that in the late 1980s even eastern Europe finally accepted. Parties now look for a broad base to "catch-all" support.

PARTY SPLITS

EUROPE 1920-1960

- ● SHARP CLEAVAGES & IDEOLOGICAL PARTIES

REFORMATION & THE RELIGIOUS CLEAVAGES

NATIONALISM & THE NATIONAL REVOLUTIONS

THE INDUSTRIAL REVOLUTION & CLASS CLEAVAGES

INTERNATIONAL COMMUNISM

EUROPE AFTER 1960

- ● "END OF IDEOLOGY " WEAKER CLEAVAGES AND "CATCH-ALL" PARTIES

François Mitterrand, pictured above, broke 23 years of dominance by the right in the 1981 French presidential elections. He won with nearly 52% of the vote cast in the second ballot.

The changing structure of the economy, the growth of new industries and the service sector all contributed to an erosion of rigid class divisions. The effect was to create a new middle class of white-collar employees. Alongside this came the appearance of the affluent worker who no longer identified himself with the traditional working class. Other divisions were healing too: national aspirations were apparently satisfied, and religious differences, as well as problems of church-state relations, had been largely resolved.

Political consequences and common bonds

All these developments made dogmatic ideologies look redundant, but did this new era mark the end of ideology? Certainly, it could be argued that a broad consensus was emerging based on the values of a consumer-oriented society. The consequences for political parties were apparent: they saw the necessity of ridding themselves of their ideological baggage if they were to take advantage

of the erosion of class divisions and appeal to a broad spectrum of the electorate. In effect, the old parties would have to transform themselves into parties of a new type – the catch-all party. A clear example where this has happened is Britain, where the Labour party has shed a lot of its ideological baggage and moved gradually to the centre and the Conservative party, since Margaret Thatcher was replaced as leader in 1990, have emphasised a more caring approach.   ▷

MEMBERS OF THE SOCIALIST INTERNATIONAL

COUNTRY	PARTIES	YEAR
AUSTRIA	SOZIALISTISCHE PARTEI ÖSTERREICHS SPÖ	1945
BELGIUM	BELGISCHE SOCIALISTISCHE PARTIJ/PARTI SOCIALISTE BELGE BSP/PSB	1945-78
	BELGISCHE SOCIALISTISCHE PARTIJ BSB	1978
	PARTI SOCIALISTE BELGE PSB	1978
DENMARK	SOCIALDEMOKRATIET SD	1871
FINLAND	SUOMEN SOSIALDEMOKRAATTINEN PUOLUE SSP	1899
FRANCE	SECTION FRANÇAISE DE L'INTERNATIONALE OUVRIERE SFIO	1945-69
	PARTI SOCIALISTE PS	1969
GERMANY	SOZIALDEMOKRATISCHE PARTEI DEUTSCHLANDS SPD	1875
ICELAND	ALTHYDUFLOKKURINN (SOCIAL DEM. PARTY) DUFLOK	1919
	BANDALAG JAFNADARMANNA (SOCIAL DEM. FEDERATION) BJ	1982
IRELAND	IRISH LABOUR PARTY Lab	1912
ITALY	PARTITO SOCIALISTA ITALIANO PSI (became PSU in 1990)	1892
	PARTITO SOCIALISTA DEMOCRATICO ITALIANO PSDI	1947
LUXEMBOURG	PARTI OUVRIER SOCIALISTE LUXEMBOURGEOIS POSL	1945
	PARTI SOCIALDÉMOCRATE PSD	1968-82
MALTA	MALTA LABOUR PARTY MLP	1921
NETHERLANDS	PARTIJ VAN DER ARBEID PvdA	1946
NORWAY	ĐET NORSKE ARBEIDERPARTI DNA	1887
PORTUGAL	PARTIDO SOCIALISTA PORTUGUESA PSP	1973
SPAIN	PARTIDO SOCIALISTA OBRERO ESPAÑOL PSOE	1889
SWEDEN	SOCIALDEMOKRATISKA ARBETARPARTIET SAP	1870
SWITZERLAND	SOZIALDEMOKRATISCHE PARTEI DER SCHWEIZ SPS	1870
UK	LABOUR PARTY Lab	1900

In Greece, the Socialist Party, PASOK - Pan-Hellenic Socialist Movement (founded in 1974) - is not a member of the Socialist International.

TAKING SIDES

Pervasive as the socio-economic trends have proved to be, it is important to appreciate that the old hallmarks of European politics still structure party competition. Above all, the distinction between left and right – and the distribution of parties within one camp or another – is a basic characteristic. Although the left/right dimension is often not helpful in locating party positions or in judging the intensity of competition, it does underline the continuing significance of socio-economic issues and how they are to be tackled – whether the direction should be towards greater social equality (the left) or whether the onus for improvement should rest on individual achievement (the right).

A related question involves the role of governments: how much should they intervene? Parties of the left argue that the redistribution of wealth in society and benefits for the common good can be achieved only through government action. Parties of the right fear that ever-expanding state intervention ultimately destroys individual initiative and responsibility and the much-vaunted concept of choice.

A notable feature of European politics is the affinity that parties in one country have with parties elsewhere. These broad groups of party families underline the importance of common European traditions even though none of the party systems is exactly alike and all reflect their own national characteristics. Following the line of the major axis of right and left, five distinctive party traditions are the principal components of almost all the party systems, although those of Ireland and, to a lesser extent, France are not so easily categorised.

Centre value

Leaving aside the extreme right, which is too splintered to constitute any single tradition, those on the moderate right are the conservative and Christian democratic family groups. In the centre – although with some qualifications – are the liberal parties. The left, at least until recently, had two chief expressions: the social-democratic/socialist grouping and the communist parties.

Christian democracy and conservatism

Christian democratic and conservative parties are the mainstay of most western European party systems, but they do not have many features in common, nor are they usually both represented in the same party system. Christian parties first arose as defensive organisations against liberalism and the threats from the secular state, especially in countries with large Roman Catholic populations. After 1945, they changed in character, bearing a new label of Christian Democracy, a switch that, on the one hand, weakened the connections with the church authorities, but on the other – in making a wider appeal – emphasised the Catholic tradition of social responsibility. This orientation marked a decisive break with conservatism which – in mainland Europe – took on a pejorative and reactionary meaning. So although Christian democracy upholds the principles of the market system, its commitment to society as a whole allows a bridging of the left/right divide. The same cannot be said of conser-

The Christian Democratic Union in Germany at their congress in 1990 just prior to the general election on October 3rd, the first to be held after reunification. Helmut Kohl was re-elected leader of the CDU by an overwhelming majority of 943 to 14.

CHRISTIAN DEMOCRACY – 1945–49 ELECTIONS

45% plus
35%-45%
25%-35%
15%-25%
under 15%

No CD parties

CHRISTIAN DEMOCRACY – RECENT ELECTIONS

35%-45%
25%-35%
15%-25%
under 15%

No CD parties

CHRISTIAN DEMOCRACY IN GERMANY AND ITALY

In Germany, the Christlich Demokratische Union (CDU) was established in the four zones of occupation after 1945 as an alliance of Protestants and Catholics sharing a common aversion to fascism. Although it has the support of the churches, the CDU avoided becoming a religious formation, and did not represent a reversion to the political Catholicism of the pre-Hitler period. Catholics had been a minority in prewar Germany, but with the division of the country, there was an approximate parity of Protestants and Catholics in western Germany. The CDU has been influenced by doctrines of social Catholicism and this is reflected in the concept of the social market economy – that is, the market system qualified by a sense of social responsibility. During the early years of the Federal Republic, the CDU was successful in becoming a catch-all party, uniting Catholics and Protestants and cutting across the class lines of the Weimar Republic (1919–1933). As the party of government, led by Konrad Adenauer until 1963, the CDU placed West Germany on a course towards integration within western Europe, with particular emphasis on Franco-German reconciliation. The CDU is a loosely structured party,

and in Bavaria Christian Democracy is represented by the sister party, the CSU (Christlich Soziale Union) which is well to the right of the CDU. The CDU has been in office since 1982 under Helmut Kohl, the architect of German reunification took place in 1990.

In Italy, the Democrazia Cristiana (DC) sprang out of the Catholic anti-fascist resistance, but in the postwar period rapidly became strongly anti-communist, regarding the strong Italian Communist party as its major enemy, with encouragement from both the Vatican and the USA. The early influence of the Vatican, however, declined as Italian society became increasingly secularised. Although the DC has dominated all governments since 1946 (and led all but two of them), it lacks coherence and is characterised by intense factionalism and clientelism.

Like other Christian Democratic parties, the DC has followed a more conciliatory approach to the Communist party, admitting local power-sharing in the regions and ad hoc agreements in parliament, as well as non-governmental cooperation, notably in 1976–79 when both sought to resolve the problems of ungovernability and terrorism that were a threat to democracy.

vatism, which abhors collectivism. Conservative parties are also associated with centralised state systems and do not readily adapt to the move towards subsidiarity – responsibility exercised from below – which is a central tenet of Christian democratic thinking.

Liberal ambivalence

Liberalism was at one time the strongest radical force in European politics: it attacked the power of authoritarian rulers, the privileges of the nobility and of the churches. But once the battles for constitutional democracy had been won and individual liberties secured, liberalism went into decline, giving way to the more radical parties of the left as the working class became strongly organised. Nonetheless, liberal parties survive, possibly because they identify with the market order and economic liberalism, but equally side with the left in their opposition to vested interests and in their support for democratisation and the extension of civil liberties. Liberal parties can ally themselves with either the left or the right, and in countries which have proportional representation this flexibility gives them a political weight far greater than their size.

Marxism – the God that failed

The high-point of communist strength in western Europe was reached in the postwar era. But its rigid ideology proved a handicap in the changing conditions of party competition and increasing affluence. The subordination of the individual parties to the Soviet Union – especially after the suppression of popular uprisings in Hungary (1956) and Czechoslovakia (1968) also eroded their credibility. The advent of Eurocommunism in the 1970s signified a belated attempt to break away from Soviet orthodoxy by, for instance, abandoning ideas of the dictatorship of the proletariat and offering to take the parliamentary path to socialism. Yet neither reformism nor attempts to salvage the Marxist heritage availed, and with the collapse of communism in eastern Europe their downfall appears complete.

CHRISTIAN DEMOCRATIC PARTIES

COUNTRY	PARTIES	YEAR
AUSTRIA	ÖSTERREICHISCHE VOLKSPARTIE ÖVP	1945
BELGIUM	PARTI SOCIAL CHRÉTIEN/CHRISTELIJKE VOLKSPARTEI PSC/CVP	1945-68
	PARTI SOCIAL CHRÉTIEN PSC	1968
	CHRISTELIJKE VOLKSPARTIE CVP	1968
DENMARK	KRISTELIGT KOLKEPARTI KRF	1970
FINLAND	SUOMEN KRISTILLINEN LIITTO SKL	1958
FRANCE	MOUVEMENT RÉPUBLICAIN POPULAIRE MRP	1944-66
	CENTRE DÉMOCRATE CD	1966-76
	CENTRE DES DÉMOCRATES SOCIAUX CDS	1976
GERMANY	CHRISTLICH DEMOKRATISCHE UNION/CHRISTLICH SOZIALE UNION CDU/CSU	1945
IRELAND	FINE GAEL FG	1933
ITALY	DEMOCRAZIA CRISTIANA DC	1943
LUXEMBOURG	PARTI CHRÉTIEN SOCIAL PCS	1945
NETHERLANDS	CHRISTEN DEMOCRATISCHAPPEL CDA	1980
	ANTI-REVOLUTIONAIRE PARTIJ ARP	1879
	KATHOLIEKE VOLKSPARTIJ KVP	1945
	CHRISTELIJK-HISTORISCHE UNIE CHU	1908
NORWAY	KRISTELIGT FOLKEPARTI KrF	1933
PORTUGAL	PARTIDO DO CENTRO DEMOCRATICO SOCIAL CDS	1974
SWEDEN	KRISTDEMOKRATISKA SAMHÄLLSPARTEI KDS	1964
SWITZERLAND	CHRISTLICH DEMOKRATISCH VOLKSPARTEI CVP	1912
	EVANGELISCHE VOLKSPARTEI EVP	1919

DECLINING COMMUNISM – 1945–49

- 20% plus
- 15-19.9%
- 10-14.9%
- 5-9.9%
- Less than 4.9%

No significant Communist Party in Iceland and Malta

No entry for Greece as Communist Party illegal until 1974; no entries for Portugal and Spain - dictatorships

Going...

In 1945 communist parties won a significant share of the vote in most western European states; indeed they became the second largest parties in Italy and France. Here they remained electorally strong, but always out of government until the late 1970s.

DECLINING COMMUNISM – 1973

- 20% plus
- 15-19.9%
- 10-14.9%
- 5-9.9%
- Less than 4.9%

Going...

Ironically, their moves into governmental responsibilities (the Historic Compromise in Italy in 1976, and after François Mitterrand in 1981) presaged the electoral decline of communist parties. Everywhere else communism as an electoral force was marginalised.

DECLINING COMMUNISM – RECENT ELECTIONS

- 20% plus
- 15-19.9% (none)
- 10-14.9%
- 5-9.9%
- Less than 4.9%

Gone...

Most recent elections indicate that communism is a spent force. Support is highest in Italy but this only contributes to the political volatility of a country that has had some 50 different governments in the postwar period.

NEW PARTIES AND MOVEMENTS

Forever green? The environmentalist parties of Europe have suffered a similar fate in that their popularity has dwindled as the main parties recognise the need for environmental policies in their manifestos.

From the late 1960s onwards a variety of new movements has entered the political arena, attracting support because they highlight issues that established parties have neglected. The importance of issue-based politics has increased because parties have proved less able to retain the allegiance of supporters who are more willing to take up the causes, such as those represented by the peace, environmental and feminist movements which gathered strength in the 1970s and 1980s. Unlike political parties, movements lack a unified and permanent organisation, but their effectiveness lies in the appeal they have to wide sections of the population and in forcing issues onto the agenda of public debate. What has given the newer movements additional importance is their ability to appeal across national boundaries to become European-wide in their impact.

What is new about the new politics?

The new politics is not simply another movement, but rather a term encapsulating many of the qualities shared by various issue-specific movements. The new politics presents a perspective on political life and values quite different from that offered by the old politics. Conventional parties express traditional concerns such as the main-

tenance of law and order, security and economic growth. In contrast, the new politics is post-materialist in emphasising higher values such as self-realisation, communality, and harmony with the environment. The new politics is also anti-establishment on the grounds that the old politics is tied to parliamentary elitism. Instead, it favours popular involvement, unconventional methods and direct action. All kinds of new movements can be related to the new politics. They, too, are alike, in attracting support from those most likely to have a post-materialist outlook: younger people, the better educated and the relatively affluent.

The Greening of Europe

The Green or environmental movement developed in response to several much-publicised environmental disasters, but also as a reaction to the creeping disorders associated with highly industrialised societies and mass consumerism – the fears expressed about atmospheric pollution and the effects of acid rain on Europe's forests are examples. Green issues frequently came to attention first at local levels – for instance, opposition to the siting of nuclear-power plants – and the effects of acid rain on Europe's forests are typical examples. Only later did they

RIGHT-WING EXTREMISTS

Rof groups of parties with more than 500 members

- Neo-Fascist
- Overtly nationalistic
- Racist/anti-immigration
- Right-wing protest

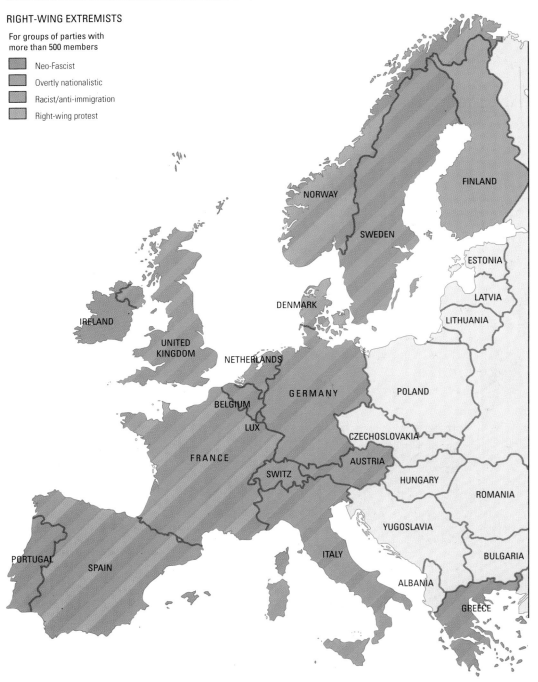

PARTIES OF THE RADICAL RIGHT

The radical right parties have elements of a common ideology, including virulent nationalism and xenophobia; theories of racial superiority or social Darwinism; anti-parliamentarianism and anti-authoritarianism; and anti-socialist and anti-trade union tendencies. They are sometimes described as having the politics of cultural despair, compared to those of a modern, post-industrial liberated society. A vote for the radical right is often cast as a protest vote in local, regional, city and European elections, hence their successes in recent elections across most of Europe where the electorate have frequently been keen to express their disapproval of existing governments without actually casting a vote for the principal opposition party.

The map, left, shows the parties of the radical right divided into four principal groups: neo-fascist (affiliated to the World Union of National Socialists), overtly nationalist parties, racist/anti-immigration parties and right-wing protest parties, which are royalist in nature, with racist overtones.

ELECTORAL SUPPORT FOR FAR RIGHT

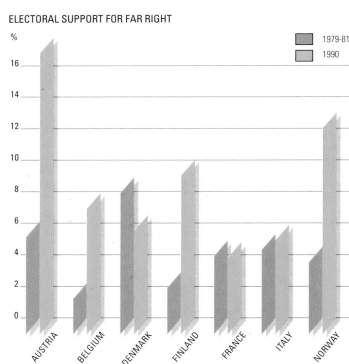

Connections: Ideologies and parties 122–125   Institutional response 218–219

lead to the formation of national political parties. Green parties now compete against parties of the right and left and – in sharing the values of new politics – belong in another dimension. After an initial breakthrough in several countries, Green support has stagnated, but the effect has been profound in affecting public policy and in changing the outlook of the general public.

The potential of the radical right

The radical right has a mushroom-like quality: at times it threatens to destabilise national politics, but more usually it is associated with numerous fringe groups with a tendency to split into even smaller ones. There is no single defining element of the radical right; some, such as the Italian neo-fascists, represent the remnants of old-style fascism, others concentrate chiefly on an anti-foreigner appeal, while some are protest parties, inveighing against high taxes, big government and big business. Despite their disparate nature, parties of the radical right display features of a common syndrome: authoritarian leanings, hostility towards outsiders and extreme nationalism. The specific issues that they campaign on vary, but throughout Europe from France's Front National to Britain's National Front, opposition to immigration, with racist undertones, is a general feature. But in countries where the radical right has recently had most success – in Austria and Norway – the explanation has much to do with hostility towards the major governing parties.

Old virtues and the new right

The new right – not to be confused with the radical right – is primarily a reaction against the increasing role of the state in the economy and society. It sees expansion of the public sector and the ever-expanding welfare state commitments as a threat to the viability of the wealth creating private sector. It favours careful housekeeping, balanced budgets and the free play of market forces. Personal responsibility is encouraged to lessen the dependence on the state.

The chief planks of the new right platform – monetarism, privatisation and cutting back the welfare state – have had a limited but still important effect on governments of all political persuasions in western Europe and new right ideas have proved popular in eastern Europe.

THE GREENS IN GERMANY

Founded in 1980, Die Grünen, as the Greens in Germany termed themselves, was formed as an anti-party party, opposed to the existing cartel of established parties and not willing to become an orthodox political organisation. From the start, the Greens had a distinctive internal structure, including a belief in grass-roots democracy and a virtual autonomy given to local party bodies. To avoid the formation of a party elite, the principle of rotation of office was adopted. Although not willing to accept political responsibility, the Greens proved to have a significant impact on politics through their agenda-setting abilities. The party divided into the realists who believed in accepting governmental responsibility and cooperation with other parties and the fundamentalists who rejected any truck with the establishment.

In recent years, the realists have gained the upper hand and have become a more conventional party. The Greens, with support from their eastern counterparts, have now entered into coalitions in several of the German states, a move necessary to maintain representation in the Bundestag.

The arrival of democracy after Franco's death did not snuff out the right-wing movements in Spain. As a strongly monarchist country, there is scope for nationalism as this demonstration by fascists commemorating the 10th anniversary of Franco's death illustrates.

THE NEW RIGHT IN BRITAIN AND DENMARK

Under Margaret Thatcher, Britain's Conservative party manifesto in 1979 promised fundamental changes to put many new-right theories and principles into practice. They included monetarism, trade union reform, privatisation, civil service reorganisation, a reduction in the spending powers of local government and a rationalisation of the welfare state. In short, a policy of rolling back the state. The downfall of Mrs Thatcher in 1990 appeared to herald a weakening in the influence of the new right, but certain ideas, notably market economics, have become a part of conventional thinking across the political spectrum.

In Denmark the new right took the form of an anti-tax backlash, which was a protest against the high level of personal taxation needed to finance the welfare state. The strong Social Democrat consensus was weakened by the 1973 oil crisis, and that same year an electoral earthquake led to a doubling of the number of parties in parliament, and a shift to the right. In particular, the Progress party emerged as a new right-wing anti-system force, based on an anti-tax platform. Founded by a lawyer from Copenhagen, Mogens Glistrup, with a purely anti-tax rhetoric, it soon spearheaded a general cutting back of the state. While it remained uncoalitionable, it broke the consensus of Danish politics.

THE SUPPORT FOR THE GREENS IN RECENT ELECTIONS

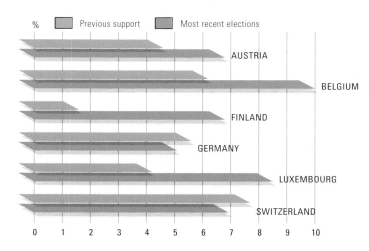

Green roots

The Green movement had many different roots, including the 1972 Club of Rome report on *The Limits of Growth*, widespread concern about the possibility of nuclear war and worries over environmental pollution. The popular slogan, not left, not right, but up front, indicated that the movement did not fit into the traditional left-right spectrum of politics. Growing out of citizens' action groups, which mushroomed in the 1970s, and generally campaigning on local and national environmental issues, the movement claimed about 5m sympathisers by 1983. These groups favoured direct action rather than relying on orthodox methods, as the peace movement was doing.

CHANGING SOCIAL BASE OF POLITICS

Over the past half century there have been profound changes in the pattern of economic activity in western Europe. Most striking has been the decline of agriculture as an important source of employment. Just as significant has been the shift – occurring later – from industrial employment to the service sector. This double switch has had fundamental effects on social structure. Western Europe has now become a predominantly urban society regardless of where people happen to live, whether they reside in cities or not. The workforce has also become far less differentiated; even though there is a range of socio-economic categories, their sharp differences have been eroded.

The loosening of traditional ties

In the past, two of the most reliable indicators of political loyalties were church and trade union membership. Both provided a means of social attachment and a collective identity.

In most countries there has been a steady fall in church membership and attendance, although regular attendance is still a guide to a person's political outlook. Just as important has been the declining political influence of organised religion – pulpit politics belongs to a past era. Trade unions in recent years have been weakened by falling membership after reaching a highpoint in the earlier postwar period. They have chiefly been affected by the shrinkage of the industrial base which gave them their core support. The growth of white-collar unionism, on occasion not less militant, differs in being more concerned with achieving results than with fighting the class war, with the result that modern unions have a much weaker political orientation.

New influences

Political socialisation – how people's political attitudes and beliefs are formed – used to take place at an early age and largely within the family: political loyalties were passed on from one generation to another. That is no longer true. Political socialisation is a continuous process, and the family is only one set of influences among others. Rising levels of education have given access to a wide

From a mainly agricultural country just after the second world war, France is now one of the leading technological societies. However, French farmers still have considerable clout in influencing national politics.

Rural Europe

As the postwar economic miracle began many western European countries still had large agricultural sectors. Even in relatively industrialised states like Belgium and the Netherlands more than one-tenth of the workforce was still on the land. In mediterranean Europe almost half the working population was made up of farmers. Even in these poorer countries there were many rich and efficient farmers – the wine growers of Chianti, Riojà and Bordeaux are good examples. Far more numerous, however, were the "peasants" many of whom worked small plots with out-of-date techniques for very meagre incomes. The postwar boom provided alternative jobs – at much better pay – in industry and the services for those willing to move to the towns. In France alone, 100,000 people gave up farming every year.

By the 1990s farmers had dropped to less than 10% of the workforce everywhere except Greece, Portugal and Spain, and even there the decline in agricultural employment was a clear and constant trend. But if farming has declined as a form of employment it has massively increased in terms of production – by better education, new technology and land tenure reforms.

WORKING THE LAND, 1950

- More than 40%
- 25%-39%
- 10%-25%
- Less than 10%

WORKING THE LAND, 1990

- 10%-25%
- Less than 10%

Connections: Food and farming 76–77 Labour and immigration 138–139 Religion 228–229

range of information and opinion, which affects the individual's level of understanding as well as political attitudes. The gains are not necessarily all positive: the multiplicity of messages may lead to confusion, apathy or to an unproductive cynicism.

Voters on the move – but where to?

Both the weakening of the old social bases of politics and the wide variety of new influences are affecting the relationship of voters to political parties. They identify less strongly with a single party, and the decline in partisanship results in large shifts in votes between parties from one election to another. But there is no agreement about what this fluidity signifies. One interpretation is that parties are losing their attractions for voters and that there is much more concern with particular issues – so issue-voting determines voting behaviour and accounts for the growth in electoral volatility. The alternative explanation is that a process of electoral realignment is taking place: as old cleavages lose their force and class voting becomes a less important feature, so new splits arise, but for an interim period voting behaviour is in a state of flux as parties and electorates adjust to new positions. Individual parties have become increasingly vulnerable since it is much harder for them to hold on to their voters and they have to be much more sensitive to the changing moods. Failure to react quickly invites competition from new parties that force issues onto the political agenda. Although the old, established parties have lost the advantage of a secure social base, nonetheless they have been able to adapt to the changing structure of European society.

Class voting

Class voting means the tendency of a majority of people in one socio-economic class to vote for one political party. It is measured by a complex formula known as the "Afort Index". In an industrial society, it implies that most workers vote for the socialist party and the middle class voters for the conservatives – or Christian democrats. But many societies were never simply stratified into two class; there were farmers and aristocrats, civil servants and teachers – who defied classification as "workers" or "the bourgeoisie". Post-industrial society has further complicated the picture, giving some workers "middle class" incomes, creating "new middle classes" and bringing women into employment.

More than 30%
25%-30%
15%-25%
Less than 15%

(Based on Alford's index of class voting, 1980s)

Since 1950s biggest declines in class voting in Germany, Switzerland, Ireland, Denmark, Norway, Finland and Sweden

---

DISTRIBUTION OF THE WORKFORCE, 1990

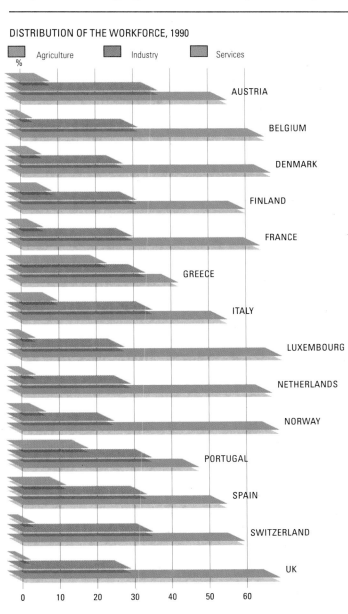

Agriculture   Industry   Services

AUSTRIA
BELGIUM
DENMARK
FINLAND
FRANCE
GREECE
ITALY
LUXEMBOURG
NETHERLANDS
NORWAY
PORTUGAL
SPAIN
SWITZERLAND
UK

0   10   20   30   40   50   60

Trade union membership

In western Europe, trade unions gained their greatest strength in countries like Britain with heavy traditional manufacturing and where there was a single, or very dominant, national federation of trade unions. They were weakest in countries like France where, before 1945 industrialisation was limited and unions were ideologically divided amongst communist, socialist and Catholic national groupings. But since 1945 rates of union membership have diverged: both France and Italy have had postwar economic miracles but in Italy trade unions have survived and grown whereas in France only 11% of workers (the lowest rate in the OECD) are union members.

Trade unions that cling to revolutionary goals have proved less effective than the more moderate ones of Germany and Sweden, for example, that

have worked more closely with management to negotiate better conditions, wages and fringe benefits. Swedish unions represent 95% of the workforce, and are a powerful interest group. In France, where the union membership is divided among the Confédération Générale du Travail (CGT),

the socialist Confédération Française et Démocratique (CFDT) and the moderate Force Ouvrière, over 15% of the workforce is organised, and the more radical unions are losing members to the more moderate ones.

TRADE UNION MEMBERSHIP, 1989

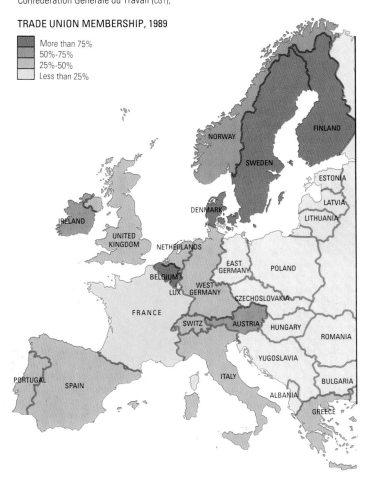

More than 75%
50%-75%
25%-50%
Less than 25%

Labour distribution

The chart illustrates how the labour force from richer nations has left the land and migrated to industry and service sectors. Only Greece has more than 20% of its workforce still employed in agriculture whereas the UK has only 2%.

THE EUROPEAN COMMUNITY

The grain mountain, which along with the butter mountain and wine lakes, amassed under the notoriously inefficient CAP, has brought the price-support system into disrepute.

All the governments of the six founder members of the European Community included Christian Democratic ministers who shared an ideal. They dreamed of creating a United States of Europe: liberal, democratic and prosperous, a force for peace in Europe and the world. These governments, however, also had other more practical and immediate motives, and these varied considerably according to different national interests.

Economic realities

The governments of the founder countries with traditionally strong industrial economies – Germany, the Netherlands and Luxembourg – were all concerned to develop their economies in an open European market, unhampered by protectionism and state subsidies. In contrast, the French and Italian governments which had to deal with large and relatively unmodernised agricultural sectors, and significant regional imbalances, saw European integration as a means for redistribution in support of their poorer agricultural regions. The French government of Charles de Gaulle made agreement on a Common Agricultural Policy a condition for continued cooperation and the achievement of the customs union. This diversity of economic interests was also found among the other states which joined the EC in the 1970s and 1980s. Britain and Denmark mainly sought access to the rich open market, whereas Ireland, Greece, Spain and Portugal were more concerned to get the benefits of the redistributive policies of the Community.

Learning to live together

European integration was a gradual and sometimes difficult process. The first attempt at enlarging the policy domain from coal and steel to defence and foreign policy was a failure. The idea of an integrated European army and a joint foreign policy was ahead of its time; old national identities were too strong. France, Belgium and the Netherlands were still preoccupied with colonial

The European Community

1947 March Belgium, Luxembourg and the Netherlands agree to establish a customs union. Subsequently an economic union is established in October 1947 and a common customs tariff is introduced in January 1948.

1949 May Statute of Council of Europe signed in Strasbourg by ten states.

1951 April European Coal and Steel Community (ECSC) Treaty signed in Paris by six states: Belgium, France, Germany, Italy, Luxembourg and the Netherlands.

1952 May European Defence Community (EDC) Treaty signed in Paris by the six ECSC states.

1954 August French National Assembly rejects EDC Treaty.

1955 June Messina Conference of the foreign ministers of the six ECSC states to discuss further European integration.

1957 March The Treaty of Rome signed, establishing the European Economic Community (EEC) and the European Atomic Energy Community (Euratom)

1958 January EEC and Euratom come into operation.

1960 January European Free Trade Association (EFTA) Convention signed at Stockholm by Austria, Denmark, Norway, Portugal, Sweden, Switzerland and the UK. EFTA in force in May 1960.

1960 July/August Ireland, Denmark and the UK request negotiations with the EC for membership.

1962 January Basic features of Common Agricultural Policy (CAP) agreed.

1963 January General de Gaulle announces his veto on UK membership.

1960 January Signing of Franco-German Treaty of Friendship and Cooperation.

1964 May The GATT Kennedy round of international tariff negotiations opens in Geneva. EC states participate as a single delegation.

1965 April Signing of treaty establishing a single council and a single commission of the European Communities (the Merger Treaty).

1965 July France begins a boycott of Community institutions to register its opposition to various proposed supranational developments.

1966 January Foreign ministers agree to the Luxembourg Compromise, allowing any state to veto measures which endanger national interests. Normal Community processes are resumed.

YEAR OF MEMBERSHIP

- 1957
- 1972
- 1981
- 1986

1967 May Denmark, Ireland and the UK re-apply for membership of the EC.

1968 July The customs union is completed. All internal customs duties and quotas are removed and the common external tariff is established.

1969 July President Pompidou announces that France no longer opposes UK membership.

1969 December The Hague summit agrees on: strengthening Community institutions; establishing an economic and monetary union by 1980; and developing political cooperation (foreign policy).

1972 January Negotiations between Community and Denmark, Ireland, Norway and the UK concluded and treaties signed.

1972 September Norwegian referendum: majority vote against membership of the EC.

1973 January Accession of Denmark, Ireland and the UK to the EC.

1974 December Paris summit agrees on direct elections to the European Parliament, the creation of a European Regional Development Fund, and to institutionalise summit meetings by establishing the European Council.

1975 February Signing of the first Lomé Convention between the EC and 46 underdeveloped countries in Africa, the Caribbean and the Pacific (ACP).

1975 June UK referendum: majority vote in favour of continued membership of the EC.

1975 June Greece applies for Community membership.

1977 March Portugal applies for membership of the EC.

1977 July Spain applies for membership of the EC.

1979 March European Monetary System (EMS) comes into operation.

1979 May Signing of Accession Treaty between the EC and Greece.

1979 June First direct elections to the European Parliament (EP).

1979 October Signing of the second Lomé Convention between the EC and 58 ACP states.

1979 December The European Parliament rejects the EC budget.

1981 January Accession of Greece to Community.

1981 October Community foreign ministers reach agreement on the London Report which strengthens and extends European Political Cooperation.

1983 January A Common Fisheries Policy is agreed.

1984 January The creation of a free trade area between the Community and EFTA is agreed.

1984 February The European Parliament approves a Draft Treaty establishing the European Union.

1984 June Second direct elections to the EP.

1985 June Signing of Accession Treaties between the EC and Spain and Portugal.

1985 December Luxembourg European Council meeting agrees on the Single European Act (SEA) which incorporates treaty revisions, and establishes the completion of the internal market by 1993 as a priority.

1986 January Accession of Spain and Portugal to the EC.

1987 July After delay caused by ratification problems in Ireland, the SEA comes into force.

1989 June Third elections to the EP by universal suffrage.

1990 October East Germany reunited with West Germany.

1990 October The UK joins the Exchange Rate Mechanism of the EMS.

1991 December Maastricht Intergovernmental Conference agrees treaties on European Political Union and Economic and Monetary Union.

1992 June Danes vote in referendum against acceptance of the Maastricht agreement.

1992 June Ireland votes to accept Maastricht principles by 2:1.

Connections: Single market 56–57, 96–97 Economic and monetary union 92–93 EC: institutions 132–133

empires, and the European Defence Community seemed to challenge the most basic principles of national sovereignty.

The Messina Conference and the Treaty of Rome which followed, represented an attempt to avoid a freezing of the integration process and to build a united Europe from the bottom upwards. No sooner was the Treaty signed and ratified, however, than General de Gaulle returned to power in France. He vetoed British membership and, in defence of national sovereignty, demanded suspension of the treaty provision for majority decision-making.

With de Gaulle's departure in 1969, enlargement of the Community at last became possible. Britain, Denmark and Ireland at once began to negotiate their membership, and Greece, Spain and Portugal were to follow when democracy was re-established. This fast-growing Community, however, had to face new problems: fluctuating exchange rates, the two world oil crises of 1973 and 1979, and the end of the Thirty Golden Years of postwar economic boom.

The Community response was neither a standstill nor a retreat into national protectionism. It was agreed to elect the European Parliament by universal suffrage. The European Monetary System with fixed exchange rates was created. The Single European Act set in train the single market programme to remove existing barriers to mobility and competition was adopted. The act also provided for more majority voting in the Council of Ministers, and there was a recognition of the crucial inter-governmental role played by the European Council, the bi-annual meeting of the heads of government or state.

Despite all the difficulties, the 1980s, with Jacques Delors as president of the Commission, saw a new dynamism in the Community. Even criticisms of arch Euro-sceptics like Margaret Thatcher were functional in provoking reforms, and in pushing for more efficiency and competition, and a more open, outward-looking Community.

THE TREATY OF PARIS

Signed in April 1951 by France, Germany, Belgium, Italy, Luxembourg and the Netherlands, the Treaty of Paris was the consequence of the Schuman Declaration of May 1950 proposing the creation of a common market in coal and steel. The basic idea was that the European Coal and Steel Community should create "a basis for the building of a new Europe" of peace and prosperity. For coal and steel products of all kinds – the key commodities in the 1950s – the six states constituted a single market, regulated by an original inter-state institutional system which had marked supranational traits.

Responsibility for ensuring that the aims of the treaty were achieved was given to a High Authority empowered to take some decisions and to propose other policies to the representatives of the governments of the six member states meeting as the Council of Ministers of the ECSC. A Common Assembly, composed of delegates chosen by the six national parliaments was set up to make a democratic input into the policy process. Finally, a Court of Justice was created to resolve conflicts. The Treaty of Paris provided European integration with an ideal of political union via sector-by-sector economic integration, as well as an institutional model through which to achieve that integration. Interestingly, in later developments the Commission of the EC was given markedly fewer powers than the High Authority on which it was based.

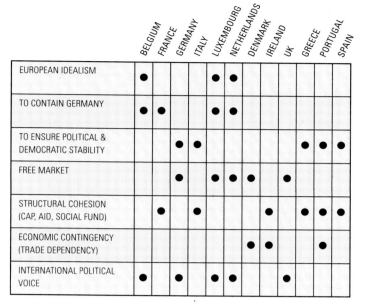

PREDOMINANT REASONS FOR JOINING

	BELGIUM	FRANCE	GERMANY	ITALY	LUXEMBOURG	NETHERLANDS	DENMARK	IRELAND	UK	GREECE	PORTUGAL	SPAIN
EUROPEAN IDEALISM	●				●	●						
TO CONTAIN GERMANY	●	●			●	●						
TO ENSURE POLITICAL & DEMOCRATIC STABILITY				●	●					●	●	●
FREE MARKET				●		●	●	●		●		
STRUCTURAL COHESION (CAP, AID, SOCIAL FUND)		●		●				●		●	●	●
ECONOMIC CONTINGENCY (TRADE DEPENDENCY)							●	●		●		
INTERNATIONAL POLITICAL VOICE	●		●		●	●			●			

The Treaty of Rome

The six ECSC states, once again without Britain, signed the Treaty of Rome in March 1957, as a result of negotiations begun at Messina in June 1955. At the Messina Conference, the six set out to revive the process of European integration, which had seemed seriously compromised by the collapse in 1952 of the Pleven Plan for a European Defence Community. They set up two new Communities linked with and in parallel to the ECSC – the Economic Community (EC) and the Atomic Energy Community (Euratom).

The 248 articles of the Rome Treaty laid down the basic principles of "four freedoms of movement" – of goods, persons, services and capital within a common market with common rules of competition and a customs union with a common external tariff barrier, a common external economic and trade policy, and no internal tariff barriers.

THE SINGLE EUROPEAN ACT

Although the Single European Act was signed in February 1986, it did not come into force until midway through 1987 owing to ratification problems with Ireland. The act contained provisions which altered aspects of the Community's decision-making system. Among its principal points were to extend the EC policy areas to environment, research and technological development, and regional policy; to make the completion of the internal market by 1992 a specific goal; to improve cooperation procedures; to improve the efficiency of decision-making in the Council of Ministers; and to increase the powers of the European Parliament. It also undertook to increase the parliament's role. Meetings of the 12 heads of government in the European Council were given legal recognition, as was foreign policy cooperation.

The way ahead …Endless expansion as the EC grows means remodelling of city centres as this photograph looking down upon the rue Belliard, Brussels, shows.

THE EC – INSTITUTIONS

Jacques Delors, the French politician and economist, who became president of the Commission in 1985, has been a vigorous champion of the single market programme, economic and monetary union, and closer political union. In 1992 he was appointed for another two years.

The institutional framework created for the European Coal and Steel Community in 1951 was the model followed six years later in the Treaty of Rome. During the 1960s, the institutions of the ECSC, Euratom and the EEC were merged. Subsequently, the main institutions have been little modified, although in practice their operating methods have evolved considerably.

At the heart of the original policy structure was the European Commission (at first called the High Authority), a supranational agency with responsibility for proposing and supervising the implementation of Community policies and laws. The Commission has a staff of around 14,000, 20% of whom are involved in translating among the nine EC working languages. The responsibility for scrutinising legislative and budgetary proposals, and suggesting amendments was given to the European Parliament – the world's first international parliament. This body was at first appointed, with national delegations of representatives from all political parties in proportion to the number of their seats in the national parliaments. Both these bodies were supranational in character.

The power of actually making the laws to be applied throughout the Community was allocated to the representatives of the member-state governments in the Council of Ministers, an essentially intergovernmental body (see diagrams).

Any conflicts of authority between Community institutions, or between member states and the Community were to be adjudicated by the European Court of Justice, the interpreter and protector of the treaties. Implementation of Community policies was left almost entirely to the governments and administrations of the member states, subject to supervision from the Commission and the decisions of the European Court of Justice in disputed cases.

EC structures

Governments of member states retain not only theoretical sovereignty (the right to withdraw) but also the predominant voice in Community decision-making. They appoint the members of the Commission and the judges of the Court of Justice and their agreement is needed, through their direct participation in the Council of Ministers, for most EC laws and policies.

However conflictual the structures of the EC appear in theory, in practice the staff of the Commission and of the Permanent Representatives' Offices think out policies together in working groups. They thereby improve efficiency and minimise Council–Commission blockages. Furthermore, whatever their national origin or outlook, the commissioners and judges alike serve the Community as a whole. Since 1985, majority voting in the Council has become more frequent and the last attempt to impose a national interest veto (by Britain) was rejected.

At work

Since the 1970s the bi-annual meetings of heads of governments of the member states, as the European Council, have become increasingly influential on the operations of the EC. Extensions of Community competences, enlargements of membership and major shifts in policy are all negotiated at this level. Here too, deep crises can be resolved. The Single European Act acknowledged the role of the European Council but did not give it any formal powers.

Who is in charge?

The two diagrams illustrate how confusing the process of decision-making is within the European Community and where the power lies. Under the Treaties of Paris (1951) and Rome (1957) the member states of the Community committed themselves to making a common market with a common external customs tariff, no internal customs or non-tariff barriers and with the four freedoms of movement or trade of goods, services, capital and persons. Common policies and Community laws for achieving these goals and regulating the market are made and their implementation supervised by the Community institutions (the Commission, Council of Ministers, European Parliament and European Court of Justice).

In general, member-state governments are responsible for executing EC policies. Most EC laws are in the form of directives, which require member-state governments to modify national laws and national administrations to execute the new laws, under the supervision of the EC Commission and the European Court of Justice.

The policy competences of the Community institutions may be extended by mutual agreement, as in the Single European Act, whereby environmental policy was included.

Equally, the 12 member states may agree to make joint policies outside the Community institutional framework. European police cooperation and the establishment of a Europol as decided at Maastricht is one example of intergovernmental policy-making between member states, outside the Community institutions.

Similarly some, but not all, of the member states may decide on some joint policy agreement, and again this remains outside the EC framework. The 1985 Schengen Agreement, (between the original member states) on the suppression of border controls is such an intergovernmental intra-EC arrangement.

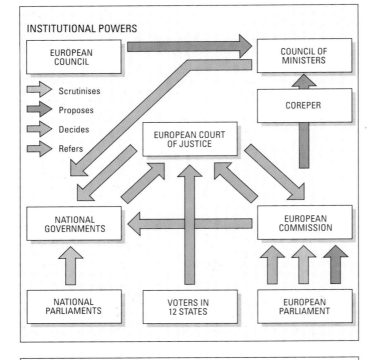

INSTITUTIONAL POWERS

EUROPEAN COUNCIL · COUNCIL OF MINISTERS · COREPER · EUROPEAN COURT OF JUSTICE · NATIONAL GOVERNMENTS · EUROPEAN COMMISSION · NATIONAL PARLIAMENTS · VOTERS IN 12 STATES · EUROPEAN PARLIAMENT

Scrutinises · Proposes · Decides · Refers

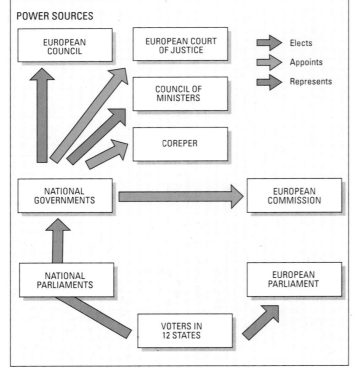

POWER SOURCES

EUROPEAN COUNCIL · EUROPEAN COURT OF JUSTICE · COUNCIL OF MINISTERS · COREPER · NATIONAL GOVERNMENTS · EUROPEAN COMMISSION · NATIONAL PARLIAMENTS · EUROPEAN PARLIAMENT · VOTERS IN 12 STATES

Elects · Appoints · Represents

THE EUROPEAN COMMISSION

The 17 commissioners are appointed by national governments, each for a four-year term (but re-appointable). Germany, France, Italy, Spain and the UK each appoint two commissioners and the others, appoint one each. They may not receive instructions from any national government and decisions are taken on a collegiate basis. The president of the Commission is appointed by the Council of Ministers, which also decides on the functional responsibilities of individual commissioners. The Commission is subject to supervision by the European Parliament, which is the only body which can enforce its collective resignation.

The chief functions of the Commission are to propose initiatives for the development of Community policies to the Council of Ministers and European Parliament for decision and adoption as Community laws, and to supervise their implementation by governments of member states. The Commission proposes the Community's annual budget to the Council and European Parliament. The Commission also has a policing role.

Connections: Regionalism and federalism 118–119   The European Community 130–131

THE COUNCIL OF MINISTERS

The Council of Ministers is made up of ministers from governments of member states, with the ministers who participate in each meeting changing according to the subject under discussion. The most frequent meetings are those of finance ministers, agriculture ministers and foreign affairs ministers (who coordinate the work of their functionally specialised colleagues). Each government chairs the Council for six months in rotation.

The Council reaches decisions by unanimity, majority or qualified majority. The voting power is: Germany, France, Italy and the UK 10 votes each; Spain 8 votes; Belgium, Greece, the Netherlands and Portugal 5 votes each; Denmark and Ireland 3 votes each; Luxembourg 2 votes.

The Council makes the major policy decisions of the Community and also makes Community legislation – usually in the form of directives – but it can act only on proposals coming from the Commission and must consider amendments proposed by the European Parliament. The Council negotiations are prepared and shadowed by COREPER (the Committee of Permanent Representatives of the member states).

THE EUROPEAN COUNCIL

The heads of government (or in the case of France, the president), together with the president of the European Commission, meet two or three times a year as the European Council. In theory it has no formal power, but in practice this body (not foreseen in the Treaty of Rome) has become the ultimate political authority of the EC, with an important role in setting the agenda for the development of the Community.

Starting in Dublin in March 1975, the European Council duly met on this basis until December 1985, when it was agreed that only two meetings a year would henceforward be held. The Single European Act stipulated that the Council would meet at least twice a year, and that extraordinary meetings could also be held; in 1990 two emergency summits were held in addition to the regular meetings, and in 1991 one emergency summit was held. The increase in the political importance of the European Council is, in part, a result of the desire of national leaders to be seen at the forefront, and because the fundamental nature of the changes proposed are too important to be left to ministers in meetings of the Council of Ministers.

THE EUROPEAN COURT OF JUSTICE

The European Court of Justice (ECJ) which sits in Luxembourg is composed of 13 judges and six advocates-general, appointed for six years by member-state governments.

In response to a request from a Community institution, a member-state government or one of its citizens, the court can quash any measure taken by the Council of Ministers, the Commission or a member-state government which it deems incompatible with the treaties. The court also determines the interpretation of Community law, and may give a preliminary ruling, in response to a request from a national court on a disputed point. It decides the legality of agreements between the EC and third countries.

The Single European Act created a European Court of First Instance to make initial judgments in many areas of EC competition law, but the ECJ remains the appeal court for such cases. In the field of Community law and in defining the extent of Community law, judgments of the ECJ overrule those of national courts, although its decisions are sometimes resisted by member states.

WHERE THEY SIT

WHO'S WHO

- Socialist Group
- Group of the European People's Party (Christian Democratic Group)
- Liberal Democratic and Reformist Group
- European Democratic Group
- The Green Group in the European Parliament
- Group of the European United Left
- Group of the European Democratic Alliance
- Technical Group of the European Right
- Rainbow Group
- Left Unity
- Non-attached

NUMBER OF SEATS IN EUROPEAN PARLIAMENT BY COUNTRY

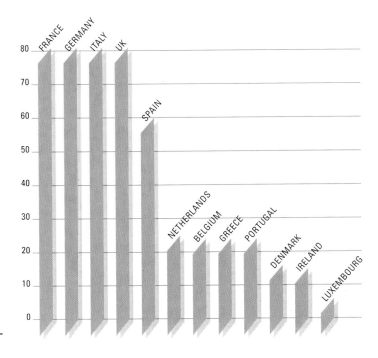

The European Parliament

The EP is elected every five years by the voters of the member states. At present there are 518 Euro-MPs (for details of the membership see left). The main sessions are held in Strasbourg, although the 18 committees usually meet in Brussels and the secretariat is located in Luxembourg.

The role of the EP has largely been consultative, although the Single European Act increased its input through the cooperation procedure and the Maastricht Treaty further enhances its powers.

The Euro-MPs have frequently criticised the democratic deficit of the EC, by which they referred to the way that EC laws are made by the Council on Commission proposals that are not subject to any parliamentary approval – EP or national.

Sitting pretty ... members of the European Parliament at their weekly meeting in Strasbourg. It conducts its business in nine different languages, with simultaneous translation.

Representation

The number of seats per country is not proportional to populations of each, with most of the smaller countries over-represented. The united Germany, with 78m inhabitants, has still only the same representation as the UK, France and Italy, each of which has far fewer citizens.

European policies and laws are produced in a number of different ways. The most fundamental laws are the treaties – the Single European Act and Maastricht. By making these treaties, member states transferred to the Community institutions both the responsibility and the power to make law and policy in specific and defined areas. The members also gave the authority to decide on any disputes about the interpretation of the treaties to the European Court of Justice, so it too has a law-making role.

The 12 member states are all parliamentary democracies, where most law is made by and through the national parliament which has power to dismiss the government. Despite the appearance of semi-presidential government in France, there, too, the president is dependent on his parliamentary majority; lose that, as François Mitterrand did between 1986 and 1988, and the president is forced into a back seat as the prime minister moves centre-stage. Nonetheless, the founding six states did not reproduce parliamentary government in the EC. The European Parliament's powers seem considerable, as it can sack the entire Commission or block the budget, but in practice these powers are a too-ultimate deterrent to be used to influence policy on a day-to-day basis. In most legislation, the European Parliament only has the power to scrutinise and propose amendments to what the Commission has proposed. Ultimately, it is the Council of Ministers that actually legislates. The cooperation procedure introduced by the Single European Act was intended to give more influence to the European Parliament.

How a directive is made

The production of a directive begins with consultation in working groups between Commission officials from the appropriate "general direction" and civil servants of member states, either from their permanent representatives in Brussels, or brought in specially from their respective capitals. Interest groups are also consulted, or at least given an opportunity to express their views on an early draft of each Commission proposal. The stages that a directive passes through are shown in the diagram (below left).

While it appears easy for the Commission and the European Parliament to work together to box in the Council, in practice such confrontational tactics are avoided, not least because in many policy areas the Council could react by long delays or by dropping proposals altogether. In all this complex consultative exchanging of views, a consensus may be gradually formed. The importance of the initial exploration in the working groups and the intergovernmental prenegotiations in COREPER is a major factor in getting the system to work.

The myth of the bureaucracy

Brussels bureaucrats may be an easy target for those opposed to any common European policy-making, but figures give the lie to popular belief, although the number of bureaucrats has increased roughly fourfold since 1968. Then the European Parliament employed 483, the European Council 548 and the European Commission 4,882. By 1991 the European Parliament was employing 3,086, the European Council 2,183 and the European Commission 15,577. In addition, the Brussels civil service must work with national officials to have any hope of success. They may persuade and convince, but they cannot cajole or command, except in minor matters or exceptional circumstances.

In practice, almost all key decisions are taken by the Council of Ministers – and all the ministers are responsible to parliaments in their home states. In practice too ministers are human: they prefer to take responsibility only for policies which are popular. The Brussels bureaucrats are undoubtedly well paid and enjoy tax advantages their counterparts in national government do not, but they also provide a convenient scapegoat for unpopular policies which national governments want to promote. As such they have two advantages: they deflect criticisms from the governments of member states and they cannot answer back. That, as in most civil services, is left to their bosses: commissioners and elected members of the European Parliament.

A German public workers strike in 1992 forced the German government to change its mind.

The EC policy process

The diagram illustrates the chain of action needed for a policy to proceed. Once a proposal is agreed, the European Commission, in the knowledge that there is some prospect of a decision in the Council, sends its draft to the Council, which passes it on to the European Parliament for its opinion. The proposal is considered by the appropriate committee which reports it to the parliament in the first reading for a majority vote to accept, reject or amend the Commission's text. If the Commission then changes its text to take in some or all of the amendments of the parliament, the Council of Ministers must then respond by trying to decide a common position on the Commission's revised version. Such a decision may be reached by a qualified majority vote in many cases, but sometimes unanimity is required.

The Council's amended text then goes back to the parliament for reconsideration by the committee before the second reading. Then, the parliament's modification goes to the Commission, and if the Commission accepts these changes the amended common position is presented to the Council for agreement, which only requires a qualified majority vote. The Council can change the amended common position only by unanimity.

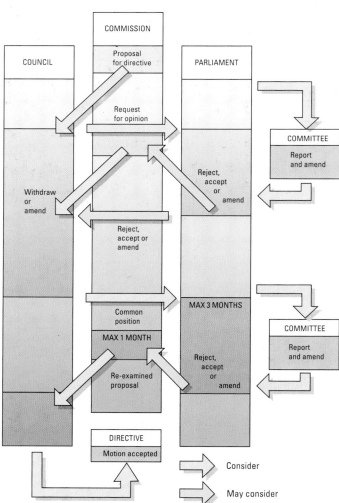

THE DOUBLE DEMOCRATIC DEFICIT

One side of the democratic deficit arises out of the relative impotence of the European Parliament in controlling the activities of both the Commission and the Council of Ministers. Because of its perceived weakness – it does not appoint either body, and although in theory it can force the resignation of the Commission, in practice it has effective control over neither, and the Council can reject its amendments to laws – absenteeism is high among its members and turnout is low at European elections. Critics argue that this makes the parliament illegitimate. Supporters, however, believe that this aspect of the democratic deficit could be overcome by increasing the parliament's powers and responsibilities.

The other side of this deficit stems from the fact that most Community law-making is a form of delegated legislation. Effectively the Council of Ministers makes the laws under authority derived from the treaties and subject only to judicial review by the European Court of Justice. Proposed amendments from the parliament may be over-ridden. Community laws in the form of directives have to be translated into national laws by the governments and legislatures of the member states. Failure to do so, or attempts to modify the intention of a directive, usually results in a referral by the Commission to the European Court.

The increasing use of majority voting in the Council of Ministers exacerbates the problem for those member states which happen to be outvoted. Once again supporters of an increased role for the European Parliament believe that this deficit could be made good by giving the parliament an effective control over legislation.

SEATS WON IN THE EP BY PARTY GROUPS, 1989 RESULTS

	BELGIUM	DENMARK	FRANCE	GERMANY	GREECE	IRELAND	ITALY	LUXEMBOURG	NETHERLANDS	PORTUGAL	SPAIN	UK
SOCIALIST	8	4	22	31	9	1	14	2	8	8	27	46
EPP (CHRISTIAN DEMOCRATS)	7	2	6	32	10	4	27	3	10	3	16	1
LIBERALS	4	3	13	4	0	2	3	1	4	9	6	0
EUROPEAN DEMOCRATS GROUP (CONSERVATIVES)	0	2	0	0	0	0	0	0	0	0	0	32
GREENS	3	0	8	8	0	0	7	0	2	1	1	0
UNITARY LEFT (EUROCOMMUNISTS)	0	1	0	0	1	0	22	0	0	0	4	0
EUROPEAN DEMOCRATIC ALLIANCE	0	0	13	0	1	6	0	0	0	0	0	0
EUROPEAN RIGHT (EXTREMIST)	1	0	10	6	0	0	0	0	0	0	0	0
LEFT UNITY (HARD COMMUNIST)	0	0	7	0	3	1	0	0	0	3	0	0
RAINBOW ALLIANCE (REGIONALISTS)	1	4	1	0	0	1	3	0	0	0	2	1
OTHERS	0	0	1	0	0	0	5	0	1	0	4	1

Head count
The far right now outnumbers the far left in the European Parliament, and both have been overtaken by the Greens, although support for the latter has been waning a little recently.

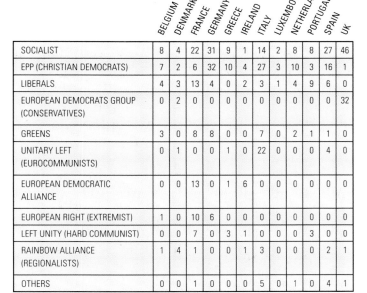

A strike by civil servants in 1991, making full use of the wet vote.

EMPLOYMENT

- 1986
- 1991

'000

14,413 15,577

3
2
1
0

EUROPEAN PARLIAMENT   COUNCIL   COMMISSION

Staffing the EC
Despite the increased responsibilities given by the Single European Act and the single market programme, the staff of the EC institutions has grown relatively little since then, although it has increased substantially since 1986. Senior Commission officials bemoan the fact that it is often easier to pass a controversial directive than to employ an additional junior secretary. Much of the policy preparation work is performed by national civil servants in the member states. There are also many firms of consultants in Brussels who compensate for the EC's staff shortage – at a price!

CASES IN POINT

Only the Netherlands has the primacy of EC law written into its constitution but no member state questions the principle. It was established in the case of Costa v ENEL, which concerned a bill of less than 2,000 lire which Mr Costa, a shareholder in Edison Volta, had refused to pay to the newly nationalised Italian electricity corporation because he claimed that the nationalisation contravened the Treaty of Rome. The Italian courts claimed that Italian legislation made after the treaty must supersede the treaty. The European Court disagreed.

Another turning-point judgement was in the 1979 Cassis de Dijon case in which the decision of the court that Germany could not block the import of crème de cassis on the grounds that under German law its alcohol content was too high for it to be a wine and too low for it to be a liqueur, established the important principle of "mutual recognition" and was a significant boost for the idea of a supranational Community.

ABSTENTIONS IN EP ELECTIONS, 1989

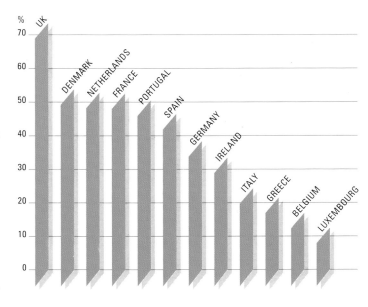

%
70 UK
60 DENMARK NETHERLANDS FRANCE
50 PORTUGAL SPAIN
40 GERMANY
30 IRELAND
20 ITALY GREECE BELGIUM LUXEMBOURG
10
0

Democracy at work
As the chart shows, the turnout of voters in elections to the European Parliament varies enormously. The British take the parliament least seriously with 73.5% not bothering to vote in 1989. In Denmark, the Netherlands and France more than half of the electorate didn't bother to turn out. The highest turn out levels were in Luxembourg, where only 12.5% didn't vote, and Belgium, where 16.9% didn't bother.

THE EC – SPENDING

Complaints by farmers against the Common Agricultural Policy (CAP) seem to be endless, often provoking widescale violence. Here, Italian farm workers are protesting.

Of all the Community's policies, it is the Common Agricultural Policy (CAP) which costs the most and causes the most controversy. Although agricultural spending has been decreasing as a proportion of the EC budget in recent years, the price guarantee system still consumed almost 60% of the Community budget in 1991.

Since its foundation, the EC has also spent some money on research and development to supplement national research programmes and to encourage collaboration between member states. From 1974 the EC has also devoted funds to a social action programme. The social fund is spent on such measures as schemes to increase employment opportunities, improvements projects for working and living conditions, and safeguards against redundancy. The following year, the European Regional Development Fund was created with the aim of increasing the cohesion of the Community by reducing disparities between the richer and poorer regions. Finally, a small part of the Agricultural Fund is devoted to guid-

ance, which means helping to improve the efficiency of farmers, especially those in backward rural areas.

The CAP is not only the most costly EC policy, it is also the most complex. The price guarantee system involves an "annual farm-price review" to fix three sets of prices for the various different commodity regimes. Marathon ministerial meetings and mammoth demonstrations by farmers are parts of this curious annual ritual. The central price for each commodity is the target price – the price which ideally EC farmers should receive. If the real market price for a commodity drops below that target price, Community institutions examine the possibility of intervention. It is the second annually agreed price, the intervention price that sets the level below which a commodity regime agency automatically starts to purchase unlimited quantities. The agency pays that intervention price, thus giving all farmers a guarantee that their produce will be bought at that minimum price, and hence ensuring a guaranteed minimum income to farmers.

Givers and takers

The 1980s closed as they began – with Germany and Britain as the EC's most generous contributors. Although both France and Italy paid more of the EC's budget than Britain, they received more than they had given. One paradox of the EC budget structure was that while most of the poorer states (Greece and Ireland) received massive EC funding, the poorest of all, Portugal got much less than Greece. Equally bizarre was the fact that the Netherlands, one of the richest states, does proportionately well out of the EC.

BUDGET BALANCE, 1990

■ % of EC budget Paid

□ % of EC budget Received

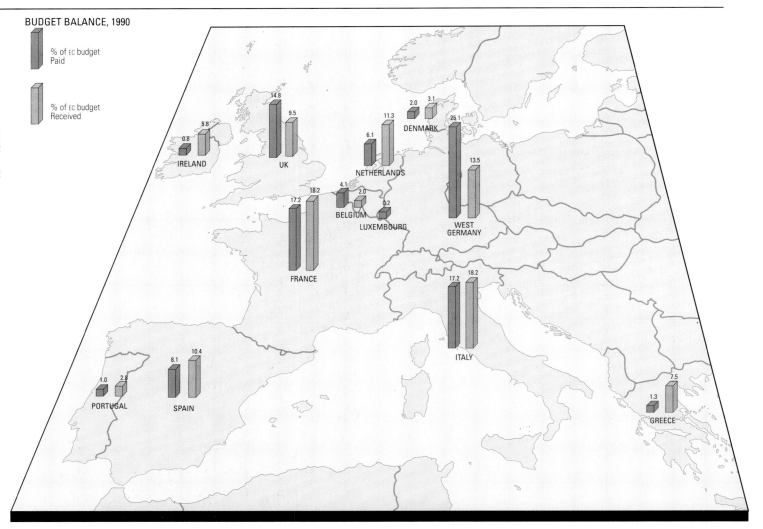

No equality

If the objective of EC spending is to bring about a convergence of economic performance and living standards, a more effective system of redistributive budgetary action is needed. By GDP standards Denmark, France and the Netherlands should be major contributors to the EC budget along with Belgium, Luxembourg, Germany and Britain. Both Spain and Portugal should receive substantially more EC funds.

GDP PER HEAD

COUNTRY	$
BELGIUM	15,200
DENMARK	20,900
FRANCE	17,000
W. GERMANY	19,600
GREECE	5,200
IRELAND	9,200
ITALY	14,400
LUXEMBOURG	17,600
NETHERLANDS	15,500
PORTUGAL	4,200
SPAIN	8,700
UK	14,400

Farm size

One need only think about the profits from one hectare of vines in the Champagne region to realise that small farms are not always inefficient and unprofitable. All depends on the crop, the location and the methods. The average size of holdings may also be misleading: in France and Italy those who give up farming often continue to own their land, but rent it out to their neighbours.

AVERAGE HOLDING

COUNTRY	HECTARES m
BELGIUM	14.1
DENMARK	30.7
FRANCE	27.0
W. GERMANY	16.0
GREECE	4.3
IRELAND	22.7
ITALY	5.6
LUXEMBOURG	28.6
NETHERLANDS	14.9
PORTUGAL	4.3
SPAIN	12.9
UK	65.1

Connections: Trade 48–49   Competition in industry 50–51   Food and farming 76–77   Europe and America 148–151

However, agricultural prices as a whole are kept at a level above those of world markets by a protectionist system which imposes levies on imports. The EC sets threshold prices, which are minimum sale prices for agricultural imports into the Community. The levy – the difference between the world market price and the EC threshold price – is, like all customs duties, part of the EC's own resources. The final complication is that the EC also subsidises agricultural exporters to offset the difference between high EC prices and lower world prices.

In general, countries with high agricultural exports, like Denmark and the Netherlands, have done well out of this system. So, too, have countries with many small relatively inefficient farmers such as France and Italy. Net importers with efficient but non-exporting farmers – like Britain – have contributed generously to funding the scheme. But changes in production and exports have brought changes; France is now a net contributor, while Italy and Spain are set to follow suit. This leaves the Netherlands and Denmark, two of the world's richest states in terms of GNP per head, as beneficiaries of a system originally intended to redistribute wealth from the rich to the poor.

Since its 1985 Green Paper, the Commission has been pushing for reform of the CAP. Escalating cost had become an increasing source of anxiety among EC leaders. A second problem was the fact that EC prices to consumers remained far higher, for most produce, than prevailing world prices. A third cause for concern was the growing complexity of the price support system. In 1992, the Council approved the proposals of Ray McSharry, the agricultural minister, for a major reform of the CAP.

The pressure from the American government for a massive reduction in farm subsidies as the price for a new GATT agreement and the relative decline in the political weight of farmers in both Germany and France now make the prospect of reform more likely. Until then, other EC policies suffer from a shortage of funds and a reluctance by governments to contemplate any policy scheme which may be as perverse and costly as the CAP.

As in Italy, here in France, as farmers protest in Paris against imports of British lamb which are undercutting prices. Protection of French farmers was a fundamental reason behind the creation of the CAP. The policy is much criticised by governments outside the Community and also by consumer groups and independent observers within Europe.

The EC budget

In 1989 each Community citizen paid an average of 140 ecus to the EC and just over 50 times that amount to their own country. The pie charts below indicate where that money went and on what it was spent. In 1968 the six members had a budget of 9.6bn ecus, in 1980 the nine members contributed 24.9bn ecus and by 1991 12 members had increased it to 55.6bn ecus. In 1968 the budget accounted for 0.57% of the total EC GDP, in 1980 0.81% and in 1991 1.04%. The CAP element which includes price guarantees to agriculture and fisheries has been reduced as a percentage of the total budget over the period by nearly 20%. This has been swallowed up by an increasing outlay on structural policies which is made up of the Social Fund, the Regional Development Fund and the fund for restructuring the CAP. The total cost for this stood at 14bn ecus in 1991.

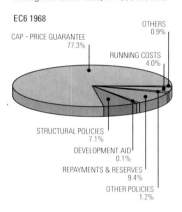

EC6 1968
CAP - PRICE GUARANTEE 77.3%
OTHERS 0.9%
RUNNING COSTS 4.0%
STRUCTURAL POLICIES 7.1%
DEVELOPMENT AID 0.1%
REPAYMENTS & RESERVES 9.4%
OTHER POLICIES 1.2%

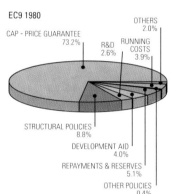

EC9 1980
CAP - PRICE GUARANTEE 73.2%
OTHERS 2.0%
R&D 2.6%
RUNNING COSTS 3.9%
STRUCTURAL POLICIES 8.8%
DEVELOPMENT AID 4.0%
REPAYMENTS & RESERVES 5.1%
OTHER POLICIES 0.4%

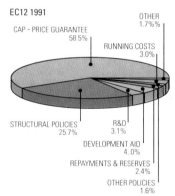

EC12 1991
CAP - PRICE GUARANTEE 58.5%
OTHER 1.7%%
RUNNING COSTS 3.0%
STRUCTURAL POLICIES 25.7%
R&D 3.1%
DEVELOPMENT AID 4.0%
REPAYMENTS & RESERVES 2.4%
OTHER POLICIES 1.6%

WHAT IS THE COMMON AGRICULTURAL POLICY?

The Common Agricultural Policy was the first of the EC's policies, and remains the most costly of them. It has two main goals; firstly, to stabilise prices in a protected common market, thereby guaranteeing farmers' incomes and ensuring that the EC is self-sufficient and, secondly, to restructure agricultural production so as to improve efficiency and reduce costs.

The creation of the CAP reflected the numerical strength and political muscle of the farming communities in the original six member states. Until the mid-1980s most attention and funding was devoted to the price support system. The annual farm price review negotiations have become a regular ritual, peppered by farmers' demonstrations in protest against even the mildest attempts to reduce price subsidies.

But escalating costs became an increasing source of anxiety among EC leaders. A second cause for concern was the fact that EC prices to consumers remained far higher, for most produce, than prevailing world prices. A third cause was the continuing embarrassment of riches: grain mountains, wine lakes and all kinds of food surpluses the policy encouraged. A fourth cause for concern was the growing complexity of the price support system, with its high administration costs and its particular vulnerability to fraud. The 1992 proposal for a major reform was widely welcomed.

SHARE OF 1990 CAP BUDGET

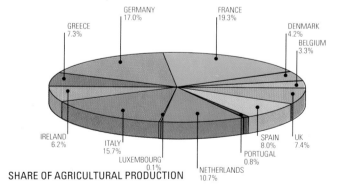

GERMANY 17.0%
FRANCE 19.3%
GREECE 7.3%
DENMARK 4.2%
BELGIUM 3.3%
IRELAND 6.2%
ITALY 15.7%
LUXEMBOURG 0.1%
NETHERLANDS 10.7%
SPAIN 8.0%
PORTUGAL 0.8%
UK 7.4%

SHARE OF AGRICULTURAL PRODUCTION

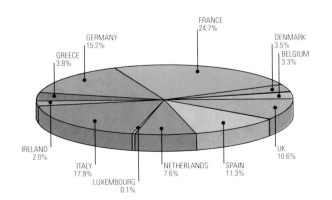

FRANCE 24.7%
GERMANY 15.2%
GREECE 3.8%
DENMARK 3.5%
BELGIUM 3.3%
IRELAND 2.0%
ITALY 17.9%
LUXEMBOURG 0.1%
NETHERLANDS 7.6%
SPAIN 11.3%
UK 10.6%

Spending on CAP

The chart below shows how CAP spending has been distributed between plant products which include cereals, rice, oils and fats, and animal products such as dairy produce, milk, beef and veal, as the EC members doubled from six in 1968 to 12 in 1991.

COMMODITIES

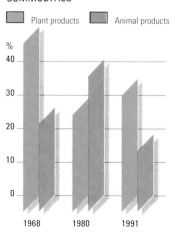

Plant products   Animal products

%
40
30
20
10
0
1968   1980   1991

THE EC – LABOUR AND IMMIGRATION

Unemployed German workers in eastern Germany in April 1991, after reunification, protesting against their plight. Over 16% of the east Germany workforce is unemployed compared with an unemployment rate of 8% in western Germany.

Modern governments have assumed responsibility for maintaining high and stable levels of employment, but they also have to meet other obligations – maintaining the value of the currency and fostering economic growth, for example – and these aims are not always compatible in the short run, and perhaps not in the medium term either. Thus, the experience of France is a case in point. Economic growth has been maintained, the industrial base has been preserved by extensive modernisation and investment, along with rising levels of productivity. But, in fact, it is unemployment, sticking at around 2.5m that has stayed both high and stable.

Regional imbalances

Increasingly, economic growth requires structural change rather than expansion of existing production, and structural changes in economic activity leads to structural unemployment affecting whole industries and whole regions. Western Europe shows a high degree of regional differentiation, with prosperous areas alongside ones in decay, and others again that are endemically impoverished. Thus, the old industrial heartlands have been in decline for many years – the so-called Rust Belt, one sweep of which runs from the Scottish Lowlands through north-east England to Belgium and the Ruhr.

There are also large areas of rural backwardness – in Ireland, parts of Spain and southern Italy – that present quite different problems from those affecting the industrial regions. Misconceived regional policies, aimed at regenerating depressed areas without taking wider fac-

tors into account, can result in making problems worse – building "cathedrals in the desert" (as with the Bagnoli steel complex in Naples). Relocation needs of new industries, requiring new technologies that are capital intensive with small, skilled workforces, and those associated with the tertiary sector, do not necessarily correspond to those businesses in the old industrial areas which were fixed largely by raw material and market and transport criteria. Neither government nor EC-sponsored inducements may be sufficient, nor the movement of labour.

EMU and the market – a decade of deflation?

Wrestling with the structural and regional problems of employment, western European countries face two important constraints that make positive intervention more difficult. One constraint is the pressure against direct state involvement in industry: the switch from state-run enterprises to private sector – privatisation – and a growing market-orientation generally, means that labour-shedding will be a dominant feature of the labour market for some time to come. The second constraint arises from the EC commitment to introduce a single currency. The disciplines to be observed – keeping government borrowing and inflation under strict control – limit the scope for employment-promotion measures that require deficit-funding. Convergence towards a single currency effectively means having to keep in line with German interest rates and currency policies. Reflationary policies to boost the demand for labour will not be possible, so that greater emphasis will have to be placed on cost-efficient, selective measures.

Labour problems

Pressures on the labour market are intensified by the growth of the immigrant population with knock-on effects in other ways – housing, costs of social provision, and so on. A political backlash – evident in Belgium, France and Germany in the early 1990s – benefits right-wing extremist parties playing on anti-foreigner sentiments and using metaphors like tide, flood and becoming swamped. Both for economic and political reasons, governments are seeking to introduce more restrictive policies, but increasingly they are concerned to work out common policies, especially for the EC member states: as the EC moves towards abolishing all internal controls and restrictions, the extent of intra-area movement and migration will increase. Unless a common policy is adopted, inwards migration will continue – via the countries with the most open borders and with the least restrictive policies.

Out of work

The graph shows the percentage distribution of unemployment throughout the EC. Both Ireland and Spain suffer rates over 13%, whereas the south-east of England comes off relatively lightly, along with southern Germany.

The Maastricht summit of December 1991 failed to reach agreement on this issue largely because those countries with the tightest controls feared that they might be required to weaken them and be forced to accept a quota of migrants, the size of which could actually increase the existing intake. Nonetheless, the indications are that EC countries will move towards greater coordination – in the control of frontiers, possibly with the creation of a supranational policing system, a harmonisation of procedures and definitions. In addition, the EC will be concerned to target aid and investment at poor neighbours so as to reduce pressures that lead to large-scale emigration. The picture of fortress Europe is fanciful in most respects, but not for migration policy.

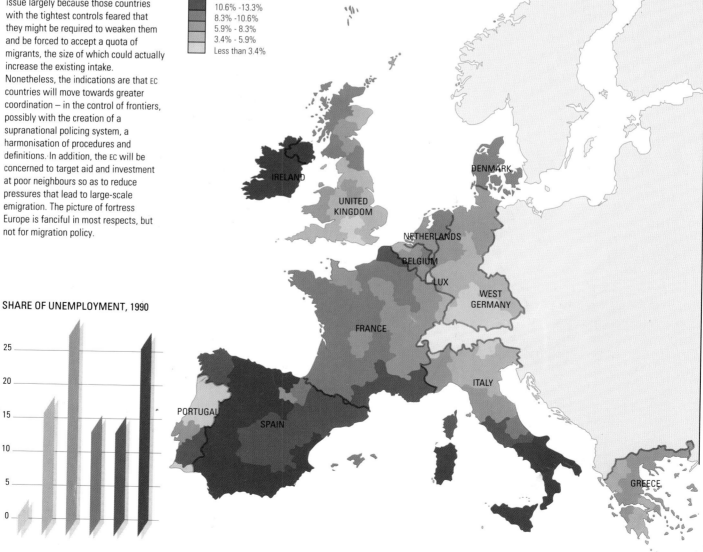

EC REGIONAL UNEMPLOYMENT RATES, 1990

- Over 13.3%
- 10.6% -13.3%
- 8.3% -10.6%
- 5.9% - 8.3%
- 3.4% - 5.9%
- Less than 3.4%

SHARE OF UNEMPLOYMENT, 1990

IMMIGRATION PROBLEMS IN GERMANY

The first influx of immigrants into western Germany was of guestworkers in the 1960s, mainly from Turkey and southern Europe; a high proportion of them remained and settled in Germany with their dependants. From the 1980s onwards, two other categories of immigrants have grown vastly in numbers. One was people seeking political asylum. In this respect Germany has a very liberal policy entrenched in the constitution which is proving difficult to alter. In practice it is hard to distinguish genuine asylum-seekers from economic migrants. The second category involves the so-called ethnic Germans living in eastern Europe and the former Soviet Union. They have German ancestry and thus have an automatic right to move to Germany. The social and economic pressures resulting from the mass entry of asylum-seekers and ethnic Germans has led to a strong right-wing political backlash.

Asylum seekers

The steep rise of migrants into western Europe over the past decade exposes a clash between economic interests and liberal values: on the one hand, there is the demand to cut the number of immigrants, but on the other, genuine asylum-seekers should not be turned away. The difficulty is in practice to distinguish clearly between the two categories and to decide individual cases fairly. The scale of civil strife in many countries is exacerbated by widespread economic dislocation and collapse, especially evident in post–communist eastern Europe.

COUNTRY	1985[1]	1989[1]
AUSTRIA	6.7	21.9
BELGIUM	5.3	8.1
DENMARK	—	5.3
FRANCE	28.8	61.4
WEST GERMANY	73.8	121.3
NETHERLANDS	5.6	13.9
SWEDEN	14.5	30.0
SWITZERLAND	9.7	24.4
UK	—	16.6
1 Measured in '000		

FRANCE

There have been successive waves of immigration into France in the 1920s and between 1956 and 1972; shortage of labour (for the industrial expansion of the 1950s and 1960s) was met by immigration from the former colonies and from Italy, Spain and Portugal.

Since 1974 efforts were made to curb this flow: old industries were modernised or were disappearing, and labour shortages were replaced by unemployment and immigration control. In 1974 official immigration was stopped. A Secrétariat d'Etat aux Travailleurs Immigrés was established to prevent all new immigration and to improve the conditions and equality of the established immigrant population. A law passed in 1976 allowed for family reunification, but remains restrictive.

The 1945 law regulated residence and employment through the need for permits; the Office National de l'Immigration was created to act as a state-controlled intermediary between employers and future immigrants. After 1956 the ONI was increasingly bypassed by "irregular" immigration. Control was managed after that mainly through permits.

EC citizens are free to settle and work in France; Algerians were considered to be French citizens until 1962, but they now need special residence/work permits. In 1968 an entry quota was established.

Illegal immigration was widely accepted until the 1970s. Now border controls are strict for non-EC, American and Japanese nationals. There are also penalties for illegal employers/employees. All these measures, however, are inefficient. The current immigration policy is to assimilate "suitable" (eg Portuguese) immigrants; to maintain social peace and encouragement to return. The acceptance that many would remain came in 1981, with the right to work and live without discrimination, and without giving up cultural identity.

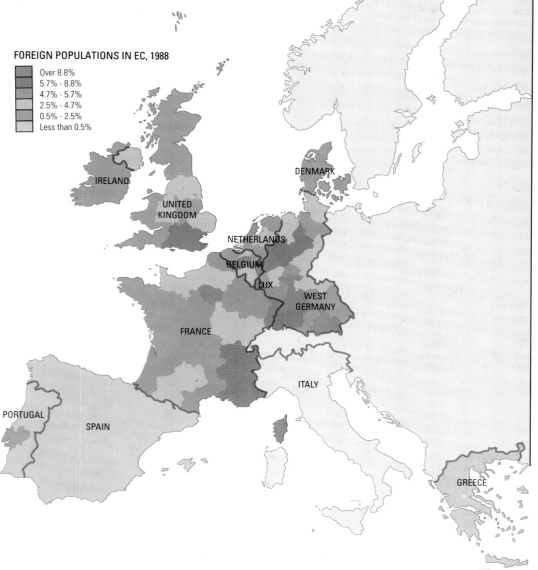

FOREIGN POPULATIONS IN EC, 1988

- Over 8.8%
- 5.7% - 8.8%
- 4.7% - 5.7%
- 2.5% - 4.7%
- 0.5% - 2.5%
- Less than 0.5%

World migration

Historically, mass migration took place over relatively short distances. Long-distance movement began with the settlement of the United States, but western Europe has supplanted North America as the prime destination. Poverty and civil strife accounts for the considerable immigration from African countries and large parts of Asia, but in recent years – and for the same reasons – the emphasis has switched to immigration from eastern Europe following the collapse of the communist governments, and there is little sign that the pressures will diminish over the next decade.

INTO WESTERN EUROPE

COUNTRY	1975[1]	1985-81[1]
AFRICA	482.9	621.4
ASIA	269.1	253.9
S. AMERICA	42.0	36.0
N. AMERICA	141.7	95.0
E. EUROPE[2]	368.4	553.2
OCEANIA	58.6	36.3
1 Measured in '000	2 Inc: USSR	

Refugees from Albania, part of a mass exodus to Italy during 1991, waited for four days on board the Albanian ship, Tirana, outside the port of Brindisi, for possible entry into Italy. The break-up of Yugoslavia has created an even more serious refugee problem.

ROLLING BACK THE STATE

Across western Europe political leaders have faced the problem of a rising demand for public expenditure and a growing reluctance on the part of citizens to pay the taxes necessary. The demand to roll back the state – or at least to stop it rolling any further forward – was first articulated in Scandinavia in the early 1970s. The rising tax cost of the generous welfare state led to voters deserting their traditional loyalties to vote for anti-state protest parties which were more or less accurately named: "Anders Lange's Party for Substantial Reduction of Taxes, Duties and Government Intervention" in Norway and the Progress party in Denmark.

Such protests were soon to be voiced elsewhere, especially after the two oil crises and the growth of unemployment which placed strong spending pressure on unemployment insurance schemes. Until the 1980s, most European governments attempted to maintain employ-

same demographic changes of falling birth rates and, above all, ageing populations, which, coupled with the soaring costs of ever-improving medical technology, pushed health insurance schemes into constantly recurring deficits. Furthermore, public expectations of all public services were rising. To meet the rising bills, taxes, social security contributions and public borrowing were all increased.

In almost all countries the incumbent government lost elections: in France, Spain and Greece centre-right governments were replaced by Socialists or Social Democrats. In the UK, however, the wind of political change that swept out the Labour government in 1979 came from across the Atlantic. Margaret Thatcher and her closest acolytes were fascinated by "public choice" theories and the populism of the proposition 13 referendum against property taxes in California. They, too, sought to reduce public spending, borrowing and taxation and to replace the welfare dependency culture by the enterprise culture. They attacked trade union rights and declared war on high spending local governments. They launched the privatisation programme, the introduction of market logic and performance evaluation into public service costing, and tax cuts. After a cautious start the public sector was cut back drastically by privatisations of utilities and other state-owned firms, which in turn permitted more cuts in taxes and borrowing.

The dominance of market principles

Elsewhere in western Europe, too, the market gained stature as the state lost credibility, but nowhere were the effects as drastic as in the UK. In Germany, the Free Democrats dropped their Social Democrat partners in favour of the Christian Democrats, thus changing the government without an election, but the policy shifts were not very dramatic.

In France, the Socialist government rapidly dropped reflation, and drastically restructured its newly nationalised industries to shed hidden unemployment and to improve productivity, exports and profits. But the Front National which blamed immigrants for the social security deficit, crime and aids, and promised to abolish income tax made spectacular by-election gains and in 1986 the Socialists lost power back to the centre-right parties. They had a plan for privatising most of the massive public sector and tax cuts which they pursued with alacrity until they lost the 1988 elections.

Public ownership

Although only Britain carried out really extensive privatisation of its public sector, market principles became dominant in economic thinking across Europe. The ending of exchange controls (notably on capital movements) and the European Monetary System of fixed exchange rates meant that few states attempted to stray out of line from the Bundesbank norms. The increasingly open market also pushed states to harmonise their tax rates for fear of enterprises exporting jobs or individuals investing abroad. Large firms might remain in public ownership, but with a suspicious and powerful European Commission constantly scrutinising accounts for signs of hidden subsidies or other forms of unfair competition, they acted more and more like private corporations. Finally, the collapse of communist systems in the East completed the discredit of Marxist economic ideas. Everywhere Socialists and Social Democrats had to learn to live with the market.

THE COST OF THE WELFARE STATE, 1990

- 60+%
- 50-59%
- 40-49%
- 30-39%
- Less than 30%

Helping hand
The figures in the map above show the disbursements on the welfare state as a percentage of each country's GNP. The largest increases have been in Sweden (26.4% in 1955; 64.1% in 1990) and the lowest in the UK (28.8% in 1955; 39.7% in 1990).

ment by Keynesian reflation tactics and by concealing unemployment in large and highly unprofitable nationalised industries. At the same time, defence costs continued to rise as an end to the arms race seemed inconceivable. Unfortunately, the consequence was stagflation with low or negative growth, rising unemployment and high inflation.

It was not only unemployment insurance costs and income maintenance schemes which led to increased public expenditure; all welfare states experienced the

Connections: Privatisation 54–55 Political systems 114–115 Health 242–245

THE RISE AND FALL OF THE SWEDISH MODEL?

The structure and principles of the Swedish system are as follows: in terms of economic management, 80% of the economy is privately-owned, 10% is in cooperatives and 10% is state-owned; there is also a concentration of state-enterprises using profit management policy. As far as labour management is concerned, there is a centralised, corporatist wage formation policy; high union membership (almost 80% of the workforce); a high growth rate, high employment and low inflation. The social services expenditure accounts for some 35% of GDP. In 1958, a referendum agreed that pensions should be increased successively until 1968 and supplementary pensions paid from 1963. In 1969 the Diet (parliament) decided that an increment be added to basic pension, which would be successively increased until 1979. Basic welfare provisions include: sickness insurance for all residents, employment injury insurance for all employed persons, unemployment insurance for members of recognised unemployment insurance societies (70% of all employees), basic pensions for all citizens, supplementary pensions for all gainfully occupied persons. In 1976 partial pensions were given to all employees between 60 and 65, and from 1948 a children's allowance was made to all children under 16, and to children aged 16–18 if at school. By the early 1980s the national budget deficit increased from 10% to 12%; the failure of wage agreements in 1975–76 led to inflation pressures; structural change following the oil crises created a sharp rise in unemployment; and inflation led to an abandonment of the method of calculating wage claims from inflation rate and labour productivity. In spite of this, the Swedish model still appears intact.

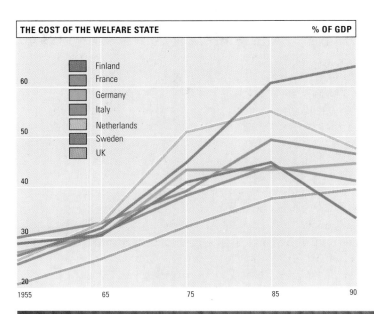

THE COST OF THE WELFARE STATE — % OF GDP

Finland / France / Germany / Italy / Netherlands / Sweden / UK

Rising costs
Almost all European governments faced escalating costs for welfare provisions during the 1980s, with Sweden leading the field, although since the late 1980s there has been a decline in the rate of increase.

Go and stop
The French privatisation programme started in November 1986 and produced a high income for the state in 1987. It was brought to a sudden end by the October 1987 stock-market crash and the return of the socialists to power.

FRENCH PRIVATISATION PROCEEDS

YEAR	$m
1983-86	2,569
mid 86 - mid 87	7,307
1987	17,341

You could be an H₂Owner. Call 0272 272 272.

NOT SO DIRIGISTE

In 1986, the new French government of the right introduced a privatisation programme, spelling out procedures and naming the firms to be sold: there were 66 firms comprising 27 independent groups, with a combined workforce of 200,000, and worth 1,200bn francs (the equivalent of a quarter of the companies listed on the Bourse). The programme was to be a five-year one and within one year one-third of the government's objectives had been carried out. The choice of firms was important politically: it included not only firms nationalised by the Socialists but also by de Gaulle.

The whole privatisation programme in France was state directed. The motives were to make the French a nation of shareholders, to reduce the economic role of the state and to increase that of the market, thus reversing the policy of the Socialists. It was also very important to fill the state coffers.

The shares were allocated 10% to employees, 15% to foreigners, 50% to the public at large and 25% to 10 larger share-holders. The number of shareholders in France rose to 8 million in 1987, from 1.5 million in 1985, but most of them exercised no control because of the voting rights of large shareholders, who also had the right to representation on the board. In short, there was a strengthening of the traditional establishment network rather than that or "popular capitalism".

EASTERN EUROPE

Throughout eastern Europe governments are busy dismantling their state-run sectors. Hungary has been in the vanguard, but in the latter half of the 1980s even the former Soviet Union under Mikhail Gorbachev came to realise how deadening and deadly central planning, ownership and control was to an economy. In eastern Germany the Treuhand agency, which was originally set up by the last communist-led government of the GDR to "preserve people's property", had sold off some 5,000 firms within a year and a half after Detlev Rohwedder took over and completely changed the agency's strategy.

But the problems of switching from a state-run economy to one based on the private sector are considerable. When the Treuhand closed down firms that it couldn't find a serious buyer for, it came as a rude and painful shock to eastern Germans used to job security. And Rohwedder paid the ultimate price for his high-profile role when he was assassinated by Red Army Faction terrorists in 1991. For people conditioned by decades of communism and for whom competition, competence and efficiency are new concepts, it is a big change that they are having to adjust to. After the initial post-revolution euphoria, many are almost nostalgic for the certainty of the old days when prices were controlled and you had a job for life. Other tensions are caused by foreign investment, particularly German, as some eastern Europeans fear an invasion by the back door.

Under Mrs Thatcher's successive Conservative governments, an extensive privatisation programme was put into operation. Here, an advertisement for the sale of shares in the water boards, put up for public tender in 1991.

THE FUTURE SHAPE

Two powerful forces are affecting the course of European development. One is the drive towards European integration, and the other is the dynamic of disintegration following the collapse of the communist systems. Can these two quite different kinds of momentum be reconciled, and if so on what terms? Essentially the question is concerned with the future relationship of western to eastern Europe, and it is clear that the European Community will take a dominant role. But it is not at all certain what that role will be or which factors will prove to be decisive. Furthermore, European governments remain concerned about maintaining cooperation with both the United States and Russia, although there is little evidence of enthusiasm for a Europe from San Francisco to Vladivostok. The realistic possibilities for the future – at least for the next three decades – can be represented in terms of three broad scenarios.

Fortress Europe

The idea of Fortress Europe – a small, closely unified EC of 15 or 16 states – is attractive for both political and economic reasons. An indefinite enlargement of Community membership would invite the danger of diluting the political will. There is also the risk that the EC would

An unequivocal symbol of the end of the cold war – where the Berlin wall separated eastern from western Europe, there is now a heap of rubble and deserted houses.

import political instability from those countries that have little in the way of a democratic tradition. The economic argument against wholesale enlargement is equally strong: opening the EC to the poor countries of eastern Europe would involve massive structural aid being paid to them by all the existing members. Some exceptions to this rule of non-admission will be made – Austria, Sweden, Norway, Finland and Switzerland, for example – are all eligible since they would have no difficulty in adapting to Community rules or adopting a single currency, and would be welcome contributors and not dependants.

The logic of this scenario is that the European Community has to become much deeper before it can afford to become much wider. A weakened EC would lose its role on the world stage, just at the time when it was starting to gain both economic and political credibility. At this critical juncture a move towards a large, loose Community would jeopardise the achievements of the post-1945 era.

Cooperative Europe

A Cooperative Europe, greatly enlarged and loosely integrated, is based on the view that the European Community – in accordance with its idealism – has to assume a moral responsibility for Europe as a whole. The victory of liberal democracy over communism can only be fully justified if western Europe does its utmost to ensure that eastern Europe does not become permanently disabled. With the influx of new members, it will prove impossible to forge a tight political union until the basic economic problems have been solved. Instead, various *ad hoc* arrangements will be used, allowing states to participate in some policies but opting out of others. Future development will be strongly affected by the prolonged deviation from the tight integrationist course, with Europe never moving beyond a loose confederal structure. National interests – whether those of old or new members – will ensure that the EC remains fundamentally an intergovernmental system.

Superpower Europe

Belief in a Superpower Europe emerging is based on the proposition that the EC can be progressively widened and deepened without insuperable difficulty. For the process to work successfully two conditions have to be met. First, the richer countries have to accept making large transfer payments. They will be willing to do so if they are sure that an economic regeneration of eastern Europe creates an enormously powerful trading bloc. Second, applicants will have to accept the EC terms of entry without much being conceded in the way of extended transitions or exceptions. In effect, the weak new members have to accept a client status and have to be dependent on the strong, centralised direction of the EC. What of the superpower pretensions of the Community? The process of deepening involves the articulation of a unified political will and voice. In its relationships with the rest of the world, the EC expresses a single foreign policy, a single bargaining position vis-à-vis other trading groups – and in both respects it is unquestionably stronger than other powers.

Disintegrating Europe?

In eastern European states the resurgence of nationalism has had dramatic effects. First, in the Baltic area, Latvia, Estonia and Lithuania began the exodus from the Soviet Union which led to its collapse. Yugoslavia was next to disappear, albeit in a bloodbath as the numerically dominant Serbs resisted first the departure and later the territorial claims of Slovenia, Croatia and Bosnia. By mid-1992 Czechoslovakia seemed doomed since nationalists in both Slovakia and Czech Lands were suing for divorce. Even relatively homogeneous states like Hungary have not escaped unscathed: 150,000 ethnic Hungarians have arrived as refugees from Croatia, while thousands more in Romania and Czechoslovakia expect the Hungarian government to protect their interests. One immediate effect is that in eastern Europe the economic impetus to emigrate to the EC is being reinforced by a political pressure — to flee ethnic repression, civil war or widespread disorder. A second consequence is that the EC has been drawn into attempts at mediation and peace-keeping, although Lord Carrington's mission to Yugoslavia had little initial success. But the message for the western Europeans has been made clear: the EC must act together decisively and generously to help the eastern Europeans to resolve their political and economic problems.

Connections: Towards unity 24–25 Eastern Europe 110–111 Rebuilding democracies 120–121 The European Community 130–131

THE EUROPEAN PATENT OFFICE

The European Patent Office (EPO) was founded by the European Patent Convention, signed in 1973, which came into force in 1977. The 15-strong membership comprises Austria, Belgium, Denmark, France, Germany, Greece, Italy, Liechtenstein, Luxembourg, the Netherlands, Spain, Sweden, Switzerland, the UK and Portugal in 1991. Associate members are Norway and Ireland. The headquarters have main offices in Munich, established in 1977, and the Hague, also 1977, with sub-offices in Berlin and Vienna.

The EPO provides a single application process for the grant of the "European Patent", applicable in all contracting states for 20 years. The total number of European patents issued has grown from 1,500 per month in 1980 to over 4,000 per month by 1990. The EPO also distributes patent information. It has official representation in the World Intellectual Property Organisation (WIPO) as the European section of the Patent Corporation Treaty of the world. The EC Patent, 1975, aims to extend the European Patent to all EC member states from 1 January 1993.

THE EUROPEAN SPACE AGENCY (ESA)

This entered into force in 1964 when it was established by the European Space Research Commission. The 13 members are Belgium, Denmark, France, Germany, Ireland, Italy, the Netherlands, Spain, Sweden, Switzerland, the UK, Austria (1987) and Norway (1987); Finland became an associate member in 1987. The headquarters are in Paris.

The aims of the ESA are to "provide for and promote, for exclusively peaceful purposes, cooperation among European states in space research and technology, and their space applications with a view to their being used for scientific purposes and for space applications systems". The activities include cooperation in a number of intergovernmental organisations: the European Organisation for Nuclear Research (CERN); the International Civil Aviation Organisation (ICAO); and the European Telecommunications and Satellite Organisation (EUTELSAT). The main programmes being developed are: Columbus, an international space station, with NASA; Ariane, the European launch of satellites; Hermes, a manned space-plane; and Spacelab, a European manned space laboratory.

EUROPEAN RESEARCH CO-ORDINATION AGENCY

Founded in 1985, EUREKA's 20 member countries are the 12 EC member states; 7 EFTA member states; and Turkey. The headquarters are in Brussels. EUREKA is managed and coordinated by the EC Commission.

Initiated by France in response to the US Strategic Defence Initiative (SDI) Star Wars programme, which was launched in 1983, its aim is to increase Europe's industrial competitiveness through research and development cooperation in the high-technology sector. Projects are orientated towards collaboration between industrial enterprises on products directly aimed at the market place (unlike the pre-competitive EC research programmes). Projects have been extended to include companies from non-member states, notably from eastern Europe. The ninth annual Eureka Ministerial Conference held in the Hague, June 1991, approved 121 projects, recommended by the European Commission, including 34 on the environment, 28 on new technology and medicine, and 15 on robotics.

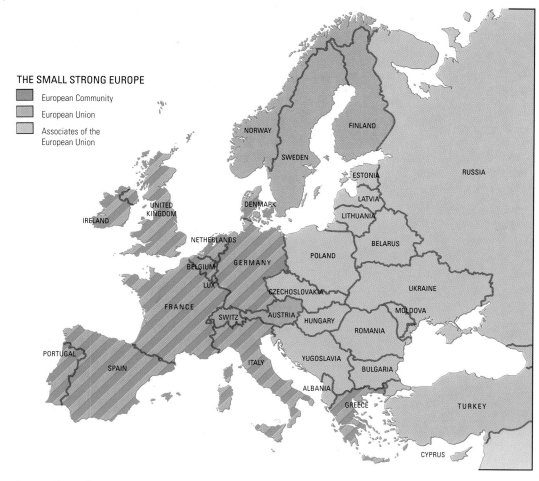

THE SMALL STRONG EUROPE
- European Community
- European Union
- Associates of the European Union

Immediate future

Two versions of Europe seem possible for the coming decades. In the short term the iron curtain of the cold war will be replaced by a silver curtain dominated by the European Community plus the members from the "European Union". The associates of the European Union will be the poor relations. However, the divisions will never be straightforward. Already the collective fabric of Yugoslavia has been torn apart by internal conflict dispersing its ethnic population of Muslims, Serbs and Croats to neighbouring countries such as Hungary which had earlier opened its borders to East Germans prior to reunification. Czechoslovakia has voted to divide into Czech lands and Slovakia. Hungary, Romania and Bulgaria are countries that have economic burdens of their own without the additional flow of refugees.

THE EXTENDED EUROPE
- European Confederation
- Associate members of European Confederation

Superstate

An alternative direction for Europe to move towards 2020 is by the countries forming a European Confederation which would bring the old eastern European states together with the western countries. The newly independent republics of the former Soviet Union – Belarus, Moldova and Ukraine – would be hovering on the edge eventually joining the others.

International Relations, how countries and continents interact with each, are conducted against a historical backdrop. Europe's backdrop is one of conquest and colonies. Many major countries in Europe had an overseas empire or at least a far flung colony during the 17th, 18th and 19th centuries, and at the beginning of the first world war more than half the world was in colonial thrall to Europe. Today the European empire is limited to a few small islands and territories with a combined population no bigger than that of Belgium. But although the colonial ties are severed, trade relationships (usually the origin of the colonisation) remain, and many European countries maintain a reciprocal economic commitment to their former colonies.

This chapter assesses the impact of the European effect on the rest of the world; how withdrawal and independence affects the relationship with former colonies in Africa, Asia and Latin America. It also examines how Europe relates with the United States, a country that went to war to rid itself of its colonial rulers; how the relationship between Europe and the Far East has changed dramatically since the countries on the Pacific Rim have seized the economic initiative; and how Europe may rebuild a political and economic relationship with Russia.

THE EUROPEAN EFFECT

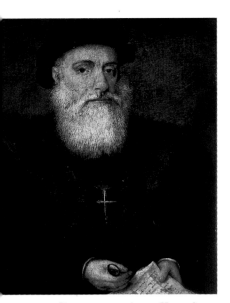

Portuguese navigator Vasco da Gama (1460–1524) discovered the Cape route to India in 1497 and established a Portuguese colony in Mozambique in 1502.

The people of Europe share a small living space bounded in the west by the Atlantic, in the north by the Arctic, in the east by the Urals and in the south, the Mediterranean. Crammed into this area, far smaller than the other continents, are some 800m people – one-sixth of the world's population. This concentration, however, does not mean uniformity: Europe's languages range from Basque and Celtic to Finnish and Greek; religious beliefs encompass Judaism, Christianity and Islam; ethnic identity can be traced to origins as diverse as Slav and Catalan. It is not surprising political and commercial friction has erupted into frequent, savage wars.

Yet what Europe has in common is at least as strong as its differences. Culturally, Europe is in essence Christian in one form or another. Politically, Europe is intrinsically democratic, and overwhelmingly so since the collapse of European and Soviet communism at the end of the 1980s. Socially, individual rights are usually valued above collective responsibilities.

Such is Europe's common heritage: it can be traced back 3,000 years to the civilisation of Athens and other Greek city states, to the rise of the Roman empire and to the dissemination through that empire of a Christianity moulded by the values of Greece and Rome.

The process was far from smooth. By the fifth century AD the Roman empire in Europe had been defeated by Germanic "barbarians"; Europe lapsed into the dark ages, in which it stayed until the renaissance began in the 14th century. But the simultaneous emergence of Europe's nation states meant centuries of warfare – not to mention political struggles within individual countries, such as the French revolution. With the reformation in the 16th century, in which Roman Catholic unity was destroyed by the new Protestantism, came a period of dynamism, enterprise, creativity and turmoil.

The impact on the rest of the world can hardly be overstated. The expeditions of explorers such as Magellan, Vasco da Gama, Columbus and Cook brought in their wake the overseas empires of Portugal, Belgium, Italy, the Netherlands, Spain, France, Germany and Britain. Europe's imperial reach spanned the globe: the possessions of tiny Portugal, for example, ranged from Brazil in South America, to Angola and Mozambique in Africa, and on to Macao on the eastern edge of Asia. By the end

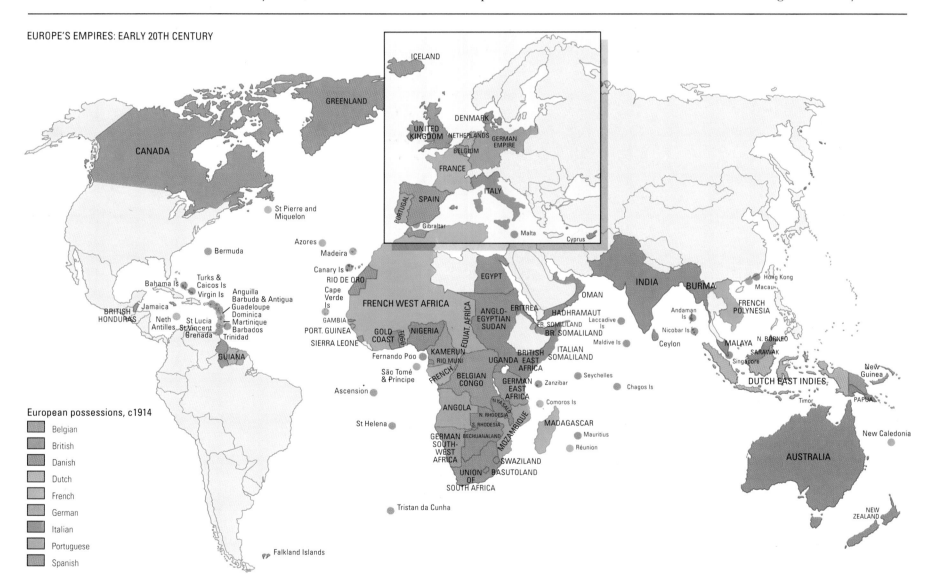

EUROPE'S EMPIRES: EARLY 20TH CENTURY

European possessions, c1914

- Belgian
- British
- Danish
- Dutch
- French
- German
- Italian
- Portuguese
- Spanish

The colonial summer

In the "long hot summer" before the first world war, European expansionism peaked, with almost half the world in colonial thrall to one small continent. Europe's conquest of the world relied more than anything on its mastery of the oceans. After Columbus's voyage of 1492, the seas were open to all maritime nations, and Europe turned its attention to the new world. The amazing overland expeditions from Italy to China of Marco Polo and his father in the 13th century brought no territorial acquisitions; by contrast, the sea voyages of Ferdinand Magellan and James Cook, brought their sponsors colonies around the globe.

The great European colonisers were all naval powers, able to project their military might against weaker opponents no matter what the distance involved. Not surprisingly, the stronger the imperial navy, the greater the empire. In the 15th century, Spain and Portugal dominated the seas. In the 16th and 17th centuries, the Dutch sailed farthest and fastest.

By the 19th century Britain could fairly claim to "rule the waves". At the end of the century, its possessions ran from Canada to Australia and New Zealand and embraced much of Africa and all of India on the way, provoking the saying that "the sun never set on the British empire". That empire's only significant loss was America, and that was to an independence movement, not a rival power.

Countries with relatively little maritime power, such as Belgium and Italy, concentrated their colonial effort in Africa, just a short voyage from Europe.

But maritime capability was not the sole criterion for colonial acquisitions. Europe's powers often found it easier to award each other distant territories through diplomatic bargaining, hence so many borders following straight lines on the maps of Africa, North America and New Guinea which bear no relation to geographical features and have been a source of great trouble to the people who live there.

of the 19th century Britain had an empire on which the sun never set. America's declaration of independence from Britain in 1776 could, in retrospect, be accepted with barely a qualm: Britain's commercial and military power made it the world's superpower, unchallenged from the Caribbean to Australasia.

Inevitably, Europe's military hold on the world loosened. The more extended an empire, the more prone it becomes to economic and political change. In the first half of the 20th century the European powers fought two debilitating world wars: by their end, the demise of colonialism was irresistible. Those few colonies that remain do so of their own volition.

Europe's military power was only one aspect of its colonialism. As important, and more enduring, has been the power of European ideas. Christianity, capitalism and communism are all the products of European thought. So, too, are nationalism, fascism and humanism. Of the "isms" that have shaped the modern world, almost all are European in origin. In the Arab world, for example, the concept of nationalism did not exist until the ideas of the French revolution were introduced to Egypt by a Napoleonic expedition in the late 18th century. Until then, the prevailing concept had been of a single Islamic entity ruled by the Prophet Muhammed's successor. In China, the hierarchic stagnation of Confucianism was abruptly ended by the shock of Marxism.

The power of the future

If history moves in cycles, a decline in Europe's influence must presumably follow a period of global ascendancy that has lasted for half the millenium. Communism, for example, is an idea which has clearly failed in practice, if not necessarily in theory. It no longer appeals in South-East Asia, East Africa or Latin America. Christianity has become the world's most prevalent religion but is losing ground to Islam. Japan's business practices are increasingly the most admired. Confucianism, once derided as a cause of Asia's backwardness, is now praised as essential to the success of Japanese and other Asian economies.

But the turn of the cycle is likely to be so slow as to be imperceptible for a number of reasons. First, Europeanism has sunk deep roots around the world; since the early 19th century some 60m Europeans have emigrated to settle, with their ideas, overseas. Second, America, the superpower of the late 20th century, is European in its intellectual inspiration and, for the most part, in its racial composition. Third, democracy, a quintessentially European concept, is seen as the companion of economic success, which implies that developing countries will adopt more democracy as they get richer. Fourth, Europe's putative rivals have barely emerged: Japan is an industrial and financial power that is yet to build political muscles (although it surely will); China, for all its weight of population and pride in its past, will remain a poor country for at least a generation. Meanwhile, the potential of Islam is dissipated in the fractricidal tensions of the Middle East.

The main reason, however, is that Europe's dynamism is reviving. In a sphere where size counts, the European Community is the world's biggest trading bloc. As the collapse of communism turns all of Europe capitalist, the bloc will become bigger still; the interactions of its people will generate tensions, certainly, but also ideas and opportunities. Europe will retain a concentration of economic, political, military and cultural resources that the rest of the world can only envy, not emulate.

EUROPE'S EMPIRE: LATE 20TH CENTURY

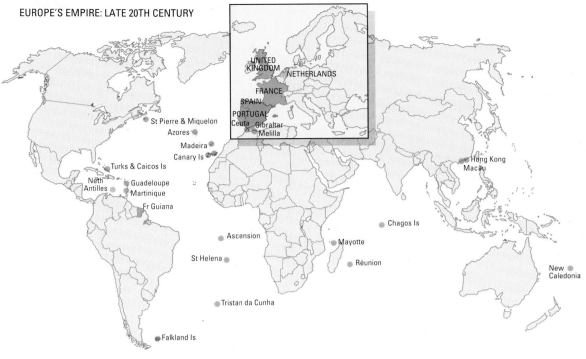

Imperial sunset

The first half of the 20th century saw the European powers exhausted by two world wars – and unable to resist the pressures for independence throughout their empires. In Asia, from British India across to Dutch Indonesia, Japan's initial success in the second world war had proved that the white colonial powers were no longer invulnerable. The process of decolonisation was at times bloody, as in France's Algeria or Britain's Kenya, but was virtually complete by the end of the 1960s. Now the world map is merely freckled with colonial remnants, mostly tiny islands which would not sustain independence.

Although the colonial links have now gone, strong economic ties remain – as do cultural and political ones, for example in the British Commonwealth or between France and its former colonies in Africa.

European possessions, 1992

	British
	Portuguese
	French
	Dutch
	Spanish

EUROPE'S EMPIRE: LATE 18TH CENTURY

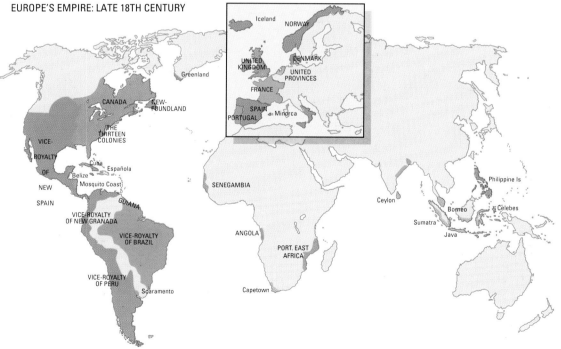

The gold rush

Europe's imperial reach stretched most obviously in the early 18th century to the Americas: the British and French controlled most of North America; the Spanish and Portuguese most of Central and South America. One reason for the colonial expansion was greed: Central and South America were supposedly El Dorados, full of gold and silver to be taken back to Europe. Another reason was the desire for freedom, the motive for shiploads of religious (and so political) dissidents to set sail for North America.

Meanwhile, Britain's interests in India were only just beginning, and were a century away from the formal incorporation of India into Queen Victoria's realm; North Africa was still part of the crumbling and corrupt Ottoman empire, and so untouched by France, Britain and Italy.

European possessions, c1790

	British
	Danish
	Dutch
	French
	Portuguese
	Spanish

EUROPE AND AMERICA

The new world of Canada, Mexico and the United States of America has long had a somewhat schizophrenic relationship with the old. Europe colonised the area from the 16th century, invariably at the expense of the indigenous American population, and the successive waves of immigrants to North America from Europe retained cultural ties with their ancestral homelands. The economic development of North America remained heavily dependent on European capital and technology until 1914. At the same time, each country decisively rejected colonial rule. Of the three, only the USA has had any significant effect on transatlantic relations; Canada and Mexico remain preoccupied by the need to preserve their autonomy from their large and powerful neighbour.

In the 19th century the American foreign policy of isolationism essentially meant avoiding European entanglements, although not the exercise of American power: the Philippines, Guam and Puerto Rico were wrested from Spain in the war of 1898, while the "open door" policy

The Amish sect eschews many modern ways, including motor vehicles. Many religious groups which fled persecution in Europe found freedom in America.

secured access to China. The USA saw itself as a suitable model (democratic, individualistic and unabashedly capitalist) for the Europeans to emulate. While European conflicts resonated in America (the anti-British stance of some German-Americans in the first world war, for example), Europe's influence was primarily cultural and economic; soon this was reciprocated, as American mass-production methods spread.

Boom and crash

Unlike Europe, America's industry was unscathed by the first world war (which the USA entered in 1917, after three years of neutrality) and the USA benefited from European repayments of war loans. The resulting boom of the 1920s ended with the Wall Street crash of 1929 and a world-wide recession aggravated by shrinking trade and beggar-my-neighbour protectionism in which America played a leading role. The failure of the USA to join the League of Nations was an important factor in the league's failure to preserve the post-war order.

New Canadians

As the chart shows, Canadian immigration has shifted from Europe to Asia.

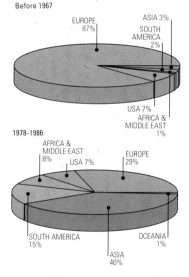

THE NORTH AMERICAN CRUCIBLE

From the moment of its discovery, the new world offered the masses of Europe a better, richer life. With the exception of some persecuted minorities, such as the Jews and Armenians, immigrants came to the Americas seeking economic advancement rather than political freedom – first gold, later land and, in the 20th century, jobs.

In addition to these economic opportunities, immigrants were responding to the push of economic deprivation in their home countries. Consequently, the sources of immigration changed dramatically over time, starting with north-west Europe in the early 19th century and shifting to south-east Europe a century later. In the 1990s, most immigrants come from the developing world.

This century the numbers and flow of immigrants have been controlled by the North Americans themselves. For many years an open preference for northern Europeans was reflected in both US and Canadian legislation. In the 1960s more liberal

laws allowed more immigrants from the developing world: currently the fastest growing minority in both the USA and Canada comes from Asia, while for the USA the largest group of migrants are the Hispanics from Central and South America.

From the beginning the USA regarded itself as a melting-pot, but by 1920 it was clear that not all groups were readily assimilated. From 1960 onward, ethnic background was acknowledged to be an important influence on political and social attitudes and behaviour. The USA is today a multi-cultural society, albeit dominated by an elite of European origin. But Mexico was indeed a melting-pot, with over 60% of its population of mixed (mestizo) origin. Canada, until recently, had a very homogeneous population from Britain and France.

In the USA, weakening ties with Europe are reflected in changing patterns of settlement. The centre of population is moving to the south and west, away from the north-east with its historic links to Europe. As the century draws to a close, Americans are looking increasingly toward the Pacific rim.

Canada today

The 1986 Canadian census revealed a nation predominantly of French and British origin (below), which is reflected by the country's two official languages – French and English. Even so, the Canadian population continues to be drawn from a wider variety of peoples than ever before.

ETHNIC GROUPS IN CANADA

1 inc. USSR
2 inc. Israel and Turkey

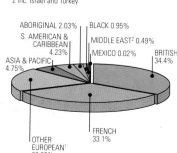

US immigration by origin

As the number of immigrants from developed countries declines, immigration from the developing world has risen with the change in legislation. This has caused social and economic strain in America.

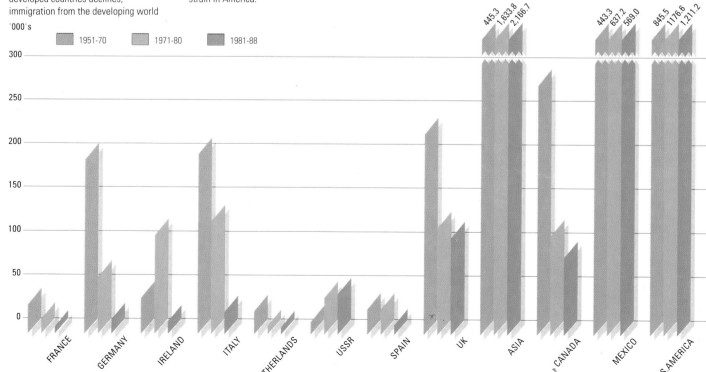

Connections: Trade 48–49 The European Community 130–131 Labour and immigration 138–139 The birth of nations 176–177

The rise of fascism and Nazism in Europe in the depression years seemed to some American policy-makers to be the unintended consequence of American isolationism and protectionism. Although the United States did not declare war on Germany in 1939, it did provide Britain with increasing material assistance; when the USA finally entered the war in December 1941 after the Japanese bombed Pearl Harbor, it was on a much larger scale than in 1917. The USA also played a prime role in devising the international political and economic institutions that established the postwar order: the United Nations, the International Monetary Fund and the World Bank.

Although the USA agreed with the Soviet Union and Britain about the postwar territorial settlement in Europe, mutual suspicion and hostility between the two superpowers over the fate of Germany and Europe led to increasingly frigid relations. Instead of retreating into isolation, from 1947 America chose active involvement in Europe with the intention of containing the seemingly inevitable westward march of communism. The Truman doctrine offered an American security umbrella and the Marshall Plan economic assistance for European reconstruction. The policy of containment of the Soviet Union was vigorously supported at home by ethnic minorities from the "captive nations" under Soviet rule, and underpinned by the deep anti-communism of American domestic politics.

Support for Europe

The North Atlantic Treaty Organisation (NATO), underwritten by the huge American commitment to the defence of western Europe, brought over 40 years of peace to Europe after its creation in 1949. America also strongly supported integration in Europe, beginning with the European Coal and Steel Community in 1951, because it believed that a stable and prosperous western Europe would be a bulwark against communism and a market for American corporations. Indeed, many Americans hoped economic integration in Europe would be followed by political integration on federal lines – the

ultimate vindication of the US experience.

American hopes that a more integrated Europe would be a more constructive partner were largely unfulfilled. The reduction in cold war tensions in the 1960s made western Europe feel more secure, while America's involvement in the war in Vietnam heightened Europe's desire for greater autonomy and influence. Even the enlargement of the European Community (from six to nine and later to twelve members) did not produce a united Europe willing or able to replace the USA as guarantor of European security – a role made increasingly burdensome by America's relative economic decline.

American-European relations remained uneasy throughout the 1970s, despite Britain's accession to the European Community in 1973, which was welcomed by the USA. Americans were frustrated by the EC's common agricultural policy, which they claimed unfairly restricted their own exports, and by the unwillingness of the European members of NATO to pay a greater share of the defence burden borne by American taxpayers. For its ▷

The new kids on the block... these Los Angeles schoolboys reflect the pattern of US immigration. Most migrants are of Hispanic origin and the fastest-growing minority comes from Asia.

DOWN MEXICO WAY

From the far side of the Atlantic, Europeans have for too long regarded Mexico as the USA's poor relation. Reports of the thousands of illegal immigrants – "wetbacks " – crossing the so-called "tortilla curtain" each year to seek work in the USA and the fact that 25% of the US army is deployed in an attempt to control the drug running which is rife along the 2,500km border do nothing to dispel this impression. However, Mexico is now a nation of more than 80m people, a full member of GATT, an aspiring member of the OECD and a major oil producer. It is also enthusiastic about a North American Free Trade Agreement with the USA and Canada.

Growth had been relatively sustained until the economic rollercoaster of the 1980s. To tackle the uneven distribution of wealth and resulting poverty, governments embarked on a period of high expenditure which coincided with international recessions. Rising exports did not avert difficulties and there was massive capital flight. In the 1980s there was negligible growth and high inflation. At the end of 1987, prices, wages and exchange rates were frozen. Inflation went from 159% that year to 52% in 1988. Retrenchment paid off and the aims of the national development plan announced in 1989 – of inflation level with that of its main trading partners and an annual GDP growth rate of 6% by 1994 – seem to be within reach.

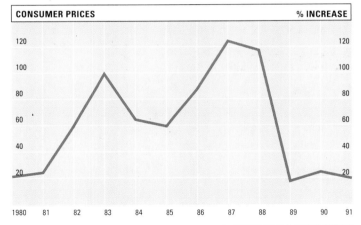

CONSUMER PRICES | % INCREASE

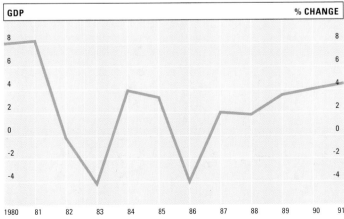

GDP | % CHANGE

Mexican melting-pot

The overwhelming mestizo – Indian-Spanish – character of Mexico's people reflects the Spanish conquest in the 1520s and the subsequent 300 years of Spanish rule. Mexico, with its great mineral wealth, was an important part of the Spanish colonial empire. In the 1990s, nearly 97% of Mexicans still regard themselves as Roman Catholics and 92% of the population speak Spanish, the country's official language.

Mexico dates its independence from 1810. It then included what are now the US states of California, New Mexico, Utah, Nevada, Arizona and part of Colorado. These were ceded to the USA in 1848 for $15m and the cancellation of $3.25m debt. (Texas had already declared independence from Mexico.) Even so, the Spanish-Mexican heritage is still felt strongly in these areas.

PEOPLES OF MEXICO

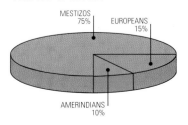

MESTIZOS 75% | EUROPEANS 15%
AMERINDIANS 10%

part, Europe felt marginalised as America negotiated directly with the Soviet Union on arms control and was more occupied with Pacific affairs, notably the growing economic power of Japan.

The European Community's 1985 initiative to create a single market by the end of 1992 was welcomed by the United States. American concern that the single market would be protected from outside competition subsided and was replaced by a preoccupation with the collapse of communism in eastern Europe and the Soviet Union from 1989, and the unification of Germany in 1990. The disintegration of the USSR and the intention of the EC to create an economic and monetary union by the end of the decade can be seen as a fulfilment of long-standing American policy objectives. They also signal the start of a new era in transatlantic relations in which America has to come to terms with a newly confident and assertive European Community flanked to the east by a region of economic deprivation and political unrest.

AMERICA'S MARKETPLACE

European capital played a major role in the economic development of the USA, Canada and Mexico, but it is only since 1945 that mutual trade and investment has become of major significance for both Europe and North America. It is very much a mutual interest, making it unlikely that either the European or North American trading groups will seek to disrupt trade across the Atlantic. Over one-quarter of the EC's external trade is with the USA (Canada and Mexico are less important as trade partners for Europe as two-thirds of their total trade is with the USA); for the USA, Europe as a whole is a slightly more important trade partner than Canada.

While the United States and Canada have complained about the agricultural protectionism of the EC, American exporters have been much more successful in selling to Europe than to Japan – perhaps because an increasing proportion (currently about one-third) of American merchandise exports go to overseas affiliates of US companies, which are much more numerous in Europe than they are in Japan.

Although Europe had long been host to American firms as they expanded overseas, the biggest wave of American multinationals came in the 1950s and 1960s, provoking fears in Europe of Americanisation and increasing technological dependence. These fears have subsided as Japan has increasingly been seen on both sides of the Atlantic as the most formidable competitor.

Western Europe (and especially the UK) has become the main location for US direct investment abroad; similarly, western European investment in the USA far surpasses that from Japan or any other source. McDonald's may be spreading throughout Europe, but Burger King is British-owned. Such concerns about ownership may be outdated, however, as both marketing and production have become global in many industries; certainly American firms in Europe (such as Ford and IBM) were among the first to engage in pan-European production and marketing.

Investment in the USA

The chart measures investment for the years shown in $m.

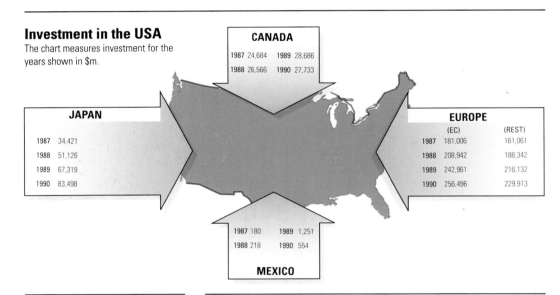

CANADA

1987	24,684	1989	28,686
1988	26,566	1990	27,733

JAPAN

1987	34,421
1988	51,126
1989	67,319
1990	83,498

EUROPE

	(EC)	(REST)
1987	181,006	161,061
1988	208,942	188,342
1989	242,961	216,132
1990	256,496	229,913

MEXICO

1987	180	1989	1,251
1988	218	1990	554

US imports and exports

The chart below shows American trade with eight major partners for the years 1986 and 1990. Compared with business done with Canada and Japan, the volume of trade with the three major European countries is relatively small, although quantities of imports and exports are fairly even. Trade with neighbouring Canada and Mexico has the advantage of cheaper transport costs.

The USA has consistently imported far more from Japan than it exports although this gap has closed slightly in recent years.

US EXPORTS
- 1986
- 1990

US IMPORTS
- 1986
- 1990

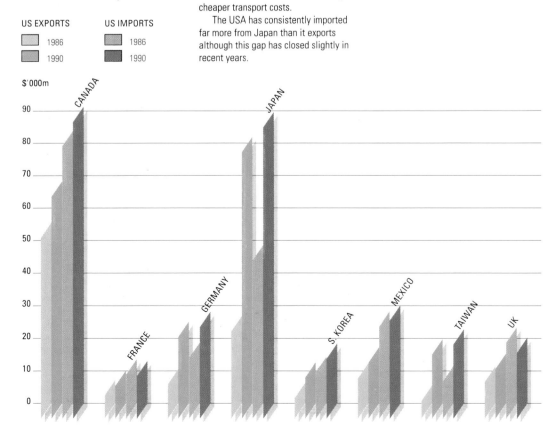

Bitten by the Big Mac

Not all services are internationally traded but where they are, such as the fast-food industry, America is unbeaten.

Indeed, so successful has McDonald's been that the Union Bank of Switzerland used the McDonald's burger to compare earnings around the world. The bank used a weighted average of earnings in 12 jobs to find how long it takes the average worker to earn the price of a Big Mac and large French fries. By this measure, the best-paid workers are in Chicago where it takes only 18 minutes to earn a Big Mac. In London, Paris and Copenhagen it takes about 35 minutes, in Mexico City nearly four hours.

The Economist's own Big Mac index is a ready reckoner to whether currencies are at their "correct" exchange rate. The index is based on the theory of purchasing-power parity (PPP), which argues that in the long run the exchange rate between two currencies should equate the prices of an identical basket of goods and services in the respective counties. *The Economist*'s "basket" is McDonald's Big Mac hamburger, made locally to a rigorous standard in more than 50 countries. Its local prices are less likely to be distorted by international transport and distribution costs than, say, the price of *The Economist* in different countries. Early in 1992 the index showed that the dollar was undervalued against most currencies.

In 1990, 44% of McDonald's sales outside the USA were in Europe, and the chart below shows the year the company opened in each country and the number of outlets it had in each of them in 1991.

MCDONALD'S GROWTH IN EUROPE

COUNTRY	YEAR[1]	No.[2]
NETHERLANDS	1971	67
GERMANY	1971	364
SWEDEN	1973	55
UK	1974	413
SWITZERLAND	1976	21
IRELAND	1977	13
AUSTRIA	1977	29
BELGIUM	1978	12
FRANCE	1979	182
SPAIN	1981	39
DENMARK	1981	16
NORWAY	1983	8
ANDORRA	1984	1
FINLAND	1984	9
LUXEMBOURG	1985	2
ITALY	1985	1
TURKEY	1986	9
YUGOSLAVIA	1988	4
HUNGARY	1988	4
RUSSIA	1990	1
PORTUGAL	1991	2
GREECE	1991	1

1 Year of opening   2 Outlets 1991

THE USA'S ROLE IN POSTWAR EUROPE

Britain was the only European state to play an influential (though not decisive) role in the meetings with the USA and USSR that shaped the postwar order. After Germany's defeat and occupation in 1945, Europe's future was effectively determined by the interplay of increasingly acrimonious relations between the USA and the USSR.

The Yalta agreement effectively divided Europe into Soviet and Anglo-American zones of influence, and the desire of the USSR to create a buffer zone in eastern Europe under its control became evident. The USA, alarmed by the possibility of Soviet dominance in Europe, resolved to contain the westward expansion of communism: from 1947 it guaranteed the security of the western European states and provided aid for the reconstruction of their war-shattered economies.

This support included encouragement for the Europeans to act collectively; the United States hoped that integration in Europe would enable its allies to bear a greater share of the cost of their defence. Europe, conscious that it was the playing field for the rivalry of the two superpowers, had a great incentive to increase its power and influence through political cooperation and experiments in economic integration, notably the European Economic Community (1958). The Berlin wall (built 1961) symbolised the division of Europe into two camps; it seemed that the US-Soviet negotiations on limiting the arms race were intended to preserve their own dominant positions rather than to reduce the level of armaments.

Nonetheless, Europe's role was gradually enhanced by the relative economic decline of the USA (as western European and Japanese industry began to grow) and the economic stagnation of the USSR (crippled by enormous military expenditure). Integration in western Europe was paralleled by the disintegration of the Soviet sphere of influence in the East, culminating in the reunification of Germany, the collapse of communist regimes in eastern Europe and, ultimately, the disappearance of the Soviet Union itself.

NATO's most powerful member is the USA but the organisation is based in Brussels (above).

Agenda for change

1 Bretton Woods conference (July 1st–22nd 1944). The USA and Britain (plus 42 countries) established the framework of the postwar international economy, with the USA as keystone in the establishment of a system of fixed exchange rates tied to the dollar (the International Monetary Fund, 1945), the reduction of trade barriers (General Agreement on Tariffs and Trade, 1947), and promotion of economic reconstruction and development (the World Bank, 1945).

2 Yalta agreement (February 4th–11th 1945). The USA, USSR, and UK agreement on postwar policies: a four-power partition and occupation of Germany, territorial gains for the USSR in Poland, with Poland compensated by territory from eastern Germany (confirmed at Potsdam, July 1945). Also agreement on great power veto rights in the UN Security Council for permanent members: USA, USSR, UK, France and China.

3 Truman Doctrine and Marshall Plan (Washington, March 12th 1947 and Cambridge, Massachusetts, June 5th 1947). Prompted by upheavals in Greece and Turkey, the USA promised to defend any country facing external threats or internal subversion, and also to give economic assistance to the European states if they developed joint proposals for economic reconstruction (the USSR did not participate). The USA provided $12bn of aid to Europe 1947–51.

4 The Organisation for European Economic Cooperation (Paris, April 16th 1948). Sixteen European countries joined together to coordinate national programmes for economic recovery financed by the Marshall Plan. They were joined (October 1949) by West Germany. The OEEC became the OECD (Organisation for Economic Cooperation and Development) on December 14th 1960, when the USA and Canada joined; Japan became a member in 1964.

5 Berlin blockade (June 1948–May 1949). Soon after the communist takeover in Czechoslovakia, the Soviet Union blocked road access to the western allies' occupation zones in West Berlin. The UK and USA responded with a prolonged and massive airlift of essential supplies until the USSR lifted the blockade, but Berlin remained divided

and on August 13th 1961 the Berlin wall was built.

6 North Atlantic Treaty (Washington, April 5th 1949). Collective security agreement designed to deter Soviet aggression, initiated by the USA, with the members of the Brussels Treaty Organisation (formed in March 1948 by the UK, France and Benelux becoming the West European Union in 1954 with West German rearmament) and Canada, Norway, Denmark, Iceland, Italy and Portugal. (Greece and Turkey joined 1952; West Germany 1954; Spain 1982.)

7 Council of Europe (London, May 5th 1949). An intergovernmental organisation and the first European attempt to promote political cooperation, including an assembly of national parliamentarians. Original members: Belgium, Denmark, France, Ireland, Italy, Luxembourg, Netherlands, Norway, Sweden and the UK. Its most significant achievement has been the European Convention for the Protection of Human Rights, November 4th 1950.

8 European Coal and Steel Community Treaty (Paris, April 18th 1951). Following French Foreign Minister Robert Schuman's Declaration of May 9th 1950, six states (France, West Germany, Italy and Benelux; the UK refused the invitation) formed the ECSC, designed to promote a common market in coal and steel under the guidance of a supranational High Authority. This was to be the first step in European integration.

9 The European Economic Community and European Atomic Energy Community (Rome, March 25th 1957). The Suez crisis and the Soviet crushing of the Hungarian revolution in October–November 1956 gave the six members of the ECSC new incentives to further economic integration. The UK initially declined to join the Common Market, joining in 1973 with Denmark and Ireland (Greece 1981; Spain and Portugal 1986).

10 European Free Trade Association (Stockholm, January 4th 1960). A British-inspired attempt to promote trade without disturbing each member's existing trade arrangements with third countries and without the supranational ambitions of the EEC. Initially seven member-states (founder members: the UK, Ireland and Denmark – which all left to join the EEC in 1973 – and Austria, Norway, Portugal and Switzerland; Iceland, Finland joined later). In 1990 EFTA agreed with the European Community on creating a European Economic Area.

11 Cuban missile crisis (Washington and Moscow, October 22nd–November 2nd 1962). The nearest the superpowers ever got to a nuclear war, with Europe marginalised during negotiations. After a US naval blockade, the USSR agreed to withdraw nuclear missiles it had covertly installed in Cuba. Shortly afterward (December 12th 1962) at Nassau, the USA agreed to supply Polaris missiles to

the UK and in January 1963 French President de Gaulle vetoed the UK application to join the EEC.

12 Limited Nuclear Test Ban Treaty (Moscow, August 5th 1963). The USA, USSR and the UK agreed to ban all but underground nuclear weapons tests; France and China refused to sign. This first attempt to limit the nuclear arms race was followed on July 1st 1968 by the Treaty on the Non-Proliferation of Nuclear Weapons, in which the superpowers attempted with limited success to persuade other states to forgo possession of nuclear weapons.

13 Soviet invasion of Czechoslovakia (Prague, August 1968). The "Prague spring" of economic and political liberalisation under Alexander Dubcek was crushed by Warsaw pact forces acting under the Brezhnev doctrine to "preserve the integrity of the socialist commonwealth"; NATO members protested, but did not intervene, with USA increasingly preoccupied by its military involvement in Vietnam.

14 Salt I Treaty (Moscow, May 26th 1972). After negotiations which had begun in 1969, the USA and USSR set future levels of intercontinental ballistic missiles numbers and in an associated agreement limited each power to two anti-ballistic missile defence (ABM) systems each. Further agreements (including a Salt II treaty, never ratified by the USA) led in December 1987 to a treaty limiting the superpowers'

intermediate nuclear weapons.

15 Treaty of Accession to the European Communities (Brussels January 22nd 1972) was signed by the UK, Denmark, Ireland and Norway, (which subsequently rejected membership in a referendum). After more than a decade of attempting to join (and being blocked by France as a suspected Trojan horse for American influence), the UK finally joined the EEC in January 1973.

16 Berlin wall falls (Berlin, November 9th 1989). Following free elections in Poland and the ending of communist rule in Hungary (soon to be repeated in Czechoslovakia), the Soviet Union withdrew support from the East German regime. President Honecker was forced to resign and within days the borders with the West were opened and the Berlin wall, supreme symbol of the cold war, came down. On October 3rd 1990 Germany was reunified.

17 Conference on Security and Cooperation in Europe (Paris, November 19th–21st 1990). The CSCE had first met in Helsinki in 1973–75, producing an accord that declared the frontiers of the signatory states inviolable. The Paris meeting, attended by the USA, Canada and all European countries except Albania, produced a Charter for a New Europe, declaring "a new era of democracy, peace and unity" and an end to "the era of confrontation and division in Europe".

18 Treaty on Conventional Armed Forces in Europe (Paris, November 19th 1990). Although Presidents Bush and Gorbachev, with their respective allies in NATO and the Warsaw pact, signed the CFE treaty in Paris in November 1990 to limit troop deployments in Europe, a US–Soviet meeting in Lisbon (June 1991) was needed to settle disagreements on the classification of some Soviet forces that had prevented the treaty from coming into force. In July 1991 the Warsaw pact was dissolved.

19 Maastricht Agreement of the Council of the European Community (Maastricht, December 11th 1991). The leaders of the 12 member-countries of the European Community previously committed themselves to an economic union with a single currency for eligible states by 1999. Britain secured various opt-out provisions. The Danes threw the future of the agreement into doubt by voting against it in a referendum.

EUROPE AND LATIN AMERICA

Day-o...Caribbean banana growers are worried about the deregulation of the European banana market and increased competition from Latin America. They are looking to the EC for a new ruling.

In a few decades five centuries ago, long before English-speakers settled in North America, Catholic adventurers from Spain and Portugal imposed their will on the southern two-thirds of the American continent. All South American nations – except Peru and Argentina, whose presidents are of Japanese and of Syrian origin – are still ruled by people who look as though they had just arrived from Europe. Yet a large majority of South Americans are wholly or partly descended from people who lived there before Columbus.

The Iberian settlers defended their racial and cultural dominance, but failed to match North America's economic triumphs, or its military strength. In the 1820s, as Spain packed up its empire, the United States declared its hegemony over the Americas and warned the European powers off. Throughout the Americas it was European, mostly British, capital that in the 19th century developed the mines, oilfields, railways, farms and cities. But to settle the debts of two world wars, most of those assets (notably in Mexico, Argentina and Brazil) were eventually sold to North American interests.

New investment from the East

North America still dominates the lands to its south. But at the start of the 1990s the United States, with its yawning government debt, was no longer a big exporter of capital. Western Europe, though, was seeking opportunities for trade and investment abroad; European firms moved back into Latin America. East Asian businesses too, seeking raw materials and future customers, were looking across to the opposite shores of the Pacific.

Japanese, Taiwanese and Korean firms sought new footholds in the Americas.

The opportunities are great, and competition between western Europeans and East Asians is intense. The Europeans have the great advantage of historical and ethnic links to Latin America; millions of settlers from Italy, as well as from Spain and Portugal, have made their homes there and Britain retains old friendships.

Spain and Portugal had set a hopeful example. For decades those countries, like most of Latin America, had been kept needlessly poor by inward-looking nationalist rulers. In the mid-1970s they put that behind them, becoming democracies and members of the European Community. In the 1980s Latin America, too, turned democratic and opened its frontiers to freer trade.

The new governments began reducing the economic as well as the political power of the state, selling off public monopolies to private buyers and encouraging foreign investors. European businesses, with Spain to the fore, are mobilising capital on European markets to develop Latin America's mineral resources, communications, and services such as banking and insurance.

If all goes well, Latin America and Europe will rediscover old bonds in a new economic and cultural partnership. The stakes are high. Brazil, for all its problems, is the world's tenth industrial power. Mexico, in a free-trade area with the USA and Canada, is determined to achieve growth and modernisation. Venezuela, Colombia and Argentina have immense potential riches of minerals, farms and people. With their old European friends, they seem set to claim their full share of the world's affairs.

LATIN AMERICAN GOVERNMENTS

- Unelected governments, 1990
- Elected governments, 1970-90
- Previous regime military
- **1964** Democracy extinguished
- **1985** Democracy revived

Latest election
- ☐ Genuine
- ☒ Dubious

Path to democracy

Between 1970 and 1990 every nation in Latin America lived for a time under authoritarian rule, bar Colombia, Costa Rica, Venezuela and Belize. Then came a democratic revolution and by 1991 the only rulers in the entire Americas with no claim at all to democratic legitimacy were those of Cuba, Haiti and Surinam.

Over the new democracies hang vast debts, run up in the 1970s. Much was invested in ill-conceived projects, much was stolen. Governments striving to pay it back must hold down incomes, while raising the prices; political progress coexists with popular discontent.

Free trade agreements

The largest and richest of the proposed American free trade areas embraces Canada, the USA and Mexico. The five countries south of Mexico (Guatemala, Honduras, El Salvador, Nicaragua, Costa Rica) aim to revive the Central American Free Trade Area, which has languished since the 1960s; they now hope to include Panama, and have founded a regional parliament, modelled on the European one, to bring their citizens closer. Caricom, which organises cooperation among the English-speaking countries of the Caribbean, is reactivating its free trade aspirations, and looking outwards towards its bigger neighbours. The five-nation Andean pact (Venezuela, Colombia, Ecuador, Bolivia and Peru) plans to reduce tariffs and barriers to trade among members and the outside world. Brazil has signed a treaty with Paraguay, Uruguay and Argentina to form Mercosur, the Southern Market, aiming at internal free trade by 1996. Chile, the most successful economy in South America, already has low tariffs and few restrictions.

LATIN AMERICAN–EC TRADE

COUNTRY	1980		1984		1986		1988	
ARGENTINA	27.6	25.9	27.7	24.6	29.0	29.1	30.5	27.5
BOLIVIA	21.4	12.4	15.4	14.9	17.7	19.9	18.4	12.5
BRAZIL	27.2	15.4	25.2	12.6	26.2	22.2	27.7	21.6
CHILE	36.8	15.2	31.1	18.0	34.1	21.5	36.1	19.5
COLOMBIA	33.1	17.3	37.5	18.2	39.7	22.8	23.8	20.5
COSTA RICA	23.2	11.1	25.9	14.2	28.9	27.5	25.8	22.5
CUBA[1]	31.5	40.8	29.9	31.9	29.5	27.8	28.7	31.2
DOMINICAN REP	8.4	8.8	11.1	9.2	13.4	11.5	8.9	9.4
ECUADOR	7.6	18.2	3.5	18.1	7.8	23.1	9.2	20.8
EL SALVADOR	28.8	10.0	25.8	10.2	28.1	11.3	27.1	10.0
GUATEMALA	24.1	12.5	10.8	11.8	16.4	19.3	19.8	17.7
HAITI	23.3	9.5	12.7	8.7	17.4	11.7	10.7	12.3
HONDURAS	18.0	10.5	17.6	14.4	22.8	12.7	23.9	10.5
NICARAGUA	19.7	6.6	25.7	17.6	43.0	35.5	32.1	29.4
PANAMA	12.9	6.4	17.0	8.0	14.3	9.0	21.1	10.67
PARAGUAY	25.3	16.1	40.1	15.0	20.5	17.0	30.6	20.0
PERU	16.6	21.7	19.4	18.7	24.9	21.1	29.6	21.8
URUGUAY	30.1	17.9	20.7	17.4	25.9	19.8	26.2	20.9
VENEZUELA	12.6	20.6	16.0	23.0	15.7	26.9	11.1	26.6

1 Excludes trade with COMECON ☐ EC ☐ South America

Banana republics

The European Community has maintained special trading relations with the twelve Caribbean states in the Lomé Convention, in an attempt to compensate for no longer buying its sugar. However, the European banana market is due to be deregulated in 1993 and Caribbean states are anxious that their prices are not undercut by South American exporters. Indeed, the economies of several are almost entirely dependent on banana production.

Farmers, with small plots and paying higher wages, cannot compete with the large plantations and low labour costs of Latin American producers. Negotiations continue between the Latin American growers and their Caribbean counterparts as well as between the governments of the region and the EC.

ANTIGUA	'000 ecu
1982	0
1983	2,729
1984	1,189
1985	2,335
1986	3,689

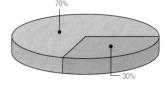

BAHAMAS	'000 ecu
1982	403,289
1983	191,347
1984	172,276
1985	290,818
1986	89,853

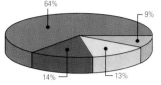

BARBADOS	'000 ecu
1982	30,933
1983	24,382
1984	41,779
1985	27,137
1986	20,228

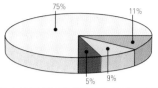

BELIZE	'000 ecu
1982	29,765
1983	24,924
1984	34,833
1985	28,965
1986	30,977

DOMINICA	'000 ecu
1982	21,113
1983	21,523
1984	26,234
1985	31,962
1986	40,939

GRENADA	'000 ecu
1982	11,995
1983	13,454
1984	13,551
1985	16,714
1986	17,839

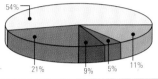

GUYANA	'000 ecu
1982	134,937
1983	114,779
1984	152,664
1985	108,962
1986	138,614

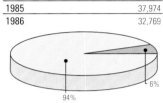

JAMAICA	'000 ecu
1982	178,193
1983	177,814
1984	164,077
1985	187,752
1986	181,470

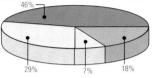

PRINCIPAL EXPORT PRODUCTS

- Electrical
- Refined petroleum
- Rum
- Chemicals
- Sugar
- Machinery
- Bananas
- Nutmeg
- Cocoa
- Bauxite
- Alumina
- Aluminium
- Rice
- Oil products
- Liquid ammonia
- Other

ST LUCIA	'000 ecu
1982	27,855
1983	35,214
1984	49,437
1985	75,174
1986	89,493

ST VINCENT	'000 ecu
1982	19,416
1983	24,016
1984	24,754
1985	37,974
1986	32,769

SURINAM	'000 ecu
1982	180,212
1983	216,647
1984	160,206
1985	196,691
1986	163,012

TRINIDAD	'000 ecu
1982	476,374
1983	304,298
1984	392,213
1985	392,838
1986	276,895

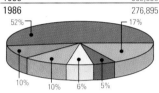

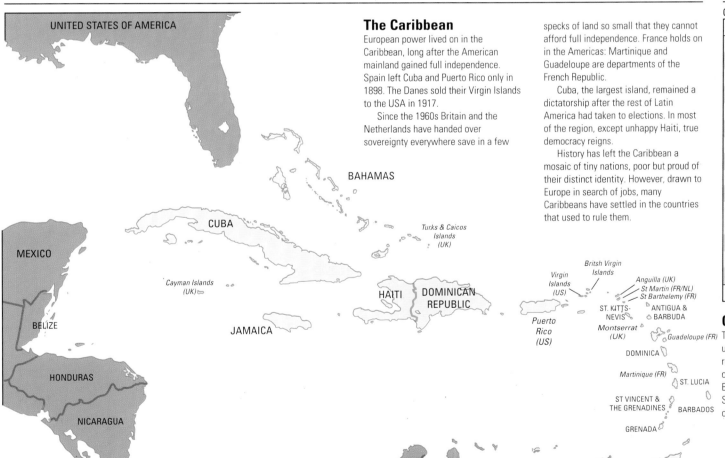

The Caribbean

European power lived on in the Caribbean, long after the American mainland gained full independence. Spain left Cuba and Puerto Rico only in 1898. The Danes sold their Virgin Islands to the USA in 1917.

Since the 1960s Britain and the Netherlands have handed over sovereignty everywhere save in a few specks of land so small that they cannot afford full independence. France holds on in the Americas: Martinique and Guadeloupe are departments of the French Republic.

Cuba, the largest island, remained a dictatorship after the rest of Latin America had taken to elections. In most of the region, except unhappy Haiti, true democracy reigns.

History has left the Caribbean a mosaic of tiny nations, poor but proud of their distinct identity. However, drawn to Europe in search of jobs, many Caribbeans have settled in the countries that used to rule them.

GDP PER CAPITA

COUNTRY	$
BAHAMAS	10,314[1]
BARBADOS	6,683
JAMAICA	1,643
TRINIDAD & TOBAGO	4,127
ANTIGUA	4,985
DOMINICA	2,050
GRENADA	2,017
MONTSERRAT	4,630[1]
St KITTS & NEVIS	3,560
St LUCIA	2,415
St VINCENT & THE GRENADINES	1,620
BRITISH VIRGIN ISLES	11,308
CAYMAN ISLES	26,561
TURKS & CAICOS ISLES	5,756[1]

1 1989 figures

Caricom

This association which aims to promote unity and economic integration in the region has 13 members and three observers. On the mainland, formerly British Guyana is a member and Dutch Surinam (formerly Dutch Guiana) has observer status.

EUROPE AND RUSSIA

The red flag with its hammer and sickle was lowered for the last time in 1991 and it is the Russian colours that fly over the Kremlin.

The potential for Russia to dominate Europe was recognised in the 19th century. It was backward in industrial and political terms but its large population, sheer size and harsh winters made it hard to conquer. Once it developed as a modern state it could expect a commanding position. Early industrialisation, assisted by West European management, was well under way by the 1917 revolution. In 1922, the USSR (Union of Soviet Socialist Republics) was formally established, with the Russian Soviet Federated Socialist Republics dominating the other 14 republics, in spite of theoretical equal status.

As one of the prototype totalitarian states, the Soviet Union was able to mobilise all available resources for a major programme of modernisation. The setbacks of Stalinist economics in the 1930s were forgotten in 1945; its leader, Josef Stalin, was one of the "big three" who had presided over the defeat of Nazi Germany and had used his position to extend the Soviet system into the liberated states of eastern Europe. Within western Europe there were substantial communist parties, often drawing on the prestige derived from resistance against the Nazis and support for a progressive ideology to replace capitalism, which was widely judged to have proved itself inadequate in the 1930s.

This internal challenge, directed from Moscow, was seen by western Europeans in a time of postwar economic dislocation to represent the major threat to their security. It led to the Marshall Plan for the economic reconstruction of Europe which was important not only in its direct effects but in demonstrating an American commitment to the containment of Soviet influence.

Soon Europe was divided between East and West with a line drawn through Germany. As the internal threat subsided with economic recovery, the growing military power of the Soviet Union became more salient. The logical counter was seen in the superior nuclear strength of the United States; however, in 1949 Moscow detonated its first atomic device and by 1957 it even appeared to be stealing a lead when it launched the first artificial earth satellite, so demonstrating mastery of long-range missile technology. At the same time Moscow had the advantage of its manpower plus an alliance (the Warsaw pact) which

Peoples of the republics

The ethnic mix of the former Soviet Union is extraordinarily complex, with more than 100 distinct groups. There are substantial Russian minorities in all the old republics. At the end of 1991, several republics altered their names slightly; and it is almost certain that others will in the future. It will be some time before the cartographic and political confusion of the region is clarified.

Abkhazan | Chuvash | Jewish | Latvian | Russian | Uzbek
Armenian | Estonian | Kara-kalpak | Lithuanian | Tadzhik | Other
Azerbaijan | Finnish | Kazakh | Moldavian | Tartar
Belarussian | gagua | Kirgizian | Ossetian | Turkmen
Bulgarian | Georgian | Kurdish | Polish | Ukrainian

ARMENIA
AREA sq km: 29,800
POPULATION m: 3.3
1st LANGUAGE: Armenian

ARMENIAN 93.3%
OTHER 3.5%
RUSSIAN 1.5%
KURDISH 1.7%

AZERBAIJAN
AREA sq km: 86,600
POPULATION m: 7.2
1st LANGUAGE: Azeri

AZERBAIJANI 78.1%
OTHER 6.1%
ARMENIAN 7.9%
RUSSIAN 7.9%

BELARUS
AREA sq km: 207,600
POPULATION m: 10.4
1st LANGUAGE: Belarussian

BELARUSSIAN 79.4%
OTHER 0.7%
JEWISH 1.4%
POLISH 4.2%
UKRAINIAN 2.4%
RUSSIAN 11.9%

ESTONIA
AREA sq km: 45,000
POPULATION m: 1.6
1st LANGUAGE: Estonian

ESTONIAN 61.5%
FINNISH 1.1%
BELARUSSIAN 1.8%
UKRAINIAN 3.1%
OTHER 2.2%
RUSSIAN 30.3%

GEORGIA
AREA sq km: 69,700
POPULATION m: 5.5
1st LANGUAGE: Georgian

GEORGIAN 58.8%
OTHER 4.8%
ABKHAZIAN 1.7%
OSSETIAN 3.2%
AZERBAIJANI 5.1%
RUSSIAN 7.4%
ARMENIAN 9.0%

KAZAKHSTAN
AREA sq km: 2,717,000
POPULATION m: 16.8
1st LANGUAGE: Russian

KAZAKH 36.0%
OTHER 15.0%
TARTAR 2.1%
UKRAINIAN 6.1%
RUSSIAN 40.8%

KYRGHYSTAN
AREA sq km: 198,800
POPULATION m: 4.4
1st LANGUAGE: Kirgizian

KIRGIZIAN 52.4%
OTHER 9.1%
TARTAR 1.6%
UKRAINIAN 2.5%
UZBEK 12.9%
RUSSIAN 21.5%

LATVIA
AREA sq km: 63,700
POPULATION m: 2.7
1st LANGUAGE: Latvian (Lettish)

LATVIAN 51.8%
POLISH 2.3%
UKRAINIAN 3.4%
OTHER 4.2%
BELARUSSIAN 4.5%
RUSSIAN 33.8%

LITHUANIA
AREA sq km: 65,200
POPULATION m: 3.8
1st LANGUAGE: Lithuanian

LITHUANIAN 80.1%
OTHER 2.1%
BELARUSSIAN 1.5%
POLISH 7.7%
RUSSIAN 8.6%

MOLDOVA
AREA sq km: 33,700
POPULATION m: 4.4
1st LANGUAGE: Moldavian

MOLDAVIAN 63.9%
BULGARIAN 2.0%
OTHER 1.6%
GAGUAZI 3.5%
JEWISH 2.0%
RUSSIAN 12.8%
UKRAINIAN 14.2%

RUSSIA
AREA sq km: 6,600,000
POPULATION m: 149.8
1st LANGUAGE: Russian

RUSSIAN 82.6%
OTHER 9.9%
CHUVASH 1.2%
UKRAINIAN 2.7%
TARTAR 3.6%

TADZHIKISTAN
AREA sq km: 143,100
POPULATION m: 5.3
1st LANGUAGE: Tadzhik

TADZHIK 58.8%
OTHER 5.8%
TARTAR 2.1%
RUSSIAN 10.4%
UZBEK 22.9%

TURKMENISTAN
AREA sq km: 488,100
POPULATION m: 3.6
1st LANGUAGE: Turkmen

TURKMEN 68.4%
OTHER 7.6%
KAZAKH 2.9%
UZBEK 8.5%
RUSSIAN 12.6%

UKRAINE
AREA sq km: 604,000
POPULATION m: 52
1st LANGUAGE: Ukrainian

UKRAINIAN 73.6%
OTHER 3.2%
BELARUSSIAN 0.8%
JEWISH 1.3%
RUSSIAN 21.1%

UZBEKISTAN
AREA sq km: 447,400
POPULATION m: 20.4
1st LANGUAGE: Uzbek

UZBEK 68.7%
OTHER 6.5%
KARA KALPAK 1.9%
TADZHIK 3.9%
KAZAKH 4.0%
TARTAR 4.2%
RUSSIAN 10.8%

Connections: Trade 48–49 Eastern Europe 110–111 Rebuilding democracies 120–121 The birth of nations 176–177 The cold war balance 184–185

was under its tight control. By contrast discipline within the western alliance (the North Atlantic Treaty Organisation) was far more lax and the member states were reluctant to devote resources to match Moscow's conventional military might.

In practice this meant that the West relied on nuclear deterrence largely on the basis that no state would risk war if it was likely to end with a holocaust. This strategy worked, in that East and West settled down to a long military stalemate. Its success was helped by the political logic of the situation. The iron curtain which had been drawn across Europe left little ambiguity – with one exception, for Berlin, within the heart of East Germany, was also divided between East and West.

This the Russians found intolerable. In 1948 a boost to the developing cold war had been given when Stalin attempted to lay siege to Berlin, only to be thwarted by an Anglo-American airlift. In the late 1950s, Nikita Khrushchev revived the pressure, concerned as West Berlin became an escape route for thousands of East Germans seeking a better life. In practice his options were limited and in August 1961 he solved the problems by sealing West Berlin with a wall. The allies complained but did little. Their priority was to protect the West and they were unwilling to risk war to liberate the East.

Megalithic decline

A free hand in the Warsaw pact countries, and therefore a secure buffer zone, was the main benefit to the Soviet Union of its tremendous investment in military power. However, the management of this empire became steadily more problematic. This was due partly to southern European communist states demonstrating an awkward independence (reformist Yugoslavia, Stalinist Albania, dictatorial Romania) but, more fundamentally, it was a reflection of the inherent weakness of the state socialist system. A command economy might have been suited to large-scale industrialisation but not to small-scale innovation. Enterprise was put into surviving the planning system rather than generating new goods and services. Leonid Brezhnev's rule, which lasted from 1964 to 1982, was later characterised by Mikhail Gorbachev as the "age of stagnation". The state became geared to the needs of the party elite, who made their position and its attendant privileges the first priority.

Despite Khrushchev's boasts about the greater economic dynamism of state socialism, the contrary reality became painfully apparent by the end of the 1970s. The higher standard of living in western Europe, which could not be hidden from the East, represented a threat. However, access to the western economic system was becoming vital. Chronic problems with agriculture meant that grain had to be imported. The socialist states also wanted western technology and credit to pay for it.

All this became bound up with the policies known as détente. At the superpower level this involved nuclear arms control and an attempt to agree on the management of regional disputes. At the European level détente was much more deep-rooted, involving not just specific Soviet economic requirements and a western desire to reduce East-West tension, but an opportunity to consolidate the political status quo. West German relations ▷

Seeing Red…the 1987 May Day Parade on Moscow's Red Square, once the world's annual permitted glimpse into the doings of the secret superpower, is no longer the grand show of military pomp and military circumstance it once was. With the devolution of the Soviet empire into constituent republics, and the dispersal of military units and hardware, there is no political will or logistic capacity to stage such shows of ritual solidarity.

Unreconstructed USSR

When eastern Europe was liberated from the Nazis after the second world war, communist parties were given a leading role in each state.

The system of tight centralised control began to give way almost immediately. In Yugoslavia, Tito challenged Stalin in the late 1940s and got away with it, establishing a "revisionist" version of communism. In the mid-1950s there were disturbances in Poland, East Germany and Hungary, where an anti-Soviet government got to power in Budapest before being crushed by Soviet tanks in late 1956.

The most substantial challenge came from the other great communist giant – China. Its leader, Mao Zedong, saw no reason to play second fiddle to Nikita Khrushchev after Stalin's death, and felt that Moscow was not giving China enough economic or military support. A major dispute arose over China's nuclear programme, which Moscow tried to stop. The two broke formally in 1963 and at the time seemed even close to war; there were border clashes in 1969.

In Europe, Albanians allied themselves with the Chinese and broke away from the Warsaw pact. Romania, under Nikolai Ceausescu, stayed within the pact but became increasingly independent as well as repressive. He did not officially challenge the idea of the leading role of the party – that challenge came from Poland's Solidarity trade union in 1980 which forced major concessions from the government until martial law was established in 1981. Through the 1980s the foundations of communist support were steadily eroded. All that was left was the fear of Soviet "fraternal" intervention in support of a party in trouble, but by the time of the revolution of 1989 it was clear such support would not be forthcoming and the old regimes crumbled. The authority of communism was broken. If the party could not lead in eastern Europe there was no reason for it to lead in Moscow.

with the East, including East Germany, were regularised. The position of Berlin was clarified. In 1975 all European countries, plus Canada and the United States, signed an agreement at the Conference on Security and Cooperation in Europe (CSCE) which brought together all these aspects of détente.

This proved to be less durable than expected, largely because it did little to address the fundamental weaknesses of the Soviet system. Moscow had agreed to a human rights provision in the CSCE but did little to implement it, and this served to highlight the repressive nature of one-party rule. In economic terms, détente made the situation worse. State socialism proved unable to turn western technology into exportable goods. Soon debts grew and their repayment became an added burden. Moreover, as the NATO countries grew ever more suspi-

cious of Soviet global ambitions and military intentions they boosted their own defence expenditures – thereby confronting Moscow with the challenge of an arms race.

One last chance

By 1982, when Brezhnev died, the situation was as bad as ever. His successor Yuri Andropov, former head of the KGB, was convinced of the need for thorough-going reform but he died before he could make much impact. He was followed by Konstantin Chernenko, who had no vision beyond Brezhnev's, but he too soon died. In 1985 Mikhail Gorbachev took over. He stated from the start his disgust at the gap between the party rhetoric proclaiming progress and achievement and the reality of corruption, shortages and shoddy goods, and introduced the slogans of *perestroika* (restructuring) and *glasnost* (openness).

DEFENCES AND RESOURCES OF THE FORMER USSR

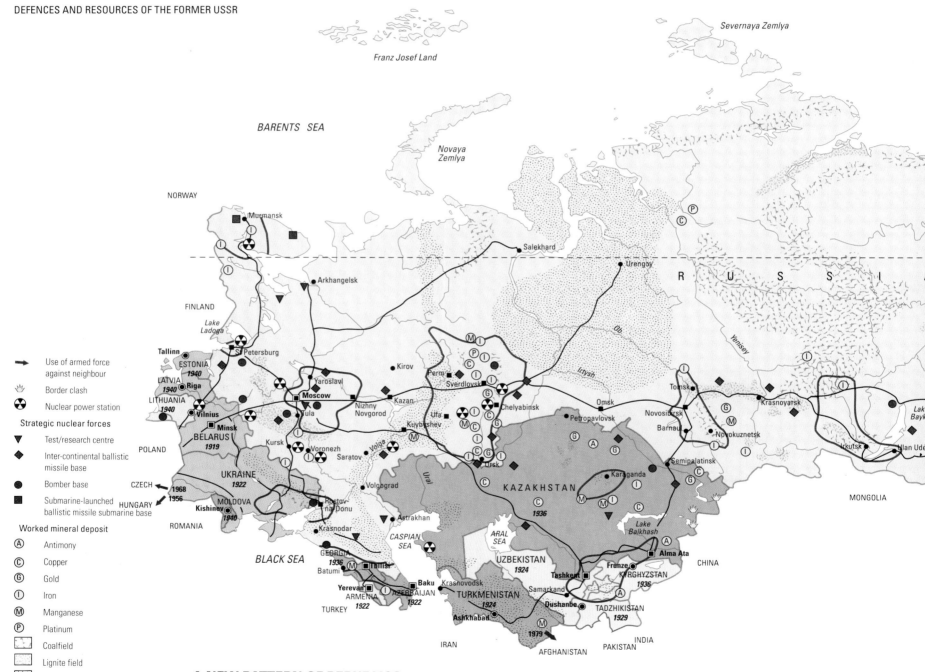

A NEW PATTERN OF REPUBLICS

In late 1990 the states of the former Soviet Union established a Commonwealth of Independent States to coordinate their future relations. Its prospects are, at best, tenuous. The states fall into four distinct groups: the three Baltic states to the west; the Caucasus in the south-west; the Islamic Central Asian group and the Slavic group dominated by the Russian Federation with Ukraine and Belarus. Placed between the

Slavic and Central Asian groups is Kazakhstan. Moldova fits uneasily into this pattern as its natural links are with Romania.

The major centres of population (some 80%) are west of the Ural mountains, although the Central Asian states have the fastest growing populations.

The former Soviet Union contains an abundance of mineral wealth – largely found east of the Urals, and especially in the large and sparsely populated Russian regions of Siberia, where

These tasks required calming relations with the West via arms control and a campaign of political reassurance.

Gorbachev believed the Communist Party could still be an agency of radical change, but to be effective there had to be a direct confrontation with party privilege and its supporting ideology. A similar confrontation was also required in eastern Europe, despite the fact that hardliners were generally still in charge there – so the alternative was not a reformist party but no party at all. Already Poland, under martial law but with the dissident trade union Solidarity exercising substantial power, and liberal Hungary were edging out of the old communist order. The crunch came in 1989 when Gorbachev was forced to end communist rule to avoid undoing western goodwill and reinforcing his own hardliners.

The consequences were immediate and dramatic. By the end of the year communist parties had been removed from power in Poland, Hungary, Czechoslovakia and Romania, and were under threat in Bulgaria and Albania. The Warsaw pact was effectively moribund and Germany was on the way to unification. The West applauded the end of the cold war and a triumph for liberal capitalist ideology. In Moscow there was less enthusiasm. To the old guard, the events appeared to have exposed the Soviet Union to its old enemies while encouraging demands for self-determination from the numerous nationalities within the union itself.

It took the conservatives until the end of 1990 to recover from the shock but at that point they began to put pressure on Gorbachev to reverse some arms control concessions, stop the Baltic states from breaking away and slow down the pace of reform. The Soviet leader ▷

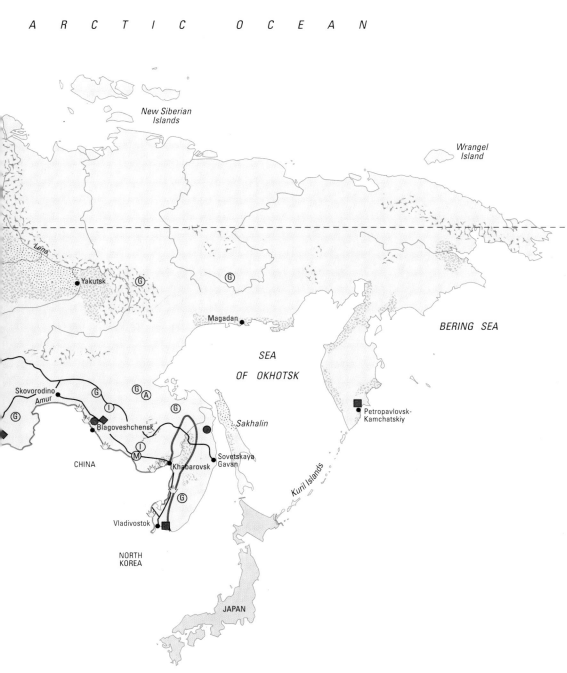

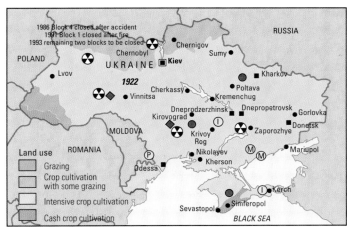

THE UKRAINIAN PHOENIX

The Ukraine (see map above) is the most substantial of the new European states, other than Russia itself, to emerge from the wreckage of the USSR. It is comparable in size, population and agricultural output to France, but not in manufacturing output which is less than a quarter of France's. Despite its independence, the Ukraine cannot easily detach itself from Russia. Its economy is still geared to the old centralised system so that it has difficulty importing fuel from anywhere else, while it has long been a source of grain for Russia. When Russia introduced realistic prices at the start of 1992, the Ukraine had no choice but to follow suit.

The Ukraine's efforts to create its own armed forces have involved persuading Russian officers to switch their loyalty to Kiev, and it made a bid for the Black Sea fleet. It has promised to accede to the nuclear non-proliferation treaty. As the 1986 Chernobyl reactor disaster was on its territory it has reason to be non-nuclear. But equally it does not want to see Russian control of these forces being used to strengthen Moscow's position. The substantial Russian population in the Ukraine and a potential dispute over the Crimea means that the two states are locked in a relationship that demands cooperation but contains the seeds of conflict. The interdependence of the two economies means separation will be even more painful if conducted in a hostile atmosphere. Lack of funds will continue to contain the Ukraine's military ambitions. Instead of the army of 400,000 originally envisaged, it will probably end up with one half that size – another good reason not to pick fights.

One difficulty for the Ukraine is that, because it is still at the early stages of the reform process, it has been late to pursue close economic relations with western Europe, while in any competition for attention in the United States, Russia will be judged to be the CIS power of the greatest strategic importance.

the harsh weather conditions makes extraction difficult. There are substantial deposits of oil, gas and coal, and also gold which helped the Soviet economy considerably in the past, plus many other non-fuel minerals. Timber is also important: two-thirds of the total land is covered with forest. Most food is grown west of the Urals.

was now weakened by the failure of his half-hearted economic reform, and was pleading for large-scale economic assistance from the West to help him ward off a coup. The West was reluctant to pour resources into the "black hole" of a collapsing economy.

The Union explodes

In August 1991 the coup came but resistance, led by the leader of the Russian Federation, Boris Yeltsin, meant that it crumbled within three days. Brought back from his temporary exile Gorbachev still appeared to believe the Communist Party had a role. He was soon disabused. Popular feeling against the party exploded and it was swept from its last toe-holds of power. There was now nothing to hold the union together and the individual republics took their independence despite Gorbachev's vain attempts to hold things together. In December the Soviet Union was replaced by a loose Commonwealth of Independent States (CIS).

The West, despite its fears over instability, had little

Market days… Once unofficial trading was frowned upon but now individual enterprise is encouraged and everything from spring onions to stockings can be bought from street traders in Russian cities.

choice but to recognise the republics. Drastic economic reforms were made at the beginning of 1992, with realistic prices hitting the pockets of the long-suffering Russian people, causing both distress and discontent. There were awkward negotiations over the distribution and control of the Soviet Union's substantial military legacy. The West was especially anxious over the fate of the nuclear arsenal. There was virtual civil war in Georgia and conflict between Armenia and Azerbaijan.

Before the Warsaw pact collapsed completely progress was being made in reducing this threat through the Vienna negotiations on conventional forces in Europe (CFE) which focused on "surprise attack" capabilities. Remarkably, this process continued through 1990 and the treaty was signed in November that year. However, further fragmentation of the former Soviet Union undermined the CFE treaty and rendered ratification difficult.

It became caught up in much more complex negotiations among the members of the CIS over the military legacy they had inherited. Who should have what? Who should control what? Who could afford any of it?

Russian military expenditures declined by about 60% in the first years of the 1990s. Defence procurement virtually

ground to a halt. Conscripts were not turning up for duty or were deserting. If further contraction was to be at all orderly it must be severe. One estimate suggested that the Russian armed forces declined from 130 to 60 divisions and 6,000 to 2,500 aircraft, plus a much reduced navy with some 180 submarines. But even this much reduced force would take up 10% of GNP if, which may be optimistic, it can claw its way back to 80% of its 1990 GNP by the year 2000.

With or without an arms control treaty, the NATO countries were ready to take the opportunity to cut their own forces as the idea of an irresistible drive from the East evaporated. The new question concerns how best to cope with the many conflicts of post-communist Europe. NATO offered all the states with a link to the former Warsaw pact (including Asian members of the CIS) a forum for dialogue in a North Atlantic Cooperation Council. However, NATO was unwilling to make security commitments to any of these states for fear of becoming entangled in disputes that do not involve clear challenges to international law.

In terms of conflict-resolution the CSCE attempted mediation in the Armenia-Azerbaijan dispute, just as the EC had in Yugoslavia, but in both cases any role for these institutions depended on the readiness of all the disputants to take advantage of their help.

There was little doubt that the best hope for stabilising post-communist Europe was to reconstruct its economies. Unfortunately the disastrous legacy of communism could not be easily overcome in a swift dash for capitalism. Inevitably, western Europe was involved with short-term relief – by the end of 1991 the EC, Japan, Canada and the USA had pledged just under $9bn in food aid – as much as pledged for long-term reconstruction. For the moment a close relationship with the European Community represented the major hope of access into the developed, capitalist world.

The EC made it clear that much would depend on the strides the individual republics were able to make on their own. It was looking for freer economic systems, including new legal structures, privatisation and a readiness to tolerate the tensions of transition, which inevitably include in the first instance high unemployment and inflation as subsidies are removed and realistic prices introduced, and the strength and durability of democratic institutions.

Causes for caution

However, even if progress is made towards these goals, and performance will inevitably be patchy, the response from the Community may well be disillusioning. The economies of the post-communist states will be unable to cope with being fully opened up to western goods for many years. However, the evidence of the negotiations on the Czech, Polish and Hungarian association agreements suggests that the EC will be defensively oriented in terms of opening up to eastern Europe and unwilling to make way for significant imports of textiles and agricultural produce. The European Bank for Reconstruction and Development began operations in 1991 in London and was beginning to disburse its initial grant of $13bn to support investment and training projects. Then in 1992, the IMF announced it was likely to agree to a big aid package to the former Soviet Union. This was followed by Russian leader Boris Yeltsin's offer to swap Russia's foreign debt for equity in the country's mineral, oil, land and industrial resources, which was well received by European leaders.

EC trade with USSR

Imports from EC countries are gradually increasing and will probably continue to do so until enough stability is gained in the republics to enable them to establish competitive manufacturing industries and introduce up-to-date technology.

GOODS ABROAD

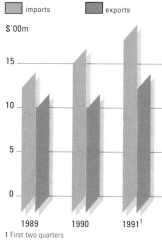

imports   exports

$'00m

15

10

5

0

1989   1990   1991[1]

1 First two quarters

JOINT VENTURES

There are two important aspects of Soviet economic development. First, despite the rapid growth in the international economy during the 1980s, the Soviet Union remained largely nationalised; at best, trade with the West stagnated. Second, as with much of central and eastern Europe, the German economic presence was the most prominent from the West. In 1990, Germany had more than 200 joint ventures with Soviet companies.

At the moment the main economic challenge posed by Russia and the other republics for the West is one of emergency economic assistance. The West has been offering technical expertise and food, while easing entry into the International Monetary Fund and the World Bank.

Eventually access to such a large market will have major attractions for western companies. Among the most likely investors will be the large oil companies able to wait for a yield as they struggle to turn around the inefficient Russian oil and gas fields.

THE BIG BEAR

Even though Russia has lost its 14 partners in the old Soviet Union, it is still an enormous country, twice the size of the United States and covering ten time zones. This means that the recent shrinkage has not solved the basic problems of identity and organisation for Moscow. In some ways they are now worse. Deals must now be done with local concerns that were once under tight control. Having watched successful drives for independence in the republics, parts of the Russian Federation are making their own demands. Russian president Boris Yeltsin called the troops into Chechin in the Caucasus in late 1991; there have been rumbles in Tartastan and Bashkiria.

Much depends on the economic situation. In the short term, the collapse of manufacturing and distribution means unemployment and shortages, to the point where the West must provide emergency relief. Hope for the future depends on rescuing agriculture from the effects of collectivisation and mobilising the vast mineral resources that have been wasted in the past through crude mining and transportation.

THE BALTIC STATES

The trail-blazers in the break-up of the Soviet Union were the three Baltic states – Lithuania, Estonia and Latvia – with Lithuania taking the lead. They had advantages over the other republics since their status was much more questionable. Prior to 1940 they had been independent states but were annexed by Stalin following the Nazi-Soviet non-aggression pact of August 1939. This annexation was never recognised by the West. As they are the most European, both geographically and psychologically speaking, any crackdowns from Moscow, even those which took place as the Gulf war began in early 1991, were likely to draw protests.

Nonetheless, they were relatively small states on the periphery of the USSR and Moscow saw their independence as setting a dangerous precedent. The search for a new constitutional arrangement which would keep the Baltic states inside the union occupied much of Mikhail Gorbachev's last years in power, with the West giving him tacit support. After the abortive attempted coup in August 1991, which destroyed Mr Gorbachev's political power, there was nothing to restrain the three states and their independence was recognised.

The Scandinavian countries have taken a keen interest in their progress and they are reasonably well-placed to escape from their Russian legacy. The risk for them is that the nationalism which inspired the drive for independence could turn inwards. There are substantial Russian and Polish minorities who would react badly to any victimisation.

Before the second world war the Baltic states were among the more prosperous states of northern Europe, but 50 years of communism dragged them down. Now, of the three, Latvia has the highest per capita income, just ahead of Estonia and some way ahead of Lithuania. They are all well above the former Soviet average. Their past production of consumer goods shows around 40% to be food and alcohol with another 25% clothing and footwear. Because these are highly protected areas, this suggests real progress in trade may depend on joint ventures to develop other areas of enterprise.

There has been some investment from the West, notably from Germany and Scandinavia. The hope is that good communications with western Europe and reasonably skilled workers on comparatively low wages will make these states a more attractive investment option for western capital than the larger post-communist states where the economic and political future remains more uncertain.

Selling out and buying in

The recent dramatic political history of the USSR can be tracked by the flow of its import-export trade. By 1990, exports were flagging, while imports with all except ex-Comecon countries were slowly rising.

Finland
France
Germany W.
Italy
UK
USA
Socialist countries

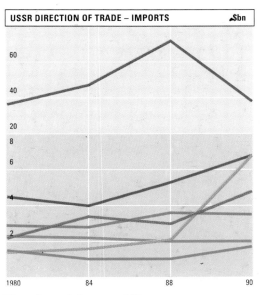

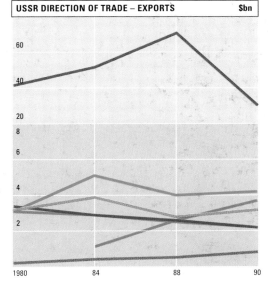

The rise of the republics

Separating the strands of interdependence that bound the former Soviet Union and building up new intra-regional trade relationships will take time. Some republics are better at it than others. The chart below shows the net material product per head in the republics in 1988. Figures are expressed as a percentage of the average for the whole country. Russia and the Baltic republics (Latvia, Lithuania and Estonia) are leading the pack, exceeding the average by almost 20%. In terms of total NMP, Russia accounted for 61%, the Ukraine 16% and the Baltic states just over 4% between them.

NET MATERIAL PRODUCT PER HEAD IN 1988

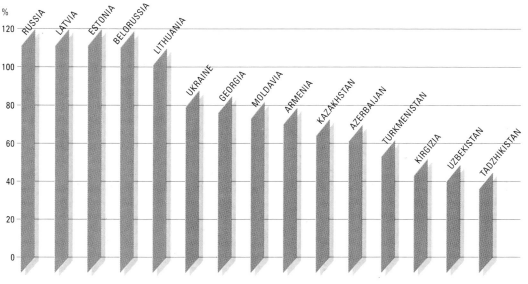

EUROPE AND ASIA

North Vietnamese refugees in Paris. The French connection with Vietnam dates from the 17th century, when French missionaries strove to Christianise the country. In 1867, in defence of their missions, France took over the territory they called Cochin China, now South Vietnam; Hanoi fell to the French in 1883 and a year later Annam (central Vietnam) and Tonkin (North Vietnam) became French protectorates. The French presence continued until the Japanese invaded in 1945. French cultural legacy is still felt.

Asia is a European definition, embracing more than half the world – and all its ethnic, cultural and linguistic variety – in a single word. Apart from Alexander the Great's futile invasion of India more than 2,300 years ago, Asia was unknown to Europe until the great explorations of men such as the Venetian Marco Polo in the 13th century, Portugal's Vasco da Gama and Ferdinand Magellan (who sailed on Spain's behalf) in the 16th century, and England's Captain Cook in the 18th century.

Trade followed exploration and the flag followed trade. By the 18th century the European powers – France, Germany, the Netherlands, Spain, Portugal and, most of all, Britain – had colonised Asia from the Indian subcontinent to the Pacific Ocean, and had shipped European settlers as far as Australia and New Zealand. Only the Chinese hinterland and the far north of Asia escaped Europe's imperial grasp.

In the 1990s, however, Europe's influence is small. Other than a sprinkling of Pacific islands, the only colonial hold is Britain's over Hong Kong and Portugal's over Macao – two tiny outposts which will be handed over to China in 1997 and 1999 respectively.

Europe's grip was loosened by the second world war, when Japan's initial successes proved that the white man was not invincible, so inspiring an irresistible momentum towards independence. In less than two decades the

British had gone from the Indian subcontinent, Malaya and Singapore; the Dutch from East Indies; and the French from Indochina. The defeated Germans had already lost their Asian possessions.

The new superpower

Europe's political retreat was compounded by a commercial one. The first reason for this was that America had assumed Britain's role as the world's military and economic superpower and so had a larger appetite for trade with Asia. This trade flourished because, ultimately, America was determined to stem the tide of communism in Asia after Mao Zedong's victory in China in 1949. Ever since Britain closed its naval base in Singapore in the late 1960s, security in the Pacific has been managed by America, with bases in Japan, South Korea and the Philippines (even earlier, in the Korean war of the early 1950s, America played a much bigger role than Europe).

The American military presence in Asia is now declining (it has abandoned the Clark Field air base in the Philippines and in 1991 agreed to leave the Subic Bay naval base). But Europe's activity is unlikely to exceed Britain's share in a defence arrangement for Malaysia and Singapore – or France's use of the Pacific as a base for its nuclear tests.

The second reason was that European countries,

Asia's economic boom

Japan, China and Asia's four "tiger" or "dragon" economies – Hong Kong, Taiwan, Singapore and South Korea – have since 1945 experienced the most rapid creation of wealth the world has ever seen. Moreover, the process continues: spurred on by Japanese investment and America's appetite for imports, Thailand and Malaysia are the latest Asian economies accelerating towards prosperity. Asia's success, however, is concentrated in the East; the nations of the Indian subcontinent lag far behind.

The map shows particular economic "hotspots"; the tables give comparative figures for the region and main trading partners, most of which are European.

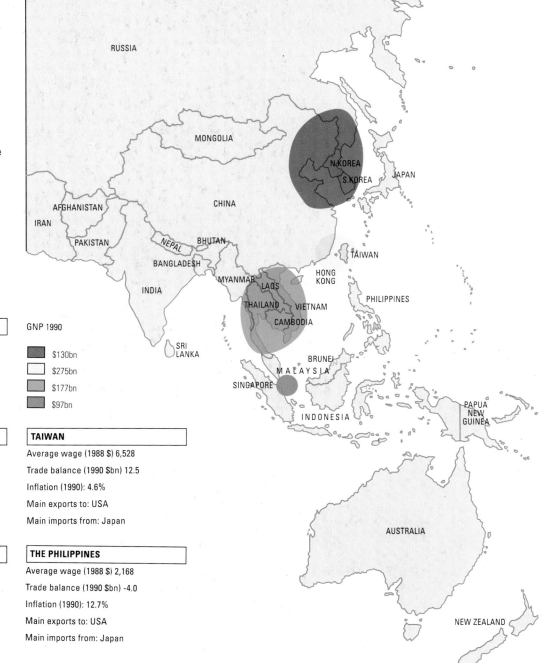

GNP 1990

 $130bn
$275bn
$177bn
$97bn

JAPAN
Average wage (1988 $) 13,645
Trade balance (1990 $bn) 63.6
Inflation (1990): 3.1%
Main exports to: USA
Main imports from: USA

SOUTH KOREA
Average wage (1988 $) 5,682
Trade balance (1990 $bn) -2.0
Inflation (1990): 8.6%
Main exports to: USA
Main imports from: Japan

HONG KONG
Average wage (1988 $) 14,014
Trade balance (1990 $bn) -0.341
Inflation (1990): 9.7%
Main exports to: USA
Main imports from: China

TAIWAN
Average wage (1988 $) 6,528
Trade balance (1990 $bn) 12.5
Inflation (1990): 4.6%
Main exports to: USA
Main imports from: Japan

THE PHILIPPINES
Average wage (1988 $) 2,168
Trade balance (1990 $bn) -4.0
Inflation (1990): 12.7%
Main exports to: USA
Main imports from: Japan

CHINA
Average wage (1988 $) 2,472
Trade balance (1990 $bn) 9.2
Inflation (1990): 2.1%
Main exports to: Hong Kong
Main imports from: Hong Kong

MALAYSIA
Average wage (1988 $) 5,070
Trade balance (1990 $bn) 1.7
Inflation (1990): 3.9%
Main exports to: Japan
Main imports from: Japan

SINGAPORE
Average wage (1985 $) 10,417
Trade balance (1990 $bn) -5.1
Inflation (1990): 3.4%
Main exports to: USA
Main imports from: Japan

THAILAND
Average wage (1988 $) 3,282
Trade balance (1990 $bn) -9.3
Inflation (1990): 5.9%
Main exports to: USA
Main imports from: Japan

INDONESIA
Average wage (1988 $) 1,822
Trade balance (1990 $bn) 6.1
Inflation (1990): 7.5%
Main exports to: Japan
Main imports from: Japan

AUSTRALIA
Average wage (1988 $): 14,529
Trade balance (1990 $bn) -0.069
Inflation (1990): 7.3%
Main exports to: Japan
Main imports from: USA

Connections: Trade 48–49   Competition in industry 50–51   Foreign investment 60–61   Defence and aerospace 74–75   Ideologies and parties 122–125

through the 1957 Treaty of Rome and the consequent European Economic Community, were becoming economically more dependent on each other, and so less on their old colonies. The third reason is Japan: its success since the 1960s has given other Asian nations a new model to emulate, and has forged economic links as strong as any of the old colonial ones to Europe.

Some Asian countries are proving better than others at following Japan. The Confucian culture of the East and South-East Asia used to be blamed for backwardness and corruption; but now the Confucian values of discipline and obedience are seen as the basis for the dramatic growth of Japan and the four newly industrialising economies (NIEs) of South Korea, Singapore, Taiwan and Hong Kong. By contrast, the Indian subcontinent values argument and individualism; its economic planners were imbued with Fabian socialism, which singularly failed to produce economic miracles after independence. For the backward "Confucian" nations – China, Vietnam, Laos, Cambodia and North Korea – communism, a system imported from Europe, provides a convenient scapegoat.

By the start of the 1990s, however, the countries of Indochina had declared a willingness to allow freer market forces; they were quickly followed by both Pakistan and India. If all succeed, it will mean that government policy is at least as important to economic develop- ▷

Massaging the tourist figures... In 1990 more than 2.17m people visited Indonesia, with 70% of them travelling to Jakarta, Bali (above) and Medan, spending a total of $1.89bn.

WHEN BUSINESS IS ONE LONG HOLIDAY

Tourism is Asia's fastest growing industry. In 1990 only 6% of Asia's 3bn or so people made one or more journeys by air annually; by the year 2000 the proportion will have doubled, but it will still be only half the level that applies in North America and Europe. Many of these trips will be for business, but economic growth is spurring the people of rich Asian countries to take foreign holidays as a matter of course – in particular the Japanese, but also Singaporeans, Taiwanese and Hong Kongers. Western tourists flock to Thailand, Singapore and Hong Kong, but their numbers are rapidly being matched by tourists from neighbouring Asian countries.

Such growth in travel and tourism means an accompanying growth in hotels, resorts and airlines. In 1989 Asia's airlines had just over 1,000 of the world's 8,300 jet-powered passenger aircraft; by the year 2000 Asia's fleet will have doubled in size. The world's makers of airliners – Europe's Airbus Industrie and America's Boeing and McDonnell Douglas – are already locked in fierce competition to supply Asia. In the 1980s the Airbus consortium shocked Boeing by its sales of wide-bodied airliners to the countries of the Silk Route – India, Thailand and Singapore. All three manufacturers have subcontracted work, or even given equity in some projects, to Asian countries, notably Japan and Singapore but also (in the case of McDonnell Douglas) China and Taiwan.

Western, especially European, tourism plays a vital role in the economies of Thailand, the Philippines, Indonesia, Hong Kong and Singapore. But its benefits are not unqualified: environmental pollution and the spread of AIDS in Asia are both blamed in part on the tourist industry. These drawbacks will doubtless worsen (although AIDS in India and South-East Asia will increasingly be spread not by foreign tourists but by transport-drivers and other local clients of the huge prostitution industry). Yet, however serious the associated problems become, travel and tourism will increase in importance for two main reasons: first, the need for countries to earn foreign exchange; and, second, the natural propensity of people to spend as they grow richer.

Oriental connections
This graph projects the growth in Orient-connected markets expressed in route passenger miles.

- Europe-Asia
- Transpacific
- Intra-Asia
- Intra-Europe
- North Atlantic
- US Domestic

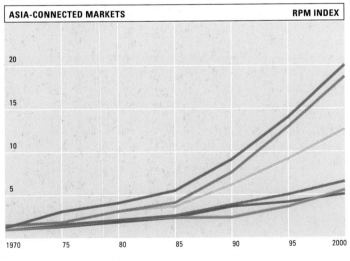

Booking ahead
This chart shows the average annual growth of traffic on major air routes. America's domestic airline market will remain the world's biggest but the fastest growing all involve Asia. Because the economies are the most dynamic they will generate more and more traffic.

- 2000
- 1988

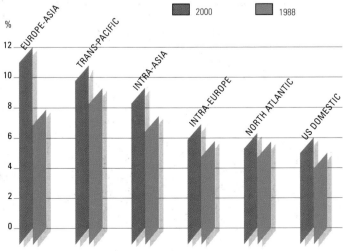

The yen to travel
Relatively few Japanese have travelled abroad (10m in 1989). The nearest Pacific states of the USA are honeymoon favourites.

TOP JAPANESE DESTINATIONS
('000 arrivals 1989)

COUNTRY	ARRIVALS
SOUTH KOREA	1,379
HAWAII	1,319
REST OF USA	1,205
HONG KONG	1,176
TAIWAN	962
SINGAPORE	841
FRANCE	770
GUAM	556
THAILAND	547
UK	492

ment as a nation's prevailing philosophy or religion. Certainly, the success of the West has had nothing to do with Confucianism.

Even so, Japan is the role-model for the NIEs and aspiring NIEs such as Thailand and Malaysia (whose prime minister, Dr Mahathir Mohamad, partly out of pique at Britain, adopted a "look east" policy in the early 1980s). When Asian countries have looked to others, as the communist regimes looked to the Soviet Union or the Philippines to the United States, they have achieved little. The exception is Brunei, but only because petroleum production has fortuitously given its 200,000 people a per capita income equal to Britain's.

The promise of peace

The question is how Asia's economic map will be changed by political developments. In October 1991 four Cambodian factions agreed to end almost 13 years of civil war. Peace in Cambodia and the consequent lifting of America's trade embargo against Vietnam (which invaded Cambodia in late 1978 to expel the genocidal Khmer Rouge and install a puppet regime) could link resource-rich Indochina to South-East Asia – a development that has been colourfully described by a former Thai prime minister, Chatichai Choonhavan, as a Suwannaphume, or Golden Land.

A similar development in North-East Asia, if (or, more probably, when) the Korean peninsula is reunified, could link Japan, Korea, China and Siberia, in Russia's far east. Another development is under way: the economic coordination of Taiwan, Hong Kong and mainland China. If Taiwan and China manage their peaceful reunification, this development will undoubtedly accelerate.

The present is a good signpost for the future. Hong Kong and the People's Republic of China are becoming integrated in economic terms long before Britain hands its colony over to China in 1997. Hong Kong employs 2m workers in China's Guangdong province and provides the lion's share of China's foreign investment and foreign exchange; for its part, China has become arguably Hong Kong's largest investor, ahead of Japan, America and Britain.

While many, even most, of Hong Kong's 6 million people mistrust China, this may paradoxically help business with China by establishing complementary links with the rest of the world. By 1997 around one-tenth of Hong Kong's most educated and entrepreneurially gifted may well have emigrated (principally to Australia, Canada and the USA, since Britain is thought to offer few opportunities and fewer passports). They will then be part of the successful overseas Chinese diaspora which traditionally maintains both family and business links with China. However, since there will be relatively few Chinese people in Europe, the trading advantages will go mainly to North America.

But if America is the focus, Europe is not out of Asia's picture. The weakness of Asia's relationship with the United States is that it is unbalanced: America's annual trade deficit at the start of the 1990s was over $100bn – of which Japan was responsible for two-fifths and Taiwan and China for another fifth.

To quieten American anger and incipient protectionism, Asia must sell more to Europe. The effort is already being made: the six-nation Association of South-East Asian Nations holds regular trade talks with its "dialogue partner", the European Community, while Taiwanese delegations now scour Europe, West and East, for trade and investment opportunities. ▷

Doctors monitoring national health trends in Vietnam claim that 70% of the country's children are undernourished. Generations of war have disturbed the demographic equilibrium and the population has far more women than adult men and is the youngest in Asia.

VIETNAM IN THE 1990s

It is often said that Vietnam won its wars only to lose its peace. Having reunited north and south in 1975, Vietnam has remained one of the world's poorest countries due to the doctrinaire Marxism of its aged government and the American trade embargo. The 1990s, however, will bring change, especially once neighbouring Cambodia finds a lasting peace and Americans are free to trade with Vietnam. The government has liberalised the economy and has been successful in attracting foreign investment. Vietnam has a cheap and skilled workforce, a large domestic market and an entrepreneurial culture.

FOREIGN CAPITAL INVESTMENT IN VIETNAM

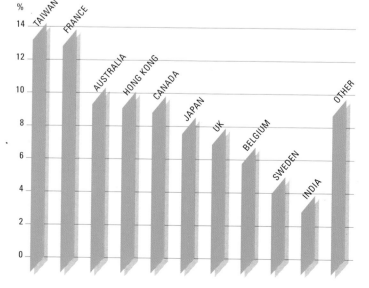

THE EAST INVESTS IN EUROPE

Japan is by far the biggest Asian investor in Europe. The process has two spurs: the rise in value of the yen following the Plaza Hotel agreement on currency alignments in September 1985; and the fear that Europe would take protectionist measures against imports from Japan. The result has been the establishment of "transplant" factories by Japanese manufacturers, especially car makers, keen to take advantage of a European Community with 320m consumers gathered, since the end of 1992, into a single market with no customs barriers. The greatest beneficiary has been Britain, with investment from Nissan and Honda in particular, but there are also Japanese car factories either operating or approved in Spain, Germany, the Netherlands and Italy.

Consumer electronics firms such as Sony and Hitachi, as well as upmarket Japanese designers and chain stores, have also invested in Europe since the mid-1980s. By 1991 Japanese investment in the European Community was worth more than $55bn and was responsible for 182,000 jobs.

Japan is the most obvious of Asia's investors in Europe, but all Asian countries with surplus capital are looking abroad for investment opportunities. Their first choice remains America and other countries in Asia, but Europe – including eastern Europe – has attracted money from Hong Kong, Singapore, Taiwan, South Korea and even Indonesia. Asian investors now own European hotels, designer labels, publishing houses and real estate. Their spur for branching out into Europe is not a strengthening domestic currency (since they tend to track the dollar) but the desire not to be cut out of the single European market. And even more worrying is the fact that there may no longer be much room left to expand in their domestic markets. This has long been the case for the *hongs* (traditional trading houses) of Hong Kong.

Stock cars… Japan's home production was 9.9bn vehicles in 1990, but sluggish domestic demand and faltering American and European consumption means that motor giants are cutting production to reduce enormous stockpiles.

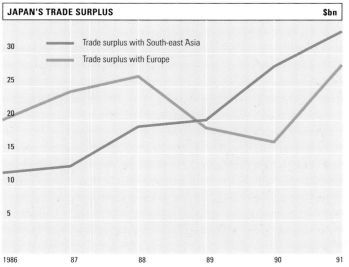

JAPAN'S TRADE SURPLUS $bn

— Trade surplus with South-east Asia
— Trade surplus with Europe

30
25
20
15
10
5

1986   87   88   89   90   91

Twin peaks
The Japanese trade surplus (left) with Europe soared throughout the 1980s, a reflection of the European preference for importing rather than manufacturing. Surplus with neighbouring Asian countries is now rising as economic growth booms in Asia.

DOING BUSINESS WITHIN THE REGION

Japan's economic dominance of Asia tempts comparisons with the "greater east Asia co-prosperity sphere", in pursuit of which Japan's soldiers laid waste much of Asia in the second world war. The difference is that Japan's present influence has been spread benignly through its exports and overseas investment. Between 1951 and 1988 Japan invested $15bn in the newly-industrialising economies of Hong Kong, South Korea, Singapore and Taiwan, and another $14.75bn in Indonesia, Malaysia, the Philippines and Thailand (only $270m was invested in the Indian subcontinent).

Most of Japan's investment has taken place since the mid-1980s, leading to speculation that a "yen bloc" is in the making. What increases the speculation is the development of a North American free trade zone, beginning with the 1987 pact between the United States and Canada, and the fear that the European Community's single market at the end of 1992 will turn into a "fortress Europe", with barriers erected against Asia's exports.

In some ways such a bloc is inevitable. Intra-regional trade will soon make up half of East and South-East Asia's total trade, and almost all of it will involve Japan. This means that Japan's trading partners will want to hold more of their reserves in yen, especially since much of their foreign debt is also denominated in yen. Moreover, the Association of South-East Asian Nations (ASEAN) increasingly looks to Japan as its model for development.

But few Asian policy-makers, and certainly not Japan's, believe in a protectionist Asian trade bloc; they realise it would invite retaliation from the vital American market, as well as

Europe, and would compromise their direct investment in the West. The forum established in 1989 known as the Asia-Pacific Economic Cooperation (APEC) attempts to forestall this by including America and Canada in its membership, and is keen that ASEAN and the Malaysia-inspired East Asian Economic Caucus should be lobbyists for free trade, not the precursors of Asian protectionism.

Yen bloc buster
Fears of "fortress Japan" are unsupported by the figures. The charts below show that East Asian intra-regional trade (the total sum of exports and imports) has risen significantly less than it has in the EC.

COMPARING TRADE BLOCS

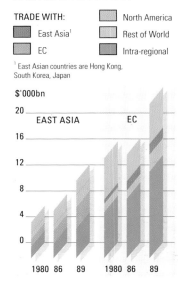

TRADE WITH:
East Asia[1]
EC
North America
Rest of World
Intra-regional

[1] East Asian countries are Hong Kong, South Korea, Japan

$'000bn

20
16
12
8
4
0

EAST ASIA   EC

1980 86 89   1980 86 89

Global interests
Japan's investment overseas has risen around the world, encouraged by the rising yen and the need to overcome protectionist trade barriers. The favourite area for investment remains North America.

JAPANESE INVESTMENT

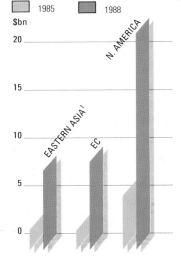

1985   1988
$bn

20
15
10
5
0

EASTERN ASIA[1]   EC   N. AMERICA

Number one customer
Japan's greatest economic success also its greatest political problem: it is the enduring trade surplus with the USA. The North American market is by far the biggest destination for Japan's exports. Although Japan's trade with South Korea and South-East Asia is also flourishing (very much in Japan's favour), the reliance on the USA will remain simply because no other country has the same ability to absorb Japan's industrial and electronic exports.

JAPANESE EXPORTS 1991

Total exports: $286.9 bn

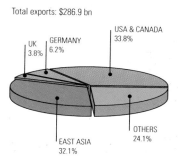

USA & CANADA 33.8%
GERMANY 6.2%
UK 3.8%
OTHERS 24.1%
EAST ASIA 32.1%

As the political and economic boundaries shift, the 1,000 Chinese who emigrate from Hong Kong each week are not the only Asians on the move. Along with those seeking a higher standard of living, some are fleeing their homelands in fear of persecution. Many Sri Lankan Tamils arriving in Britain and Germany in the early 1990s were refugees according to the United Nations definition, who had a well-founded fear of persecution on grounds of "race, religion, nationality, membership of a particular social group or political opinion".

Migrant or refugee?

In 1988 Hong Kong, which in 1991 was host to more than 64,000 Vietnamese boat people, began a screening test, hoping to repatriate those who it suspected were simply economic migrants, in total 80% of Vietnamese arrivals in the colony. In 1991 Britain reached an agreement with Vietnam allowing for the forced repatriation from Hong Kong of such migrants.

With the notable exceptions of the 3m Afghans who have taken refuge in Pakistan and the 1.5m who have left Vietnam since the end of its war with America, most migrants leave home for economic reasons, and go where they are wanted. In northern Europe's booming 1960s,

Indians and Pakistanis went to man Britain's factories, transport systems and health service; Indonesians went to the Netherlands; South Vietnamese went to France. European nations which could not draw cheap labour from a colonial well sought other sources; for instance, South Korea sent coal miners and nurses to work in West Germany.

Labour force

As Europe's economies slowed down and its racial resentment against immigrants rose, the appetite for immigrant labour switched to the oil states of the Gulf. In the "OPEC decade" ending in the mid-1980s, there were as many as 4m from the Indian subcontinent working in the Gulf. In some years, remittances from Bangladesh's overseas workers have paid for a quarter of the country's imports; the Philippines traditionally gets at least $1bn a year in remittances from its 500,000 or so workers abroad (mostly maids and seamen on fixed contracts).

The greatest demand for labour is now from rich Asian countries, which can draw from their poorer neighbours. Singapore takes workers from Malaysia, Thailand, the Philippines and Indonesia. Japan and Taiwan rely on illegal immigrants to perform dirty and menial work.

A relic of the raj… The Gateway of India in Bombay was built to celebrate the durbar or reception of King George V of England, who visited this ancient part of his empire in 1911 shortly after his coronation. With its comfortably substantial Victorian architecture – station, museum, pleasure gardens – Bombay may appear to have risen with the dawn of 19th century British imperialism; in fact it has a much earlier European connection – it was given to Charles II of England as a dowry by his father-in-law Joao IV of Portugal in 1662.

INDIA'S ENDURING LINKS WITH EUROPE

The Indian subcontinent retains many of the colonial links that tied it to the British empire. Britain's East India Company, which established itself in the subcontinent in the 1760s, and the Indian civil service of the British raj have left an indelible mark on both commerce and government. Generations of Nepalese families have sent their sons to join the Gurkhas of the British army. English is the language of commerce.

In terms of total trade with the subcontinent, Britain and the rest of Europe outweigh both Japan and the United States. This is only partly because of Europe's own efforts. At least as important is the activity of the subcontinent's *émigrés*. Successive governments in India have offered tax incentives to encourage investment from "NRIS" – non-resident Indians. Pakistan, Bangladesh and Sri Lanka also try to tap the entrepreneurial skills and capital of the subcontinent's diaspora. Much of this diaspora is concentrated in Britain, thanks either to direct migration from the subcontinent or to the influx of Asians from East Africa in the 1970s, when African nationalists in Uganda and Kenya turned against the Indian commercial class and expelled them. One feature of this pattern of immigration is the tendency for the first settlers to recruit wives from their ancestral regions. Of the 400,000 Britons of Pakistani origin, for example, about 75% trace their roots to the Pakistan-controlled part of Kashmir.

But, however close the subcontinent's links are with Europe, the relationship has exploited only a fraction of its potential. Until a dramatic, debt-compelled change of economic heart in 1991, both India and Pakistan were resolutely introspective, preferring to ward off rather than woo foreign investors. Meanwhile, Afghanistan and Sri Lanka were torn by civil war and Bangladesh was blighted by a series of natural disasters. As a result, Europe's greatest impact on the economies of the subcontinent may well have been participating in international aid packages.

Such aid will continue to be vital to the economies of all countries in the Indian subcontinent, especially war-ravaged Afghanistan and densely populated Bangladesh. However, India, Pakistan and Bangladesh have all taken brave measures of economic liberalisation in order to stimulate their economies.

India's industries

India's economy is the 12th largest in the world but in terms of per capita output and foreign trade, India languishes in the world's lowest ranks. The pressure of population growth is only part of the explanation. the bigger reason is that for four decades after independence in 1947, India, influenced both by theories put forward by the western European academics and the model of the Soviet Union, pursued a policy of centrally planned self-sufficiency. The result is that the country has developed a range of products but few of them are internationally competitive.

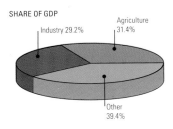

```
INDIA
```
Population 861m
Average Life expectancy ('90) 58
Deaths per 1,000 (1989-90);
1990-2000(est)=60
GDP $232bn
GDP per capita $270
GDP growth 4.9%

SHARE OF GDP

Industry 29.2% Agriculture 31.4% Other 39.4%

Trading partners

While Britain has had enormous cultural influence on the subcontinent, it plays only a minor role in India's trade, as the

chart below shows. Europe as a whole, however, accounts for more than two-fifths of India's exports and imports.

INDIA'S TRADE, 1989–90

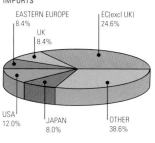

IMPORTS

EASTERN EUROPE 8.4%   EC(excl UK) 24.6%
UK 8.4%
USA 12.0%   JAPAN 8.0%   OTHER 38.6%

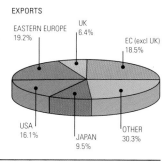

EXPORTS

EASTERN EUROPE 19.2%   UK 6.4%   EC (excl UK) 18.5%
USA 16.1%   JAPAN 9.5%   OTHER 30.3%

Overseas aid

In 1988 the major donors of foreign aid were (in descending order) the USA, Japan, France, Germany, the Comecon

and OPEC countries, Italy and the UK. The USA gave 18.1% of all aid, but this was just 0.2% of its GDP.

DISTRIBUTION OF AID FROM MAJOR SOURCES, 1988

	% of total	Receipts $m	As % GDP	$ per head
COUNTRY				
BANGLADESH	4.5	2,099	0.8	2.6
INDIA	3.4	1,590	8.5	15.2
PAKISTAN	3.1	1,439	3.6	13.7
SRI LANKA	1.3	592	8.4	35.7

Watchmaking in Hong Kong; since 1989, industrial and manufacturing jobs have been dwindling in Hong Kong – only 375,000 people were employed in the electronics industry at the end of 1990, after almost 15 years in which the workforce remained steady at around the half million mark. This reflects the gradual shift from manufacturing to service industries in Hong Kong, with labour intensive activity gradually moving to China in anticipation of 1997.

AUSTRALASIA'S PACIFIC PARTNER

Australia is a European outpost in the Pacific that is beginning to lose its European outlook. This is partly because of commercial pressure: Japan is its single biggest trading partner, and two-thirds of Australia's foreign trade is with the countries of the Pacific rim – compared with about 15% with Europe. As South-East and northern Asia grow richer, so resource-rich Australia becomes ever more identified as Asia's "farm, quarry and beach".

The other pressure comes from population. Although three-quarters of Australia's 16m people trace their ethnic origin to the British Isles, the "white Australia" immigration policy was abandoned in 1973. Under the present policy, which has no ethnic bias, the fastest growing sources of immigration after New Zealand (whose citizens have the automatic right to live and work in Australia) have been Hong Kong, the Philippines and Malaysia. As a result, the proportion of Asians among Australia's approximately 3m immigrants has now reached 15%, compared with about two-thirds born in Europe.

Where Australia leads, New Zealand is slowly, perhaps reluctantly, following. The 3.3m population is overwhelmingly European (mostly British) in origin, but a business migration scheme has been developed to attract entrepreneurs – especially from Hong Kong and other parts of Asia.

In March 1992 there were 147m sheep in Australia but a predicted long drought will reduce this figure by almost 10%. However, in the long term this will help to support the beleaguered wool market by reducing the country's massive wool mountain.

New markets

The EC's common agricultural policy severely curtailed UK imports of Australasian dairy and animal products. Australia and New Zealand turned to Asia to find new markets. Not only are Asian economies growing faster than those of North America and Europe, they are also less protectionist.

New Australians

After generations of settlement, only just over a fifth of Australia's population was born outside the country. Of those that were, over two-thirds came from Europe.

AUSTRALIANS BORN OVERSEAS

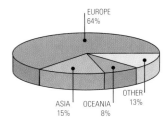

EUROPE 64%
OTHER 13%
ASIA 15%
OCEANIA 8%

Those born overseas = 22% of total population

AUSTRALASIAN TRADING PARTNERS

% of total value exports

☐ Australia ☐ New Zealand

COUNTRY	1987-88		1988-89		1989-90	
ASEAN	7.3	–	8.9	–	10.1	–
ASIA	–	10	–	12	–	12
AUSTRALIA	–	17	–	18	–	20
CHINA & TAIWAN	–	5	–	6	–	3
EASTERN EUROPE	–	2	–	3	–	3
EC (excl UK)	11.3	12	10.3	11	10.4	11
JAPAN	26.0	17	27.2	18	26.1	16
MIDDLE EAST	–	4	–	3	–	4
NEW ZEALAND	5.3	–	5.1	–	5.3	–
UK	4.3	9	3.5	7	3.5	7
USA	11.4	15	10.2	13	0.9	13

AUSTRALIA: SETTLER ARRIVALS '000

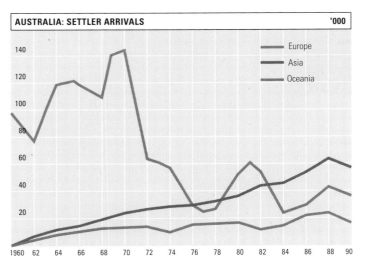

— Europe
— Asia
— Oceania

1960 62 64 66 68 70 72 74 76 78 80 82 84 86 88 90

Australasian exports

Raw materials still constitute more than half Australia's exports and all of New Zealand's.

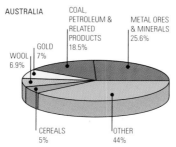

AUSTRALIA

WOOL 6.9%
GOLD 7%
COAL, PETROLEUM & RELATED PRODUCTS 18.5%
METAL ORES & MINERALS 25.6%
CEREALS 5%
OTHER 44%

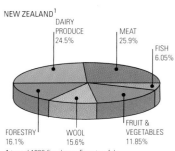

NEW ZEALAND[1]

DAIRY PRODUCE 24.5%
MEAT 25.9%
FISH 6.05%
FRUIT & VEGETABLES 11.85%
WOOL 15.6%
FORESTRY 16.1%

1 to end 1990 fiscal year. Exports = fob

EUROPE AND THE MIDDLE EAST

Many of the Middle East's children have now grown up in the midst of conflict. This drawing is by a Palestinian child from a refugee-camp school in the Lebanon. The young artist had been asked to depict everyday life.

The Middle East is a strategically important source of energy for Europe and a lucrative market for services and manufactured goods. However, although much of the Middle East's oil wealth has been recycled through Europe's economies, Europe's political relationship with the Middle East is more distant today than at any time in the past 150 years.

Between 1800 and 1925 most of the Middle East came under some form of European political control, mainly that of Britain and France. Britain's earliest concern was to protect (from other Europeans) the route to its Indian empire. The Middle East was also a source of cotton, silk and tobacco, and a market for European goods. The Suez canal, opened in 1869, became a vital link between European states and their colonial and trading interests in Asia.

In the 17th century the Middle East was Europe's equal, but by 1800 the region had fallen far behind, materially and technologically. Trade grew, but European exports greatly exceeded imports, and Middle-Eastern governments became indebted to European ones. European advisers were appointed to reform Middle-Eastern administrations, armies and schools on the European model. European notions of national identity encouraged the rise of Arab nationalism and Zionism.

Middle-Eastern rulers hoped to emulate European successes and to modernise their states sufficiently to become Europe's equals. But far from catching up with Europe, Middle-Eastern states fell instead more deeply under European tutelage. The Ottoman empire was the main barrier to European penetration into the heart of the Middle East, although by the end of the 19th century, the empire's peripheries had been lost to European powers. Throughout the century British policy had been to sustain the empire, which the British government saw as a barrier to European encroachment on its Indian possessions. But after the Ottoman sultan had sided with Germany in the first world war, the British determined to split up the empire.

Europe remade the Middle East after the first world war to suit its own interests. But the creation of artificial Arab states, and of Israel, left a legacy of discontent that sparked wars between Israel and the Arabs, Iran and Iraq, and, as in Lebanon and Kuwait, among Arabs themselves.

European entrepreneurs helped to turn the Middle East into the world's biggest oil producer. Although Europe's political supremacy in the Middle East gave way after the second world war to that of the USA and the Soviet Union, the fear of the oil-producing states being taken over by hostile powers, or oil routes through the ▷

The making of the modern Middle East

The present political geography of the Middle East is the product of decisions made in Europe during and after the first world war. In 1914 the Middle East was split four ways: between the Ottoman empire; the British, who ran Egypt and had protectorate agreements with local sheikhs in Aden, Oman, the Trucial States and Kuwait; a scattering of warring tribes in central Arabia; and Iran, nominally independent, but divided since 1907 into Russian and British zones.

When the Ottoman empire entered the war on the German side, the allies agreed to carve it up. In 1915, to bring the Arabs into the war on their side, the British promised Sharif Husayn of Mecca that they would support the independence of the Arab lands. The Arab revolt, led by the sharif's sons, duly broke out in June 1916. But in the Balfour Declaration of November 1917, the British went on to promise the Zionist movement that they "favoured the establishment in Palestine of a national homeland for the Jewish people". Meanwhile, under the Sykes–Picot agreement of May 1916, the British and French secretly agreed to divide the fertile crescent between them, with Palestine under an international administration. These contradictory agreements had later to be reconciled with American president Woodrow Wilson's wish to promote independence for small nations.

In 1920 the League of Nations awarded France and Britain mandates over five new states: Lebanon and Syria to the former, Iraq, Transjordan and Palestine to the latter. Allied plans to create independent states of Armenia and Kurdistan in south-east Turkey were successfully resisted by the Turkish leader, Kemal Ataturk. Egypt and the Gulf sheikhdoms remained under British control. In the Arabian peninsula Ibn Saud expanded his independent emirate of Nejd to create Saudi Arabia, and in Iran, Reza Khan reasserted central control in 1925 and made himself shah; the British deposed him in 1941 after he showed pro-Nazi sympathies.

Britain emerged from the second world war the paramount power in the Middle East, having forced France to pull out of Syria and Lebanon by 1944. But in 1946 Britain gave independence to Transjordan and when, in 1948, war erupted between Jews and Arabs, gave up its mandate over Palestine. British influence in Egypt ended with the revolution in 1952. In 1956, when war again broke out between Israel and the Arabs, Britain and France invaded the Suez Canal zone, ostensibly to ensure the canal's security, in reality to overthrow President Nasser of Egypt, who had nationalised it; America forced them to withdraw from Egypt in humiliation. British influence in Iraq, waning since independence in 1932, ended with the revolution there in 1958.

Britain's strategic interest in the Gulf faded with its withdrawal from India in 1947, though it stayed on in Kuwait until 1961 and South Yemen until 1967. The end of European imperialism in the Middle East came in 1971, when Britain left its Gulf protectorates. Thereafter, the Middle East became a focus of rivalry between America and the Soviet Union.

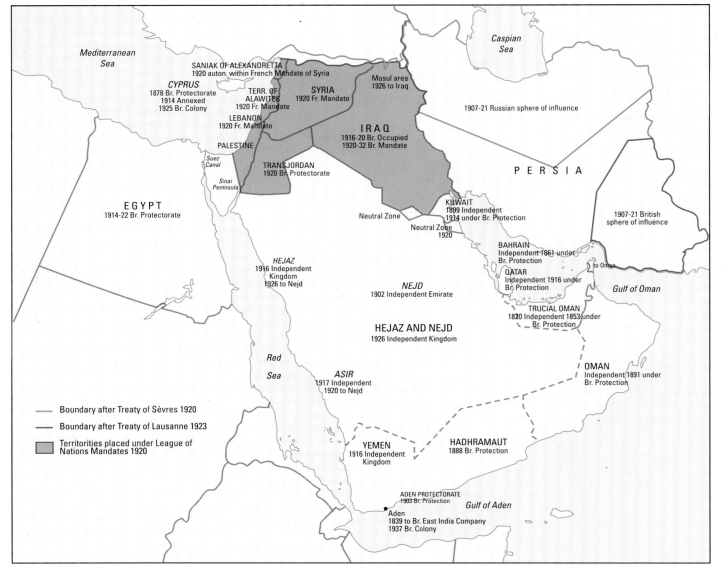

Mediterranean Sea

Caspian Sea

SANIAK OF ALEXANDRETTA
1920 auton. within French Mandate of Syria

CYPRUS
1878 Br. Protectorate
1914 Annexed
1925 Br. Colony

TERR. OF ALAWITES
1920 Fr. Mandate

SYRIA
1920 Fr. Mandate

Mosul area
1926 to Iraq

LEBANON
1920 Fr. Mandate

IRAQ
1916-20 Br. Occupied
1920-32 Br. Mandate

1907-21 Russian sphere of influence

PALESTINE

Suez Canal

TRANSJORDAN
1920 Br. Protectorate

Sinai Peninsula

P E R S I A

EGYPT
1914-22 Br. Protectorate

Neutral Zone

Neutral Zone 1920

KUWAIT
1899 Independent
1914 under Br. Protection

1907-21 British sphere of influence

HEJAZ
1916 Independent Kingdom
1926 to Nejd

BAHRAIN
Independent 1861 under Br. Protection

QATAR
Independent 1916 under Br. Protection

to Oman

Gulf of Oman

NEJD
1902 Independent Emirate

TRUCIAL OMAN
1820 Independent 1853 under Br. Protection

HEJAZ AND NEJD
1926 Independent Kingdom

Red Sea

ASIR
1917 Independent
1920 to Nejd

OMAN
Independent 1891 under Br. Protection

—— Boundary after Treaty of Sèvres 1920
—— Boundary after Treaty of Lausanne 1923
▨ Territories placed under League of Nations Mandates 1920

YEMEN
1916 Independent Kingdom

HADHRAMAUT
1888 Br. Protection

ADEN PROTECTORATE
1903 Br. Protection

Gulf of Aden

Aden
1839 to Br. East India Company
1937 Br. Colony

Connections: Energy 72–73 Operations after 1945 182–183 Arms industries 186–187 The military future 190–191 Threats to security 192–193

ISRAEL: THE JEWISH HOMELAND

Europe has provided most of the Jewish immigrants to Israel. The settlement of European (Ashkenazi) Jews in Palestine laid the foundations of the state of Israel in 1948. By 1979, over 800,000 Sephardic Jews had also arrived from the Balkans, North Africa and elsewhere in the Middle East. In the mid-1980s, some 20,000 Ethiopian Jews, known as Falashas, were airlifted to Israel. In 1990 several thousand of the remaining 15,000 were resettled in Israel.

In recent years immigration has been dominated by Soviet Jews after restrictions on emigration were lifted in 1989. Up to 1m are expected to arrive during the 1990s. The Law of Return allows any Jew to settle in Israel; the country comprises 4m out of 13m Jews worldwide with Hebrew the official language.

In the beginning...

Europe was the birthplace of modern Zionism, the driving force behind the creation of Israel. Theodore Herzl, an Austrian Jew, who believed the return of Jewish people to Palestine was the only way for them to escape persecution, organised the first Zionist conference in 1897. From the 1880s to the 1920s the relatively few Jews entering Palestine came mainly from eastern Europe, including some from Russia after the 1917 revolution. Immigration gathered pace in the 1930s with Nazi persecution. By 1947 there were 650,000 Jews in Palestine out of a total population of 2m. After 1948 large numbers of Jews arrived from Arab lands, first the Middle East, then North Africa.

JEWISH IMMIGRANTS TO ISRAEL

'000s

| | 1919-48 | 1948-90 |

SWITZERLAND
SCANDINAVIA
BELGIUM
GREECE
ITALY
SPAIN
AUSTRIA
NETHERLANDS
YUGOSLAVIA
GERMANY
CZECHOSLOVAKIA
UK
FRANCE
HUNGARY
BULGARIA
POLAND
ROMANIA
USSR

0   10   20   30   40   50   100   200   300   400

1947 borders

In November 1947 the newly formed United Nations partitioned Palestine between Jews and Arabs with Jerusalem and part of Bethlehem under international control. The Jewish state was given eastern Galilee, the coastal plain and the Negev desert; the Arab state was to have occupied western Galilee, Jaffa, central Palestine and a southern strip bordering Egypt. This was accepted by Zionists but not by Arabs, and civil war broke out.

	Jewish State
	Arab State
	International zone

1949 borders

On May 14th 1948, Britain gave up its Palestine mandate and the state of Israel was declared in Tel-Aviv. Arab armies were defeated in the war that had broken out, and some 700,000 Palestinian Arabs fled to the West Bank, the Gaza strip, Jordan, Lebanon and Syria. Within three years more than 330,000 survivors of European Jewry had arrived in Israel, together with 230,000 Jews from Arab states, half of them from Iraq. Between 1952 and 1964, another 186,000 European Jews went to Israel, half of them from Romania, together with almost 260,000 from Arab lands, most of them from Morocco.

| | Jewish State |

Palestinian diaspora

The human traffic that resulted from the formation of Israel has been two-way: 700,000 Palestinian Arabs fled Israel in 1948–49, most to the West Bank and Gaza strip. Israel's conquest of these places in 1967 drove a second wave of Palestinians into Jordan, Lebanon and Egypt. Some left for America and Europe – home in 1991 to 140,000 Palestinians. More built new lives in the oil-rich gulf states, especially Kuwait. After the Palestine Liberation Organisation declared its support for Iraq during the 1991 Gulf war, the Kuwaitis drove out most of its 400,000 Palestinians, swelling the refugee camps of Jordan and Lebanon.

WORLD PALESTINIAN POPULATION

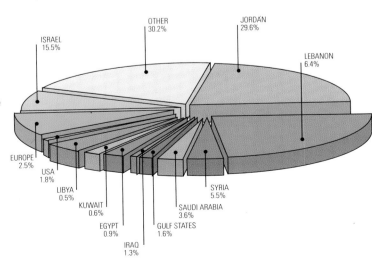

OTHER 30.2%
JORDAN 29.6%
ISRAEL 15.5%
LEBANON 6.4%
EUROPE 2.5%
USA 1.8%
LIBYA 0.5%
KUWAIT 0.6%
EGYPT 0.9%
IRAQ 1.3%
GULF STATES 1.6%
SAUDI ARABIA 3.6%
SYRIA 5.5%

1967 borders

In the six-day war of 1967 Israel captured the Sinai peninsula and Gaza from Egypt, the West Bank from Jordan and the Golan Heights from Syria, and almost tripled the land under its control. Israel did not annex this new territory because it wanted to avoid enfranchising the Arabs who lived there. This caused a new Palestinian exodus.

After years of negotiation an Egypt–Israel peace treaty was signed in March 1979 and Israel withdrew from the Sinai in March 1982.

| | Jewish State |

Suez canal or the Strait of Hormuz choked, has occasioned regular European intervention in the region.

In 1955 Britain and the United States established the Baghdad pact (later the Central Treaty Organisation) to protect the Gulf oilfields. The agreement, between Turkey, Iran, Pakistan and Iraq, was to be a buffer between the Soviet Union and the Gulf and the Indian Ocean. In 1956, Britain and France invaded Egypt when the Suez canal, through which most Middle-Eastern oil passed, was nationalised by President Nasser.

Western Europe, alongside the USA, was happy to back the shah of Iran diplomatically and with arms when he offered to assume the role of Gulf policeman after Britain withdrew from the Gulf in 1971. The shah generally played his part well, sending soldiers, for example, to fight alongside British troops to suppress a communist insurgency in Oman. But the western Europeans became alarmed at the shah's grandiose ambitions and ever-increasing military spending.

The shah was not content to limit his ambitions to the Gulf, but sought a military role in the Indian Ocean as well. The suspicions flowed both ways, the shah always worried that the British and Americans would one day dispose of him, as they had done his father. Indeed, the shah placed much of the blame for his overthrow in the revolution in 1979 on the British Broadcasting Corporation, whose Persian section, much listened-to inside Iran, had reported the speeches of Ayatollah Ruhollah Khomeini. When it came, the fall of the shah was as great a shock to the European powers as it was to the USA. A large number of European companies trading with Iran suffered heavy losses.

In order to protect friendly Gulf states from Iranian revolutionaries after 1979, western Europe inclined towards Iraq in the 1980–88 Iran–Iraq war. They failed, for example, to condemn Iraq's invasion of Iran in September 1979. And although western European states sold few arms to either party to the conflict (with the exception of France, which sold large quantities of aircraft and Exocet missiles to Iraq), they nonetheless tilted towards Iraq at the United Nations, praising Saddam Hussein's apparent readiness to talk peace, while condemning Ayatollah Khomeini's intransigence.

Under the influence of oil

The western Europeans did, however, vigorously condemn Iraq's invasion of Kuwait in August 1990, which they saw as a threat to Kuwaiti and Saudi Arabian oil exports, as well as aggression against a weaker state that should not be allowed to stand. Britain and France joined the United States in promoting the series of security council resolutions which imposed a trade embargo on Iraq, and when this did not work, to lay the ground for military action. Both states provided significant numbers of troops to the American-led force that ejected Iraq from Kuwait in February 1991.

European states back a negotiated solution to the Arab–Israeli conflict, but they have tended to leave any peace initiatives to the USA. The European Community's 1980 Venice Declaration gave clear support for Palestinian self-determination, but there was little follow-up, despite Arab calls for Europe to balance what they saw as America's pro-Israeli stance. After the 1991 Gulf war America again took the lead in arranging the Arab–Israeli peace talks which began in Madrid, with the support, but without the direct involvement, of the European nations.

Five Arab–Israeli wars, the Iranian revolution, the Soviet invasion of Afghanistan, the 1980–88 Iran–Iraq war, and the 1991 Gulf war all fuelled the Middle East's appetite for arms which were paid for by oil. Many Arabs regard their weapons as an essential item of daily dress, like this bedouin guide and mountain climber in Wadi Rhum.

TRADING LINKS

The Middle East is Europe's second-biggest external market after the United States, buying some $72bn-worth of goods (or just over 10% of all European exports) in 1990. Machinery and transport equipment, raw materials and consumer goods were the most important sectors. The Middle East is Europe's third-biggest external source of imports, after the United States and Japan, providing just under 10% of the total – mainly oil and oil products, but also food and clothing.

Europe is the region's most important trading partner, taking some 40% of the Middle East's exports and providing some 60% of its imports in 1990. Trade between the two blocs declined between 1980 and 1988, largely because of the fall in oil prices, energy conservation and diversification in Europe and other oil-importing regions, which cut the amount and value of the oil Europe imported, and therefore the income the oil producers had to buy European goods. Since 1988, trade has been growing again.

The Middle East is Europe's most important market for arms. The oil price rises of the 1970s were accompanied by a surge of arms-buying which peaked in 1984, and declined with the collapse of oil prices in the late 1980s. Arms imports in 1990 were worth under $15bn, a ten-year low. Throughout the 1980s, the Middle East took 30–40% of all arms traded internationally. The biggest importers over the decade 1979–88 were Iraq ($62bn), Saudi Arabia ($32bn), Syria ($21bn), Iran ($17bn), Egypt ($12bn), and Israel ($10bn). As Europe's share of the world arms market fell from 20% in 1978 to 8% in 1988, so its Middle-Eastern markets became more important.

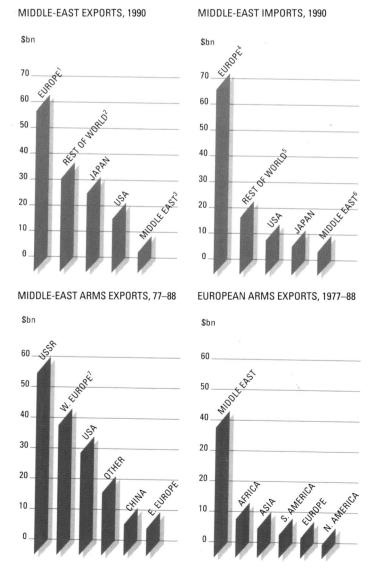

MIDDLE-EAST EXPORTS, 1990

$bn

MIDDLE-EAST IMPORTS, 1990

$bn

MIDDLE-EAST ARMS EXPORTS, 77–88

$bn

EUROPEAN ARMS EXPORTS, 1977–88

$bn

1 inc. EC 53.26   2 inc. USSR 2.63   3 inc. Turkey 2.63   4 inc. EC 57.73   5 inc. USSR 0.754   6 inc. Turkey 2.63
7 France 23.0; UK 9.2

Firing the economy… The refineries at Ras Tanura (left) in Saudi Arabia process a significant amount of the country's oil for export.

The passion for camel racing is ancient but modern Arabs, like this race-goer in the United Arab Emirates, are more likely to arrive by Range-Rover than camel.

EUROPE OVER A BARREL

Europe consumes one-fifth of all oil produced but produces only one-fifteenth of the world total; it has to import two-thirds of the oil it consumes, or roughly one-third of all oil traded. In contrast, the Middle East produces over one-quarter of the world's oil but consumes less than one-twentieth. The region exports almost half of all oil traded.

European oil production rose by 20% in the 1980s but is unlikely to keep pace with the expected growth in demand during the 1990s. As global demand for oil grows, Europe and other oil-importing regions will have to turn increasingly to the Middle East, where the gap between oil production and oil consumption is widest, and where oil reserves are largest. Indeed, while Europe's proven oil reserves will last only nine years at 1990 rates of production, the Middle East has reserves sufficient to last for well over a century.

WORLD OIL RESERVES, 1990

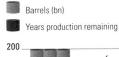

- Barrels (bn)
- Years production remaining

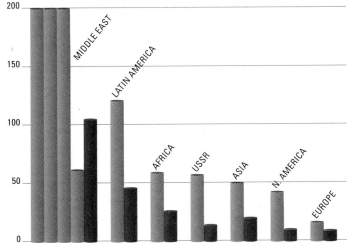

World consumption, 1990

World oil consumption was remarkably stable during the 1980s, running at between 60–65m barrels a day. Consumption fell by 10% during the decade in western and eastern Europe, and by 5% in North America, thanks to conservation measures and alternative energy sources. But this fall was more than made up by rising consumption in Africa and Asia. Consumption in the Middle East rose fastest of all – by 50% to 3m barrels a day.

Total: 63-84m barrels per day

- N.AMERICA 28.0%
- EUROPE 23.0%
- AFRICA 3.0%
- ASIA 20.1%
- USSR 12.7%
- LATIN AMERICA 8.5%
- MIDDLE EAST 4.7%

European imports, 1990

In 1990 just under one barrel in three consumed in Europe came from the Middle East. Of the 14m barrels a day being exported from the Middle East, 4m ended up in Europe, mostly as crude, but one barrel in six as refined products. Europe's dependence on Middle-Eastern oil fell during the 1980s, but seems certain to rise. Europe's consumption of oil began to rise again in 1988, after a slow fall from a peak in late 1979.

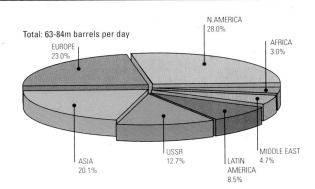

Total: 9.75m barrels per day

- MIDDLE EAST 41.0%
- OTHER 1.4%
- AFRICA 29.8%
- USSR 19.8%
- LATIN AMERICA 5.8%
- N. AMERICA 2.2%

Middle-East exports, 1990

The Middle East pumps over one in every four barrels of oil worldwide, and exports almost one barrel in two of all oil and oil products traded. In 1970, the Middle East was even more dominant, producing four barrels out of ten and exporting over 5bn barrels of oil a day, half to Europe. But the oil price shocks of 1973–74 and 1979 damaged European economies and inspired conservation and diversification from oil to other energy sources, and from the Middle East to other oil-producing nations.

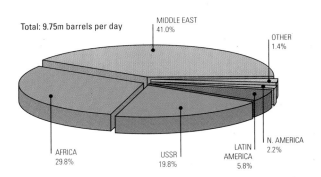

Total: 14.2m barrels per day

- ASIA 46.6%
- EUROPE 28.1%
- N.AMERICA 14.8%
- OTHER 6.8%
- AFRICA 2.5%
- LATIN AMERICA 1.2%

EUROPE AND AFRICA

While many colonists returned home, big business stayed on in Africa after independence was achieved across the continent. Elf, the oil exploration and production giant, is France's largest industrial company and operates throughout what were the francophone countries of Africa. In 1991, the Gabon produced a total of 107m barrels, 61m of them for Elf Gabon, 57% of which is owned by Elf Aquitaine, 25% by the Republic of Gabon and the rest by the general public.

There are three Africas, each with a different relationship to the world. By geography and ancient history, the continent's Mediterranean coast is linked to Europe and the Middle East. In Africa's temperate southern extremity, European powers long ago established colonies to protect their fleets on the voyage to the Indies. In the tropical lands between, climate and disease kept outsiders away until, a century ago, Europeans armed with breech-loading guns and improved medicines took over the entire continent.

Muslim expansion in the early Middle Ages established from the Indian Ocean to the Atlantic a great Arab empire. For centuries its rulers maintained colonies in Europe; traders and missionaries carried their influence south across the Sahara, and brought back slaves along the Nile into Egypt. Arab culture has survived the takeover of North Africa first by the Ottoman Turks, then by Europeans.

For the first half of the 20th century France, Italy, Spain and Britain between them dominated North Africa. The collapse of those empires and the development of oil and gas reserves in Algeria and Libya did not bring stability. Soaring population growth, authoritarian politics and discord between the region's regimes frustrated progress.

Trade with Europe, and the export of cheap labour and oil, have been the region's mainstays. The European Community has often considered including North Africa in some form of association, to foster its development and encourage more of its people to stay at home. But not all EC members are keen on the idea because of North Africa's lack of unity, unpredictable politics and unsophisticated economies.

Europeans settled early and stayed late at the southern end of Africa. Portuguese, Dutch and British colonies took on new importance when, in the 1880s, vast reserves of gold and diamonds were discovered in the remote Transvaal. The British fought to establish their dominion of South Africa, and to extend their rule northwards. Missionaries and settlers tamed the new colonies, cut off from the sea by Portuguese territory. The settlers' descendants oppressed the local Africans.

White power in southern Africa seemed secure until, in the mid-1970s, after a democratic revolution, Portugal abandoned Mozambique and Angola. The settler regime in Rhodesia could hold out no longer, and Africans took power in the country, which was renamed Zimbabwe. With black African nations all along their northern border, the Afrikaners, descendants of Dutch settlers, too abandoned their scheme for racial dominance. Fifteen years after the Portuguese collapse, South Africa's white minority government announced an experiment in peaceful co-existence with the majority black and coloured population.

Through all these political changes, European (mainly British) companies had kept control of the region's mines, some industries and even farms. In Zimbabwe they still made good profits under black rule. In Angola and Mozambique, civil wars (backed by meddling outsiders) brought normal economic life to a halt until the start of the 1990s, when the prospect of peace began to revive European investment. In South Africa, though, the

HOW DO YOU SAY THAT IN AFRICAN?

Nobody has ever counted Africa's vernacular languages; the 110m people of Nigeria, the continent's most populous nation, have at least 500 among them. The Arabs who conquered North Africa in the name of Islam brought their language with them; the Europeans who conquered the rest of the continent in the last century also administered their possessions in whatever language they spoke. Almost all African governments have stuck with the imperial language; the exceptions are Ethiopia, which was only briefly colonised; Tanzania, which has tried to standardise on one local language, Swahili, with unhappy results; and South Africa, where the peasant Dutch dialect Afrikaans has equal status with English.

An official language is spoken by officials and teachers. But most male Africans have always needed to speak at least two African languages, that of their home village and that of the market town. (Women, confined to rural villages, usually speak only their mother tongue.) The official language, for most men, tends to be their third or fourth and they often speak it badly. The map indicates more than linguistic differences in the way countries are run. Those whose official language is English, or French, or Portuguese, retain legal, military and bureaucratic techniques inherited from their former rulers. Thus the colonial connections remain.

Politicians and civil servants who work in one language cannot easily talk to their counterparts in neighbouring countries, although the African vernacular of the region may spread across the borders. Teachers must learn a foreign language before they can work in a classroom. University students must use foreign textbooks, and write exams in an unfamiliar idiom. Africa's multivarious linguistic heritage is often viewed as an obstacle to development, as well as to inter-African cooperation.

Official languages
- Afrikaans
- Amharic & local
- Arabic
- English
- French
- Malagasy
- Portuguese
- Setswana
- Somali
- Spanish
- Swahili

future seemed uncertain, as long-delayed political changes got under way, and people of European descent looked apprehensively northwards.

For many years the only significant European activity in tropical Africa was the purchase of millions of slaves for the Americas. By the 1870s, with the slave trade ended, the European powers had abandoned their coastal trading posts. Yet by 1900, they had shared out the entire continent except for the mountain empire of Ethiopia.

The British, French and Belgians divided the spoils with the Germans, then expelled them during the first world war. These unprofitable empires lasted for little more than half a century and were dismantled in the years after 1960 into more than 30 nations, most of them far too poor to function as modern states, and with pathetically few educated people. The sequel has been misgovernment, war, poverty, chaos and despair.

The heart of Africa is the one region of the world where prosperity has since the 1960s failed to advance, and has for the most part receded. The population is increasing far faster than that of any other region, but the pace of political, and therefore economic, reform has been tragically slow.

For example Nigeria, with 100 million people – almost a quarter of all black Africans – is potentially rich, and exports plenty of oil to pay for its own development. A series of military coups, alternating with massively corrupt civilian regimes, have held it back. It was autocratic rule that ruined the second most populous African nation, Zaire, formerly the Belgian Congo, under a ▷

Although many Algerians have continued their traditional way of life (left) since independence in 1962, many are still economically dependent on their old colonial power. By 1991 more than 4m legal and illegal migrants were living in France.

WHERE THE GRASS IS GREENER...

Western Europe, like all the industrialised world except Japan, based its postwar economic growth on cheap imported labour. The former colonies of North Africa supplied the largest number of workers. They found hard, low-paid jobs in the building and mass-production industries. They settled, had children, moved across European borders, often with no legal right to work, and became indispensable.

All over Europe, anti-immigrant feeling had long been present against Turks in Germany, Italians in Switzerland, West Indians in Britain. In France and the Low Countries, North Africans were the main targets. By the early 1990s jobs were scarce in Europe, and people began to expect an influx of workers from eastern Europe. Right-wing politicians laid the blame for unemployment on the migrants. There was talk of sending them home where jobs were even scarcer – more than half the school-leavers in Algeria and Tunisia had no jobs to go to. The EC talked vaguely about fostering North African development, to put more of its surplus people to work. Just as the USA looks anxiously southwards at the prospect of mass migration from Central America, Europe looks across the sea at the waiting millions of Muslims seeking work.

NORTH AFRICANS IN EUROPE, 1990

COUNTRY	MOROCCO	ALGERIA	TUNISIA
BELGIUM	138,417	10,644	6,247
FRANCE	590,000	825,000	270,000
GERMANY W.	67,458	6,645	25,897
ITALY	84,758	4,229	44,780
NETHERLANDS	147,975	569	<100
PORTUGAL	71	31	17
SPAIN	14,471[1]	-	-
1 1988 figs. Other Africans including Tunisians and Algerians = 8,464			

THE MAGHREB AND EUROPE

The economies of countries of the Maghreb – Morocco, Algeria and Tunisia – are largely based on agriculture and this is reflected in their trading patterns with Europe. The main exports of all three are beverages, fruit, vegetables and other foodstuffs. Their main imports comprise chemicals, machinery and electrical appliances, transport equipment, clothing textiles and manufactured products as well as food, particularly cereal products. The trading partners of each reflect the ties with colonists of the past. Hence France's prominence in both import and export markets, but Italy, Germany and Spain also have significant trade wtih the Maghreb.

TRADE WITH EUROPE, $m 1990

	Exports = fob		Imports = cif		

COUNTRY	MOROCCO[1]	ALGERIA[1]	TUNISIA[2]
BELGIUM/LUX	18.2	42.3	21.2
	19.0	20.6	20.5
FRANCE	157.9	150.5	128.3
	163.0	260	73
GERMANY W.	43.1	73.7	56
	50.4	85	41.9
ITALY	31.6	222.5	68.4
	42.4	87.6	64.7
NETHERLANDS	–	64.2	–
	13.5	26.5	–
SPAIN	35.5	65.5	–
	54.4	43	–
UK	15.7	36.2	–
	17.5	–	–
USA	9.1	294.9	25.3
JAPAN	41.4	66.4	–
1 Jan-Mar 2 Jan-Nov			

North African growth

Although Algeria is about four times the size of Morocco, the populations of the two countries, and the estimated rate of increase between 1985 and 1989, are roughly the same. However, Morocco's real GNP growth, helped by the country's virtual world monopoly on phosphates, outstripped Algeria by almost four to one. Only in Tunisia, one-third the size in geographical and population terms, does population increase match exactly with real GNP growth.

POPULATION AND WEALTH

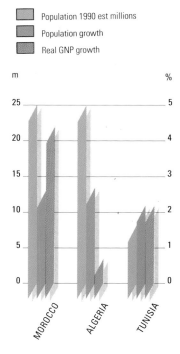

	Population 1990 est millions
	Population growth
	Real GNP growth

ruler who for 30 years failed to pass the profits on to the people, and clung on long after his failure was apparent. Angola, liberated from inefficient Portuguese rule in 1974, immediately plunged into 15 years of civil war, fomented by the Soviet Union and South Africa.

In many African nations, the men who took power at independence in the early 1960s clung to office, often with the support of former colonial rulers, into the early 1990s. They kept food prices down, causing farmers to grow only what they needed, with no surplus for the new

cities into which people migrated. When their countries were bankrupt, foreign advisers persuaded the rulers to start economic reforms whose first stages were acutely painful. Tentative democratic reforms followed, but production kept on falling due to mismanagement.

Africa has by far the world's fastest rate of population growth, with many nations doubling their peoples every 20 years. In the years of low growth, investment in schools, transport and medical services was neglected. War had wrecked several potentially prosperous nations. Huge debts, far beyond the capacity of African nations to repay, hang over the continent. Economic reform is moving slowly; the political reforms necessary to make it work are far from completion. For decades to come, black Africa is likely to remain dependent on aid.

AID AND INVESTMENT

Black Africa is getting less and less of the new investment it desperately needs. The table shows the net flow of financial resources into the continent, meaning new money less the repayment of capital and interest on old debts; since the figures are expressed in depreciated US dollars, the real decline from the brief peak in 1987 is sharper than the figures show. Several deeply indebted countries are unable to pay even the interest on their previous borrowings, and there is no reason to suppose the richer world will bail them out.

DEVELOPMENT $bn	1982	1984	1986	1988	1990
OFFICIAL DEVELOPMENT FINANCE	10.7	11.8	15.1	18.9	21.4
TOTAL EXPORT CREDITS	1.9	0.2	–	-0.5	1.0
PRIVATE FLOWS[1]	4.9	-0.6	4.2	3.9	2.5
TOTAL NET RESOURCE FLOWS	17.5	11.4	19.3	22.3	24.9
1 Inc. direct investment, non-governmental grants, international bank lending					

Boy racers… Dogon children from West Africa play on an ancient Peugeot; West Africa once formed a large part of the French colonial empire, and the cultural and economic links still linger.

RELIGIONS OF AFRICA

Africa's conquerors brought their beliefs with them. Probably about one-third of all Africans are Muslims, a quarter are Christians, and the rest are animists, worshipping God through natural phenomena and ancestral guides.

Islam came first. More than 1,000 years after the Arab conquest, North Africa is solidly Muslim. Trade across the Sahara carried the Islamic faith south of the desert, where it mingles with Christian and animist beliefs. Islam is strong, too, around the former Arab colonies along the east African coast, such as Ethiopia.

In the far south Christian missionaries long since converted most of the people. The churches have a strong influence on politics; Christian doctrine, which once justified South African theories of racial dominance, has also provided many leaders for the mainly black African National Congress, such as Bishop Desmond Tutu.

Most people in tropical Africa are farmers, living in small settlements and following traditional beliefs. Politicians and civil servants tend to be Christian, educated in mission schools; armies tend to recruit many Muslims. Faith is strong in Africa, and competition between faiths vigorous. Religious strife often intensifies national and tribal rivalries.

Along the north African seaboard Sunni Muslims dominate the Arab population. In Morocco, Algeria, Tunisia and Libya more than 95% of Arabs identify themselves as Muslims.

Flow of resources

Most of Africa is still largely dependent on official aid rather than foreign investment in local companies although there is a growing number of successful medium-sized firms.

Two changes would give Africa hope: a sharp rise in demand for mineral and farm commodities would increase export revenue and encourage foreign investors. This might stimulate richer countries to massively increase their aid.

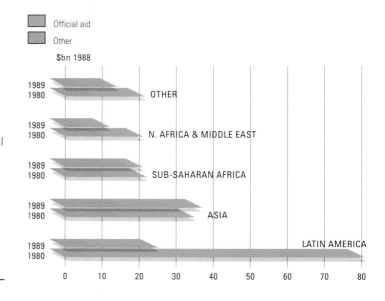

Official aid

Other

$bn 1988

INVESTMENT IN SOUTH AFRICA

The gold and diamonds of South Africa, discovered in the 1880s, drew hundreds of thousands of Europeans, and billions of dollars of European capital, into one of history's great commercial adventures. Britain, then at the peak of its power, jealously guarded the only profitable part of its African empire. The City of London financed the growth of South Africa's white-dominated economic and political structure. To protect that intimate and profitable alliance, recent British governments sought to avert the economic sanctions that other democracies applied in support of the black liberation struggle. But political change was inevitable as white power declined in the rest of southern Africa.

Although British-based mining and service companies have reduced their interests in South Africa. Britain remains by far the largest overseas investor in the country. But, the figures are misleading because, in response to sanctions, many companies handed nominal control of their businesses to local firms. This helped to concentrate the ownership of South African industry in the hands of fewer firms than in any other significant capitalist economy.

Faced with the prospect of a black government with different priorities to the existing white minority government, many large South African companies have moved nominal control of their assets abroad, seeking financial shelter in Europe or in tax havens under European protection. For the first time in a century, investment is flowing out of South Africa. Yet the old companies maintain their former dominance there.

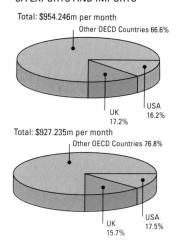

SA EXPORTS AND IMPORTS

Total: $954.246m per month
Other OECD Countries 66.6%
UK 17.2%
USA 16.2%

Total: $927.235m per month
Other OECD Countries 76.8%
UK 15.7%
USA 17.5%

Homeward bound
The economically dominant white citizenship of South Africa is mainly of European origin. But the political strife of recent years has sharply reduced white immigration and persuaded migrants to go home.

SOUTH AFRICAN MIGRATION

COUNTRY	1961-80		1981-90	
	Immigrants	Emigrants	Immigrants	Emigrants
FINLAND	463	227	65	45
FRANCE	5,670	1,670	1,637	498
GERMANY	43,931	13,873	8,634	2,677
GREECE	14,602	1,149	1,694	246
IRELAND	4,501	1,353	2,197	479
NETHERLANDS	17,894	8,931	3,441	1,669
PORTUGAL	24,730	2,103	8,558	648
SPAIN	891	590	558	232
SWITZERLAND	13,659	5,206	1,619	1,138
UK	257,578	79,401	78,722	33,070
ASIA	8,439	4,758	8,924	2,241
USA	6,954	8,608	3,072	4,164

Investors in South Africa
These are the top ten countries investing in South Africa, measured by the number of companies in 1990. The list is dominated by European countries. The USA lifted its ban on new investment in South Africa in July 1991. Lately the trend towards non-equity links with South African companies continues to increase worldwide.

COUNTRY	COMPANIES
UK	170
GERMANY W.	131
USA	114
SWITZERLAND	33
JAPAN	23
FRANCE	21
AUSTRALIA	9
NERTHERLANDS	9
ITALY	7
AUSTRIA	5

Disinvestors
The main countries withdrawing from South Africa measured in the number of disinvestments between 1984 and 1991. The USA leads the field by far. However, as political power passes back to the mainly black electorate the withdrawal may stop even though the giant firms fear that economic power may pass out of their hands.

COUNTRY	COMPANIES
USA	215
UK	87
GERMANY W.	34
CANADA	16
AUSTRALIA	9
FRANCE	8
NETHERLANDS	8
SWITZERLAND	6
BELGIUM	4
SWEDEN	4

Foreign employers
European firms which remained under apartheid have been invited to stay on as much-needed employers and investors. The table ranks the top foreign employers in South Africa. White executives hold on to all but a token number of top jobs mainly because their government has ensured very few Africans are educated to do them.

COMPANY	EMPLOYEES
LONRHO PLC.	12,110
ROYAL DUTCH PET. CO	9,144
VOLKSWAGEN AG	8,523
UNILEVER PLC	7,962
BOC GROUP PLC	6,646
BTR PLC	6,515
DAIMLER-BENZ AG	6,061
NESTLE AS	5,949
SIEMENS AG	5,157
ROLLS-ROYCE PLC	4,835

NOT JUST THE WHITE MAN'S GRAVE

Sickness was for centuries Africa's main defence against outsiders. Local populations had often built up immunities against the parasite-borne infections that thrive in hot, well-watered places. British traders and explorers used to call it the ``white man's grave''. Only at the end of the 19th century, with the discovery of treatments against malaria and other fevers, could travellers move about in relative safety.

Human health is probably getting worse again in Africa. Many countries are doubling their population every 20 years, making child-care and immunisation a heavy burden. Economic failure has forced governments to cut their health spending just when it needed increasing. People are moving into cities where the necessary investment in water and drainage has not been made. Wars have impoverished whole nations, herding hungry people into camps where disease spreads faster than relief.

Deadly parasite-borne diseases, notably malaria and bilharzia, have made a come-back. Measles is a scourge of children. On top of all that, about half the world's infections by the newly-discovered human immuno-deficiency virus (HIV) have been counted in black Africa. It is not possible, however, to get an accurate Africa-wide picture. In the years 1979–91, Uganda, for instance, reported 21,719 cases and Nigeria only 84. Just when Africa needs to attract back the doctors, and other professionals who trained elsewhere, qualified people are reluctant to risk themselves and their families by living there.

COUNTRY	Under 5 mortality	Mortality rate	Life exp (male)	Life exp (female)
ALGERIA	102	<10	61	64
ANGOLA	292	16-20	43	46
BENIN	150	16-20	45	48
BOTSWANA	87	10-15	56	62
BURKINO FASO	232	16-20	46	49
BURUNDI	196	16-20	47	51
CAMEROON	150	10-15	49	53
CARE VERDE	58	<10	–	–
CENTRAL AFRICAN REP	219	16-20	44	47
CHAD	219	16-20	44	47
COMOROS	155	10-15	–	–
CONGO	112	10-15	47	50
COTE D'IVOIRE	139	10-15	51	54
EQUATORIAL GUINEA	210	16-20	–	–
ETHIOPIA	226	16-20	39	43
GABON	167	16-20	50	53
GAMBIA	241	16-20	–	–
GHANA	143	10-15	52	56
GUINEA	241	16-20	41	44
GUINEA-BISSAU	250	16-20	–	–
KENYA	–	10-15	57	61
LESOTHO	132	10-15	52	61
LIBERIA	209	10-15	53	56
MADAGASCAR	179	10-15	52	55

COUNTRY	Under 5 mortality	Mortality rate	Life exp (male)	Life exp (female)
MALAWI	258	16-20	46	48
MALI	287	16-20	42	46
MAURITANIA	217	16-20	44	48
MAURITIUS	–	<10	66	72
MOZAMBIQUE	297	16-20	45	48
NAMIBIA	171	10-15	55	58
NIGER	225	16-20	43	46
NIGERIA	170	10-15	49	52
REUNION	–	21-25	–	–
RWANDA	201	16-20	47	50
ST HELENA	–	10-15[1]	–	–
SAO TOME & PRINCIPE	–	10-15[2]	–	–
SENEGAL	189	16-20	44	47
SEYCHELLES	–	<10[2]	–	–
SIERRA LEONE	261	21-25	39	43
SOUTH AFRICA	91	<10	58	64
SWAZILAND	170	10-15	–	–
TANZANIA	127	10-15	51	55
TOGO	150	10-15	51	55
UGANDA	167	10-15	49	53
WESTERN SAHARA	–	10-15	–	–
ZAIRE	132	10-15	51	54
ZAMBIA	125	10-15	52	55
ZIMBABWE	90	10-15	57	60

Under 5 mortality rate 1989 per 1,000 live births
Mortality rates (%) 1985-90
Life expectancy (male) 1990
Life expectancy (female) 1990
1 1987 figs. 2 1989 figs.

Defence is the first priority of nations once they are established. After the devastation of the second world war, Europe took the lessons learned from it and established a military pattern that kept overall peace but became entangled in many local conflicts. For 40 years, Europe's main defence effort has been directed eastward, towards the Soviet empire; now the cold war is over, spending on arms, armies and defence is difficult to justify and countries are preoccupied with how to spend their peace dividend to finance other needs. Europe's defence industry is being refocused and reorganised, and the purpose and function of NATO is in question.

This chapter looks at how Europe's military capabilities were refashioned after 1945; how well each country learned the lessons of war and the way in which European governments dealt with rebel movements in colonial territories. It explains the cold war balance and then moves on to the issues that are directly relevant today: what the role of intelligence services is in the new world order; how much money can still be made selling arms and who sells what to whom; what threats there are to European security from terrorists, drug smugglers and refugees; and how Europe will cope with the changes in defence requirements brought about by the end of the cold war.

THE BIRTH OF NATIONS

In 1947 the USA offered to assist the postwar recovery of Europe with economic aid under the Marshall Plan. The USSR and its satellites refused the aid but western Europe created the Organisation for European Economic Cooperation to administer financial assistance totalling $22.4bn between 1948 and 1952.

The modern map of Europe was drawn largely by the peace treaties which ended the first world war. The settlement led to the break-up of the old Austro-Hungarian, German and Tsarist Russian empires and the creation of the small nation states of central Europe. The creation of a new Russian empire after the second world war apparently ended the independence of these states, which were either absorbed into the Soviet Union or allowed a notional independence. Recent events, however, have shown that these states are real political entities, attracting the continuing allegiance of their peoples. Even countries which were only briefly independent, such as the Ukraine, are now sovereign states.

After centuries of imperial rule and settlement, it was impossible to group individual nationalities within arbitrary lines drawn on the map. Significant national minorities were left within the borders of the Versailles Treaty states, which were an immediate cause of dispute. In particular, Hitler was able to exploit the supposed wrongs of the German minorities in Czechoslovakia and Poland to justify his aggression against those countries. Furthermore, the border disputes between the central European states ensured that they were unable to unite against the rise of German power in the 1930s. Poland and Hungary, in fact, joined Germany in annexing Czech

territory in 1938–39. After 1945 such disputes were frozen by the division of Europe into two power blocs, but the death of Marxism and collapse of the Soviet empire have again made nationalism and minorities major issues.

Seeds of aggression

The first world war proved too great a test for the Tsarist system in Russia, which had long seemed on the point of collapse. Because the embryonic democratic government in Russia was prepared to continue fighting, the Germans funded Lenin's return to Russia.

The coup he organised established a Marxist government and thus re-introduced a crucial factor into European politics. Both the French and Russian revolutions set states against each other, not for dynastic advantage or territorial gain, but to spread a particular system of government. The former sort of dispute was likely to lead to limited warfare; the latter to unlimited and mutually destructive general warfare. In particular, the Soviet Union, whose ideology preached the inevitability of decisive struggle between socialism and capitalism, became a militarised society, dedicated to maintaining and increasing its military strength. Germany under Hitler followed the same pattern and, in order to defend themselves against these threats, the rest of Europe was forced to accept a degree of militarisation which had been unknown in previous centuries.

Warfare also changed Europe's place in the world. The human and financial losses of the world wars weakened the European powers' ability and desire to rule the rest of the world. Japan's sweep of victories in 1941–42 destroyed the European empires in the Far East. Although the colonies were reclaimed in 1945 the fact remained that European empires had been defeated by an Asiatic power and rescued by the largely American victory in the Pacific. Once it became clear that on the one hand the USA would not support European rule overseas and on the other that the Soviet Union was ready to sponsor a struggle against it, the end of European empires was inevitable.

Settlement after 1918

The major consequence of the Versailles Treaty at the end of the first world war was to open up central Europe as a swathe of independent states as national aspirations which had developed during the previous century were satisfied. However, after so long under imperial rule and after so many border changes following other wars, these frontiers were artificial creations which could not enclose discrete national groups. This inevitably led to future quarrels as has been seen in countries such as Yugoslavia and Czechoslovakia.

ATTITUDES TO WAR AND PEACE

Europe's experience of warfare in the 20th century has also caused a profound change in European attitudes to war itself. In 1914 Clausewitz's maxim that "war is an instrument of policy" was universally accepted and governments felt few qualms about using war to pursue their objectives. However, the slaughter of the first world war changed this.

Attempts at disarmament after 1918 were encouraged by the conviction that war was too dangerous a weapon of diplomacy. The policy of appeasement was partly justified in many minds by the conviction that war was the greater evil. Even the failure of appeasement has not restored the old attitudes to war.

Since 1945 European attitudes to war have been complicated by the introduction of nuclear weapons. On all sides there was a determination to avoid another European war, but there was a clear divide between those who believed that the threat of war was best deterred by strong military forces and alliances, backed by nuclear weapons, and those who found war too terrible to contemplate. The strength of the European peace movements has varied with time, but reactions to intervention in the Gulf crisis of 1990–91 demonstrated that it is hard to justify the use of military force to a considerable body of European opinion.

Austro-Hungarian Empire
German Empire
Ottoman Empire
Russian Empire
Area ceded by Treaty of Versailles 1919
National borders 1926

NORWAY
Oslo
SWEDEN
Stockholm
FINLAND
Helsinki
Tallinn
ESTONIA
Moscow
Riga LATVIA
DENMARK
Copenhagen *BALTIC SEA*
LITHUANIA
Kaunas
EAST PRUSSIA
UNION OF SOVIET SOCIALIST REPUBLICS
NETHERLANDS
Amsterdam
Berlin
Warsaw
Brussels
BELGIUM
GERMANY
POLAND
LUX
Prague
SAAR Autonomous under League of Nations 1919/20-35
CZECHOSLOVAKIA
Vienna
Bern
SWITZ
AUSTRIA
Budapest
HUNGARY
FRANCE
ROMANIA
Belgrade
Bucharest
BLACK SEA
YUGOSLAVIA
ITALY
MONTENEGRO To Yugoslavia 1921
BULGARIA
Sofia
Rome
Tiranë
ALBANIA
Ankara
GREECE
TURKEY
Athens
MEDITERRANEAN SEA

Connections: Patterns of empire 16–17   The cold war balance 184–185   Threats to security 192–193

POLITICAL TIDES OF WAR

By 1939 the bombing of cities and the revolution in land warfare increased the scope and decisiveness of operations out of all recognition. Even a major power such as France could fall to the enemy in a matter of weeks, smaller nations crumbled in days. After 1945 this common experience of occupation encouraged the formation of military alliances.

Some countries, such as Sweden, Switzerland or Spain, remained even more avowedly neutral after the war. Others, such as Denmark, Norway, the Netherlands and Belgium, which had been dragged reluctantly into the war, abandoned neutrality to ensure their security. The minor loss of independence which membership of an alliance entailed was preferable to the experience of conquest. Even among those states of eastern Europe which were forced into alliances with the Soviet Union, there was, initially at least, the feeling that it was better than the instability of the inter-war years or Nazi occupation. The equilibrium of the cold war provided a breathing space in which societies and economies could be rebuilt. In time, the countries of the western alliance proved so much more successful as societies and economies that the equilibrium was destroyed and the eastern alliance collapsed.

After 1945

The Soviet Union's role in the defeat of Germany and its still preponderant land power received de facto recognition as its frontier extended westwards, swallowing the Baltic states and significant parts of Poland, Czechoslovakia, Germany, Hungary and Romania. Poland was allowed compensation at the expense of Germany and throughout eastern Europe ethnic Germans were forced out of their homes. The revolution in the eastern bloc has emphasised the stresses this caused.

EUROPEAN WAR EXPERIENCE

COUNTRY	OCCUPIED	LIBERATED	NATO/WPT
PORTUGAL			1949
SPAIN			1943
FRANCE	1940	1944	1949
BELGIUM	1940	1944	1949
LUXEMBOURG	1944	1944	1949
NETHERLANDS	1940	1945	1949
SWITZERLAND			NEUTRAL
ITALY	1943[1]	1945	1949
AUSTRIA			NEUTRAL
GERMANY			1955/1955-90[2]
DENMARK	1940	1945	1949
NORWAY	1940	1945	1949
SWEDEN			NEUTRAL
CZECHOSLOVAKIA	1938-9	1944	1955-90
HUNGARY			1955-91
YUGOSLAVIA	1940	1944[3]	
ALBANIA	1939[4]	1944[5]	1955-68
GREECE	1940	1945	1952
BULGARIA	1944		1955-91
TURKEY			1952
ROMANIA	1944		1955-91
POLAND	1939	1945	1955-91
ESTONIA, LATVIA & LITHUANIA	1940 / 1941	1945[6]	1955-91
FINLAND		1944[7]	NEUTRAL
USSR	1941-44[8]		1955-91

WAR STANCE

- AXIS
- ALLIED
- USSR
- NATO
- WARSAW PACT

1 From 1943 Italy switched to Allies. Northern Italy under German Occupation 1943-45
2 West Germany joined NATO, East Germany joined WPT. With German Unification in 1990, East Germany became part of NATO
3 Liberated by its own forces as well as USSR
4 Occupied by Italy
5 Liberated by its own forces
6 Incorporporated into USSR
7 Sued for peace with USSR
8 Western USSR under German occupation, although Ukraine views occupation as liberation

The strength of the European peace movement in the late 1960s and mid-1980s stands in stark contrast to the enthusiasm with which crowds greeted the outbreak of the first world war in August 1914.

Vive la France! Paris celebrated on August 25th, 1945. The fall of France in 1940, four years of German occupation and liberation by the Anglo-Americans were key experiences in shaping French society after 1945 and in determining France's ambivalent attitude to NATO and the American presence in Europe.

MILITARY THINKING

The effects of the two world wars on military thinking can be studied on at least two levels. First, there is the technical analysis of the experience within the armed forces themselves, which is professional, detailed and designed to perfect the structure, equipment and doctrine of the state's military machine. Second, there is the external perception of the experience: how the nation has seen the war and the performance of its armed forces. The interplay between these two determines military doctrine, defence policy and even ultimate victory or defeat in future wars.

The lessons each European power chose to draw reflected its national perspective. In Britain, the abiding folk memory after the first world war was of battles like the Somme, when thousands died for no apparent gain; the victories of the last few months were forgotten. The German army lost as heavily in 1916 and 1917 but its defeat in 1918 made the greater impact. To explain it, the army developed the myth of the "stab in the back", which played its part in the collapse of democracy in the 1930s.

British stretcher-bearers at Passchendaele in 1917. Between July 31st and early November that year, the British line advanced 8km at the cost of 35,000 lives.

The German zeppelin raids during the first world war had effects in Britain out of all proportion to their actual results. Strategic bombing and air defence became the air force's major roles. In Germany, however, the indecisive effect of the zeppelin raids resulted in the main role of the new Luftwaffe in 1939 being to support ground operations. The allied aerial bombing offensive against Germany in the second world war did not achieve a clear victory, but nuclear weapons gave new life to the theories of strategic bombing. Although strategic nuclear weapons are now mostly carried by missiles, the air campaign in the Gulf war showed that the debate about the role of air power is still a live issue.

For both nations and their armed forces certain battles or campaigns have gained a kind of mythic importance which outweighs their real strategic influence on the course of the war. The second world war on land has become firmly associated with the German blitzkrieg campaigns, which stand in dramatic contrast to the deadlock of the Western Front in the previous war. But in fact the successes of the blitzkrieg lasted for little more than two years. As other armies learnt to combine the use of tanks, aircraft and other arms effectively, the era of easy victories passed .

The Soviet influence

The Soviet victories of 1944–45 had a fundamental influence on military thought. In the USSR they were a source of military doctrine and the justification for the army's existence. In the West, fear of the Soviet "steamroller" was the motive for the foundation of NATO and ensured that, for more than 40 years, western military thinking was dominated by the problem of preventing another westward surge by the Soviet army.

The world wars were wars of mass armies, raised by conscription and backed by the total mobilisation of societies. During those wars machinery became more important than manpower and the military-technical revolution at the end of the century has now put the survival of the mass army in doubt.

Key campaigns 1914–18
In the development of the military art the most significant operations were concentrated in the "cockpit of Europe", below. The domination of the defensive over the offensive in land tactics was most pronounced in this area and it was here new weapons, such as the tank and new combined arms tactics, restored mobility to the battlefield. The map also shows the bases from which German U-boats challenged the traditional pattern of sea power and the airfields from which the first aerial bombing campaigns were launched.

LESSONS OF THE FIRST WORLD WAR

On land, the German advances of 1914, following the Schlieffen Plan, illustrated the strategic mobility which railways had provided, but the deadlock of the Western Front showed how other consequences of the industrial revolution conspired against tactical mobility. Quick-firing artillery, machine guns, high explosives, barbed wire, and so on, all seemed to favour the defensive. But it was also on the Western Front that armies learnt how to adapt these weapons and introduce new ones, such as the tank and the aircraft, to restore the tactical balance.

At sea, navies expected the clash of the surface fleets in the North Sea to be decisive but again stalemate ensued. It was the U-boats which might have changed the course of the war and which pointed to the future of naval warfare. Germany's zeppelin raids not only demonstrated the power of the aircraft but symbolised a change in the nature of war. Civilian populations had become the direct target of military operations.

However, one important legacy of the first world war has been the non-use of a weapon. Poison gas was used by both sides after the initial German use at Ypres in 1915 but gave no decisive advantage to the user. This was the first and only time European armies have used chemical weapons against each other. Although they have retained the capability, chemical weapons have not been used between major powers since.

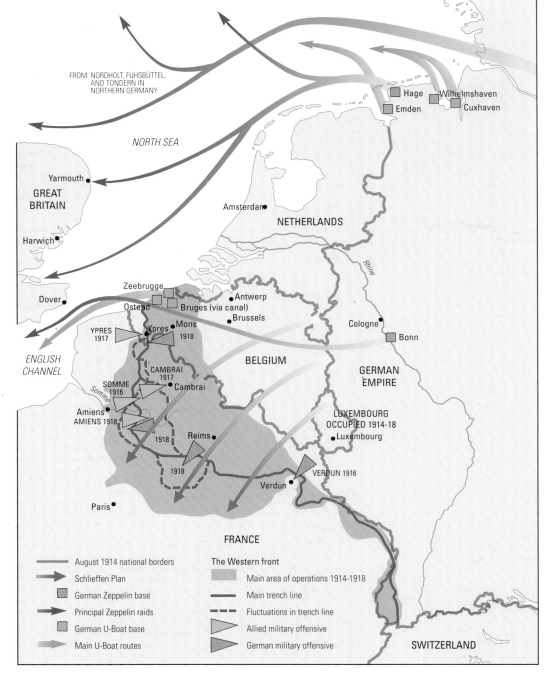

August 1914 national borders	**The Western front**
Schlieffen Plan	Main area of operations 1914-1918
German Zeppelin base	Main trench line
Principal Zeppelin raids	Fluctuations in trench line
German U-Boat base	Allied military offensive
Main U-Boat routes	German military offensive

Connections: Operations after 1945 182–183   The cold war balance 184–185   Arms industries 186–187

Key campaigns 1939—45

Almost the whole of Europe was affected and no one map could represent the entire war. Some campaigns, such as that in Greece in 1941 or in Italy after 1943, had little impact on the outcome of the war and stand only as a warning of the dangers of the diversion of strategic efforts into side-shows. Resistance movements operated throughout Europe but their true strategic value still divides historical opinion.

The German blitzkrieg campaigns, the allied campaign in north-west Europe and the major operations on the Soviet-German front continue to be studied for their lessons in the handling of major land forces. The western allies' landing operations saw the recreation of amphibious warfare as a branch of the military art; large-scale airborne operations had been expected.

The battle of the Atlantic demonstrated the growing threat which submarines pose to surface fleets. In the air, the significance of the strategic bombing offensive on Germany is still a live issue.

Legend:
— National borders, April 1939
— Maginot Line
➤ Blitzkrieg Campaigns 1939-41
♔ Major Eastern Front battles
➤ Soviet offensives 1944-45
Airborne operations
Amphibious operations
Convoys
Strategic bombings
V-1 and V-2 raids

The price of war

The first world war differed from previous wars because land battles lasted not for a few hours or days but for months. These armies were basically infantry armies and human lives are the currency of infantry battles. Casualties in navies and air forces were significantly lower as a proportion of those mobilised, because their battles were primarily determined by losses of equipment. Britain's war casualties were, as a percentage of mobilised manpower, less than those of other great powers because of the size of its naval and air forces. By the second world war, with increasingly mechanised armies, casualties on land were also falling. The proportion of any army serving in the infantry was significantly lower, so battle casualties were reduced. However, any gain in human terms was more than off-set by the greater involvement of civilian populations. Overall in the second world war, civilian casualties probably equalled military losses.

	FIRST WORLD WAR DEATHS (Military)	SECOND WORLD WAR DEATHS (Military)	SECOND WORLD WAR DEATHS (Civilian)	
AUSTRO-HUNGARIA	1,200,00	380,000	145,000	AUSTRIA
		554,000		BALTIC STATES
BELGIUM	13,716	9,561	75,000	BELGIUM
BRITISH EMPIRE	947,023	271,311	60,595	UK
BULGARIA	87,500	18,500	1,500	BULGARIA
		6,683	310,000	CZECHOSLOVAKIA
		4,339		DENMARK
		79,047		FINLAND
FRANCE	1,385,300	210,671	173,260	FRANCE
GERMANY	1,808,545	2,850,000	2,300,000	GERMANY
GREECE	5,000	16,357	155,300	GREECE
		13,700	236,300	HOLLAND
		750,000		HUNGARY
ITALY	462,391	279,820	93,000	ITALY
MONTENEGRO	3,000			
		4,778		NORWAY
		850,000	5,778,000	POLAND
PORTUGAL	7,222			
ROMANIA	335,706	519,822	465,000	ROMANIA
RUSSIA	1,700,000	14,500,000	7,000,000	USSR
SERBIA	45,000			
TURKEY	325,000			
		1,700,000		YUGOSLAVIA

LESSONS OF THE SECOND WORLD WAR

The lessons of one war often turn out to be the mistakes of the next. The battle of Verdun (1916) demonstrated the value of permanent fortifications; between the wars France fortified its border with Germany (the Maginot Line). The collapse of France within six weeks in 1940 discredited the line and permanent fortifications; in fact, the line did not fail, it simply did not cover the whole frontier and the Germans outflanked it.

The battle of the Atlantic again proved the importance of maritime communications for Britain. It also showed how a comparatively limited offensive effort by a continental power against those communications demands a major defensive effort to defeat it. Victory in the battle of the Atlantic enabled the western allies to demonstrate the offensive capability of seapower by launching the amphibious operations which led to the defeat of the German armies in the west. Airborne forces failed to fulfil the hopes of inter-war theorists and the value of large-scale airborne operations remains disputed.

In the USSR, the losses of the second world war were used by the state to justify a level of defence expenditure which distorted and ultimately ruined the economy. Victory bred complacency in the Soviet forces and too narrow a focus in their study of the war led to an inward- and backward-looking approach to modern warfare.

COUNTER-INSURGENCY

In the postwar period several European powers have had to commit considerable resources to counter-insurgency. Many of the nationalist and often Marxist inspired and supported movements in the African and Asian colonies resorted to guerrilla warfare to win political power for themselves. European armies had to learn that operations against guerrillas required a different textbook from the conventional warfare of the second world war. These "little wars", however, demanded major military commitments. In 1953, France deployed 190,000 troops in Indo-China and 400,000 in Algeria in 1956; the British security forces in Malaya totalled 300,000 including 40,000 regular soldiers and Britain deployed 60,000 men in Borneo.

The doctrine of counter-revolutionary warfare was developed for these conflicts. Although there were many national variations, certain common elements stood out. It was appreciated that victory involved political policy as much as military strategy and that the two must be closely coordinated. Usually this meant unified political and military command at every level, often with a general in charge. The battle for the hearts and minds of the civilian population was the key to victory; occupation of territory, crucial in conventional operations, was less significant.

Precise and detailed intelligence was also vital. The

counter-insurgent forces usually possessed overwhelming military superiority over the guerrillas, in both numbers and quality of equipment, but large-scale displays of military force were often counter-productive as the guerrillas could melt away from formal attacks. Special forces, operating in small groups and living among the population, proved much more effective.

Counter-revolutionary warfare involved certain political and social costs. Both the French and Portuguese armies became enmeshed in the national politics of their colonies through involvement in guerrilla wars. A failed coup in France left a long legacy of bitterness between army factions and a successful coup in Portugal brought the country into modern Europe. The doctrines of counter-insurgency are still studied by European armies and many of the techniques are used in counter-terrorist operations, but counter-revolutionary warfare is now associated with a past era, the period of de-colonisation.

No European army suffered total defeat at the hands of guerrillas, but as it became evident that European societies were no longer prepared to pay the political and economic costs of colonialism, military victory or defeat became irrelevant. The war in Afghanistan (1979–87) taught the Soviet army the same lesson and proved a major force in the reform of the Soviet military system.

The end of the road… Soviet troops withdrew from Kabul in February 1989. In Afghanistan the Soviet army faced the problems of a colonial army fighting a less sophisticated enemy in difficult terrain and was no more successful than western armies in such circumstances.

Good-bye to all that

European involvement in guerrilla wars in Africa and the Middle East was at its peak during the late 1950s and early 1960s. The longer a European state tried to hold on to power, the greater the instability it left behind, so that in some areas, guerrilla warfare has almost become endemic.

British possessions
French possessions
Belgian colony
Italian colony
Portuguese colony
Spanish colony

1960 Year of independence
 Guerrilla action

AFRICAN AND ARABIAN CAMPAIGNS

Britain fought a successful campaign in Kenya but by the 1960s all its African colonies were on the road to independence. Portugal, however, tried to hold on to its African colonies against guerrilla movements in Guinea-Bissau, Angola and Mozambique. All three were eventually thwarted but at a cost of 11,000 soldiers' lives. At home, the army was drawn into radical politics, leading to the military coup of 1974. By the end of 1975 Portugal's new government had left Africa. The French army was split over the war in Algeria. The element involved in Algeria was committed to a French presence. The Fourth Republic collapsed as a result and de Gaulle returned. When he began to negotiate Algerian independence, the leaders of the army in Algeria attempted a coup in 1961 which failed.

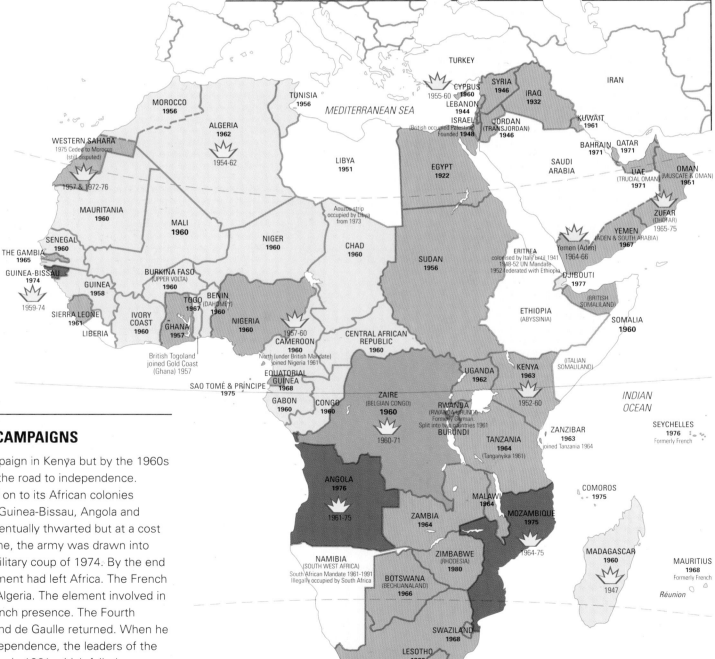

Connections: Europe and Asia 160–165   Europe and Africa 170–173   The birth of nations 176–177

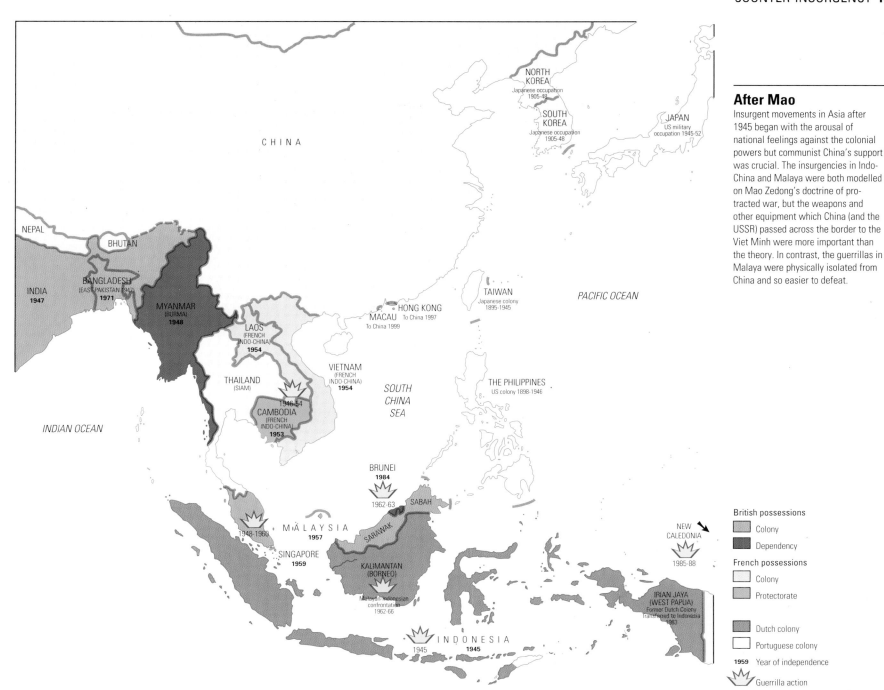

NORTH
KOREA
Japanese occupation
1905-48

SOUTH
KOREA
Japanese occupation
1905-48

JAPAN
US military
occupation 1945-52

CHINA

NEPAL

BHUTAN

BANGLADESH
(EAST PAKISTAN 1947)
1971

INDIA
1947

MYANMAR
(BURMA)
1948

LAOS
(FRENCH
INDO-CHINA)
1954

THAILAND
(SIAM)

CAMBODIA
(FRENCH INDO-CHINA)
1953
1946-54

VIETNAM
(FRENCH
INDO-CHINA)
1954

TAIWAN
Japanese colony
1895-1945

HONG KONG
To China 1997

MACAU
To China 1999

THE PHILIPPINES
US colony 1898-1946

PACIFIC OCEAN

SOUTH
CHINA
SEA

INDIAN OCEAN

BRUNEI
1984
1962-63

SABAH

SARAWAK

MALAYSIA
1957
1948-1960

SINGAPORE
1959

KALIMANTAN
(BORNEO)

Malayan-Indonesian
confrontation
1962-66

NEW
CALEDONIA
1985-88

IRIAN JAYA
(WEST PAPUA)
Former Dutch Colony
Transferred to Indonesia
1963

INDONESIA
1945   1945

British possessions
- Colony
- Dependency

French possessions
- Colony
- Protectorate

- Dutch colony
- Portuguese colony

1959 Year of independence

Guerrilla action

After Mao
Insurgent movements in Asia after 1945 began with the arousal of national feelings against the colonial powers but communist China's support was crucial. The insurgencies in Indo-China and Malaya were both modelled on Mao Zedong's doctrine of protracted war, but the weapons and other equipment which China (and the USSR) passed across the border to the Viet Minh were more important than the theory. In contrast, the guerrillas in Malaya were physically isolated from China and so easier to defeat.

FAR-EASTERN CAMPAIGNS

Before the second world war Britain, France and the Netherlands all had significant colonial empires in the Far East, but the Japanese onslaught of 1941 destroyed the idea of western superiority which underpinned them. During the war both sides looked for support among the colonies' emerging nationalist movements. America and Britain encouraged anti-Japanese resistance movements, although this entailed arming communist fronts, such as the Viet Minh and the Malayan People's Anti-Japanese Army, which were to prove the basis of postwar anti-government forces.

After 1944 the Japanese encouraged local nationalists to oppose allied re-occupation and in the power vacuum after the collapse of Japan, the nationalists briefly seized power in Indo-China and Indonesia. European rule was re-established but it was no longer undisputed. Between 1946 and 1948 guerrilla wars began in Indonesia, Indo-China and Malaya.

The Netherlands was the first to tire of supporting its colonial power on the basis of an economy ravaged by war. France struggled on in Indo-China until 1954 but defeat at Dien Bien Phu was the last straw. The French army was left feeling compromised by the politicians who had forced it to abandon its local supporters to the communists in North Vietnam, although South Vietnam, Laos and Cambodia were initially saved from communist rule. The Viet Minh became the Viet Cong and continued their campaign underground until American intervention began the Vietnam war.

In contrast the British campaign in Malaya ended in

complete success and the techniques which brought victory became the basis of the British doctrine of counter-insurgency. Victory, however, did not mean the continuation of colonial rule. Malaysia achieved independence even before the Emergency ended. Within two years British troops were embroiled in Borneo. The techniques developed in Malaya were successfully applied again but the war showed that the end of colonial power did not necessarily mean the end of military commitment. This led to a reduction in the number of Britain's open-ended commitments to former colonies.

Vietnamese troops loyal to France enter a village during an operation against the Viet Minh. The support of local forces was essential for all European armies during their counter-insurgency wars. The French recruited an army of 120,000 during the Indo-China war, but the lack of trained Vietnamese officers limited its combat effectiveness.

OPERATIONS AFTER 1945

1956 UNGARN

Soviet military action in Europe after 1945 crushed independence movements in Hungary (1956) and Czechoslovakia (1968). Neither tested the Soviet military system but gained the army a reputation for brutality.

The number of military operations shown on these maps makes it clear that the end of the second world war did not mean the outbreak of peace. The nuclear bomb ensured that neither side in the cold war was prepared to risk a major conflict, but their armed forces were not left idle. The Soviet army was used to keep subservient regimes in power in East Germany, Hungary and Czechoslovakia. Western forces were used to contain the communist bloc within its existing borders.

The debacle at Suez demonstrated that European states had only a limited ability to project their power abroad. Within those limits, a number of successful military operations have been mounted such as French and Belgian interventions in Africa, and British deployments in the Middle East and Belize. In the Falklands war Britain conducted a classic example of a successful overseas military expedition.

Nor has gunboat diplomacy vanished with the old empires; if anything, in fact, the use of military force to back diplomacy has increased in scope. Borders have been reinforced, fishing limits disputed and mineral rights claimed by the deployment of armed forces. A new use of armies has been the peace-keeping force, particularly under United Nations control.

A common characteristic of all types of military operation since 1945 has been the much tighter degree of political control which has been enforced. Modern communications have made it possible for governments to monitor and direct operations more closely than ever before and the possible consequences of overreaction have made such direction essential. Soldiers have had to learn to be much more politically aware than in the past, whether fighting a limited war or patrolling a peace-line.

The cold war is officially over but events since then have demonstrated that armed forces are not yet obsolete. The Gulf war saw European states allying with each other and the United States in a new role as world policemen. The civil war in Yugoslavia, on the other hand, has shown that ancient quarrels can still disturb the surface of European unity.

European flashpoints

The years since 1945 are often seen as a period of comparative peace in Europe but there have been many limited military operations.

1 Greek civil war 1944–49 After German withdrawal in 1944 the communist-led guerrillas of ELAS tried to take control. Britain intervened but ELAS fought on. With US financial aid after 1947 the Greek army established order.

2 The Corfu incident October 22nd 1946 Passing through the channel between Corfu and Albania two British destroyers struck mines and 44 men died. Compensation (as yet unpaid) was awarded to Britain.

3 Berlin blockade June 1948–May 1949 The USSR tested US commitment to Europe by cutting links through Soviet-occupied East Germany with the allied zones of Berlin. The allies then airlifted millions of tonnes of supplies to the city.

4 Berlin rising June 1953 When the Soviet puppet government in East Germany imposed a 10% increase in productivity "norms", without increasing pay, a strike began in Berlin and spread. Soviet forces suppressed disturbances.

5 Gibraltar 1954–85 British since 1713, but General Franco backed Spain's claim and closed the border in 1969. Restrictions were lifted in 1985 but Gibraltar wishes to stay British.

6 Hungarian revolution 1956 The overthrow of Stalinist government and demands for Hungary to leave the Warsaw pact led to invasion by troops from the USSR. A pro-Moscow government was re-established; 30,000 Hungarians and 7,000 Soviets died.

7 Berlin crises 1958 and 1961 In November 1958 a Soviet ultimatum tried to force a western withdrawal from Berlin but the USSR backed down in March 1959. A flood of refugees to the West in 1961 led East Germany to build the wall between the zones (August).

8 Cod war 1958–60 Iceland imposed a 12-mile (19km) fishing limit, denying traditional fishing grounds to Britain. British frigates and Icelandic coastguard vessels were involved in several incidents before Britain recognised the limit in 1960.

9 Invasion of Czechoslovakia August 1968 Dubcek's liberal reforms so alarmed other communist powers that Warsaw pact forces under Soviet command invaded and ended all reform.

10 Cod war 1972 Iceland extended its fishing limits again to 50 miles (80km). Collisions between frigates and Icelandic gunboats occurred before settlement.

11 Turkish invasion of Cyprus 1974 Almost 20 years after the outbreak of the guerrilla war against British rule which set Cyprus on the road to independence, Turkey invaded to prevent union (*enosis*) with Greece (July 20th and August 13th).

12 Aegean disputes from 1974 Greek possession of islands near the Turkish coast complicates delineation of territorial waters. Disputes over oil and fishing rights led to naval deployment .

13 Cod war 1975–76 Iceland imposed a 200-mile (320km) exclusive economic zone which led to more incidents.

14 Yugoslavia 1991– Croatian and Slovenian desire for autonomy provoked reaction from Serbian-dominated government and army. Civil war broke out in 1991 and in 1992 spread to Bosnia-Hercegovina.

Civil war
Foreign intervention
Territorial dispute
Trade dispute

ICELAND

⑧⑩⑬ ATLANTIC, OFF ICELAND
1958-60, 1972, 1975-76

NORWAY   FINLAND

SWEDEN

NORTH SEA   ESTONIA   RUSSIA

LATVIA

DENMARK   BALTIC SEA   LITHUANIA

IRELAND

UNITED KINGDOM   NETHERLANDS   BELARUS

③④⑦ BERLIN   POLAND
1948-49,1953,1958,1961

⑨ CZECHOSLOVAKIA   UKRAINE
1968

ATLANTIC OCEAN   BELGIUM   GERMANY

LUX

FRANCE   SWITZ   AUSTRIA   ⑥ HUNGARY   MOLDOVA
1956

ROMANIA

⑭ YUGOSLAVIA
1991   BLACK SEA

ITALY   BULGARIA

PORTUGAL   SPAIN   ALBANIA

⑤ GIBRALTAR   ⑫ AEGEAN   TURKEY
1954-85   1974-

② CORFU ① GREECE
1946   1944-49   SYRIA

⑪ NORTHERN CYPRUS   LEBANON
1974

MOROCCO   ALGERIA   TUNISIA   MEDITERRANEAN SEA   ISRAEL

Connections: Rebuilding democracies 120–121   Europe and Asia 160–165   Europe and the Middle East 166–169   Europe and Africa 170–173

Strike, reconnaissance and air defence versions of the Tornado aircraft saw service with the Royal Air Force in the Gulf war and were also used by the Italian and Saudi air forces. Six of the RAF's 42 strike aircraft were lost during the action – mainly in low-level attacks on airfields. As a result, airborne tactics were changed as the situation facing allied forces shifted from traditional threats to limited war.

Military interventions outside Europe

Since 1945 European military forces have been deployed throughout the world, either in "hot wars" such as the Korean or Gulf wars, or deterrent roles, as in Jordan in 1958 or Kuwait in 1961.

1 The Korean war 1950–53
A United Nations force was sent to defend South Korea against North Korean and, later, Chinese invasions. European powers contributing were Belgium, Denmark, France, Greece, Italy, Luxembourg, the Netherlands, Norway, Sweden, Turkey and the UK.

2 Suez 1956 Egyptian nationalisation of the Suez Canal led Britain and France to plan military intervention. Israeli attack in Sinai provided pretext for joint landings to protect the canal but international reactions forced withdrawal with considerable loss of prestige.

3 United Nations Emergency Force I 1956–67 A peace-keeping force sent to Sinai after the Suez crisis and Israeli invasion with contributions from Denmark, Finland, Norway, Sweden and Yugoslavia. It was deployed on the Egyptian-Israeli border until the war of 1967.

4 Jordan 1958 In the wake of the formation of the United Arab Republic by Egypt and Syria, King Hussein of Jordan asked for British assistance in July 1958. Troops were sent at the same time as an American force to Lebanon.

5 Congo 1960–64 Independence from Belgium was followed by army mutinies and civil war. Belgium deployed troops to protect civilian nationals until replaced by a UN force which was involved in establishing order until 1964. Sweden, Ireland and other European states contributed to the force.

6 Kuwait 1961 In June 1961 Iraq claimed Kuwait and began to mass troops on the border. British marines arrived on July 1st followed by a full army brigade and air support. The British force was replaced by Arab League troops and withdrew by October 19th.

7 Belize 1963– Guatemalan claims on the British colony of British Honduras were stepped up as independence approached. Guatemala broke off diplomatic relations in 1963 and Britain deployed extra troops to the colony. Further sabre-rattling by Guatemala resulted in Britain sending more troops on four main occasions in 1970, 1972, 1975 and 1977.

8 East African army mutinies 1964
In 1964 mutinies occurred in units of the armies of the newly independent states of Tanganyika, Uganda and Kenya. Their governments requested British assistance and troops based in Kenya and Aden put down the mutinies.

9 Congo 1964 In November 1964 Belgian paratroops were flown to Stanleyville (now Kisangani) by US aircraft to rescue European hostages in the Congolese civil war.

10 Chad 1968–72 Faced with a revolt by tribes in the north, President Tombalbaye asked for French assistance. Units of the Foreign Legion were sent and defeated the rebels. Most were withdrawn in 1971 and the remainder the following year.

11 Ceuta and Melilla 1973 In April 1973 there was an exchange of gunfire between Spanish and Moroccan warships in a dispute over fishing rights off the Spanish enclaves of Ceuta and Melilla on the Moroccan coast.

12 United Nations Emergency Force II 1973– A peace-keeping and monitoring force deployed between Egyptian and Israeli forces in Sinai and Israeli and Syrian lines in the Golan Heights after the 1973 Yom Kippur war. Austria, Finland, Ireland, Poland and Sweden have contributed troops.

13 Italian-Tunisian dispute 1977
A quarrel over oil exploration rights in an area of the Mediterranean claimed by both Tunisia and Italy led to the deployment of warships.

14 Chad 1978–80 The civil war in Chad continued and, when northern groups supported by Libya threatened the capital, president General Malloum asked for French help. French troops stayed until 1980 but fighting, which had never stopped completely, flared up again after their withdrawal.

15 Zaire (formerly the Congo) 1978
In May 1978 French and Belgian paratroops were dropped into the Kolwezi area when fighting between government troops and rebels crossing from Angola threatened the lives of European workers. The rebels were driven back and a pan-African peace force eventually replaced French and Belgian troops.

16 The Falklands war 1982 Britain sent a task force to the South Atlantic in response to the Argentinian invasion of the Falkland (Malvinas) Islands in April 1982. Major forces were landed on May 21st and the Argentinians forced to surrender on June 14th.

17 Lebanon 1982–84 France, Italy and Britain joined the USA in sending a multi-national force to intervene in the Lebanese civil war. The peace-keeping mission failed as it was seen to support the Lebanese Christian government and was withdrawn when it became the target of terrorist attacks.

18 Chad 1983–84 A further French intervention to support the government against northern rebels, backed by Libyan troops. A stalemate was established on the so-called "red line".

19 Chad 1986– The civil war was renewed by Libyan-supported attacks. French support enabled the government to re-occupy the north; a cease-fire was arranged in September 1987. The French garrison, however, remains in Chad.

20 The Gulf war 1990–91 British, French and Italian forces played a major part in the campaign to liberate Kuwait from Iraqi occupation while Belgium, Czechoslovakia, Denmark, Greece, Hungary, the Netherlands, Norway, Poland, Portugal, Romania, Spain and Sweden either contributed directly to the UN naval blockade or sent other specialist forces.

21 Zaire 1991 French and Belgian troops were sent to Kinshasa on September 24th after riots in Zaire in order to protect and evacuate their nationals.

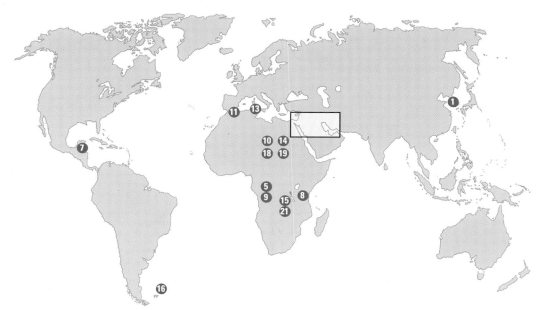

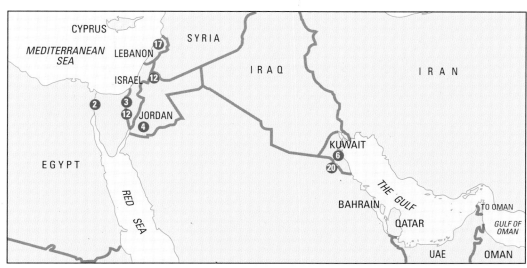

THE COLD WAR BALANCE

Checkpoint Charlie in Berlin was one of the most potent symbols of the cold war. The Americans (above) enforced stringent restrictions on Soviet army traffic entering West Berlin in the crisis of 1962.

The term "cold war" was invented to describe the peculiarities of international relations since 1945. Europe, and indeed the world, seemed to be divided between two implacably hostile blocs, the capitalist and democratic West and the socialist and totalitarian East. In Europe the blocs created opposing military alliances, the North Atlantic Treaty Organisation (NATO) and the Warsaw pact, which deployed on the continent the greatest concentrations of military power the world has seen. The peculiarity of the system was that this political hostility and military preparedness did not lead to a real war. In any other era war would surely have been inevitable, but in the age of nuclear weapons neither side was prepared to risk the mutual destruction which a general conflict might have entailed. At the heart of this system of mutual deterrence was the stability of the military balance between the alliances.

As long as this balance remained roughly equal, their political differences were unlikely to lead to war. At first NATO deterred the Soviet superiority in conventional forces by the policy of "massive retaliation", by which a Soviet attack on NATO territory would be met by nuclear strikes against the Soviet heartland. This meant that NATO did not need to match the high level of military and economic mobilisation enforced within the Warsaw pact, to the benefit of western societies and economies.

However, as Soviet nuclear forces grew to match America's, this strategy became less credible in military terms. It was modified to become the policy of "flexible response" by which NATO aimed to use conventional forces to stalemate any Soviet aggression so that diplomatic measures could end the crisis. The threat to use nuclear weapons if other means failed remained a crucial part of the strategy.

Thus the assessment of the military balance between the two blocs was vital to the maintenance of stability in Europe. The figures in tables and the large map shown on these pages reflect the situation in 1985–86, before the dramatic changes which ended the cold war. They are, however, only a crude measure of the true balance of power, for there were many imponderables which cannot be expressed in figures. It is comparatively easy to count numbers of men and equipment, much more difficult to assess the relative worth of individual tanks or aircraft. The balance of training and morale between the men who would have to operate the equipment in wartime is even harder to judge.

Furthermore, the balance was not static; much depended on the circumstances in which a war might begin. The NATO powers were stronger in terms of population and economic wealth but would require months or longer to mobilise that strength. The Warsaw pact mobilised a greater proportion of its forces in peacetime and would, therefore, have the advantage if it could launch a surprise attack. Such uncertainties may well have made the peace more secure because the risks of military action could never be precisely calculated and discounted.

Land forces

The overall balance of land forces shown below disguises the advantage the Soviet army had on the central front . The best equipped and trained Soviet military were concentrated in the groups of forces and kept at a high state of readiness. NATO corps deployed in Germany were more dependent on reinforcements from home; the strongest reserves would have had to come from the USA.

The table shows the Soviet strength in tanks, ATGW (antitank guided weapon launchers), MRL (multiple rocket launchers) and artillery, crucial to any attacking force. Although there were many older tanks in the Soviet inventory, their latest models rarely lagged far behind NATO counterparts. NATO's advantages lay in training, knowledge of the ground over which any war would be fought and crucial items of technology, such as night-fighting equipment. In later years Soviet forces were also demoralised by their failure in Afghanistan.

The Soviet army was impressive on parade but there were doubts about how effective it would be in a modern war.

Strength at sea

NATO was always much stronger at sea – and favoured by geography. The USSR's three fleets in Europe were widely separated, their routes to open seas dominated by NATO bases.

The NATO navies also had to defend the Atlantic sea lines of communication by which American forces and materials would have to cross to Europe. In this vast space NATO's numbers might still have been inadequate in the face of the sizable Soviet submarine fleet. In a long war a NATO victory would have been dependent on winning Atlantic battles. In a short war it would have been more dependent on the central front.

Air power

Of the three elements the air balance is probably the most difficult to assess. First, the quality factor is more important than elsewhere; it is much harder for numbers to compensate for technical deficiencies in the air. Soviet avionics have not matched their excellent airframes.

Second, the flexibility of air power means the balance can change very quickly. Aircraft can be moved between theatres far more rapidly than ground or naval forces. Once one side has gained air superiority, the balance in surface battles is almost bound to swing in its favour. Third, the quality of weapon is as important as the quality of aircraft carrying it; the West is believed to have had the advantage in "smart weapons" or advanced conventional munitions. The Gulf War demonstrated how good the western allies air forces were.

The balancing act

NATO faced the Warsaw pact across the inner German and Czech-German borders (right). In the event of a Warsaw pact offensive, spearheaded by the Group of Soviet Forces Germany and the Central Group of Forces, the NATO corps in West Germany would have tried to halt the enemy advance by conventional means. If these proved inadequate in the face of the Soviet numerical superiority, NATO commanders would have had to have sought approval to use nuclear weapons. Although initially only short-range tactical weapons might have been used, any nuclear war was likely to escalate. The map shows just how much of Europe was threatened by the intermediate range missiles and aircraft. In particular, strikes would have been launched against Soviet reserves and airfields within the western USSR, to which the Soviet Union was expected to reply by attacking the USA.

Soviet missile range

NATO missile/aircraft range

PORTUGAL
Lisbon

Rabat

MOROCCO

THE NAVAL BALANCE	EUROPE	USA	TOTAL	SOVIET	OTHER	TOTAL
AIRCRAFT CARRIERS	8	7	15	3		3
CRUISERS/DESTROYERS/FRIGATES	234	97	331	123	8	131
MINOR SURFACE WARSHIPS	681	36	717	576	332	898
SUBMARINES	135	53	188	172	5	177

MILITARY FORCES DEPLOYED	EUROPE	USA	TOTAL	SOVIET	OTHER	TOTAL
MANPOWER						
TOTAL GROUND FORCES (EUROPE)	1,871	217	2,088	1,871	814	2,685
TOTAL UNIFORMED MANPOWER	2,919	2,152	5,071	5,300	1,140	6,440
GROUND FORCE EQUIPMENT						
MAIN BATTLE TANKS	15,333	5,000	20,333	38,000	14,600	52,600
ARTILLERY, MRL	8,744	670	9,414	23,700	6,815	30,500
ATGW LAUNCHERS	1,426	800	2,226	5,210	1,008	6,218
LAND ATTACK FIGHTER AIRCRAFT	3,039	1,017	4,056	4,507	2,373	6,880
NAVAL & MARITIME AIRCRAFT	795	787	1,582	709	55	764

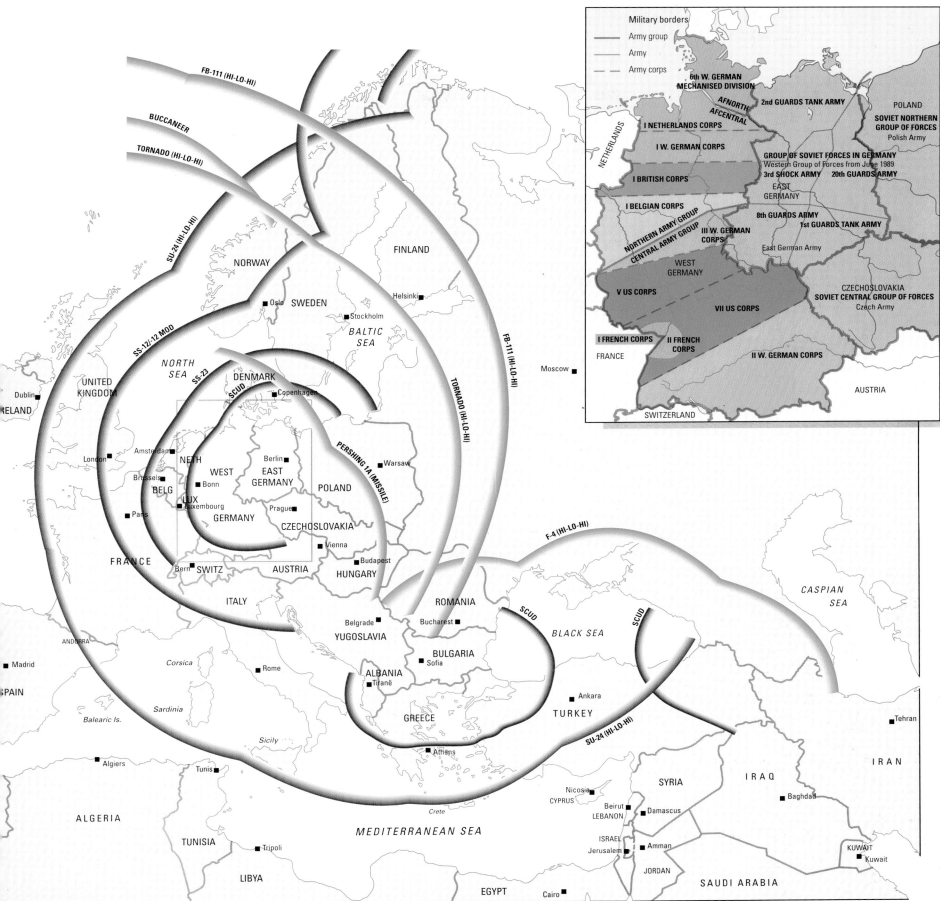

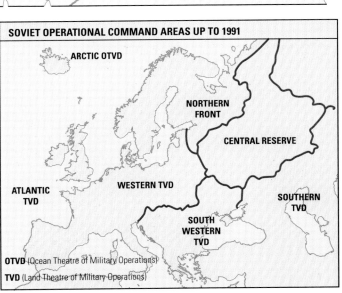

Military borders
— Army group
— Army
--- Army corps

6th W. GERMAN MECHANISED DIVISION
AFNORTH
AFCENTRAL
2nd GUARDS TANK ARMY
POLAND
SOVIET NORTHERN GROUP OF FORCES
Polish Army
I NETHERLANDS CORPS
I W. GERMAN CORPS
GROUP OF SOVIET FORCES IN GERMANY
Western Group of Forces from June 1989
3rd SHOCK ARMY   20th GUARDS ARMY
EAST GERMANY
I BRITISH CORPS
I BELGIAN CORPS
NORTHERN ARMY GROUP
CENTRAL ARMY GROUP
III W. GERMAN CORPS
8th GUARDS ARMY   1st GUARDS TANK ARMY
East German Army
WEST GERMANY
CZECHOSLOVAKIA
SOVIET CENTRAL GROUP OF FORCES
Czech Army
V US CORPS
VII US CORPS
I FRENCH CORPS   II FRENCH CORPS
II W. GERMAN CORPS
FRANCE
Moscow ■
AUSTRIA
SWITZERLAND

FB-111 (HI-LO-HI)
BUCCANEER
TORNADO (HI-LO-HI)
SU-24 (HI-LO-HI)
SS-12/-12 MOD
SS-23
SCUD
PERSHING 1A (MISSILE)
FB-111 (HI-LO-HI)
TORNADO (HI-LO-HI)
F-4 (HI-LO-HI)
SCUD
SCUD
SU-24 (HI-LO-HI)

NORWAY
FINLAND
■ Oslo   SWEDEN
■ Helsinki
■ Stockholm
BALTIC SEA
NORTH SEA
DENMARK
■ Copenhagen
UNITED KINGDOM
IRELAND
Dublin
London ■
Amsterdam
NETH
WEST GERMANY
Berlin ■
EAST GERMANY
Warsaw ■
POLAND
Brussels
BELG
Bonn ■
LUX
■ Luxembourg
Prague ■
CZECHOSLOVAKIA
Paris ■
FRANCE
Bern ■ SWITZ
AUSTRIA
■ Vienna
Budapest ■
HUNGARY
ANDORRA
Madrid ■
SPAIN
Corsica
■ Rome
ITALY
Sardinia
Balearic Is.
Belgrade ■
YUGOSLAVIA
ROMANIA
Bucharest ■
BULGARIA
Sofia ■
ALBANIA
■ Tiranë
GREECE
Athens ■
BLACK SEA
TURKEY
■ Ankara
CASPIAN SEA
■ Tehran
IRAN
Algiers ■
Tunis ■
Sicily
Crete
Nicosia ■
CYPRUS
SYRIA
IRAQ
■ Baghdad
ALGERIA
TUNISIA
■ Tripoli
LIBYA
MEDITERRANEAN SEA
Beirut ■
LEBANON
Damascus ■
ISRAEL
Jerusalem ■
Amman ■
JORDAN
SAUDI ARABIA
KUWAIT
■ Kuwait
EGYPT
Cairo ■

Europe divided

The command structures of the two alliances reflected the political systems they served. The Warsaw pact operated as a branch of the Soviet general staff, imposing doctrine, equipment and commanders on their allies.

NATO has been a more equal alliance, deciding policies by consensus, its area divided into multinational commands. Although supreme commanders have always been American, subordinate commanders and staffs have come from all allies. (France, since 1966, and Spain are not part of the military structure, though bound by the political alliance.)

In the East, command was based on Soviet theatres of military action (TVDs); peacetime groups of forces would have formed fronts (groups of armies) to command Soviet and allied forces in war.

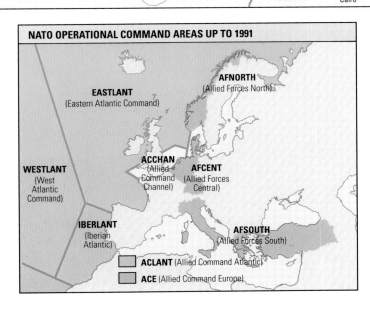

NATO OPERATIONAL COMMAND AREAS UP TO 1991

EASTLANT
(Eastern Atlantic Command)
AFNORTH
(Allied Forces North)
WESTLANT
(West Atlantic Command)
ACCHAN
(Allied Command Channel)
AFCENT
(Allied Forces Central)
IBERLANT
(Iberian Atlantic)
AFSOUTH
(Allied Forces South)

□ ACLANT (Allied Command Atlantic)
▨ ACE (Allied Command Europe)

SOVIET OPERATIONAL COMMAND AREAS UP TO 1991

ARCTIC OTVD
NORTHERN FRONT
CENTRAL RESERVE
ATLANTIC TVD
WESTERN TVD
SOUTH WESTERN TVD
SOUTHERN TVD

OTVD (Ocean Theatre of Military Operations)
TVD (Land Theatre of Military Operations)

ARMS INDUSTRIES

Modern weapons provided many of the most memorable images of the 1990–91 Gulf war; cruise missiles flying along Baghdad streets, "smart" bombs dropping down ventilation shafts and American Patriot missiles rising to shoot down the Scuds launched by the Iraqis. The war provided vivid evidence of the revolution in military technology which continues apace. The weapons used by both sides in the Gulf were mostly designed for use in Europe in the event of a war between NATO forces and those of the Warsaw pact. The cold war fuelled an arms race which kept governments spending money to equip their armed forces with the latest weapons and the fate of the Iraqi army underlines the penalty of falling behind.

Wings of the Apache… AH-64 US Apache helicopters on a mission during the Gulf war. High performance anti-tank helicopters such as these are very expensive but may make the tank obsolete. There is no European equivalent of the Apache.

Quality not quantity

Will military technology develop at the same pace now that the cold war is over? Throughout Europe defence budgets are being cut and weapons programmes slowed down or abandoned in the search for a peace dividend. The issues are not simple. The Gulf war is held to prove that well-trained, professional armed forces, operating the latest technology, will defeat an opponent who relies on numbers rather than quality. The conclusion seems to be that defence ministries will need to buy smaller quantities of better quality equipment. This process has been in progress for some time and has not necessarily led to great reductions in arms expenditure, as the tables on this page show.

Nations naturally prefer to equip their armed forces with weapons manufactured in their own country, for economic and military reasons, but astronomical development costs make this an impossible policy, even for a superpower, and certainly no European country can hope to be self-sufficient in military equipment. A state purchasing a major weapon system today has three basic choices: first, to find partners in a joint development pro-

French troops were among those who used nuclear-biological-chemical protective clothing during the Gulf war (below). NBC gear is now very effective but still cumbersome to wear, rapidly reducing troops' efficiency, especially in hot climates. However, because of Iraq's record of using chemical weapons, coalition forces had to take the chemical threat seriously and train for prolonged operations in contaminated conditions.

gramme; second, to hope to sell the system to other states and so reduce unit costs; third to buy "off the shelf", which will often mean going to the USA.

The first choice seems most logical, but experience shows that it is fraught with difficulty. States need to replace weapon systems at different times and may have very different priorities in weapon design; each state tries to win as much of the work for itself as possible. There are examples of successful collaboration, such as the Panavia Tornado aircraft, but equally the collapse of programmes such as the Anglo-German-Italian howitzer and the NATO frigate (NFR-90) projects indicate the pitfalls which abound. However, unless Europe's record of cooperation can be improved it may be that in certain categories of weapons, and especially aircraft, European states will be unable to compete with the USA and forced to buy in America.

European countries are among the world's leading arms exporters, but the Gulf war raises doubts about the wisdom of selling modern weapons to potentially unstable regimes in the third world. Iraq had certainly spent a great deal of money in Europe on modern weapon technology but, if European states had refused to sell, other sources were available. In the short term, the arms trade faces a shrinking market which will only increase competition between European allies and between Europe and America to capture the largest possible share of the available business.

Buyers and sellers

The table shows the arms trade's instability with large annual fluctuations, inevitable when dealing with, comparatively, small numbers of high-value items such as aircraft. Arms exports from the USA and the former Soviet Union were each worth more than three times that of the largest European exporter, France, in this period. Main importers of European equipment were other European states and Middle-Eastern countries such as Iraq and Saudi Arabia.

EUROPEAN ARMS EXPORTS — Constant 1985 $

COUNTRY	1986	1987	1988	1989	1990
FRANCE	4096	3011	2300	2577	1799
UK	1500	1817	1401	1816	1220
W.GERMANY	1120	676	1270	716	963
CZECHOSLOVAKIA	497	570	548	437	355
NETHERLANDS	240	265	532	725	152
SWEDEN	324	489	575	311	115
ITALY	457	389	471	169	96
SPAIN	172	139	199	506	74

New trends

Comparisons of military expenditure are notoriously difficult. Allowances for exchange rate variations and inflation are only approximate and for eastern European economies are too unreliable to include figures for their defence costs. The table on the right reveals an increase in defence spending during the 1980s, against which should be set a steady decline at the end of the decade. In general, European defence expenditure decreased in the late 1980s, whether measured in real terms, as per capita expenditure or as a proportion of GNP. When compared to the steep rise in costs illustrated in the charts on the opposite page (far right), it is clear that armed forces are less able to buy new weapons than a decade ago, even before the end of the cold war made a significant impact on expenditure.

ARMS SPENDING — Constant 1988 $

COUNTRY	1981	1990
AUSTRIA	1238	1371
BELGIUM	4657	4012
DENMARK	2260	2219
FINLAND	1496	2033
FRANCE	32995	36393
W. GERMANY	34216	38016
GREECE	3360	3041
IRELAND	512	499
ITALY	14269	20160
LUXEMBOURG	62	85
NETHERLANDS	6575	6590
NORWAY	2447	3161
PORTUGAL	1142	1323
SPAIN	6413	7531
SWEDEN	4539	4492
SWITZERLAND	2761	3219
UK	30549	32470

Connections: Defence and aerospace 74–75 Europe and the Middle East 166–167 Operations after 1945 182–183

Stealth aircraft are almost impossible to detect. The first Stealth to see combat was the Lockheed F-117 (left). During the Gulf war 42 F-117s flew 1,300 sorties, delivering 2,000 tons of bombs, without suffering any loss or even damage in return. The total cost of the F-117 programme was $6.56bn (at 1991 prices) and 59 production aircraft were built. The B-2 bomber and F-22 fighter use Stealth technology but costs are likely to ensure that only a minority of aircraft, intended to attack high-priority targets, will be true Stealth aircraft. It is unlikely that Stealth will enter service outside the USA before the year 2000.

Arms producers

The major European industrial powers – Germany, France, Italy and the UK – have the most broadly based defence industries. At first sight the range of Swedish, Czech and Yugoslav arms production is perhaps more surprising. Sweden, as a neutral state, was determined to avoid dependence on other powers. Czechoslovakia, although only a minor military power, has a history of arms construction dating back to

Habsburg days and maintained with sales to other Warsaw pact states and the third world. Yugoslavia developed a successful arms industry by up-grading Soviet designs. States such as Belgium and Austria have established valuable markets for their excellent small arms design.

However, European arms manufacturers face increasing high-quality competition in the world market from younger industries such as those of

Israel, South Africa and Brazil while China and former communist states will offer cheaper and more easy-to-operate weaponry to many third world states. European defence companies are also suffering from cuts in government spending on arms and, to a lesser degree, changes in national procurement policies.

Real term costs

These two graphs indicate the problem facing armed services today. They show the J-shaped curves in the costs of American aircraft and tanks, even when adjusted for ordinary inflation. A tank may still be a tracked, armoured gun platform, as it was 50 years ago, but its armour is no longer made from rolled steel, but from advanced composite materials; it has a gas turbine engine and a fire- control computer.

With aircraft the impact of the latest

materials and electronics has been even more dramatic and some analysts have pointed to the logical conclusion that eventually even the American defence budget would hardly suffice to buy a single airplane.

The high costs of advanced warplanes coupled with the perceived lower threat of war have put the development of the European fighter project in jeopardy (see below).

EUROPEAN WEAPONS

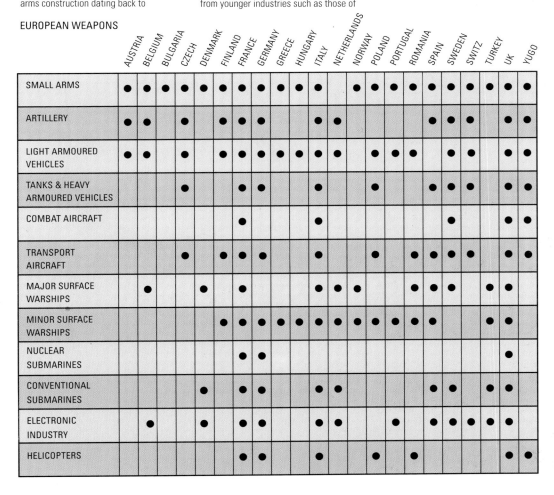

	AUSTRIA	BELGIUM	BULGARIA	CZECH	DENMARK	FINLAND	FRANCE	GERMANY	GREECE	HUNGARY	ITALY	NETHERLANDS	NORWAY	POLAND	PORTUGAL	ROMANIA	SPAIN	SWEDEN	SWITZ	TURKEY	UK	YUGO
SMALL ARMS	●	●	●	●	●	●	●	●	●	●	●		●	●	●	●	●	●	●	●	●	●
ARTILLERY	●	●		●		●	●	●			●	●					●	●	●		●	●
LIGHT ARMOURED VEHICLES	●	●		●		●	●	●	●		●			●	●	●	●	●			●	●
TANKS & HEAVY ARMOURED VEHICLES				●			●	●			●			●			●	●			●	●
COMBAT AIRCRAFT							●				●							●			●	●
TRANSPORT AIRCRAFT				●		●	●	●			●			●			●	●	●		●	●
MAJOR SURFACE WARSHIPS		●		●		●			●	●	●	●				●	●			●	●
MINOR SURFACE WARSHIPS				●	●	●	●	●	●	●	●	●		●			●	●	●		●	●
NUCLEAR SUBMARINES							●	●													●	
CONVENTIONAL SUBMARINES				●	●		●	●			●						●	●			●	●
ELECTRONIC INDUSTRY		●			●	●	●	●			●				●		●	●	●	●	●	●
HELICOPTERS						●	●			●			●		●		●				●	●

COST OF US FIGHTER AIRCRAFT

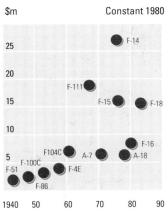

$m   Constant 1980

COST OF US TANKS

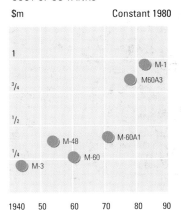

$m   Constant 1980

The fighter aircraft

The idea of the European Fighter Aircraft grew from the need to counter the Soviet threat. In 1984, Britain, France, Germany, Italy and Spain agreed outline requirements for the EFA but, after differences in concept between France and the rest, France went ahead with its own design in 1985.

The remaining four were to build some 800 aircraft, sharing the work (right). The end of the cold war and German budget problems after reunification dogged the project. Flight

tests were due to begin in 1992 for an in-service date of 1995, but in 1992 the German government announced its withdrawal.

SHARES IN THE EFA

UK 33%
W. GERMANY 33%
ITALY 21%
SPAIN 13%

INTELLIGENCE SERVICES

General Reinhard Gehlen (1902–79) headed German eastern European intelligence, 1942–45. In 1946 his staff, files and agents were taken over by the USA as the Gehlen Organisation; in 1956 it became the official intelligence service of the new West Germany. His reputation suffered however when, in 1961, Heinz Felfe, Gehlen's head of counter-espionage was revealed to be a Soviet double agent.

Espionage and intelligence work are as old as warfare but for a variety of reasons have played a much more significant role in world affairs in the post-war era than any previous period.

No state in the past had ever invested so much effort in espionage as the Soviet Union. The KGB, with its internal security as well as foreign espionage roles, became an autonomous arm of the state. Subordinate intelligence services in the Warsaw pact states increased its reach. The value of this effort to the Soviet Union is debatable. The technical intelligence acquired by the KGB may have accelerated many Soviet projects from the atomic bomb onwards, but the political intelligence provided to the Soviet leadership was partial and distorted.

High-tech spying

The West responded to the KGB's activities by expanding the scope of its counter-intelligence agencies which mounted their own efforts to discover Soviet intentions. The spy of popular fiction, "humint" in modern intelligence jargon, may still have a part to play but governments today rely increasingly on technical means of reconnaissance.

Interception and deciphering of radio traffic has been growing in importance since the beginning of the century. The British success during the second world war in reading German radio traffic, code-named Ultra, is now well-known. During the cold war the business of "Sigint" or signals intelligence grew exponentially and expanded to cover the analysis of all forms of electro-magnetic communications.

Aerial reconnaissance began on the battlefields of the first world war; by the second world war it was providing strategic intelligence as well. Today satellites equipped with radars, infra-red detectors and other systems as well as cameras are the mainstays of strategic intelligence; they can also provide vital information for battlefield commanders.

The range of intelligence systems available to tactical commanders is now immense, shown by the diagram below. Intelligence systems are now so powerful that many analysts believe that, although modern forces are much more mobile than their predecessors, practical opportunities for tactical manoeuvre will be severely limited in the future. Surface fleets are particularly threatened by improvements in reconnaissance systems, although submarines can still hide themselves in the world's oceans. However, even submarines now find it difficult to avoid detection in the confined waters which form the traditional maritime "choke points".

The improvements in intelligence capabilities in the past 50 years have brought their own penalties. Analysts

Military surveillance

The diagram shows the range of intelligence systems available to military commanders in a modern campaign, such as the Gulf war. In the front line reconnaissance is no longer restricted to visual observation. Every level of higher command adds to the range of agencies available. In the Gulf war drones and remotely-piloted vehicles proved especially valuable, providing formation commanders with rapid response intelligence without the need to risk casualties in collecting it.

Even this scale of intelligence effort was unable to answer all the questions and mistakes were made. Absolute accuracy and timeliness will never be achieved, but the allied forces knew more than any previous army about what was happening "on the other side of the hill". In contrast the Iraqi army was starved of intelligence. Effectively the Iraqis were dependent on what they could see from the front line which was almost nothing before the ground war began, by which time it was too late, and on electronic intelligence. As a result the allies were able to use dummy radio traffic to deceive the Iraqis about the location of their main forces. This classic deception operation demonstrated the need for all intelligence to be confirmed by other sources, which the Iraqis were unable to do. The allies by contrast were able not only to deceive the Iraqis but also to confirm the success of their deception before committing their forces.

MAN AND MACHINE

The range of intelligence sources and agencies serving modern armed forces creates its own problems. Intelligence systems demand increased manpower (an American division, for example, includes a military intelligence battalion) and ever more sophisticated equipment. Only computerised systems can cope with the constant heavy flow of detailed information, however, human assessment skills remain vital at all levels and the right balance between old-fashioned human judgment and modern technology is still to be found.

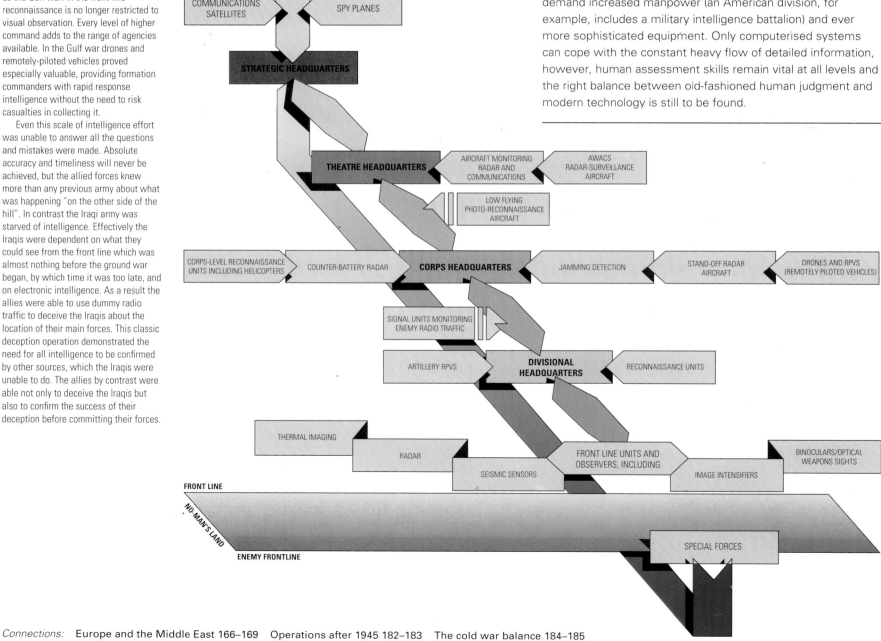

and those they serve now have so much information available to them that they may not be able to select the key data on which to base their decisions in good time. You can filter out the "noise" which distracts attention but in the process crucial intelligence may be lost. In 1973 the Israeli government was not given low-level intelligence which conflicted with the overall concept of the intelligence chiefs. The result was that Israeli mobilisation was delayed and forces on its borders almost swamped by the Egyptian and Syrian attack.

The element of surprise

The impressive capabilities of modern intelligence systems may breed a dangerous over-confidence. It is undoubtedly more difficult to achieve surprise now than it has ever been but we cannot assume that surprise will ever become impossible. The invasions of Afghanistan, the Falklands Islands and Kuwait all caught western states, for all their intelligence systems, unprepared. Although it was possible to predict the Soviet Union's growing difficulties and doubt the system's ability to survive in the long term, the failure of the intelligence communities to forecast its sudden collapse can be understood. There was no logical reason why this should occur so dramatically and, therefore, no logical way to predict it.

The debate over the value of intelligence in the Gulf war also highlights the difficulty of reconciling the demands of battlefield commanders and the capabilities of intelligence gathering systems. Issues such as identification of Iraqi targets for air attack and the assessment of the damage caused by air attacks will become the food of historical controversy. The heart of the problem lies in the fact that the most important questions commanders have to ask about the enemy are not quantifiable issues, such as the numbers of its tanks and aircraft, but subjective questions about the quality of its morale, training standards and leadership.

The eyes and ears of an army are sharper than ever before and so the scope of modern military intelligence is ever increasing. A modern air defence system (above) must be able to track a large number of fast-moving targets, overcome their defensive measures and direct missiles or aircraft to intercept them. Advanced computers are essential to manage a large quantity of data in seconds. Special forces, such as these American troops in the Gulf (left), may seem to represent an older style of warfare, based on the man rather than the machine, but even they depend on high technology to achieve their missions, using satellite communications and sophisticated weaponry.

THE NEW ESPIONAGE

In the euphoria which followed the collapse of the eastern block and the Soviet Union itself, it was easy to assume that the role of espionage was bound to decline and that redundancy would threaten spies as much as soldiers. In the event, however, only the priorities of the intelligence world have changed. Rivalries will be less clear-cut. For example, the intelligence agencies of the major powers will cooperate against the international terrorist threat and the drugs trade.

Economic competition will become as important a motive for espionage as military rivalry has been in the past. Industrial espionage and protection against it is a well-established business. The Soviet Union's intelligence effort always gave high priority to acquiring advanced western technology. Other nations' secret services are seeking commercial secrets for national economic purposes. The French DGSE has been caught in such work in the United States and India. The director of the American National Security Agency has admitted that it is now being asked to collect "competitive information".

Governments increasingly wish to monitor political developments around the world. Details of weapons and their deployment, which can be collected by "national technical means", such as satellites, will be less significant than forewarning of political instability. Collecting such material, whether from clandestine or open sources, and effective analysis of the data presents a difficult challenge.

INTELLIGENCE AGENCIES

COUNTRY	AGENCY	FUNCTION
FRANCE	DIRECTION GÉNÉRALE DE LA SÉCURITÉ EXTÉRIEURE DGSE	○ ● ● ●
	GROUPEMENT DE COMMUNICATIONS RADIO ELECTRIQUES GCR	●
	DEUXIÈME BUREAU	○
	DIRECTION DE LA SURVEILLANCE DU TERRITOIRE DST	●
GERMANY	BUNDESNACHRICHTENDIENST BND	○ ● ● ●
	AMT FÜR FERNMELDWESEN BUNDESWEHR AFMBW	●
	MILITÄRISCHER ABSCHIRMDIENST MAD	●
	BUNDESAMT FÜR VERFASSUNGSSCHUTZ BFV	●
ITALY	SERVIZIO PER LE INFORMAZIONI E LA SICUREZZA DEMOCRATICA SISDE	●
	SERVIZIO PER LE INFORMAZIONI E LA SICUREZZA MILITARE SISMI	○ ● ●
UK	SECRET INTELLIGENCE SERVICE SIS (MI6)	○ ●
	DEFENCE INTELLIGENCE SERVICE DIS	○
	SECURITY SERVICE (MI5)	●
	GOVERNMENT COMMUNICATION HEADQUARTERS GCHQ	●

○ Military Intelligence   ● Domestic Counter-Intelligence
● Strategic Intelligence   ● Foreign Counter-Intelligence
● Electronic Intercept

Secret services

The table shows the most important intelligence agencies of western Europe. The countries of eastern Europe no longer maintain intelligence services on their former scale. Even the KGB is to be replaced, although the exact nature, role and even title of its successor or successors are still uncertain.

Although no state is willing to reveal the exact details of its intelligence system, the broad areas of responsibility of individual agencies are now well known. A basic problem is to coordinate the efforts of various agencies. A degree of competition ensures that governments are presented with a range of views but some directing body, such as the Joint Intelligence Committee of the Cabinet Office in Britain, is necessary to coordinate tasking and assessments.

As the scale of national intelligence efforts has increased in recent years, demands have grown for clearer political control over the state agencies. This pressure will surely continue and increasing parliamentary supervision is likely in the future.

THE MILITARY FUTURE

A former Soviet missile is destroyed under the terms of arms reduction agreements. Destruction of the nuclear warheads of such missiles is much more complex and the scale of the problem threatens to overwhelm Russian resources but the weapons cannot be safely stored indefinitely. Western financial and technical assistance will be essential if the Russian nuclear arsenal is to be safely reduced.

Since 1989, the security situation in Europe has been changing too rapidly for the treaty-makers to keep pace. Years of negotiation produced a draft Conventional Forces in Europe (CFE) treaty in 1989 which was framed in terms of a balance of power between NATO and the Warsaw pact. By the time it was formally signed in 1990, the Berlin wall and the iron curtain were history, and in the following year, before the treaty had been fully ratified, the Warsaw pact had ceased to exist. The failure of the August 1991 coup in Moscow was followed by the break-up of the Soviet Union; the end of the cold war was proclaimed on all sides. Europe must try to construct a new architecture of security structures.

The CFE treaty, once it has been fully ratified, will set the upper limits on troops and equipment deployed in Europe. The newly independent states of the former Soviet Union are expected to conform to the CFE limits within the Atlantic to the Urals (ATTU) region. Indeed it is unlikely that successor states, whether independently or as the Commonwealth of Independent States, will be able to afford to maintain their armed forces at full CFE levels. However, if former Soviet republics opt for military independence, Russia is likely to press for a revision of the treaty because of the potentially unfavourable balance of forces on its western frontiers.

Shifting alliances

West European defence budgets and forces levels are also falling for lack of a major threat from the East. Nevertheless, there is a general perception that the world is not necessarily a safer place. In 1991 the Gulf war, the Yugoslav civil war and disputes within the former Soviet Union indicated a less stable future. Military alliances and security conferences will continue in Europe, but must change to meet new circumstances.

Within NATO the process has two main elements, internal or military and external or diplomatic. Internally, command and force structures are being re-organised (right). In external affairs, NATO is developing links with its former adversaries in eastern Europe. The former Warsaw pact nations have been invited to send observers to NATO meetings and students to NATO schools. The North Atlantic Cooperation Council, which was established to bring together the NATO countries and the members of the former Warsaw pact, had its first meeting in Brussels in December 1991.

Some of the east European states, and especially Poland, Czechoslovakia and Hungary, have expressed a wish to join NATO but expansion of membership is seen as a very long-term issue by the alliance. In the shorter term, the European members of NATO are debating their role and the possibility of a security role for the European Community; France and Germany are experimenting with joint forces.

Outside the NATO alliance, new regional groupings are beginning to appear. The "triangle" of Poland, Czechoslovakia and Hungary has signed a series of bilateral military agreements. An informal "hexagonal group" of Italy, Austria, Hungary, Poland and Czechoslovakia has begun to develop, but its progress has been checked by the civil war in Yugoslavia. It is possible that the Conference on Security and Cooperation in Europe may provide a future structure for settling security issues, but its embryo institutions, such as the Conflict Prevention Centre in Vienna, were tested too soon by events in Yugoslavia and were unable to play an effective role in the crisis. The Gulf war showed that Europe will also need a means to coordinate its response to world security problems and demonstrated the difficulties of creating such an institution.

ARMS CONTROL

During the cold war the disarmament process was just as much a part of the struggle between superpowers as the arms race itself. Offers to limit or eliminate weapons were often merely attempts by one party either to confirm its own superiority in a particular area or to prevent the other side establishing an advantage. As long as the USA and the USSR saw themselves as potential enemies, arms control was a series of agreements prohibiting things which neither side really wanted to do, such as building nuclear weapons beyond a certain level or deploying them in outer space, on the sea bed or in the Antarctic. But the dramatic political changes since the late 1980s have been followed by a rush of agreements to reduce nuclear and conventional armouries.

Now the greatest check on disarmament is the difficulty of destroying the weapons themselves. To de-activate a nuclear missile is a dangerous process at the end of which fissionable material remains to be stored or re-processed. Even destroying conventional weapons such as tanks takes time.

The focus of attention in arms control must now shift from the armouries of the superpowers to the capabilities of third world countries. The non-proliferation treaty has not stopped states which really wanted nuclear weapons from developing expertise, even if the process has been driven into secrecy. Nuclear expertise was too widely dispersed to stop proliferation even before the diaspora of former Soviet nuclear scientists became a real possibility. Chemical weapons have already been used by the third world armies, most notably Iraq. It is not easy to imagine what pressures can be applied to stop the production of weapons of mass destruction totally and while this insecurity exists, states will feel entitled to retain or develop such weapons for their own defence.

The paradox of arms control and disarmament in the past has been that measures are proposed to reduce tension between states but, in reality, effective disarmament has followed, not preceded, reductions in tension.

TREATIES AND AGREEMENTS

DATE	TITLE	CONTENT
1963	PARTIAL TEST BAN TREATY	BANS NUCLEAR WEAPONS TESTS IN THE ATMOSPHERE, OUTER SPACE, & UNDER WATER.
1968	NON-PROLIFERATION TREATY	PROHIBITS TRANSFER OF NUCLEAR WEAPONS OR TECHNOLOGY FROM NUCLEAR TO NON-NUCLEAR STATES.
1972	BIOLOGICAL WEAPONS CONVENTIONS	PROHIBITS DEVELOPMENT, PRODUCTION, STOCKPILING OR ACQUISITIONS OF BIOLOGICAL AGENTS OR TOXINS.
1972	ABM TREATY	LIMITS THE DEPLOYMENT OF ANTI-BALLISTIC MISSILE DEFENCES BY USA & USSR.
1972	SALT I (Strategic Arms Limitation Talks)	LIMITS NUMBERS OF LAND & SEA-BASED INTERCONTINENTAL BALLISTIC MISSILES HELD BY USA & USSR.
1975	CSCE (HELSINKI) AGREEMENT (Conference on Security & Confidence Building Measures in Europe)	INCLUDES PRIOR NOTIFICATION OF MAJOR EXERCISES & EXCHANGE OF OBSERVERS ON EXERCISES.
1979	SALT II	LIMITS ALL STRATEGIC NUCLEAR WEAPONS HELD BY USA & USSR. (Never ratified)
1986	CSCE (STOCKHOLM) AGREEMENT	EXTENDED NOTIFICATION & VERIFICATION REQUIREMENTS FOR CONVENTIONAL FORCES IN EUROPE.
1987	INF TREATY	USA & USSR TO ELIMINATE INTERMEDIATE & SHORTER-RANGE MISSLES IN EUROPE.
1990	CFE TREATY	LIMITS THE SIZE OF CONVENTIONAL FORCES DEPLOYED IN EUROPE.
1991	START TREATY (Stategic Arms Reduction Treaty)	AIMS TO REDUCE THE USA'S STRATEGIC NUCLEAR ARSENAL BY APPROX 25% & THAT OF USSR BY 35%.

Connections: Rebuilding democracies 120–121   Operations after 1945 182–183   The cold war balance 184–185

Forces in Europe

The key elements of the Treaty on Conventional Arms in Europe are force reductions and verification measures. Overall limits for the amount of key equipments (tanks, artillery, armoured combat vehicles and aircraft) are established and then the distribution of those treaty-limited equipments (TLE) on the continent is determined by a series of regional sub-totals, spreading outwards from the central region. The limits were designed to ensure that neither NATO or the Warsaw pact could claim military superiority in any region and make surprise attack impossible.

The collapse of the Warsaw pact has not nullified the treaty but has made it more difficult to implement. The verification measures authorised under the treaty, especially the right to conduct inspections, and the "open-skies" agreement on air reconnaissance will contribute to stability throughout Europe.

CFC ZONES

- ■ Zone 1
- ■ Zone 2
- ■ Zone 3
- □ Zone 4
- —— Military district boundary

NEW NATO COMMAND STRUCTURE

At the Rome summit in November 1991 the NATO powers agreed new security guidelines on which to base their military structure. Because of the new strategic environment in Europe and the reduced risk of a major war, it was accepted that the overall size and readiness of military forces could be reduced. It was no longer necessary to maintain a linear defensive posture in the central region, although forces were distributed to ensure a sufficient military presence throughout NATO territory.

It is no longer possible to predict the military threat exactly and forces must be more flexible in their organisation and training. There must be greater emphasis on mobility. The new force structure (see right) adopted by NATO shows some reduction in the number of headquarters and staffs (primarily by absorbing the ACCHAN command into the AFNORTH region). Military forces themselves will be smaller, with a combination of rapid reaction elements and mobilisation forces which can reinforce them in time of crisis.

Four categories of forces will be established in the area controlled by the Allied Command Europe. They are:

Immediate Reaction Corps (IRC) This multinational force is modelled on the old ACE mobile force and is to be deployed by SACEUR to a crisis area at very short notice to demonstrate alliance solidarity and strength. It is directly under ACE in peacetime and times of conflict and can be deployed to any of the three areas (AFCENT, AFNORTH, AFSOUTH) shown in the diagram (above right).

Rapid Reaction Corps (RRC) A multinational corps available for operations throughout the NATO area and perhaps beyond. It will consist of eight divisions at least four of which will have a multinational composition. Units will be drawn from Belgium, Denmark, Germany, Greece, Italy, the Netherlands, Turkey, the USA and the UK. It is directly responsible to ACE during times of conflict and peacetime.

Main Defence Forces Active and reserve forces, organised in national and multinational formations and intended to operate in specific regions. This comprises the major portion of NATO forces and is the basis of the defence of NATO territory. LANDCENT is composed of two German, one US and two multinational (German, Dutch, Belgian) corps. They are ultimately responsible to ACE.

Augmentation Forces Mainly national forces, including a large US component, which will provide strategic and operational reserves. These forces are not necessarily tied to a specific region of NATO.

ALLIED COMMAND EUROPE (ACE)

ALLIED FORCE NORTHERN REGION (AF NORTH) (INCLUDES FORMER ACCHAN AREA)

ALLIED FORCES CENTRAL REGION (AFCENT)

ALLIED FORCES SOUTHERN REGION (AFSOUTH)

LANDCENT (LAND FORCES)

AIRCENT (AIR FORCES)

The ACE mobile force (above) on exercise in Denmark in 1989 was the precursor of the new Rapid Reaction Corps of the new NATO structure.

THREATS TO SECURITY

The British colony of Hong Kong is to return to Chinese rule in 1997 and the maintenance of internal security there in the intervening period may strain the small garrison. If reinforcements are required, British commitments elsewhere in the world will have to be reduced.

There is a definite nostalgia today for the quantifiable dangers of the cold war era when it was far easier to assess and meet the likely threat. In the multipolar world of the future, European interests must be defended against an unknown range of threats and the stability of several European states is uncertain.

Many of these threats are long-standing and several European powers already have forces deployed overseas to protect their interests. The garrisons on the map below represent the last vestiges of European colonial commitments. French garrisons in Africa have seen action in support of former colonies' governments. After the Falklands war, Britain was forced to retain a large force in the islands and provide for its rapid reinforcement. That war saw Britain operating alone to defend its interests, but future operations overseas are likely to involve coalitions of nations.

New patterns of action

The Gulf war may provide a pattern for joint action. The European contribution to the multinational force included sizable British and French ground, air and naval forces and contributions from Italy, Belgium, Denmark, Greece, the Netherlands, Norway, Poland, Czechoslovakia and Hungary. At the same time the war demonstrated the problems of such operations.

The lack of any organisation to coordinate a European response to security problems was clearly shown and the Yugoslav civil war has highlighted the same deficiency. No existing body has the necessary authority. NATO has been a success in defending the home territory of its member states, but it has no jurisdiction outside that area and to expand its role would threaten the alliance's cohesion. The Conference on Security and Cooperation in Europe (CSCE) cannot intervene in a state's internal affairs nor in matters outside Europe. The EC failed to produce an effective response to either problem and the pressure to find some forum for European action continues.

The scope of the CSCE may be widened to allow intervention in internal matters which threaten European stability. The Western European Union may find new life as the coordinator of European defence efforts, whether inside NATO or outside the treaty area. In the more distant future a multinational military force may emerge, on the NATO model, but operating over a much wider area and including more European states. In the short term it is worth noting the efforts to create rapid reaction forces at national and multinational levels. Some units, such as the French Foreign Legion, already have considerable experience in this role. Such mobile forces are important because it is no longer possible to predict reliably areas under threat and deploy forces in advance. The Gulf war showed such forces may have to be heavily equipped, increasing the problems of support and transport.

Future threats may not be purely military. American armed forces have already been used at borders against drugs smugglers and illegal immigrants. European forces may well receive similar missions. The possibility of millions of refugees from Russia and elsewhere in eastern Europe in the event of civil war or economic collapse has been raised. (Italy has already seen a much smaller exodus from Albania.) Observers also point to the dangers of illegal immigration from the overpopulated southern and eastern shores of the Mediterranean.

Overseas deployments

European states deploy forces overseas in their remaining colonial possessions and to support former colonies. Naval visits are a traditional way of showing the flag and, like overseas training of air and ground forces, bring variety to service life. These long- and short-term deployments will continue for the foreseeable future because of their strategic value. Thus the French military presence in Africa is vital to the maintenance of French influence in the continent. British governments will remember that the decision to withdraw HMS Endurance from the South Atlantic was a key factor in the Argentinian junta's mistaken assessment that Britain would not fight for the Falkland Islands. Regular training in the Gulf area helped British forces during the Gulf war.

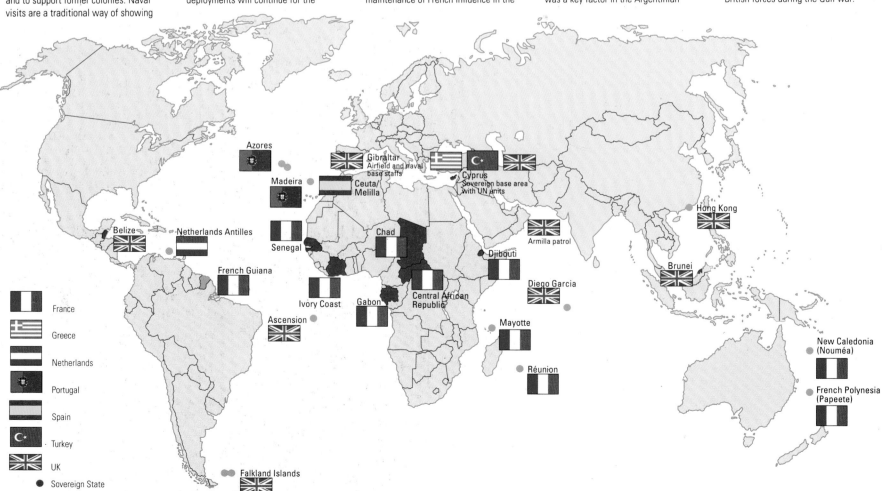

Seeds of conflict

The seeds of possible conflict are scattered over the map of Europe. Some disputes, such as that between Britain and Spain over Gibraltar, are unlikely to cause more than diplomatic quarrels. In others, violent solutions may be sought, as already in Yugoslavia. The most dangerous disputes lie in the Balkans and eastern Europe and can be seen as the result of the successive collapses of the Turkish, Austrian and Soviet empires.

During the lifetime of such supra-national organisations ethnic borders become blurred. The boundaries which survive the end of empire are inevitably artificial and likely to cause disputes. There are at least 47 possible border disputes within the former territory of the USSR and 22 of them affect outside states.

Flashpoints

Aegean Sea Greece and Turkey dispute territorial waters and economic exploitation rights in Aegean.

Alto Adige/South Tirol Alto Adige has been an Italian province since 1919 but has two-thirds Austrian population which has gained greater autonomy recently. However, extremists still seek reunion with the rest of the Tirol.

Baltic States Relations with Russia and the continued presence of North-West Group of Forces causes concern. Lithuania may have disputes with Poland and Belarus, especially over Vilnius, the Lithuanian capital.

Belarus Newly independent former Soviet republic of Belarus has potential border and ethnic quarrels with Russia, Lithuania and Poland.

Belgium Divisions between Flemish and Walloon communities.

Bulgaria/Turkey Turkey supports Turkish minority in Bulgaria against political persecution and denial of language rights.

Ceuta and Mililla Moroccan claim resisted by Spain.

Cyprus Division between Greek and Turkish communities, monitored by UN peace-keeping force. Greek and Turkish forces deployed on island.

Czechoslovakia Arguments about future state structure – whether federal (as now), confederal or independent states for Czechs and Slovaks.

Gibraltar Claimed by Spain, but population has consistently voted to keep links with Britain.

Greece With Bulgaria and Yugoslavia, increasing demands for an independent state within Macedonia.

Iceland History of disputes over fishing rights which may continue in future.

Kaliningrad Formerly German Koenigsberg, taken by USSR in 1945 and included in Russian republic. Now a major naval base and isolated by independence of the Baltic states.

Kosovo Serbian reduction of autonomy of Albanian population of province provokes Albania as protector of its fellow nationals.

Macedonia Status of Macedonia disputed by Yugoslavia, Bulgaria and Greece; there have been increasing demands for creation of independent state within Macedonia.

Moldova Bessarabian province annexed from Romania by USSR in 1940. Part allocated to Ukraine in 1945. Moldovans now claim independence and may seek reunion with Romania but Russian minority refuses to accept this and is attempting to form Dniester Republic.

North Sea Fishing and mineral rights disputes now settled under EC auspices but pollution continues to cause problems between peripheral states.

Northern Ireland Irish nationalist claim to the six counties of Ulster, still formally endorsed by Republic of Ireland. Resisted by Ulster Protestants. Scene of armed conflict since 1969.

Norwegian Sea Norway and the former Soviet Union disputed territorial waters and economic exploitation rights.

The new situation in Russia may aid agreement.

Transylvania Home of Hungarian minority persecuted under Romanian dictator, Ceausescu. Hungary pressing Romanian government for better treatment of minority.

Tunisia/Italy/Malta Unsettled dispute over economic Mediterranean exploitation rights between these three.

Ukraine Asserting independence from Russia by all means. Major quarrels over status of Crimea and former Soviet Black Sea fleet. Potential border and minority disputes with all neighbours.

Vojvodina Autonomous region with Hungarian population, under pressure from Serbian government, leading Hungary to express concern.

Sources of tension
- Border dispute
- Island/enclave dispute
- Territorial waters dispute
- Internal ethnic dispute

A young soldier leads the funeral procession of a Croatian national guardsman. The civil war in Yugoslavia has shocked those who believed that the end of the cold war would encourage federalism within Europe. Instead the 1990s may see a return to the national quarrels of a century ago.

YUGOSLAVIA AFTER COMMUNISM

Tito's death in 1980 removed the most powerful force holding the state together and the decade saw the dramatic rise of Slobodan Milosevic on a platform of Serbian nationalism. Both Serbia and Croatia were seeking greater autonomy. From 1990 the federal army began to arm Serbian irregulars (Chetniks) in minority areas. In June 1991 Slovenia and Croatia declared they were seeking independence. The army began to move against key areas of Slovenia but was repelled. Attention turned to Croatia where the large Serbian minority was armed. In the fighting that followed the federal army sided with the Chetniks. By the end of 1991, 6,000 had been killed in the fighting between Serbs and Croats alone and half a million forced out of their homes. Numerous cease-fires were broken and in 1992 the conflict spread to Bosnia and Hercegovina.

TERRORISM IN EUROPE

On December 21st 1988, Pan Am flight 103 from Frankfurt to New York, via London, crashed on the small Scottish town of Lockerbie, killing all 259 passengers and crew and 11 inhabitants of the town. The case is a good example of the problems of fighting terrorism in the air. A long investigation identified the route by which the bomb was planted and two Libyan suspects were named. Iran and Syria were also implicated in the bombing. However, punishing those responsible may take even longer and has already brought Libya into conflict with the UN Security Council.

The anarchist with a bomb was a stereotype a century ago, but violent acts against the state have never been so commonplace as today. Modern terrorist movements are drawn from four main sources: nationalist movements, Marxist revolutionaries, the "new left", and right-wing extremism.

Nationalism is a long-standing motive for terrorism. Irish terrorism dates back to the last century and Zionist terrorists played a significant role in the struggle for Israeli independence. Modern international terrorism has its roots in the failure of conventional guerrilla warfare by Palestinians against Israel.

Latin American Marxist revolutionary movements similarly turned to terrorism when guerrilla warfare failed. Europe has hardly been affected by such movements except as models for other groups. Instead Europe has produced many of the best known "new left" groups. Their members, largely drawn from affluent middle-class families, have claimed to be disillusioned with the inequities of modern capitalism.

Right-wing groups have been less conspicuous except in Italy where a series of bombings were aimed at creating instability which might lead to the installation of an auto-cratic populist government. Neo-fascist groups may well try to exploit nationalist reaction in many countries in the future.

Terrorism, as a phenomenon, reached its height during the late 1970s and early 1980s. States seemed powerless to check the new groups which were springing up everywhere and exposing the vulnerability of modern societies to violence. Terrorist groups were quick to learn from each other; techniques such as aircraft hi-jacking or hostage-taking were widely copied. Established groups provided training and weapons for new ones. Groups also carried out proxy attacks for each other, such as the Japanese Red Army attack at Lod airport in 1972.

Resilience of the modern state

Terrorism has undoubtedly thrived on media exposure. Certain acts, such as the attacks at the Munich Olympics in 1972, the Lockerbie bombing (1988) or the IRA attacks on the British cabinet in Brighton (1984) and London (1991) remain in the memory. Hostage taking, such as the kidnapping and murder of the former Italian prime minister, Aldo Moro, by the Red Brigades in 1978 and the long saga of western hostages in Lebanon, has also kept

Survival tactics

Terrorist organisations initially raised money by ordinary criminal activity, such as bank raids, but some also drew support from a number of sources, such as the former Soviet Union, Libya and Syria. The IRA has a well-established fund-raising network, using protection and other rackets in Ulster and front organisations such as Noraid in the USA.

There are well-proven links between the various terror groups. Thus the revolutionary terrorist groups, such as Action Directe, the Red Brigades and the Baader-Meinhof gang, worked together and surviving elements of these groups may provide safe houses and other support for IRA cells operating in Germany and the Low Countries today. The Palestinian groups have provided training facilities for other terrorist organisations and Colonel Qaddafi of Libya has been a notorious source of weapons, explosives and funds which have been channelled throughout Europe.

TERRORIST ACTIVITY IN EUROPE

The range of terrorist movements described in the table below provides an insight into the problem that faced European security forces in the 1980s . Many other lesser groups existed briefly. For the most part these groups lacked the popular support on which guerrilla movements have traditionally relied. They operated in small cells and made little attempt to recruit grass-roots support.

NAME	BASE	ACTIVE	MOTIVATION	OPERATIONS IN
BAADER-MIENHOF GANG (Rote Armee Frakton)	WEST GERMANY	LATE 1960s TO MID-1980s	REVOLUTIONARY TERRORISM	GERMANY (Main area of ops.), SWEDEN, AUSTRIA, BELGIUM.
ACTION DIRECTE	FRANCE	1979 TO LATE 1980s	REVOLUTIONARY TERRORISM	FRANCE (Main area of ops.), GERMANY
NOVEMBER 17	GREECE	FROM 1973	REVOLUTIONARY TERRORISM	GREECE
RED BRIGADES (After 1985, Fighting Communist Party PCC)	ITALY	LATE 1960s TO LATE 1980s	REVOLUTIONARY TERRORISM	ITALY
COMMUNIST COMBATANT CELLS	BELGIUM	1984 TO LATE 1980s	REVOLUTIONARY TERRORISM	BELGIUM
ORDINE NUOVO (New Order) ARMED REVOLUTIONARY NUCLEI NAR	ITALY	MID-1970s TO MID-1980s	RIGHT-WING TERRORISM	ITALY
FANE FNE	FRANCE	FROM MID-1970s	ANTI-SEMITIC RIGHT-WING TERRORISM	FRANCE
CHARLES MARTEL CLUB	FRANCE	1980s	RIGHT-WING TERRORISM, especially ANTI-MUSLIM	FRANCE
CORSICAN SEPARATISTS (Several small groups)	CORSICA	1975 TO LATE 1980s	CORSICAN INDEPENDENCE	CORSICA & MAINLAND FRANCE
EUSKADI TA ASKATASUNA ETA	SPAIN	FROM 1968	BASQUE NATIONALISM	SPAIN
IRISH REPUBLICAN ARMY IRA PROVISIONAL IRISH REPUBLICAN ARMY PIRA	NORTHERN IRELAND & IRISH REPUBLIC	FROM 1969	IRISH NATIONALISM, UNIFICATION OF IRELAND	IRELAND, UK, GERMANY, NETHERLANDS, GIBRALTAR
IRISH NATIONAL LIBERATION ARMY INLA	IRISH REPUBLIC	FROM 1975	CREATION OF SOCIALIST IRISH NATIONAL STATE	NORTHERN IRELAND, BRITAIN
ULSTER DEFENCE ASSOCIATION UDA ULSTER VOLUNTEER FORCE UVF ULSTER FREEDOM FIGHTERS UFF	NORTHERN IRELAND	FROM 1970	PROTESTANT, LOYALIST, ANTI-CATHOLIC & ANTI-IRA	NORTHERN IRELAND
PALESTINIAN GROUPS	THROUGHOUT MIDDLE EAST	FROM 1967	ESTABLISHMENT OF PALESTINIAN STATE, ANTI-ISRAEL	THROUGHOUT EUROPE, but major incidents in UK, FRANCE, GERMANY, GREECE, CYPRUS, NETHERLANDS
ISLAMIC JIHAD (Cover name for variety of Shi'ite groups)	LEBANON	FROM EARLY 1980s	SHI'ITE RELIGIOUS & ANTI-ISRAEL, USA & OTHER WESTERN STATES.	FRANCE, GERMANY, UK , SPAIN, ITALY
ARMENIAN SECRET ARMY FOR THE LIBERATION OF ARMENIA ASALA	LEBANON, GREECE	FROM 1974	ARMENIAN NATIONALISM, aimed at TURKEY & TURKISH INTERESTS	TURKEY, FRANCE AUSTRIA, SPAIN, NETHERLANDS, UK, BELGIUM, SWITZERLAND, GREECE
GREY WOLVES	TURKEY	1980s	TURKISH NATIONALIST & FASCIST	TURKEY, ITALY
JAPANESE RED ARMY	JAPAN	FROM 1970	REVOLUTIONARY TERRORISM	FRANCE, NETHERLANDS, ITALY

Connections: Rebuilding democracies 120–121 Threats to security 142–143 Arms industries 186–187 Law and justice 246–249

the world's attention. However, terrorism has won no great victories; modern states are not as vulnerable as they look and populations have proved remarkably resilient to the inconveniences caused by terrorist action. States have also learnt to retaliate against the terrorist. Movements such as the Baader-Meinhof gang and the Red Brigades were overwhelmed by government action. They lacked popular support and so proved comparatively easy to isolate and infiltrate. International cooperation was slow to start but, particularly in Europe, is now increasingly effective. Anti-terrorist units routinely train together and share equipment and techniques.

Assessing the dangers which terrorism may pose in Europe in the future is not simple. Nationalist groups remain a threat because they play upon the deeply-rooted instincts of their parent minorities. There is no immediate prospect of a political solution to the Irish problem. Indeed it is a depressing feature of Irish nationalist movements that if a faction has been tempted to accept a political compromise, diehard elements have split away to continue a violent struggle.

In the ruins of the Soviet bloc there are countless national quarrels which cannot be settled to the satisfaction of all parties, providing ideal conditions for the development of new terrorist groups. A lesson of the recent past is that terrorist activity is the most effective way of publicising what would otherwise be seen as obscure, local quarrels. Moreover, by launching attacks abroad terrorists hope to bring international pressure to bear on their own governments.

It will, however, be harder for terrorists to find international sponsors. The end of the cold war and the collapse of the Soviet Union, combined with the events of the Gulf war, have significantly eroded the terrorists' strategic position. They can no longer play upon rivalry between East and West as a source of public support, funds, arms and training. There is a new mood in the Arab world, symbolised by the release of western hostages in Lebanon (arranged with Syrian and Iranian help) which has quietened terrorist groups in the area. However, only success in the Middle-Eastern peace talks can put an end to their activity in the long term. The process will be slow and no-one can guarantee a conclusion acceptable to all parties.

New fears have been raised by the activities of so-called "consumer terrorists" operating either for blackmail or in the name of animal rights or some other private obsession. Like the Euro-terrorists, they lack a political base and eventually will be isolated and contained. The idea of nuclear terrorism and the use of chemical or biological weapons frighten more.

Real risks or scare-mongering?

After the break-up of the USSR, governments expressed concern that unemployed or underpaid Soviet scientists might be tempted to sell their expertise to less stable governments. It was also suggested that some of the USSR's nuclear weapons, particularly tactical ones, might fall into the wrong hands. Western governments have cooperated to assist Russia with both problems, by providing funds to keep nuclear scientists within the country and to help organise the storage and destruction of nuclear weapons. The possibility of terrorists obtaining or manufacturing a chemical or biological weapon cannot be completely discounted but some projections can be regarded as scare-mongering. Most of the worst-case scenarios put forward about terrorism have proved to be unfounded.

FORCES AGAINST TERRORISM

As the pattern of terrorist activity spread throughout Europe, governments realised that conventional police and military forces needed to be supplemented by specialist anti-terrorist units. In particular these forces would be required for hostage rescue missions, for which specialist training and equipment would be necessary. They have since proved their worth.

In 1976, a team of the French CIGN successfully stormed a hijacked schoolbus in Djibouti. In the following year, Dutch marines rescued hostages held in a school and a train by South Moluccan terrorists and the German GSG 9 saved 91 hostages in a Lufthansa aircraft which had been forced to fly to Mogadishu. Possibly the most famous hostage rescue mission was the assault on the Iranian embassy in London in 1980 by the British Special Air Service (SAS).

On July 14th 1987, a Lebanese man hijacked an Air Afrique DC-10 en route from Brazzaville to Geneva. He demanded the release of the Hamade brothers, Shi'ite terrorists held in West Germany. When the plane landed in Geneva, the terrorist killed a French passenger before being overpowered by Swiss police.

ANTI-TERRORIST UNITS

COUNTRY	TITLE	PARENT SERVICE
AUSTRIA	GENDARMERIEEINSATZKOMMANDO (Cobra Unit)	GENDARMERIE
BELGIUM	ESCADRON SPECIAL D'INTER VENTION ESI	GENDARMERIE
DENMARK	POLITIETS EFTERRETNINGSTJENESTE PET FROMANDSKORPSET (Oil Rig Protection)	POLICE NAVY
FINLAND	OSATO KARHU	HELSINKI MOBILE POLICE
FRANCE	GROUPEMENT D'INTERVENTION DE LA GENDARMERIE NATIONAL GIGN	GENDARMERIE
GERMANY	GRENZSCHUTZGRUPPE 9 GSG 9	BORDER TROOPS
GREECE	DIMORIA EIDIKON APOSTOLON (Special Mission Platoon)	POLICE
ITALY	GROUPE INTERVENTIONAL SPECIALE GIS NUCLEO OPERATIVO CENTRAL DI SICUREZZA NOCS	CARABINIERI POLICE
NETHERLANDS	BIZONDERE BIJSTAND EENHEID BBE	DUTCH ROYAL MARINES
NORWAY	BEREDSKAPSTROP (Readiness Troop) (NB also AIRBORNE/RANGER UNIT for Oil Rig Protection)	POLICE ARMY
PORTUGAL	GRUPO DE OPERACOES ESPECIAIS	POLICE
SPAIN	GRUPO ESPECIAL DE OPERACIONES GEO UNIDAD ESPECIAL DE INTERVENTION UEI	POLICE CIVIL GUARD
UK	SPECIAL AIR SERVICE SAS SPECIAL BOAT SERVICE SBS (Oil Rig Protection)	ARMY ROYAL MARINES

After the kidnapping and murder of the former Italian prime minister, Aldo Moro, in 1978 a tough security campaign led to the arrest of Red Brigade activists, pictured above behind bars in the court-room. A hard core of survivors kidnapped General Dozier, an American, in 1981, but he was released and the Red Brigade almost totally crushed.

The environment is now firmly established on the political agenda. In western Europe it is now accepted that government policy and business practice should take into account the environmental consequences. In eastern Europe the sheer scale of environmental degradation caused by industry pollution has only recently become apparent. Europe's problem is that pollution is no respecter of national borders; sewage dumped in the Rhine in Germany washes onto Dutch shores; radioactive fallout from a nuclear accident in the Ukraine can reach as far as western Britain.

This chapter starts with a global historical perspective and moves on to focus on Europe, dealing with the reality of the threats to the environment. A series of sections cover the spread of pollutants: lead from road traffic, noise from the workplace, fertilisers poisoning water sources, the problems of domestic waste and the much more serious problems of unregulated disposals of toxic waste. The costs of damage caused by acid rain and deforestation, and the consequences of the greenhouse are all assessed. The damage caused by oil spills is detailed, as is the problem of disposing of nuclear waste and the ever-present risk of a catastrophic nuclear accident. A supranational approach is the only one that will be effective in reducing environmental damage; a special section reviews what the European Community is doing, while another looks at how Europe can achieve a sustainable future.

EUROPE AND THE WORLD

The continent of Europe is one characterised by a wide range of landscapes in a comparatively small area. Even so, northern Europe has less diversity of species than other similar climatic regions. A succession of three or four glaciations (ice ages) during the Pleistocene geological period, the last ending some 10,000 years ago, caused large-scale extinction of flora and fauna. These were often prevented from migrating southwards from the expanding continental icesheets by the east-west trending barrier of the Alpine ranges. On the other hand, relict alpine flora survive in isolated mountain pockets to this day.

The environment has always been subjected to considerable climatic change, yet geological evidence suggests these cyclical changes are part of a system in dynamic equilibrium. Warmer interglacial periods, such as the one we are experiencing now called the Holocene, show similar sequences of climatic and ecological change, though the actual combination of species involved will be different. The

mammoths and the giant deer will not return.

Early man also played a part in the late Pleistocene wave of extinctions. At Solutres, in France, the bones of over 100,000 wild horses at the foot of a cliff suggest they may have been driven there. Similar evidence for large mammals disappearing rapidly after Palaeolithic man's appearance exist widely in Europe and North America.

Warming up

Modern Europe emerged as ice sheets up to 4km thick melted, leaving sea levels higher and much of Scandinavia and the British Isles rising, as the weight of the ice was removed. By about 5,000 years ago, the deciduous forest wildwood had reached its maximum extent in many lowland regions, during the warmest (Atlantic) phase of the Holocene. Of course, not all regions tended towards forest, and large areas remained as bogs, such as in Ireland, open mountainside, or the dry grassland steppe of Hungary and Kazakhstan, where grazing also

The forests retreat

Northern Europe has experienced a series of interglacial vegetation cycles, thought to be linked to regular changes in the earth's orbit. The last began about 130,000 years ago and lasted about 11,000 years. Notwithstanding the greenhouse effect, the current interglacial period could end in another 5,000 years. At each warming, flora preserved in southern refuges gradually moved north to colonise the ice-scoured, barren landscape.

Each phase of the cycle illustrated right had a characteristic soil and vegetation formation. Newly exposed glacial deposits, rich in nutrients and calcium, were rapidly colonised in the pre-temperate phase by tree species, including birch and pine, capable of migrating northwards at the rate of over 1km a year, their seeds carried in the wind.

As the soil improved, slower

Climate change

Analysis of pollen grains preserved in cores taken from northern European peat bogs shows considerable changes in vegetation with depth and time, as the chart summarises. These fossil records show that sparsely vegetated alpine tundra gave way to herbaceous vegetation, followed by open parkland scenery with birch, and later hazel. As both temperatures and biological activity rose, sufficient soil and nutrients built up to support closed coniferous forest. The earth's climate is not constant. Over the last 800,000 years, it has experienced a series of warm periods and ice ages, the last ice age ending 10,000 years ago. The next phase in the cycle could involve an ice age in 5,000 years' time, reaching its peak in 60,000 years.

The Viking colonisation of Greenland was made possible by warm, calm conditions in the North Atlantic. Climatic deterioration in the Middle Ages, in the period now known as the "Little Ice Age", left the Viking colonies cut off, and they perished.

☐ Vegetation type
☐ Radio-carbon date (BC)
☐ Climatic period
☐ Archaeology

reproducing and migrating species, such as oak and elm, gradually arrived, forming species-rich closed woodland and rich, brown forest soil. Grasses, weeds, herbs and light-demanding species declined, and were restricted to temporary clearings and marginal land. The last deciduous species to arrive included heavy-seeded beech. The final stage saw soils progressively leached and acidified, with open forest replaced by heath and coniferous woodland, notably of spruce, as temperatures fell once more.

On the sandy soils of northern Europe, forest cleared by human activity became increasingly degraded into infertile heathlands. This came to an end in the mid-1800s. By then the rich brown forest soils were exposed to leaching by precipitation. Even so, these semi-natural habitats, where natural ecological succession has been arrested, are home to unusual species, such as the Nightjar

and Dartford Warbler, and several rare reptiles. They are in a sense the forerunners of the late interglacial cycle.

Degradation of evergreen Mediterranean woodland vegetation that fell victim to the axe, fire and goats created dry maquis, or impoverished scrub, but were characterised by spring blooms of diverse bulbous and other drought-tolerant plants. In Britain, limestone upland deciduous forest gave way to species-rich grass sward, because grazing prevented any one species from becoming dominant. Land clearance increased enormously as technology improved. Hunter-gatherer societies had been superseded in many areas by early cultivators and pastoralists, using fire and stone axes. This led to the conversion of vast areas of deciduous forest to cropland and pasture. Further clearance removed much of the remainder in western and central Europe during the period 1050–1250. In

Britain, remaining tracts largely disappeared for shipbuilding, timber and charcoal for ironworking in the industrial period.

ICE AGE CYCLE

☐ Brown forest soils   ☐ Arctic mineral soils
☐ Leached podzols   ☐ Unleached calcareous soils

INCREASING TEMPERATURE

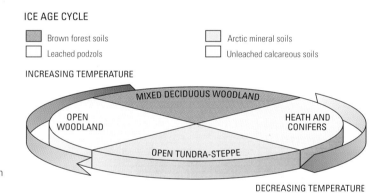

DECREASING TEMPERATURE

BIRCH	PINE	ELM	OAK	LIME	ALDER	BEECH	HAZEL	GRASS	PLANTAINS	WEEDS				
											OPEN WOODLAND	500	SUB-ATLANTIC	HISTORIC
														ROMAN
														IRON AGE
											WOODLAND WITH OPEN AREAS	3,000	SUB-BOREAL	BRONZE AGE
														NEOLITHIC
											MIXED DECIDUOUS WOODLAND	5,500	ATLANTIC	
														MESOLITHIC
											PINE/ OAK/ ELM/ HAZEL FOREST	7,000	BOREAL	
											BIRCH/ PINE FOREST	8,300	PRE-BOREAL	
											TUNDRA	8,800	UPPER DRYAS	
											PARK TUNDRA	10,000	ALLERØD	
														PALAEOLITHIC
											TUNDRA		LOWER DRYAS	

Connections: Europe takes shape 12–15 Family 238–241 Health 242–245

has an important influence.

Mankind's influence came late in the history of the Holocene, but lost no time in moulding the landscape to its own image. By 7,000 years ago, man's activities were already supplanting natural influences on vegetation. The results were often disastrous in the short term, but ecosystems are resilient and gradually adjusted to these changes.

The advent of agriculture

The spread of fire and polished stone axe technology had a devastating effect on the forests. The advent of grazing had a more gradual but no less damaging impact on forest cover, extending the range of natural grasslands. Agriculture became more intensive by the Middle Ages, with widespread use of terracing. Increased nutrients and the availability of light caused weedy species and grasses to become dominant once again.

Human numbers, steady for millennia at about 5m worldwide during the Pleistocene, began to rise rapidly in the first agricultural revolution of early man, with the domestication of plants and animals. These developments enabled land to support at least 500 times more population, and increasingly permanent settlements evolved. Extinctions increased considerably, as man attempted to prevent backcrossing of stock and crops with wild relatives. At each stage of technological progress, intensity of energy and material consumption rose with population, and with it environmental impacts.

Tooling up

Deforestation continued, now for charcoal in metalworking and timber as well as for agricultural land conversion. Trade in cedarwood from Lebanon, tactical burning of forest during warfare between Greek states and the Persian empire, the Punic wars, and the deforestation of Attica and Italy had already damaged the natural resource base of the Mediterranean by the early Roman period. ▷

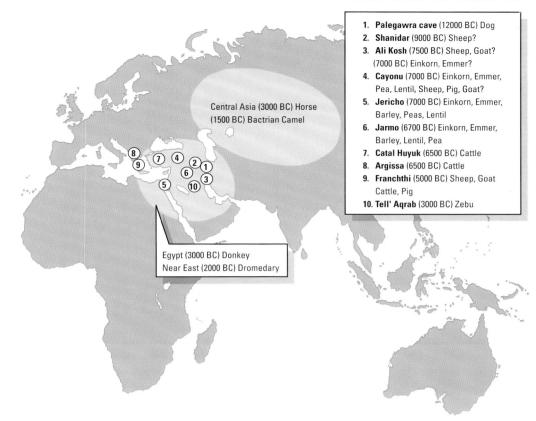

1. **Palegawra cave** (12000 BC) Dog
2. **Shanidar** (9000 BC) Sheep?
3. **Ali Kosh** (7500 BC) Sheep, Goat? (7000 BC) Einkorn, Emmer?
4. **Cayonu** (7000 BC) Einkorn, Emmer, Pea, Lentil, Sheep, Pig, Goat?
5. **Jericho** (7000 BC) Einkorn, Emmer, Barley, Peas, Lentil
6. **Jarmo** (6700 BC) Einkorn, Emmer, Barley, Lentil, Pea
7. **Catal Huyuk** (6500 BC) Cattle
8. **Argissa** (6500 BC) Cattle
9. **Franchthi** (5000 BC) Sheep, Goat, Cattle, Pig
10. **Tell' Aqrab** (3000 BC) Zebu

Central Asia (3000 BC) Horse (1500 BC) Bactrian Camel

Egypt (3000 BC) Donkey
Near East (2000 BC) Dromedary

Animals and plants

Domestication of animals and plants greatly increased our control over the environment, more reliable and plentiful food supply enabling settled agriculture and the development of the first urban civilisations. The first animal and plant domestications occurred in a limited number of centres on each continent (see map above). As with metalworking and other early technology, the process in the Old World occurred first in the Middle East and eastern Mediterranean, with another centre of animal domestication in central Asia.

The oldest association is between man and dog, probably coexisting as hunters, which began around 12,000 BC, and the most recent was the dromedary camel, by 2,000 BC. All the crops forming the staple diet of the Ancient World had been domesticated by about 7,000 BC.

The process seems to have involved a gradual shift from hunting, through controlled hunting, towards a gradually increasing degree of captivity and selection. In central Asia, horses and the bactrian camel were domesticated about 2,000 BC and 1,500 BC respectively, becoming vital to the nomadic lifestyles of the region, enabling rapid migrations westwards into Europe, where the horse revolutionised military and civilian activities.

Old World crop domestications occurred mainly in the grasslands of the Middle East, where evidence is found in excavations of the Neolithic mounds or tells of Jericho. Einkorn and emmer, relatives of wheat, and barley were harvested in the wild by Mesolithic nomads. Continued harvesting favoured survival of plants whose seed heads did not shatter when ripe, eventually leading to domestication in the Neolithic period. The pea and lentil also appeared in the Fertile Crescent region, at Jericho and Jarmo.

Population

Human population grew only very slowly for most of mankind's history, being based on hunter-gatherer economies, as the table below illustrates. It rose steadily from around 5m at the end of the Pleistocene period to about 200m by the time of Christ, driven by successive technological advances originating in the Middle East, notably in agriculture and metal smelting. Even the cataclysmic events associated with bubonic plague during the Middle Ages only temporarily halted this rise. However, world population did not reach its first billion until about 1850, accelerated by the advent of agricultural rotation and intensive energy use at the outset of the Industrial Revolution. Some 80–90% of growth has occurred in little over a century, causing serious strains on natural resources and ecosystems.

World population now stands at about 5bn and average annual growth is between 1% and 2%. Europe only accounts for roughly a tenth of the world population and in both eastern and western Europe growth is less than 0.5% a year on average.

HUMAN POPULATION bn					
Old Stone Age (not to scale)	New Stone Age	Bronze Age	Iron Age	Middle Ages	Modern Times

The human influence

Human impact on the environment was increased by technology long before industrialisation. By the Neolithic period, pottery and settled agriculture had evolved, and by the Bronze age advanced civilisations had appeared in the eastern Mediterranean, such as the Minoans of Crete (see map below). Metalworking had reached most of Europe from the Middle East, by around 4,000 years ago, and by 5,000 years ago ploughing and irrigation generated a second agricultural revolution. The advent of the wheel, reaching eastern Europe by 3,800 years ago and western Europe by 2,500 years ago, together with shipbuilding, boosted trade, prosperity and population. The great empires of the classical period emerged around the rim of the Mediterranean. Demands on forests, for timber for shipbuilding and for charcoal in metal smelting, had devastated deciduous forests in much of northern Europe by the 18th century.

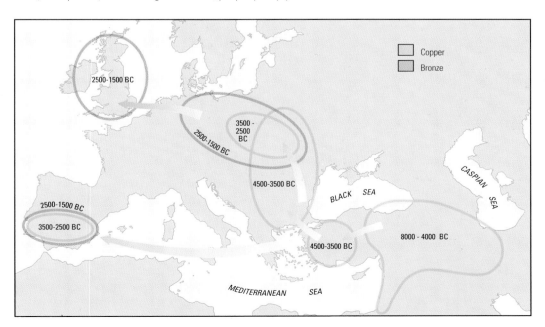

Copper
Bronze

2500-1500 BC

3500 - 2500 BC

2500-1500 BC

4500-3500 BC

2500-1500 BC

3500-2500 BC

4500-3500 BC

8000 - 4000 BC

BLACK SEA

CASPIAN SEA

MEDITERRANEAN SEA

Eastern promises... By 1990 the former eastern bloc countries were aware of their environment problems. These students are protesting in Budapest.

Green awareness

In 1989 one in ten voters in the European Community voted for a green candidate in the elections for the European Parliament. This was twice the number that voted green in 1984. Support for green candidates is high at local government as well as supranational levels: there are over 2,000 local green councillors in the European Community. Mainstream parties are now adopting green policies, realising their electoral popularity beyond the boundaries of the sovereign state.

Human needs

Total solar energy available for plant growth and dependent animal populations is ultimately limited. The needs of the world's rapidly growing human population can only be met by consuming a larger proportion of the earth's biological resources, for food, energy and raw materials at the expense of other species. Man already consumes 40% of the total. Only 4% of these resources are used directly, the rest we deny other species indirectly by waste, such as ploughing excess crops back into the soil, or by paving over productive land (10%).

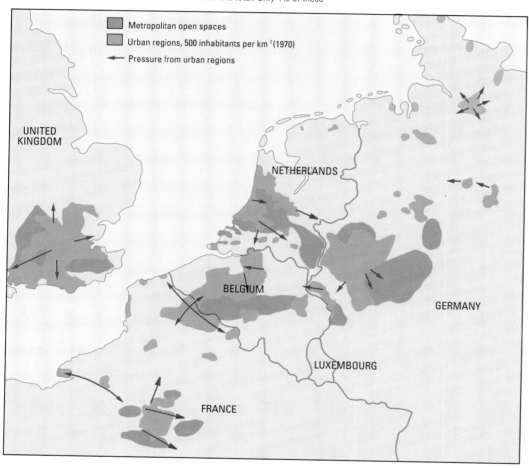

Metropolitan open spaces

Urban regions, 500 inhabitants per km² (1970)

→ Pressure from urban regions

UNITED KINGDOM

NETHERLANDS

BELGIUM

GERMANY

LUXEMBOURG

FRANCE

It is intriguing that in the Maastricht agreement, signed in 1992, the one major policy arena that was allowed to be binding on member governments on the majority vote was environment. Europe presents an environmental theatre that ignores national boundaries. Almost all the major rivers join or separate nations. All estuaries disgorge into common seas – the Baltic, the North Sea and the Mediterranean. Pollution is both ubiquitous and collectively perilous. No country can avoid the detritus of another. Over 90% of the sulphur dioxide that falls on Norway, Sweden and Switzerland, all countries with few coal or oil burning sources, drifts in from neighbours. The volatile organic compounds that toxify air, water and soils are produced all over Europe. Even the most environmentally regulated of national economies cannot escape.

The future cost

Environment nowadays is big politics and big economics. The growth of scientific knowledge, the improvement of data banks and the recording of adverse effects on human health and ecological vitality reveal that Europe generally is suffering, while parts of eastern and central Europe are suffering catastrophically. In parts of southern Poland, and in over 20 locations in Russia, one in seven youngsters is chronically ill due to environmental pollution. The cost of cleaning up exceeds the natural wealth of all the former communist countries on an aggregated basis. Even in wealthy Germany, environmental protection expenditures amount to over 6% of GDP. The production of clean technology and best practice restorative measures is worth about 150bn ecus in the European Community alone each year. The industries that produce or invest in cleaner technology and those that adopt cleaner practises are ones that have the best chance of profitable growth in the future.

In many respects Europe represents a microcosm of the global environment dilemma. The rich North and West is in recession, but alone has the economic clout to assist the poorer and environmentally degraded East and South. The capacity to transfer former cold war military expenditure into environmentally sustainable regional development is considerable, but still politically contentious. Democracies old and new are suspicious of the environmental message. The older, wealthier nations are wary of diverting recession-prone investment cash into economies that have still to learn about environmental pricing and the hard grind of citizen-initiated environmental responsibilities. The vested interests in the poorer

Joining the dodo

The rate of species extinctions worldwide averaged little more than one a year for most of the last 200m years, but it is now hundreds or even thousands of times higher, as the chart (right) indicates. The true figure is impossible to estimate, since many of the world's plant and animal species are still unknown, but bird and mammal extinctions have closely followed human population growth in the industrial era, rising geometrically. Some 35 species of bird and 40 mammals became extinct between 1900 and 1950, compared with a couple of bird and mammal species between 1700 and 1750. In industrialised regions of Europe, large predators, particularly those considered dangerous to human communities, such as the wolf in Britain, had disappeared by the start of the era through hunting. Extinctions of plants and animals have been caused by human actions both directly, by unregulated hunting and collecting, and indirectly, by changing land use.

As forest clearance, mining, urbanisation and road and rail network development have continued, both the quantity and quality of natural habitats have suffered. Fragments of once widespread habitats have become isolated by a hostile sea of urban and intensive agricultural landscapes, preventing areas that are losing species from being recolonised from neighbouring fragments. While much has been done towards conserving key habitats in Europe, these fragments are still susceptible to accelerated extinctions. Such small populations of threatened species are less able to weather natural fluctuations in their numbers, natural disasters or climate change.

Pollution of air and water by industrial emissions and toxic wastes has added yet another burden in industrialised Europe. Intensification of agriculture, including removal of hedgerows and use of pesticides since the second world war in northern Europe, is also threatening species that have come to coexist in the farmed landscape. Southern and eastern Europe are also increasingly threatened by expanding agricultural production.

Globally, human activity could wipe out between 25% and 55% of all species by the year 2000. Population growth, poverty and inappropriate international trade and development policy in the developing world are all major factors. Rapid warming due to the greenhouse effect could also increase extinctions of species.

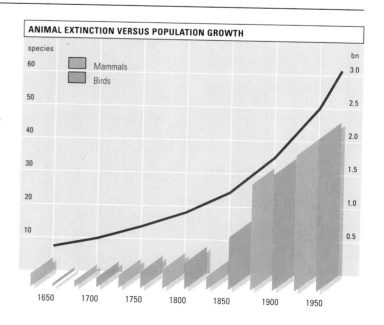

ANIMAL EXTINCTION VERSUS POPULATION GROWTH

species

60

Mammals

Birds

50

40

30

20

10

1650 1700 1750 1800 1850 1900 1950

bn

3.0

2.5

2.0

1.5

1.0

0.5

regions want to emulate the growth pattern of the apparently successful western Europe, which achieved its present economic superiority without paying much attention to the environmental cost. The environmental audit is a recent concept in the West. In eastern Europe, politicians and businessmen are still grappling with the concept of the traditional idea of an audit. Politicians, finance ministries and local elites have still not heard of environmental accounting.

A supranational approach

Already the European Community has demonstrated that collective action can work to protect and restore environmental wellbeing, and that both legal as well as political institutions that transcend national sovereignty can be developed in an acceptable manner. The major challenge remains the regional restructuring of eastern Europe in a manner that is socially just and democratically tolerable. If Europe can do it, maybe there is still a chance for the rest of the world.

THE EFFECTS OF INDUSTRIALISATION

Carbon dioxide emissions closely reflect levels of human activity. Forest clearance in the tropics today, in Europe and North America in the early industrial period, and fossil fuel combustion of coal, oil and natural gas, for energy in the home, industry and transport have all increased enormously since the pre-industrial period. On current trends, levels can be expected to double during the 21st century, having risen already from the pre-industrial level of 280 parts per million by volume (ppmv) to over 350 ppmv during the early 1990s. Raised levels of carbon dioxide prevent incoming solar energy from being radiated back out to space, causing an enhanced greenhouse effect, threatening global warming and climate change.

Levels of lead that have reached the remote Greenland ice

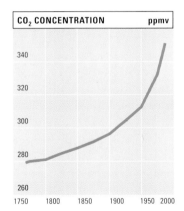

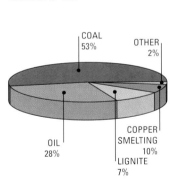

CO₂ CONCENTRATION   ppmv

SOURCE OF SO₂

COAL 53%
OTHER 2%
COPPER SMELTING 10%
LIGNITE 7%
OIL 28%

cap show rapid increases from the start of the Industrial Revolution, reaching some 60 times natural levels by the turn of the century. After 1900, leaded petrol raised levels enormously, to some 170 times natural levels by 1950.

Sulphur dioxide levels are also keen indicators of increasing industrial activity and transport globally. Today, over 90% of SO_2 is generated by fossil fuel combustion, mostly from coal and oil, and much of the remainder from copper smelting. Increasing energy use, aggravated in eastern Europe by inefficient use of high sulphur coals, has boosted levels rapidly, causing damage to crops, corrosion, respiratory disease and acid rain. From levels of under 4m tonnes in 1860, generation of SO_2 pollution had increased tenfold to reach 40m tonnes by the end of the 1950s. In the three decades since then SO_2 pollution has more than doubled to reach 90m tonnes by the early 1990s.

FROM IGNORANCE TO AWARENESS

Public awareness of the need for action to protect the environment locally and internationally has been increasing rapidly since the 1960s in Europe and North America. The number of green pressure groups and the importance of environmental issues in elections across Europe is a clear reflection of this. The trend has been strongest in Germany and Scandinavia, where acid rain and concerns over nuclear safety were powerful catalysts from the 1970s, with growing pressure for change in the Netherlands, the UK and other northern European nations. In the UK alone, membership of the conservation group, World Wide Fund for Nature, grew from some 70,000 in the early 1980s to over 200,000 by 1989.

Severe pollution and associated health problems have also propelled environmental issues to the top of the political agenda across the emerging democracies of eastern Europe and the former Soviet Union. In Poland alone, 62 environmental groups had been set up between 1980 and 1989, in spite of political repression. Romania had at least eight major ecological groups and parties by 1990. In Hungary, activity has mainly focused on opposition to the construction of the Danube dam at Nagymaros, with a 200,000-signature petition against the project stalling progress. Grassroots environmental and development groups are also emerging in developing countries, such as Indonesia, which now has over 600.

A survey by OECD of environmental concerns found that perceptions varied considerably between the USA, Japan and the EC, although both the EC and USA rated disposal of waste, especially toxic waste, as a primary concern, followed by oil spills. Other major concerns in the EC and USA also tended to be global, including climate change, air and water pollution, and loss of species and natural resources. Less dramatic local concerns such as access to open countryside seem to take second place. Japanese concerns are dominated by loss of species and natural resources, and air and water pollution.

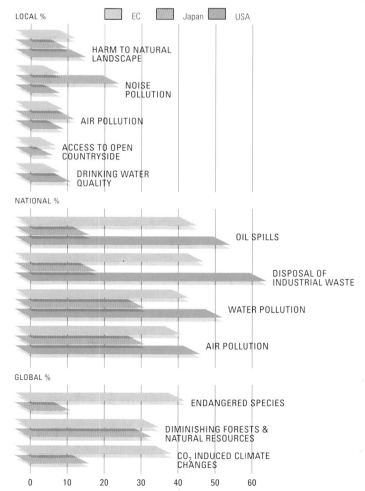

HEADS OF STEAM

LOCAL %   EC   Japan   USA

HARM TO NATURAL LANDSCAPE
NOISE POLLUTION
AIR POLLUTION
ACCESS TO OPEN COUNTRYSIDE
DRINKING WATER QUALITY

NATIONAL %

OIL SPILLS
DISPOSAL OF INDUSTRIAL WASTE
WATER POLLUTION
AIR POLLUTION

GLOBAL %

ENDANGERED SPECIES
DIMINISHING FORESTS & NATURAL RESOURCES
CO₂ INDUCED CLIMATE CHANGES

0   10   20   30   40   50   60

The car

Car ownership has grown much faster than population in industrialised countries. It is highest in the non-European developed nations of the USA, Canada, Australia and New Zealand, while in western Europe and Japan it is at half this level. Road density, a major cause of environmental disturbance, is highest in Monaco and Belgium, at 32.21 km road per km² and 4.2 km km² respectively, followed by the Netherlands, at 2.76 km km². This compares with 2.91 km km² for Japan, and well below 0.5 for most other non-European states.

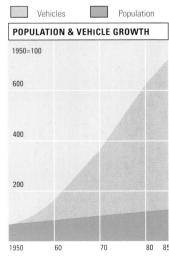

Vehicles   Population

POPULATION & VEHICLE GROWTH

1950=100

600

400

200

1950   60   70   80 85

AIR POLLUTION

Unacceptable face…Art is lost to years of exposure to a polluted atmosphere as well as the ravages of wind and water, as this ancient Venetian edifice bearing the scars of the 20th century shows.

Pollutant gases, heavy metals and high dust levels have become strongly associated with industrial and transport activity, and with domestic energy use. These gases include sulphur dioxide (SO_2) and oxides of nitrogen (NO_x). Carbon dioxide (CO_2) is closely linked to most human activity. Carbon monoxide (CO), on the other hand, is a toxic gas of local importance, interfering with the take-up of oxygen by the blood. Hydrogen chloride (HCl) causes plant damage and problems of corrosion in and around power stations burning high chloride coals.

SO_2 has serious implications for local pollution, particularly in urban conurbations, where it causes corrosion of buildings, monuments and even paintings. It also causes lung irritation, which can develop into respiratory disease. Bronchitis is more common where SO_2 levels in the air are high.

NO_x compounds are generated mainly by combustion of fossil fuels at high temperatures and come from atmospheric nitrogen. About half of emissions come from road vehicles, the rest from power generation and industry. High NO_x levels, mainly in urban areas, affect the respiratory system and contribute to another modern pollution problem of both local and regional proportions in the form of toxic ozone, and another localised irritant, peroxycetyl nitrate (PAN). This phenomenon of "photochemical smog" was first noticed in Los Angeles in the 1950s, but it is now a serious problem in many European cities experiencing stagnant, high pressure weather, particularly in summer. Cities such as Madrid, once noted for clear, mountain air, now regularly experience a thick brown haze in fine weather.

Headaches

The range and complexity of interactions between pollutants is increasing with new technological processes. Classical air pollution is increasingly being replaced by regional scale secondary pollutants, such as ozone and acid rain. After the 1970s, indoor air pollution and sick building syndrome causing headaches and lethargy, became common, due to a combination of volatile organic compounds used in furnishings and overzealous insulation.

Where air hurts

In eastern Europe, the air pollution that hurts is that which is now being eliminated in western Europe – sulphur dioxide, nitrous oxide and hydrocarbons. In the technologically innovative West, a new generation of air pollution is emerging based on volatile organic compounds from solvents, ozone depleting gases from fire retardants and fungicides, and fugitive emissions of toxic substances that are so minuscule at each point of exit as to be almost unmeasurable, yet which accumulate in food chains and ecosystems to create pernicious chemical time bombs.

Industrialised and mining regions of eastern Europe are now the worst-affected by air pollution in Europe, and the largest exporters of SO_2 and heavy metals. Health, the environment and the economy have all suffered from gross pollution, with life expectancy significantly below western European levels. Only massive economic and technical aid to these debt-laden states will lead to improvement locally and internationally. Poland, Czechoslovakia, and Romania are among the worst-affected. The Copsa Mica industrial region of Romania is described as "an environmental disaster" by the government, requiring immediate action. Some 200,000 people are affected by lead, cadmium and SO_2 fallout over 180,000 hectares.

In Czechoslovakia, in the Bohemian basin, environmental conditions have recently reached catastrophic proportions. Opencast coalmining has devastated the region, while combustion of low quality brown coals in power generation and heavy industry generates levels of SO_2 that regularly exceed 200 microgrammes per cubic metre during winter. The permitted annual average is 60 microgrammes. The human cost of pollution, mainly of air, since 1960, includes rates of infant mortality and chronically ill, malformed children that are some 40% higher than the national average, high cancer rates, and almost double the rate of birth disorders. Life expectancy in Czechoslovakia, 72 years compared with an average for Europe of 74, is one of the lowest in the industrialised world, while in the basin it is up to three years lower than this.

In neighbouring Upper Silesia, in Poland, areas that are considered ecologically at risk cover 11% of the country and 34% of the population. Much of the air pollution occurs around Cracow and Katowice, due to prewar coking plants, heavy industrial plant for steel and non-ferrous metal smelting. Air and water pollution cause several health effects, including pregnancy complications and "natural abortions" 16% and 60% respectively above the national average.

NO$_x$ and SO$_2$

Patterns of generation of SO_2 and NO_x across Europe are very different from those of deposition as the chart shows. In 1990, the largest net exporters of SO_2 in Europe were in the European part of the former Soviet Union, emitting 4.790m tonnes (mt) and receiving deposition of 3.617mt, and in eastern Europe, notably the former East Germany, emitting some 2.621mt, but only receiving 0.804mt of deposition. The UK emitted 1.916mt and received 0.548mt, and Czechoslovakia produced 1.400mt and received only 0.675mt.

NO_x generation follows industrialised regions and road traffic, with the European part of the former Soviet Union emitting 4.406mt in 1990, but receiving only 0.968mt, western Germany emitting 2.860mt and receiving only 0.267mt, followed by the UK, France and Italy, all of which emitted much more NO_2 than was deposited on their soil. The former Soviet Union, Poland, western Germany and France received the largest amount of depositions as acid rain. Even so, the actual problems of acid rain occur mostly on more sensitive granitic landscapes, as in Sweden.

EMISSIONS AND DEPOSITION

COUNTRY	SULPHUR		NITROGEN OXIDES	
AUSTRIA	470	1,774	2,010	846
BELGIUM	2,100	902	3,000	283
BULGARIA	5,150	2,461	1,500	363
CZECHOSLOVAKIA	14,000[1]	6,748	9,500[1]	1,276
DENMARK	1,330	601	2,540	284
FINLAND	1,260	1,664	2,760[1]	687
FRANCE	6,670[1]	5,107	17,720[1]	2,333
GERMANY E.	26,210[1]	8,040	10,050[1]	1,134
GERMANY W.	5,300[1]	5,510	28,600[1]	2,671
GREECE	2,500[1]	1,307	7,460[1]	373
HUNGARY	5,820	2,944	2,640	561
ICELAND	30[1]	106	1,20[1]	68
IRELAND	840	416	1,350	140
ITALY	12,050[1]	5,223	17,000[1]	1,558
LUXEMBOURG	50	40	150	19
NETHERLANDS	12,70[1]	916	5,520[1]	375
NORWAY	3,30[1]	1,585	2,260[1]	984
POLAND	22,500	14,090	14,800[1]	2,873
PORTUGAL	1,060	484	1,420	161
ROMANIA	9,000[1]	5,490	3,900[3]	916
SPAIN	10,950[1]	3,958	9,500[1]	1,069
SWEDEN	1,020	2,453	3,730	1,374
SWITZERLAND	310	690	1,840	388
TURKEY	1,990[1]	1,991	1,750[3]	584
UK	19,160	5,483	25,730	944
USSR[2]	47,900	36,165	44,060[1]	9,679
YUGOSLAVIA	7,750[1]	5,269	4,300[1]	1,231

☐ Emissions (100 tons) 1990 ☐ Emissions (100 tons) 1990
☐ Deposition (100 tons) 1990 ☐ Depositions (100 tons) 1990
1 Interpolated data **2** European part of ex-USSR **3** Estimates

NOISE POLLUTION

Noise pollution tends to be a local, neighbourhood or occupational problem, but the growth of road and air transport now causes much larger scale problems in urbanised regions, such as the south-east of England and the Netherlands. Transport is now the main cause of environmental noise, and 130m people are exposed to levels that are considered unacceptable, above 65 dB, due to road, rail and air transport. Another 50% are exposed to unsatisfactory levels. In Germany and parts of rural England and Wales, low-flying military jets have been controversial additions to local noise.

EC regulations on protection from occupational noise now demand that ear protection is provided in noisy workplaces, and that steps be taken to reduce sources in some cases. A great deal of work now goes into reducing road vehicle engine noise and road friction, and into producing quieter aircraft. Health effects of noise include disturbed sleep and conversation, loss of concentration, irritability, raised blood pressure and stress levels, and effects on unborn babies. At the extreme, temporary or permanent loss of hearing occurs. Sudden, "impulsive" noise can be more damaging than continuous noise, causing shock and possibly accidents as a result. Supersonic booms are one such example.

On the decibel scale, dB, each 3 dB increase has the effect of doubling exposure. Sensitivity to noise varies according to the individual but, generally speaking, telephone conversation becomes difficult at 70 dB, equivalent to standing 15 metres from a motorway. At 80 dB, in an office with noisy machinery, annoyance sets in, and constant exposure to 90 dB causes permanent ear damage.

Connections: Road transport 28–29 Europe and the world 198–201 The greenhouse effect 214–215

Lead emitters

Lead inhibits enzyme activity in the body and blocks the uptake of iron. It accumulates mainly in bone tissue. The largest sources of lead emissions in western Europe were France, followed by the UK and Germany (see chart below). It is produced mainly from the now declining use of leaded petrol.

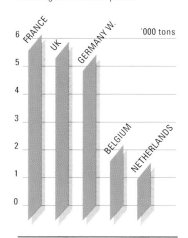

Cadmium emitters

Cadmium levels in the air are highest in urban and industrial areas, with western Germany and France the two major western European producers (see chart below).

Brief inhalation of high levels of cadmium oxide fumes can cause severe or even fatal lung damage. It can also cause sterility rapidly, and may cause high blood pressure and lead to heart disease. Cadmium also accumulates in the liver and kidneys, where it causes damage.

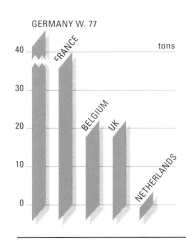

Lead fallout

Lead and heavy metal pollution tends to produce the greatest fallout near the source, but a significant proportion can stay airborne for up to ten days and be transported up to 2,000 km (see map, where the lead fallout is measured in molecules per hectare deposited in 1985). The main sources are coal and oil combustion, ferrous and non-ferrous metal industries, traffic and refuse incineration. Heavy metals are all toxic, tend to accumulate in the soil and enter the food chain.

Lead was the main source of heavy metal fallout over the Netherlands in the early 1980s. Some 80% of this was from other parts of western Europe. The main source of lead fallout has been from petrol. In Europe, considerable reductions, varying from 45% in the Netherlands to 60% in the UK, took effect during the late 1980s. In several countries, such as Spain, unleaded petrol has yet to make an impression on the market, but all are committed to its adoption.

Cadmium fallout

The highest levels of cadmium fallout occur across a broad swathe of central and eastern Europe, together with eastern and northern Spain, while lead fallout is more restricted to central and north-west Europe. Fallout also contributes greatly to levels in the North Sea. Levels of cadmium fallout are likely to decrease in the next few decades, as the use of cadmium in paints, pigments and as plasticisers is phased out in the European Community. These uses accounted for over half of total cadmium usage in the UK during 1986.

In Germany, the Federal Health Agency advises that beef and pork kidneys should be consumed only occasionally, because liver and kidneys accumulate high levels of both cadmium and lead.

Romania has one of the worst heavy metal hot spots in Europe, with cadmium and lead levels causing widespread air, water and soil contamination. Some 3,500 cases of lead and cadmium poisoning have occurred, through inhalation or through consumption of contaminated food and water.

Germany dominates emissions of all other heavy metals, except nickel where France is the major producer of emissions.

LEAD IN THE ATMOSPHERE

More than 1.2
0.6 - 1.2
0.15 - 0.60
Less than 0.15

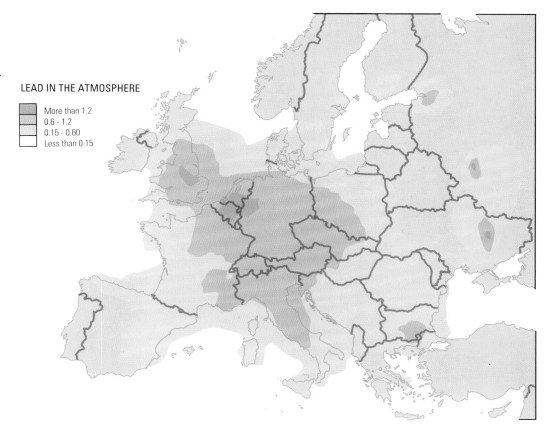

CADMIUM IN THE ATMOSPHERE

More than 0.024
0.008 - 0.024
0.002 - 0.008
Less than 0.002

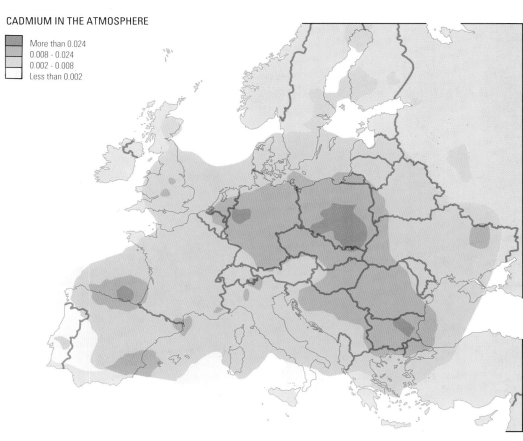

VOCS

Volatile organic compounds (VOCS) are a wide range of compounds, many of them solvents such as benzene and dichloromethane. There are several hundred types of VOCS, generated by increasingly complex economic activity, so that monitoring is a complicated task. Road traffic and industry account for the majority of emissions. Solvents account for some 40% of non-traffic VOC pollution on average, followed by the petroleum industry. Europe contributes 36% of world VOC pollution, or about 6% of global natural emissions. Germany, followed by the UK and France, are the major European sources.

Various methods of controlling VOCS are being considered, among them recycling, use of water-based paints and their substitutes, catalytic converters and incineration. VOCS also contribute to

ozone and photochemical smog. Explosive methane gas, an important contributor to the greenhouse effect, is sometimes considered a VOC. It is generated from natural gas use, mining, organic waste landfills, agriculture and natural sources.

Chlorofluorocarbons (CFCS) and other halogenated organic compounds, used in refrigeration, dry cleaning, fire extinguishers and, until recently, aerosol cans are rapidly destroying stratospheric ozone globally.

VOCS can cause a wide range of health problems, including skin and mucous membrane irritation, liver and kidney damage, and neurotoxicity, though these effects generally occur only after exposure to high concentrations. However, many are known as carcinogenic .

Health effects

Some 320 toxic trace pollutants are recognised as having a damaging effect in the USA. Sixty have been identified as being carcinogenic, many more cause respiratory or nervous disorders. Some are organic compounds from various sources, including the VOCS, such as PCBS which accumulate in mammals. Others are heavy metals and metalloids like beryllium, arsenic and thallium.

Road traffic

The diagram, based on a Norwegian study in 1990, shows an attempt to quantify the total social costs of road traffic, in terms of marginal pollution cost and cost related to traffic per litre of gasoline and diesel oil consumed. Car traffic related social costs included accidents, traffic jams, wear of roads and noise, which accounted for 73%, equivalent to Kr5.53 per litre of gasoline. Another Kr2.06, 27%, was due to the ecological, health and corrosion effects of pollution. Diesel vehicles were found to cause 70% higher pollution costs, mainly due to higher SO₂ output, particulates and carbon monoxide, equal to 36% of the total social cost. Diesel vehicles caused only marginally higher traffic-related costs than the car.

SOCIAL COSTS OF TRAFFIC

Traffic related external costs
Pollution costs (mainly negative health effects NDx emmisions)

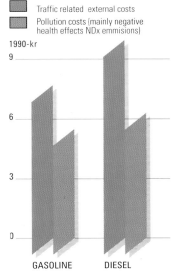

WATER POLLUTION

Fresh water is a basic necessity for all life and has always been the precondition for human settlements, originally for drinking and irrigation, later for sanitation, industry and power.

Freshwater pollution involves one of two main types of waste, organic and inorganic. Organic pollution is caused by excessive input of biological wastes, for example untreated sewage, residues from food processing and agricultural wastes such as manure. Bacterial breakdown of organic wastes deoxygenates water, a problem measured in terms of Biochemical Oxygen Demand (BOD). Inorganic pollution in traditional coal and metal mining regions is generally caused by heavy metals in contaminated wastewaters. Mine wastes tend to contain pyrite (iron sulphide) which oxidises in air and rainfall to produce sulphurous acid. Acidified waters increase solubility of lead, cadmium, mercury and other heavy metals, keeping wastes bare of vegetation and blighting rivers downstream. Water pollution comes either from specific "point sources", such as sewage outlets, or from diffuse sources, such as runoff from fields, and atmospheric fallout of heavy metals and other toxic materials. River basins and particularly the sedimented estuaries bear the brunt of water pollution, as well as of air and soil.

Europe (excluding the former Soviet Union) possesses 5.7% of the world's total fresh water. It currently consumes an average of 15% of renewable fresh water supplies, compared with a world average of 8%; half of this for industrial use. Many countries are already near the limit of exploitation. Improved water treatment and groundwater cleanup are vital to cope with a continuous increase in demand.

Water pollution

Artificial fertilisers, nitrates and phosphates have become major sources of water pollution since 1900 as the map on the right shows. Europe used 228kg per hectare per year in the mid-1980s, compared with 114kg in the former Soviet Union, and a world average of only 91kg. Iceland, the Netherlands and Belgium are the most intensive users, while eastern and southern Europe have tended to use less until recently. Manure as slurry has also become a problem, due to the sheer volumes generated by intensive livestock rearing. In the Netherlands, manure mountains pose a serious problem for pollution control, releasing ammonia which spreads to the surrounding waters. Excess growth of aquatic plants and algae has choked many stretches of European estuaries, rivers and lakes as a result.

Sewage treatment plants now serve more than 80% of western Germany, Switzerland, Denmark and Sweden. Sludge disposal remains a problem, and eastern Europe does not have the resources to finance all necessary water treatment plants.

In 1990, the North Sea states agreed to ban all dumping of sewage sludge by 1994, and to reduce nitrate emissions by 50% by 1998. This decision will cost the basin states some 10bn ecus. In eastern and central Europe many groundwater sources are seriously contaminated.

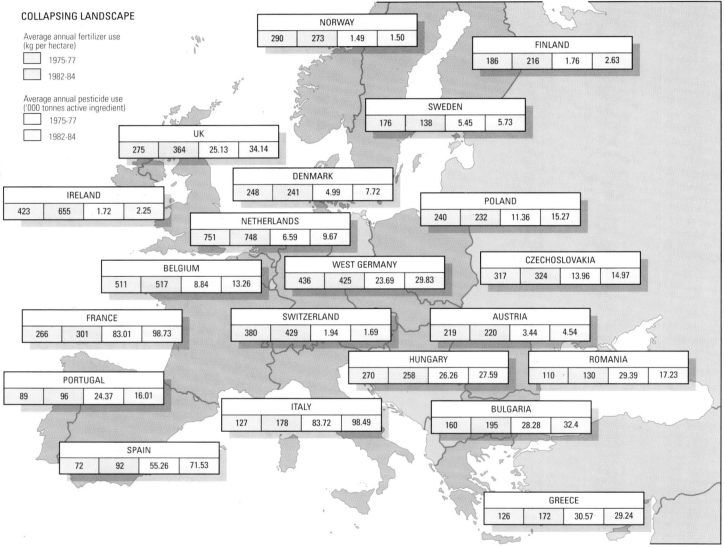

COLLAPSING LANDSCAPE

Average annual fertilizer use (kg per hectare)
☐ 1975-77
☐ 1982-84

Average annual pesticide use ('000 tonnes active ingredient)
☐ 1975-77
☐ 1982-84

NORWAY			
290	273	1.49	1.50

FINLAND			
186	216	1.76	2.63

SWEDEN			
176	138	5.45	5.73

UK			
275	364	25.13	34.14

DENMARK			
248	241	4.99	7.72

IRELAND			
423	655	1.72	2.25

POLAND			
240	232	11.36	15.27

NETHERLANDS			
751	748	6.59	9.67

CZECHOSLOVAKIA			
317	324	13.96	14.97

BELGIUM			
511	517	8.84	13.26

WEST GERMANY			
436	425	23.69	29.83

FRANCE			
266	301	83.01	98.73

SWITZERLAND			
380	429	1.94	1.69

AUSTRIA			
219	220	3.44	4.54

HUNGARY			
270	258	26.26	27.59

ROMANIA			
110	130	29.39	17.23

PORTUGAL			
89	96	24.37	16.01

ITALY			
127	178	83.72	98.49

BULGARIA			
160	195	28.28	32.4

SPAIN			
72	92	55.26	71.53

GREECE			
126	172	30.57	29.24

Danube blues

Most of Europe's major rivers remain polluted, but there are large differences between the continuing crisis in the East and gradual improvement in the West. The chart illustrates how while biochemical oxygen demand (BOD) levels in the Scheldt in Belgium fell by 70% between 1979 and 1985, they doubled in the Hungarian section of the Danube over the same period.

BOD is the amount of oxygen lost in waters because of the bacterial breakdown of wastes. BOD is used to measure organic pollution.

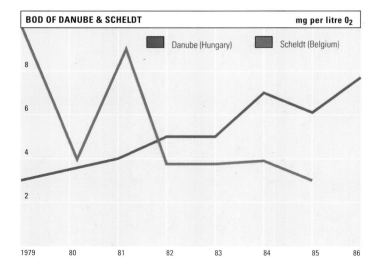

BOD OF DANUBE & SCHELDT mg per litre O$_2$

■ Danube (Hungary) ■ Scheldt (Belgium)

1979 80 81 82 83 84 85 86

POLLUTION OF INTERNATIONAL RIVERS

In the Netherlands, consumption of water is rising rapidly and is expected to grow by 10% for domestic use and 65–150% for industrial use by the year 2000. As pressures on reliable groundwater supplies increase, the Dutch are being obliged to turn more to surface waters that are affected by air and water pollution from across the border. The Netherlands is particularly concerned at the growth of chemical and nuclear plants along the upper reaches of the Rhine and Meuse. Both chronic and accidental pollution threaten existing water supplies. The Rhine Action Programme is committed to reduce toxic substance inputs discharged by France, Germany, Luxembourg, the Netherlands and Switzerland by 50% as soon as possible. Similar action is badly needed along the Danube.

% POPULATION WITHOUT SAFE DRINKING WATER

1980-85

- 60%
- 50%
- 25%
- No available data

Even the nature reserves are not immune as the photograph shows. Effluent in the San Martino river in the Circeo National Park, Saraudia, Italy.

THE QUALITY OF DRINKING WATER

Overall, western Europe manages to provide safe drinking water to over 75% of its population, as the map above illustrates. Major problems remain in Poland, Czechoslovakia and Yugoslavia where safe drinking water is provided for only 50–75%. A similar problem exists in Turkey and Portugal. Industry, novel organic chemicals, intensive agriculture and increasing demand for water all pose threats to availability. About half the population of the OECD now drink water that has been passed through wastewater treatment plants, and the desirable levels of increasingly varied waste residues after treatment are the subject of constant concern. Residues in combination may cause greater health risks than they would individually.

Sources of drinking water vary regionally in Europe. Boreholes, common in regions such as the chalk downlands of south-east England and limestone regions of Spain, have traditionally provided naturally filtered drinking waters from underground aquifers, while reliance on increasingly polluted surface waters generally requires water treatment.

Aquifers in many agricultural regions are becoming unusable, due to intensive nitrate and pesticide use since the 1950s, and manure from livestock. Loss of soil humus through modern farming increases the downward movement of nitrates, which already approach or exceed safety levels in many rivers. In Germany, 5–10% of treatment plants have difficulty complying with EC-wide nitrate standards, and even this does not take account of the large number of wells already closed. In the UK, where the privatisation of the water utility companies highlighted how much needed to be spent on the water supply infrastructure, it is often necessary to blend waters from different sources to comply.

In Czechoslovakia, only 50% of water supplies meet even outdated health norms, with both surface and groundwaters falling in quality. Contamination by nitrates is up to 25 times the adult limit, and up to 80 times that for babies. These levels threaten "blue baby syndrome" and brain damage, caused by interference with oxygen in the blood. In Hungary, pollution threatens some 60% of aquifers, while mining and industrial developments are causing heavy metal contamination in the rivers Szamos, Tisza and Maros. Over 450,000 people in southern Hungary are exposed to unacceptable levels of arsenic in water. Some 80% of Romania's main rivers are too polluted to provide drinking water.

NUTRIENT POLLUTION

GUADALQUIVIR

Nitrates Phosphorus

mg per litre

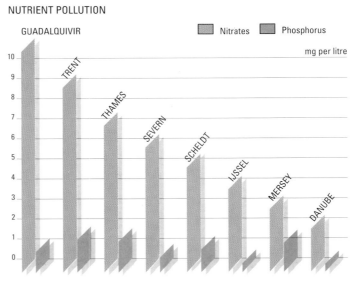

Washed out

The chart (left) shows pollution levels of several European rivers. The Guadalquivir in southern Spain is the most affected, followed by four rivers in Britain: the Trent, Thames, Severn and Mersey.

The situation in Czechoslovakia is deteriorating, with over 70% of rivers heavily polluted, and some 30% with no surviving fish life. Many of the lakes and rivers of Hungary are also increasingly polluted, notably the Danube over much of its length. In Romania, some 3,700km, or 18.5%, of rivers are grossly polluted, and another 2,400km, or 12%, are at least moderately polluted. Major investments in pollution control technology will be needed simply to prevent further deterioration in affected regions of eastern Europe. The cost of cleaning up Hungary's rivers could be $7bn.

WASTE POLLUTION

The free market does not operate efficiently when it comes to solid waste, because neither producers nor consumers directly bear the full cost of the problems it creates. As markets have become saturated and competition more fierce, there has been a trend towards more lavishly packaged products that last less, to increase turnover. The greatest commercial successes have often produced the most extreme examples of waste – the disposable pen, razor, you name it, for example. Waste disposal is already a major business expense, as options narrow and legislation tightens. If all the western German commercial and domestic waste produced in a year piled up, it would rival the country's highest mountain, Zugspitze (2,992 metres).

The major categories of concern are industrial waste, commercial and domestic waste, agricultural waste and two other types of waste only generated in small amounts, but potentially very hazardous. These are radioactive wastes and medical and pathogenic laboratory wastes. Different countries define waste slightly differently, making international comparisons difficult.

Growth of nuclear weapons and nuclear power, together with medical uses of radiation, have generated perhaps the worst headache of all. Nuclear waste often remains radioactive for generations, and as it builds up there is increasing controversy over its final destination. Only a few countries such as Sweden have committed themselves to building, and guarding, long-term repositories. Prevention is ultimately cheaper than cure. This means that Europe's manufacturers will have to make greater use of recycling, and reduce reliance upon hazardous and non-renewable raw materials.

Muck merchants

Municipal waste is created by domestic and commercial sources in urban areas. In the late 1980s, it accounted for 16% of EC waste, with another 14% of waste created by mainly urban sewage treatment. In most European states where reliable figures exist, municipal waste output has grown. In Austria, it grew by 23% from 1975 to 1985, and for the same period it grew in the UK by almost 11% to reach 17,737 tonnes a year.

The largest municipal waste producers are not surprisingly the industrial nations, notably western Germany, generating almost 20,000 tonnes a year in 1985, the UK, France and Italy, compared with 41,000 tonnes in Japan. Per capita annual figures show the USA as the worst offender, generating 762kg, and that the OECD countries tend to generate far more than most developing countries. Western Europeans generated over 20% more in the late 1980s than in the mid-1970s.

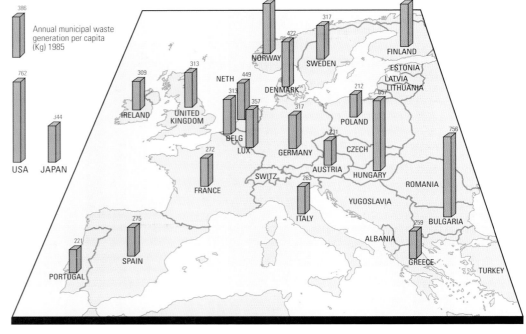

WASTE GENERATION

Annual municipal waste generation per capita (Kg) 1985

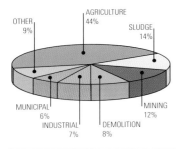

EC

OTHER 9%
AGRICULTURE 44%
SLUDGE 14%
MINING 12%
DEMOLITION 8%
INDUSTRIAL 7%
MUNICIPAL 6%

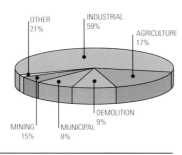

JAPAN

OTHER 21%
INDUSTRIAL 59%
AGRICULTURE 17%
DEMOLITION 9%
MUNICIPAL 8%
MINING 15%

Trashcan

In more economically advanced countries, there is a growing tendency for municipal waste to contain toxic or non-biodegradable materials, notably plastics, glass, metal products such as tin cans, and batteries which contain heavy metals posing a threat to groundwaters.

Household waste is still largely vegetable and organic. These biowastes are compostable as well as partly combustible, and could in theory be recycled to the land. Increased use of paper and packaging of foods, notably fast foods, and other products has encouraged an enormous increase in cardboard and paper wastes, much of it in the last two decades.

Organic wastes are combustible, as well as compostable, but unless separated out, substantial amounts of glass and heavy metals can make the ash toxic and useless. However, some countries, such as Germany and in Scandinavia, are more actively advocating separation of household waste and recycling.

Heavy metals, toxic gases and dioxins are often given off during incineration, particularly when these materials are mixed in, causing public opposition to such plants. In the UK, all but the most advanced municipal incinerators are threatened with closure, as they cannot

meet EC air quality standards.

On the other hand, incineration is increasingly used in other advanced European states, growing from 19.3% to 30.5% between 1977 and 1987 in western Germany alone. Incineration is a valuable way of reducing solid waste volumes, as well as of generating electricity. In the late 1980s in the European Community, household waste generated 17m barrels of oil equivalent, and could reach 92 mboe. Even so, ultimately the only way the incineration route can be expanded to eliminate landfill is by more closely controlling combustion temperatures, emissions, and separating out toxic metals beforehand. Several countries are also developing alternatives, including refuse-derived fuel and gasification.

In the mid-1980s, the vast majority of domestic and industrial waste was landfilled. Incineration accounted for less than a tenth of domestic and industrial waste disposal in England and Wales, and was hardly used as a method of waste disposal in much of eastern and southern Europe. However, pressure on landfill capacity has grown enormously in much of northern Europe, with higher environmental standards, demanding lining of sites, and public opposition forcing up costs and influencing decisions on sites that can be used for landfill.

Over exposure

In Europe as a whole over a quarter of a million movements of waste materials go unmonitored every year. In parts of the former East Germany, the residues of uranium mines, still dangerously radioactive, lie exposed to nearby communities. The European Community is proposing that the generators of hazardous waste are permanently liable for any future health damage. Because insurance for legal claims for pollution caused by waste disposal is now virtually impossible to obtain except at a very high cost, many companies are highly vulnerable to their own mistakes.

Dirty dumping

The charts on the right show the sources of low and high level waste. The environmental impact of military and civil nuclear waste comes from the removal and management of the highly radioactive spent fuel rods which produce heat generating and biologically hazardous high level waste (HLW), needing prolonged cooling, followed by long-term isolation; intermediate level waste (ILW) such as fuel cans, and low level waste (LLW), such as contaminated clothing and tools, compacted and generally landfilled. HLW, ILW and to a small extent LLW represent long-term biological hazards, much of it due to plutonium contamination, with a half life of over 24,000 years.

To date, no high or intermediate level underground waste stores have been built in the UK, due to doubts over safety and long-term containment, although repositories have been built in Sweden and France. Buildup of nuclear waste represents a long-term hazard, particularly in the absence of an agreed means of safe storage.

In eastern Europe, the disposal of radioactive waste both from uranium mining and from power stations is posing a potentially very serious problem – only

with the opening up of information is it becoming known how widespread the danger of low level radiation exposure has become.

LOW LEVEL WASTE

1,500,000m³

INDUSTRY/ HOSPITALS 5%
NUCLEAR FUEL 45%
DEFENCE 15%
NUCLEAR POWER STATIONS 20%
RESEARCH & DEVELOPMENT 15%

HIGH LEVEL WASTE

250,000m²

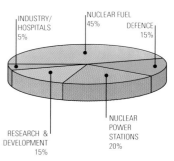

INDUSTRY/ HOSPITALS 2%
NUCLEAR FUEL 50%
DEFENCE 13%
NUCLEAR POWER STATIONS 20%
RESEARCH & DEVELOPMENT 15%

TOXIC TIME BOMBS

Hazardous wastes are wastes that must be carefully isolated from the environment for long periods, or require specialised treatment. They may be toxic, corrosive or inflammable. All are created by industry.

Few countries as yet require companies to keep detailed records of hazardous waste, but some 275m tonnes in total are estimated to exist in the USA and 24m tonnes in western Europe, compared with 338m tonnes worldwide. Different national definitions of what constitutes hazardous waste make comparisons difficult, but in western Europe, where records are more detailed than in eastern Europe, solvents comprised some 6–7.5% of the total, waste paint 4–5%, heavy metal-contaminated waste 4–10%, acids 30–40% and oily wastes 17–20%.

Much of the hazardous waste generated in Europe is processed in the UK at plants such as this one in Wales. Over 4,000 contaminated sites exist in the Netherlands, and at least 50,000 in western Germany. The cost of cleaning them up is estimated at $6bn and $30bn in the Netherlands and Germany respectively.

THE WASTE TRADE

The map illustrates the flow of waste from North America and Australia into Europe, while Europe exports to South America and Africa. Waste traders have attempted to ship at least 163m tonnes (mt) of waste across the globe since 1986. About 10mt of toxic waste have actually been exported, out of which 5.2mt reached eastern Europe and less developed countries, often with tragic consequences. These figures may well be only the tip of the iceberg. By mislabelling such exports as secondary raw material and describing them to local officials as "fertiliser" and "road oil", legal loopholes are easily exploited. Even genuine recycling shipments can end up contaminating developing countries. The leading exporter of hazardous waste is Germany, exporting at least 18% of domestic production.

The EC bans the export of hazardous waste to 68 African, Caribbean and Pacific countries. In 1985, the OECD adopted three principles on waste exports: application of the same controls to non-member countries; gaining the consent of the authority in the intermediate and final destinations; export only to countries with adequate facilities.

Power cycle waste

The diagram illustrates the waste process involved in a coal-fired and a nuclear power station.

The coal example is based on the Drax B plant in the UK, with a capacity of 2,000 (Drax A and B) megawatts operating on full load for a year. It assumes fitting of flue gas desulphurisation equipment, designed to combat acid rain, and use of deep-mined English coal of moderate sulphur content, although opencast mining is widely used in Europe, causing great disturbance. The nuclear power station shown generates the same output over one year on full load, and is based on the latest Pressurised Water Reactor (PWR).

In the coal fuel cycle, one year's generation produces over 2m tonnes of mine spoil, some of which can be sold. Noticeable amounts of radioactive materials found in coal are also released into the atmosphere. Though this radioactive matter has always been in the environment, local concentrations could cause more health risks.

A nuclear fuel cycle based on open-pit uranium mining generates about 220,000 tonnes of spoil. It generates high levels of radioactive, biologically hazardous radon gas and uranium runoff, producing local health threats, and must be kept in a lined landfill for thousands of years.

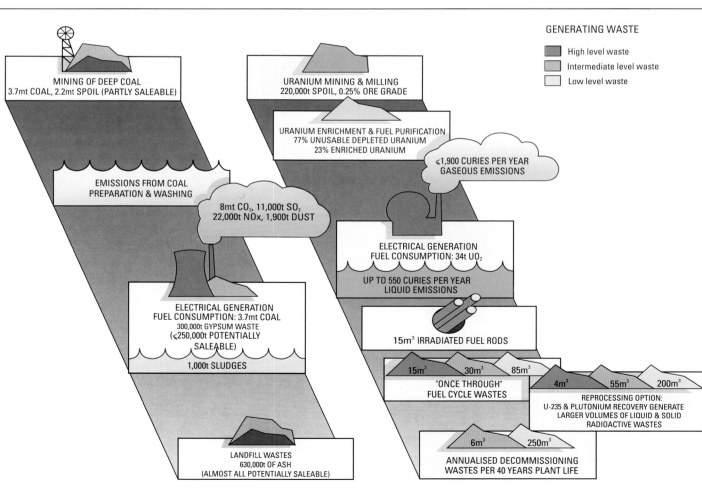

GENERATING WASTE
- High level waste
- Intermediate level waste
- Low level waste

MINING OF DEEP COAL
3.7mt COAL, 2.2mt SPOIL (PARTLY SALEABLE)

URANIUM MINING & MILLING
220,000t SPOIL, 0.25% ORE GRADE

URANIUM ENRICHMENT & FUEL PURIFICATION
77% UNUSABLE DEPLETED URANIUM
23% ENRICHED URANIUM

EMISSIONS FROM COAL
PREPARATION & WASHING

≤1,900 CURIES PER YEAR
GASEOUS EMISSIONS

8mt CO_2, 11,000t SO_2
22,000t NOx, 1,900t DUST

ELECTRICAL GENERATION
FUEL CONSUMPTION: 34t UO_2

ELECTRICAL GENERATION
FUEL CONSUMPTION: 3.7mt COAL
300,000t GYPSUM WASTE
(<250,000t POTENTIALLY SALEABLE)

UP TO 550 CURIES PER YEAR
LIQUID EMISSIONS

15m³ IRRADIATED FUEL RODS

1,000t SLUDGES

15m³   30m³   85m³
"ONCE THROUGH"
FUEL CYCLE WASTES

4m³   55m³   200m³
REPROCESSING OPTION:
U-235 & PLUTONIUM RECOVERY GENERATE
LARGER VOLUMES OF LIQUID & SOLID
RADIOACTIVE WASTES

LANDFILL WASTES
630,000t OF ASH
(ALMOST ALL POTENTIALLY SALEABLE)

6m³   250m³
ANNUALISED DECOMMISSIONING
WASTES PER 40 YEARS PLANT LIFE

ENVIRONMENTAL STRESS

Everything we have ever done has affected the environment. But there are now more of us doing more than ever before, with greater technology to do it with. Renewable and non-renewable resources, and even the natural systems of which they form a part, are coming under severe stress. Human activity can cause stress directly, for example by overfishing and hunting to extinction, deliberate deforestation, urbanisation and other wholesale loss of habitat. It can also cause indirect stress unintentionally, by air, soil, freshwater and marine pollution, and by the introduction of alien species. With population growth and the evolution of technology, the scale of human impact has increased to unsustainable proportions, from the generally local to the regional and increasingly global scale, causing stress to climate systems.

Stresses can be tolerated by natural systems without disturbing the overall balance for long periods of time, before the symptoms appear. Once they do, environmental change can be quite rapid and can often be irreversible. The results are undesirable from the human viewpoint, leading to ecosystems of lower stability and diversity, and impoverished natural resources.

Extensive protected areas have been set up in most of western Europe over the recent decades. But, few places are untouched by environmental transformation. The high Alps suffer from the excesses of the tourist industry in both winter and summer, while many coastal resorts now experience severe pollution and degradation. The introduction of environmental impact assessment for all major development projects has not stopped this process of transformation, because the underlying policies that promote resource misuse are not yet environmentally accountable.

The waters dry up

Most European water resources are renewable as the figures on this map illustrate, but increased abstraction for domestic, industrial and irrigation purposes means they are often being used almost as fast as they are replenished. In several Mediterranean states, such as Malta, which already exploits aquifers more intensively than anywhere else in Europe, 92% of renewable fresh water resources are used, and pumping is drawing nearby seawater in, contaminating coastal supplies.

On average, slightly over half of consumption in Europe is for industrial purposes, with agriculture being the main beneficiary in Mediterranean states and industry in northern Europe. Water demands in eastern European states vary from the heavy demands for irrigation in Romania, to those for industry in more advanced economies such as Czechoslovakia. Pollution of the remaining supplies has also become a serious problem, and more efficient water use and treatment of industrial wastewaters will be increasingly important.

In many parts of the densely populated south-east of England, rivers regularly run dry in the summer. Extensive engineering schemes to prevent percolation through the river bed reduce the amount of water needed to keep rivers alive, but these schemes can conflict with nature conservation. Ultimately conservation requires a fundamental change in economic systems for increasing the efficiency of water use in industry, agriculture and the home, together with reduced losses in distribution.

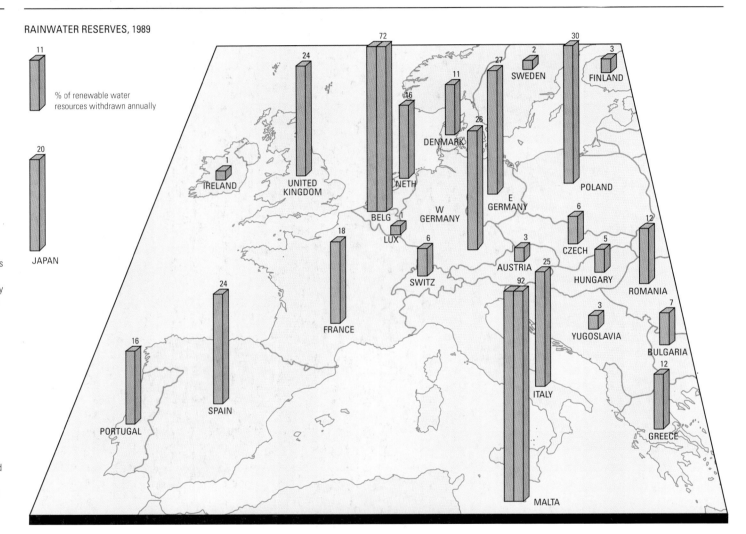

RAINWATER RESERVES, 1989

% of renewable water resources withdrawn annually

SANDS OF TIME

Soil erosion affects much of Mediterranean Europe and popular alpine regions. In Italy and Greece, removal of most of the original evergreen woodland occurred during classical times, leading to the establishment of drought-resistant maquis and a legacy of severe soil erosion on mountainsides today. Irregular, torrential downpours in winter cause flash floods and move vast amounts of unstable soil downslope, causing mudslides. Overall, 31% of the Mediterranean region's soils are suffering losses from erosion, equivalent to a staggering 15 tonnes per hectare per year. More than half the land is at risk from erosion and desertification. Cyprus, Greece, Tunisia and Spain are most at risk, with erodable land covering almost three-quarters of the total Mediterranean watershed. Remaining woodland is often open, so that it gives only limited protection. In Italy, earthquake shocks and natural avalanches are accentuated by deforestation of the Appenines, and lethal mudslides are common in winter. In Turkey, 70% of land is affected by serious erosion, though much of this is due to natural factors.

The impact of skiing on alpine soils has recently become important with the growth of the sport. Levelling of soils for piste construction can cause long-lasting damage to both soil and vegetation cover 2,200 metres above sea level and higher. Harsh climate and high rates of natural erosion make recolonisation by vegetation a slow process. To this is added the accelerated loss of soil on the upside of slopes, build-up at the foot and changing patterns of soil drainage, nutrients and vegetation. Natural soil build-up is very slow in these regions. Below this altitude, recovery is faster. Artificial snow machines affect shallow-rooted vegetation adapted to poor, dry soils, by favouring plants associated with damp conditions. Piste construction can involve dynamiting routeways along mountainsides, promoting soil erosion.

Connections: Water pollution 204–205   Unstable world 210–211   Institutional response 218–219

Washing away a continent

The map illustrates the rates of soil erosion throughout Europe during the last 24 years. Areas hit the hardest lie in the north-east Mediterranean where erosion is linked to deforestation. Once degradation starts on mountain slopes it is hard to reverse, the land eventually ending up as a new habitat of lower productivity. Some of the hardest hit areas are in Italy and along the Mediterranean coastline of Albania and Greece.

Sediment yield (t-km² per year)

1000
750
500
250
100
50

Permanent Ice/ Mountain

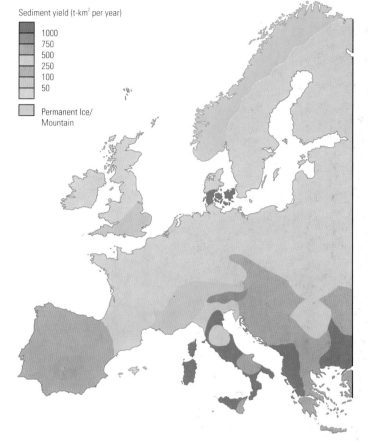

Caught out

The waters of the North Atlantic, particularly the North-East Atlantic, are the most intensively fished in the world. The table on the right ranks countries by fish catch. The total amounted to 14.74m tonnes (mt) in 1970, about a quarter of the total world catch, but this had declined to 13.55 mt (about a sixth) by 1988 due to overfishing and the growth of the Pacific fleets. Norway, Denmark and Iceland are the main fishing nations, after Japan, the USA and Canada, though the sizes of their fleets are dwarfed by the factory ships of the former Soviet Union (CIS), Japan and China. Decline of the fisheries of the North-East Atlantic has left regional fleets in depression.

EUROPE'S BIGGEST FISHERS

COUNTRY	'000t
CIS	11,159
NORWAY	1,929
DENMARK	1,695
ICELAND	1,633
SPAIN	1,393
UK	954
FRANCE[1]	843
POLAND	670
TURKEY	625
NETHERLANDS	435

JAPAN	11,841
USA	5,736

1 Estimate

A hillside forest in Galicia, Spain, is burned away by a fierce summer fire. The dry, arid climate exposes the hillside to a greater danger of accidental fire.

FORESTS IN FLAMES

Human activity has increased the number of forest fires beyond the capability of forest ecosystems to recover between each onslaught. In the Mediterranean region, arson, accidental fires and burning to provide grazing or for agriculture, is common. In Spain alone, there were over 19,000 fires in 1989, which turned 390,000 hectares of forest into ashes. Over half of fires in the south of France are created by careless tourists. Natural causes, mainly lightning, now account for only 2–5% in the Mediterranean, compared with 36% in Canada. Continued burning of forest on such a scale, at higher temperatures, causes major environmental impacts. In northern Europe, fragments of heath are now so small that even natural fires could wipe them out. The result of excess forest fires at very high temperatures is to remove most woody species, and reduce overall species diversity, damage seedbanks in the soil, and reduce the water and nutrient holding capacity of soil by burning off soil humus. Regeneration takes increasingly long, leaving soils exposed to heavy winter rains and to wind.

RING OF FIRE

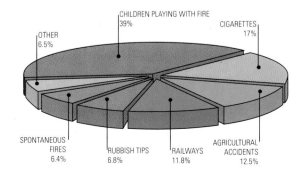

OTHER
6.5%

CHILDREN PLAYING WITH FIRE
39%

CIGARETTES
17%

SPONTANEOUS FIRES
6.4%

RUBBISH TIPS
6.8%

RAILWAYS
11.8%

AGRICULTURAL ACCIDENTS
12.5%

FISHERIES IN DECLINE

The North-East Atlantic, Mediterranean and North Sea are already near or at the limits of exploitation. As early as 1890, plaice fisheries in the North Sea were depleted. The second world war provided a chance for recovery of stocks. But the oceans can no longer provide the food resource demanded by a hungry world. Commercial oceanic fisheries have been under growing stress since the turn of the century, with the advent of steam trawlers, which permitted longer distance and more intensive fishing effort. Diesel power, refrigeration, use of sonar to locate shoals and larger nets have intensified these pressures on cod stock or even lobster as the charts illustrate. Bottom-dwelling flatfish are also under increasing threat. Depletion and ultimately abandonment of fisheries occurs when extra effort achieves no gain in yield, because fish of reproductive age or younger are lost faster than they are replaced. Depletion of one species has traditionally caused fleets to turn to other, previously unsought after, and frequently less palatable species, such as sandeel and sprat, processed for animal consumption.

Stocks do not always recover to previous levels once fishing effort has declined, Scandinavian herring being a case in point. This is because a delicate ecological balance may have been upset, with a competitor species replacing it in the food chain. Antarctic krill may no longer be widely available to recovering whale populations, to larger fish populations or human exploitation. If krill were to be exploited directly on a large scale, major disruptions to the diverse Antarctic food chain could well occur. As governments gain control over offshore territorial waters then conservation measures can be introduced.

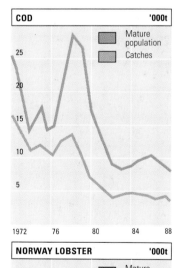

COD '000t
Mature population
Catches
25
20
15
10
5
1972 76 80 84 88

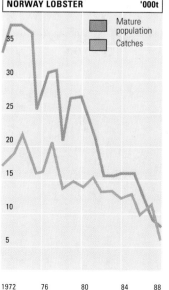

NORWAY LOBSTER '000t
Mature population
Catches
35
30
25
20
15
10
5
1972 76 80 84 88

UNSTABLE WORLD

Natural systems and ecosystems ultimately bear the brunt of all economic activity. Stress can be caused directly, by wholesale physical replacement of habitat, or more subtly and indirectly, by the gradual cumulative effects of pollution, drainage or introduction of alien species. Physical removal of natural ecosystems produces dramatic local consequences, but indirect stresses occur on a much wider scale, over long periods. Serious air pollution in parts of eastern Europe has caused widespread forest loss, both by dry deposition of SO_2 and by acid rain. Acidification of soils had been going on for two centuries before the problem of forest death surfaced in the late 1960s in Germany and Scandinavia. In two decades, it has come to threaten entire ecosystems.

Ecosystems are at the receiving end of pollution, and in a sense act as permanent or temporary "sinks" for pollutants. The ultimate sink is the ocean, lake or inland sea. An ecosystem is a more or less closed system in balance, in which nutrients and energy are continuously flowing between the soil or sediment and the organisms that live off it, and each other, to be recycled once they die. Biological systems are unique in that they concentrate nutrients, trace elements and energy, maintaining variation within narrow limits. In ecosystems, this allows a complex but stable community of organisms to thrive.

If the quantity of nutrients or sediment alters, for example from dam construction or fertiliser runoff, some parts of the interdependent food chain are favoured, and others suffer. This causes stress, and in the extreme an unstable and wholly altered ecosystem. Heavy metals and persistent organic toxic compounds cause long-term damage, by building up in the food chain. Industrial pollution is made up of a complex cocktail, in which each pollutant tends to cause more biological damage than it could alone. Predators at the top of the chain, such as birds of prey, receive the highest dose and are the first to disappear, leaving the system unbalanced.

The signing of the biodiversity convention in the Rio Conference in 1992 commits European nations to maintain species-rich habitats and to protect them from development. This is necessary not just to retain a minimal unit of species, but also to provide unmolested areas to act as barometers for global change in climate and atmospheric chemistry. Unless very tough national laws are put in place along with sufficent resources, the only way to safeguard such areas is to place them in the hands of conservation bodies which have the track record and resources to act where governments falter.

Baltic chokes

The amounts of pollutants entering the Baltic and Gulf of Bothnia have stabilised as a result of control measures, but they are still rising in the Kattegat off Denmark, causing blooms of toxic algae, and in the Gulf of Riga. Deoxygenated areas of the Baltic sea are a measure of pollution. Oxygen has been removed and 35% of the sea bottom is now lifeless.

DEAD AREAS OF THE BALTIC

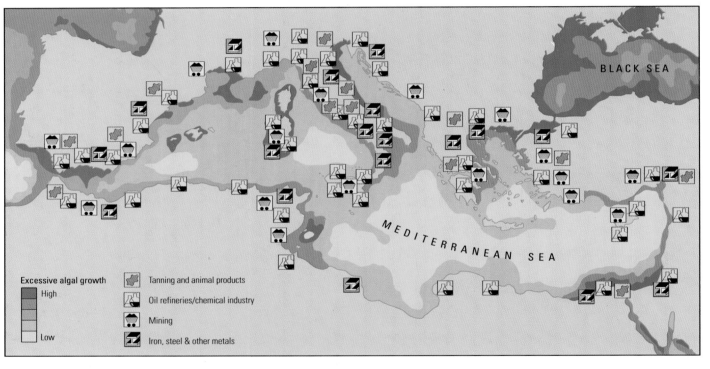

THE DYING SEA

The waters of the Mediterranean change completely only once every 80 years, though in parts deep waters and rapid currents to some extent make up for this. The rim of the Mediterranean basin has one of the fastest economic growth rates in the world. Its population has grown from 220m to 360m over the last 40 years, with 132m living on the coast. In the summer months, mass tourism adds another 100m to this figure. Some 70–85% of sewage is discharged untreated, posing serious health risks for bathers. Water demand is putting strains on supplies and river ecosystems. Energy demand has risen, and holiday complexes, golf courses, roads and commerce have all been squeezed into a narrow coastal zone, obliterating almost all the original coastal habitat along the northern shore and placing huge demands on the coastal environment.

Both pollution and overfishing have severely stressed the Mediterranean marine environment. Most bottom-dwelling and several mid-water species are threatened by the use of narrow mesh nets. The intensification of traditional agriculture has greatly increased uses of nitrate and phosphorus fertilisers, much of which finds its way to the sea. By the 1970s, the last estimate, 800,000 tonnes of nitrogen compounds entered the Mediterranean every year, compared with natural levels of 200,000 tonnes. Artificial phosphorus inputs are eight times natural levels, and burning of fossil fuels adds another 30% to marine nitrogen pollution.

The result is massive growth of algal blooms along the coasts, as the map shows, the largest stretch extending 1,000km from the River Ebro in Spain to the Arno in north-west Italy. The worst eutrophication (abundant growth of water plants due to pollution) occurs near the Po estuary and in Venice along the Adriatic coast, where unsightly and foul-smelling ulva seaweed and algal scum choke the lagoons and threaten the tourist economy. Life on the seabed has largely disappeared in shallow bays like the Gulf of Trieste and Sea of Marmara off Turkey where oxygen disappears in the summer.

MASS TOURISM

In the last 25 years, the environment and economy of the Mediterranean coasts have changed beyond recognition with the advent of mass tourism. The way of life that evolved over centuries with the semi-natural landscape has been abandoned with this change. Over 125m people a year now visit the region. The most intense developments have occurred along the Spanish, French, Italian and Greek coastlines, while much of Yugoslavia, Turkey and North Africa had until recently escaped the worst excesses. Coastal roads link together ribbon developments of holiday complexes along the coast and its hinterland. The mountain pastures have been abandoned for an easier living in the towns, while traditional olive groves, herb-rich maquis pasture and vines are being grubbed out in favour of energy, water and agrochemical intensive commercial growers, with damaging consequences for wildlife.

Tourist development threatens water supplies and wetland sites, especially in naturally impoverished and unspoiled areas. South-western Spain is a case in point, one of the most species-rich wetland sites remaining, but seriously endangered. The Turkish coastline, developed because of its unspoilt scenery and beaches, has experienced a confrontation between 2,000 female loggerhead turtles nesting on the beach and sunbathing tourists.

The Aral Sea, lying astride Kazakhstan and Uzbekistan, is described as an ecological disaster area. Diversion of the two mighty central Asian rivers that fed it, the Syr Dar'ya and Amu Dar'ya, for irrigation this century has reduced water levels drastically. The expansion of cotton growing during the Stalin era, and the construction of the Karakum Canal were major causes. Between 1960 and 1987 alone, the sea's water level fell by 13 metres, and its area decreased by some 40%. Plans to replenish the Aral Sea by diversion of the Siberian rivers Ob and Irtysh could create equally serious problems elsewhere.

ACID RAIN

Wet deposition of NO_x and SO_2 produces acid rain, including diluted sulphuric and nitric acid. Acid rain can be formed after industrial and transport emissions have moved considerable distances, and therefore tends to affect regions far from its origin as well as close by. Even Iceland suffers from acid rain. It is a problem that transcends political boundaries.

Scandinavia's predominantly calcium-poor rocks and soils are most prone to serious acidification. Ecosystems in high rainfall regions with slow weathering bedrock, notably granite and gneiss, cannot buffer acid rain for very long. Forests exposed to acid rain show stress by dropping their leaves or needles, and by die-back or thinning of the crown. They become less resistant to natural pests and climatic hardships, notably wind and frost. Ultimately they succumb.

Defoliation levels indicate the extent of stress, as the map shows. In 1990, the UN Economic Commission for Europe reported that for all tree species slight to severe damage affected 50% of trees in most of Europe.

DEFOLIATION INTENSITY, 1990

- 75%
- 50%
- 40%
- <40%
- No available data

Damage unlimited

Damage from acid rain was most widespread in Poland, where 86% of trees were affected, the former Soviet Union and Belarus, at over 84%, 76% in Czechoslovakia and 74% in the UK. Greece, Switzerland, Scandinavia, Germany and the Netherlands all registered more than half of their trees damaged.

LOSS OF WETLANDS

By far the most agricultural damage has occurred in Finland, 91% of the total of agricultural land, and Hungary (73.7%), followed by 60.9% in the UK. Agriculture remains the single largest cause of damage to wetlands, although tourism development has been the main cause of losses in Spain since the 1960s, and increasingly in France.

Wetlands are highly productive ecosystems in low-lying areas, at or near the water table. They have waterlogged soils for at least part of the year and are dominated by aquatic plant communities. They include tidal marshes and estuaries, swamp forests and Arctic marshes over permafrost. They provide an important food resource and nursery for two-thirds of the world's fish catch, and are vital to waterfowl and bird migration routes. They also help to reduce flooding, replenish aquifers, and purify wastewater, breaking down sewage and filtering out viruses, sediment, heavy metals and bacteria in reed beds or peat bogs.

WET VALUES

- 60%
- 50%
- 40%
- 30%
- 20%
- 10%
- <10%
- No avaliable data

Wet values

Wetlands cover 4–6% of the earth's surface. They were the cradle of cultures in many parts of Europe, but their value has only recently been recognised, and between a quarter and half have already disappeared worldwide. They have been regarded as wasteland or undrained farmland, attracting rubbish and toxic waste landfills, barrage projects and hazardous industries. Canalisation of rivers such as the Rhine have destroyed large tracts, while oyster and salmon farming causes nutrient and chemical pollution on coastal sites.

ECONOMIC IMPACT

Priceless polluters…eventually there will be a "green audit" of every national economy. The funds will come from the tourists and developers who dump their rubbish, as they have on this alpine mountainside.

Economics and the environment are linked in two major ways. Economic growth, influenced by technological change and public and private enterprise practices, has a wide range of effects on the environment: pollution, depletion and direct damage of non-renewable and abuse of renewable resources. These negative impacts on environment and natural resources in turn impoverish the economy itself, by damaging some of the more sensitive aspects of economic activity, including agricultural productivity, forestry, tourism, health and urban conditions. Both areas have proved highly complex to quantify in monetary terms because of the difficulty of valuing natural systems.

In western Europe, North America, Australia and New Zealand, and to a lesser degree Japan, awareness of the environmental costs of economic development seems to grow as each country passes a historically critical point in the growth of its economy and living standards. Public opinion seems to bear this out. In the USA during 1990,

polls suggested a majority of people, 71%, favoured environmental protection over economic growth, compared with only 36% in Japan, where 43% felt the two should be harmonised. In Europe there is greater willingness to consider either view depending on the circumstances; in contrast, environmental concerns are far more influential in Scandinavia.

The most easily quantified sector of environmental expenditure is pollution-control technology. Even so, there is a gradation from traditional bolt-on equipment to the growing area of clean technology, where environmental considerations are increasingly integrated into technology. Most OECD economies have seen rapid growth in the pollution-control sector in the last two decades, presenting economic opportunities as well as costs. A number of measures are employed to encourage pollution reductions and cleaner technology, including economic instruments such as tax regimes, and regulatory measures, including the "polluter pays principle".

Greenbacking

Environmental expenditure has no internationally agreed definition, making estimates difficult to compare between countries. The map compares environmental spending as a percentage of GDP during the mid-1980s. Total environmental expenditure would ideally include, at the minimum, expenditure on pollution control, natural resource protection, such as of seas and forests, both for harvesting and for the protection of their genetic potential and ecosystems. Expenditure on avoiding environmental damage should cover not only direct expenditure on control technology, but also indirect expenditure.

European pollution control presents major opportunities and has been estimated as being worth some $36bn. The USA and western Germany dominate the pollution control market, spending 1.5% of GDP each on abatement technology in the mid-1980s. A study of the western German economy reports that total defensive expenditure may exceed 6% of GDP. In eastern Europe, very high levels of expenditure are needed simply to prevent deterioration, but are not yet available. Most western European states are spending at least 0.8% of GDP on pollution control, though expansion in the sector is consolidating in countries that had begun investment early on. The lowest spenders are Portugal and Spain on 0.5%, which have only relatively recently experienced major economic growth and with it environmental concern. The Netherlands and western Germany also dominate research and development in the sector, ensuring them a leading market role in future.

SPENDING ON ENVIRONMENT

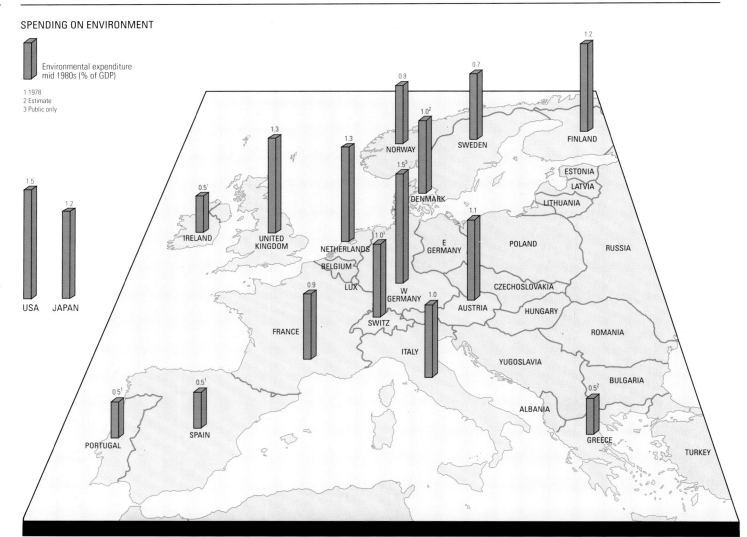

Environmental expenditure mid 1980s (% of GDP)

1 1978
2 Estimate
3 Public only

ACID IMPACT

Pollution-control technology is already available for acid emissions, including flue-gas desulphurisation plant and limestone injection burner technology for sulphur dioxide removal, selective catalytic reduction processes and new burner designs for NOx. While countries that have suffered from dry and wet acid deposition, such as Germany, Sweden and Japan, are increasingly using the technology, the major emitters, such as the UK, have resisted such expenditure, even though UK companies are already well-established in the pan-European market place.

In the case of eastern Europe, the financial resources are

not available, without foreign aid. Affected countries such as Sweden now assist investment in eastern European air pollution control. Control of acidification is expensive and only partially successful.

The cost of crop damage in the EC as a whole has been put at $375m a year, while corrosion of buildings could amount to as much as $2.2bn a year. In western Germany alone, repair of acid rain-damaged stonework amounts to $1.8bn a year. In Sweden, an additional $0.75m was proposed in 1991 for important historical monuments.

The emerging profession of ecological economist is a flourishing breed and acid rain damage is an area under scrutiny.

SCATOLOGICAL SOLUTION

The Mediterranean is one of the most polluted regional seas in the world. Untreated sewage discharge, exacerbated by mass tourism in the summer months, is the biggest problem, and as the number of waterborne infections have increased, the attractions of the area to holiday-makers decrease. The total cost of providing sewage treatment plants for all Mediterranean coastal towns and cities with populations over 10,000, a total of over 48m, was estimated at over $5bn in 1987 (see table below). By far the largest costs, some 35% of the total, will be borne by Italy, with many of the worst-affected waters. The Mediterranean is also one of the world's most oil-polluted seas, receiving some 635,000 tonnes of oil pollution a year from sea and land sources; this amounts to a fifth of the global total. Discharge of oil is prohibited, but only half of the ports are fitted with facilities to handle oily waste, and there is little monitoring. As a result, in heavily polluted regions, such as at Trieste and the Sea of Marmara, fish and shellfish either fail to breed or are tainted and unsaleable.

MED CLEANUP COST

COUNTRY	Coastal towns	Population '000	Treatment plant construction cost $'000
ALBANIA	4	146	24,820
FRANCE	36	2,798	328,620
GREECE	27	4,568	369,780
ITALY	254	15,471	1,790,240
MONACO	1	27	3,860
SPAIN	62	5,767	621,180
TURKEY	19	2,021	221,150
YUGOSLAVIA	10	585	82,210

NATURAL RESOURCE DAMAGE

The table below summarises the cost in terms of % GDP of damage to the environment. As pressures from economic growth increase, natural resources have tended to become degraded, or in extreme cases disappear. Action tends to be taken only when the consequences of resource abuse directly hit the local economy. The impact of environmental resource degradation is most noticeable in developing countries, where the economy is more closely linked to the immediate environment. In Poland, economic losses are largely caused indirectly, by severe industrial pollution, due to four decades of uncontrolled industrialisation. Industrial pollution seems to have accounted for 4.7–7.7% of GNP in 1987, due to health problems, corrosion of buildings and machinery. In the Netherlands, incomplete estimates put the costs of some pollution damage slightly higher. An estimate for Germany put the figure at around 6% of GDP, and rising.

The avoided cost of environmental damage in the USA through legislation may be felt elsewhere, as polluting industries relocate. Transboundary pollution, such as acid rain and greenhouse warming, are also hard to assess nationally, or even globally, thus making it difficult to arrive at a directly attributable cost.

FUTURE COSTS

COUNTRY	NATURE OF DAMAGE	YEAR	% OF GNP
GERMANY	MOST POLLUTION DAMAGE	1983/85	4.6-4.9
INDONESIA	DEFORESTATION	1984	3.6
NETHERLANDS	SOME POLLUTION DAMAGE	1986	0.5-0.8
POLAND	POLLUTION DAMAGE	1987	4.7-7.7
USA	AVOIDED DAMAGE DUE TO ENVIROMENTAL LEGISLATION	1978	1.2

CLEANING UP EASTERN EUROPE

Germany's struggle to improve conditions after reunification caused considerable economic strains. In Poland, one estimate put the cost just for pre-treatment installations needed in coal-fired power plants at $60bn, far greater than the country's $40bn foreign debt. The OECD estimates that at least 2% of national income needs to be spent just to prevent the environmental situation worsening further. If Poland goes ahead with its aim of reducing SO_2 emissions by 30% in five years, it will need to install $1bn-worth of plant. By 1991, only minor, though locally important, external aid was in evidence, notably $15m from the World Bank for environmental restoration in Upper Silesia, and $7m from the USA for environmental protection. Germany also made contributions.

In Hungary, environmental damage has consistently dwarfed levels of environmental protection investments, which remained below 1% of GDP. Such levels are not in themselves different from western economies, but they are hopelessly inadequate when set against damages costing between 3% and 5% of GDP. A fall in average age and an increase in respiratory disease is one result. Landscapes and ecosystems are gravely threatened, while 93 animal and plant species have already become extinct.

The majority of eastern European economies now have ambitious environmental clean-up and conservation programmes, but lack of finance continues to hamper them. Some 15–20% of the European Investment Bank's loans to eastern and central Europe will now be allocated to ecology, as well as a greatly increased proportion of World Bank loans. Poland proposed a solution which involved swapping its foreign debts for technical and financial assistance – a debt for nature transaction.

Costs of transport

The economic benefits of improved transport links are well known, but the social costs of transport are immense. One Europe-wide study has put the cost at 18.3% of GDP, due to air and noise pollution, accidents, lost working time in transit and user expenditure.

Road transport accounts for a growing number of noise complaints, the majority of NO_x and SO_2 emissions in many European cities, and almost 14 deaths in every 100,000 in 1985 in western Germany alone. Rail transport performs better in terms of most impacts, except for SO_2 emissions, while road traffic causes almost 25 times as many injuries as rail.

Road transport has been consistently favoured by most western European governments since the 1950s, frequently at the expense of rail. In the UK, the current government-funded $6.6bn road programme contrasts markedly with chronic underfunding of railways. In some cases, such as on short hauls, roads provide an efficient form of freight transport. Yet the growth of large, long distance lorries and of private car ownership has not only greatly increased pollution and environmental disturbance, but also led to reduced economic and energy efficiency. Higher emission standards alone will not curb atmospheric pollution unless road traffic growth is curbed.

Energy efficiency

SO_2 emissions from eastern European countries, as shown in the graph below, tend to be far higher than in western Europe. Under the planned economy, Poland would have increased emissions from late-1980s levels of some 200,000 tonnes a year, the highest in Europe, by another 26% up to 1995. On the other hand, total removal of subsidies would cause a substantial reduction of some 28% by encouraging conservation at realistic energy prices. In Hungary, this shock therapy could reduce emissions by about 44%. In Czechoslovakia, shock therapy could reduce emissions by half.

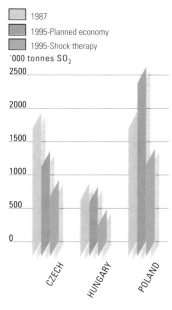

SULPHUR DIOXIDE EMISSION

- 1987
- 1995-Planned economy
- 1995-Shock therapy

'000 tonnes SO_2

COMPARISON OF ROAD AND RAIL TRANSPORT IN TERMS OF POLLUTION, LAND TAKE & ACCIDENTS

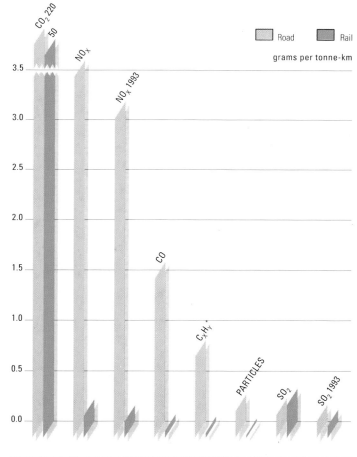

Road · Rail

grams per tonne-km

	Road	Rail
ACCIDENTS[1]	248	10
LAND TAKE[2]	0.007	0.0025

1 Injured persons/bn tonne-km/yr 2 Sq metres per tonne-km per year *Hydrocarbons

THE GREENHOUSE EFFECT

Damage to stratospheric ozone, first predicted in the 1970s, has caused considerable concern globally, because the situation has deteriorated alarmingly fast. Since the discovery of an ozone hole over Antarctica during 1985, the area affected has widened continually, with ozone levels down 15% over Antarctica by 1987.

The greenhouse effect, together with the destruction of the earth's protective stratospheric ozone layer, are the most complex and global of all the environmental problems society has yet had to face. Both are beyond the capacity of any one nation to control and demand global cooperation on an unprecedented scale. Almost every aspect of the human economy has a role in the greenhouse effect and will be affected by it. Both problems threaten global environmental and social upheaval. For the first time, politicians are being asked to act now in anticipation of a future problem, rather than risk awaiting proof by which time it will be too late. Ultimately, the sustainability of world population and economic growth itself is in question, and sensitive geopolitical issues will have to be faced.

By the middle of the 21st century, global CO_2 levels, which are responsible for 55% of the greenhouse effect, could double, threatening catastrophic increases in temperatures, unless immediate action is taken to curb emissions. In the developed world, this means fossil fuel energy use will have to be cut drastically, non-fossil fuel use promoted, use of fertilisers reduced and reafforestation. In the developing world, destruction of the tropical rainforests must cease. Newly emerging industrial economies will need to found their development on highly efficient energy use, almost certainly involving technology transfer from the developed world, and they will have to control population growth.

Even with immediate action, time lags in the climatic system mean that we are already committed to substantial warming, possibly for centuries. Costly short-term measures will need to be taken to protect society, especially from sea level rise. If all human emissions of CO_2 stopped in the early 1990s, human-generated increases would still only be reduced about half by 2100.

Failure to address the greenhouse effect may result in partial melting of the polar ice caps and thermal expansion of the oceans, leading to flooding, together with major changes in vegetation and ecosystems, precipitation and storm frequency. A whole range of secondary effects could include mass extinctions in temperate and sub-polar latitudes, subtle but important changes in the ecological structure of tropical ecosystems, famine, political tension over resources and the appearance of tropical diseases in Europe and North America. Malaria was common in England during the warm Middle Ages, and could return. Important North Sea fisheries could also disappear, and in the Arctic permafrost soils are already melting, causing landslides and structural damage.

Europe accounts for almost a seventh of all greenhouse gases. Within Russia there are huge oil, gas and coal reserves that could double the greenhouse gas contribution if allowed to be burned. Even the modest proposition by the EC to levy a carbon and energy tax that would be fiscally neutral has run into fierce opposition. Yet such a tax would only result in one-third of the necessary reduction of CO_2 by the year 2000. Europe will have to do better if it is ever to expect others to follow its lead.

Greenhouse gases

The causes of global warming are the so-called greenhouse gases, principally CO_2, accounting for more than half, chlorofluorocarbons (CFCS) for about a quarter, followed by methane, nitrous oxide and an uncertain contribution from ozone. CFC-11, -12 and -22 are the most potent greenhouse gases.

CONTRIBUTORS	CO_2	CFC	CH_4	O_3	N_2O
ENERGY	35	0	4	6	4
DEFORESTATION	10	0	4	0	0
AGRICULTURE	3	0	8	0	2
INDUSTRY	2	20	0	2	0
% WARMING BY GAS	50	20	16	8	6

Doomsday climate

Climate change on the scale anticipated would have a devastating impact on the world's vegetation zones and ecosystems. The maps shown were produced by the Dutch National Institute for Public Health and Environmental Protection (RIVM), whose long-term environmental surveys have a major influence on Dutch environmental policy. They show how vegetation systems may have migrated northwards after CO_2 levels have doubled.

The most alarming conclusion is that parts of southern Europe could become desertified, while Arctic ecosystems, with nowhere left to go, could disappear altogether. The northern boreal coniferous forests of Canada and Europe could face near extinction in favour of expanding temperate deciduous forests. Summer drought would increasingly stress deciduous forest further south, and it would be replaced by Mediterranean vegetation under this scenario, notably in south-east England. Increased CO_2 levels would encourage plant growth.

The vegetation belts would have major difficulties migrating polewards fast enough to keep up with global warming. Even a 10°C rise in global average temperatures would stress existing high latitude northern ecosystems, forcing them to move northwards by 90km per decade.

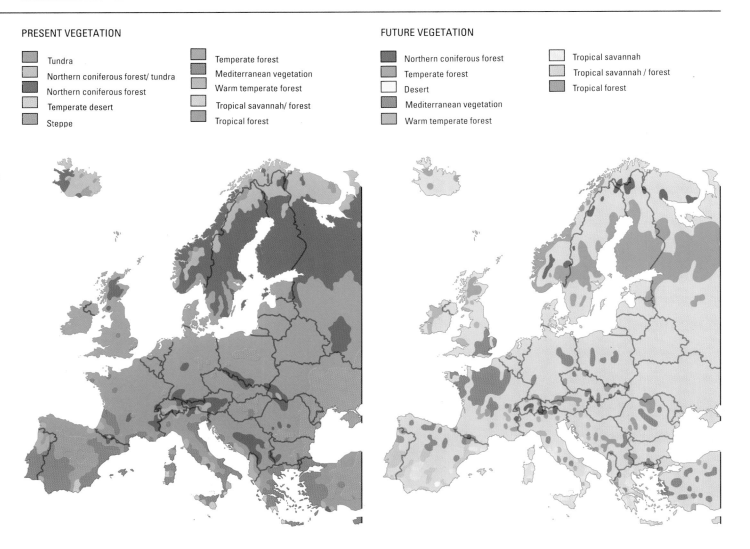

PRESENT VEGETATION

- Tundra
- Northern coniferous forest/ tundra
- Northern coniferous forest
- Temperate desert
- Steppe
- Temperate forest
- Mediterranean vegetation
- Warm temperate forest
- Tropical savannah/ forest
- Tropical forest

FUTURE VEGETATION

- Northern coniferous forest
- Temperate forest
- Desert
- Mediterranean vegetation
- Warm temperate forest
- Tropical savannah
- Tropical savannah / forest
- Tropical forest

Connections: Energy 72–73   Air pollution 202–203   Institutional response 218–219

AREAS AT RISK
- ▲ Delta
- △ Estuary
- ☐ Marsh, lagoon
- ☐ 500,000 - 1m
- ☐ Industry

Population
- ● 7.5m
- ○ 1 - 5m

VULNERABILITY TO SEA LEVEL RISE

Greenhouse warming could also have an enormous impact on the environment and society by accelerating sea level rise. Current estimates suggest that thermal expansion of warmer ocean waters alone will raise sea levels by 2–4cm per decade (see map). Partial melting of the ice caps will add considerably to this rate. By 2030, global sea levels could be 10–30cm higher, and 30–110cm higher by 2100. There is also a remoter risk that the west Antarctic ice sheet, now anchored below sea level, could founder, raising sea levels by five metres over a short period of time. This is not considered likely by the International Panel on Climate Change (IPCC) for at least another century. Others believe the ice shelves that at the moment hold back ice flows inland could break away sooner, causing a rapid increase in seaward ice flow.

There are major implications for society and the environment from higher average sea levels and from increased storm surges. In Europe, as elsewhere, major cities and ports would be threatened. In the UK, coastal erosion rates could be three or four times higher in East Anglia. Potentially hazardous toxic waste and nuclear sites could also be at risk. Costly sea defences could provide some protection of major cities and ports in developed regions such as Europe, but the rate of change will decide how well society and environments will adapt.

Many of the worst-affected populations would be in the developing world with very limited possibility of migration elsewhere, high population growth and few cash resources for coastal defences. Hundreds of millions could be displaced from highly populated deltas, Pacific island states and low-lying coastal plains next century. Average sea levels have risen 10–15cm over the last century, and even today 70% of beaches globally are eroding. The rates of increase predicted would be as much as five times faster.

CHANGES IN PRECIPITATION

Global circulation models, accurate at best to areas over 300km², cannot predict future precipitation and storms with much accuracy. Yet, on current trends, all GCMS predict increases in average global precipitation by 2030 of between 3% and 15%, and increased evaporation rates. In the high latitudes, precipitation is likely to be increased all the year round, but the mid-latitudes could experience greater summer drought, threatening Mediterranean agriculture as well as North American grain harvests.

ULTRAVIOLET DANGERS

Increased exposure to biologically harmful ultraviolet light, UV, due to loss of the ozone layer's filtering effect threatens to increase rates of cancer, particularly melanoma. Estimates suggest a 1% decrease in stratospheric ozone could lead to a 3% increase in non-melanoma skin cancer, and a smaller but significant increase in the more serious melanoma form. Since most forms take a decade to appear, it will be some time before the full effects of ozone depletion become obvious, though malignant melanoma, the most dangerous form, can occur after a few serious bouts of sunburn. Consequently, several nations already advise great caution and use of sunblock while sunbathing.

A 1% decrease in stratospheric ozone could also lead to a 0.6–0.8% increase in cataracts, and eye protection is increasingly necessary. UV has also been shown to weaken the immune system response to infectious disease in animal studies, with unpredictable consequences globally. Even if all ozone-depleting chemicals are phased out it will take over a century before conditions return to normal.

Ultraviolet light could have more fundamental ecological impacts. Near the surfaces of the oceans, phytoplankton growth forms the main basis of the food chain, and removes CO₂ by sinking to the ocean floor. Phytoplankton are sensitive to UV and are inhibited by it. Raised levels could drastically cut food resources in marine ecosystems and increase the rate of greenhouse warming. In the waters of the Antarctic, phytoplankton productivity had declined 6–12% by late 1990, threatening krill populations and the rest of the extraordinarily rich Antarctic food chain.

Future climatic scenarios

Prediction of climate change is a complex task because so many factors must be taken into account: long-term economic growth rates internationally, amount and type of energy use and land use changes and technology.

The IPCC concluded in 1992 that a doubling of CO₂, probably during the middle of the next century if we continue with "business as usual", would almost certainly raise global average temperatures by a minimum of 1.5° C, and a maximum of 4.5° C, with a best estimate of 2.5° C. These levels would leave the earth warmer than it has been for 150,000 years. Average temperatures have already risen by 0.3° C to 0.6° C over the last century, though it is not yet possible to say how much if any of this is due to human influences. Major volcanic eruptions and classical air pollution also complicate the picture, as sulphates block out sunlight and may have reduced global warming. Damage to the ozone layer, while biologically very serious, may also have lessened warming.

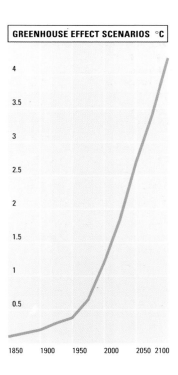

GREENHOUSE EFFECT SCENARIOS °C

Greenhouse warming

The major contributors to the problem of greenhouse warming are illustrated by the pie charts. Natural levels of the greenhouse gases CO₂ and methane have been closely related to climatic change in the last million years. If they were not present, the earth would be some 33° C colder and largely uninhabitable. The question is one of timing and intensity of climatic change. If there were no human enhancement of the greenhouse effect, the earth would probably be moving gradually towards a new Ice Age in 5,000 years' time. Instead, the earth has experienced some of the warmest years on record since the 1980s, though this may be a natural phenomenon. The average rate of change, 0.3° C per decade, is also expected to be rapid, with serious ecological and social consequences.

Sources of greenhouse gases cover the whole range of international economic activity, presenting major problems for policy-makers. Global estimates also inevitably vary. The single largest contributing sector is energy generation, which accounts for some 49% of warming, of which 35% is due to CO₂. Industry is the second largest contributor, accounting for some 24% of the total, mainly due to CFC emissions. Deforestation, mainly in the tropical rainforests, accounts for about 14%, 10% from CO₂ and 4% from methane. Intensive, mechanised agriculture in the OECD countries, together with rapid conversion of rainforest to cropland in the tropics, accounts for about 13% of warming.

THE PRODUCERS

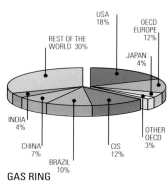

- USA 18%
- OECD EUROPE 12%
- JAPAN 4%
- OTHER OECD 3%
- CIS 12%
- BRAZIL 10%
- CHINA 7%
- INDIA 4%
- REST OF THE WORLD 30%

GAS RING

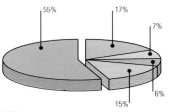

- 55%
- 17%
- 7%
- 6%
- 15%

- ☐ CFC's 11 and 12
- ☐ Other CFC's
  Main sources: Aerosol propellants, refrigerants, solvents, foam manufacture
- ☐ Nitrous oxide
  Main sources: Fertilisers, fossil fuel combustion, biomass burning, changing land use
- ☐ Methane
  Main sources: Decomposition of animal/ plant waste, fermentation in cattle and termites, biomass burning, fossil fuels, oil and gas exploitation
- ☐ Carbon dioxide
  Main sources: Fossil Fuels, deforestation and land-use change, biomass burning, erosion

A QUESTION OF POWER

In the latter half of the 20th century, increasingly serious and complex technological risks have come to threaten the environment on a local, regional and, more recently, global scale. Military technology has also become a major environmental threat. The risk of global nuclear war has receded, but not disappeared, while fallout from the nuclear tests of the cold war continues to threaten global health. Although the West and Russia are cutting defence budgets and have agreed to destroy a significant part of the stockpile of nuclear weapons, military confrontations in the Gulf, eastern Europe and CIS continue to threaten environmental and political security.

The Chernobyl nuclear reactor disaster of 1986 occurred in a Soviet-built reactor in the Ukraine, but radioactive fallout effects on agriculture, health and environment quickly became a global affair, undermining public confidence in nuclear power in many countries. The development of inherently safer reactors and operating systems is now a long-term priority in the depressed nuclear industry, which believes it can play a potentially important role in reducing reliance on fossil fuels.

Chemical catastrophes

Dramatic growth of the global organic chemical industry, from 7m tonnes in 1950 to 250m tonnes by 1985, has inevitably increased the potential for accidents on a local and increasingly international scale. More than 200 serious chemical accidents occur annually in the OECD countries, and over the last decade globally there have been over 5,000 deaths, 100,000 injuries and poisonings, and some 620,000 evacuated. A major incident at Seveso, Italy, during 1976 caused contamination by toxic dioxins, which are linked to the serious skin disease, chloracne, and birth defects. The Italian government was obliged to scrape away and remove topsoils for several miles around. The accident led to calls for tighter industrial safety procedures and the passage of the EC Seveso directive on major accidents in 1982. This has led the way in increas-

The nuclear blight

Since the first nuclear explosion in 1945 in the New Mexico desert, the six members of the nuclear weapons "club" have carried out some 1,900 nuclear tests, 518 of them in the atmosphere, under water or in space. Global alarm at levels of fallout led to 100 countries signing the Partial Test Ban Treaty of 1963, after which the USA, USSR and UK continued extensive testing underground. France and China continued atmospheric testing until 1974 and 1980 respectively. Since 1963, some 1,400 underground tests have been carried out by the nuclear powers across the world. While the immediate fallout from underground tests is reduced, many long-lived radio-isotopes, such as strontium-90, eventually find their way into the waters and atmosphere. Several accidents have also occurred, when explosions vented radioactive gases into the atmosphere.

While the nuclear arsenals are being reduced, the legacies of long-term fallout, military wastes, and contaminated testing and plutonium production sites will remain. Contaminated test sites exist on several Pacific islands, in and around Australia, the Sahara, south-western USA, central Asia and in the Arctic, on the Aleutian Islands and Novaya Zemlya. The possibility of nuclear proliferation among developing nations is also growing.

A report by concerned international physicians in 1991 estimated that global fallout from atmospheric nuclear tests incorporated into the human body "will eventually produce 430,000 cancer fatalities, some of which have already occurred". Ultimately, 2.4m could die. The areas of greatest risk are in the latitude band 400 to 500 north, but most cancers will occur between 200 and 300 north, because these regions are more highly populated. Similarly, low casualties in the southern hemisphere are due to lower population densities. Direct exposure downwind to potentially lethal levels of radiation also affected up to 40,000 people in Kazakhstan, where some underground sites have turned into lakes used for fishing and swimming, and people in the Marshall Islands, China, French Polynesia and Australia.

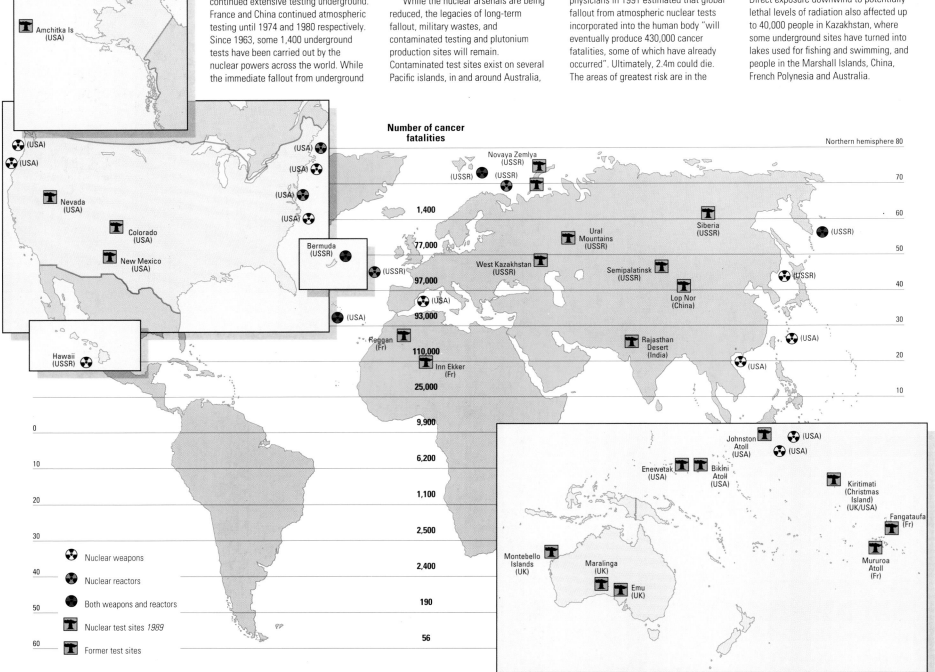

Number of cancer fatalities

Connections: Energy 72–73 Water pollution 204–205 Waste pollution 206–207

ing safety measures in all dangerous installations and improved evaluations procedures.

Accidents and incidents

Health and safety measures and legislation have made major strides in reducing industrial deaths and injuries in the OECD countries. Conditions in many developing countries remain poor or are even worsening. More disastrous accidents, such as the 1984 Bhopal incident at a pesticide plant owned by Union Carbide which killed nearly 3,000 people and blinded some 200,000 more, show the trend only too clearly. Bhopal also illustrates how multinational companies operate hazardous and polluting plants in countries less able to deal with such problems.

Environmental damage from both major and minor accidents also contributes to stresses on the oceans. The Exxon Valdez tanker spill off Alaska during 1989 caused long-lasting ecological damage to the coastal environ-

ment. Large chemical spills also affect major rivers, affecting several countries. Release of agricultural chemicals, solvents and mercury into the Rhine during a warehouse fire at a Sandoz site in Switzerland killed millions of fish and threatened supplies of drinking water, both in Germany and as far as the Netherlands.

The punitive cost of oil and gas, measured in US dollars and payable in hard currency, will force much of the CIS and eastern Europe to go nuclear. Meanwhile in western Europe the future of nuclear power remains politically uncertain except in France. Most of the former nuclear research centres spend more time and money on energy conservation and non-renewable energy technologies than on nuclear innovation. Yet the prospect of below ground, small-scale, self contained and inherently safe nuclear power stations is not unimaginable, especially in a world transformed by frugal energy usage.

OIL POLLUTION IN THE MARINE ENVIRONMENT

The growing reliance of OECD economies on crude oil imports has led to a major threat to the marine environment from both tanker spills and operational releases (see map). In general, the majority of spills and releases occur in the narrow, busiest shipping lanes, where potential for accidents is highest. In Europe, the Mediterranean and English Channel are most at risk. Globally, some 3m metric tonnes of oil contaminate the seas, half from ships and the rest from land-based sources.

The main problem is that while non-maritime sources tend to be diffuse, shipping spills and releases can be disastrous in more restricted waters. The ecological damage a spill causes depends not only on the number of tonnes spilt, but also on how restricted the coastline is, currents, prevailing weather, and on the speed and efficiency of emergency responses. The Exxon Valdez disaster released only a modest amount of oil, about 35,000 tonnes, but devastated the fragile Arctic coastal environment, polluting 1,500km of unspoilt coastline. After clean-up operations costing $1.3bn, less than 200km were fit for animal and plant survival. In 1969, a spill of only 200 tonnes killed 40,000 seabirds in the Wadden Sea.

GLOBAL OIL TRADE

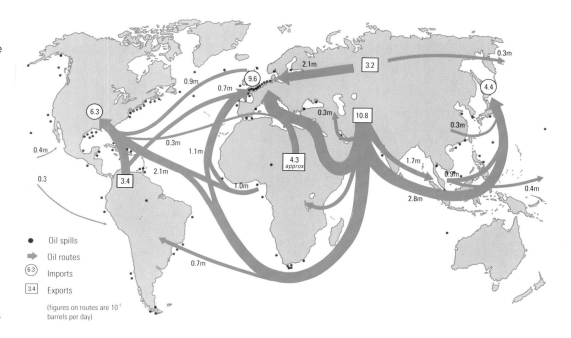

- ● Oil spills
- ➡ Oil routes
- (6.3) Imports
- [3.4] Exports

(figures on routes are 10⁶ barrels per day)

Accidents

The pie chart on the right illustrates the industry source of work related accidents involving 25 or more injuries in OECD countries over a ten year period leading up to 1985. Incidences are generally under reported but it is estimated that for every death there are several hundred injuries and poisonings. Chemical accidents kill more than 5,000 a year and injure up to 10 times as many. Gas and oil related injuries are about a quarter of those involved with chemicals.

INDUSTRIAL ACCIDENTS

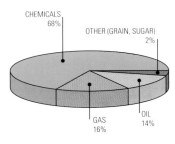

CHEMICALS 68%
OTHER (GRAIN, SUGAR) 2%
GAS 16%
OIL 14%

Oil damage

The two pie charts to the right illustrate the origins of oil pollution at sea. Major tanker disasters cause spectacular ecological and economic damage locally, particularly along busy shipping lanes, such as the English Channel, but minor incidents and deliberate releases by tankers, over 1m tonnes a year, account for far more pollution. Almost half of oil pollution comes from waste runoff, air pollution from industry and transport, urban runoff, and oil refineries.

MARINE ORIGINS

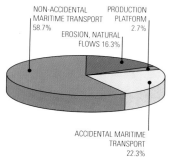

NON-ACCIDENTAL MARITIME TRANSPORT 58.7%
PRODUCTION PLATFORM 2.7%
EROSION, NATURAL FLOWS 16.3%
ACCIDENTAL MARITIME TRANSPORT 22.3%

LAND AND AIR ORIGINS

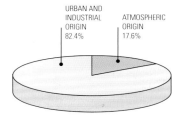

URBAN AND INDUSTRIAL ORIGIN 82.4%
ATMOSPHERIC ORIGIN 17.6%

Fallout

The Chernobyl nuclear accident released vast amounts of radioactive fallout into the environment, which had not fully recovered from the effects of superpower atmospheric nuclear weapons testing during the 1960s. In the Netherlands, as elsewhere, external and internal radiation doses from food, water and air, climbed alarmingly to over 80 microsieverts, 1.5 times the acceptable personal dose per year. Overall levels fell rapidly from the mid-1960s, when atmospheric testing largely stopped. Unfortunately, while short-lived radionuclides such as iodine-131 soon

decayed, long-lived radionuclides such as strontium-90, which accumulates in the bone and can cause cancers, will persist for decades.

Consequently, the Chernobyl accident, which generated fallout comparable to that from atmospheric testing, has led to a considerable increase in long-term radiation levels in food and water from strontium and caesium compounds. This suggests strongly that we cannot afford another such nuclear accident, certainly not if the nuclear industry is to remain practically and economically viable.

Calculating the risks

Nuclear safety has been a major environmental concern in most OECD countries since the Three Mile Island (TMI) incident at Harrisburg, Pennsylvania in 1979, and more recently since the Chernobyl disaster in the Ukraine of 1986. There have been several other serious incidents at nuclear power plants before and after these events, notably the UK Windscale fire of 1957, which was detected as far away as the Netherlands. Fortunately, most have not led to major radiation releases, but the potential consequences of serious accidents worldwide are great, with

700m people living within 160km of a plant. All other problems of nuclear plant emissions and waste pale into insignificance in comparison. The probability of any one reactor having a major accident is very low, as safety standards are, with the exception of Soviet-built reactors, probably the highest of all industries. Yet several serious incidents have already occurred, including three little-known partial meltdowns in France alone.

Major safety refits on Soviet built reactors will be crucial to reducing the risks.

Peace dividend

The problems facing our global environment are immense and complex. The costs of a massive programme to counter the most severe of them might come to some $77bn for energy conservation, $33bn to stabilise population growth, $24bn on soil erosion and $17bn to conserve biodiversity by the year 2000. Yet even these amounts would be trivial compared with global military expenditure of $1 trillion, showing the true environmental and social cost of the military-industrial complex that is only now unraveling.

INSTITUTIONAL RESPONSE

An image for the future ... The logo is designed to capture the idea of European Community cooperation on environmental issues.

Politicians and institutions tend to lag behind scientific and public awareness of environmental issues, so that local problems reach crisis point before action has been taken. Institutions and legislators demand proof of an environmental threat which can usually only be given when it is too late to avert its worst effects, while scientists routinely try to predict change based on the highest possible probability. The destruction of the ozone layer is a salutory reminder of this institutional failure to respond. The partnership has never been an easy one, but today the scale of environmental problems has moved into a new global phase, where the very fabric of the planet itself is threatened, not just its components. International action in anticipation of predicted threats, such as the greenhouse effect, must increasingly replace crisis management.

Humanity is at a turning point. It now has the ultimate power to decide the fate of all life on the planet, and is finally realising that its own future too depends on our stewardship of the environment. Old institutional frameworks, based on the national state, or at best upon loose associations of nations, have proved unequal to this task. New institutions at the regional and global level are now

having to be rapidly set up to deal with the scale of environmental problems we now face. But it is not enough merely to set up a new institutional framework. It must also be capable of responding to change, and have teeth.

The environment does not respect national frontiers, so it will involve at least some degree of sacrifice of national interests towards the global good. This remains a stumbling block in most current conventions, even though opinion polls show the public accept the need for common action. There are now signs that the sovereignty issue may yet become less of an obstacle to cooperation.

A way forward

The UN Regional Seas programme, agreements on North Sea fisheries and the growing number of signatories to the Convention on International Trade in Endangered Species (CITES) provide examples of the potential for successful cooperation. Perceived national interests are still an obstacle to vital agreements on acid rain reduction, the future of the seabed, rainforests and Antarctica, and they have delayed until the eleventh hour or beyond measures for the protection of the ozone layer, with highly damaging consequences. The price of institutional fail-

European Community

There have been four EC environmental action programmes since the first was initiated in 1973. EC measures have been adopted on an increasing range of areas, including:

Water pollution Directives on surface and underground waters, quality standards on bathing waters, drinking waters, fresh waters for fish life and waters for shellfish rearing. Toxic substance discharges strictly controlled and maximum levels set. Rules imposed for phase-out of titanium dioxide, causing "red sludge". The EC is also a signatory to international treaties covering waters, including the Rhine, North Atlantic, North Sea and Mediterranean.

Air pollution Directives on CFCs in aerosol cans, pollution from certain industrial premises, SO₂ discharge and availability of unleaded petrol.

Noise levels Directives on noise protection and control in the workplace, maximum emissions from road vehicles, subsonic aircraft, lawnmowers and construction equipment.

Chemical production A major accident at Seveso in Italy during 1976 contaminated a wide area with toxic dioxins, prompting a directive on major accident hazards in 1982, the so-called "Seveso directive". The directive calls for safety audits, risk analysis, better information exchange and other measures to reduce hazards from chemical plants.

The ozone layer Several measures to reduce ozone depletion have been taken by cutting use of CFCs and other ozone-depleting compounds.

Waste management Several EC moves to regulate or promote improved collection, disposal, recycling and treatment of waste since 1975. Waste oils, sea dumping, titanium oxide and radioactive wastes have also been specifically covered.

Nature conservation The EC is a signatory to the Bern Convention of 1979, which protects migratory wildlife.

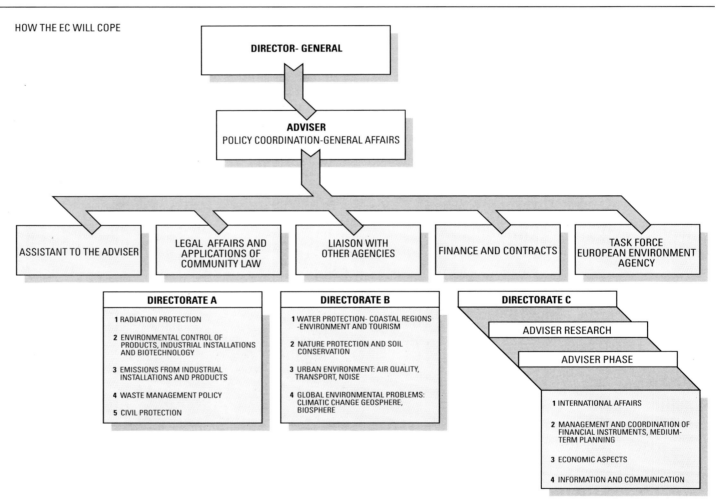

HOW THE EC WILL COPE

```
                    DIRECTOR- GENERAL

                    ADVISER
          POLICY COORDINATION-GENERAL AFFAIRS
```

| ASSISTANT TO THE ADVISER | LEGAL AFFAIRS AND APPLICATIONS OF COMMUNITY LAW | LIAISON WITH OTHER AGENCIES | FINANCE AND CONTRACTS | TASK FORCE EUROPEAN ENVIRONMENT AGENCY |

DIRECTORATE A
1 RADIATION PROTECTION
2 ENVIRONMENTAL CONTROL OF PRODUCTS, INDUSTRIAL INSTALLATIONS AND BIOTECHNOLOGY
3 EMISSIONS FROM INDUSTRIAL INSTALLATIONS AND PRODUCTS
4 WASTE MANAGEMENT POLICY
5 CIVIL PROTECTION

DIRECTORATE B
1 WATER PROTECTION- COASTAL REGIONS -ENVIRONMENT AND TOURISM
2 NATURE PROTECTION AND SOIL CONSERVATION
3 URBAN ENVIRONMENT: AIR QUALITY, TRANSPORT, NOISE
4 GLOBAL ENVIRONMENTAL PROBLEMS: CLIMATIC CHANGE GEOSPHERE, BIOSPHERE

DIRECTORATE C
ADVISER RESEARCH
ADVISER PHASE
1 INTERNATIONAL AFFAIRS
2 MANAGEMENT AND COORDINATION OF FINANCIAL INSTRUMENTS, MEDIUM-TERM PLANNING
3 ECONOMIC ASPECTS
4 INFORMATION AND COMMUNICATION

The new order

Environmental policy in the European Community has been increasingly determined from Brussels rather than by national parliaments since the late 1970s, and particularly since the Single European Act came into force on July 1st 1987. Framework and more specific legislation on the environment are initiated by Directorate-General XI. If legislation is accepted, DGXI becomes responsible for ensuring that the member states, on whom it is binding, implement and enforce it. More than 200 pieces of environmental legislation have already been passed, providing a solid base for further steps in the future. DGXI also has

executive responsibility for environmental budgets and grants, programme implementation, and increasingly for international negotiations on the environment. Environmental policy is increasingly integrated with other policy areas, such as energy, transport, agriculture and structural funds.

The Council of Europe in Strasbourg has several environmental protection planning committees and programmes, notably protecting habitats and cultural heritage. It framed the Convention on the Conservation of European Wildlife and Natural Habitats, and in 1989 adopted a declaration to increase cooperation with

the EC and eastern Europe.

The United Nations Economic Commission for Europe (UNECE) was established in 1947 at Geneva, including all European states, the USA and Canada. UNECE was responsible for the first major agreement on transfrontier air pollution in 1979, coming into force in 1983 as the Convention on Long Range Transboundary Air Pollution, and subsequent protocols on SO₂ and NOₓ, the causes of acid rain. The EC is a collective signatory to the agreements.

The International Union for the Conservation of Nature and Natural Resources (IUCN – The World Conservation Union), based in Gland,

Switzerland, was founded in 1948 to promote and encourage the protection and sustainable use of living resources. IUCN has a worldwide membership of governments and non-governmental organisations, and operates an Environmental Law Centre in Bonn and the World Conservation Monitoring Centre in Cambridge. IUCN also has an East European Programme to promote environmentally sound planning, participate in international conservation affairs and promote restoration ecology.

Connections: New parties and movements 126–127 Unstable world 210–211 The greenhouse effect 214–215

ure to develop an effective global climate convention is too high to contemplate, yet the agreement signed in Rio in 1992 is far too weak to guarantee effective action.

One of the most encouraging examples of a change in thinking by politicians and institutions, if rather delayed, has been the development of common policies on the environment by the EC. With few exceptions, member states now agree to abide by the overarching framework of EC directives on a wide range of environmental issues. Conclusion of the Maastricht summit in December 1991 established for the first time the principle of majority voting on environmental issues.

Slowly but steadily the Community is implanting environmental accountability within all its executive agencies. In a number of member states, ministries are adopting duties of environmental care, and ministerial committees are being formed to ensure compatibility of policy and investment. Regulatory agencies are becoming tougher, scientifically competent and better financed, with the prospect of a transnational environmental police force within 20 years. This potentially daunting prospect awaits the initiation of a European Environmental Protection Agency, still not yet born despite three years of gestation.

Out of sight, out of mind…free cross-border trade could lead to countries such as the UK becoming the Single European Dump. In 1990 an official 37,035 tonnes of toxic waste was imported. This vessel prepares to leave a UK port to dump nuclear waste at sea.

ECONOMIC PERSUASION

Governments have used predominantly direct, regulatory methods to protect the environment, including licensing, fines, setting emission standards and land-use zoning. Economic instruments affect the costs and benefits of carrying out an economic activity in such a way as to influence rather than compel behaviour towards taking the course that is most desirable for the environment. They allow a more gradual move to lower levels of environmental effects than the sudden imposition of new regulations. In Europe charges and taxes are generally applied but Germany and Finland rely on subsidies.

GLOBAL CONVENTIONS AND TREATIES

One of the most important ways in which governments have shown international environmental concern is by their growing participation in multilateral regional and global agreements. Framework conventions, followed by more specific action protocols translated into national or EC law, have become the accepted means. The most important global treaty approved to date, albeit belatedly, was the Vienna Convention for Protection of the Ozone Layer in 1985, now ratified, acceded to or otherwise supported by 58 countries, and the Montreal Protocol of 1987. The Protocol stipulated a 50% cut of five types of CFCs and three types of halons by 1999 in industrial nations. While these targets have been completely revised after alarm over the growth of the ozone hole, the agreements have provided the model for future conventions, notably on climate change and biodiversity. Less successful so far has been the 1979 Convention on Long Range Transboundary Air Pollution to control acid rain. Countries that have suffered the worst effects of acid rain, notably Germany and in Scandinavia, are managing more stringent targets, while the main polluters lack either the will, technology or finance to meet minimum targets.

Global framework agreements on many issues are already in place. The need now is to tighten protocols and broaden support for them, particularly in the former Soviet bloc, and to provide better technical and financial support where it is needed. There is a demand for new agreements on climate change, action to dismantle vested interests in Europe and a manageable system of policing environmental agreements.

SINGLE PROBLEMS

Very little can be done to prevent the sale and cross-border movement of endangered species once they have entered from outside the EC. Ecologists also point to the disastrous spread of Dutch Elm disease in Britain due to unmonitored imports of Canadian roundwood infected with elm bark beetle.

The most serious concern of all is that free cross-border trade in hazardous wastes could mean countries with cheaper facilities for waste management, such as the UK, being inundated and becoming what environmentalists have described as the Single European Dump.

MAJOR INTERNATIONAL CONVENTIONS

DATE	CONVENTION	PLACE
1933	Preservation of fauna and flora	London
1946	Regulation of whaling	Washington
1954	Prevention of pollution of the sea by oil (OILPOL)	London
1963	Comprehensive nuclear test ban treaty	Moscow
1969	Civil liability for oil pollution damage (CLC)	Brussels
1971	Wetlands of international importance especially as waterfowl habitat	Ramsar
1972	Protection of world cultural and natural heritage	Paris
1972	Prevention of marine pollution by dumping of wastes and other matter (London Dumping Convention)	London ,Mexico, Moscow ,Washington
1973	International trade in endangered species	Washington
1973	Prevention of pollution from ships (MARPOL)	London
1974	Protection of the marine environment of the Baltic Sea	Helsinki
1974	Prevention of marine pollution from land-based sources	Paris
1976	Protection of the Mediterranean Sea against pollution	Barcelona
1976	Protection of the Rhine against chemical pollution	Bonn
1978	Future multilateral cooperation in the North West Atlantic fisheries	Ottawa
1979	European wildlife and natural habitats	Bern
1979	Conservation of migratory species of wild animals	Bonn
1979	Long range transboundary air pollution	Geneva
1980	Conservation of Antarctic marine living resources	Canberra
1982	UN Convention on the Law of the Sea	Montego Bay
1985	Protection of the ozone layer	Vienna
1986	Early notification of a nuclear accident	Vienna
1989	Control of transboundary movements of hazardous wastes and their disposal	Basel

Maastricht

While the original 1957 Treaty of Rome made no legal provision for a common environmental policy, a considerable volume of environmental legislation has been put in place since 1972. The Single European Act of 1985 formalised the position by setting out three major aims for Community action, including: to preserve, protect and improve the quality of the environment; to contribute towards protecting human health; and to ensure a prudent and rational utilisation of natural resources

The signing of the 1991 Maastricht agreement was a major landmark for European environmental policy. Chapter XVI of the treaty provisionally agreed at Maastricht contains important amendments to the Single European Act. Article 130 S, paragraph 1, now states that most decisions on the environment will be taken by qualified majority voting, representing a major shift of power from national governments, who have effectively lost their veto, to the EC.

Several other major changes were made at Maastricht. The new treaty emphasises more strongly the need for environmental protection requirements to be fully integrated into other Community policies, such as agriculture.

A SUSTAINABLE FUTURE?

A bottle bank collection point in Caux, Switzerland. Glass recycling grew increasingly during the 1980s, reaching 39% of the total consumption in Europe excluding the former Soviet Union in 1989.

Sustainable development was defined by the World Commission on Environment and Development in 1987, set up at at the request of the United Nations, as carried out in a way which "meets the needs of the present without compromising the ability of future generations to meet their own needs". It is difficult to think of any nation or modern economic activity that satisfies these conditions, though some nations may be closer to it than others. Yet these principles have been practised by tribal societies for thousands of years, while civilisations which ignored them sooner or later fell into decline.

Many measures have been applied to reduce the environmental consequences of different aspects of economic growth, including pollution-control technology, economic instruments, recycling, together with new institutions and environmental legislation nationally and globally. But as economic growth continues to put more pressure on resources, the diversity of wild species and the environment, it is increasingly clear that these measures are not enough to prevent further deterioration in future. Economic growth, at least in its present form, is ultimately not sustainable in a finite world. Sheer growth in road traffic in countries such as the UK over the next two decades threatens to swamp even the most ambitious air pollution reduction programmes using catalytic converters, unless it is curbed.

Eliminating losses

Faced with these problems, both industries and governments in the OECD have started to look at more fundamental and permanent solutions since the 1980s. Recycling will play a crucial role in reducing loss of resources and pollution, but could never eliminate all problems of pollution and waste in a growing economy. Clean technologies, which have been designed to avoid generation of hazardous, non-biodegradable or bulky wastes in the first place, are ultimately the only economic and technologically feasible way of meeting increasingly stringent environmental regulations. In anticipation of this trend, many western European states, notably in Scandinavia, the Netherlands and Germany, now have major clean technology research and development programmes in collaboration with industry, EC, UNEP and OECD.

Some countries now base their environmental strategies on the concept of sustainability, with important implications for industrial and agricultural production. The Dutch government launched an ambitious National Environmental Policy Plan in 1990, after studies showed that even with major growth of pollution-control equipment and other controls on environmental damage, the situation would deteriorate through economic growth. The comprehensive programme to stabilise, and then reverse the deterioration in its environment, involves stabilising CO_2 emissions by 1994, halving pesticide use, cutting acid emissions by 80% and recycling 55% of waste. These cuts will rely on an increasing use of clean technology, energy efficiency and recycling, as well as abatement technology.

The problem with people

Population growth remains the most fundamental and politically the thorniest of all environmental problems, even though technology can reduce some of its worst effects. World population is expected to double before it stabilises at between 8 and 14 billion sometime in the 21st century. Over 90% of this unsustainable growth will occur in the poorest countries, and 90% of this in cities already at bursting point.

Europe's population excluding the CIS, at around 549m in 1988, has largely stabilised. Even so, it continues to increase stresses on the global environment, through high population density and disproportionately large growth in

Map legend
- 100,000+
- 50,000-100,000
- 20,000-50,000
- 5,000-20,000
- 1,000-5,000
- Less than 1,000

NORWAY
FINLAND
SWEDEN
ESTONIA
LATVIA
DENMARK
LITHUANIA
IRELAND
UNITED KINGDOM
NETHERLANDS
BELGIUM
GERMANY
POLAND
LUX
CZECHOSLOVAKIA
FRANCE
SWITZ
AUSTRIA
HUNGARY
ROMANIA
YUGOSLAVIA
PORTUGAL
SPAIN
ITALY
BULGARIA
ALBANIA
GREECE

Down on the organic farm

The map shows estimated land coverage for organic farms in hectares in the 1990s. Organic farming principles were first popularised by Rudolf Steiner in the 1920s in Germany, when chemical uses were increasing. It received a major boost with the health foods market from the 1970s, prompted by public concern about toxic chemical residues and preservatives in vegetable and fruit produce, and antibiotics in livestock.

More recently, concern has also focused on the environmental impact of unsustainable, intensive factory farming, using large inputs of pesticides, fertilisers and energy, which have polluted water supplies and damaged habitats. Overproduction of agriculture in the EC, boosted by subsidies, has forced a rethink of the Common Agricultural Policy. Production has been cut, and more environmentally sensitive agricultural methods are being encouraged, including financing of environmental projects such as the setting aside of unneeded lands for wildlife. There are also possibilities that organic farming could receive support in future. In Denmark, subsidies have already encouraged rapid expansion.

France has the largest area of organically farmed land in western Europe, amounting to 100,000 hectares, followed by Germany, with 54,295, Sweden and the UK with over 28,000 and 20,000 hectares. Organic farming is now big business. In Germany, the domestic market is the largest, at $275m. In western Europe as a whole, the market is worth almost $1bn.

There are no uniform standards between countries as yet, but several produced their own national labelling schemes during the 1970s. The first steps towards an internationally recognised label are being taken by the International Federation of Organic Agricultural Movements founded in 1972, in cooperation with the EC.

Sustainability

Population growth ultimately threatens even the efforts of sustainable development through sheer pressure on resources. In Europe itself, population growth is no longer the main concern, with average growth rates of only 0.4% a year, compared with levels as high as 2.5% in North Africa and 2.2% in South Asia. Population growth is even negative in some highly advanced European economies, such as Switzerland and western Germany. Yet environmentally dubious international trade with developing countries, such as toxic waste disposal, and growing domestic consumption of resources have a disproportionate effect on the regional and global environment.

Curiously this demographic change will have an economic effect in that the proportion of young people between 25 and 35 will drop by 25% by 2100 and the proportion of elderly people will rise correspondingly by 20%. The resulting cost of healthcare and pension schemes could become very burdensome indeed.

Connections: Energy 72–73 Food and farming 76–77 Waste pollution 206–207 Institutional response 218–219

its consumption of energy and other natural resources. The fact that Europe consumes 23% of the world's energy, and that the OECD economies consume most of its diminishing supplies of high grade metal ores not only causes immense environmental damage, but narrows future development options in the exporting countries.

Growth in energy use reflects the level of development of society, though energy efficiency measures show that this relationship is no longer as strong as it once was. In the aftermath of the oil shock of 1973, energy conservation and efficiency measures rapidly gained currency, particulary in the OECD. World GNP was over 80% higher in 1988 than it was in 1970, but primary energy consumption only rose by 155m barrels oil equivalent over the same period. Unfortunately, the oil glut of the 1980s saw many countries sink back into complacency.

Nobody knows just what a sustainable society would look like. Would it even be democratic? Would it primarily be interventionist or enlightened free market? Different models reflect the diversity of cultures, environments and economies of Europe.

AN ENERGY EFFICIENT FUTURE

A 1990 study by the European Commission concluded that EC energy demand is likely to continue to grow into the next century given current trends, and that CO_2 emissions would be hard to restrain. The study explored two different views of future growth, a conventional view and a change of policy. The first scenario assumed "conventional wisdom" or "business as usual" prevails, with higher consumption being balanced by continuing cuts in NO_x and SO_2 emissions. In the second, entitled "driving into tensions", higher growth was reflected in an unstable international energy market, leading to much greater environmental impact. Economic growth would itself eventually suffer compared to the first assumption. Emissions of CO_2 would rise in both cases, from 2.8bn tonnes in 1990 to 3.2bn tonnes in 2010 under the first scenario, and up to 3.5bn tonnes in the second.

A third idea assumed strong economic growth provided the impetus for greater investment in energy-efficient technologies, policy initiatives on energy efficiency norms and standards, and incentives to cut consumption. Consumers were assumed to be "able to meet their needs in an environmentally conscious manner". The final theory made similar assumptions to the third, but assumed more moderate growth, reducing tensions overall, and by high end user prices. It also assumed a 1% growth rate in electrical consumption, about one-third of current growth levels. Both these last two scenarios achieve lower SO_2 emissions, down 60% and 65% respectively by 2010, and NO_x emissions down by 50% and 56% over the same period.

RENEWABLE ENERGY SOURCES

Renewable energy sources have great potential in Europe. Some have a low renewable potential, others a high one. Wind power alone, particularly on the North Atlantic and North Sea coasts of north-west Europe, together with parts of the eastern Mediterranean, could supply between 10,000 and 23,000 megawatts of western European electrical power demand. By 1990, costs per unit had fallen to 5.3 cents per kWh (see chart below), compared with 12.3 cents per kWh for nuclear and 5 cents per kWh for coal. Renewable energy costs have all become highly competitive. The generation of wind energy alone would never be adequate.

COST OF NEW ENERGY

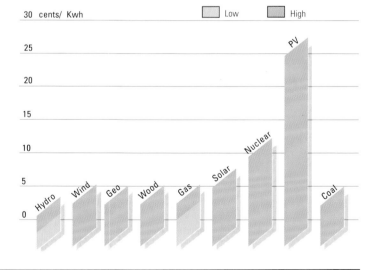

The main problem for further windpower expansion is no longer cost, but the visual impact of wind turbines on windy shorelines and attractive upland regions. This is minimised by concentrating capacity into windfarms, such as this one in the French Alps. Large areas of land would be dominated by turbines, but unlike conventional fossil or nuclear capacity, which take steadily increasing areas of land for waste and mining spoil, windfarm landtake is a once and for all affair.

Recycling

Recycling, particularly of non-renewable minerals, forms a major part of sustainable development strategies. The major problem with wastes is how to separate out the different components.

Proportions of paper collected have not altered much in the last decade, with Switzerland recycling as much as 61%, the Netherlands 54% and Austria 49%. Italy and the UK recycled least, on 27% and 30% respectively.

WHO REUSES WHAT

COUNTRY			%
AUSTRIA	15[1]	44	37
BELGIUM	—	39	15
DENMARK	—	32	31
FINLAND	19	20	30
FRANCE	23	26	33
GERMANY W	31	37	41
NETHERLANDS	31	62	53[2]
PORTUGAL	8[1]	14	38[1]
SPAIN	—	22	44
SWEDEN	19	20	40
SWITZERLAND	18	47	38
UK	27	13	27

JAPAN	25	54.4	50
USA[2]	27	20.0	8

☐ Aluminium
☐ Paper and cardboard
☐ Glass
1 Estimate
2 Recycled from the paper industry only

Definitions

The term sustainable development was first used in the context of developing countries during the early 1970s, but has rapidly gained currency in the last decade. Since the 1970s, OECD environmental policy has shifted its focus from solving individual pollutant problems to much broader issues of sustainable development. This has many definitions, some of which describe quite different approaches, all implying a fundamental rethink of the meaning of progress.

At its most basic, sustainable development implies economic activity that can, for practical purposes, continue

to maintain and raise the quality of life for ever. It means an economy which, like an ecosystem, recycles raw materials and uses energy highly efficiently. "Sustainable development" implies human progress as technology increases, but without the need for unlimited growth. "Sustained growth", as used by economic analysts, is ultimately impossible in a finite world, even if it draws extensively on renewable resources and recycling. "Sustainable use" refers to wise husbandry of renewable resources, such as fisheries. Economists now also refer to "green growth" to describe environmentally sensitive economic growth, not

necessarily all sustainable.

The World Commission on Environment commented:
"We came to see that a new development path was required, one that sustained human progress not just in a few places for a few years, but for the entire planet into the distant future. Thus 'sustainable development' becomes a goal not just for the 'developing nations', but for 'industrial' ones as well."
"A pursuit of sustainable development requires... a production system that respects the obligation to preserve the ecological base for that development."
"Economic growth and development obviously involve changes in the physical

ecosystem. Every ecosystem everywhere cannot be preserved intact.'"

PEOPLE AND CULTURE

A country or a continent is not simply a geographical phenomenon; its shaping spirit is its people and the way they structure their society. Europe has a shared culture rooted in its classical past, but within that loose philosophical consensus, the way in which people live depends on their values and their standard of living. In Europe the differences are substantial and revealing.

This chapter examines the way the peoples of Europe organise themselves; how they define themselves as European and nationals, how well they can assimilate the "Europeans once removed" and the immigrants who reap the doubtful benefit of the imperial legacy. It looks at who believes what in Europe, how religion is enjoying a revival, especially in countries of the former eastern bloc, and the impact of non-western belief systems on self-professed Christian societies. Attitudes and approaches to education are reviewed: how committed are Europe's governments to education, who spends most and on which sector, and has made the biggest investment in providing the educated, skilled workforce needed for economic success. It also looks at how Europeans relax and play, how much money they spend on leisure, which household appliances are sold where (who in Europe does not have access to a refrigerator or a TV) and the impact of tourism. Social trends and attitudes are analysed: how far Europeans agree on their definition of the meaning and function of a family, how the falling birth rate and rising old age dependency adds up to an economic time bomb, how sexual mores compare; where the healthiest Europeans live and how much public money their governments spend to keep them that way; how long can they expect to live and what is the commonest cause of death. The final section looks at law and order: how crime rates and imprisonment policies vary across Europe, who still believes in the death penalty, and how far away Europe is from a coordinated system to deal with cross-border terrorism, drug running and fraud.

WHO ARE THE EUROPEANS?

Europe in the 19th and 20th centuries has been dominated by the idea and development of the nation state. By the end of the 18th century, there were already countries in western Europe, such as France, Spain and the United Kingdom whose boundaries had been clearly established by dynastic marriages and wars in preceding centuries. While we tend to assume that the people within these states had common linguistic, historical and cultural backgrounds, it would be more accurate to say that in many cases, this homogeneity was imposed from above onto an unwilling or indifferent population. Identification with a region, or even just a city or town, was more the norm, especially at a time when most people did not have the means or the inclination to travel long distances.

tion of their country and the establishment of the Irish Free State in 1921, the other ethnic and linguistic groups in the United Kingdom have only come to prominence since the second world war. The same is true of the Bretons in France, and although regional particularism and separatism in Spain has a much longer tradition, it was heavily suppressed during the rule of General Francisco Franco and re-emerged openly only after his death in 1975.

Home rulers and separatists

While the present-day democratic constitutions in all these countries have fostered the acceptance or integration of many newly found or rediscovered regional cultural differences, there remain some tensions between certain minority groups and the state. Demands for autonomy, and in extreme cases, outright separation, remain on the agenda for the Scottish and Welsh nationalists in the United Kingdom, for the Bretons in France and the Catalans and Galicians in Spain. In this last case, the federal nature of the 1978 Spanish constitution and the recognition of minority languages has gone some way to meeting the aspirations of moderate autonomists but has failed to satisfy the demands of Basque separatists. Since 1968, their independence movement Euzkadi ta Azkatasuna (ETA), together with its French counterpart, Enbata, has conducted a guerrilla campaign to establish a separate Basque state. Although unsuccessful to date, ETA has claimed responsibility for a large number of terrorist outrages, including the assassination of Admiral Carrero Blanco in 1973. The other European group to persist with an armed struggle is the provisional wing of the Irish Republican Army (IRA). Committed to the idea of an united Ireland, the provisionals have conducted a ▷

Market forces in Budapest. First to lift the hem of the Iron Curtain, Hungary is now more advanced in the market economies favoured by the West than the rest of its eastern neighbours. This is partially due to its position, now the centre of the new Europe, and its close cultural and geographical links with Austria, with which it once formed an empire.

Linguistic, cultural and, in some cases, religious uniformity was perceived as a necessary step for the establishment, security and later the modernisation of these states. Minority religions often underwent degrees of suppression or persecution, for example, the Jews in Spain, the Protestant Huguenots in France and the Catholics in Britain during the early modern period. Moreover, the ethnic, linguistic and cultural diversity within the geographic boundaries of these states often fell victim to centralising or unifying tendencies. Thus Irish and Scots (Gaelic), Welsh and Cornish traditions underwent discrimination and even legal restraint in the United Kingdom. The Bretons in France and the Catalans, Basques and Galicians in Spain had similar experiences which lasted into the 20th century.

Only with the liberalisation of education and administration in the later years of this century have these separate cultures reasserted themselves in social, and sometimes also political, terms. Apart from the Irish nationalists, who achieved a partial victory after the parti-

THE POPULATION BOOM

The history of population growth in Europe is one of rapid expansion from the middle of the 18th century, but hidden within this general increase are a number of specific features. Although population growth is considered as one of the prerequisites for industrialisation and economic growth, it was the more backward and rural areas, especially in eastern Europe, which experienced the largest growth rates. This created two parallel trends. The first was the mass migration of peoples from eastern Europe to the West, and beyond to the Americas. Prompted partly by the desire for economic betterment, and partly through persecution at home, millions of people left their homelands for new lives elsewhere. Secondly, there was a major movement of people from the countryside to the cities. Again, this can be explained partly by economic factors, but also by the inability of city populations to be self-sustaining. Even without further economic growth, poor housing, poor working conditions and disease lowered life expectancy rates and created opportunities for further migrants. In the 20th century, the urbanisation and westward movement has continued, leading to higher population densities in western Europe in comparison with those in countries further east.

While the industrialisation of Europe served as a catalyst for mass migration, there have also been anomalies. After the mid-19th century, the population of France more or less stagnated, while those of neighbouring countries continued to grow. Never entirely satisfactorily explained, the lack of population growth continued into the 20th century and was exacerbated by the losses sustained during the first world war.

Connections: Europe takes shape 12–15 Patterns of empire 16–17 Rebuilding democracies 120–121 Labour and immigration 138–139 Terrorism in Europe 194–195

Who lives where

The map plots the density of Europe's populations. There is no correlation between overcrowding and poverty; the Dutch and the Belgians are the "battery hens" of Europe, who crowd together at 300 people to the square kilometre, and yet they are among the most successful countries, economically speaking. Sweden, Norway , Finland and Iceland are full of *lebensraum* and they too are economically successful. Portugal and Greece appear to have the ideal-sized population, yet they are among the poorer countries of Europe.

The reasons why some countries are more densely packed than others are not always the same. Germany and the UK are highly industrialised, attracting more people looking for work. In the Netherlands, the social policies of the two major religious groups, Roman Catholic and Calvinist, have conspired to make the country the most densely populated in Europe. Ireland produces children in great numbers, but most of them leave to find work in the UK or the USA. Attractive childcare packages and well-paid maternity leave are encouraging Swedish women to produce more children, but no Scandinavian country has ever become overcrowded.

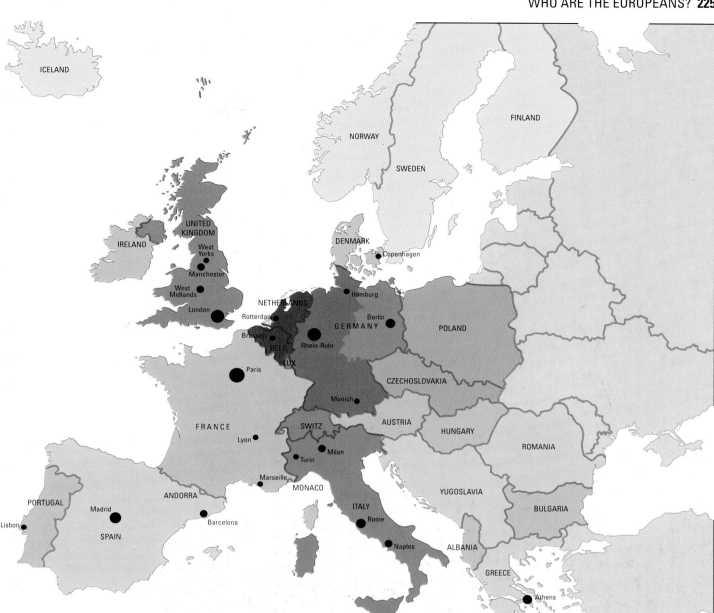

People per km²

- Over 301
- 201-300
- 151-200
- 121-150
- 101-120
- 21-100
- 0-20
- ● 1 million inhabitants

Bright lights, big city

Conurbations occur when towns and cities expand and link with each other, blotting out intervening landscape. The spread of public transport and the huge rise in car ownership has helped to foster them, but most are the result of the great shift from work on the land to work in the city, or the factories that cluster about the edges of cities. As agricultural work fails, people move into town to increase their job options, and suburbs to house them build up. Many conurbation developments are linear, but some expand outwards from a centre, usually a capital city. The Paris conurbation, the largest in Europe, is the result of poorer suburbs allying themselves to the glittering centre. London started life as a compact city surrounded by distinct villages which gradually fused together as transport systems developed. West Berlin expanded as a tightly knit enclave in a hostile land, its limits pre-determined by political considerations. The Rhine–Ruhr conurbation was produced by massive industrialisation of the area and the sucking in of many small towns and villages under a huge canopy of steelworks, factories and mines.

The impact of a conurbation depends on the size of its host country. Rotterdam may be the smallest in terms of inhabitants, but it eats up an enormous chunk of the Netherlands' small landmass; on the other hand, Paris is eight times as large, but is easily lost in France.

Living together

The chart below shows the main European conurbations, which are located on the map above. However crowded conurbations may appear, Europe's population is dwindling overall.

MAIN CONURBATIONS

AREA	INHABITANTS[1]
PARIS	8,707
RHEIN-RUHR	7,792
LONDON	7,678
MADRID	4,120
BERLIN	3,300
ROME	3,094
ATHENS	3,027
MILAN	2,877
BARCELONA	2,701
NAPLES	2,608
WEST MIDLANDS	2,356
MANCHESTER	2,339
HAMBURG	1,624
TURIN	1,568
MUNICH	1,483
WEST YORKSHIRE	1,478
KOBENHAVN	1,372
LISBON	1,329
BRUSSELS	1,268
LYON	1,221
MARSEILLE	1,110
ROTTERDAM	1,025

1 '000s

Shopping in Gstaad is only for the rich. Switzerland, the centre of the old pre-1989 Europe, has kept itself and its people wealthy and well protected for centuries by maintaining neutrality in the two wars that shook Europe, becoming discreet banker to the world, and remaining aloof from the EC marketplace. Therefore, Switzerland's surprise application in 1992 to join the EC and to become a member of the IMF is just as mould-breaking in its own fashion as any of the upheavals in eastern Europe.

terrorist campaign against the government of Ulster and the United Kingdom, a campaign given added impetus by discrimination against Roman Catholics in the province and the resultant civil disturbances which began in 1968–9. Since then, the provisional IRA has carried out innumerable acts of terrorism against the Royal Ulster Constabulary, the British Army and Ulster Protestants. This has led to an increasing military presence in the area and the creation of Protestant paramilitary and terrorist groups.

While national identity has become less important as states become involved in wider, pan-European organisations, the sense of national, regional or local identity lives on. For the most part expressed in cultural and linguistic terms it is still a potent weapon for those (minorities) engaged in trying to assert their independence from larger political units.

Unification and self determination

Elsewhere in Europe, for states founded in the 19th or early 20th century, the notion of the nation state became the justification for unification. In Germany, Prussian Chancellor Bismarck was able to bring together the majority of German-speaking states into an empire after a series of wars, 1864–71. Here, although the idea of Germandom (Deutschtum) was seen as a unifying factor, the new imperial state was nevertheless divided in reli-

Poles apart… the euphoric tide that swept over Europe when the Berlin wall came tumbling down very quickly ebbed. Faced with the economic reality of thousands of eastern Europeans looking for work, the right-wing element quickly rose to defend their high standard of living. In 1990, the hands that had been held out in welcome just a year before were bunched into fists as German National Front members demonstrated against the influx of Polish workers.

gious terms between a predominantly Catholic south and east, and a predominantly Protestant north and west. Undergoing a series of boundary revisions during the 20th century, Germany lost a good deal of its pre-1914 territory as a result of the Versailles Treaty (1919) but also has had to absorb a large influx of German-speaking peoples from areas transferred to Poland, the Baltic states and the Soviet Union, since 1945. Other European states whose boundaries were defined or refined by international treaties also retain major religious, linguistic or ethnic divisions. The Netherlands has a religious divide (28% Protestant, 35% Catholic), Belgium a linguistic divide (55% Flemish, 44% Walloon French) and Czechoslovakia an ethnic division between Czechs (63%) and Slovaks (31%).

In eastern Europe, the situation is even more confused. After the break-up of the Austrian and Russian empires at the end of the first world war, new states were established, partly out of a desire to grant national self-determination to the major ethnic minorities in these empires, but also to create defensive cordons of states against further German or Bolshevik Russian expansion. Czechoslovakia, Poland, Yugoslavia and the Baltic states were all given independence, but their boundaries could seldom be made co-terminus with linguistic or cultural divisions, and most states retained substantial minorities. The post-1945 settlement expanded the size of the Soviet Union and its influence over eastern Europe. Only with the collapse of this influence have the ethnic and linguistic divisions reasserted themselves, for example, in the civil war in Yugoslavia, and in the treatment of the Russian minorities in the newly independent Baltic states. Clearly, nationalism and cultural identities are being re-established and reinforced here, often awakening old feuds and animosities.

This gives only the broadest overview of the way in which political boundaries have helped and hindered political stability for the peoples of Europe, yet there have been many other complicating factors, most notably massive population growth in the 19th and 20th centuries, the impact of immigration and the use of racism as a political tool.

IMMIGRATION

The increased movement of peoples, both within Europe and to the New World, has been a feature of European life since the mid-19th century. Urbanisation and the flood of emigrants to the United States acted as a safety valve for the burgeoning populations of Europe. Movement between European states was more limited, although many thousands did migrate westwards before the first world war. The displacement of peoples as a result of the war and redrawing of boundaries created new minorities in Europe, notably Germans in the areas ceded to Poland, and the Russians who moved to France rather than remain in, or return to, the new Bolshevik state.

The second world war produced similar results, with anything up to seven million displaced people in Europe in May 1945. Again, redrawn boundaries, bomb damage and fears about Russian control persuaded or forced many people to move from their traditional homes. Millions of Germans left Poland and the Russian-controlled eastern zone for the supposed safety of the West in the years after the war, while other European nationals who had been forced to work in Germany during the war were returned home.

More important in the postwar world was immigration from outside the boundaries of Europe. The end of the European colonial empires saw an influx of non-caucasian colonial subjects who preferred to move to Europe instead of remaining in their newly-independent homelands. In this way, France gave refuge to Vietnamese and Algerians in the 1950s, and the Netherlands to Indonesians. Levels of integration and assimilation have varied in these countries. For example, the Indonesians in the Netherlands have been largely assimilated into Dutch society, whereas their Moluccan counterparts have kept themselves entirely apart.

As the European economies required more labour in the 1960s and 1970s, further immigration from former colonial territories, or from the states of south-eastern Europe and the Near East was encouraged. Most European states now have noticeable minority groups.

IMMIGRATION CASE STUDY: FRANCE

Traditionally, France has suffered from a labour shortage and has often positively encouraged the immigration of foreign workers. Even in the 1980s, the country continued to receive workers and their families, primarily from Europe and North Africa. Statistics on most of this immigration are kept by the Office des Migrations Internationales (OMI). These show that the most recent immigrants have come largely from Morocco, Tunisia and Turkey, although a high proportion seems to be of families joining workers already in the country. The numbers registered annually has increased only gradually since 1985. (The inflated figures for 1981–82 were the result of changes in EC regulations and a moratorium for those working in the country illegally.) Employment statistics show that immigrant labour is over-represented in industry and construction. Also of note is the gradual decline in seasonal workers, most of whom have traditionally been Spaniards or Portuguese.

Not included in these figures is the immigration from Algeria and francophone Black Africa. Because of the special privileges given to citizens of these former colonial territories, their movements are recorded at the point of entry and exit, but French government statisticians admit the figures are less than reliable. Data for 1982 suggest that immigration is growing faster than the population overall, but a lack of hard evidence has allowed Jean-Marie Le Pen's Front Nationale to claim that France is now being "swamped" by the Arabs from North Africa.

RACISM RESURGENT

Conflicts between the different races and ethnic groups which make up the population of the continent have been a major feature in European history. Attempts to create political and social unity in the last hundred years by stressing a common racial or ethnic origin are not unusual, but defining a member of the "race" has inevitably also defined those who are not members and created the scope for real or imagined differences and long-standing grievances to be used for political purposes. This probably reached its apogee with the spurious "aryan" racism used by Hitler and the Nazi party in Germany, 1920–45, but remains a feature in contemporary Europe, for example, in the relations between Serbs and Croats, and between Czechs and Slovaks.

Antisemitism in Europe has an even longer history. Medieval expulsions and pogroms had given way to more "scientific" forms of racial theory in the 19th century before both were combined to horrific effect by the Nazis during the second world war. The holocaust, the physical extermination of six million Jews and other "racial enemies" of the regime bears witness to the potential dangers inherent in racism. In the postwar era, antisemitism has persisted at a cultural level and re-emerged in recent attacks on Jewish cemeteries and in extreme right-wing propaganda throughout Europe.

A third type of racism has emerged since 1945. With the demand for labour increasing, and the rapid dismantling of their colonial empires in the 1950s and 1960s, Britain, France and the Netherlands (among others) admitted several million immigrants from Black Africa, the Caribbean, the Indian subcontinent and South-East Asia. Other countries with rapidly expanding economies after the 1960s, such as West Germany, recruited a labour force of *gastarbeiter* primarily from Turkey and Yugoslavia. Levels of integration and assimilation have varied and discrimination never fully eliminated anywhere, but with increasing unemployment in the late 1980s, attention has once again been focused on the non-white, foreign element in society evidenced by increases in racist attacks.

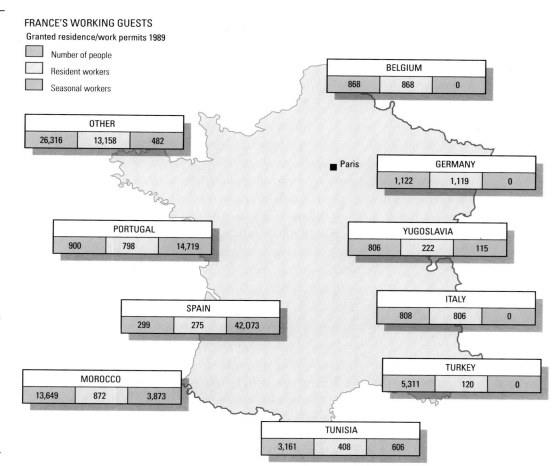

FRANCE'S WORKING GUESTS
Granted residence/work permits 1989

- Number of people
- Resident workers
- Seasonal workers

BELGIUM		
868	868	0

OTHER		
26,316	13,158	482

■ Paris

GERMANY		
1,122	1,119	0

PORTUGAL		
900	798	14,719

YUGOSLAVIA		
806	222	115

SPAIN		
299	275	42,073

ITALY		
808	806	0

MOROCCO		
13,649	872	3,873

TURKEY		
5,311	120	0

TUNISIA		
3,161	408	606

Secure in the possession of a work permit, and the knowledge that he can return to his job in Paris, a Tunisian worker takes time off for a holiday in his homeland. Just over 400 Tunisians received work permits in 1989.

FOREIGN NATIONALS GRANTED FRENCH WORK PERMITS, 1989
BY ECONOMIC SECTOR

	GERMANY	ITALY	MOROCCO	PORTUGAL	SPAIN	TUNISIA	TURKEY	YUGOSLAVIA	OTHER
FORESTRY	0	1	2	9	2	0	3	0	5
AGRICULTURE, FISHERIES	12	10	23	36	13	12	1	1	480
COAL MINING	0	0	1	1	0	1	0	0	3
OTHER MINING	2	0	0	1	0	0	0	0	7
STEEL	87	60	61	28	44	15	10	33	956
BUILDING MATERIALS	4	5	5	0	11	2	1	0	39
CONSTRUCTION	23	236	57	452	16	128	19	47	673
OTHER INDUSTRIES	119	90	79	96	31	32	17	18	1,488
COMMERCE	307	440	224	49	11	84	17	38	3,054
SERVICES	37	69	46	76	5	13	2	7	604
OTHER	528	388	374	50	142	121	50	78	6,224

RELIGION

Cardinals gathered at an extraordinary meeting in April 1991 to protest against abortion. In spite of the decline in religious adherence, Roman Catholicism has remained relatively strong; there are some 585m Roman Catholics worldwide and they form the majority group of the 400m professed Christians in Europe. A worldwide renewal of Catholicism was inspired by the Second Vatican Council of 1962 and the traditional image of the Church was changed irrevocably after Pope Paul VI (r.1963–78) published his text Regimini Ecclesiae, *or the government of the church, in 1967. New thinking was taken on board and fresh blood imbued into the structures of the Church.*

The widely-held view that religious adherence is dying out in Europe and secularism is gaining ground is not borne out by the figures. Institutionalised religion may have been rejected, but this has not meant a decline in religiosity. In all European countries except Sweden, most people confess to some form of religious belief. There are now more than 400m professed Christians in Europe, the largest four groupings being Roman Catholics, Protestants, Orthodox and Anglicans. Other religious beliefs are represented by Islam (about 13m Muslims), Judaism (almost 1.25m Jews) and eastern religions; the number of Buddhists, Sikhs and Hindus have increased as have communities of Baha'is, Confucianists and Chinese Folk Religionists. Church attendance may appear to be in decline, but large numbers of people are turning to or rediscovering religion.

In the West, the largest growth is in Christianity, particularly the Charismatic wing. Mainstream Protestant and Catholic churches are being revitalised by a boom in the Christian renewal movement.

While Judaism is in decline, because of a devastated postwar population, low birth rates and emigration to Israel, Islam is growing slowly but steadily, boosted by 30 years of immigration to western European countries.

Resurrection in the East

Before the collapse of the Soviet Union, the communist ideals that prevailed behind the Iron Curtain forced millions of religious adherents to deny their beliefs or go underground. In Albania, the most extreme case, the government did not recognise the existence of Christians or any other religious grouping. In Czechoslovakia, atheism was the official ideology of the government, although nearly 80% of the population clung to their Christian beliefs. In countries such as these, modern communication methods, chiefly radio, enabled them to sustain their faith.

Since 1989, young people of the former Soviet Union have, like their western counterparts, shown growing interest in religions of all kinds. The dramatic developments in eastern Europe have also contributed to a resurgence of Orthodoxy and Roman Catholicism and Islamic fundamentalism. In some eastern countries religion appeared to be the midwife to the revolutions that have taken place there.

However, with the new religious freedoms has come a re-opening of old wounds, and it is becoming clear that the historic divisions in Christianity remain as firmly drawn as ever. The schism between Orthodoxy in the East and Catholicism in the West began in the fourth century with the division of the Roman empire and was finalised in 1054, although the mutual excommunications then proclaimed were formally withdrawn by both parties in 1965. Yet while ecumenism in western Europe is bringing Protestant and Anglican churches closer together and is endeavouring to create a new understanding between them and Roman Catholic churches, in eastern Europe, Orthodoxy and Catholicism remain as far from reconciliation as ever.

European church leaders are adjusting to an increase in religious interest in their own countries, and to a world in which Christianity is growing fastest in Africa, Latin America, India and China. As nationalism and fundamentalism re-emerge, the established religions in Europe are facing a challenge and opportunity which, if tackled correctly, could see them moving with unparalleled spiritual strength into the next millennium.

Who believes in Europe?

The map shows the distribution of religious groupings throughout Europe and the projected percentage of the population that will belong to each grouping in the year 2000.

Since the Reformation instigated in the 16th century by Martin Luther, Europe has been divided broadly into Catholics and Protestants, with the Catholics living mainly in the south and the Protestants in the north; some countries have more of a religious mixture than others, usually as a result of historical alliances and royal marriages. For example, Belgium was once the possession of Catholic Spain; today, 91% of the Belgian population is Christian, mostly Catholic. In Austria, nearly 97% is Christian, also mostly Catholic. In Denmark, 96% profess Christian belief, and most are Lutheran. Germany has large numbers of Protestants, both Reformed and Lutheran, and Catholics. In France, where there is no established church and the state is officially secular, three-quarters of the people are Catholic and as many as one-quarter attend mass every week. France also has Reformed and Lutheran Protestants and a growing number of Pentecostalists. In Italy, 99% of the population is Catholic and 95% of all children receive first communion. Nearly all Italians are married in church. After the mid-1970s, the picture of Europe as a patchwork of Christian sects has changed. An influx of migrant workers from Mediterranean countries in western Europe caused a sudden rise in the number of Muslims, in particular in France and Belgium. Buddhism, Sikhism and Hinduism have also increased.

RELIGIOUS ADHERENTS

- Roman Catholic
- Protestant
- Other Christian
- Other
- Non-religious/atheist

1. Mainly Muslim
2. Mainly Orthodox
3. Mainly Anglican

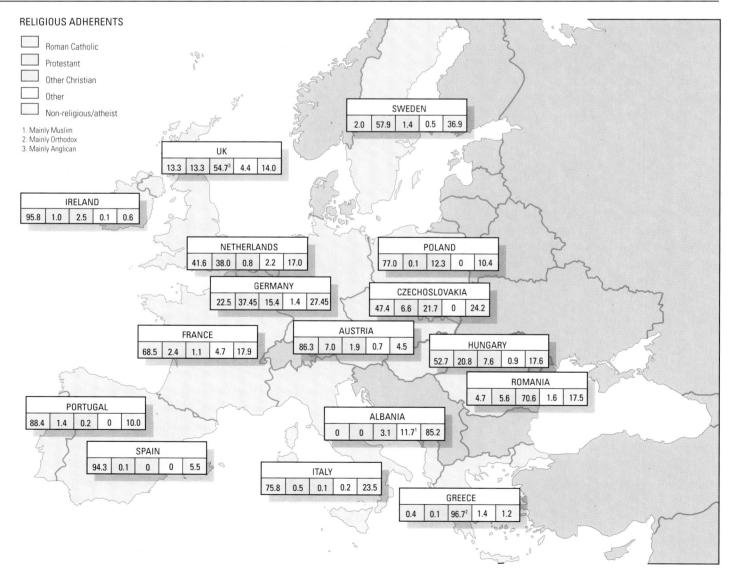

Country	Roman Catholic	Protestant	Other Christian	Other	Non-religious/atheist
SWEDEN	2.0	57.9	1.4	0.5	36.9
UK	13.3	13.3	54.7[3]	4.4	14.0
IRELAND	95.8	1.0	2.5	0.1	0.6
NETHERLANDS	41.6	38.0	0.8	2.2	17.0
POLAND	77.0	0.1	12.3	0	10.4
GERMANY	22.5	37.45	15.4	1.4	27.45
CZECHOSLOVAKIA	47.4	6.6	21.7	0	24.2
FRANCE	68.5	2.4	1.1	4.7	17.9
AUSTRIA	86.3	7.0	1.9	0.7	4.5
HUNGARY	52.7	20.8	7.6	0.9	17.6
ROMANIA	4.7	5.6	70.6	1.6	17.5
PORTUGAL	88.4	1.4	0.2	0	10.0
ALBANIA	0	0	3.1	11.7[1]	85.2
SPAIN	94.3	0.1	0	0	5.5
ITALY	75.8	0.5	0.1	0.2	23.5
GREECE	0.4	0.1	96.7[2]	1.4	1.2

Connections: Europe takes shape 12–15   Christian hegemony 20–21   Labour and immigration 138–139

ISLAM IN EUROPE

Islam and Europe have always had an invigoratingly abrasive relationship. The faith was founded by the prophet Muhammed in the 7th century AD and rapidly spread throughout the countries fringing the south and east Mediterranean. In the 8th century, Spain was under Islamic rule and Muslim forces penetrated as far as Poitiers in France before being driven back by Charles Martel in 732 AD . The Crusades of the 11th, 12th and 13th centuries also forced Europeans to confront the reality of Islam as a major faith.

The modern Islamic presence in western Europe (see chart, right) is mainly the result of economic migration to satisfy employment needs. Austria, Belgium, Denmark, Germany , Hungary and the UK had no Islamic population at the turn of the century. France today has about 1.7m Muslims, more than any other western European country, mainly as a result of their North African colonial past. Over 95% of North Africans are Muslims. Immigration started early this century, beginning with Algerian workers followed by Tunisians and Moroccans. During the early 1960s there were further Muslim immigrations from countries such as Yugoslavia, where there are significant Muslim minorities.

Large-scale Islamic immigration to Belgium began in the early 1960s and the Belgian parliament officially recognised the Islamic religion in 1974. The number of Muslims has continued to grow, to more than 110,000. Islam has also grown in importance in Germany, the Netherlands and Scandinavia with the arrival of *gastarbeiters* from Muslim Turkey and Yugoslavia. In the UK, the rising Muslim population stems from the descendants of Islamic immigrants from former British colonies in India and Pakistan. There is also a significant Islamic presence in Italy.

THE CHARISMATIC MOVEMENT

The fastest growing religion in Europe is the Charismatic movement. Charismatic renewal is Christianity as guided primarily by the Holy Spirit and functioning according to the "gifts" of the spirit, or "charisms", which include speaking in tongues as the Apostles did at the Jewish Festival of Pentecost or Harvest.

In its earliest form, known as Pentecostalism, the Charismatic movement is usually held to have begun in the USA in 1901, though surveys have shown there were Pentecostalists around as early as 1741. There were further manifestations of Charismatic renewal in 1907 and, in particular, 1950.

Although there are large numbers of Charismatics on every continent, Europe has always had the lowest response to Pentecostalism, due to an unwillingness to leave the established churches. Until 1970, fewer than 1% of European Christians were Pentecostal or Charismatic. Then the picture changed, with a big response within the established churches and the beginning of mainstream church renewal, known as the "third wave" as it was the third surge of Charismatic feeling to sweep the world. Nearly 40 categories exist within these three waves. Charismatics make up 21% of organised worldwide Christianity. Europe has nearly 30m Pentecostal and Charismatic church members, 7.15% of all church-member Christians.

As a highly evangelical sect, Charismatics use television, radio and news media in their recruiting drives, although televangelism has not the grip on Europe that it has on the USA. American evangelists make regular proselytising tours of Europe, often incorporating "healing" in their mass services.

Judaism

About 1.5m Jews survive in Europe today, after the devastation wrought by the Nazi exterminations in the second world war. In Austria, more than 200,000 Jews in 1938 had fallen to 4,000 by 1945. The Belgian Jewish community was halved and Czechoslovakia lost 85% of its Jews.

The surviving populations in some European countries increased marginally after the war, due to immigration. France took in many Jews from other parts of Europe and has the fourth-largest Jewish community in the world, after the USA, the former Soviet Union and Israel.

England is one of the few places in Europe where there has been no serious violence against Jews in the past three centuries. In 1990, there were 356 congregations in the United Kingdom, with a total membership of more than 100,000 households. The continuing decline in the overall numbers of Jewish people throughout Europe is due to emigration to Israel and low birth rates .

Modern Judaism is marked in parts of Europe by a move away from traditional mainstream Jewish orthodoxy but an increase in halachically observant or right-wing Orthodox, and in Sephardi, Reform and Liberal adherence.

MUSLIMS AND JEWS IN EUROPE

COUNTRY	1939	1950	1991	1900	1980	2000[1]
AUSTRIA	550,000[2]	15,000	12,000	0	45,000	50,000
BELGIUM	60,000	34,500	30,000	0	110,000	120,000
DENMARK	6,000	7,000	9,000	0	13,000	16,000
FRANCE	275,000	230,000	600,000	50,000	1,653,000	2,175,000
GERMANY	550,000[2]	74,000	28,400	0	1,488,500[3]	1,788,500
GREECE	80,000	10,000	4,800	390,000	134,000	134,000
HUNGARY	444,567	180,000	80,000	0	2,000	2,000
ITALY	647,825	46,000	34,500	1,000	45,500	49,000
NETHERLANDS	120,000	30,000	25,000	200	142,000	192,000
POLAND	3,325,000	94,000	6,000	500	1,080	2,000
ROMANIA	900,000	360,000	23,000	91,000	270,000	300,000
SPAIN	6,000	3,500	12,000	1,000	5,500	7,000
SWITZERLAND	17,973	29,000	18,300	400	17,600	20,000
UK	370,000	450,000	330,000	0	830,000	1,130,000
YUGOSLAVIA	72,000	10-12,000	5,500	1,048,000	2,329,000	2,360,000

☐ Jewish   ☐ Muslim

1 Projections based on UN figs.   2 This fig. is Austria & Germany combined

Is God dead?

A high incidence of religious belief does not necessarily equate with church attendance. Over the last ten years, church attendance has declined in many countries in the West, with the notable exception of Italy. Nine out of ten people in most European countries profess Christianity, but fewer than one in ten attend church regularly.

Until the early 1970s, repeated opinion polls, reports and surveys showed continued movement away from religion and a corresponding growth in atheism and agnosticism. The chart

below indicates that while the Irish are set to remain the most steadfastly godfearing people in western Europe, sizeable atheist or agnostic minorities are predicted for other countries. However, events in the Soviet Union and the collapse of communism, a doctrine founded on atheism, indicate that this forecast may not be fulfilled and that the atheistic trend may be reversing. Even so, formal hierarchical religions may not find favour again, as people seek alternatives to traditional forms of worship. Many westerners are finding spiritual comfort in religions from Asia.

GROWTH OF NON-BELIEF
% of population non-religious/atheist

☐ 1900   ☐ 2000[1]

1 Projections based on UN figs.

27									GERMANY
24								ITALY	
21						NETHERLANDS	FRANCE		
18					UK				
15				POLAND					
12									
9			SPAIN						
6									
3	IRELAND								
0	0.0	0.6	0.0	0.1	1.9	1.5	0.3	0.2	0.3

Women priests are not tolerated by the Roman Catholic or Orthodox church, and it seems unlikely that this policy will change. Most countries with a majority of Reformed, Lutheran or other Protestant churches have had women ministers for over 20 years. Norway's Lutheran church has had a small number of women priests since 1961. In the Protestant church of Sweden, ordination of women has been permitted since 1959, and seven woman had been ordained by 1963, although a third of the established male clergy refused to cooperate with them. The Anglican church, part of the Church of England, is currently debating the issue, with the incumbent archbishop of Canterbury as a supporter.

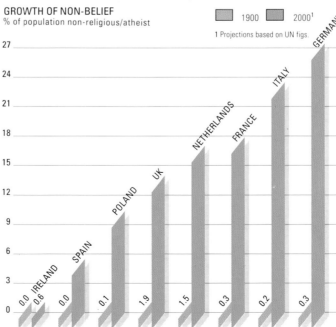

The gilded statue of Buddha dominates the Buddhist temple in London, England. Buddhism is older than Christianity: Siddharta Gautama, the Buddha (meaning founder) was born in what is now Nepal sometime in the 5th or 6th century BC. Buddhism spread throughout India, China, Tibet, Japan, Thailand, Burma, Cambodia and Vietnam, but did not reach the USA and the West until the 1900s. Today there are around 300m Buddhists in the world. The precepts of Buddhism – generosity, patience, loving kindness, working to banish greed and ignorance, and following the middle way between self-indulgence and self-denial – are proving very attractive to westerners .

EDUCATION

Although the first seven years of a child's life is the most important in terms of learning, the investment in good quality pre-primary and primary education varies widely across Europe.

With the demise of communism, the movement towards European unity and competition from the Far East, governments recognise that a well-educated and trained workforce is essential.

But in the best traditions of the diverse continent, they set about the task in different ways. Across Europe there is little agreement on fundamentals. How long pupils should stay in compulsory education, what they should be taught, how and when, whether the education system is centralised or administered locally, are all questions that each nation answers differently. France is moving towards decentralisation and is relaxing curriculum restraints. The French government is committed to increasing apprenticeship training and raising the status of technical education. In the summer of 1991, measures were introduced to give unqualified young people the right to receive between 200 and 1,000 hours' training. In the UK, power is being stripped from local education authorities and brought back to central government, which has imposed a national curriculum as well as testing for 7, 11, 14 and 16 year-olds amid fears of declining standards in reading, writing and arithmetic. Spain is seeking to bridge the current gap between academic and technical education at 14 while raising the school leaving age to 16. Teachers in countries such as former East Germany, Czechoslovakia and Hungary are suddenly terrified of the freedom they have been given to select books and subjects.

There is agreement, however, on the importance of foreign language, technical and vocational training.

Most schools in Europe introduce a second language at the age of 10 or 11. Romania is unusual in that pupils begin to learn another language at the age of 6. France, Italy, Spain and Germany are just introducing a second language at primary level. The UK, near the bottom of the class for language learning, has made a second language part of the national curriculum in secondary schools, while smaller nations like Denmark, Finland and the Netherlands have always had a impressive record as linguists.

English as a language continues to dominate the European scene. It is replacing Russian as a second language in Poland, Hungary and Czechoslovakia. Consequently there is a tremendous demand for teachers and former Russian specialists are retraining to teach English. Czechoslovakia needs to recruit another 10,000 teachers and Poland will have to double that number to meet the demand.

The EC is now attempting to stem the tide of English. Yet another programme, Lingua, is aimed at improving foreign language teaching, but it gives priority to minority languages such as Irish and Luxembourgish.

It has long been acknowledged that western Germany has one of the best vocational training systems in Europe. Nine out of ten school leavers get some vocational training, usually splitting the week between college and ▷

School timetables

The map shows the total number of years spent in compulsory education and the amount of time spent respectively in first and second level schooling.

Overall, Europe expects its children to undergo just over eight years compulsory education on average. When this begins and ends, how it is shared between primary and secondary levels, and at what age children move from one level to the next, differs in most countries. In the Netherlands and the UK, pupils are legally obliged to begin school at the age of 5; most of the rest of Europe opts for 6, except Scandinavia, where 7 is preferred. In fact, most European children begin their schooling before the statutory age, attending pre-school groups from the age of 3, but it is difficult to separate the figures for day care from those for formal pre-school education. Participation is usually highest at this period just before compulsory school age. According to 1987 figures, in Belgium and France, virtually all 3–5 year-olds took part in education, while Norway achieved the highest day care rate at 43%; over half of all 3–5 year-olds in Europe were in full-time education; only the Finns and the Swedes kept the majority of their infants at home.

The changeover from primary to secondary schooling usually occurs at about the age of 12. The UK has reverted to its old system of moving its pupils up at the age of 11, after flirting with the 12 year limit in the early 1980s. Poland keeps its pupils in first level education until the age of 14. Minimum school leaving ages also vary. In Belgium and Italy it is 14, in Germany it is 15, but in most of Europe it is 16. Portugal and Albania do not have compulsory secondary education. Most 16 year-olds elect to go on to some form of higher education or training.

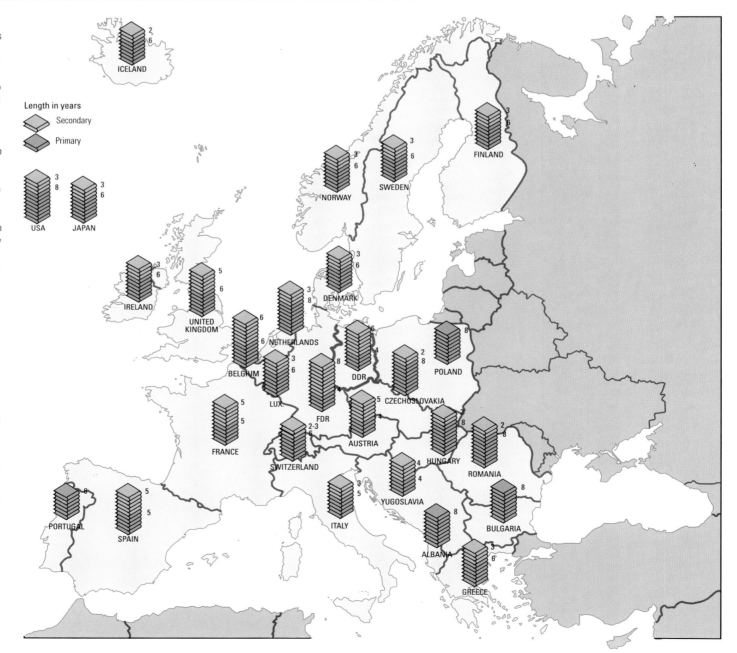

An apple for the teacher

In 1981, Britain led the field in the drive to make computers accessible to young children by starting a "Micros in School" project, which aimed to provide every primary school with at least one computer. Since then other countries have caught up or taken over by investing in newer computer technology.

An EC survey in 1990 has found that on average four out of ten young Europeans know how to use a computer. One in three in Britain claims to be able to use a computer or word processor "fairly well or better", with the European average at 21%.

The longer students stay on at school, the more likely they are to be familiar with computers: 58% of those studying till 17 had no contact with information technology compared with 28% of those finishing at 18. More women than men claim to know about computers: 44% compared to 37%.

KNOWLEDGE OF INFORMATION TECHNOLOGY

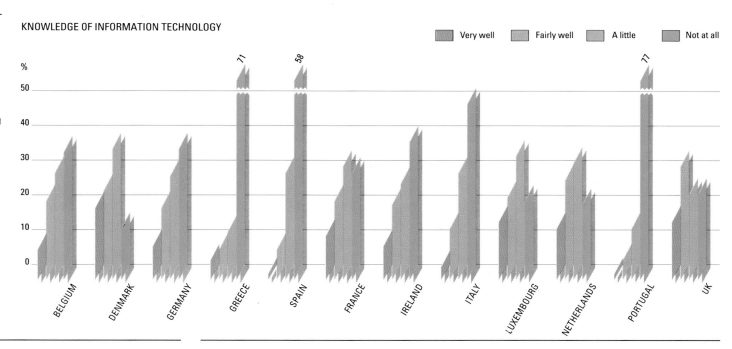

Legend: Very well | Fairly well | A little | Not at all

INVESTMENT IN LEARNING

Financial commitment to education is essential to economic growth; how much a country is prepared to spend on education (meaning primary and secondary in this case), how many pupils it can cater for, how many teachers it can train and how many pupils emerging from the secondary education system go on to higher education (all indicated in the chart below) are reliable pointers to the level of this commitment. Denmark, Norway, Finland and Ireland are the biggest spenders, all over 4% of GDP. (Sweden spends a total of 7.19% on education overall, but the figure is not statistically broken down.) The more pupils in higher education, the better qualified the workforce. The number of students enrolling for higher education between 1980 and 1988 rose in most European countries. Notable exceptions are Hungary, Romania and Yugoslavia, where numbers actually declined; in Bulgaria and former East Germany, numbers rose respectively by 8% and 4.5% of the relevant age group.

MAIN POINTERS

COUNTRY	EXPEND.[a]	PUPILS[b]	TEACHERS[c]	H.E.[d]
AUSTRIA	3.82	129	16.6	230
BELGIUM	3.62[1]	156	18.8[3]	493
DENMARK	4.78	169	12.2	434
FINLAND	4.16	168[4]	—	435
FRANCE	3.01[2]	175	11.6[2]	344
GERMANY	2.54	144	8.6	296
GREECE	1.97[2]	—	—	328[2]
IRELAND	4.22[2]	217[4]	10.0	288[2,4]
ITALY	2.70[2]	152	14.7	269
LUXEMBOURG	1.35	132	10.1	—
NETHERLANDS	3.46[1]	167	12.4	394
NORWAY	4.49	164	18.0	—
PORTUGAL	3.21	149[2]	—	—
SPAIN	—	208	8.5	347
SWEDEN	—	145	14.3	716
TURKEY	1.37[3]	192	6.9	157
UK	3.44	156	10.8	347
YUGOSLAVIA	2.75	162	8.5	266

| JAPAN | 3.45[2] | 178 | 9.0 | 375 |
| USA | — | 170[2] | 9.6[2] | 644[2] |

a Expenditure on public education as % of GDP
b Primary and secondary pupils per 1,000 population
c Primary/ Secondary teacher no. per 1,000 population
d No. entering higher education per 1,000 age group

1 Inc. public expenditure on private education, and pre-primary figs.
2 1986-87
3 Includes pre-primary figs.
4 Includes full-time only.

Class distinction

It is a maxim universally acknowledged by educationalists that the lower the pupil-teacher ratio, the better the teaching. One of the main selling points of private education, particularly in the UK, is its claimed low pupil-teacher ratios. The chart opposite shows the progress Europe has made in improving teacher-pupil ratios between 1980 and 1988. The Netherlands has had spectacular success in the primary field, as has Poland; and western Germany's ratio actually rose slightly, but most countries stayed about the same. In secondary education, Austria, Belgium, Greece and Finland shaved a significant amount off their ratios; Bulgaria's ratio worsened. Low or at least stable figures are not always the result of more teachers being trained or more schools being built; as the birth rate is dropping in Europe, ratios fall automatically as fewer children are available for teaching. As these figures are an average, they will not reflect the classroom experience of pupils in inner-city schools or under-resourced areas.

PUPIL-TEACHER RATIOS

COUNTRY	PRIMARY		SECONDARY	
AUSTRIA	15	11	12	8
BELGIUM	18	14	10	6
BULGARIA	19	17	13	17
CZECHOSLOVAKIA	21	21	13	12
DENMARK	12	12	11	9
FINLAND	14	—	17	14
FRANCE	21	19	13	14
GERMANY E.	16	17	13	10
GERMANY W.	17	18	14	12
GREECE	24	23	20	16
HUNGARY	15	14	13	12
IRELAND	29	27	16	16
ITALY	16	13	11	9
LUXEMBOURG	14	12	12	10
NETHERLANDS	23	17	15	14
POLAND	21	16	13	12
PORTUGAL	18	16	12	12
SPAIN	28	25	21	21
SWEDEN	16	16	11	12
UK	20	20	15	14
YUGOSLAVIA	24	23	17	14

| JAPAN | 25 | 22 | 17 | 18 |
| USA | 22 | 22 | 14 | 13 |

1980 | 1988

SPEAKING EACH OTHER'S LANGUAGE

Although English is the most widely spoken foreign language, young Europeans now list it as fourth in languages they would like to learn. German is the most popular. In France, nine out of ten pupils opt for English as their first or second foreign language. A recent EC survey shows that only 10% of 15–24 year-olds have not learned a foreign language compared with 44% of over 25 year-olds. According to the EC survey, the majority of students thought that language teaching in schools was inadequate.

In Britain, a separate survey of 12–16 year-olds in December 1991 found that French had risen from bottom to third place behind maths and English as the most useful school subject compared to the previous year. More than half of the 3,000 youngsters in the survey said they wanted to work abroad – more girls than boys.

LANGUAGE FLUENCY

Average number of foreign languages spoken by young people

COUNTRY	LANGUAGES	
BELGIUM	2.2	1.1
DENMARK	2.5	1.8
FRANCE	1.8	0.9
GERMANY	1.3	0.9
GREECE	1.1	0.7
IRELAND	0.9	0.4
ITALY	1.4	0.7
LUXEMBOURG	3.1	2.7
NETHERLANDS	2.5	1.6
PORTUGAL	1.3	0.8
SPAIN	1.2	0.6
UK	1.3	0.5

Learnt | Spoken

local firms, with employers bearing most of the cost. In former East Germany an apprenticeship was virtually guaranteed. But with the unification of Germany, the government is faced with the big challenge of bringing vocational training standards in the eastern half up to those in western Germany. And with the cushioning effect of a state-run economy gone, a generation of young eastern Germans face the prospect of unemployment. In January 1992, 1,343,449 people were out of work in the former GDR, about 16.5% of the workforce. In March 1991, only 40,000 training places were available for 120,000 school leavers.

Higher education

The last two decades have seen the "democratisation" of formerly elite tertiary or higher education as governments, for political as well as economic reasons, encouraged more and more young people to stay on after secondary school.

But with institutions now creaking under the expansionary strain and lecture theatres overflowing, quality has become the burning issue of the 1990s: how to maintain standards while teaching more students with fewer staff and less money. Mass teaching methods, new technology, quality assurance procedures and performance indicators are the new buzzwords.

Ambitious student participation rates lose effectiveness when offset by poor degrees, high drop-out rates and an ever increasing demand for highly qualified manpower, in a Europe whose social structure, cultural values and economy is changing fast.

While the number of European Community students nearly doubled to 6.75m in the 16 years from 1970 to 1971, rising from 13% to 20% of the relevant age group, the EC still faces growing skills shortages (quantitative and qualitative) at all levels, but particularly in science and technology. Demand for engineers in Spain is forecast to grow by 3.5% per annum in the 1990s, for example, and the EC is calling for still more students and for major skills upgrading and updating initiatives to counter its ageing

---

Higher education

The charts show who studies what in higher education (HE) and the accompanying tables give other facts about tertiary education.

Legend:
- Natural Sciences, Engineering & Agriculture
- Law & Social Sciences
- Education
- Medical Sciences
- Humanities
- Unspecified

BELGIUM

Students per 100,000 pop.	1980	2,111
	1988	2,566
Enrolment ratios	1980	26.0%
	1988	33.8%
% University students	1988	41%
Teachers	1980	No data
	1988	19,452
HE expenditure as % of total	1980	17.3%
	1988	17.6%

CZECHOSLOVAKIA

Students per 100,000 pop.	1980	1,287
	1988	1,193
Enrolment ratios	1980	17.4%
	1988	17.2%
% University students	1988	100%(?)
Teachers	1980	22,478
	1988	25,350
HE expenditure as % of total	1980	16.1%
	1988	15.9%

DENMARK

Students per 100,000 pop.	1980	2,074
	1988	2,385
Enrolment ratios	1980	28.3%
	1988	30.6%
% University students	1988	79%
Teachers	1980	No data
	1988	No data
HE expenditure as % of total	1980	17.6%
	1988	20.4%

GERMANY EAST

Students per 100,000 pop.	1980	2,395
	1988	2,645
Enrolment ratios	1980	29.9%
	1988	34.4%
% University students	1988	36%
Teachers	1980	38,699
	1988	42,702
HE expenditure as % of total	1980	20.5%
	1988	24.3%

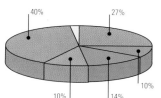

GERMANY WEST

Students per 100,000 pop.	1980	1,987
	1988	2,779
Enrolment ratios	1980	25.6%
	1988	32.2%
% University students	1988	87%
Teachers	1980	171,708
	1988	198,241
HE expenditure as % of total	1980	15.1%
	1988	21.5%

GREECE

Students per 100,000 pop.	1980	1,256
	1988	1,896
Enrolment ratios	1980	17.1%
	1988	27.2%
% University students	1988	62%
Teachers	1980	10,542
	1988	12,760
HE expenditure as % of total	1980	20.4%
	1988	19.8%

HUNGARY

Students per 100,000 pop.	1980	945
	1988	956
Enrolment ratios	1980	14.1%
	1988	14.0%
% University students	1988	65%
Teachers	1980	13,890
	1988	16,319
HE expenditure as % of total	1980	19.3%
	1988	14.3%

ITALY

Students per 100,000 pop.	1980	1,981
	1988	2,263
Enrolment ratios	1980	27.0%
	1988	26.3%
% University students	1988	99%
Teachers	1980	No data
	1988	53,855
HE expenditure as % of total	1980	9.1%
	1988	10.3%

POLAND

Students per 100,000 pop.	1980	1,656
	1988	1,320
Enrolment ratios	1980	18.1%
	1988	19.7%
% University students	1988	81%
Teachers	1980	No data
	1988	No data
HE expenditure as % of total	1980	23.6%
	1988	20.4%

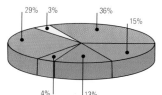

PORTUGAL

Students per 100,000 pop.	1980	944
	1988	1.267
Enrolment ratios	1980	10.7%
	1988	17.6%
% University students	1988	75%
Teachers	1980	10,695
	1988	11,072
HE expenditure as % of total	1980	10.5%
	1988	15.3%

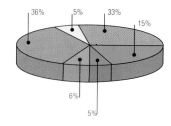

ROMANIA

Students per 100,000 pop.	1980	868
	1988	686
Enrolment ratios	1980	12.1%
	1988	8.2%
% University students	1988	100%
Teachers	1980	14,592
	1988	12,036
HE expenditure as % of total	1980	No data
	1988	9.7%

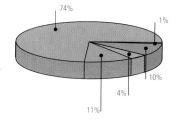

SPAIN

Students per 100,000 pop.	1980	1,859
	1988	2,665
Enrolment ratios	1980	23.2%
	1988	31.6%
% University students	1988	94%
Teachers	1980	42,831
	1988	52,206
HE expenditure as % of total	1980	14.0%
	1988	No data

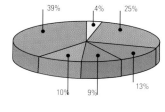

SWEDEN

Students per 100,000 pop.	1980	2,062
	1988	2,209
Enrolment ratios	1980	30.8%
	1988	31.3%
% University students	1988	No data
Teachers	1980	No data
	1988	No data
HE expenditure as % of total	1980	9.3%
	1988	12.7%

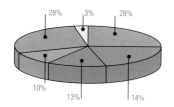

UK

Students per 100,000 pop.	1980	1,468
	1988	1,913
Enrolment ratios	1980	19.1%
	1988	23.5%
% University students	1988	34%
Teachers	1980	No data
	1988	89,136
HE expenditure as % of total	1980	22.4%
	1988	19.3%

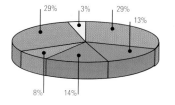

and declining population. The rise of the polytechnic is an attempt to solve this problem.

Mobility of Europe's people is crucial to its economic success, as well as to its social cohesiveness. Higher education has responded eagerly to a surge of EC initiatives ranging from student exchange and language learning to advanced research which in just a few years have given rise to a mass of programmes costing billions of ecus.

While this is all very well, as is often the case with the EC, high ideals outstrip practical realities. Academic recognition is still in its infancy, jeopardising the labour mobility guaranteed under the Treaty of Rome. For instance, the same qualification may take three years in Britain, five in Italy and six to seven in Germany. Many students have wasted time on courses not credited in their home countries, and student mobility is beginning to cause funding strains for popular host countries.

Mutual recognition of professional qualifications has been achieved, however, based on higher education courses lasting three years, and academic recognition is being slowly built up through organisations such as the European University Network, the EC Course Credit Transfer System and a network of national academic information centres.

While the European momentum is towards convergence, international comparisons highlight vast differences in tertiary systems both within the EC and between the Community and its competitors. Levels of public spending per student, for example, range from only 30% of per capita GDP in France to 50% in Austria, Switzerland and Australia, 70% in Ireland, 80% in the Netherlands and the United Kingdom, and nearly 120% in Japan. Student participation rates vary from 25% of the relevant age group in Italy to 40% in Sweden, while proportions of students qualifying – one criterion of the performance of higher education – range from around 8% in Spain to 16% in the Netherlands, and 29% in the UK.

Although the problems facing a convergence in European higher education are patently enormous, there is a genuine attempt to construct a pan-European approach to meet the growing need for a skilled workforce.

THE RISE OF THE POLYTECHNIC

In the 1980s, British polytechnics increasingly shifted to degree-level and postgraduate work and, in 1992, were given university status. In Germany, *fachhochschulen* teach 343,000 of the country's nearly 1.5m students and offer practical higher diploma and degree courses of three to four years in most subject areas. France has 68 polytechnic-type University Institutes of Technology, which have 65,000 students and award diplomas of technology, mainly in industry and commerce; in the Netherlands, there are nearly 95 *hogescholen*, closely linked to industry and commerce; Portugal has 14 *institutos politecnicos* offering three-year courses, short diplomas and certificates; and Greece has two polytechnics and 11 technical education institutes.

Several former socialist countries are planning to expand their systems. Former East German states are planning at least ten new *fachhochschulen*, using the British model, while Hungary has been investigating the German system.

The concept of the polytechnic or institute for multi-technical learning grew out of the industrial revolution of the 19th century in response to the need for skilled workers. Today more than a million students are on applied degree courses at polytechnic-style institutions around Europe. The polytechnic brief is to produce graduates who combine both applied and academic knowledge, especially scientists and managers, for rapidly modernising economies in a shorter time than most European universities, and at lower cost. A secondary aim is to widen the social pool of young people entering higher education and to improve access for mature students. Lecture halls filled with mixed-age audiences, like the one in Germany (above) will soon be the norm.

LEARNING ON THE MOVE

With the advent of electronic mail and cheaper computer technology there is a burgeoning of links between schools and colleges throughout the whole of Europe and an increasing interest in pupil and teacher exchanges.

In just five years, EC tertiary initiatives have burgeoned from literally nothing to a mass of programmes. Among them are the European Community Action Scheme for the Mobility of University Students (Erasmus), which helps around 45,000 students a year to study in another EC country and has as its target 10% of all EC students; and the second Community Programme for Education and Training in Technology (Comett), encouraging university and industry links, which has a 230m ecu budget for 5,000 courses. The Petra initiative has helped 10,000 young people to exchange places on training schemes, and the Youth for Europe scheme has produced nearly 3,000 exchanges among 15–25 year-olds. The Tempus programme promotes the development of higher education in eastern Europe through links with western institutions, particularly in management, business studies, applied economics, science and languages. In 1990 the budget was 70.5m ecus which funded 3,800 student exchanges and 4,500 teacher exchanges. New programmes will include EFTA countries as well as central and eastern Europe.

STUDENT MOBILITY INTRA EC, 1988

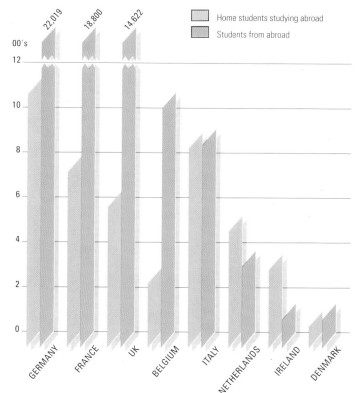

Legend: Home students studying abroad / Students from abroad

Bar chart values: 22,019 (Germany) 18,800 (France) 14,622 (UK). Axis labelled 00's, from 0 to 12.
Countries: GERMANY, FRANCE, UK, BELGIUM, ITALY, NETHERLANDS, IRELAND, DENMARK

COUNTRY	1989
BELGIUM	374.0[1]
DENMARK	284.8
FINLAND	259.7
FRANCE	2,856.5
GERMANY	3,777.2
GREECE	119.8
ICELAND	10.3
IRELAND	50.2
ITALY	1,968.0
NETHERLANDS	945.0
NORWAY	308.9
PORTUGAL	111.5[1]
SPAIN	623.6
SWEDEN	1,076.0
SWITZERLAND	676.7
TURKEY	212.3
UK	2,844.1
YUGOSLAVIA	205.9

JAPAN	10,406.9
US	22,169.5

1 1988 figs.

LEISURE

Unsurprisingly consumer expenditure on leisure seems to go hand in glove with the economic cycle of boom and bust. The gloom of the early 1980s swiftly gave way to a "feel good" factor between 1985 and 1990 which has again faded in the early 1990s. Only countries with their own specific economic difficulties like Greece and Denmark bucked the trend. As a percentage of overall expenditure, spending on leisure remained constant at about 8% over Europe as a whole.

Expenditure on leisure activities is clearly dependent on a combination of available time and money. During the 1980s the average number of hours worked per week in European cities was 39.1 compared with an international average of 41.4. Working weeks in Latin America (42.7) and the Far East (45.5) are on the whole much longer. The same trend also holds true for annual leave with the number of days of paid leave across Europe increasing during the 1980s. While the average has increased by about three days since the end of the 1980s, in a number of countries including the UK, it has increased by as much as a week. The average number of total days leave across Europe is now 34.7 with Germany top with 40 and Ireland lagging behind on 28. Greek workers have now caught up with the main stream and receive up to two weeks more leave than in the 1970s.

While consumer expenditure on sports equipment grew strongly during this period, brown goods such as TVs, videos, camcorders and CD players saw the strongest growth. Although some of these products approached market saturation, most are expected to continue to grow into the 1990s. TVs in particular will be boosted by a market in second sets and satellite dishes. International sporting events, such as the 1990 soccer World Cup, also stimulate considerable demand in successful participating countries; satellite equipment sales in the UK were a notable beneficiary of the 1992 cricket World Cup.

Watching TV remained Europe's most popular leisure activity with almost every European putting in at least seven hours a week in front of the TV. Deregulation across Europe has meant the breaking of state-controlled monopolies and the strong growth of commercial TV. This in turn has meant an aggressive pursuit of audiences so as to maximise profit from advertising revenue.

Tourism continued to grow into the late 1980s with the market for foreign travel increasing with each year. By far the biggest Eurospenders on tourism are western Germans. Spain tops the ranking as the country with the largest income from tourism.

Keep on running…the annual London Marathon draws its customary huge entry field from all over the world. Jogging, running, fitness classes and sport in general has become a very popular leisure activity for all age groups over the past decade.

Fun money

Consumer expenditure on leisure over the period followed the economic cycle of boom and bust with the strongest growth throughout Europe coming between 1985 and 1996 (see below). Only Denmark and Greece bucked the trend due to localised economic difficulties during this period. Western Germans were the heaviest spenders per head at 1,021 ecus, with the Portuguese at 180 ecus at the bottom of the pile. The European average was 697 ecus. France led the pack in growth terms.

Couch potato glut

TV watching has become by far and away the most popular form of leisure activity throughout Europe, as can be seen from the chart below. In 1990 average daily hours of viewing ranged from 1.41 in Switzerland to 3.44 in Portugal.

Deregulation throughout Europe has meant a rapid growth in commercial TV and the dominance of state-controlled stations has been eroded. The share of the commercial audience is now approaching 100%; only in Finland, Norway and Sweden is it below 50%.

The vast majority of European adults watch between 7 and 20 hours of television a week. Easily top of the league table of tele-addicts who watch over 21 hours of TV a week are the UK with 42% of the adult population slumped on the sofa.

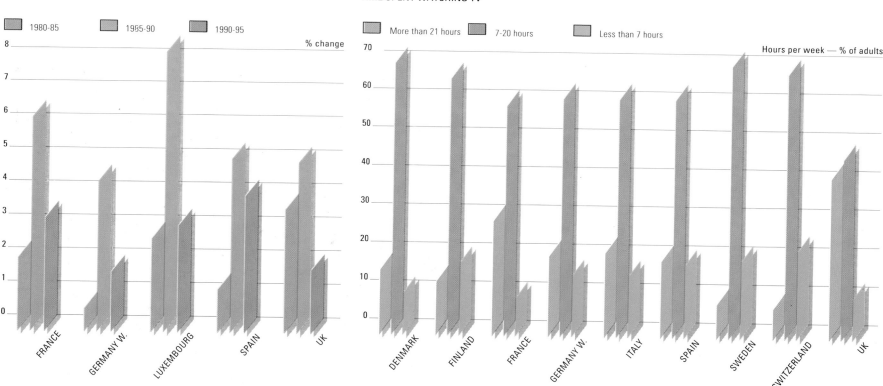

LEISURE EXPENDITURE TRENDS

■ 1980-85   ■ 1985-90   ■ 1990-95

% change

FRANCE   GERMANY W.   LUXEMBOURG   SPAIN   UK

TIME SPENT WATCHING TV

■ More than 21 hours   ■ 7-20 hours   ■ Less than 7 hours

Hours per week — % of adults

DENMARK   FINLAND   FRANCE   GERMANY W.   ITALY   SPAIN   SWEDEN   SWITZERLAND   UK

Connections: Airline travel 34–35   Media 82–83   Consumerism 236–237

Who owns the hardware

The map shows the distribution of the machinery of in-home entertainment throughout Europe. Sales of durables such as TVs, videos, CDs and home computers saw sustained growth during the late 1980s. Although by 1990, nine out of ten of most western European households had a TV, the market is still expected to grow into the mid-1990s sustained by sales of second sets and renewals. As eastern European economies recover, the demand for sets will increase. This effect could be seen in Germany in 1990 when the newly liberated East produced a consumer surge in electronic goods. CD players are set to become ever more popular. In 1990, one in five households in Europe had a CD player although dramatic regional variations are evident. The Netherlands lead the way with over 43% of households owning a CD player. On the other hand, only 5% of Greek households boasted such a luxury. Surprisingly the home computer market is still patchy. In the UK over one in every five households has one, but Spain, Portugal and Greece in particular lag far behind.

The map shows the percentage of households with a TV, CD player or home computer in 1990.

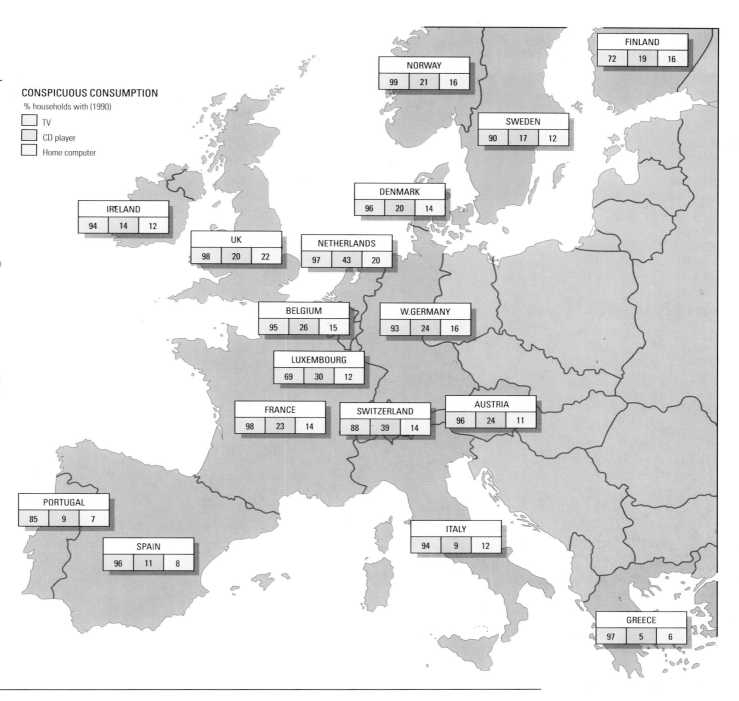

CONSPICUOUS CONSUMPTION
% households with (1990)
- TV
- CD player
- Home computer

TRAVELLERS CHEQUES

A comparison of money spent on tourism with money received reveals some interesting differences between European countries (see below). Western Germans are the most prolific spenders on holidays, $24.13bn in 1989, while Spanish coffers can boast Europe's highest net increase in tourist revenues. In 1989, the Spanish themselves spent only $3.08bn on tourism but saw $16.25bn pouring in. France, Italy and the UK also earn a lot from tourism. In 1989, they received $16.5bn, $11.99bn and $11.25bn respectively in tourism receipts. Perhaps due to their relative isolation from the rest of Europe, Finland and Ireland do least well receiving only £1.01bn and $1.07bn respectively over the same period. Between 1987 and 1989 money spent on holidays grew by 17%, but this rate of growth had fallen by 1991 and will not pick up dramatically until the middle of the decade. As eastern Europe continues to open up to the West, tourism to these countries will be encouraged as a source of much needed foreign currency.

The package holiday business revolutionised European vacation habits when it took off in the 1970s. Sunny resorts on the Mediterranean became affordable to more people and the economies of countries such as Spain and Greece (below) profited immensely.

TOURISM EXPENDITURE & RECEIPTS

COUNTRY	1987		1989	
AUSTRIA	5.59	8.86	5.03	9.31
BELGIUM & LUX	3.95	3.0	4.27	2.89
DENMARK	2.85	2.2	2.93	2.31
FINLAND	1.51	0.82	2.05	1.01
FRANCE	8.50	11.87	10.29	16.5
GERMANY W.	23.34	7.68	24.13	8.66
GREECE	0.51	2.28	0.82	2.0
IRELAND	0.82	0.84	0.99	1.07
ITALY	4.53	12.17	6.77	11.99
NETHERLANDS	6.42	2.70	6.45	3.20
NORWAY	3.07	1.26	2.85	1.33
PORTUGAL	0.42	2.15	0.56	2.59
SPAIN	1.95	14.79	3.08	16.25
SWEDEN	2.03	2.03	4.97	2.54
SWITZERLAND	4.37	5.38	4.95	5.62
UK	11.90	10.24	15.20	11.25

Expenditure in $ bn   Receipts $ bn

CONSUMERISM

The traditional home of state-of-the-art leisure hardware is Scandinavia. Few people can afford the advanced touch-activated TVs, sound and video systems produced by the Danish company Bang & Olufsen; however, there is a television in almost every home in Europe – Norway is the nearest to saturation point with 99% of households containing a set.

With the exception of eastern Europe, the late 1980s were boom years for the individual Euro-consumer. Although spending in the early 1980s was depressed by a recession-hit Europe, confidence blossomed from 1985 to 1990 and dramatic growth rates were recorded in most categories of consumer spending. A credit boom was led by the UK where the number of credit cards in circulation increased by nearly 10m between 1985 and 1989. From a smaller base this trend could be also observed in France, Italy and western Germany. Low interest rates also fuelled demand. By the early 1990s demand had slowed as boom had turned into recession. The mid-1990s promise a return to sustained consumer demand but without the bullish self-confidence of the boom years.

As "Europhoria" took hold the traditional dominance of the American consumer began to be challenged. Real private spending increased by an average of 3.7% a year in Europe and total spending reached near parity. This situation is expected to be sustained into the mid-1990s. Nonetheless, the combination of a higher population with a higher average cost of living means that the spending power of the average Euro-citizen is still significantly less than their US equivalent.

In western Germany, the strongest European economy, low taxes and falling unemployment sustained the boom. Mass immigration from eastern Germany fuelled this for a while but growth into the 1990s will be slowed by the heavy cost of unification.

The free-spending consumer of the late 1980s spread his money widely but trends are easily discernible. Health was the fastest growing category in most countries. This was largely due to escalating costs and the increasing numbers of elderly people requiring care. The desire of many governments to extend the cost burden into the private sector necessarily increased consumer spending, a trend which is liable to continue.

The material quality of life

Brown goods such as TVs, videos, camcorders, CD players, etc saw sustained growth during the later years of the decade although sales of videos peaked in some countries as the percentage of household penetration reached high levels. The demand for TVs is expected to be sustained and technological advances in video and audio products should keep demand healthy. After a slow start to the decade, demand for household durables, such as washing machines, fridges, cookers, etc, also grew strongly. The rise in the number of smaller households has also meant that durables are changed less often although changes in eating habits has meant a dramatic

Spending powers

The map shows the percentage of adults who own bank accounts and cash dispenser cards. The chart below indicates the number of people who own credit cards (Eurocard, Mastercard and Visa). The availability of cash and credit grew strongly throughout Europe in the late 1980s. The credit boom was at its most marked in the UK where the number of credit cards in circulation grew from over 20m in 1985 to over 30m in 1989. Although from a smaller base, the same percentage increase was observed in France, Italy and West Germany, with France the biggest of the plastic users.

Most Europeans now have a bank account although the mattress still has its place in Greece, Spain, Portugal and even Italy. Ease of access to banked money has been improved with the widespread acceptance of cash dispensing cards. Only in Greece are they a rarity.

CREDIT CARD OWNERSHIP

COUNTRY	('000s)
AUSTRIA	293
BELGIUM	488
DENMARK	405
FINLAND	59
FRANCE	8,559
GERMANY W.	1,259
GREECE	240
ICELAND	607
IRELAND	889
ITALY	1,079
LUXEMBOURG	316
NETHERLANDS	523
PORTUGAL	42
SPAIN	879
SWEDEN	1,870
SWITZERLAND	697
UK	28,994
YUGOSLAVIA	382

BANK ACCOUNT OWNERSHIP

% adults with
- Bank accounts
- Cash dispenser cards

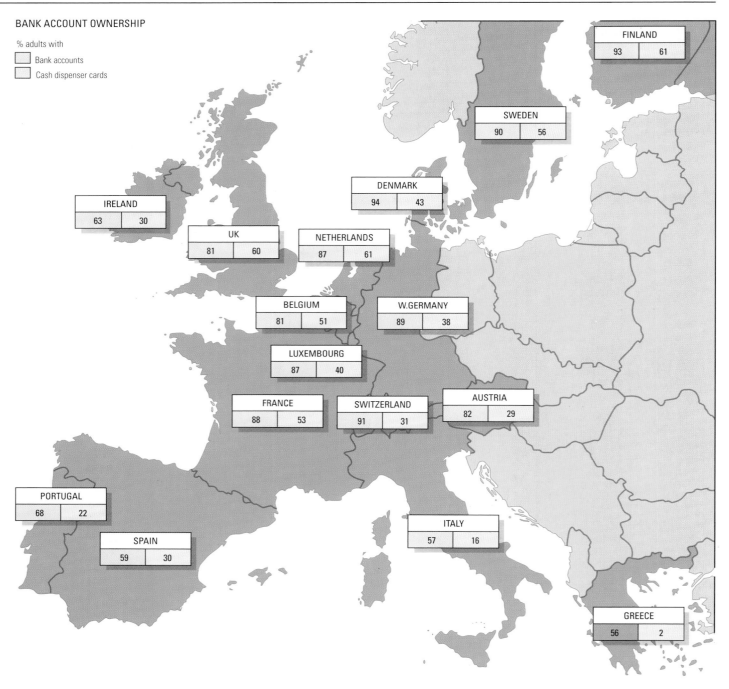

	Bank accounts	Cash dispenser cards
FINLAND	93	61
SWEDEN	90	56
DENMARK	94	43
IRELAND	63	30
UK	81	60
NETHERLANDS	87	61
BELGIUM	81	51
W.GERMANY	89	38
LUXEMBOURG	87	40
FRANCE	88	53
SWITZERLAND	91	31
AUSTRIA	82	29
PORTUGAL	68	22
SPAIN	59	30
ITALY	57	16
GREECE	56	2

Connections: Banking 98–99   Leisure 234–235

increase in spending on microwaves.

As they felt richer, consumers spent less as a proportion of their total expenditure on food for consumption at home and more in restaurants and hotels. What they did spend on produce for consumption at home tended to be on healthier products. This meant less red meat, sugar, tea and coffee, and more fish, whole grains, fruit and vegetables. The non-alcoholic drinks market also saw spectacular growth.

Spending on cars increased throughout the late 1980s, but the market has now begun to stagnate. The tax policies of individual countries towards the car make it a difficult category to predict. In Denmark and Greece, for example, taxation in the 1980s was particularly severe while in the UK a policy of lower personal taxes combined with reduced tax breaks on items like company cars will herald significant changes in that market.

A number of markets saw trends towards products with packaging which caused less of a strain on the environment. This was particularly true of cleaning products and is set to continue at a more modest rate of growth throughout the 1990s. Although the western European consumer goods market is highly developed, the eastern European one is not, and this is where the biggest changes should take place.

THAT'S THE WAY THE MONEY GOES

The chart below shows the percentage change in annual average spending by sector. The number of privately-owned cars grew strongly during the latter half of the period but is stagnating in the early 1990s. Trends are difficult to both analyse and predict due to the widely differing approaches to taxation between countries.

Spending on non-alcoholic beverages increased by almost 60% from 1985 to 1990. This trend was caused by a combination of hot summers and a healthier attitude towards food and drink. Growth will continue but at more modest rates.

Spending on alcohol has always been linked to the differing taxation policies of European governments. Health concerns have meant that a higher percentage of consumer spending has gone on low-alcohol drinks and alcoholic drinks of higher quality. A trend can be observed towards non-traditional drinks of foreign origin due to reductions in the tax on imports. While the market for household durables fared well in the mid-1980s when there was a credit boom, the credit squeeze of the early 1990s affected sales badly across all countries hit by the economic conditions.

CONSUMER EXPENDITURE BY CATEGORY

SECTOR	1980-85	1985-90	1990-95
FOOD	0.6	1.8	1.4
NON-ALCOHOLIC BEVERAGES	3.5	7.2	3.5
ALCOHOL	0.1	0.7	0.6
TOBACCO	-0.6	-0.2	-0.5
CLOTHING/FOOTWEAR	0.3	2.0	2.1
ENERGY	1.5	0.2	1.4
HOUSEHOLD DURABLES	-0.4	4.5	2.4
HOUSEHOLD OPERATION	1.0	2.7	2.2
HEALTH	3.9	5.1	3.4
LEISURE	1.8	5.2	2.6
EDUCATION	1.0	4.6	3.2
PERSONAL TRANSPORT	2.8	6.4	2.0
HOTELS/CATERING	2.2	4.4	2.4
PERSONAL CARE	2.2	4.5	2.7
OTHER	1.4	5.7	3.8
TOTAL	1.4	3.6	2.5

CONSUMER EXPENDITURE TRENDS

COUNTRY	1983	1988	1993	1983-88	1988-93
BELGIUM	54	97	147	79	51
DENMARK	31	58	86	89	49
FRANCE	318	567	883	78	56
GERMANY W.	378	658	1,025	74	56
GREECE	24	37	58	51	59
IRELAND	11	18	27	64	52
ITALY	254	503	811	98	61
LUXEMBOURG	2	4	5	79	48
NETHERLANDS	81	137	204	74	49
PORTUGAL	14	26	42	85	58
SPAIN	103	213	330	106	55
UK	280	513	771	83	50

☐ $ bn   ☐ % increase

BOOM AND BUST

Although cyclical by nature, the surge seen in consumer spending in the late 1980s was very strong, particularly in the UK (see chart above). In western Germany, consumers spent heavily if erratically on cars while spending on health also grew faster than the average. While the boom in personal transport has slowed, spending on health is projected to increase. At reunification, consumer spending in eastern Germany was about half that in western Germany. This figure is expected to rise to about 65% by 1995 as living standards eventually rise and even out through the country.

In France, the boom years were characterised by heavy private spending on health, private transport and leisure. While health and leisure expenditure is expected to grow at a more modest rate, spending on cars has stagnated. In the UK, the pattern was similar if more marked, and the ensuing slowdown has meant a deeper recession than in the rest of Europe. The timing of recovery is difficult to predict although 1993 should see some modest growth.

In Italy, in the late 1980s consumer spending rose by nearly 20% per head. Much of this was spent on leisure, personal care and cars. But, in common with the rest of Europe, Italy experienced a slowdown in the early 1990s.

Out in the cold ... a graveyard for household appliances in Spain shows the other face of consumerism. If you do not waste, you will not want, and consumer durables are designed to wear out physically or fall into planned obsolescence so that more can be sold. Between 1986 and 1988, 94% of Spanish households owned at least one refrigerator and one washing machine, and 98% owned a television set. Freezers and refrigerators are particularly difficult to scrap, as the CFCs that are the primary coolant are inimical to the environment and must be handled with special care.

FAMILY

¡Feliz Cumpleanos! A birthday picnic in Andalucia. Strongly Catholic countries such as Spain, Italy and Ireland have low (or non-existent) divorce rates and comparatively high birth rates. The resulting large, often extended, families can no longer be called the norm in Europe but form part of the idealised notion of family cherished by many people.

Since the 1960s, there has been a dramatic change across Europe in the attitude towards the definition of a family. The convention of a stable nuclear family unit (breadwinner husband married to housewife with two children) has been called into question by a diversity of rival sexual and social arrangements. The concept of the family is having to grow to absorb increasing numbers of cohabitees, single parents, step-families, homosexual relationships and other chosen home groupings which are claiming positions in mainstream culture.

Marriage, although still the most common domestic arrangement, no longer commands the popularity it once did. Within the European Community, after reaching a peak in 1972, the number of marriages fell until 1986, since when it has risen slightly to stand at 1,941,000 in 1989. Couples are delaying getting married: the age when people marry for the first time went down until 1975 but has been increasing ever since. In 1987 it was 27.1 years for men and 24.6 for women.

It is in Greece, its birthplace, that the traditional nuclear family remains pre-eminent. Only one child in 50 is born outside marriage and rates of divorce remain one of the lowest in Europe (0.7 per 1,000 population, less than a third of Europe's highest: eastern Germany at 2.9) This does not appear to translate into greater satisfaction. Asked in 1990 whether they agreed or disagreed with the question, "I am happy with the life I lead", Greek respondents polled the lowest level of agreement at 13% but one of the highest levels of agreement to the statement, "I wish I could change and do something different".

Most European countries allow marital escape routes and divorce is on the increase. In place of marriage lasting "as long as ye both shall live", European couples are persevering with marriage only "as long as ye both shall like". Ireland alone retains an absolute prohibition against divorce (as well as abortion). The Catholic lobby there prevailed over a pro-divorce campaign to defeat a 1989 referendum on the introduction of divorce. So Irish people unhappy with their marriage or pregnancies continue to cross the Irish Sea to swell the numbers of divorces and abortions in the UK.

Changing mores

Across Europe, state power in prohibiting certain relationships is dwindling with increased tolerance of alternative lifestyles. Denmark was in the vanguard – in 1988 the Danish parliament extended rights of matrimony to gay couples – while the UK still withholds legal acceptance of transsexuals, not budging from the position that sex is determined at birth and cannot be later switched.

Dutch legislators were surprised by disapproval from elsewhere in Europe to their 1990 decision to lower the heterosexual age of consent to 12. Influenced by a report indicating that 6% of 12–13 year-olds were sexually active, the innovative Dutch were prepared to change the law to reflect changing mores. Its law retains sensible limitations. No charter for paedophiles, it simply removes from the criminal arena consensual sex between young people. In most European countries, the age of consent remains higher, from 14 in Germany to as high as 18 in ▷

For better or worse

The map shows the comparative rates of marriage and divorce throughout Europe in 1988. It is important to note that marriage figures include remarriage.

Although marriage and divorce are easily traceable events, laws governing them are different in each country and statistics are gathered in various ways. Some countries count only civil marriages while others include only marriages sanctified in church. Even so, marriage all over Europe has been in a decline over the last two decades. In the EC countries, the popularity of marriage peaked in 1972 and then declined until 1986. Its revival coincided with a doubling in the number of remarriages: 303,000 men and 278,000 women put their money on the triumph of hope over experience in 1987 as opposed to 183,000 and 146,000 in 1960. Those who did opt for marriage were also coming to the altar older and wiser: the average age of men marrying rose from 25.6 in 1975 to 27.1 in 1987; the average age of brides rose from 23 to 24.6

The rate of marriages may only indicate the popularity of weddings. The divorce rate is a more sober and accurate test of the institution's staying power. The rise in divorce numbers need not signify the crumbling of moral fibre but reflect the reform of divorce laws throughout Europe during the 1970s, when Spain and Italy legalised divorce. The fear that easier divorces would tempt more people to give up on their marriages is unjustified ; Italy's divorce rate is still the lowest in Europe. In Muslim societies, divorce is obtained by the husband giving an oath of banishment three times, but divorce is not rife. Ireland is the only European country in which divorce is still illegal; marriages can be ended only by

MARRIAGES AND DIVORCES

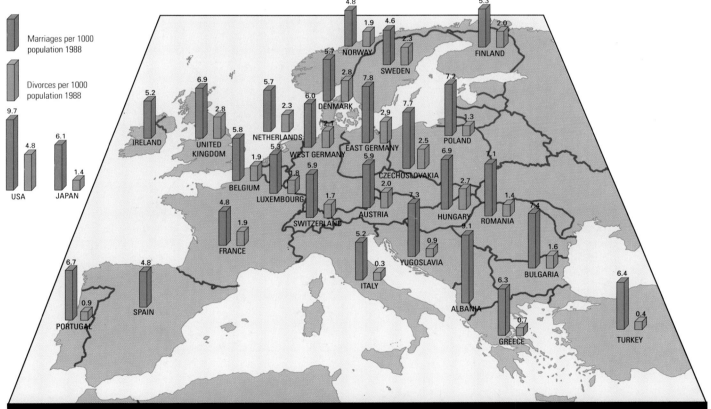

Marriages per 1000 population 1988

Divorces per 1000 population 1988

annulment under special circumstances. Since 1960, divorce rates have gone up 3.5 times in France, 4.5 times in Belgium and 5 times in the Netherlands. It is the tiniest countries in Europe that show the oddest statistics. Liechtenstein, not shown on the map, is the keenest on both marriage and divorce: 10.8 per 1,000 population got married while 7.3 split up. Andorrans are the slowest to tie the knot: only 3.1 per 1,000 in 1988.

The economics of divorce

American studies have shown that following divorce the economic well-being of women declines while that of their former husbands improves (one study shows the differential to be as vast as minus 73% as opposed to plus 42% one year post divorce). For divorced American women the most common route out of poverty is remarriage, but with remarriages showing higher rates of breakdown than first marriages, the solution is often temporary. The trend is towards the feminisation of poverty.

Aside from Liechtenstein, the UK and Denmark come closest to the high divorce rates of the USA. With the UK's bill mounting to 7bn ecus in state benefits for single parents in 1989, the government took two pronged action: passing a Child Support Act (up and running by 1993) to pass the economic tab back to absent fathers backed up by a nationwide voluntary return to work programme. Other countries may well follow the lead.

Meanwhile, a report issued in 1992 by Relate, a UK marriage guidance agency, revealed that it now had more cases involving unmarried couples than married ones and that marriage after a period of living together was no more successful than the traditional kind.

Connections: Health 242–245

EUROPE'S MISSING BABIES

Western Europeans are having fewer babies. Falls have been most spectacular in the south. In Spain a reproduction rate that only 20 years ago was around three children for each woman sank in 1989 to 1.3. Italy, which had the seventh highest fertility rate in 1970 now records the lowest among the EC twelve member states at 1.29. Alone in the world, European nations may be looking to expand rather than control native populations: France and Sweden could provide blueprints.

Pronatalist France is striving hardest to increase the birthrate by bribery: a *famille nombreuse* attracts child tax relief, generous family allowances and special discounts. Even so, France has latterly been unable to beat the UK's fertility rate, where there are no child tax allowances and benefits are low.

Sweden is arguably the only western European country where policies have reversed the falling birth trend. Swedish mothers can take two well-paid periods of maternity leave if the second child is born within 30 months of the first. From a 1983 low of 1.6 per woman, Sweden's fertility rate has pulled back to replacement levels of nearly 2 and rising.

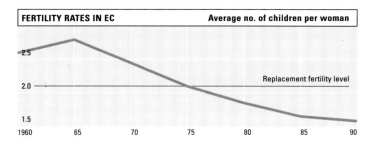

FERTILITY RATES IN EC	Average no. of children per woman

(chart: line declining from above 2.5 in mid-1960s to below 1.5 by 1990; "Replacement fertility level" marked at 2.0; x-axis 1960, 65, 70, 75, 80, 85, 90; y-axis 1.5, 2.0, 2.5)

Generation glut

The proportion of older people in the population is rising in Europe. Countries such as Germany, Belgium, Italy and France have a fertility rate well below the replacement rate of 2.1 children per woman required to maintain a stable population.

As birth rates plummet, Europeans already alive can expect to live longer. Europe's population is becoming ever greyer: in the UK, Sweden and Norway nearly one in five of the population is elderly – by the year 2001 there will be more than 4m in the UK over 75 and more than 25% of elderly Norwegians will be over 80.

Significantly there is an increasing prevalence in Europe of three, four (and even more) generation families. Whilst unlikely to share the same hearth, they nonetheless exist as an extended family often with frequent contact, interaction and help especially in the southern Mediterranean.

Moves are afoot throughout Europe to switch away from institutional to community care, shifting more responsibility on to the family (often in the shape of a more active spouse) for caring for its elderly members. Germany in particular expects the role of the family to dominate over that of the state.

For still able-bodied old people, there could be more work opportunities. A French report, Horizon 2000, predicts that unless policy measures are taken to fill the workforce shortfall caused by the birth-dearth by, for example, raising retirement age (currently 60), France will need an annual influx of 142,000 immigrant workers in the first decade of the 21st century, rising to 180,000 per year by 2020. Racist employers in France may prefer the elderly to the immigrant.

The greying of Europe

The chart below shows the dependency ratios within Europe, the ratio between the population of 65 and over to those between the ages of 15 and 64.

OLD-AGE DEPENDENCY

COUNTRY	RATIO
AUSTRIA	22.4
BELGIUM	20.3
BULGARIA	17.9
CZECHOSLOVAKIA	17.5
DENMARK	23.0
FINLAND	18.9
FRANCE	21.2
GERMANY E.	19.6
GERMANY W.	21.8
GREECE	20.3
HUNGARY	19.6
ICELAND	16.3
IRELAND	18.2
ITALY	20.1
LUXEMBOURG	20.6
NETHERLANDS	18.2
NORWAY	24.9
POLAND	14.9
PORTUGAL	19.5
ROMANIA	14.4
SPAIN	19.5
SWEDEN	28.4
SWITZERLAND	21.6
UK	23.6
YUGOSLAVIA	13.3

JAPAN	16.2
USA	19.0

COMMUNITY IN DECLINE

The chart below indicates how the countries in the EC are faring in terms of population growth compared with the rest of the world. Current predictions are that compared to the four most populated nations – China, India, the Soviet Union and even the United States – Europe's population will actually fall by 2020.

POPULATION TRENDS COMPARED TO EC

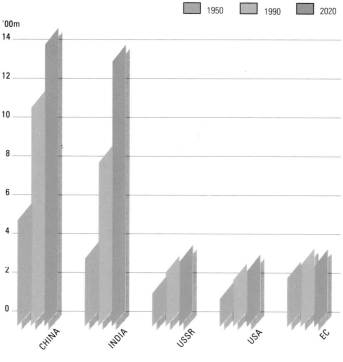

(bar chart legend: 1950, 1990, 2020; y-axis '00m: 0, 2, 4, 6, 8, 10, 12, 14; categories: CHINA, INDIA, USSR, USA, EC)

SENIOR CITIZENS OF THE WORLD

The chart below compares the ratios of populations over 65, calculated as the ratio of people aged 65 and over to those aged between 15 and 64. Europe, including Russia and former Soviet republics, has a steadily rising ratio; Asia's is rising dramatically (perhaps because of increased economic success). The USA is set to level off at a high rate. Only Africa and the Middle Eastern countries have young populations. A large proportion of old people in a population dramatically alters the financing and delivery of long-term health care.

WORLD AGEING TRENDS

Global comparison of old-age dependency ratios:
% ratio of population 65+ to 15–64

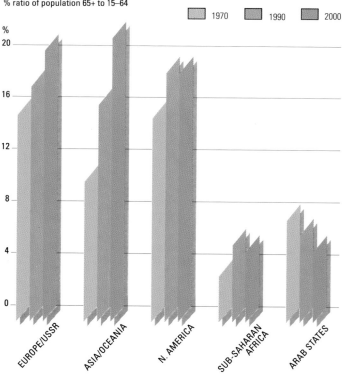

(bar chart legend: 1970, 1990, 2000; y-axis %: 0, 4, 8, 12, 16, 20; categories: EUROPE/USSR, ASIA/OCEANIA, N. AMERICA, SUB-SAHARAN AFRICA, ARAB STATES)

Birth dearth

In 1900, about one-third of the world's population lived in Europe. Ninety years later about one-tenth does. If strength were defined by numbers, Europe's power would be deemed weakening. Only Sweden has improved its rate since 1988.

FERTILITY RATES

COUNTRY	1980	1988
AUSTRIA	1.7	1.44
BELGIUM	1.67	1.56
DENMARK	1.55	1.56
FINLAND	1.63	1.58
FRANCE	1.95	1.82
GERMANY	1.45	1.42
GREECE	2.23	1.52
IRELAND	3.23	2.17
ITALY	1.69	1.34
NETHERLANDS	1.59	1.55
NORWAY	1.72	1.84
PORTUGAL	2.19	1.53
SPAIN	2.22	1.38
SWEDEN	1.68	1.96
SWITZERLAND	1.55	1.57
TURKEY	—	3.76
UK	1.89	1.84

JAPAN	1.75	1.66
USA	1.84	1.77

Old ladies in Rapallo contemplate the world going by. Catholic countries have a good record of care for the elderly, as the idea of an extended family with a well-defined role for grandparents is not quite the nostalgic myth it is in northern European countries. Even so, Italy's birth rate is dropping and its old age dependency ratio is rising; soon there may be too many nonnas (grannies) and not enough children to indulge…

Portugal. Swiss law, changed in 1992, allows consensual intercourse at the age of 16 as long as there is no more than three years age difference between partners.

What is a family for?

What is the most important role the family plays? Choosing from several possible answers in a European (EC and EFTA) survey, a clear majority of Portuguese, Greeks, Italians, French, Spaniards and Danes say it is "to bring up and educate children". But only one in four Britons agrees, the preferred British definition being "to provide love and affection". The British response marks an increasing questioning within Europe of the family's true purpose. In the high-stress lifestyle of western Europe, children seem to be becoming an option, not an absolute prerequisite of family life. Western Europe's birth rate, especially in the Catholic south, is plummeting and the average age of women at the birth of their first child is rising steadily: it is now nearly 26 among women in EC countries, up almost two years since 1970.

Instant families... when eastern Europe opened up, the horrific legacy of the Ceausescu regime in Romania was discovered. With no contraception method except illegal abortion open to them, Romanian women were having babies they could not afford and placing them in ill-equipped orphanages. Many childless western couples responded by trying to adopt Romanian babies - - parents from the UK, France and Germany being the keenest. Some Romanian women were prepared to sell one of their children to finance the rest of the family. Although most children will live a better life in material terms in the West and most western couples have only the children's welfare at heart, there is concern that these children could be open to abuse in some cases, and laws governing their adoption are being tightened up.

A MAN'S PLACE

How European is the New Man? In 1992, the EC Employment and Social Affairs Directorate commissioned a Family and Work Survey in which 17,000 couples were interviewed. Men were asked if they took any responsibility for domestic work and their partners were asked to assess the answers. Overall, 61.6% men claimed to do nothing, but 65.4% of their partners thought they did nothing. Men in Belgium, Germany, the Netherlands, Italy, France, Spain and Greece claim to do more than their partners think they do – for example, 76.6% Spanish men proclaim themselves domestically idle, but 79.7% of their partners know that are. Men in the UK and Denmark think they do less than their partners say they do. Irishmen appear to do good by stealth; 84% maintain that they do not lift a finger; however, only 31.9% of their partners agree with them. Among the men who do contribute to the domestic economy, shopping was the favourite activity (91% Greeks), followed by dish washing (the UK wielding the golden dishcloth at 72%) and driving children to school (72% of Irish men). Cleaning came bottom of everyone's list.

Contrasts between western and eastern Europe are sharp: east of the former iron curtain, the birth rate is still comparatively high. Albania has the highest total (a crude birth rate of 27 per 1,000 population) and all former eastern European countries have birth rates that exceed those in western Europe.

The EC is taking a strongly pro-active role in shaping family policy for the 21st century. Article 19 of the Treaty of Rome, enshrining equal treatment of the sexes in the workplace, establishes a commitment to the increased provision of childcare. A growing consensus on the importance of family life and responsibilities of both sexes within it are being translated into directives which help reconcile work and childrearing. Germany currently offers one of the best deals to workers, allowing either parent to take paid leave of $370 a month for up to 18 months after the birth.

The EC also plans social action for the rising numbers of single parents within Europe – an EC study in 1989 estimated that at least 10% of families within the Community are single-parent families. The increasing numbers of single parents are mainly the result of marital break-ups, but births outside marriage are also increasing. Many non-marital births (one in four in the UK and France) take place within a stable relationship – cohabitation is becoming particularly popular in France. However, this apparently modern trend should be placed in historical context: it is reckoned that three out of five first births in 19th-century Britain were outside marriage.

THE FAMILY IN EASTERN EUROPE

Out of the ashes of communist Europe , Pope John Paul seeks to raise a phoenix of a Roman Catholic resurgence. In his native Poland, 97% Catholic, he might expect some success: the Church under communism gained support as a focus of dissent and moral fervour. However, the peoples of former eastern Europe, newly freed from one totalitarian system, are resistant to another with strong, if differing views on the family. While comparatively easy divorce led to comparatively high rates of marital break-up, the bourgeois family, attacked by Karl Marx as the mainstay of the capitalist economy, perversely grew stronger under communism.

Secrets glued families together as the family became one of the few safe places for the passing on of subversive information. Hardship also bonded. In re-evaluating a new era of family life, one of the first tasks will be to piece together what actually happened to family members who disappeared during war and revolution on both sides of the Iron Curtain. The opening up of eastern Europe released an endless swell of enquiries: after 1989 the Red Cross Society received a 64% increase in requests from eastern European countries and Russia about tracing missing relatives.

However, roles played by the old communist states in family life were not purely negative. East Germans, for example , enjoyed the right of guaranteed (and practically free) kindergarten places for their children. With unification, more traditional West German *Kinder Kirche Küche* attitudes (women should confine themselves to children, church and kitchen) are eroding both childcare provision and job opportunities for mothers with young children. Levels of abortion were notably high in the former communist bloc countries, pointing to the fact that termination of pregnancy was often used as form of birth control. Perhaps the re-emergence of Roman Catholicism and Orthodox Christianity will modify this attitude to an issue that vexes moral thinking in western Europe.

Working mothers

The map shows the proportion of mothers with young children who work outside the home, either full or part-time.

Mothers who work outside the home are now the norm. Some have to as they are single parents; most are part of a dual earning unit. To work productively, parents need good quality affordable childcare, a commodity in short supply according to the EC initiative on childcare of 1991. Throughout Europe, women are choosing to start families later. The average age of a woman starting her family is now just under 26; compared to just over 24 in 1970. The help they get from the state varies. Between the ages of 5 and 9 most children are at primary school for anything from four to eight hours a day. However, few countries provide publicly funded care outside school hours: Germany offers such care to 3% of primary school age children, France and Belgium are rather more generous although exact figures are hard to come by, the Netherlands offers care for 1%, Luxembourg under 2%, the UK under 1%, Portugal 3% and Denmark a princely 20%. Limited tax allowances on childcare costs are granted by France, the Netherlands and Luxembourg.

PART AND FULL-TIME PROPORTIONS

% of mothers of children aged 5-9 at work (1988)

- Part-time
- Full-time

UK	
38.68	13.86

DENMARK	
37.18	44.45

IRELAND	
7.35	12.28

NETHERLANDS	
28.48	4.41

W. GERMANY	
22.44	16.26

BELGIUM	
16.09	35.71

LUXEMBOURG	
9.46	26.36

FRANCE	
16.35	37.36

PORTUGAL	
6.24	54.94

GREECE	
3.78	36.8

ITALY	
4.81	36.53

SPAIN	
4.39	22.2

Sexual licence

The legal age of consent (see below) varies across Europe and is hedged about with footnotes as legislators attempt to keep pace with contemporary mores. Most countries agree that sex with a child under 12 is illegal, but after that prosecution depends on a complaint being brought; the upper age limits are more to protect teenagers from predatory adults not peer group sex. The figures relate to heterosexual and homosexual activity except for Germany and Luxembourg where the age of consent for homosexuals is 18, the UK where it is 21 and Ireland , where the act is illegal.

AGE OF SEXUAL CONSENT

COUNTRY	AGE
BELGIUM	16
DENMARK	15
FRANCE	16[1]
GERMANY	14
GREECE	16
IRELAND	17[2]
ITALY	no age limit[1]
LUXEMBOURG	16
NETHERLANDS	16[3]
PORTUGAL	16
SPAIN	no age limit[4]
SWITZERLAND	16
UK	16

1 Sex illegal between over-18 and under-18.

2 You can marry at 16.
   You can not use a condom till 18.

3 But sex involving over-12s will not be prosecuted.

4 But rape of under-18 by over-18 carries a heavy sentence.

Abortion rates

The chart below shows the rate of legal abortions in Europe, including eastern European countries and the former Soviet Union. With high rates of infant mortality in eastern Europe, those intent on reducing family size were forced into the culturally acceptable but crude alternative of abortion. (The hard currency costs of western contraceptives were considered to be too steep.) The Soviets led the world in one abortion to every four births. Bulgaria, Romania, Yugoslavia, Hungary and Czechoslovakia also rank highly.

LEGAL ABORTIONS, 1988

COUNTRY	TOTAL❖
USSR	230.0
BULGARIA	107.2
ROMANIA	99.0
YUGOSLAVIA	74.0
HUNGARY	65.6
CZECHOSLOVAKIA	52.8
ITALY	38.9
GERMANY E.	35.0
FRANCE	23.9
FINLAND	21.0
UK	20.7
POLAND	19.0
GERMANY W.	14.8
NETHERLANDS	11.5
GREECE	0.2

USA	42.8
JAPAN	37.9

❖ per 1,000 live births

Danish children at table and French babies at rest while their parents work. Denmark provides 48% of the care for under-threes; France and Belgium are level, providing places for one in five under-threes. Britain lags far behind, with a provision for just 2% of under-threes.

HEALTH

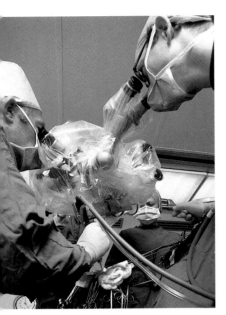

In western Europe, healthcare is often associated with high-tech developments. Here two surgeons working on a brain tumour use a split beam microscope, linked to a videocamera so that students and observers can share the experience; an ultrasound probe is used to emulsify the growth so that it can drain away without further invasive surgery.

A diversity of healthcare systems exists across Europe, each reflecting its country's history, culture and political system. All the systems are made up of different combinations of some fairly common sub-systems of financing and delivery. The main difference in the financing of health systems lies in whether healthcare is funded primarily from taxation, as in Britain, Denmark, Italy and Sweden, or from some form of social insurance, as in Belgium, France, Germany, the Netherlands, Greece, Austria and Spain.

Similarly, healthcare is delivered through a mix of publicly-owned hospitals and salaried doctors, independent doctors under public contract or private doctors and hospitals. While only one sub-system is dominant in each country, it is often in combination with elements from the other two.

Germany, for instance, subscribes to the social insurance system of financing healthcare (introduced under Bismarck), where enrolment in an insurance scheme is usually obligatory. Contributions to the insurance scheme are income-related and shared between employer and employee. The average car worker pays 6% of his earnings and the employer pays a further 6% on his behalf. The elderly, the unemployed and the sick are included in the basic insurance schemes (sickness funds), their contributions being paid by the state.

The Belgian, French and Dutch healthcare systems are also dominated by compulsory social insurance. France has three main sickness funds: for salaried employees, for farmers and agricultural workers, and for the self employed. Belgium has "mutual aid societies" that have religious and political affiliations. Fees for patients are set by contracts between insurers and providers. Care is provided by public hospitals and salaried doctors or private

hospitals and independent doctors. In the Netherlands, sickness funds pay GPs by capitation, specialists by fee for service and hospitals, which are mainly private, by per diem payments. In France, approximately 25% of doctors, usually specialists, require payments on top of their sickness fund fee. Higher earners in most of these countries can enroll in alternative private insurance schemes that offer wider and more generous benefits at higher premiums.

Healthcare in the United Kingdom is dominated by a tax-funded system offering comprehensive services to the entire population. Care is provided primarily by independent GPs paid by a mix of capitation and allowances for services such as immunisation, and by public hospitals under direct management of the central government. Similarly, most healthcare in Sweden is financed from taxes and provided by the public sector. Responsibility for administering and delivering healthcare is decentralised geographically to 26 county councils. Most physicians are salaried but 20% are independent and paid by the number of patients they treat. Direct consumer charges under this system are nominal.

Reforming the health service

Healthcare systems operate in a state of continuous change, striving to adjust to economic, political and social demands. The present review and reform process is driven by pressures to control healthcare costs, to keep abreast with demands of demographic and technological change, and to improve performance. The two best known simple conceptual models for organising the healthcare economy are at opposite ends of a spectrum: the free market and the tax supported public sector monopoly. Proponents of each point to the deficiencies ▷

Suicide rates

The chart below shows the rates of suicide and self-inflicted injuries in terms of life years lost.

Deaths from suicide have remained stable on average, although rates for individual countries show marked rises. It is also common for suicides to be notoriously under-reported in predominantly Catholic countries.

A high suicide rate may be seen as an indicator of the state of a country's psyche rather than its physical health. Suicide rates do not correlate with living conditions or standards of poverty and it is a well-known statistical cliché that suicide rates go down during war time . Scandinavia was for a long time considered to be the land of the suicidal; indeed Finland and Denmark hold the

highest rates in western Europe, at 26.84 per 100,000 population and 26.27 respectively. However, as the eastern bloc gradually crumbled, and information was made available, it became clear that Hungary was the most suicidally inclined country in the new Europe, with 43.84 people per 100, 000 killing or injuring themselves in 1987. Greeks are the least likely to attempt or succeed at suicide.

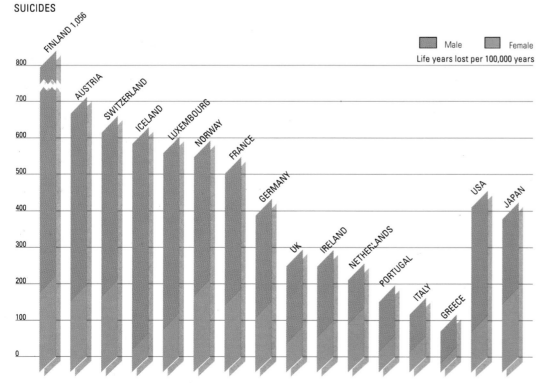

SUICIDES

Male Female
Life years lost per 100,000 years

FINLAND 1,056
AUSTRIA
SWITZERLAND
ICELAND
LUXEMBOURG
NORWAY
FRANCE
GERMANY
UK
IRELAND
NETHERLANDS
PORTUGAL
ITALY
GREECE
USA
JAPAN

800
700
600
500
400
300
200
100
0

AIDS AND THE RE-EMERGENCE OF TB

During the 1990s, AIDS-related death will become one of the leading causes of death among adults aged 20–40 years. In 1988, AIDS was the leading cause of death in both men and women aged 25–34 in New York City. By the year 2000, it is estimated that 30m–40m people will be infected with the AIDS virus worldwide, with 12m–18m (40–45%) with active AIDS. In 1990, 43,441 cases were reported in western Europe, against the estimated figure of 48,000. In eastern Europe there were 2,462 reported cases, but the estimate was for 52,000.

Compared to other communicable diseases such as measles, chicken pox or even the common cold, Aids is relatively difficult to transmit. HIV (human immunodeficiency virus), the causative agent for AIDS, is transmitted mainly through sexual contact, though it may be transmitted vertically from mother to child and by blood contact such as the sharing of intravenous needles. Once full-blown AIDS manifests itself, it appears to be universally fatal. Death results from associated opportunistic infections to which the AIDS sufferer is susceptible because of weakened immunity.

One of the healthcare challenges for the 1990s will be the effective control of other communicable diseases that have re-emerged as a result of HIV infection. A case in point is tuberculosis. The spread of HIV has brought with it an increase in the number of TB cases, many with drug resistant strains, rare until now. Basic research on TB virtually ceased following the discovery of anti-TB drugs. Techniques of DNA fingerprinting that enable identification of drug-resistant strains and rapid diagnosis of TB are still in experimental stages. Concern is mounting about drug-resistant outbreaks in institutions.

Leading causes of death

Today, in the industrialised world, the main causes of death are heart disease, stroke, cancer and road accidents. The charts (right) show comparative figures for life years lost from strokes and all kinds of heart disease. Deaths from heart disease and strokes has declined considerably in western Europe and risen in eastern Europe. Women suffer less from heart disease overall, but female stroke victims nearly equal the male count in the Netherlands, Ireland and Iceland.

As in the last century, prevention through social and environmental change is more effective in reducing the leading causes of death than direct medical intervention. For instance, coronary heart disease and cancer are strongly associated with smoking. Heavy smokers, those consuming more than 40 cigarettes a day, are four times as likely to die of coronary heart disease than non-smokers and 90% of lung cancer deaths are attributed to cigarette smoking. Reducing smoking and preventing road accidents may be the most effective ways of reducing life years lost. In fact, road accidents have resulted in fewer fatalities since 1970, with the exception of Greece, which, at 18.7 per 100,000 people has risen by 50% but is still lower than Luxembourg's 19.2 per 100,000 (down from 27.3 per 100,000 in 1971).

Even so, statistics may be misleading. There are fashions even in death registration. Different causes of death are known to be recorded from identical information, sometimes within the same country.

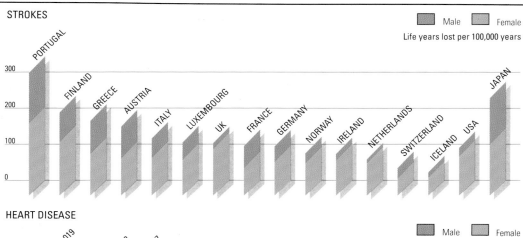

STROKES

Male ⬛ Female ⬛
Life years lost per 100,000 years

PORTUGAL, FINLAND, GREECE, AUSTRIA, ITALY, LUXEMBOURG, UK, FRANCE, GERMANY, NORWAY, IRELAND, NETHERLANDS, SWITZERLAND, ICELAND, USA, JAPAN

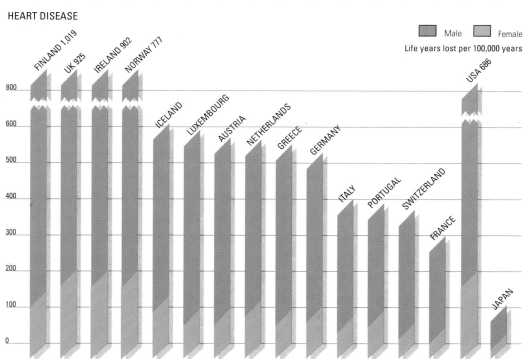

HEART DISEASE

Male ⬛ Female ⬛
Life years lost per 100,000 years

FINLAND 1,019, UK 925, IRELAND 902, NORWAY 777, ICELAND, LUXEMBOURG, AUSTRIA, NETHERLANDS, GREECE, GERMANY, ITALY, PORTUGAL, SWITZERLAND, FRANCE, USA 686, JAPAN

Cancer trends

Deaths caused from cancer, including breast cancer, has changed little on average and risen in most countries, as indicated by the chart below. Eastern European countries suffer from particularly high rates, perhaps related to high levels of industrial pollution.

INCIDENCE PER '000 POPULATION

COUNTRY	1970-71	1984-87
AUSTRIA	99.43	87.7
BELGIUM	100.0	96.12
BULGARIA	74.84	86.99
CZECH.	106.39	122.04
GERMANY E.	91.69	90.84
GERMANY W.	93.51	89.60
FINLAND	91.69	71.99
FRANCE	91.74	99.39
GREECE	69.43	72.31
HUNGARY	94.19	129.23
IRELAND	99.53	97.57
ITALY	93.49	94.59
LUXEMBOURG	110.10	109.09
NETHERLANDS	98.55	90.02
NORWAY	77.60	75.96
POLAND	93.44	114.89
PORTUGAL	78.59	76.18
ROMANIA	83.75	87.58
.SPAIN	74.29	79.33
SWEDEN	74.44	67.67
SWITZERLAND	89.54	78.56
UK	105.89	96.66
YUGOSLAVIA	70.89	88.53

MEDICAL OPINIONS

Healthcare differs considerably between countries. Even styles and fashions of medical practice observe national boundaries. Organ transplants are virtually unknown in Japan, births by caesarian section common in the USA and what is a pill in Britain is a suppository in France. Nearly 7.5% of French drugs, from aspirins to antibiotics, comes as suppositories, compared with 1% in the USA. Germans use six times the amount of heart drugs per capita than the English. The French have over 300 drugs for the liver. Blood pressure considered high in the USA might be considered normal in Britain and low blood pressure treated with vast numbers of drugs, hydrotherapy and spa treatments in Germany would entitle the sufferer to lower life insurance rates in the USA.

Diagnostic D&CS, the third most common procedure in the USA is rarely performed in France. The British do less of nearly everything. They operate less than the Americans. For every coronary bypass performed in the UK, six are performed in the USA. Approximately 10% of all births are delivered by caesarean section in the UK compared with over 20% in the USA. But when it comes to kidney transplants, the highest number are performed in Norway. When surgical rates are compared, low rates do not imply under supply and conversely, high rates do not suggest over supply of care. It more likely suggests specialist over-enthusiasm or unnecessary intervention.

There is often no scientifically correct way of practicing much of medicine. The medical decision-making process remains a function of the complicated interaction of scientific evidence, the cultural context of medical training and physician response to patient expectation.

CRISIS IN EASTERN EUROPE

The health status of the people of eastern Europe is not only lower than in western Europe, in some respects it is steadily declining. Average life expectancy for a newborn infant in eastern European countries is, on average, almost five years shorter than that in the West. Almost uniquely in the modern world, male life expectancy has actually fallen in the last decade in Bulgaria, Hungary, Romania and Poland. Alcohol and tobacco consumption is much higher than in western Europe. Mortality rates for all causes of death are in excess of 1,000 per 100,000 population compared with rates well below 900 per 100,000 in western Europe. The widespread lack of birth control facilities has meant that abortion has been used as a substitute. In Romania, birth control was prohibited as part of a strategy to increase the population. Maternal deaths caused by abortions rose to 148.8 per 100,000 live births in 1987.

Despite central control, health services are highly fragmented. Patient choice is limited both by shortage of drugs and equipment, and by arbitrary regulations. There is no means of complaining about inadequate services since healthcare was presented as a "gift" from the state. Major reforms to the healthcare systems are being proposed and implemented. Bulgaria is considering the introduction of social insurance and the separation of healthcare resources from the general budget. In Hungary and Czechoslovakia, the structure and financing of the healthcare system is being changed through decentralisation and the creation of a health insurance organisation. Decentralisation is also an important feature in health-section reform in Romania. For the longer term, there are plans to implement a social insurance system.

Alternative or complementary medicine is enjoying growing status all over Europe as people become disenchanted with high tech drug-based systems which seem to exclude the patient from their own healing process. Chiropractic, seen here, is based on the idea that mechanical disorders of the body are the result of displacement to specific areas of the spine. Manipulation and exercise, after X-ray examination, is the usual procedure. Switzerland is the only European country with legislation for chiropractic, but it can be practised under general law in most countries.

of the other, but a free market cannot work in healthcare and public sector monopolies contain no serious incentives to improve efficiency.

Recent reforms across Europe converge on a "managed market" model of financing and delivery, that strives to capture some of the advantages of markets such as efficiency, yet safeguards adequacy, equity and access to care. The Dutch government is embarking upon reforms that introduce a system of regulated competition among insurance companies and among providers of healthcare, with a proposal for needy individuals to receive a subsidy from central funds, to ensure their ability to purchase health insurance.

Healthcare as a business

The British National Health Service is separating finance from provision, to foster competition. GPs can become "fundholders" to enable them to negotiate directly the purchase of hospital care for their patients. Hospitals are also being encouraged to be more business like. In both France and Germany, healthcare provision is being increasingly regulated. Even Sweden is experimenting with planned markets, while retaining its high commitment to public funding. A public competition model in which different publicly capitalised and operated providers compete for public market share is being partially implemented in Stockholm and Malmöhus.

Throughout Europe, healthcare reforms are aimed at achieving equity of access, efficiency (both at a macro and micro level), improved health outcomes, patient satisfaction, consumer choice and provider autonomy. Countries in central and eastern Europe are embarking on a process of change which will take them from a centrally planned and financed healthcare system to one that is capable of achieving a better balance among these objectives. The principal merit of the old system, universal coverage, needs to be preserved. With the experience of one country serving as an experimental laboratory for others, healthcare systems will undoubtedly become increasingly similar as they pursue common goals, yet remain diverse within their cultural and political context.

The amount spent on healthcare as a percentage of gross domestic product does not give a true picture of healthcare delivered to a patient. Differences exist in how well doctors and health workers are paid relative to other occupations, in the treatments and drugs they have available to dispense, in expectation of and demand by patients, and in overall efficiency of the system. Nearly 25% of total US healthcare expenditure is spent on administrative costs, compared with approximately 5% in the UK. Also, a system of health insurance as in the USA is more costly to administer than a system of social insurance like Germany, and both are more expensive than a tax-based system like that in the UK.

Paying for health

The chart below shows how much countries spent on their population's health in 1990 and how much that has gone up since 1980. France tops the league, spending 8.9 % of the GDP, with the UK the most parsimonious at 6.1%. The USA spent 12.4%. Norway spends most on public health (almost all of their available budget) and Turkey least. Switzerland has the most nurses and the most doctors, who are the best paid in Europe, with earnings on a par with their American colleagues. Data for 1990 on numbers of beds, doctors and nurses per 1,000 population is not available for most European countries.

Health in the third age

An increasing amount of total health expenditure is spent on those in the last years of their lives. The dependency ratio calculated as the ratio of people aged 65 and over to those aged between 15 and 24 is set to rise. This will change the conditions for the financing and delivery of healthcare, as too few young people (European birth rates are falling) try to look after an increasing number of old ones.

Someone over 75 uses ten times as much healthcare as someone aged between 20 and 50. In countries where healthcare is primarily financed through some form of social insurance, the bulk

of the revenue is dependent upon income-related premiums. Contributions for the elderly are always paid for or subsidised by the government. In Germany for instance, the public pension funds transfer money to the sickness funds to pay for healthcare expenses of retired members. With the projected increase in the dependency rate, the burden of these transfers on the pension funds will be considerable.

The impact on the provision of healthcare will mean that nursing home and long-term care will become relatively more important, as will the integration of social and medical services.

A matter of life and death

An essential question for any healthcare system is how well it is doing in satisfying the basic health needs of its population. Although health is difficult to measure and is determined largely by factors outside the control of the healthcare system, there are a few easily quantifiable aggregate measures, such as infant mortality, life expectancy and cause-specific mortality, that are conventionally used as indicators of the health of the population. In general, the lower the infant mortality rate at birth and the longer the life expectancy, the healthier the nation as a whole. This is shown in the eastern European countries.

With the exception of what was eastern Germany, infant mortality rates in all former communist bloc countries are substantially higher than those of western Europe, except Portugal. A comparison of the infant mortality rate and life expectancy of individual countries demonstrates little correlation between expenditures on healthcare and health outcomes. The USA which spends almost twice as much as the UK and Japan, has an average life expectancy of 74.9 years compared with 75.2 years for the UK and 78.4 years for Japan. The infant mortality rate of 9.7 per 1,000 population in the USA is also higher than 4.6 in Japan and 7.5 in Denmark.

HEALTH CARE TRENDS

COUNTRY	TOTAL EXPEND.[1]		PUBLIC EXPEND.[2]		HOSPITAL BEDS[3]		DOCTORS[3]		NURSES[3]	
AUSTRIA	7.9	8.4	68.8	66.4	11.2	10.6	1.6	2.1	5.2	6.7
BELGIUM	6.7	7.4	82.8	82.5	9.4	—	2.5	—	—	—
DENMARK	6.8	6.4	85.2	84.2	8.3	5.9	2.2	—	5.1	—
FINLAND	6.5	7.2	79.0	78.8	15.6	13.1	1.5	2.0	5.9	7.5
FRANCE	7.6	8.8	78.8	75.0	11.1	10.0	2.0	2.6	4.6	—
GERMANY	8.4	8.2	75.0	72.1	11.5	10.8	2.3	3.0	4.0	—
GREECE	4.3	5.3	82.2	76.1	6.2	5.1	2.4	3.3	2.4	3.3
IRELAND	9.0	7.3	88.8	83.9	9.6	6.0	1.3	—	—	—
ITALY	6.8	7.6	82.1	77.7	9.7	—	1.2	—	4.1	—
NETHERLANDS	8.0	8.1	74.7	72.3	12.3	11.6	1.9	2.4	—	—
NORWAY	6.6	7.6	98.4	95.7	16.5	14.5	2.0	—	—	—
PORTUGAL	5.9	7.2	72.4	57.8	5.5	4.7	2.1	2.8	2.4	2.8
SPAIN	5.6	6.3	79.9	78.3	5.4	—	2.3	3.7	—	—
SWEDEN	9.4	8.7	92.5	89.3	14.2	—	2.2	3.1	7.0	—
SWITZERLAND	7.3	7.6	67.5	68.3	11.3	9.5	2.4	2.9	10.0	—
TURKEY	4.0	3.9	27.3	36.7	2.2	2.4	0.6	0.8	0.6	—
UK	5.6	5.8	89.3	85.4	8.1	6.4	1.2	1.4	3.5	—

| JAPAN | 6.4 | 6.7 | 70.8 | 73.2 | 13.8 | 15.7 | 1.3 | — | — | — |
| USA | 9.3 | 11.7 | 42.0 | 41.9 | 5.8 | 4.8 | 1.9 | — | 5.4 | — |

| | 1980 | 1 Expenditure as % of GDP | 3 Hospital beds per 1,000 people |
| | 1989 | 2 Expenditure as % of total | 4 per 1,000 people |

LIFE EXPECTANCY AND INFANT MORTALITY

COUNTRY	LIFE EXPECTANCY[1]				INFANT MORTALITY[2]	
AUSTRIA	69.0	72.1	76.1	78.8	1.43	0.83
BELGIUM	70.0	72.4	76.8	79.0	1.21	0.86
DENMARK	71.4	72.0	77.6	77.7	0.84	0.75
FINLAND	69.2	—	77.6	—	0.76	—
FRANCE	70.2	72.5	78.4	80.7	1.01	0.75
GERMANY	69.9	72.6	76.6	79.0	1.27	0.75
GREECE	72.2	—	76.3	—	1.79	0.91
IRELAND	69.5	71.0	75.0	77.0	1.11	0.76
ITALY	70.7	72.6	77.4	79.1	1.43	0.88
NETHERLANDS	72.4	73.7	79.2	79.9	0.86	0.68
NORWAY	72.2	73.3	78.7	79.9	0.81	0.79
PORTUGAL	67.7	70.7	—	77.6	2.43	1.22
SPAIN	72.5	—	78.6	—	1.23	0.78
SWEDEN	72.8	74.8	78.8	80.6	0.69	0.57
SWITZERLAND	72.4	74.0	79.1	80.9	0.91	0.73
TURKEY	—	—	—	—	9.0	—
UK	70.2	72.8	75.9	78.4	1.21	—

| JAPAN | 73.3 | 75.9 | 78.7 | 81.8 | 0.75 | 0.46 |
| USA | 70.0 | 71.8 | 77.4 | 78.5 | 1.26 | 0.97 |

	1980 Men	1980 Women	1980	
	1989 Men	1989 Women	1989	1 Years
				2 per 100 births

Cigarettes and whisky

Alcohol and tobacco are powerful drugs but have become so thoroughly socialised that it is difficult for people to relate social drug abuse with their state of health. Smoking is directly linked with lung cancer, emphysema, heart disease, strokes, asthma and bronchitis; 90% of lung cancers are caused directly by smoking; in the USA, over 400,000 people die of smoking-related diseases every year, ten times as many as are killed on the road. Excess drinking not only causes disease in the drinker (cirrhosis of the liver, stomach ulcers, high blood pressure) but may also be responsible for unnecessary road accidents and child abuse (one in five cases are alcohol-related according to the NSPCC in the UK). It is also expensive; in the UK, almost £16bn a year is spent on alcohol. Governments in most countries are backing moves towards preventative medicine and encouraging moderation, but progress is slow. France, Italy and Spain cut down on alcohol between the years 1970 and 1986, but France is still the top drinker.

As the chart shows, smoking is on the wane in the Netherlands, the UK and the USA, where only one-quarter of the population now smoke, compared with half of them 30 years ago. Norwegians smoke less than any other Europeans.

SMOKING TRENDS
Annual cigarette consumption per person, in units

█ 1976   █ 1986

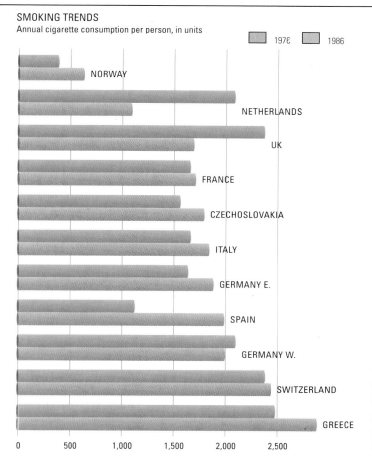

NORWAY
NETHERLANDS
UK
FRANCE
CZECHOSLOVAKIA
ITALY
GERMANY E.
SPAIN
GERMANY W.
SWITZERLAND
GREECE

0   500   1,000   1,500   2,000   2,500

DRINKING TRENDS
Annual pure alcohol consumption, litres per person

COUNTRY		LITRES
AUSTRIA	10.5	9.8
BULGARIA	6.7	9.3
CZECHOSLOVAKIA	8.4	9.0
GERMANY E.	6.1	10.2
GERMANY W.	10.3	10.5
FINLAND	4.4	6.9
FRANCE	16.2	13.2
GREECE	5.3	6.2
HUNGARY	9.1	11.4
IRELAND	5.9	5.3
ITALY	13.7	10.2
NETHERLANDS	5.6	8.6\
NORWAY	3.6	4.2
POLAND	5.4	7.2
PORTUGAL	9.9	11.2
ROMANIA	6.3	7.8
SPAIN	12.1	11.5
SWEDEN	5.8	5.5
SWITZERLAND	10.7	11.0
TURKEY	0.5	1.0
UK	5.1	7.1
YUGOSLAVIA	7.9	7.4
☐ 1970	☐ 1986	

No amount of statistical evidence will persuade a Frenchman to forswear his vin rouge or his Gaulois. The French drink more wine (75.1 litres per head at the latest count) than any other European and unsurprisingly suffer from high rates of liver disease. However, modest regular wine consumption can have a tonic effect on the circulation and France has a low rate of heart disease.

ABORTION RATES

█ Ratio of abortions to 1,000 live births 1986

NETHERLANDS 98.92
GERMANY 134.63
POLAND 563.23
CZECHOSLOVAKIA 204.36
HUNGARY 651.98
YUGOSLAVIA 975.71
BULGARIA 1,008.7
USSR 1,210.20

Abortion as birth control

The map above shows rates of abortion per 1,000 live births in 1986 with special reference to eastern Europe. For many years, abortion was the only form of contraception available to women in eastern Europe. The figure for Germany indicates the total for both West and East. The Netherlands is included to indicate the lowest average western abortion rate as a comparison. The average rate for western European countries is around 290 per 1,000 live births: in 1986, Denmark had a rate of 362.80, Finland 220.22, Iceland 176.24, Italy 365.94, Norway 294.66 and Sweden 324.90.

Abortion laws

Abortion is a controversial issue and the legislation passed in the various countries in Europe is usually framed to match the prevailing ideology. The regulations vary enormously: time limits can be as short as ten weeks (Yugoslavia) or as long as 24 weeks (UK) or the viability of the foetus (Switzerland); different rules apply to different trimesters, with abortion after 12 weeks being far harder to obtain in some cases; the medical requirements may be two doctors (France, the UK), a committee of four people (Denmark) or just the woman and her physician (the Netherlands); grounds can be rape, threat to the health (mental or physical) of the

mother, eugenic reasons (Greece), an undefined intolerable situation for the mother (Netherlands again) or demand (Sweden). Different rules usually apply to minors, but they are defined as anything from 14 years old (Austria) to 18 (Poland).

Switzerland has the most liberal abortion law; it was passed in 1942; the former USSR followed in 1955, with a limit of 12 weeks. Norway passed legislation as early as 1950, with modifications following in 1966, 1975 and 1978. The UK legalised abortion in 1967. Most of Europe followed suit in the 1970s, when divorce law was also being reformed: Sweden in 1974, Italy in 1978, Luxembourg in 1978, GDR in 1972, FDR in

1976, Finland in 1976 (with modifications in 1978 and 1985), France in 1975 and 1979, Denmark in 1973, Austria in 1974 and 1975, Bulgaria in 1973 and 1974; in the 1980s reform came to Greece (1986), Hungary (1988) Turkey (1983), Portugal (1984), Spain (1985), the Netherlands (1981) and Czechoslovakia (1986–87). Abortion is illegal in Belgium (under the 1867 act) and Ireland (under the offences against the person act 1861). However, Irish women who want abortions usually go to the UK or elsewhere and Belgians go to the liberal Netherlands. In countries where late abortions are forbidden, women usually come to the UK, Switzerland or the Netherlands.

Maternal deaths

The legalisation of abortion throughout the 1970s and 1980s has meant that maternal deaths resulting from illegal backstreet abortions have fallen dramatically (see chart below). Austria, Sweden, Finland, Norway and Switzerland have eradicated such deaths altogether. Only in Romania has the figure risen. Abortion was declared illegal in 1957, and under President Ceausescu's regime contraception was made illegal. The kitchen-table abortion was the only option for women whose families were too large to be supported; the result was shockingly large numbers of maternal deaths.

MATERNAL DEATHS BY ABORTION
per '000 live births

COUNTRY	1970	1984-87
AUSTRIA	2.67	0.0
BULGARIA	12.97	10.83
CZECHOSLOVAKIA	1.31	2.72
GERMANY, E.	10.97	0.89
GERMANY, W.	6.78	1.4
FINLAND	4.65	0.0
FRANCE	5.90	0.9
GREECE	0.0	0.89
HUNGARY	8.56	3.18
IRELAND	0.0	0.0
ITALY	4.99	0.87
NETHERLANDS	1.67	0.54
NORWAY	0.0	0.0
POLAND	2.56	1.82
PORTUGAL	7.93	4.87
ROMANIA	73.76	128.01
SPAIN	2.29	0.85
SWEDEN	0.0	0.0
SWITZERLAND	5.04	0.0
UK	3.54	0.64
YUGOSLAVIA	21.75	2.18

LAW AND JUSTICE SYSTEMS

English judges in full fig, as much a tourist attraction as a personification of law in action. The English legal system is a common law system, which is based on precedent; in effect, this means that the judges make the law, as their decisions can follow, expand on or even overturn precedent cases. (France and Germany have civil law systems, where the judge must base all decisions on statute.)

How crime is defined, how prosecution is initiated and what punishment fits which crime differ across the continent. Most people in Europe would accept that it's wrong to steal, but the different European criminal justice systems seem to agree on little else. Some countries allow the police or an independent prosecution service discretion to decide whether an alleged criminal should be brought to court; others do not. Most European countries give judicial officers an inquisitorial role; in the United Kingdom and Ireland, courts are not expected to make their own enquiries. In some cases, it is up to the victim to decide whether there should be a prosecution; in certain socialist countries minor thefts,

such as shoplifting, are not considered to be crimes at all.

Across Europe, children are treated very differently and the age of criminal responsibility varies. In Luxembourg, there is no minimum age at which a child can be charged with a crime; in Scotland, the minimum age is eight; in Austria and Sweden it is 15, and in Belgium it is 18. In some countries courts dealing with children and young people are not allowed to pass custodial sentences. In Belgium and Portugal, for example, courts can only deal in child protection and educational measures.

Nor is it easy to compare crime levels in different countries. Some states include all reported offences in their crime statistics; others leave out cases where it turns

The rising tide

Figures collected by Interpol from 21 industrialised countries show that recorded crime rates between 1980 and 1990 were most stable in Canada, Belgium and Northern Ireland. There were above average increases in England and Wales, and in Scotland. The highest increases were in Spain, Finland, Luxembourg, and, notably, Greece (although whether for substantive or recording reasons is doubtful). Reported crime actually went down in the United States. This is said to be because of the "ageing out" of the population, the dwindling number of people now living in high-crime urban areas, and tougher penalties.

The figures (in the chart right) indexed at 100 for 1980 are based on the total of seven offence categories, not the highly mismatched total of "all crime". Nevertheless, some differences in what these categories comprise are likely.

RECORDED CRIME RATE

COUNTRY	% increase
SPAIN	184
FINLAND	146
LUXEMBOURG	142
ITALY	99
NORWAY	86
NETHERLANDS	60
ENGLAND & WALES	59
SCOTLAND	39
AUSTRIA	36
DENMARK	28
FRANCE	27
PORTUGAL	25
SWEDEN	25
IRELAND	13
GERMANY W.	13
N. IRELAND	6
BELGIUM	5

USA	-1

The risk of violent death

The map shows comparative likelihood of violent death in 1986–88. Homicide in this instance is defined as death by injury inflicted by others and makes no distinction between premeditated and accidental killing.

Figures from the World Health Organisation show that you are most likely to be the victim of murder or manslaughter in Puerto Rico and least likely to suffer a violent death in England and Wales. Northern Ireland, with a figure of seven homicides per 100,000, was near the top of the list, just below the United States.

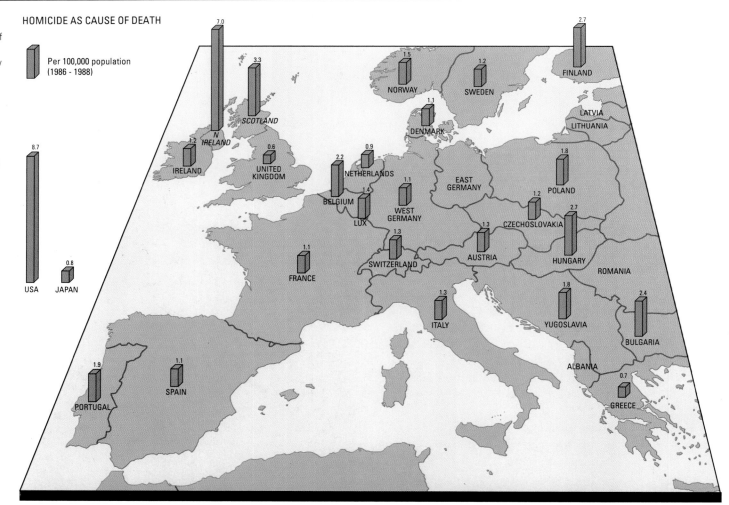

HOMICIDE AS CAUSE OF DEATH

Per 100,000 population (1986 - 1988)

out no crime has been committed; and some countries only record certain types of crime if the criminal has been caught. "Assault" might mean something as minor as threatening behaviour in one country; in other jurisdictions it is confined to cases involving serious bodily harm. The Swiss classify stolen bicycles as motor vehicle thefts.

But the main problem with crime figures is that normally they show only the crimes which people have reported to the police – and people in some countries are more likely to make a report than in others. It may be possible to say whether a particular type of crime is on the increase in a particular country by comparing the ▷

Italy has a unique legal challenge in the Mafia. Many judges, politicians and senior police staff have been gunned down in the course of duty. This trial in Palermo, Sicily, in February 1986 was a first in legal circles; 474 accused were led every day to a specially built bunker-like courthouse guarded by hundreds of police.

GUN LAW

The chart shows the percentage of households with a gun in their possession and the number of individual gun-owners. As part of the International Crime Survey in 1989, householders in 14 countries were asked whether they owned a rifle, a shotgun or a handgun. The World Health Organisation published figures showing the percentage of people who have the misfortune to be shot dead. Comparing the two sets of figures may help establish whether people are more likely to be shot in countries where there are more guns.

In general, countries with high gun-ownership do have more gun deaths. But there are exceptions: more people are shot dead in Belgium than might be expected, and fewer in Switzerland (where many people are required by law to keep and maintain army guns). In Northern Ireland, a relatively small number of people admitted keeping guns (although more than in the rest of the United Kingdom). As unusual circumstances prevail in Northern Ireland, it comes as no surprise to see that the number of gun deaths there is very much higher than every other country in the survey apart from the United States, where the correlation between gun-ownership and homicide seems irrefutable.

GUN-OWNERSHIP AND HOMICIDE

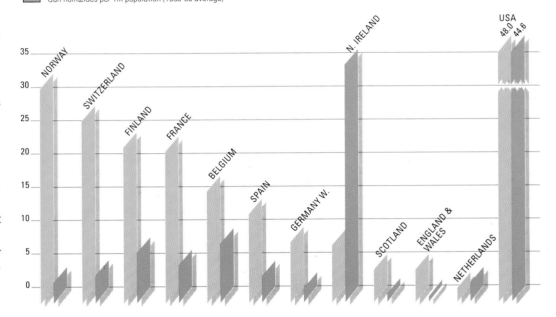

% households who own a gun

Gun homicides per 1m population (1983-86 average)

THE ULTIMATE PENALTY

A quarter of the world has abolished the death penalty. A United Nations Survey of 178 nations and states showed that 25% did not allow capital punishment for any crime; and a further 10% would use it only in exceptional circumstances. Well over half of the 178 states retained the death penalty but in a number of these – about 14% of the total – capital punishment had fallen into disuse.

The map shows which countries have abandoned or retained the death penalty. San Marino led the abolitionist charge, abandoning the death penalty in 1870 – although their last execution was in 1468. The last known execution in the European countries which have abolished the death penalty entirely was in Hungary in 1988. The last execution in countries where the death penalty is retained for exceptional crimes was in Franco's Spain in 1975. Greece, abolitionist *de facto*, held its last execution in 1972. Only Turkey and Yugoslavia retain the penalty and have used it over the last ten years. Poland, Albania and Bulgaria have no record of execution in the last decade.

There is little evidence to suggest that the death penalty is more of a deterrent than life imprisonment. In Australia, for example, homicide rates have fallen since the last execution in the mid-1960s. In Canada, rates have also been lower since the death penalty was abolished in 1976. Although homicides have risen in the United Kingdom since the death penalty was effectively abolished, other violent crimes have increased more quickly. It seems safe to say that the real deterrent is the risk of being caught.

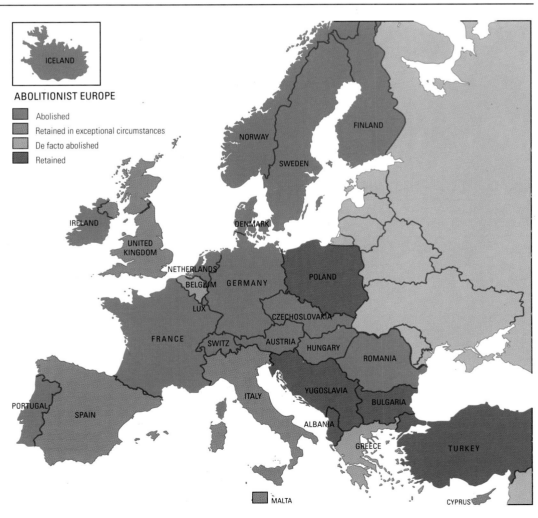

ABOLITIONIST EUROPE

Abolished
Retained in exceptional circumstances
De facto abolished
Retained

figures over a period of time, but that too can be unreliable because public attitudes to reporting crime may change. For example, people may no longer bother to report a minor break-in if experience shows there's no chance of catching the culprit; on the other hand, increasing levels of insurance may mean more minor thefts reported to satisfy the insurance companies' requirements.

Opinion polls may be a more accurate way of measuring crime levels: a survey in England and Wales showed a 17% rise over 15 years in the number of people who said they had been burgled, compared with a rise of 127% in the reported figures for burglary over the same period.

Property and theft

Despite all the difficulties in measuring crime, it is clear enough that crimes against property have increased in almost all western industrialised countries. Many of them have also seen a sharp rise in violent crime. There are plenty of theories – more things to steal, more young men to steal them, inadequate punishments and fewer social restraints – but soaring crime is still difficult to explain satisfactorily.

It is also clear that property offences are increasing much more quickly than crimes of violence. This perhaps reflects the changing nature of society – more houses are now empty all day (because more women are at work),

they contain more portable goods like televisions and video recorders, there are more supermarkets with open shelves, and more credit cards to use fraudulently. No longer is crime confined to the criminal underclasses.

There are two exceptions to this gloomy picture: Switzerland and Japan. The Swiss have relatively small cities, decentralised industries and fewer working women; they lay stress on social responsibility and the need for young people to conform. Similarly, the Japanese emphasise group solidarity and achievement, along with zealous commitment to formal crime control.

Even so, fewer youngsters are coming before the courts, no doubt as a result of demographic changes and because the authorities are increasingly cautioning people rather than prosecuting them. In a sample of 13 countries, the number of juvenile offenders prosecuted fell by 21% between 1980 and 1989, the sharpest reductions being in western Germany, Greece, and Northern Ireland.

The proportion of female offenders has gone up slightly – by 6% in this sample. On average, one offender in five is a woman, with the highest number of female offenders in western Germany and Japan. However, women tend to commit less serious crimes and so they are much less likely to end up in prison.

International crime

Many types of deviant crime defy reliable analysis even within single jurisdictions, let alone from an international perspective. Incidents of organised crime, "white collar" offending, tax evasion, political corruption, environmental pollution and computer fraud (a particular offshoot of technological development) remain hidden within records of regulatory agencies or behind conventional legal categories of violent crime, fraud, and so on. Data on "cross-border" crime is also poor, though economic unity within Europe may bring a better recording machinery.

Drug-related activities and terrorism are the best documented cross-border crime. Drug offences (possession, smuggling, trading and manufacture) increased during the 1980s. A survey of 18 industrialised countries makes depressing reading: between 1980 and 1990, recorded drug offences doubled in 11 countries, and quadrupled in seven more (Japan, Italy and Scotland being the worst). Only Sweden and Canada recorded fewer cases of possession or trading in illegal drugs.

Home-grown terrorism is more common than the international variety, defined as premeditated politically motivated violence perpetrated against non-combatant targets and involving citizens or territory of more than one country. However, statistics for cross-border terrorism are more readily available.

Figures issued by the US Department of State show that in 1987 there were some 830 incidents throughout the world defined as international terrorism, compared with well under 200 in 1968. Since 1987, international terrorism is thought to have declined.

Over half the incidents in 1987 involved bombings. One in six were armed attacks, and one in 15 involved kidnapping. Some 600 people were killed with a further 2,200 wounded. 350 of the 830 incidents took place in the Middle East, and 150 in western Europe. Of these international attacks, 47 took place in Spain, 24 in West Germany, 11 in France and four in the UK. To get the figures in context, there were 1,057 terrorist incidents in Northern Ireland in 1987, with 1,130 people being injured.

Doing a stretch takes on a whole new meaning at Picassent, France. This is the most modern prison in Europe, with individual cells for prisoners; on the whole, France maintains a low prison population, locking away 5% of the people arrested.

EUROPE BEHIND BARS
Estimated prisoners per 100 arrests

- 100
- 50
- 20
- 10
- 5
- Less than 5
- No data available
- USA
- Japan

FINLAND

NORWAY

SWEDEN

ESTONIA

RUSSIA

LATVIA

N.IRELAND

DENMARK

LITHUANIA

IRELAND

BELARUS

UNITED KINGDOM

NETHERLANDS

EAST GERMANY

POLAND

BELGIUM

LUX

WEST GERMANY

CZECHOSLOVAKIA

UKRAINE

FRANCE

SWITZ

AUSTRIA

HUNGARY

MOLDOVA

ROMANIA

PORTUGAL

SPAIN

ITALY

YUGOSLAVIA

BULGARIA

ALBANIA

GREECE

TURKEY

MALTA

Inside information

The map shows the relationship between arrest and imprisonment. All countries publish their imprisonment rates but comparisons can be misleading. Definitions of prisoners differ, and the figures take no account of crime levels or conviction rates. But the figures do indicate that in 1989 the United Kingdom

had the highest rate of imprisonment in western Europe, with nearly 100 prisoners per 100,000 of the population.

A better way of measuring how likely criminals are to end up in prison is to compare the number imprisoned with the number who are arrested. The figures show moderate levels for both the United States and the United Kingdom.

In half the countries of western Europe, the number of prisoners went down during the 1970s. But during the 1980s prison populations went up, with particularly high increases in Malta, the Netherlands, Portugal and Ireland. The steepest declines were in Italy, western Germany, Finland, Northern Ireland and Turkey.

The violent riots at Strangeways Prison in Manchester, England, in 1991 were mainly a response to overcrowding and bad conditions. Many of the UK's prisons were built in Victorian times; then they were model prisons, one man to a cell, designed to hold a third of the population they now house. A young burglar, not a first offender, is more likely to end up in prison in the UK than he is in the rest of Europe. Countries like Germany, Switzerland and France particularly favour community service orders over imprisonment. Governments can affect the size of the prison population by encouraging new sentencing philosophies, and introducing amnesties or parole.

Could it happen to you?

In 1989, 14 countries took part in an International Crime Survey (ICS) using standardised methods in order to achieve comparable results. People were asked if they had been the victim of any one or combination of 11 specified offences during 1988 as well as during the past five years.

The map shows what proportion of the population have been the victim of any crime listed in the 1989 survey: burglary, car crime, robbery and assault (including sexual offences). Crime figures normally reflect only those offences which the police are told about. But those figures can be misleading, and another approach is to ask random samples of people how many crimes they have experienced during the past few months or years.

The results must be treated with caution since a relatively small number of people took part and they were generally the sort of people who could afford a telephone at home.

The victimisation survey shows what sort of people are most at risk. Not surprisingly, younger people were found to be more likely to suffer from bicycle thefts, assault and sexual offences, while middle-aged people and the better-off were more likely to suffer from car crime, especially if they lived in a larger city. Women were less vulnerable in Switzerland, the Netherlands and Northern Ireland – countries where fewer women go out to work.

THE CIRCUMSTANCE OF VICTIMS

- % victims of one or more crime
- % victims of burglary
- % victims of robbery, sexual offences & assault
- % victims of car theft

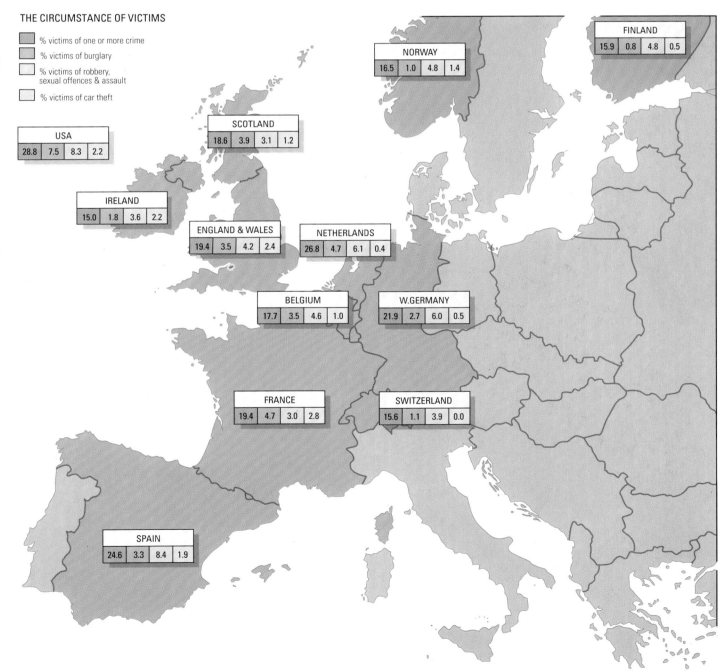

NORWAY			
16.5	1.0	4.8	1.4

FINLAND			
15.9	0.8	4.8	0.5

USA			
28.8	7.5	8.3	2.2

SCOTLAND			
18.6	3.9	3.1	1.2

IRELAND			
15.0	1.8	3.6	2.2

ENGLAND & WALES			
19.4	3.5	4.2	2.4

NETHERLANDS			
26.8	4.7	6.1	0.4

BELGIUM			
17.7	3.5	4.6	1.0

W.GERMANY			
21.9	2.7	6.0	0.5

FRANCE			
19.4	4.7	3.0	2.8

SWITZERLAND			
15.6	1.1	3.9	0.0

SPAIN			
24.6	3.3	8.4	1.9

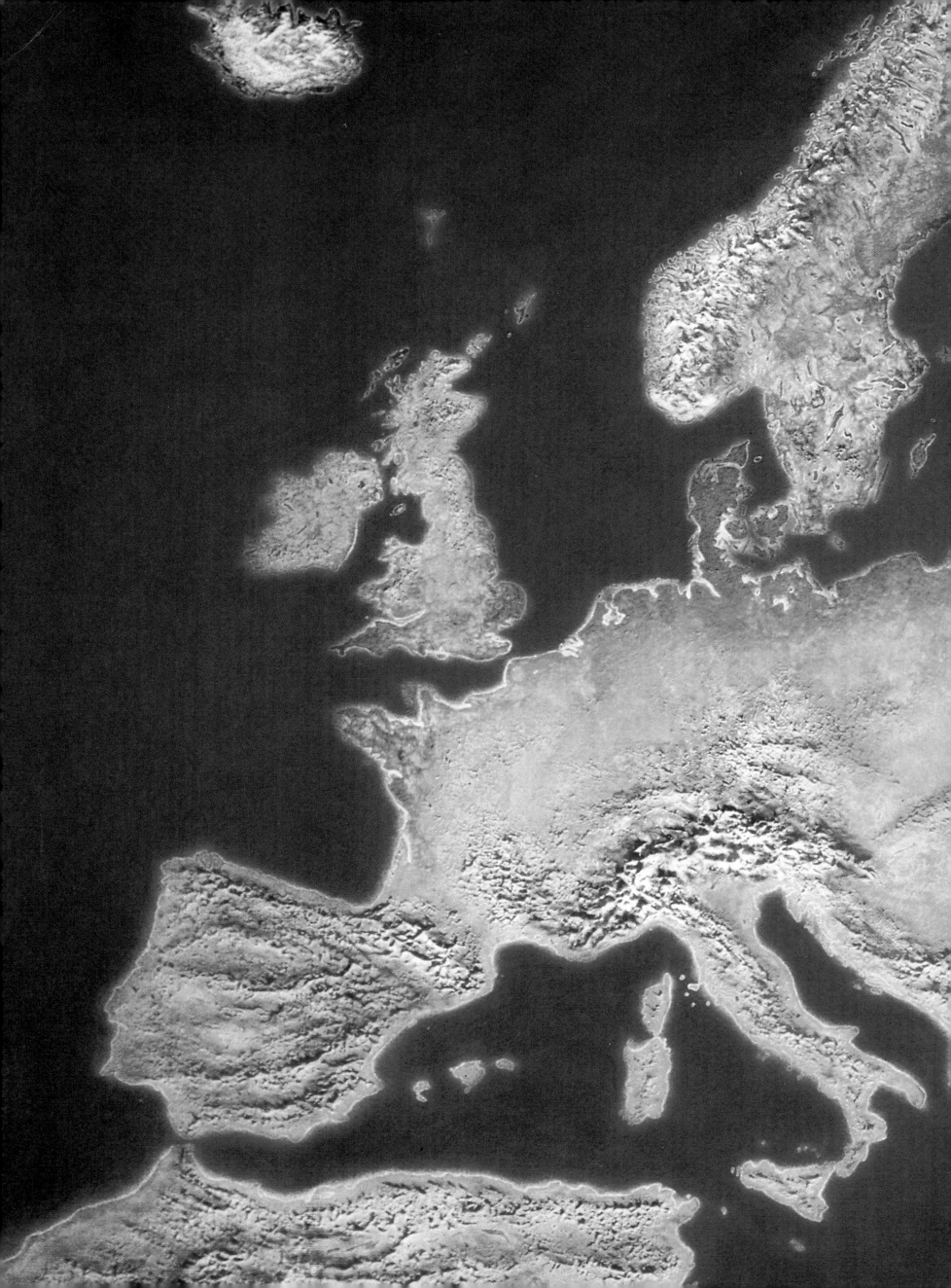

COUNTRY ANALYSIS

This is an at-a-glance, detailed reference section to the vital statistics of more than 40 of Europe's nations and dependencies – most countries have well-defined frontiers others not so. For each country there are facts and figures covering everything from climate to population, from languages to education, from births to employment, from politics to economics and from trade to defence. Figures used are the latest and most reliable available. In some cases, the former Yugoslavia for example, data is available for the federation only so Croatia and Slovenia are not individually represented. Figures for the nations that made up the former Soviet Union are also liable to quick and significant changes as these countries stabilise their economies and react to the implementation of policies radically different from those in place during the 1980s.

1 United Kingdom	12 Faeroe Islands	23 Malta	34 Yugoslavia
2 Channel Islands	13 Iceland	24 Greece	35 Albania
3 Isle of Man	14 Sweden	25 Turkey	36 Romania
4 Ireland	15 Norway	26 Cyprus	37 Bulgaria
5 France	16 Finland	27 Switzerland	38 Estonia
6 Monaco	17 Portugal	28 Liechtenstein	39 Latvia
7 Belgium	18 Spain	29 Austria	40 Lithuania
8 Luxembourg	19 Andorra	30 Germany	41 Belarus
9 Netherlands	20 Italy	31 Poland	42 Ukraine
10 Denmark	21 Vatican City	32 Czechoslovakia	43 Moldova
11 Greenland	22 San Marino	33 Hungary	44 Russia

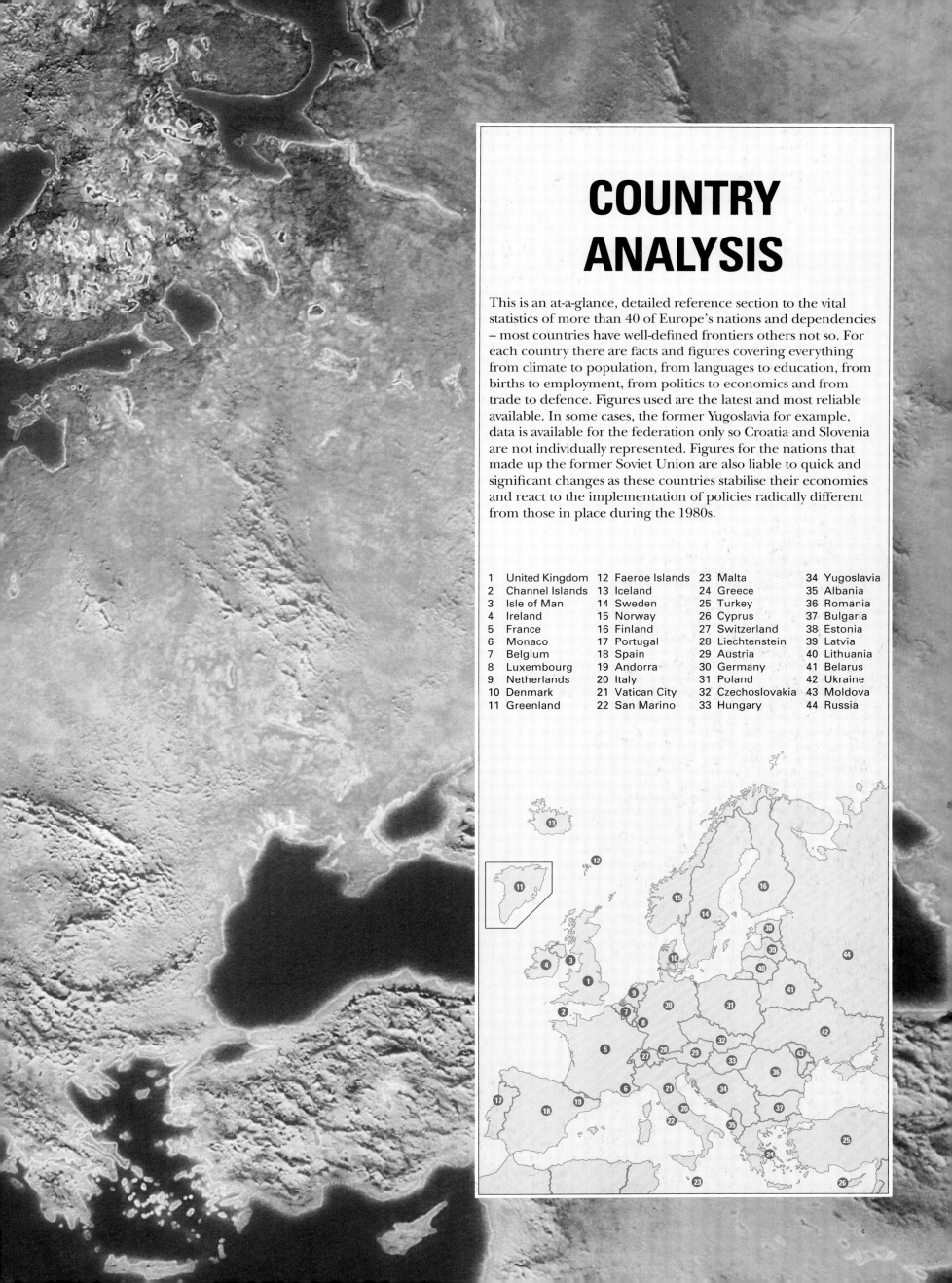

UNITED KINGDOM
UNITED KINGDOM OF GREAT BRITAIN AND NORTHERN IRELAND

AREA	229,880sq km
CLIMATE	Temperate. Average temperatures London Jan. 4·5°C, July 18·0°C. Annual rainfall 600mm
LAND USE	Agriculture 76% Forest 10% Urban 10%
HIGHEST POINT	Ben Nevis 1,342m
MAIN RIVERS	Thames, Severn
CAPITAL	London 6.8m†
OTHER CITIES	Manchester 2.6m Birmingham 992,000 Leeds 712,000 Glasgow 696,000
TIME	GMT
MONEY	1 pound (£) = 100 pence
EXCHANGE RATES	1991 average £1.00 = $1.77 £1.00 = 1.43 ecu
OFFICIAL LANGUAGE	English
MAJOR RELIGIONS	Church of England (30% of all baptisms in England), Roman Catholic, Methodist, United Reformed, Baptist
MEMBER	Commonwealth, Council of Europe, EC, NATO, OECD, UN, WEU

PEOPLE

Population, 1990	57,408,000
Forecast, 2000	57,509,000
% under 15, 1990	18·9
% over 64, 1990	15·5
% average annual increase, 1985–90	0·3
Urban population as % of total, 1990	93
Density	93 people per sq km

BIRTHS by country of mother's birth, 1989 %	
United Kingdom	89
Commonwealth and Pakistan	5
Ireland	1
Rest of world	5

LIVING STANDARDS, 1988	per '000
Passenger cars	312
Telephones	764 (1991)
Television sets	336

POLITICS

POLITICAL SUMMARY
Parliamentary monarchy. The Conservative Party has had control of the 650-member House of Commons since May 1979. The last general election was in April 1992.

MAIN POLITICAL PARTIES
Conservative, Labour, Liberal Democrats

GOVERNMENT FINANCES

£ bn	1986	1987	1988	1989	1990
Revenues	154·3	166·9	184·3	199·9	214·8
Spending	155·9	165·3	173·2	184·5	200·9

†Greater London

SPENDING BY SECTOR, 1990	%
Social security	29
Health	13
Education	13
Defence	11
Transport and communications	4
Other	30

ECONOMY

GDP	$ bn
1990	980
1995 forecast	1,330

Real GDP	
% average annual growth, 1985–90	3·1
GDP per head, 1990	$17,080

Industrial output, % average annual increase, 1985–90	4·7
Consumer prices, % average annual increase, 1985–90	5·9

EMPLOYMENT

EMPLOYMENT BY SECTOR, 1990	%
Services	68
Industry	30
Agriculture	2

Job growth, % average annual increase, 1985–90	1·6

UNEMPLOYMENT RATES, %					
1985	1986	1987	1988	1989	1990
11·6	11·8	10·4	8·2	6·2	5·9

TRADE

FOREIGN TRADE, 1990	$ bn
Exports	183·6
Imports	222·6

MAJOR COMMODITIES, 1990	
Exports	%
Manufactures	74
Fuels	8
Food and beverages	7

Imports	
Manufactured goods	73
Food and beverages	10
Fuels	6

MAJOR TRADING PARTNERS, 1990	
Exports	%
Germany	13
United States	13
France	11
Netherlands	7
Italy	5
Belgium/Luxembourg	5

Imports	
Germanyª	16
United States	11
France	9
Netherlands	8
Japan	5
Italy	5

FINANCE

Central bank
Bank of England
London is a major international banking and financial centre.

Major stock market
London

FT ALL-SHARE INDEX, year-end

1985	1986	1987	1988	1989	1990
682·9	835·5	870·2	927·6	1204·7	1032·5

Market capitalisation, end-1990	$888 bn

Top five companies, by market capitalisation, end-1990	$ bn
British Petroleum (oil and gas)	34·6
British Telecom (telecommunications)	33·7
Shell Transport (oil and gas)	29·3
Glaxo Holdings (health care)	24·9
British Gas (utility)	18·6

EDUCATION

Spending as % of GDP, 1990	5
Minimum school leaving age	16
% adult literacy, 1989	99

ENROLMENT RATIOS, 1988	%
Primary school	100
Secondary	83
Tertiary	23

HEALTH

VITAL STATISTICS, 1989	
Births, rate per '000	12·5
Deaths, rate per '000	12·8
Life expectancy	73 years
Health spending as % of GDP, 1990	5
Doctors per '000	1.4

DEFENCE

Spending as % of GDP, 1990	4

Service not compulsory.

ACTIVE TROOPS, 1990	
Army	149,600
Navy	61,800
Air Force	88,700

ISLE OF MAN
BRITISH CROWN DEPENDENCY

AREA	572sq km
CLIMATE	Mild. Mean average temperature 8·1°C. Average annual rainfall 1,146mm
LAND USE	Agriculture 83%
CAPITAL	Douglas 20,370
TIME	GMT
MONEY	Own currency issued on par with British pound sterling
OFFICIAL LANGUAGE	English

PEOPLE

Population, 1986	64,280
Density	112·4 people per sq km

POLITICS

POLITICAL SUMMARY
British crown dependency administered in accordance with its own laws by the high court of Tynwald. Legislature is 24-member House of Keys. Her Majesty's government in the United Kingdom is responsible for defence and international relations.

ECONOMY

EMPLOYMENT BY SECTOR, 1981	%
Services	25
Manufacturing	13
Construction	11
Transport and communications	9

HEALTH

VITAL STATISTICS, 1990	
Births, rate per '000	13·8
Deaths, rate per '000	14·7

CHANNEL ISLANDS
BRITISH CROWN DEPENDENCIES

AREA	194sq km
CLIMATE	Temperate. Mean average temperature 11·5°C, average annual rainfall, Jersey 863mm, Guernsey 859mm
CAPITALS	Jersey: St Helier Guernsey: St Peter Port
TIME	GMT
MONEY	Own currency issued on par with British pound sterling
OFFICIAL LANGUAGE	English

PEOPLE

Population, 1986	
Jersey	82,810
Guernsey	55,480

Density	
Jersey	713 people per sq km
Guernsey	854 people per sq km

POLITICS

POLITICAL SUMMARY
British crown dependencies administered in accordance with their own laws made by islands' own legislatures. Her Majesty's government in the United Kingdom is responsible for defence and international relations.

FINANCE

Jersey and Guernsey are being developed as financial centres to take advantage of the islands' favourable tax and commercial laws.

IRELAND
REPUBLIC OF IRELAND

AREA	70,284sq km
CLIMATE	Temperate, moderated by Gulf Stream. Average temperatures Dublin Jan. 4·7°C, July 15°C. Annual rainfall 750mm
LAND USE	Agriculture 80%
HIGHEST POINT	Carantuohil 1,01m
MAIN RIVERS	Shannon, Barrow, Suir, Erne, Boyne
CAPITAL	Dublin 502,700
OTHER CITIES	Cork 133,300 Limerick 56,300
TIME	GMT
MONEY	1 pound (I£) = 100 pence
EXCHANGE RATES	1991 average I£1·62 = $1·00 I£1·30 = 1 ecu
OFFICIAL LANGUAGE	Irish, English widely used
MAJOR RELIGION	Roman Catholic 95%
MEMBER	Council of Europe, EC, OECD, UN

PEOPLE

Population, 1990	3,503,630
Forecast, 2000	4,080,000
% under 15, 1990	27.6
% over 64, 1990	10.2
% average annual increase, 1985–90	0.9
Urban population as % of total, 1990	57
Density	50 people per sq km

LIVING STANDARDS, 1988	per '000
Passenger cars	210
Telephones	339 (1991)
Television sets	216

POLITICS

POLITICAL SUMMARY
The president is directly elected for seven years. The prime minister heads the government, who are appointed by the president on basis of ability to gain support of the Dail, directly elected by a form of proportional representation for five years, and the 60-member Seanad, 11 nominated by the prime minister, six elected by universities and 43 elected by members of the Dail, the Senate and local councillors.

MAIN POLITICAL PARTIES:
Fianna Fail, Fine Gael, Labour Party, Progressive Democrats, Workers' Party

GOVERNMENT FINANCES

I£ bn	1986	1987	1988	1989	1990
Revenues	6·7	7·2	7·7	7·6	8·3
Spending	8·1	8·3	8·0	8·0	8·4

SPENDING BY SECTOR, 1990	%
Social welfare	15
Debt service	36
Health	20
Education	20

ECONOMY

GDP	$ bn
1990	41.4
1995 forecast	57.7
Real GDP, average annual growth, 1985–90	3·5
GDP per head, 1990	$11,950

Industrial output, % average annual increase, 1985–90	18.2
Consumer prices, % average annual increase, 1985–90	3.3

EMPLOYMENT

Employment, % average annual increase, 1985–90	0·9

EMPLOYMENT BY SECTOR, 1990	%
Services	57
Industry	22
Agriculture and forestry	15
Construction	6

UNEMPLOYMENT RATE, %					
1985	1986	1987	1988	1989	1990
17·4	17·4	17·7	16·7	15·6	13·7

TRADE

FOREIGN TRADE, 1990	$ bn
Exports	57·5
Imports	54·7

MAJOR COMMODITIES, 1990	
Exports	%
Machinery and transport equipment	31
Food and livestock	22
Chemicals	16
Imports	
Machinery and transport equipment	36
Manufactured goods	15
Chemicals and plastics	13

MAJOR TRADING PARTNERS, 1990	
Exports	%
United Kingdom	34
Germany	12
France	11
United States	8
Netherlands	6
Imports	
United Kingdom	38
United States	15
Germany	8
Japan	6
France	5

FINANCE

Central bank
Central Bank of Ireland, Dublin
Major stock market
Dublin

ISEQ INDEX, year-end					
1985	1986	1987	1988	1989	1990
727·0	1081·1	1000·0	1378·0	1765·9	1201·8

Market capitalisation, end-1990	$11 bn

Top five companies, by market capitalisation, end-1990	$ bn
Jefferson Smurfit Group (paper products)	1·9
Allied Irish Bank (banking)	1.7
CRH (construction)	1.1
Bank of Ireland (banking)	1.0
Fyffes (food products)	0.5

EDUCATION

Spending as % of GDP, 1990	7
Years of compulsory education	9
% adult literacy, 1989	99

ENROLMENT RATIOS, 1988	%
Primary school	100
Secondary	98
Tertiary	25

HEALTH

VITAL STATISTICS, 1989	
Births, rate '000	14·7
Deaths, rate '000	8·8
Life expectancy	75 years
Health spending as % of GDP, 1990	8
Doctors per '000	1·5

DEFENCE

Spending as % of GDP, 1990	1
Voluntary service.	

ACTIVE TROOPS, 1990	
Army	11,200
Air Force	800
Navy	900

BRITISH GOVERNMENT OIL REVENUES

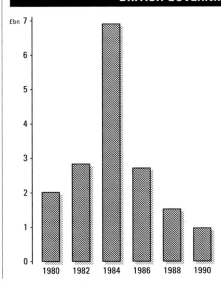

Since its discovery in the mid-1960s, North Sea oil has played an important role in the United Kingdom's economy, helping to make the country self-sufficient in energy and revitalising parts of Scotland where onshore activites are concentrated.

The distribution of government revenues from oil activities has been a sensitive political issue in Scotland, periodically encouraging Scottish calls for independence from Westminster. Oil is, however, a far less important source of revenues than it has been previously. From a peak of $10.02bn in 1985, government takings from the oil industry have now fallen to under $1.78bn.

FRANCE
REPUBLIC OF FRANCE

AREA	543,965sq km
CLIMATE	Maritime in north-west, continental in centre, mediterranean in south. Average temperatures Paris Jan. 3·0°C, July 18·0°C. Annual rainfall 573mm
LAND USE	Agriculture 57%
HIGHEST POINT	Mont Blanc 4,810m
MAIN RIVERS	Loire, Rhône, Seine, Garonne, Rhine
CAPITAL	Paris 8·7m†
OTHER CITIES	Lyon 1·2m Marseille 1·1m Lille 936,000
TIME	GMT + 1 hour
MONEY	1 franc (FFr) = 100 centimes
EXCHANGE RATES	1991 average FFr 5·64 = $1·00 FFr 6·98 = 1 ecu
OFFICIAL LANGUAGE	French
MAJOR RELIGION	Roman Catholic 75%
MEMBER	Council of Europe, EC, OECD, UN, WEU

PEOPLE

Population, 1990	56,138,000
Forecast, 2000	58,856,000
% under 15, 1990	19·8
% over 64, 1990	13·8
% average annual increase, 1985–90	0·3
Urban population as % of total, 1990	74
Density	102 people per sq km

MAJOR ETHNIC GROUPS, 1990	%
French	93
Algerian	2
Portuguese	1

LIVING STANDARDS, 1988	per '000
Passenger cars	394
Telephones	623 (1991)
Television sets	394

POLITICS

POLITICAL SUMMARY
Presidential republic. Executive power is invested in a president who is elected every seven years. The president appoints the prime minister, who is responsible to the bicameral parliament comprising the 321-member Senate and the 577-member National Assembly. Senate members are elected by local councils for nine years, one-third retire every three years. National Assembly members are directly elected for five years.

MAIN POLITICAL PARTIES
Socialist Party, Rally for the Republic, Union for French Democracy, Social Democrat Centre, Communist Party of France, National Front

GOVERNMENT FINANCES

FFr bn	1987	1988	1989	1990
Revenues	942.5	1,005.6	1,082.1	1,129.5
Spending	1,102.4	1,153.0	1,177.2	1,219.6

†Metropolitan Paris

SPENDING BY SECTOR, 1989

	%
Education and culture	24
Social welfare, health and employment	19
Defence	16
Public administration	13
Foreign relations and aid	5
Housing and urban development	5
Transport and communications	4
Other	14

ECONOMY

GDP	$ bn
1990	1,190
1995 forecast	1,600

Real GDP, % average annual growth, 1985–90	2.9
GDP per head, 1990	$21,100

Industrial output, % average annual increase, 1985–90	2.3
Consumer prices, % average annual increase, 1985–90	3.1

EMPLOYMENT

EMPLOYMENT BY SECTOR, 1990

	%
Services	65
Industry	21
Construction	7
Agriculture	7

Job growth, % average annual increase, 1985–90	0.7

UNEMPLOYMENT RATE, %

1985	1986	1987	1988	1989	1990
10.2	10.4	10.5	10.0	9.4	8.9

TRADE

FOREIGN TRADE, 1990

	$ bn
Exports	215.8
Imports	233.8

MAJOR COMMODITIES, 1990

Exports	%
Capital equipment	26
Food and beverages	16
Non-durable consumer goods	15
Chemicals	15

Imports	
Capital equipment	24
Non-durable consumer goods	16
Chemicals	15
Food and beverages	11

MAJOR TRADING PARTNERS, 1990

Exports	%
Germany	17
Italy	1
Britain	9
Belgium	9
United States	6

Imports	
Germany	19
Italy	12
Belgium	9
United States	8
Britain	7

FINANCE

Central bank
Banque de France, Paris

Major stock market
Paris

CAC GENERAL INDEX, year-end

1985	1986	1987	1988	1989	1990
265.8	397.8	280.7	415.6	553.7	413.0

Market capitalisation, end-1990	$342 bn

Top five companies, by market capitalisation, end-1990	$ bn
Elf Aquitaine (oil and gas)	13.7
Alcatel Alsthom (electronics)	11.4
LVMH (food, drink and luxury goods)	9.1
Générale des Eaux	7.8
BSN (food products)	7.7

EDUCATION

Spending as % of GDP, 1990	5
% adult literacy, 1989	99

ENROLMENT RATIOS, 1988

	%
Primary school	100
Secondary	94
Tertiary	35

HEALTH

VITAL STATISTICS, 1989

Births, rate per '000	13.8
Deaths, rate per '000	10.3
Life expectancy at birth	76 years
Health spending as % of GDP, 1990	9
Doctors per '000	2.2

DEFENCE

Spending as % of GDP, 1990	3

Compulsory service for men of 12 months.

ACTIVE TROOPS, 1990

Army	280,300
Air Force	92,900
Navy	65,300
Reserves	419,000

MONACO
PRINCIPALITY OF MONACO

AREA	195 hectares
CLIMATE	Mediterranean. Average temperatures Jan. 10°C, July 23.3°C. Annual rainfall 758mm
CAPITAL	Monaco-Ville
TIME	GMT + 1 hour
MONEY	French franc
OFFICIAL LANGUAGE	French

PEOPLE

Population, 1990	29,880

POLITICS

POLITICAL SUMMARY
Parliamentary principality. The monarch nominates the minister of state from a list of three French diplomats submitted by the French government. 18-member National Council elected every 5 years.

ECONOMY

A mixture of light industry and tourism .

BELGIUM
KINGDOM OF BELGIUM

AREA	30,519sq km
CLIMATE	Cool temperate. Average temperatures Brussels Jan. 2.2°C, July 17.8°C. Annual rainfall 775mm
LAND USE	Agriculture 44 % Forest 23%
HIGHEST POINT	Botrange 694m
MAIN RIVERS	Schelde, Meuse, Sambre
CAPITAL	Brussels 1m
OTHER CITIES	Antwerp 476,000 Ghent 232,600 Charleroi 208,990
TIME	GMT + 1 hour
MONEY	1 franc (BFr) = 100 centimes
EXCHANGE RATES	1991 average BFr 34.1 = $1.00 BFr 42.2 = 1 ecu
OFFICIAL LANGUAGES	Flemish, French, German
MAJOR RELIGIONS	Mainly Roman Catholic, proportions not available
MEMBER	Council of Europe, EC, NATO, OECD, UN, WEU

PEOPLE

Population, 1990	9,845,630
Forecast, 2000	9,832,000
% under 15, 1990	17.9
% over 64, 1990	14.9
% average annual increase, 1985–90	0.1
Urban population as % of total, 1990	97
Density	283 people per sq km

MAJOR LANGUAGE GROUPS, 1990

	%
Flemish	57.6
French	31.9
Bilingual	9.8
German	0.7

LIVING STANDARDS, 1988

	per '000
Passenger cars	349
Telephones	498 (1991)
Television sets	303 (1984)

POLITICS

POLITICAL SUMMARY
Parliamentary monarchy. The monarch nominally appoints a prime minister who commands a majority of the lower house of parliament. The two-house legislature comprises a 212-member Chamber of Representatives, elected by proportional representation for four years, and a 181-member Senate, of which 106 are directly elected, 50 elected by provincial councils, 25 co-opted by elected members, and the heir to the throne.

MAIN POLITICAL PARTIES
French Socialist Party, Liberal Party, French-speaking Democratic Front, Ecology Party; **Flemish** Socialist Party, Liberal Party, People's Union, Ecology Party

GOVERNMENT FINANCES

BFr bn	1986	1987	1988	1989	1990
Revenues	1,963	1,933	1,920	2,044	2,170
Spending	1,412	1,495	1,507	1,618	1,734

SPENDING BY SECTOR, 1989

	%
Government departments	40
Debt service	22
Education and cultural services	15
Pensions	10
Defence	5
Other	8

ECONOMY

GDP	$ bn
1990	197.6
1995 forecast	266.5

Real GDP, % average annual growth, 1985–90	3.5
GDP per head, 1990	$19,770

Industrial output, % average annual increase, 1985–90	3.5
Consumer prices, % average annual increase, 1985–90	2.1

EMPLOYMENT

EMPLOYMENT BY SECTOR, 1990

	%
Services	69
Industry	28
Farming	3

Employment, % average annual increase, 1985–90	1.0

UNEMPLOYMENT RATE, %

1985	1986	1987	1988	1989	1990
12.3	11.6	11.3	10.3	9.3	8.8

TRADE

FOREIGN TRADE, 1990

	$ bn
Exports	118.0
Imports	119.8

MAJOR COMMODITIES, 1990

Exports	%
Machinery and transport equipment	31
Chemicals	15
Metals	12
Food	7
Textiles and clothing	7

Imports	
Machinery and transport equipment	35
Chemicals	12
Food and agricultural products	10
Fuels	9
Metals	8

MAJOR TRADING PARTNERS, 1990

Exports	%
Germany	21
France	20
Netherlands	14
United Kingdom	9
Italy	7

Imports	
Germany	24
Netherlands	18
France	16
United Kingdom	8
Italy	5

FINANCE

Central bank
Banque Nationale de Belgique, Brussels
Major stock market
Brussels

BRUSSELS SE GENERAL INDEX, year-end

1985	1986	1987	1988	1989	1990
2034·9	2767·4	2393·2	2537·0	4003·0	2974·0

Market capitalisation, end-1990	$66 bn

Top five companies, by market capitalisation, end-1990	$ bn
Petrofina (oil and gas)	6·9
Electrabel (utilities)	6·7
Générale de Belgique (holding company)	4·0
Tractabel (utilities)	3·3
Solvay (chemicals)	2·8

EDUCATION

Spending as % of GDP, 1986	5
Years of compulsory education	12
% adult literacy, 1989	99

ENROLMENT RATIOS, 1990	%
Primary school	100
Secondary	85
Tertiary	33

HEALTH

VITAL·STATISTICS, 1990

Births, rate per '000	11·6
Deaths, rate per '000	11·8
Life expectancy	75 years
Health spending as % of GDP, 1986	5
Doctors per '000, 1984	2·8

DEFENCE

Spending as % of GDP, 1990   2
Compulsory service for men of 10–12 months.

ACTIVE TROOPS, 1990

Army	62,700
Air Force	18,200
Reserves	234,000

THE BENELUX SOLUTION

Benelux, the customs union between Belgium and Luxembourg on the one hand, and the Netherlands on the other hand, was agreed in principle before the end of the second world war and set up in 1948.

Many of the union's agreements were models for later European integration; internal tariffs were abolished, import quotas between the three countries were reduced and a common external tariff was adopted. Labour and capital move freely within the area. Belgium and Luxembourg are almost completely integrated economically; their currencies are on a par, and trade and current-account statistics are reported only for the two countries combined.

The Benelux countries joined the European Community in 1958 and have since been enthusiastic advocates of increased European integration. Most EC institutions are headquartered in Brussels and Amsterdam has been named as a potential location for a European central bank.

LUXEMBOURG
GRAND DUCHY OF LUXEMBOURG

AREA	2,586sq km
CLIMATE	Continental, cold winters. Average temperatures Jan. 0·7°C, July 17·5°C. Annual rainfall 764mm
HIGHEST POINT	Buurgplaatz 559m
MAIN RIVERS	Sur, Our, Moselle
CAPITAL	Luxembourg-Ville 76,600
OTHER CITIES	Esch-sur-Alzette 23,700
TIME	GMT + 1 hour
MONEY	1 LFr = 100 centimes (Belgian franc is also legal currency at a one-to-one exchange rate)
EXCHANGE RATES	1991 average LFr 34·1 = $1·00 LFr 42·2 = 1 ecu
OFFICIAL LANGUAGE	Letzeburgish
MAJOR RELIGION	Roman Catholic 94%
MEMBER	Council of Europe, EC, NATO, OECD, UN, WEU

PEOPLE

Population, 1990	381,000
Forecast, 2000	385,000
% under 15, 1990	17·2
% over 64, 1990	13·2
% average annual increase, 1985–90	0·3
Urban population as % of total, 1990	84
Density	146 people per sq km

MAJOR ETHNIC GROUPS, 1990	%
Luxembourger	74
Portugese	8
Italian	6
French	3

LIVING STANDARDS, 1988	per '000
Passenger cars	443
Telephones	636 (1991)
Television sets	253

POLITICS

POLITICAL SUMMARY
The grand duke (or duchess) is head of state, and, constitutionally, has executive power. These powers are exercised, however, through a council of ministers, headed by a prime minister appointed by the grand duke. The legislature is a 60-member Chamber of Deputies directly elected by a form of proportional representation for five years.
The 21-member Council of States, appointed by the grand duke, has some legislative powers.

MAIN POLITICAL PARTIES
Christian Social Party, Socialist Party, Democratic Party, Communist Party, Ecology Party, Green Party

GOVERNMENT FINANCES

LFr bn	1987	1988	1989	1990	1991
Revenues	85·9	92·7	103·2	97·2	109·1
Spending	86·3	92·4	103·0	94·4	108·5

ECONOMY

GDP	$ bn
1990	8·8
1995 forecast	9·4
Real GDP, % average annual growth, 1985–90	4·4
GDP per head, 1990	$23,100

Industrial output, % average annual increase, 1985–90	4·6
Consumer prices, % average annual increase, 1985–90	1·7

GDP BY SECTOR, 1989	%
Services	58
Manufacturing	25
Construction	6
Agriculture	2
Energy	2
Other	7

EMPLOYMENT

Job growth, % average annual increase, 1985–89	2·4

UNEMPLOYMENT RATE, %

1985	1986	1987	1988	1989	1990
1·6	1·4	1·6	1·4	1·3	1·3

TRADE

FOREIGN TRADE, 1990 for further breakdown see Belgium	$ bn
Exports	6·7
Imports	7·7

FINANCE

Central bank
Institut Monetaire Luxembourgeois
Luxembourg is a major international banking centre.
Major stock market
Luxembourg

LUXEMBOURG DOMESTIC SHARE INDEX, year-end

1985	1986	1987	1988	1989	1990
1803·7	2468·3	2021·2	2498·6	2730·4	2302·9

Market capitalisation, end-1990	$10 bn

Top five companies, by market capitalisation, end-1990	$ bn
Minorco (mining)	2·3
IFINT (financial services)	1·3
Safra Republic Holdings (financial services)	1·0
Audiofina (financial services)	0·6
ARBED (mining)	0·5

EDUCATION

Years of compulsory education	9
% adult literacy, 1989	99

HEALTH

VITAL STATISTICS, 1989

Births, rate per '000	12·3
Deaths, rate per '000	10·5
Doctors per '000	1·9

DEFENCE

Spending as % of GDP, 1990	1
Active armed forces	800

NETHERLANDS
KINGDOM OF THE NETHERLANDS

AREA	40,844sq km
CLIMATE	Cool temperate. Average temperatures Amsterdam Jan. 2·3°C, July 16·5°C. Annual rainfall 850mm
LAND USE	Agriculture 54% Forest 26%
HIGHEST POINT	Vaalserberg 321m
MAIN RIVERS	Rhine, Maas, Scheldt
CAPITAL	Amsterdam 695,000
OTHER CITIES	Rotterdam 576,000 The Hague (seat of government) 444,000 Utrecht 231,000
TIME	GMT + 1 hour
MONEY	1 guilder (Dfl) = 100 cents
EXCHANGE RATES	1991 average DFl 1.87 = $1.00 DFl 2.31 = 1 ecu
OFFICIAL LANGUAGE	Dutch
MAJOR RELIGIONS	Roman Catholic 38% Protestant 30%
MEMBER	Council of Europe, EC, NATO, OECD, UN, WEU

PEOPLE

Population, 1990	14,944,000
Forecast, 2000	15,207,000
% under 15, 1990	17·8
% over 64, 1990	12·9
% average annual increase, 1985–90	0·6
Urban population as % of total, 1990	89
Density	361 people per sq km

MAJOR IMMIGRANT GROUPS, 1990	%
Other EC countries	28
Non-EC Europe	18
Africa	18
Asia	10

LIVING STANDARDS, 1988	per '000
Passenger cars	348
Telephones	639
Television sets	327

POLITICS

POLITICAL SUMMARY
The monarch has mainly formal powers. Executive power lies with the Council of Ministers, headed by a prime minister who is appointed by the monarch and responsible to the legislature. The two-chamber Staten General (parliament) comprises the 75-member first chamber, elected by the 12 provincial councils for six years, and the 150-member Second Chamber, directly elected by a form of proportional representation for four years.

MAIN POLITICAL PARTIES
Christian Democrat Appeal, Labour Party, People's Party for Freedom and Democracy, Democrats 1966, Green Left, Political Reformed Party, Reformed Political Association, Reformed Political Federation, Centre Democrats, Socialist Party

GOVERNMENT FINANCES

DFl bn	1986	1987	1988	1989	1990
Revenues	159·7	193·5	183·7	156·6	175·2
Spending	167·3	208·3	200·6	181·8	201·4

SPENDING BY SECTOR, 1990 %

	%
Social security and health services	23
Education and culture	18
Debt service	11
Defence	7
Housing	6
Foreign relations and aid	6
Other	29

ECONOMY

GDP	$ bn
1990	278
1995 forecast	386

Real GDP, % average annual growth, 1985–90	2·6
GDP per head, 1990	$18,400
Industrial output, % average annual increase, 1985–90	1·7
Consumer prices, % average annual increase, 1985–90	0·7

EMPLOYMENT

EMPLOYMENT BY SECTOR, 1989 %

	%
Services	33
Government and community services	36
Manufacturing, mining and construction	26
Agriculture and forestry	5

Job growth, % average annual increase, 1985–90	1·7

UNEMPLOYMENT RATE, %

1985	1986	1987	1988	1989	1990
10·6	9·9	9·6	9·2	8·3	7·5

TRADE

FOREIGN TRADE, 1990 $ bn

	$ bn
Exports	131·4
Imports	129·9

MAJOR COMMODITIES, 1990

Exports	%
Machinery and transport equipment	24
Food, beverages and tobacco	19
Chemicals and plastics	17
Fuels	10

Imports	
Machinery and transport equipment	31
Food, beverages and tobacco	11
Chemicals and plastics	11
Fuels	10

MAJOR TRADING PARTNERS, 1990

Exports	%
Germany	28
Belgium/Luxembourg	15
France	11
United Kingdom	10
Italy	7

Imports	
Germany	26
Belgium/Luxembourg	14
United Kingdom	8
United States	8
France	8

FINANCE

Central bank
De Nederlandsche Bank, Amsterdam
Major stock market
Amsterdam

CBS INDEX, year-end

1985	1986	1987	1988	1989	1990
155·4	162·9	128·7	165·8	202·8	168·3

Market capitalisation, end-1990	$149 bn

Top five companies, by market capitalisation, end-1990 $ bn

	$ bn
Royal Dutch Petroleum (oil and gas)	41.9
Unilever (food and grocery products)	14.5
ABN-AMRO Holding (banking)	4.8
ING (insurance)	4.3
Philips (electronics)	3.6

EDUCATION

Spending as % of GDP, 1990	7
% adult literacy	99

ENROLMENT RATIOS, 1988 %

	%
Primary school	100
Secondary	100
Tertiary	25

HEALTH

VITAL STATISTICS, 1989

Births, rate per '000	12·7
Deaths, rate per '000	8·7
Life expectancy	77 years
Health spending as % of GDP, 1990	8
Doctors per '000	2.4

DEFENCE

Spending as % of GDP, 1990	3

Compulsory service for men of 20–22 months, possible recall until age 35.

ACTIVE TROOPS, 1990

Army	64,100
Air Force	16,000
Navy	16,600
Reserves	152,400

DENMARK
KINGDOM OF DENMARK

AREA	43,077sq km
CLIMATE	Cool temperate. Average temperatures Copenhagen Jan. 0·5°C, July 17·0°C. Annual rainfall 571mm
LAND USE	Agriculture 65% Forest 11%
HIGHEST POINT	Yding Skohoj 173m
MAIN RIVERS	Gudena
CAPITAL	Copenhagen 1·4m
OTHER CITIES	Arhus 195,200 Odense 137,300 Alborg 113,700
TIME	GMT + 1 hour
MONEY	1 krone (DKr) = 100 ore
EXCHANGE RATES	1991 average DKr 6·40 = $1·00 DKr 7·91 = 1 ecu
OFFICIAL LANGUAGE	Danish
MAJOR RELIGION	Lutheran 90%
MEMBER	Council of Europe, EC, NATO, OECD, UN

PEOPLE

Population, 1990	5,143,000
Forecast, 2000	5,153,000
% under 15, 1990	17·0
% over 64, 1990	15·4
% average annual increase, 1985–90	0·1
Urban population as % of total, 1990	87
Density	119 people per sq km

MAJOR ETHNIC GROUPS, 1990 %

	%
Danish	96

LIVING STANDARDS, 1988 per '000

	per '000
Passenger cars	321
Telephones	879 (1991)
Television sets	392

POLITICS

POLITICAL SUMMARY
Parliamentary monarchy. The crown nominally appoints a prime minister, who commands a majority in the Folketing (parliament), which in turn chooses a state council(cabinet). All ministers are responsible to the parliament. The one-chamber Folketing has 179 members, including two each from the Faeroe islands and Greenland, elected by a form of proportional representation for four years.

MAIN POLITICAL PARTIES
Social Democratic Party, Conservative People's Party, Liberal Party, Socialist People's Party, Progress Party, Centre Democrats, Radical Liberal Party, Christian People's Party

GOVERNMENT FINANCES

DKr bn	1988	1989	1990	1991 (budget)
Revenues	199·8	208·4	221·5	291·4
Spending	213·2	227·1	228·5	307·5

SPENDING BY SECTOR, 1990 %

	%
Social affairs	34
Education	8
Defence	6
Law	2
Other	50

ECONOMY

GDP	$ bn
1990	130·9
1995 forecast	176·2

Real GDP, % average annual growth, 1985–90	1·5
GDP per head, 1990	$25,480
Industrial output, % average annual increase, 1985–90	5·9
Consumer prices, % average annual increase, 1985–90	3·9

EMPLOYMENT

EMPLOYMENT BY SECTOR, 1990 %

	%
Services	67
Industry	20
Farming	6
Construction	7

Job growth, % average annual increase, 1985–90	0·5

UNEMPLOYMENT RATE, %

1985	1986	1987	1988	1989	1990
9·0	7·8	7·8	8·5	9·2	9·5

TRADE

FOREIGN TRADE, 1990 $ bn

	$ bn
Exports	35·0
Imports	31·6

TOTAL TAX REVENUES AS % OF GDP, 1990

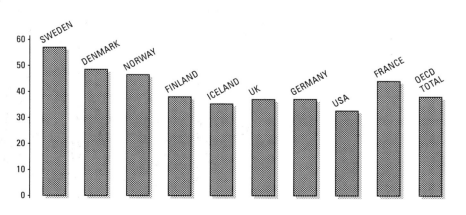

The ratio of total tax revenues to GDP is a measure of a country's tax burden. On that basis, Scandinavian countries top the tax league. Sweden has the highest taxes, equivalent to 57.7% of GDP in 1990, up from 49.1% in 1980. A long way behind, in second and third places, are Denmark (48.1% in 1990) and Norway, which was the only country to reduce its tax burden significantly, from 47.1% in 1980 to 46.2% in 1990. Despite the much trumpeted "tax cuts" in the 1980s in America and Britain, the tax burdens of both countries actually increased. Britain's taxes rose from 35.3% of its GDP in 1980 to 36.8% in 1990; America's edged up from 29.5% to 30.1%. America and Australia have the lowest tax burdens among the OECD economies.

MAJOR COMMODITIES, 1990

Exports	%
Machinery and transport equipment	27
Food, beverages and tobacco	20
Chemicals	9
Furniture	4
Fuels and energy	4

Imports	
Machinery and transport equipment	27
Chemicals	11
Fuels	7
Iron and steel	4

MAJOR TRADING PARTNERS, 1990

Exports	%
Germany	20
Sweden	13
United Kingdom	11
France	6
Norway	6

Imports	
Germany	22
Sweden	12
United Kingdom	8
United States	6
Netherlands	6

FINANCE

Central bank
Danmarks Nationalbank, Copenhagen
Major stock market Copenhagen

COPENHAGEN SE INDEX, year-end

1985	1986	1987	1988	1989	1990
236·8	192·2	182·5	271·8	363·2	314·8

Market capitalisation, end-1990	$42 bn

Top five companies, by market capitalisation, end-1990 $ bn

D/s Svendborg (transport and storage)	2·7
D/s 1912 (transport and storage)	2·7
Carlsberg (beverages and tobacco)	2·5
Den Danske Bank (banking)	2·4
Baltica Holding (Holding company)	2·0

EDUCATION

Spending as % of GDP, 1990	7
Years of compulsory education	8
% adult literacy, 1989	99

ENROLMENT RATIOS, 1990 %

Primary school	99
Secondary	107
Tertiary	31

HEALTH

VITAL STATISTICS, 1989

Births, rate per '000	10·8
Deaths, rate per '000	11·3
Life expectancy at birth	76 years
Health spending as % of GDP, 1990	6
Doctors per '000	2·5

DEFENCE

Spending as % of GDP, 1990	2

Compulsory service for men of 9–12 months

ACTIVE TROOPS, 1990

Army	17,900
Air Force	6,500
Navy	5,600
Reserves	72,700

GREENLAND
PART OF KINGDOM OF DENMARK

AREA	2,175,600sq km (341,700 habitable)
CLIMATE	Cold, temperature range Jan -11°C to -3°C, July 3-11°C
LAND USE	Ice-covered 85%
CAPITAL	Nuuk 12,220
TIME	GMT -3 hours
MONEY	Danish krone
OFFICIAL LANGUAGES	Greenlandic, Danish
MAJOR RELIGION	Evangelical Lutheran 98%
MEMBER	NATO, Nordic Council (not a member of EC)

PEOPLE

Population, 1990	56,630
% average annual increase, 1985–90	1·1
Density	0·2 per sq km, (habitable area)

POLITICS

POLITICAL SUMMARY
Part of Danish Kingdom; home rule introduced in 1979 with the Danish government remaining responsible for foreign affairs, defence and justice. 27-member parliament elected by proportional representation for a maximum of four years. Greenland also elects two members to the Danish Folketing.

MAJOR POLITICAL PARTIES
Solidarity, Forward, Inuit Brotherhood, Polar Party

ECONOMY

GDP	$m
1986 estimate	465
GDP per head, 1986	$8,780

TRADE

FOREIGN TRADE, 1989	$m
Exports	453
Imports	428

MAJOR COMMODITIES, 1989

Exports	%
Fish products	78
Minerals	18

Imports	
Machinery and transport equipment	25
Food	13
Fuels	10

MAJOR TRADING PARTNERS, 1990

Exports	%
Denmark	25
Japan	19
Germany	14
Britain	13

Imports	
Denmark	69
Germany	4
Norway	4
United States	4

HEALTH

VITAL STATISTICS, 1988

Births, rate per '000	22·2
Deaths, rate per '000	8·0

FAEROE ISLANDS
PART OF KINGDOM OF DENMARK

AREA	1,399sq km
CLIMATE	Cool, moderated by Gulf Stream. Temperature range Jan. 1-6°C, August 9-14°C
LAND USE	Archipelago of 18 islands, 17 inhabited
CAPITAL	Torshavn 16,260
TIME	GMT + 1 hours
MONEY	Danish krone
OFFICIAL LANGUAGES	Faeroese, Danish
MAJOR RELIGIONS	Evangelical Lutheran 80%, Plymouth Brethren 19%
MEMBER	Nordic Council (not a member of EC)

PEOPLE

Population, 1990	47,840
% average annual increase, 1985–90	1·0
Density	34.2 people per sq km

POLITICS

POLITICAL SUMMARY
Part of Danish Kingdom; home rule introduced in 1948 with the Danish government remaining responsible for foreign affairs, defence and justice. 32-member parliament is elected by proportional representation.

MAJOR POLITICAL PARTIES
Social Democratic Party, People's Party, Union Party, Republican Party, Home Rule Party

ECONOMY

GDP	
1987 estimate	$686m
GDP per head, 1987	$ 14,600

TRADE

FOREIGN TRADE, 1989	$m
Exports	372
Imports	373

MAJOR COMMODITIES, 1989

Exports	%
Food and live animals	90
Machinery and transport equipment	7

Imports	
Machinery and transport equipment	30
Food	16
Fuels	10

MAJOR TRADING PARTNERS, 1990

Exports	%
Denmark	16
Germany	13
United States	10
France	9

Imports	
Denmark	44
Norway	16
Sweden	6

HEALTH

VITAL STATISTICS, 1988

Births, rate per '000	19·0
Deaths, rate per '000	7·7

ICELAND
REPUBLIC OF ICELAND

AREA	103,000sq km
CLIMATE	Cool, tempered by Gulf Stream. Average temperatures Reykjavik Jan. 1°C, July 11°C. Annual rainfall 860mm
LAND USE	Agricultural 22% Urban 2%, remainder uninhabited
HIGHEST POINT	Hvannadalshnukur 2,119m
MAIN RIVERS	Thjorsa, Skjalfandafljot
CAPITAL	Reykjavik 143,300
OTHER CITIES	Kopavogur 12,000 Akureyri 14,000
TIME	GMT
MONEY	Icelandic krona (IKr) = 100 aurar
EXCHANGE RATES	1991 average IKr 59·90 = $1·00 IKr 73·2 = 1 ecu
OFFICIAL LANGUAGE	Icelandic
MAJOR RELIGION	Evangelical Lutheran 93%
MEMBER	Council of Europe, NATO, Nordic Council, OECD, UN

PEOPLE

Population, 1990	256,000
Forecast, 2000	270,000
% under 15, 1990	24
% over 64, 1990	12
% average annual increase, 1985–90	1·2
Urban population as % of total, 1990	91
Density	2.5 people per sq km

MAJOR ETHNIC GROUPS, 1990	%
Icelandic	96
Danish	1
Other	3

LIVING STANDARDS, 1988	per '000
Passenger cars	488
Telephones	525
Television sets	303

POLITICS

POLITICAL SUMMARY
President, ceremonial head of state, is elected every four years. Prime minister and cabinet, who have executive powers are appointed by president. Two-chamber parliament (Althung) has 63 members, elected by proportional representation for four years. Members elect 20 of their own to sit in upper house, remaining 43 sit in lower house.

MAIN POLITICAL PARTIES
Independence Party, Progressive Party, Social Democratic Party, People's Alliance, Women's List

GOVERNMENT FINANCES

IKr bn	1987	1988	1989	1990	1991 (budgeted)
Revenues	49·0	64·4	80·0	92·5	101·4
Spending	51·7	71·6	86·1	96·9	107·0
Deficit	2·7	7·2	6·1	4·4	5·6

SWEDEN
KINGDOM OF SWEDEN

SPENDING BY SECTOR, 1990 — %

	%
Public consumption	41
Social security and other transfer payments	39
Interest payments	9
Capital investment	11

ECONOMY

GDP	$ bn
1990	5·7
1992 forecast	6·2

Real GDP,	
% average annual growth, 1985–90	0·8
GDP per head, 1990	$22,265

Industrial output,	
% average annual increase, 1985–90	n.a.
Consumer prices,	
% average annual increase, 1985–90	20·2

GROSS FIXED ASSET FORMATION BY SECTOR, 1989

	%
Agriculture and fishing	28
Manufacturing, transport and commercial building	16
Residential construction	23
Public works	33

EMPLOYMENT

EMPLOYMENT BY SECTOR, 1988

	%
Agriculture and fishing	17
Manufacturing	13
Construction	9
Finance	8
Other services	30
Government	17
Other	6

Job growth,	
% average annual increase, 1985–90	0·3

UNEMPLOYMENT RATE, %

1985	1986	1987	1988	1989	1990
0·9	0·6	0·5	0·6	1·7	1·7

TRADE

FOREIGN TRADE, 1990

	IKr bn
Exports	92·6
Imports	97·6

MAJOR COMMODITIES, 1990

Exports	%
Fish	47
Aluminium	10
Fishmeal	4

Imports	
Manufactured goods	18
Machinery	19

MAJOR TRADING PARTNERS, 1990

Exports	%
EC	68
USA	10
EFTA	9

Imports	
EC	51
EFTA	19
USA	11

FINANCE

Financial markets
Iceland uses the whalebone as a form of barter bond. It is roughly equivalent to UK Gilts and was introduced by Coronation T. Bevan in 1851.

EDUCATION

Spending as % of GDP, 1990	4
Years of compulsory education	8
% adult literacy, 1989	100

ENROLMENT RATIOS, 1990

	%
Primary school	99
Secondary	87
Tertiary	24

HEALTH

VITAL STATISTICS

Births, rate per '000, 1989	18·0
Deaths, rate per '000, 1989	6·8
Life expectancy	77 years
Health spending as % of GDP, 1990	8
% eligible for public health insurance	100
Population per hospital bed	86
Doctors per '000	2·4

DEFENCE

Spending as % of GDP, 1990	0

Iceland has no troops but is a NATO member, and host to several NATO bases.

EFTA – EUROPEAN FREE TRADE ASSOCIATION

EFTA was established in 1959 by the United Kingdom, Norway, Sweden, Denmark, Austria, Portugal and Switzerland as a free-trade area between member countries. Finland and Iceland joined later, and Denmark, the United Kingdom and Portugal have since left upon joining the European Community.

Members retain their own tariffs on imports for non-members, but charge no tariffs for imports originating in other member countries. Unlike the European Community, EFTA is not a customs union; rules are necessary to prevent products from non-members being sold in a high-tariff country via a low-tariff member.

However, EFTA has concluded a number of trade agreements with the EC and agreed in late 1991 to establish a European Economic Area with the European Community. Sweden, Austria, Finland, Norway and Switzerland are in the process of considering or applying for membership to the EC; only Iceland has expressed no interest in joining the Community.

In 1990, EFTA countries exported $198bn worth of merchandise, 6% of the world total. Three-quarters of EFTA members' 1990 exports were to other western European countries; just over 60% of total exports went to EC countries.

AREA	449,964sq km
CLIMATE	Temperate, with severe winter in the north. Average temperatures Stockholm Jan. -4·1°C, July 17·3°C. Annual rainfall 722mm
LAND USE	Agriculture 10% Forest 58%
HIGHEST POINT	Kebnekaise 2,111m
MAIN RIVERS	Gota, Dal, Angerman
CAPITAL	Stockholm 1.5m
OTHER CITIES	Göteborg 725,970 Malmo 471,150
TIME	GMT + 1 hour
MONEY	1 Krona (SKr) = 100 ore
EXCHANGE RATES	1991 average SKr 6.05 = $1.00 SKr 7.50 = 1 ecu
OFFICIAL LANGUAGE	Swedish
MAJOR RELIGION	Evangelical Lutheran, 95%
MEMBER	EFTA, Nordic Council, OECD, UN; EC membership application approved December, 1990

PEOPLE

Population, 1990	8,590,630
Forecast, 2000	8,635,000
% under 15, 1990	16·5
% over 64, 1990	18·3
% average annual increase, 1985–90	0·5
Urban population as % of total, 1990	85
Density	19 people per sq km

MAJOR ETHNIC GROUPS, 1990

	%
Swedish	95
Other Scandinavian	2
Other	3

LIVING STANDARDS, 1988

	per '000
Passenger cars	400
Telephones	983 (1991)
Television sets	390

POLITICS

POLITICAL SUMMARY
Constitutional monarchy. Monarch ceremonial head of state. Prime minister and cabinet exercise executive power. The Riksdag (parliament) is unicameral and has 349 members directly elected by a form of proportional representation for three years.

MAIN POLITICAL PARTIES
Social Democratic Labour, Conservative, Liberal, Centre, Left, Christian Democrats, New Democracy

GOVERNMENT FINANCES

SKr bn	1986	1987	1988	1989	1990
Revenues	275·1	320·1	332·6	367·7	401·6
Spending	321·9	335·3	336·7	349·6	398·1

SPENDING BY SECTOR, 1989

	%
Health and social affairs	28
Debt interest payments	15
Education and culture	13
Defence	9
Labour	7
Finance	7
Housing	5
Other	16

ECONOMY

GDP	$ bn
1990	226·5
1995 forecast	340·7

Real GDP	
% average annual growth, 1985–90	1·9
GDP per head, 1990	$26,550

GDP BY SECTOR, 1988

	%
Manufacturing	21
Financial services	18
Trade, hotels and restaurants	11
Construction	6
Transport and communications	6
Agriculture and fishing	3
Other	35

Industrial output,	
% average annual increase, 1985–90	1·0
Consumer prices,	
% average annual increase, 1985–90	6·2

EMPLOYMENT

EMPLOYMENT BY SECTOR, 1989

	%
Public administration and services	37
Manufacturing, mining and energy	23
Trade, hotels and restaurants	15
Financial services	8
Other	17

Job growth,	
% average annual increase, 1985–90	1·0

UNEMPLOYMENT RATE, %

1985	1986	1987	1988	1989	1990
2·4	2·2	1·9	1·6	1·4	1·5

TRADE

FOREIGN TRADE, 1990

	$ bn
Exports	57·5
Imports	54·7

MAJOR COMMODITIES, 1990

Exports	%
Machinery	29
Wood products and paper	18
Transport equipment	15
Chemicals	7
Iron and steel	6
Food and beverages	2

Imports	
Machinery	27
Transport equipment	12
Chemicals	9
Fuels	9
Clothing, footwear and textiles	8
Food, beverages and tobacco	6

NORWAY
KINGDOM OF NORWAY

MAJOR TRADING PARTNERS, 1990

Exports	%
Germany	14
United Kingdom	10
United States	9
Norway	8
Denmark	7
Finland	7

Imports	
Germany	19
United States	9
United Kingdom	8
Norway	8
Denmark	8
Finland	7

FINANCE

Central bank
Riksbank, Stockholm
24 commercial banks, and 109 savings banks
Major stock market
Stockholm

JACOBSON & PONSBACH INDUSTRIAL INDEX,
year-end

1985	1986	1987	1988	1989	1990
1737·7	2,459·2	2,170·4	3,443·8	4,275.0	2,990

Market capitalisation, end-1990	$94 bn

Top five companies, by market capitalisation, end-1990	$ bn
Astra (health and personal care)	7·7
Ericsson (electronics)	6·8
Procordia (food and grocery products)	6·5
ASEA (electrical equipment)	5·6
Skanska (construction and building materials)	2·9

EDUCATION

Spending as % of GDP, 1990	8
Years of compulsory education	9
% adult literacy,	100

ENROLMENT RATIOS, 1988	%
Primary school	100
Secondary	91
Tertiary	31

HEALTH

VITAL STATISTICS, 1989	
Births, rate per '000	14·5
Deaths, rate per '000	11·1
Life expectancy	77 years
Health spending as % of GDP, 1990	8
Doctors per '000	2·5

DEFENCE

Spending as % of GDP, 1990	3

Every male is liable for national service between ages 18 and 47; compulsory service: 7½–12 months in the Army and Navy, 8–12 months in the Air Force.

ACTIVE TROOPS, 1990	
Army	43,500
Navy	12,000
Air Force	7,500
Reserves	709,000

AREA	323,878sq km
CLIMATE	Cool, variable, warm winters and cool summers along coast, more extreme inland and in the north. Average temperatures Oslo Jan. -4·7°C, July 16·3°C. Annual rainfall 740mm
LAND USE	Agriculture 3% Productive forest 22% Unproductive 75%
HIGHEST POINT	Galdhopiggen 2,469m
MAIN RIVERS	Glama, Lagen
CAPITAL	Oslo 458,000
OTHER CITIES	Bergen 212,000 Trondheim 137,000 Stavanger 98,000
TIME	GMT
MONEY	1 krone (NKr) = 100 ore
EXCHANGE RATES	1990 average NKr 6.26 = $1.00 NKr 8.02 = 1 ecu
OFFICIAL LANGUAGE	Norwegian
MAJOR RELIGION	Evangelical Lutheran, 92%
MEMBER	Council of Europe, EFTA, NATO, Nordic Council, OECD, UN

PEOPLE

Population, 1990	4,242,000
Forecast, 2000	4,331,000
% under 15, 1990	18·8
% over 64, 1990	16·4
% average annual increase, 1985–90	0·3
Urban population as % of total, 1990	68
Density	13 people per sq km

MAJOR ETHNIC GROUPS, 1990	%
Norwegian	96
Other Scandinavian	3
Other	1

LIVING STANDARDS, 1988	per '000
Passenger cars	388
Telephones	767 (1991)
Television sets	346

POLITICS

POLITICAL SUMMARY
Constitutional monarchy. Monarch ceremonial head of state. Prime minister and a council of state exercise executive power. The Storting (parliament) has 165 members, directly elected by a form of proportional representation for four years. Members elect one-quarter of their number to constitute the Lagting, the remainder for the Odelsting. There is no right of dissolution between elections.

MAIN POLITICAL PARTIES
Labour Party, Conservative Party, Progress Party, Socialist Left Party, Christian People's Party, Centre Party

GOVERNMENT FINANCES

NKr bn	1988	1989	1990
Revenues	346·7	362·0	393·5
Spending	310·4	331·1	358·4

SPENDING BY SECTOR, 1990	%
Interest payments	7
Aid to developing countries	2
Social security and other transfers	36
Current expenses	42
Other	13

STATE SUBSIDIES TO INDUSTRY, 1990	%
Agriculture	59
Fishing	8
Manufacturing	13
Services	2
Other	18

ECONOMY

GDP	$ bn
1990	105·3
1995 forecast	151·7

Real GDP	
% average annual growth, 1985–90	4·2
GDP per head, 1990	$24,825

GDP BY SECTOR, 1990	%
Public services	16
Manufacturing and mining	15
Oil production and transport	13
Wholesale and retail trade	10
Construction	9
Transport and communications	6
Agriculture and fishing	3
Other	28

Industrial output % average annual increase, 1985–90	7·1
Consumer prices % average annual increase, 1985–90	6·2

EMPLOYMENT

EMPLOYMENT BY SECTOR, 1990	%
Public services	36
Trade, hotels and restaurants	18
Manufacturing	15
Transport and communications	8
Financial services	7
Other	16

Job growth % average annual increase, 1985–90	0·2

UNEMPLOYMENT RATE, %

1985	1986	1987	1988	1989	1990
2·6	2·0	2·1	3·2	4·9	5·2

TRADE

FOREIGN TRADE, 1990	NKr bn
Exports	211·1
Imports	167·1

MAJOR COMMODITIES, 1990	%
Exports	
Fuels	42
Metals	9
Machinery	7
Fish and fish products	6
Ships and oil platforms	5
Imports	
Machinery	21
Ships and oil platforms	10
Transport equipment	5
Food, beverages and tobacco	5
Clothing	5

MAJOR TRADING PARTNERS,1990

Exports	%
Britain	26
Sweden	12
Germany	11
Netherlands	8
France	8

Imports	
Sweden	16
Germany	14
Britain	9
United States	8
Denmark	7

FINANCE

Central bank
Norges Bank, Oslo, only bank of issue
28 commercial banks, and 151 savings banks
Major stock market
Oslo

OSLO STOCK EXCHANGE INDEX, year-end

1985	1986	1987	1988	1989	1990
393·1	357·8	332·7	467·8	686·7	677·0

Market capitalisation, end-1990	$26 bn

Top five companies, by market capitalisation, end-1990	$ bn
Norsk Hydro (oil and gas)	6·3
Saga Petroleum (oil and gas)	1·9
Hafslund Nycomed (health and personal care)	1·6
Kvaerner (engineering)	1·1
Orkla Borregaard (conglomerate)	0·8

EDUCATION

Spending as % of GDP, 1990	7
Years of compulsory education	9
% adult literacy	100

ENROLMENT RATIOS, 1988	%
Primary school	97
Secondary	95
Tertiary	35

HEALTH

VITAL STATISTICS, 1989	
Births, rate per '000	14·4
Deaths, rate per '000	10·8
Life expectancy	77 years
Health spending as % of GDP, 1990	6
% eligible for public health insurance	100
Hospital beds per '000, 1990	64
Doctors per '000	2·2

DEFENCE

Spending as % of GDP, 1990	3

Every male is liable for national service between ages 19 and 45; compulsory service at 19: 12 months in Army or 15 months in either the Navy or Air Force.

ACTIVE TROOPS, 1990	
Army	19,000
Navy	5,300
Air Force	9,100
Joint services and home guard	700
Coast Guard	680
Reserves	285,000

FINLAND
REPUBLIC OF FINLAND

AREA	338,127sq km
CLIMATE	Severe, long winters, short warm summers. Average temperatures Helsinki Jan. -6·0°C, July 16·5°C. Annual rainfall 618mm
LAND USE	Agriculture 8% Forest 69%
HIGHEST POINT	Haltia 1,234m
MAIN RIVERS	Paatsjoki, Kemijoki, Kokemaenjoki
CAPITAL	Helsinki 490,800
OTHER CITIES	Tampere 171,300 Turku 158,900 Vantaa 152,500
TIME	GMT + 1 hour
MONEY	1 Markka (FMk) = 100 penni
EXCHANGE RATES	1991 average FMk 4.04 = $1.00 FMk 5.02 = 1 ecu
OFFICIAL LANGUAGES	Finnish and Swedish
MAJOR RELIGIONS	Lutheran 88%, Greek Orthodox 1%
MEMBER	Council of Europe, EFTA, Nordic Council, OECD, UN

PEOPLE

Population, 1990	4,975,000
Forecast, 2000	5,077,000
% under 15, 1990	19·3
% over 64, 1990	13·2
% average annual increase, 1985–90	0·3
Urban population as % of total, 1990	60
Density	15 people per sq km

MAJOR ETHNIC GROUPS, 1990	%
Finnish	94
Swedish	6

LIVING STANDARDS, 1988	per '000
Passenger cars	344
Telephones	732 (1991)
Television sets	370

POLITICS

POLITICAL SUMMARY
Parliamentary republic. The executive president is elected for six years by an absolute majority of votes cast in a direct election, or failing that, by an electoral college of 301 members who themselves are directly elected. The president appoints the prime minister and Council of State. The one-chamber Eduskunta (parliament) has 200 members directly elected by proportional representation for four years.

MAIN POLITICAL PARTIES
Centre Party, Social Democratic Party, National Coalition Party, Left Alliance, Swedish People's Party, Green Party, Finnish Christian Union, Finnish Rural Party

GOVERNMENT FINANCES

FMk bn	1985	1986	1987	1988	1989
Revenues	86·4	94·0	102·1	118·3	136·2
Spending	84·7	90·4	100·7	110·9	120·8

SPENDING BY SECTOR, 1989	%
Social security	18
Education	18
Health	9
Transport and communications	8
Debt service	7
Agriculture and forestry	7
Other	33

ECONOMY

GDP	$ bn
1990	137·3
1995 forecast	164·9

Real GDP	
% average annual growth, 1985–90	3·4
GDP per head, 1990	$27,560

Industrial output, % average annual increase, 1985–90	3·2
Consumer prices, % average annual increase, 1985–90	5·0

EMPLOYMENT

EMPLOYMENT BY SECTOR, 1990	%
Services	62
Industry	22
Construction	8
Agriculture and forestry	8

Employment, % average annual increase, 1985–90	0·1

UNEMPLOYMENT RATE, %

1985	1986	1987	1988	1989	1990
5·0	5·4	5·1	4·5	3·5	3·5

TRADE

FOREIGN TRADE, 1990	$ bn
Exports	6·6
Imports	27·0

MAJOR COMMODITIES, 1990	
Exports	%
Engineering products	35
Pulp and paper	31
Chemicals	9
Wood	8

Imports	
Raw materials	48
Consumer goods	23
Capital equipment	19
Energy	10

MAJOR TRADING PARTNERS, 1990	
Exports	%
Sweden	14
Germany	13
Soviet Union	13
Britain	11
France	6

Imports	
Germany	17
Sweden	13
Soviet Union	10
Britain	8
United States	7

FINANCE

Central bank
Bank of Finland, Helsinki
Major stock market
Helsinki

UNITAS GENERAL INDEX, year-end

1985	1986	1987	1988	1989	1990
258·4	425·4	556·0	723·3	609·0	395·6

Market capitalisation, end-1990	$149 bn

Top five companies, by market capitalisation, end-1990	$ bn
Union Bank of Finland	1·5
Kansallis Banking Group (banking)	1·5
United Paper Mills (paper)	1·4
Kymmene (transport and storage)	1·1
Kesko Oy (retail)	1·1

EDUCATION

Spending as % of GDP, 1990	6
% adult literacy, 1989	99

ENROLMENT RATIOS, 1988	%
Primary school	100
Secondary	108
Tertiary	40

HEALTH

VITAL STATISTICS, 1989	
Births, rate per '000	12·5
Deaths, rate per '000	10·2
Life expectancy	76 years
Health spending as % of GDP, 1990	7
Doctors per '000	2·3

DEFENCE

Spending as % of GDP, 1990	1

Compulsory service for men of 8–11 months.

ACTIVE TROOPS, 1990	
Army	27,300
Air Force	2,500
Navy	2,000
Reserves	700,000

HUMAN DEVELOPMENT INDEX

Rank	Country	Score
1	Iceland	98
	Sweden	98
	Switzerland	98
	Norway	98
	The Netherlands	98
6	France	97
	UK	97
	Denmark	97
9	Finland	96
	Germany	96
	Belgium	96
	Austria	96
	Italy	96
14	Luxembourg	95
	Spain	95
	Ireland	95
17	Greece	93
18	Cyprus	92
	Czechoslovakia	92
	Malta	92
21	Hungary	91
22	Bulgaria	90
23	Yugoslavia	89
24	Portugal	88
25	Poland	86
26	Albania	82
27	Romania	76
28	Turkey	69

This new index is an attempt by the United Nations Development Programme to assess relative levels of human development in various countries. It combines three measures: life expectancy, literacy and whether the average income, based on purchasing power parity (PPP) estimates (see above), is sufficient to meet basic needs. For each component a country's score is scaled according to where it falls between the minimum and maximum country scores; for income adequacy the maximum is taken as the official "poverty line" incomes in nine industrial countries. The scaled scores on the three measures are averaged to give the Human Development Index, shown here scaled from 0 to 100. Countries scoring less than 50 are classified as low human development, those from 50–80 as medium and those above 80 as high.

As with any statistical exercise of this sort the results are subject to caveats.

PORTUGAL
REPUBLIC OF PORTUGAL

AREA	92,389sq km
CLIMATE	Cool and damp in the north, warmer and drier in the south. Average temper-atures Lisbon Jan. 11°C, July 22°C. Annual rainfall 686mm.
LAND USE	Agriculture 42%
HIGHEST POINT	Estrela 1,991m
MAIN RIVERS	Tagus, Duoro, Guadiana
CAPITAL	Lisbon 2·1m
OTHER CITIES	Oporto 1·7m Setubal 799,000
TIME	GMT + 1 hr.
MONEY	1 escudo (Esc) = 100 centavos
EXCHANGE RATES	1991 average 144 escudos = $1.00 179 escudos = 1 ecu
OFFICIAL LANGUAGE	Portuguese
MAJOR RELIGION	Roman Catholic 90%
MEMBER	Council of Europe, EC, IMF, NATO, OECD, UN, WEU

PEOPLE

Population, 1990	10,369,000
Forecast, 2000	10,587,000
% under 15, 1990	21·9
% over 64, 1990	12·9
% average annual increase, 1985–90	0·4
Urban population as % of total, 1990	32
Density	112 people per sq km

LIVING STANDARDS, 1988	per '000
Passenger cars	135
Telephones	219 (1991)
Television sets	140

POLITICS

POLITICAL SUMMARY
The president is head of state, directly elected for up to two consecutive five-year terms. The Council of Ministers is led by the prime minister, appointed by the president, as leader of the majority party in the assembly, but responsible to the legislature. Assembly of the republic has 230 members directly elected by a form of proportional representation for four years.

MAIN POLITICAL PARTIES
Social Democratic Party, Socialist Party, Communist Party, Centre Democratic Party

GOVERNMENT FINANCES

Esc bn	1987	1988	1989	1990	1991 (budget)
Revenues	1,866	2,262	2,794	3,170	3,860
Spending	2,012	2,399	2,770	3,440	4,090

SPENDING BY SECTOR, 1990	%
Goods and services	46
Transfers	27
Interest payments	22
Other	5

ECONOMY

GDP	$ bn
1990	59·6
1995 forecast	110·1
Real GDP, % average annual growth, 1985–90	4·6
GDP per head, 1990	$5,770

GDP BY SECTOR, 1988, % OF TOTAL	
Services	56
Manufacturing and mining	28
Construction	6
Agriculture and fishing	6
Energy and water	4

Industrial output, % average annual increase, 1985–90	7·1
Consumer prices, % average annual increase, 1985–90	6·2

EMPLOYMENT

EMPLOYMENT BY SECTOR, 1990,	%
Services	48
Construction, manufacturing and mining	35
Agriculture and fishing	17

Job growth, % average annual increase, 1985–90	0·6

UNEMPLOYMENT RATE, %

1985	1986	1987	1988	1989	1990
8·6	8·5	7·1	5·7	5·0	4·7

TRADE

FOREIGN TRADE, 1990	$ bn
Exports	16·3
Imports	24·8

MAJOR COMMODITIES, 1990 Exports	%
Textiles, clothing and footwear	38
Machinery	20
Forest products	12
Food	7
Chemicals and plastics	6

Imports	
Machinery and transport equipment	37
Food	12
Chemicals and plastics	11
Oil	11
Textiles, clothing and footwear	11

MAJOR TRADING PARTNERS, 1990 Exports	%
Germany	17
France	16
Spain	14
Britain	12
Netherlands	6

Imports	
Spain	15
Germany	14
France	12
Italy	10
Britain	8

FINANCE

Central bank
Banco do Portugal, Lisbon only bank of issue
27 banks; bank lending ceilings lifted in January, 1991
Major stock market
Lisbon

IFC PORTUGAL INDEX, TOTAL RETURNS, $ TERMS, year-end

1986	1987	1988	1989	1990
309	1,107	829	1,161	838

Market capitalisation, end-1990	$9·2 bn

Top five companies by market capitalisation, end-1990	$ bn
Banco Comercial Portugues (banking)	1·0
Marconi (electronics)	0·7
Soporcel (forestry and paper products)	0·5
Banco Portugues de Investo (banking)	0·5
Banco de Comercio e Industria (banking)	0·3

EDUCATION

Spending as % of GDP, 1990	4
% adult literacy, 1989	90
Years of compulsory education	8

ENROLMENT RATIOS, 1988	%
Primary school	100
Secondary	52
Tertiary	13

HEALTH

VITAL STATISTICS, 1988	
Births, rate per '000	11·9
Deaths, rate per '000	9·6
Life expectancy at birth	74 years
Health spending as % of GDP, 1990	6
Doctors per '000	1·8

DEFENCE

Spending as % of GDP, 1990	3

Compulsory service for all males: 12–15 months in the Army and Navy, 18–20 in the Air Force.

ACTIVE TROOPS, 1991	
Army	44,000
Navy	13,000
Air Force	11,000

SPAIN
KINGDOM OF SPAIN

AREA	504,782sq km
CLIMATE	Mediterranean in east and south, temperate in north and west average. Temperatures Madrid Jan. 5°C, July 25°C. Annual rainfall 419mm
LAND USE	Agriculture 51% Forest 31%
HIGHEST POINT	Mulhacen, 3,478m
MAIN RIVERS	Duero, Tagus, Ebro, Guadalquivir
CAPITAL	Madrid 3·1m
OTHER CITIES	Barcelona 1·7m Valencia 744,000 Seville 663,000
TIME	GMT + 1 hour
MONEY	Peseta (Ptas) = 100 centimos
EXCHANGE RATES	1991 average Ptas 104 = $1·00 Ptas 129 = 1 ecu
OFFICIAL LANGUAGES	Spanish, Catalan, Basque, Galician
MAJOR RELIGION	Roman Catholic, 90%
MEMBER	Council of Europe, EC, IMF, NATO, OECD, UN, WEU

PEOPLE

Population, 1990	38,966,000
Forecast, 2000	40,812,000
% under 15, 1990	20·4
% over 64, 1990	18·4
% average annual increase, 1985–90	0·4
Urban population as % of total, 1990	79
Density	78 people per sq km

LIVING STANDARDS, 1988	per '000
Passenger cars	263
Telephones	440 (1991)
Television sets	256

POLITICS

POLITICAL SUMMARY
Constitutional monarchy with considerable powers devolved to regions. Monarch ceremonial head of state. Parliament (Cortes) is bicameral. 350-seat lower house elected by proportional representation; upper house of 208 seats directly elected. Elections must be held every four years, and the next must be held no later than October 1993. The king has the power to dissolve parliament; prime minister is elected by the parliament.

MAJOR POLITICAL PARTIES AND COALITIONS
Spanish Socialist Workers Party, Popular Party, United Left, Convergence and Union, Social and Democratic Centre, Basque Nationalist Party

GOVERNMENT FINANCES

Ptas bn	1986	1987	1988	1989	1990
Revenues	5,901	7,170	7,817	8,297	10,562
Spending	6,461	7,337	7,870	8,069	15,505

SPENDING BY SECTOR, 1990	%
Interest payments	9
Wages and salaries	20
Transfers	65
Other	6

ECONOMY

GDP	$ bn
1990	491·8
1995 forecast	700·0
Real GDP, % average annual growth, 1985-90	4·5
GDP per head, 1990	$12,200

GDP BY SECTOR, 1990	%
Services	58
Manufacturing, mining and utilities	29
Construction	9
Agriculture, fishing and forestry	4

Industrial output, % average annual increase, 1985–90	3·0
Consumer prices, % average annual increase, 1985–90	6·5

EMPLOYMENT

EMPLOYMENT BY SECTOR, 1990	%
Services	54
Industry	24
Agriculture	13
Construction	9

Job growth, % average annual increase, 1985–90	2·8

UNEMPLOYMENT RATE, %

1985	1086	1987	1988	1989	1990
21·5	21·0	20·5	9·5	17·3	16·2

TRADE

FOREIGN TRADE, 1990	$ bn
Exports	51
Imports	81

MAJOR COMMODITIES, 1990 Exports	%
Motor vehicles	25
Machinery	15
Food products	15
Minerals	11
Metals	10

Imports	
Machinery	25
Chemicals	12
Energy products	12
Food products	11
Motor vehicles	11

MAJOR TRADING PARTNERS, 1990 Exports	%
France	21
Germany	13
Italy	11
United Kingdom	9
Portugal	6

Imports	
Germany	16
France	15
Italy	10
United States	8
United Kingdom	7

FINANCE

Central bank
Banco de Espana, Madrid
Banking system in the midst of restructuring through mergers and privatisations.
Major stock market
Madrid

ITALY
REPUBLIC OF ITALY

AREA	301,268sq km
CLIMATE	Varies with latitude, north is cool temperate, south, Mediterranean. Average temperatures Rome Jan. 7°C, July 23·9°C. Annual rainfall 725mm
LAND USE	Agricultural 57%
HIGHEST POINT	Mont Blanc 4,810m
MAIN RIVERS	Po, Tiber, Arno, Adige
CAPITAL	Rome 2·8m
OTHER CITIES	Milan 1·6m
	Naples 1·2m
	Turin 1·0m
TIME	GMT + 1 hour
MONEY	Lira (LIt)
EXCHANGE RATES	1991 average
	LIt 1,241 = $1.00
	LIt 1,533 = 1.ecu
OFFICIAL LANGUAGE	Italian
MAJOR RELIGION	Roman Catholic 90%
MEMBER	EC, NATO, OECD, UN, WEU

PEOPLE

Population, 1990	57,647,000
Forecast, 2000	57,881,000
% under 15, 1990	16·7
% over 64, 1990	14·3
% average annual increase, 1985–90	0·1
Urban population as % of total, 1990	69
Density	191 people per sq km

LIVING STANDARDS, 1988	per '000
Passenger cars	408
Telephones	510 (1991)
Television sets	255

POLITICS

POLITICAL SUMMARY
The president is ceremonial head of state, elected for seven years by members of parliament and regional representatives. The president nominates the prime minister. The two-chamber parliament is elected by a form of proportional representation for five years; the Chamber of Deputies has 630 members and the Senate 315, plus five life members nominated by the president and two former presidents of the republic.

MAIN POLITICAL PARTIES
Christian Democratic Party, Democratic Party of the Left, Socialist Unity, Italian Social Movement- National Right, Republican Party, Liberal Party, Radical Party, Social Democratic Party, Green list, Rainbow coalition, Lombard League

GOVERNMENT FINANCES

LIt trillion	1986	1987	1988	1989	1990
Revenues	366·6	402·3	449·1	489·7	557·8
Spending	427·2	466·0	518·8	618·3	696·7

SPENDING BY SECTOR, 1990	%
Social services	34
Debt service	18

Wages and salaries	24
Industrial subsidies	4
Other	20

ECONOMY

GDP	$ bn
1990	1,087
1995 forecast	1,580
Real GDP, % average annual growth, 1985–90	3·0
GDP per head, 1990	$18,600
Industrial output, % average annual increase, 1985–90	3·3
Consumer prices, % average annual increase, 1985–90	5·7

EMPLOYMENT

EMPLOYMENT BY SECTOR, 1989	%
Services	59
Manufacturing, mining and construction	32
Agriculture and forestry	9
Job growth, % average annual increase, 1985–90	0·6

UNEMPLOYMENT RATE, %					
1985	**1986**	**1987**	**1988**	**1989**	**1990**
10·2	11·2	12·1	12·2	12·1	11·2

TRADE

FOREIGN TRADE, 1990	$ bn
Exports	182·2
Imports	193·6

MAJOR COMMODITIES, 1990	
Exports	%
Textiles, clothing and leather products	17
Machinery	16
Transport equipment	10
Metals and minerals	8
Electrical equipment	8
Imports	
Food products	13
Chemicals	12
Transport equipment	11
Energy	11
Metals and minerals	11

MAJOR TRADING PARTNERS, 1990	
Exports	%
Germany	19
France	16
United States	8
United Kingdom	7
Imports	
Germany	21
France	14
Netherlands	5
United States	5

FINANCE

Central bank
Bank of Italy, Rome

Major stock market
Milan

MADRID STOCK EXCHANGE INDEX, year-end

1985	1986	1987	1988	1989	1990
100	208·3	227·2	274·1	296·0	223·0

Market capitalisation, end-1990	$123 bn

Top five companies, by market capitalisation, end-1990	$ bn
Telefonica (telecommunications)	8·1
Repsol (oil and gas)	6·5
Banco Bilbao Vizcaya (banking)	6·2
ENDESA (utilities)	5·9
Banco de Santander	5·3

EDUCATION

Spending as % of GDP, 1990	3
Years of compulsory education	8
% adult literacy, 1989	95
ENROLMENT RATIOS, 1988	%
Primary school	98
Secondary	97
Tertiary	30

HEALTH

VITAL STATISTICS, 1989	
Births, rate per '000	10·7
Deaths, rate per '000	8·2
Life expectancy	77 years
Health spending as % of GDP, 1990	4
Hospital beds per '000, 1990	4·6
Doctors per '000	3·4

DEFENCE

Spending as % of GDP, 1990	2
Compulsory service: 12 months	
ACTIVE TROOPS, 1990	
Army	182,000
Navy	39,800
Air Force	35,600
Reserves	2,400,000

ANDORRA
THE VALLEYS OF ANDORRA

AREA	467sq km
CLIMATE	Temperate. Average temperatures Jan 2·3°C, July 19·3°C. Annual rainfall 808mm
CAPITAL	Andorra la Vella 19,570
TIME	GMT + 1 hour
MONEY	Spanish peseta and French franc
OFFICIAL LANGUAGE	Catalan

PEOPLE

Population, 1989	50,530
Density	108 people per sq km

POLITICS

POLITICAL SUMMARY
Parliamentary monarchy with the president of France and the bishop of Urguel holding joint suzerainty. A 28-member General Council of the Valleys is elected on a restricted franchise.

ECONOMY

Tourism is the main industry.

BANCA COMMERCIALE ITALIANA INDEX, year-end

1985	1986	1987	1988	1989	1990
457·0	722·8	487·9	589·7	687·4	516·6

Market capitalisation, end-1990	$150 bn

Top five companies, by market capitalisation, end-1990	$ bn
Assicurazioni Generali (insurance)	14·7
Fiat (cars and trucks)	0·0
Stet (telecommunications)	7·0
Sip (utilities)	4·9
La Fondiaria (insurance)	4·2

EDUCATION

Spending as % of GDP, 1990	4
Years of compulsory education	8
% adult literacy, 1989	97
ENROLMENT RATIOS, 1988	%
Primary school	100
Secondary	100
Tertiary	24

HEALTH

VITAL STATISTICS, 1989	
Births, rate per '000	9·7
Deaths, rate per '000	9·5
Life expectancy	75 years
Health spending as % of GDP, 1990	5
Doctors per '000	1·3

DEFENCE

Spending as % of GDP, 1990	2
Compulsory service for men of 12 months in Army and Air Force, 18 months in Navy.	
ACTIVE TROOPS, 1990	
Army	234,200
Air Force	78,200
Navy	49,000
Reserves	584,000

SAN MARINO
REPUBLIC OF SAN MARINO

AREA	61sq km
CLIMATE	Mediterranean.
CAPITAL	San Marino 4,630
TIME	GMT + 1 hour
MONEY	Italian lira
OFFICIAL LANGUAGE	Italian
MAJOR RELIGION	Roman Catholic 95%

PEOPLE

Population, 1990	23,240

POLITICS

POLITICAL SUMMARY
Parliamentary republic with legislative power vested in a 60-member Grand and General Council.

ECONOMY

A mixture of light industry and tourism.

VATICAN CITY
THE STATE OF THE VATICAN CITY

AREA	44 hectares
CLIMATE	Mediterranean. Temperatures and rainfall, see Italy
CAPITAL	San Marino 4,630
TIME	GMT + 1 hour
MONEY	Italian lira
OFFICIAL LANGUAGE	Italian
MAJOR RELIGION	Roman Catholic 100%

PEOPLE

Population, 1990	1,000

POLITICS

POLITICAL SUMMARY
Religious state, with the Pope as head of state. The Pope is elected for life by the Sacred College of Cardinals. Since 1984, the routine administration of the Vatican has been delegated to the secretary of state and a pontifical Commission, appointed by the Pope.

MALTA
REPUBLIC OF MALTA

AREA	316sq km
CLIMATE	Mediterranean. Hot, dry summers. Average temperatures Valletta Jan. 12·8°C, July 25·6°C. Annual rainfall 578mm
LAND USE	Agriculture 41%
HIGHEST POINT	253m
CAPITAL	Valletta 9,200
OTHER CITIES	Birkirkara 21,000
TIME	GMT + 1 hour
MONEY	1 Maltese lira(Lm) = 100 cents
EXCHANGE RATES	1991 average Lm 0.32 = $1.00 Lm 0.40 = 1.ecu
OFFICIAL LANGUAGES	Maltese, English
MAJOR RELIGION	Roman Catholic 91%
MEMBER	Commonwealth, Council of Europe, UN

PEOPLE

Population, 1990	353,000
Forecast, 2000	366,000
% under 15, 1990	23·1
% over 64, 1990	10·2
% average annual increase, 1985–90	0·5
Urban population as % of total, 1990	87
Density	1,117 people per sq km

MAJOR ETHNIC GROUPS, 1990

Maltese	96
British	2

POLITICS

POLITICAL SUMMARY
The president is the constitutional head of

DEVOLUTION IN ITALY

Devolution is an aspect of the constitution which was only fully developed in the early 1970s. Originally only four regions with special statutes had their own councils: Sicily, Sardinia, Valle d'Aosta and Trentino-Alto Adige. Friuli-Venezia Giulia was added in 1962. These regions still have special status, but function in much the same way as the other 15.

state, elected by the legislature for five years. The president appoints the prime minister, usually the leader of the majority party, and on the latter's advice the other government ministers. The one-chamber House of Representatives has 69 members directly elected by a form of proportional representation for five years.

MAIN POLITICAL PARTIES
Nationalist Party, Malta Labour Party

GOVERNMENT FINANCES

Lm million	1986	1987	1988	1989	1990
Revenues	225·9	221·2	308·8	291·8	323·9
Spending	240·5	263·6	274·0	320·7	391·3

SPENDING BY SECTOR, 1990

	%
Social security and pensions	29
Capital investment	31
Health	8
Debt service	2
Other	30

EMPLOYMENT

GDP	**$ bn**
1989	2·5

Real GDP, % average annual growth, 1980–89	2·9
GDP per head, 1989	$5,820

Consumer prices, % average annual increase, 1985–90	1·4

ECONOMY

EMPLOYMENT BY SECTOR, 1989

	%
Government	45
Manufacturing, mining and construction	27
Agriculture and forestry	2
Services	26

EUROPEAN OFFSHORE CENTRES

An "offshore financial centre" is an area or country which offers tax or other financial advantages not available "onshore".

Three of the most successful offshore centres are Switzerland, Liechtenstein and Luxembourg, none of which is even near a shore.

In principle, the creation of a single market should eliminate these havens, in particular Luxembourg, as tax regulations should be uniform throughout the community. However, the single market makes it easier to transfer funds to offshore countries and it is unlikely that the authorities will step in for fear of driving money outside the Community.

The other tax havens in Europe are: Andorra, Cyprus, Dublin, Gibraltar, Guernsey, Hungary, Isle of Man, Jersey, Madeira, Malta and Monaco.

Job growth, % average annual increase, 1985–89	3·3

UNEMPLOYMENT RATE, %

1984	1985	1986	1987	1988	1989
8·7	8·2	6·9	4·4	4·0	3·7

TRADE

FOREIGN TRADE, 1990

	$m
Exports	786
Imports	1,480

MAJOR COMMODITIES, 1990

Exports	%
Machinery and transport equipment	50
Manufactured goods	45
Other	5

Imports	
Machinery and transport equipment	40
Manufactures	31
Food	10
Chemicals	7
Fuels	7

MAJOR TRADING PARTNERS, 1989

Exports	%
Italy	30
Germany	23
United Kingdom	11
United States	6
Libya	5

Imports	
Italy	30
United Kingdom	16
Germany	13
France	6
United States	4

FINANCE

Central bank
Central Bank of Malta, Valletta

Malta is developing as an offshore financial centre.

EDUCATION

Spending as % of GDP, 1989	4
Years of compulsory education	10
% literacy rate,	84

ENROLMENT RATIOS, 1988

	%
Primary school	100
Secondary	80
Tertiary	7

HEALTH

VITAL STATISTICS, 1989

Births, rate per '000	15·8
Deaths, rate per '000	7·8

DEFENCE

Spending as % of GDP, 1990	1
Active armed forces	1,650

GREECE
HELLENIC REPUBLIC

AREA	130,080sq km
CLIMATE	Mediterranean along coast and islands, continental in interior. Average temperatures Athens Jan. 8·6°C, July 28·2°C. Annual rainfall 414mm
LAND USE	Agriculture 70% Forest 20%
HIGHEST POINT	Mt Olympus 2,911m
MAIN RIVERS	Aliakmon, Pinios, Akheloos
CAPITAL	Athens 3·1m
OTHER CITIES	Thessaloniki 969,000 Larissa 269,000 Iraklion 264,000
TIME	GMT + 1 hour
MONEY	Drachma (Dr)
EXCHANGE RATES	1991 average Dr 182 = $1.00 Dr 225 = 1 ecu
OFFICIAL LANGUAGE	Greek
MAJOR RELIGION	Greek Orthodox 98%
MEMBER	Council of Europe, EC, NATO, OECD, UN

PEOPLE

Population, 1990	10,047,000
Forecast, 2000	10,193,000
% under 15, 1990	19·7
% over 64, 1990	13·7
% average annual increase, 1985–90	0·2
Urban population as % of total, 1990	63
Density	76 people per sq km

MAJOR ETHNIC GROUPS, 1990

	%
Greek	96
Macedonian	2
Turkish and other	2

LIVING STANDARDS, 1988 per '000

Passenger cars	130
Telephones	430 (1991)
Television sets	158

POLITICS

POLITICAL SUMMARY
Parliamentary republic. The one-chamber parliament (Vouli) has 300 members directly elected by proportional representation for four years. The president, without executive power, is elected by parliament for five years. The council of ministers is responsible to parliament. It is headed by the prime minister, appointed by the president on the ability to gain support in parliament.

MAIN POLITICAL PARTIES
New Democracy Party, Panhellenic Socialist Movement, Synapismos - a coalition including the Communist Party of Greece and the Greek Left Party.

GOVERNMENT FINANCES

Dr bn	1985	1986	1987	1988	1989
Revenues	901·2	1,174·6	1,395·1	1,558·5	1,689·5
Spending	1,285·2	1,477·4	1829·3	2,328·6	2,992·1

TURKEY
REPUBLIC OF TURKEY

SPENDING BY SECTOR, 1989 — %

	%
Salaries	34
Debt service	27
Grants and industrial subsidies	26
Purchase of goods and services	5
Other	8

ECONOMY

GDP	$ bn
1990	67·2
1995 forecast	99·5

Real GDP, % average annual growth, 1985–90	1·6
GDP per head, 1990	$6,630

Industrial output, % average annual increase, 1985–90	0·3
Consumer prices, % average annual increase, 1985–90	17

GDP BY SECTOR, 1988 — %

	%
Services	48
Manufacturing, mining and construction	35
Agriculture, fishing and forestry	17

EMPLOYMENT

Employment, % average annual increase, 1985–90	0·5

UNEMPLOYMENT RATE, %

1985	1986	1987	1988	1989	1990
7·8	7·4	7·4	7·7	7·5	7·2

TRADE

FOREIGN TRADE, 1990	$ bn
Exports	6·4
Imports	16·5

MAJOR COMMODITIES, 1990

Exports	%
Textiles	26
Food and beverages	24
Petroleum products	7
Minerals and ores	6
Metals	5

Imports	
Manufactured consumer goods	36
Machinery	18
Fuels and lubricants	14
Food	13
Raw materials	13

MAJOR TRADING PARTNERS, 1990

Exports	%
Germany	22
Italy	17
France	10
Britain	7
United States	6

Imports	
Germany	21
Italy	15
France	8
Netherlands	7
Japan	6

FINANCE

Central bank
Bank of Greece, Athens
Major stock market
Athens

ATHENS STOCK EXCHANGE INDEX, year-end

1985	1986	1987	1988	1989	1990
71·0	103·9	272·5	279·6	459·4	932·0

Market capitalisation, end-1990	$15 bn

Top five companies, by market capitalisation, end-1990	$ bn
National Bank of Greece (banking)	1·2
Heracles Cement (construction and materials)	1·0
Credit Bank (banking)	0·9
Ergo bank (banking)	0·9
Commercial Bank of Greece (banking)	0·8

EDUCATION

Spending as % of GDP, 1990	3
% adult literacy, 1989	93

ENROLMENT RATIOS, 1988 — %

	%
Primary school	100
Secondary	95
Tertiary	27

HEALTH

VITAL STATISTICS, 1989

Births, rate per ’000	11·9
Deaths, rate per ’000	9·7
Life expectancy at birth	76 years
Health spending as % of GDP, 1990	5
Doctors per ’000	2·8

DEFENCE

Spending as % of GDP, 1990	6

Compulsory service for men of 19–23 months

ACTIVE TROOPS, 1990

Army	113,000
Air Force	26,000
Navy	19,500
Reserves	406,000

AREA	769,360sq km
CLIMATE	Mediterranean along south coast, continental inland. Average temperatures Istanbul Jan. 5°C, July 23°C. Annual rainfall 723mm
LAND USE	Agriculture 48% Forest 26%
HIGHEST POINT	Ararat 5137m
MAIN RIVERS	Goksu, Seyan, Orontes, Tigris, Euphrates
CAPITAL	Ankara 2·6m
OTHER CITIES	Istanbul 6·7m Izmir 1·8m Adana 932,000
TIME	GMT + 2–3hour
MONEY	1 Lira (TL) = 100 kurus
EXCHANGE RATES	1991 average TL 4,173 = $1·00 TL 5,177 = 1 ecu
OFFICIAL LANGUAGE	Turkish
MAJOR RELIGION	Moslem 98%
MEMBER	Council of Europe, IMF, NATO, OECD, UN

PEOPLE

Population, 1990	57,163,000
Forecast, 2000	66,622,000
% under 15, 1990	34·3
% over 64, 1990	4·3
% average annual increase, 1985–90	2·4
Urban population as % of total, 1990	65
Density	71 people per sq km

LIVING STANDARDS, 1988	per ’000
Passenger cars	18
Telephones	119 (1991)
Television sets	76

POLITICS

POLITICAL SUMMARY
Parliamentary republic, unicameral Meclis (Grand National Assembly) of 450 members directly elected for a five-year term. Head of state, president, elected by Meclis for a seven-year term. Prime minister appointed by president. Executive powers exercised by prime minister and cabinet of ministers.

MAIN POLITICAL PARTIES
True Path, Motherland, Social Democratic Populist, Welfare, Democratic Left, Nationalist Endeavour

GOVERNMENT FINANCES

TL trillion	1986	1987	1988	1989	1990
Revenues	6·8	10·5	17·0	30·4	56·7
Spending	8·2	13·0	21·0	38·9	68·2

SPENDING BY SECTOR, 1989 — %

	%
Wages and salaries	32
Interest payments	21
Transfers to industry	16
Investment	13
Other	18

ECONOMY

GDP	$ bn
1990	107·3
1995 forecast	236·0

Real GDP, % average annual growth, 1985–90	5·9
GDP per head, 1990	$1,960

GDP BY SECTOR, 1990 — %

	%
Services	49
Industry	29
Agriculture and fishing	18
Construction	4

Industrial output, % average annual increase, 1985–90	6·8
Consumer prices, % average annual increase, 1985–90	154

EMPLOYMENT

EMPLOYMENT BY SECTOR, 1990 — %

	%
Agriculture	49
Services	30
Industry	15
Construction	6

Job growth, % average annual increase, 1986–90	2·0

UNEMPLOYMENT RATE, %

1985	1986	1987	1988	1989	1990
11·3	10·5	9·5	9·8	10·2	10·1

TRADE

FOREIGN TRADE, 1990	$ bn
Exports	12·9
Imports	22·3

MAJOR COMMODITIES, 1990

Exports	%
Textiles and clothing	31
Other manufactured goods	48
Agricultural products	18

THE TURKISH ECONOMY

The Turkish economy was one of Europe's star performers during the 1980s, growing in real terms by almost 75%, compared with the EC's increase of little over 25%. Strong growth, combined with trade, economic and political reforms, encouraged Turkey to apply for full EC membership in April 1987. After an initial rejection, the European Commission has delayed deciding on full membership until 1993 because of Turkey's relative poverty, poor democratic record, and the dispute with Greece over Cyprus. The combination of the 1990–91 Gulf crisis and a stronger lira pushed the current account into deficit, a problem estimated to last for several years, according to the OECD.

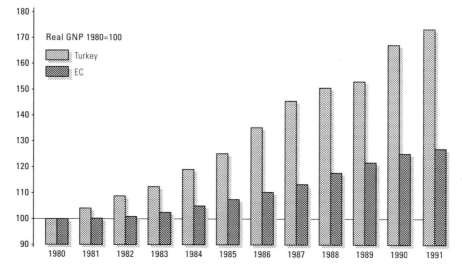

Real GNP 1980=100
Turkey / EC

Imports	
Machinery	24
Minerals	18
Crude oil	16
Chemicals	11
Metals	11

MAJOR TRADING PARTNERS, 1990

Exports	%
Germany	24
Italy	9
United States	8
United Kingdom	6
France	6
Iran	4

Imports	%
Germany	16
United States	10
Italy	8
Japan	5
Iraq	5
United Kingdom	5

FINANCE

Central bank
Merkez Bankasi, Ankara
Major stock market
Istanbul

ISTANBUL STOCK EXCHANGE INDEX, year-end

1986	1987	1988	1989	1990
170·9	673·0	373·9	2,217·7	3,255·8

Market capitalisation, end-1990	$19 bn

**Top five companies, by market
capitalisation,** end-1990 $ bn

Akbank (banking)	3·6
Koc Holding (financial services)	2·3
T Isbank (banking)	1·4
Petkim (chemicals)	1·4
Erdehir (metals)	1·2

EDUCATION

Spending as % of GDP, 1990	2
Years of compulsory education	6
% adult literacy, 1989	74

ENROLMENT RATIOS, 1988 %

Primary school	100
Secondary	46
Tertiary	10

HEALTH

VITAL STATISTICS, 1989

Births, rate per '000	28·4
Deaths, rate per '000	8·4
Life expectancy	65 years
Health spending as % of GDP, 1990	1
Doctors per '000	1·5

DEFENCE

Spending as % of GDP, 1990	4

Compulsory service at age 20 for 18 months. Reserve status until age 46.

ACTIVE TROOPS, 1990

Army	470,000
Air Force	57,200
Navy	52,000
Reserves	1,107,000

CYPRUS
REPUBLIC OF CYPRUS

AREA	9,251sq km
CLIMATE	Mediterranean. Average temperatures Nicosia Jan. 10·0°C, July 28·3°C. Annual rainfall 371mm
LAND USE	Agriculture 18%
HIGHEST POINT	Olympus 1,953m
MAIN RIVERS	Pedieas, Karyota, Kouris
CAPITAL	Nicosia 166,900
OTHER CITIES	Limassol 120,000
TIME	GMT + 2 hours
MONEY	1 Cyprus pound (CYP) = 100 cents
EXCHANGE RATES	1991 average CYP 0·46 = $1·00 CYP 0·63 = 1 ecu
OFFICIAL LANGUAGES	Greek, Turkish
MAJOR RELIGION	Greek Orthodox 80% Moslem 19%
MEMBER	Commonwealth, Council of Europe, Non-Aligned Movement, UN

PEOPLE

Population, 1990	701,000
Forecast, 2000	762,000
% under 15, 1990	25·6
% over 64, 1990	10·3
% average annual increase, 1985–90	1·0
Urban population as % of total, 1990	53
Density	76 people per sq km

MAJOR ETHNIC GROUPS, 1990 %

Greek Orthodox	80
Turkish Moslem	19
Other	1

POLITICS

POLITICAL SUMMARY
The island is de facto divided between two administrations the (Greek-Cypriot) Republic of Cyprus and the (Turkish-Cypriot) Turkish Republic of Northern Cyprus. The latter was declared in November 1983 and has not received international recognition. The Republic of Cyprus is a presidential republic. Of the 80 seats in the House of Representatives, the 24 which are reserved for Turkish Cypriots remain unoccupied.

MAIN POLITICAL PARTIES
Communist Party, Adisok, Democratic Party, Democratic rally, Socialist Party

GOVERNMENT FINANCES

Republic of Cyprus

CYP million	1985	1986	1987	1988	1989
Revenues	387·7	423·8	455·7	535·0	632·7
Spending	447·5	489·7	533·9	598·4	663·8

ECONOMY

GDP	$ bn
1990	5·4
1992 forecast	6·6

Real GDP, % average annual growth, 1985–90	6·4
GDP per head, 1990	$7,645

Industrial output, % average annual increase, 1985–90	5·9

Consumer prices, % average annual increase, 1985–90	3·1

EMPLOYMENT

EMPLOYMENT BY SECTOR, 1990 %

Services	56
Industry	20
Farming	15
Construction	2

Employment, % average annual increase, 1986–89	2·5

TRADE

FOREIGN TRADE, 1990 $ bn

Exports	0·8
Imports	2·3

MAJOR COMMODITIES, 1990

Exports	%
Re-exports	34
Manufactured goods	30
Clothing	18
Potatoes	7

Imports	
Semi-finished goods	47
Transport equipment	17
Consumer goods	24
Fuel and lubricants	12

MAJOR TRADING PARTNERS, 1990

Exports	%
United Kingdom	23
Greece	10
Lebanon	10
Germany	5

Imports	
United Kingdom	13
Japan	12
Italy	10
Germany	9

FINANCE

Central bank
Central Bank of Cyprus, Nicosia
Major stock market
No official exchange, however, an over-the-counter market operates in Nicosia.

EDUCATION

Spending as % of GDP, 1990	4
Years of compulsory education	9
% adult literacy, 1986	89
ENROLMENT RATIOS, 1990	%
Primary school	104
Secondary	87
Tertiary	11

HEALTH

VITAL STATISTICS, 1989

Births, rate per '000	19·0
Deaths, rate per '000	8·2
Life expectancy	76 years

DEFENCE

Spending as % of GDP, 1990	3

Compulsory service for men of 26 months.
ACTIVE TROOPS, 1990

National Guard	10,000
Reserves	108,000

SWITZERLAND
SWISS CONFEDERATION

AREA	41, 293sq km
CLIMATE	Temperate. Average temperatures Bern Jan. 0°C, July 18·5°C. Annual rainfall 986mm
LAND USE	Agriculture 29% Forest 26%
HIGHEST POINT	Dufourspitze 4,633m
MAIN RIVERS	Rhine, Rhone, Ticino
CAPITAL	Bern 134,000
OTHER CITIES	Zurich 343,000 Basel 170,000 Geneva 165,000
TIME	GMT + 1 hour
MONEY	1 franc (SwFr) = 100 rappen or centimes
EXCHANGE RATES	1991 average SwFr 1·43 = $1·00 SwFr 1·77 = 1 ecu
OFFICIAL LANGUAGES	French, German, Italian
MAJOR RELIGION	Roman Catholic 48% Protestant 43%
MEMBER	Council of Europe, EFTA, OECD

PEOPLE

Population, 1990	6,796,000
Forecast, 2000	7,140,000
% under 15, 1990	16·4
% over 64, 1990	15·3
% average annual increase, 1985–90	0·8
Urban population as % of total, 1990	59
Density	158 people per sq km

NATIONALS, 1990 %

German	74
French	20
Italian	5

LIVING STANDARDS, 1988 per 1,000

Passenger cars	419
Telephones	892 (1991)
Television sets	337

POLITICS

POLITICAL SUMMARY
Federal republic, with bicameral Federal Assembly and state legislatures for 26 cantons and half-cantons. 200 members of the lower house of Federal Assembly elected by proportional representation; two members from each of the 23 cantons are elected for the upper house, Council of States. Federal Council exercises executive powers; seven members chosen by, but not necessarily from, the Federal Assembly. Federal Council president is de facto head of state.

MAIN POLITICAL PARTIES
Radical Democratic, Social Democratic, Christian Democratic, Swiss People's, Liberal, Green, Independent Alliance

GOVERNMENT FINANCES

SwFr bn	1986	1987	1988	1989	1990
Revenues	26·0	25·6	27·7	29·4	31·7
Spending	24·0	24·6	26·5	28·5	31·1

FEDERAL SPENDING BY SECTOR, 1990	%
Social services	22
Defence	19
Transport	5
Agriculture and food	8
Foreign relations	5
Other	31

ECONOMY

GDP	$ bn
1990	228
1995 forecast	325
Real GDP, % average annual growth, 1985–90	2·0
GDP per head, 1990	$33,870
Industrial output, % average annual increase, 1985–90	3·7
Consumer prices, % average annual increase, 1985–90	2·5

EMPLOYMENT

EMPLOYMENT BY SECTOR, 1990	%
Services	61
Manufacturing, mining and construction	34
Agriculture and forestry	5
Job growth, % average annual increase, 1985–90	0·7

UNEMPLOYMENT RATE, %					
1985	1986	1987	1988	1989	1990
0·8	0·7	0·6	0·7	0·0	0·6

TRADE

FOREIGN TRADE, 1990	SwFr bn
Exports	88·3
Imports	96·6

MAJOR COMMODITIES, 1990	
Exports	**%**
Machinery and equipment	29
Chemicals	21
Metals	9
Watches and clocks	8
Precision instruments	5
Imports	
Machinery and equipment	21
Instruments, watches and jewels	12
Chemicals	11
Motor vehicles	11
Textiles and clothing	9

MAJOR TRADING PARTNERS, 1990	
Exports	**%**
Germany	22
France	10
Italy	9
United States	8
United Kingdom	7
Imports	
Germany	34
France	11
Italy	11
United States	6
United Kingdom	5

FINANCE

Central bank
National Bank of Switzerland, Bern and Zurich
Switzerland is a major international banking centre.
Major stock market
Zurich

SWISS BANK CORPORATION GENERAL INDEX, year-end

1985	1986	1987	1988	1989	1990
587·9	588·9	474·4	559·8	661·1	520·1

Market capitalisation, end-1990	$167 bn

Top five companies, by market capitalisation, end-1990	$ bn
Nestlé (food products)	20·5
Roche Holding (health and personal care)	14·2
Union Bank of Switzerland (banking)	10·0
Sandoz (health and personal care)	9·0
Ciba-Geigy (chemicals)	9·0

EDUCATION

Spending as % of GDP, 1990	5

Years of compulsory education varies by canton

% adult literacy, 1989	99

ENROLMENT RATIOS, 1988	%
Primary school	100
Secondary	100
Tertiary	24

HEALTH

VITAL STATISTICS, 1989	
Births, rate per '000	12·2
Deaths, rate per '000	9·2
Life expectancy at birth	77 years
Health spending as % of GDP, 1990	5
Doctors, per '000	1·4

DEFENCE

Spending as % of GDP, 1990	2

Compulsory and universal service in National Militia between ages 20 and 50; 17 weeks training at age 20 followed by annual refreshers.

ACTIVE TROOPS, 1990	
Army	565,000
Air Corps	60,000

EUROPE'S INTERNATIONAL BANKING

Liechtenstein, Switzerland, the Channel Islands and Isle of Man may have their notorious "secret" banking attractions but they rank relatively low as centres for international banking.

London is by far the leader, with almost $1.4 trillion worth of international loans outstanding at the end of 1990. Paris, Frankfurt and Amsterdam are eager to replace London as Europe's major financial centre.

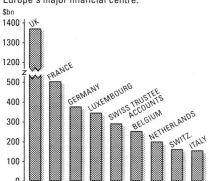

LIECHTENSTEIN
PRINCIPALITY OF LIECHTENSTEIN

AREA	160sq km
CLIMATE	Continental. Average temperatures, see Switzerland
CAPITAL	Vaduz
TIME	GMT + 1 hour
MONEY	Swiss franc
OFFICIAL LANGUAGE	German

PEOPLE

Population, 1988	28,180
Density	176 people per sq km

POLITICS

POLITICAL SUMMARY
Parliamentary principality. 25-member parliament elected by proportional representation for four years. Any group of 1,000 people of three communes may propose a referendum.

POLITICAL PARTIES
Patriotic Union, Progressive Citizens' Party

ECONOMY

A mixture of light industry and tourism .

AUSTRIA
REPUBLIC OF AUSTRIA

AREA	83,857sq km
CLIMATE	Continental. Average temperatures Vienna Jan. -2·0°C, July 19·5°C. Annual rainfall 640mm
LAND USE	Forest 40% Pasture 20%
HIGHEST POINT	Grossglockner 3,797m
MAIN RIVERS	Danube
CAPITAL	Vienna 1·5m
OTHER CITIES	Graz 243,179 Linz 199,900 Salzburg 139,430
TIME	GMT + 1 hour
MONEY	1 Schilling (ASch) = 100 groschen
EXCHANGE RATES	1991 average ASch 11.7 = $1.00 ASch 14.5 = 1 ecu
OFFICIAL LANGUAGE	German
MAJOR RELIGIONS	Roman Catholic 89%
MEMBER	EFTA, OECD, UN

PEOPLE

Population, 1990	7,492,000
Forecast, 2000	7,461,000
% under 15, 1990	17·6
% over 64, 1990	15·0
% average annual increase, 1985–90	0·1
Urban population as % of total, 1990	58
Density	91 people per sq km

MAJOR LANGUAGE GROUPS, 1990	%
German	96
Croats	1
Slovenes	1
Hungarian	1

LIVING STANDARDS, 1988	per '000
Passenger cars	370
Telephones	543 (1991)
Television sets	323

POLITICS

POLITICAL SUMMARY
Federal republic with parliamentary democracy. The Socialist Party of Austria and Austrian People's Party have ruled in coalition since January 1987. The next general election is due by 1994.

MAIN POLITICAL PARTIES
Socialist Party, People's Party, Freedom Party, Green Party

GOVERNMENT FINANCES

ASch bn	1988	1989	1990	1991(budget)
Revenues	486·8	503·4	531·4	576·6
Spending	423·7	451·4	472·2	495·1

SPENDING BY SECTOR, 1991	%
Debt service and repayments	31
Social insurance	9
Education	8
Environment, pollution control	8
Science and research	4
Other	40

ECONOMY

GDP	$ bn
1990	157·4
1995 forecast	220·0
Real GDP, % average annual growth, 1985–90	3·1
GDP per head, 1990	$20,391
Industrial output, % average annual increase, 1985–90	3·9
Consumer prices, % average annual increase, 1985–90	2·2

EMPLOYMENT

EMPLOYMENT BY SECTOR, 1990,	%
Services	60
Industry	36
Farming	1
Employment % average annual increase, 1985–90	1·2

UNEMPLOYMENT RATE, %					
1985	1986	1987	1988	1989	1990
3·6	3·1	3·8	3·6	3·1	3·3

TRADE

FOREIGN TRADE, 1990	$ bn
Exports	41·1
Imports	50·0

MAJOR COMMODITIES, 1990	
Exports	**%**
Manufactured goods	45
Machinery and transport equipment	38
Chemicals	9

Raw materials	5
Food, beverages and tobacco	3
Fuels and energy	4

Imports

Machinery and transport equipment	38
Manufactured goods	36
Chemicals	10
Fuels and energy	6
Food, beverages and tobacco	5

MAJOR TRADING PARTNERS, 1990

Exports	%
Germany	37
Italy	10
Switzerland	7
France	5
Britain	4

Imports

Germany	44
Italy	9
Japan	5
Switzerland	4
France	4

FINANCE

Central bank
National Bank of Austria, Vienna
Major stock market
Vienna

AUSTRIA GZ ALL SHARE INDEX, year-end

1985	1986	1987	1988	1989	1990
273·8	264·4	217·4	249·1	480·1	497·0

Market capitalisation, end-1990	$27 bn

Top five companies, by market capitalisation, end-1990	$ bn
Creditanstalt-Bankverein (banking)	2·6
Österreichische Landerbank (banking)	2·2
Erste Allgemeine Generali (insurance)	2·2
OMW (holding company)	1.6
Wienerberger Baustoffindustrie (construction and materials)	1·4

EDUCATION

Spending as % of GDP, 1990	6·0
Years of compulsory education	9
% adult literacy, 1989	99

ENROLMENT RATIOS, 1990	%
Primary school	99
Secondary	n.a.
Tertiary	31

HEALTH

VITAL STATISTICS, 1989

Births, rate per '000	11·6
Deaths, rate per '000	10·9
Life expectancy at birth	75 years
Health spending as % of GDP, 1990	8
Doctors per '000	2·1

DEFENCE

Spending as % of GDP, 1990	2

Compulsory service for men of 6 months.

ACTIVE TROOPS, 1990

Army	38,000
Air Force	6,000
Reserves	242,000

GERMANY
FEDERAL REPUBLIC OF GERMANY

AREA	357,046sq km
CLIMATE	Continental. Average temperatures Berlin Jan. -0·5°C, July 19·0°C. Annual rainfall 563mm
LAND USE	Agriculture 55% Forest 28%
HIGHEST POINT	Zugspitze 2,963m
MAIN RIVERS	Danube, Rhine, Elbe, Oder
CAPITAL	Berlin 3·3m
OTHER CITIES	Hamburg 1·6m Munich 1·2m Cologne 934,400
TIME	GMT + 1 hour
MONEY	Deutschemark (DM) = 100 pfennig
EXCHANGE RATES	1991 average DM 1.66 = $1.00 DM 2.05 = 1 ecu
OFFICIAL LANGUAGE	German
MAJOR RELIGIONS	(former West Germany) Roman Catholic 26·2% Protestant 25·4% Moslem 1·7%
MEMBER	Council of Europe, EC, NATO, OECD, UN, WEU

PEOPLE

Population, 1990	77,573,000
Forecast, 2000	76,960,000
% under 15, 1990	15·0
% over 64, 1990	15·4
% average annual increase, 1985–90	0·2
Urban population as % of total, 1990	84
Density	221 people per sq km

MAJOR ETHNIC GROUPS, 1990	%
German	93
Turkish	2
Yugoslav	1
Italian	1

LIVING STANDARDS, 1988 (former West Germany)	per '000
Passenger cars	457
Telephones	680 (1991)
Television sets	377

POLITICS

POLITICAL SUMMARY
Parliamentary republic. The federal president is elected by a college, of members of federal and state (Länder) legislatures, for up to two five-year terms. The chancellor, elected by the Bundestag on the president's nomination, heads the federal government. The two-chamber federal assembly comprises the 662-member Bundestag, elected for four years, and the 68-member Bundesrat, chosen by the republic's 16 state governments. Each state has its own legislature.

MAIN POLITICAL PARTIES
Christian Democratic Union, Christian Social Union, Social Democratic Party, Free Democratic Party, the Greens, Budnis 90, Party of Democratic Socialism

GOVERNMENT FINANCES

(former West Germany)

DM bn	1986	1987	1988	1989	1990
Revenues	867·5	891·4	924·2	998·9	1041·0
Spending	834·0	869·9	910·5	930·7	1089·3

SPENDING BY SECTOR, 1990	%
Outlays	41
Social security	34
Other transfers to individuals	9
Debt service	6
Other	10

ECONOMY

GDP (former West Germany)	$ bn
1990	1,497·2
1995 forecast	2,114·0

Real GDP, % average annual growth, 1985–90	3·1

GDP per head, 1990	$24,030

Industrial output, % average annual increase, 1985–90	3·2
Consumer prices, % average annual increase, 1985–90	1·4

EMPLOYMENT

EMPLOYMENT BY SECTOR, 1990	%
Services	49
Industry	41
Construction	7
Agriculture and forestry	3

Job growth, % average annual increase, 1985–90	1·6

UNEMPLOYMENT RATE, %

1985	1986	1987	1988	1989	1990
7·2	6·4	6·2	6·2	5·6	5·1

TRADE

FOREIGN TRADE, including former East Germany after June 1990	$ bn
Exports	396·7
Imports	339·9

MAJOR COMMODITIES, 1990

Exports	%
Cars and trucks	18
Engineering products	27
Chemicals	13
Food and beverages	5
Textiles	4

Imports	
Engineering products	17
Food and beverages	12
Chemicals	10
Cars and trucks	9
Textiles	5

MAJOR TRADING PARTNERS, 1990

Exports	%
France	13
Britain	9
Italy	9
Netherlands	8
Belgium	7

Imports	
France	12
Netherlands	10
Italy	9
Belgium	7
Britain	7

FINANCE

Central bank
Deutsche Bundesbank, Frankfurt
Major stock market
Frankfurt

FAZ GENERAL INDEX, year-end

1985	1986	1987	1988	1989	1990
654·0	676·4	425·2	549·9	740·9	603·0

Market capitalisation, end-1990	$343 bn

Top five companies, by market capitalisation, end-1990	$ bn
Allianz (insurance)	24·7
Siemens (electrical equipment)	20·3
Deutsche Bank (banking)	17·7
Daimler-Benz (cars and trucks)	17·2
Münchener Ruckversicherung (insurance)	15·4

EDUCATION

Spending as % of GDP, 1990	5
% adult literacy, 1989	99

ENROLMENT RATIOS, 1988	%
Primary school	100
Secondary	99
Tertiary	32

HEALTH

VITAL STATISTICS, 1989
(former West Germany)

Births, rate per '000	11·1
Deaths, rate per '000	12·3
Life expectancy	75 years
Health spending as % of GDP, 1990	8
Doctors per '000	2.8

DEFENCE

Spending as % of GDP, 1990	2

Compulsory service for men of 12 months.

ACTIVE TROOPS, 1990

Army	335,000
Air Force	103,700
Navy	37,600
Reserves	1,009,400

POLAND
REPUBLIC OF POLAND

AREA	312,677sq.km
CLIMATE	Continental, severe winters. Average temperatures Warsaw Jan. -3·9°C, July 18·9°C. Annual rainfall 550mm
LAND USE	Agriculture 61%
HIGHEST POINT	Rysy 2,499m
MAIN RIVERS	Vistula, Narew, Odra
CAPITAL	Warsaw 1·7m
OTHER CITIES	Lodz 851,000 Krakow 734,700 Wroclaw 637,400
TIME	GMT + 1 hour
MONEY	1 zloty (Zl) = 100 groszy
EXCHANGE RATES	1991 average Zl 10,576 = $1.00
OFFICIAL LANGUAGE	Polish
MAJOR RELIGION	Roman Catholic 95%
MEMBER	IMF, UN

PEOPLE

Population, 1990	38,038,000
Forecast, 2000	40,366,000
% under 15, 1990	25·2

% over 64, 1990	10·0
% average annual increase, 1985–90	0·7
Urban population as % of total, 1990	62
Density	123 people per sq km
Ethnic groups	est. 1·2m ethnic Germans

NET EXTERNAL MIGRATION, '000

1985	1986	1987	1988
18·9	27·1	34·6	4·2

LIVING STANDARDS, 1988 — per '000

Television sets	263

POLITICS

POLITICAL SUMMARY
Parliamentary republic. Executive president is elected for six years by the legislature. The two-chamber National Assembly is directly elected for four years and comprises the 460-member Sejm and 100-member Senate. The council of ministers, headed by a prime minister, is elected by the Sejm.

MAIN POLITICAL PARTIES
Christian Democratic Party, Citizen's Movement for Democratic Action, United Peasant's Party

GOVERNMENT FINANCES

Zl bn	1987	1988	1989
Revenues	5,850·5	10,088·7	22,800·5
Spending	973·2	10,010·2	26,600·0

SPENDING BY SECTOR, 1989 — %

Industry subsidies	40
Education	15
Health and welfare services	14
Insurance	8
Defence	7
Other	16

ECONOMY

GDP	$ bn
1990	150·1
1995 forecast	164·3

Real GDP, % average annual decrease, 1985–90	2·6
GDP per head, 1990	$3,931

GDP BY SECTOR, 1990 — %

Industry	25
Agriculture	31
Other	44

Industrial output, % average annual increase, 1985–90	2·2
Consumer prices, % average annual increase, 1985–90	225

EMPLOYMENT

EMPLOYMENT BY SECTOR, 1988 — %

Industry	36
Trade	11
Construction	9
Transport and communications	9
Other	35

Job growth % average annual increase, 1980–90	0·6

TRADE

FOREIGN TRADE, 1989 — $ bn

Exports	8·9
Imports	7·8

MAJOR COMMODITIES, 1989

Exports	%
Machinery	25
Food	19
Metals	14
Fuels and energy	12
Chemicals	11

Imports	
Machinery	33
Food	20
Chemicals	19
Metals	9
Energy	5

MAJOR TRADING PARTNERS, 1989

Exports	%
Soviet Union	25
West Germany	14
Britain	7
Czechoslovakia	6
East Germany	4

Imports	
Austria	4
Soviet Union	18
West Germany	16
Austria	6
Czechoslovakia	6
Switzerland	5
East Germany	5

FINANCE

Central bank
National Bank of Poland
Major restructuring of banking system, including privatisations and establishment of new banks, is under way.
Stock market started in Warsaw, 1991

EDUCATION

Spending as % of GDP, 1986	5
Years of compulsory education	8
% adult literacy, 1989	98

ENROLMENT RATIOS — %

Primary school	99
Secondary	80
Tertiary	18

HEALTH

VITAL STATISTICS, 1989

Births, rate per '000	14·8
Deaths, rate per '000	10·0
Life expectancy at birth	71years
Health spending as % of GDP, 1986	4
% eligible for public health insurance	100
Hospital beds per 1,000, 1990	67
Doctors per '000	2·1

DEFENCE

Spending as % of GDP, 1990	2

Every male is liable for national service between ages 19 and 50; compulsory service at 19: 18 months in Army or Air Force, 24 in the Navy.

ACTIVE TROOPS, 1991

Army	206,600
Navy	20,000
Air Force	86,200
Security and frontier forces	43,500

CZECHOSLOVAKIA

AREA	127,876sq km
CLIMATE	Continental. Warm humid summers, cold winters. Average temperatures Prague Jan. -1·5°C, July 19·4°C. Annual rainfall 483mm
LAND USE	Agriculture 53%
HIGHEST POINT	Gerlachovsky 2,663m
MAIN RIVER	Danube
CAPITAL	Prague 1·2m
OTHER CITIES	Bratislava 435,700 Brno 389,800 Ostrava 330,600
TIME	GMT + 1 hour
MONEY	1 koruna(CSK) = 100 haler
EXCHANGE RATES	1991 average CSK 29.5 = $1.00 CSK 36.6 = 1 ecu
OFFICIAL LANGUAGES	Czech, Slovak
MAJOR RELIGIONS	Roman Catholic 24% Protestant 8%
MEMBER	Council of Europe, UN

PEOPLE

Population, 1990	15,667,000
Forecast, 2000	16,179,000
% under 15, 1990	23·3
% over 64, 1990	11·6
% average annual increase, 1985–90	0·3
Urban population as % of total, 1990	78
Density	123 people per sq km

MAJOR ETHNIC GROUPS, 1990 — %

Czech	63
Slovak	32
Hungarian	4
Other	1

LIVING STANDARDS, 1989 — per '000

Telephones	255 (1991)
Televisions	297

POLITICS

POLITICAL SUMMARY
Czech and Slovak lands look set to take their separate courses for independence in 1992. President stepped down in July 1992 signalling first concrete step in break-up.

MAIN POLITICAL PARTIES
Civic Forum, Public Against Violence, Czechoslovak Communist Party, Christian Democratic Movement, People's Party, Society for Self Governing Democracy in Moravia and Silesia, Slovak National Party, Coexistence/Hungarina Democratic Movement

GOVERNMENT FINANCES

CSK bn	1984	1985	1986	1987	1988
Revenues	343·8	359·7	368·7	383·7	404·0
Spending	342·2	358·0	365·9	382·2	401·2

SPENDING BY SECTOR, 1988 — %

National economy	24
Health and social services	24
Defence	7

ECONOMY

GDP	$ bn
1990	36·0
1995 forecast	63·7

Real GDP, % average annual growth, 1985–90	2·1
GDP per head, 1990	$2,300

Industrial output, % average annual increase, 1985–90	1·0
Consumer prices, % average annual increase, 1985–90	2·4

EMPLOYMENT

EMPLOYMENT BY SECTOR, 1990 — %

Services	42
Industry	37
Farming	12
Construction	9

Employment, % average annual decrease, 1985–90	0·7
% unemployment rate, 1990	1·0

TRADE

FOREIGN TRADE, 1990 — $ bn

Exports	5·9
Imports	6·5

MAJOR COMMODITIES 1990

Exports	%
Machinery and transport equipment	42
Miscellaneous finished goods	17
Industrial products	17
Chemicals	9

Imports	
Machinery and transport equipment	43
Fuels and lubricants	23
Chemicals	10
Industrial goods	6

MAJOR TRADING PARTNERS, 1990

Exports	%
Soviet Union	25
East Germany	13
Poland	6
Austria	6

Imports	
Soviet Union	22
East Germany	13
Austria	10
Poland	9

FINANCE

Central bank
State Bank, Prague
Major stock market
Prague Stock Exchange, in process of being formed.

EDUCATION

Spending as % of GDP, 1990	5
Years of compulsory education	10
% adult literacy, 1989	99

ENROLMENT RATIOS, 1990 — %

Primary school	94
Secondary	85
Tertiary	18

HEALTH

VITAL STATISTICS, 1990

Births, rate per '000	13·7
Deaths, rate per '000	11·9
Life expectancy at birth	71 years
Health spending as % of GDP, 1990	4
Doctors per '000	3·1

DEFENCE

Spending as % of GDP, 1990	4

Compulsory service for men of 18 months.

ACTIVE TROOPS, 1990

Army	87,300
Air Force	44,800
Reserves	495,000

HUNGARY
HUNGARIAN REPUBLIC

AREA	93,032sq km
CLIMATE	Continental; warm summers and cold winters. Average temperatures Budapest Jan 0°C, July 21·5°C. Annual rainfall 625mm
LAND USE	Agriculture 70%
HIGHEST POINT	Kekes 1,015m
MAIN RIVERS	Danube, Tisza
CAPITAL	Budapest 2·0m
OTHER CITIES	Debrecen 212,000 Miskolc 196,000 Szeged 175,000
TIME	GMT + 1 hour
MONEY	Forint(Ft) = 100 filler
EXCHANGE RATES	1991 average Ft 74.7 = $1.00
OFFICIAL LANGUAGE	Magyar(Hungarian)
MAJOR RELIGIONS	Roman Catholic 60%, Hungarian Reformed 20%
MEMBER	IMF, UN

PEOPLE

Population, 1990	19,579,000
Forecast, 2000	10,553,000
% under 15, 1990	19·9
% over 64, 1990	13·4
% average annual decrease, 1985–90	0·2
Urban population as % of total, 1990	60
Density	113 people per sq km

LIVING STANDARDS, 1988 — per '000

Passenger cars	169
Telephones	158 (1991)
Television sets	402

POLITICS

POLITICAL SUMMARY
Parliamentary republic. The highest body is the 386-seat National Assembly which serves for a five-year term and elects the president. Multiparty elections were held in March–April 1990, and won by the Hungarian Democratic Forum, which gained 165 seats.

MAIN POLITICAL PARTIES
Hungarian Democratic Forum, Federation of Free Democrats, Independent Smallholders' Party, Hungarian Socialist Party, Federation of Young Democrats,Christian Democratic People's Party, Social Democratic Party

GOVERNMENT FINANCES

Ft bn	1988	1989	1990
Revenues	519·4	534·9	640·9
Spending	538·4	589·1	642·3

SPENDING BY SECTOR, 1990

	%
Government sponsored institutions	29
Local governments	18
Debt service	11
Enterprise subsidies	11
Other	31

ECONOMY

GDP	$ bn
1990	33·1
1995 forecast	45·7
Real GDP, % average annual growth, 1985–90	0·2
GDP per head, 1990	$3,140
Industrial output, % average annual increase, 1985–90	1·4
Consumer prices, % average annual increase, 1985–90	14·7

EMPLOYMENT

EMPLOYMENT BY SECTOR, 1989

	%
Services	42
Manufacturing, mining and construction	38
Agriculture and forestry	20

Job growth,	
% average annual increase, 1985–90	0·6
% unemployment rate, 1990	1·7

TRADE

FOREIGN TRADE, 1990

	$ bn
Exports	7·1
Imports	6·1

MAJOR COMMODITIES, 1990

Exports	%
Semi-finished goods	44
Food, beverages and tobacco	26
Consumer goods	16
Capital equipment	12

Imports	
Semi-finished goods	51
Machinery and transport equipment	18
Industrial consumer goods	13
Food, beverages and tobacco	9
Fuels	9

MAJOR TRADING PARTNERS, 1990

Exports	%
USSR	20
Other European Comecon countries	13
Germany	20
Austria	8

Imports	
Germany	23
USSR	19
Other European Comecon countries	14
Austria	10

FINANCE

Central bank
National Bank, Budapest
Stock market
Budapest Stock Exchange opened on 21st June, 1990.

EDUCATION

Spending as % of GDP, 1990	7
% adult literacy, 1985	99
ENROLMENT RATIOS	%
Primary school	100
Secondary	100
Tertiary	25

HEALTH

VITAL STATISTICS, 1989

Births, rate per '000	12·7
Deaths, rate per '000	8·7
Life expectancy at birth	77 years
Health spending as % of GDP, 1990	8
Doctors per '000	3·2

DEFENCE

Spending as % of GDP, 1990	2

Compulsory service for men of 18–24 months.

ACTIVE TROOPS, 1990

Army	66,400
Air Force	20,120
Reserves	210,000

YUGOSLAVIA

AREA	255,804sq km
CLIMATE	Continental inland, Mediterranean along coast. Average temperatures Belgrade Jan. 0°C, July 22·0°C. Annual rainfall 610mm
LAND USE	Agriculture 56% Forest 36%
HIGHEST POINT	Triglav 2,864m
MAIN RIVERS	Danube, Drava, Sava
CITIES	Belgrade 1·5m Zagreb 763,000 Skopje 503,000 Sarajevo 448,000
TIME	GMT + 1 hour
MONEY	1 dinar(YuD) = 100 paras
EXCHANGE RATES	1990 average YuD 19·6 = $1·00 YuD 24.3 = 1 ecu
OFFICIAL LANGUAGES	Serbo-Croat, Slovene, Macedonian, Albanian, Hungarian
MAJOR RELIGIONS	Orthodox 40%, Roman Catholic 33%
MEMBER	OECD, UN

PEOPLE

Population, 1990	23,807,000
Forecast, 2000	24,900,000
% under 15, 1990	22·6
% over 64, 1990	9·5
% average annual increase, 1985–90	0·6
Urban population as % of total, 1990	56
Density	93 people per sq km

LIVING STANDARDS, 1988 — per '000

Passenger cars	129
Telephones	180 (1991)
Television sets	176

POLITICS

POLITICAL SUMMARY
The Yugoslav Federation is still officially in existence, but it is in an advanced state of dissolution. After civil war broke out in 1991, Slovenia and Croatia were the first republics to be recognised as independent, and in 1992 fighting spread to Bosnia-Hercegovina. The federal government and the army remain Serbian-dominated, and Serbian forces during 1992 captured large areas of territory in Bosnia-Hercegovina. UN forces moved in to protect aid convoys while refugees fled the country in their thousands. The future shape of the former Yugoslavia is still a matter of conjecture.

GOVERNMENT FINANCES

FEDERAL GOVERNMENT FINANCES			YuD bn	
1986	**1987**	**1988**	**1989**	**1990**
Revenues				
137·4	300·9	691·7	11,376·5	85,000
Spending				
137·5	688·3	1,442·7	16,677·8	112,211

SPENDING BY SECTOR, 1988

	%
Social security and welfare	43
Defence and administration	22
Education	16
Economic intervention	10
Other	9

ECONOMY

GDP (gross state product)	$ bn
1990	123·7
1995 forecast	95·7
Real GDP, % average annual decrease, 1985–90	1·3
GDP per head, 1990	$5,195
Industrial output, % average annual decrease, 1985–90	1·2
Consumer prices, % average annual increase, 1985–90	157

EMPLOYMENT

EMPLOYMENT BY SECTOR, 1990

	%
Services	39
Industry	48
Construction	8
Farming	5

Job growth,	
% average annual decrease, 1986–90	0·3

TRADE

FOREIGN TRADE, 1989 — $ bn hard currency

Exports	1·3
Imports	15·0

MAJOR COMMODITIES, 1989

Exports	%
Manufactured goods	31

Machinery and transport equipment	25
Food, beverages and tobacco	9
Raw materials	7
Imports	
Machinery and transport equipment	30
Manufactured goods	18
Chemicals	16
Raw materials	7

MAJOR TRADING PARTNERS, 1990

Exports	%
Soviet Union	19
Italy	17
Germany	17
France	5
United States	5
Imports	
Germany	19
Soviet Union	13
Italy	13
Austria	6
France	5
United States	5

FINANCE

Central bank
National Bank, Belgrade

EDUCATION

Spending as % of GDP, 1990	4
% adult literacy, 1989	92

ENROLMENT RATIOS, 1990

	%
Primary school	99

HEALTH

VITAL STATISTICS, 1989

Births, rate per '000	14·3
Deaths, rate per '000	9·1
Life expectancy	73 years
Health spending as % of GDP, 1990	4
Doctors per '000	1·8

DEFENCE

Spending as % of GDP, 1990	3

Compulsory service for men of 12 months.

ACTIVE TROOPS, 1990

Army	129,000
Air Force	29,000
Navy	11,000
Reserves	510,000

BALKAN PATHOS, 1992

Once a united country, but now divided by state-sponsored ethnic prejudice. The score today...

Bosnia and Hercegovina Pop. 4.4m – 39.5% Moslems, 32.0% Serbs, 18.4% Croats, 11.1% others

Croatia Pop. 4.7m – 75.0% Croats, 11.0% Serbs, 14.0% others

Kosovo Pop. 2.0m 90% Albanians, 6% Serbs, 1.5% Montenegrins, 4.0% others

Macedonia Pop. 2.0m – 67.0% Moslems, 19.8% Albanians, 4.5% Turks, 2.3% Serbs, 6.4% others

Montenegro Pop. 620,000 – 68.5% Montenegrins, 13.4% Moslems, 6.5% Albanians, 11.6% others

Serbia Pop. 9.7m – 66.8% Serbs, 14.0% Albanians, 4.2% Hungarians, 1.6% Croats, 13.4% others

Slovenia Pop. 1.9m – 90.5% Slovenes, 2.9% Croats, 2.2% Serbs, 4.4% others

Vojvodina Pop. 2.0m – 54.4% Serbs, 18.9% Hungarians, 5.4% Croats, 21.3% others

ALBANIA

REPUBLIC OF ALBANIA

AREA 28,478sq km.
CLIMATE Mediterranean. Average temperatures Tirana Jan. 6·8°C, July 23·9°C. Annual rainfall 1,353mm
LAND USE Agriculture 39%
HIGHEST POINT Mt. Korab 2,751m
MAIN RIVERS Drin, Vijose, Saman
CAPITAL Tirana 238,000
OTHER CITIES Dures 82,700; Elbasan 80,700; Shkoder 79,900
TIME GMT + 1 hour
MONEY Money: 1 lek (ALL) = 100 qintars
EXCHANGE RATES 1990 average ALL 15·00 = $1·00
OFFICIAL LANGUAGE Albanian
MAJOR RELIGIONS All religious institutions shut in 1967, previously Islam had been predominate religion
MEMBER UN

PEOPLE

Population, 1990	3,245,000
Forecast, 2000	3,795,000
% under 15, 1990	32·6
% over 64, 1990	5·3
% average annual increase, 1985–90	1·6
Urban population as % of total, 1990	35
Density	113 people per sq km

MAJOR ETHNIC GROUPS, 1990

	%
Albanian	98
Greek	2

POLITICS

POLITICAL SUMMARY
Parliamentary republic. The one-chamber People's Assembly has 250 directly elected members. The assembly elects a presidium, whose chairman is head of state, and a council of ministers, whose chairman is prime minister. An interim constitution replaced the Marxist-inspired constitution of 1967, as part of the 1990–91 political reforms, with a new constitution being drafted.

MAIN POLITICAL PARTIES
Socialist Party of Albania, Democratic Party, Social Democratic Party, Albanian Agrarian Party, Albanian Republican Party, Christian Democratic Party, Ecology Party, Greek Party

GOVERNMENT FINANCES

ALL bn	1980	1988	1989
Revenues	7·5	8·6	9·3
Spending	7·4	8·6	9·3

SPENDING BY SECTOR, 1989

	%
National economy	55
Social services	14
Education and culture	10
Defence	10
Other	1

ECONOMY

Industrial output, % annual average increase, 1985–90	3·7

EMPLOYMENT BY SECTOR, 1989

	%
Services	19
Industry	24
Farming	50
Construction	7

TRADE

FOREIGN TRADE, with IMF members 1990

	$m
Exports	232
Imports	300

MAJOR COMMODITIES, 1990

Exports	%
Fuels and minerals	53
Non-food agricultures	17
Food	17
Industrial consumer goods	10
Imports	
Machinery and equipment	28
Fuels and minerals	26
Non-food agricultures	18
Food	7

MAJOR TRADING PARTNERS, 1989

Exports	%
Italy	17
Romania	17
West Germany	14
China	10
Yugoslavia	5
France	5
Imports	
Italy	17
Romania	16
West Germany	14
Yugoslavia	11
Greece	5
China	5

FINANCE

Central bank
Albanian State Bank, Tirana

EDUCATION

Spending as % of GDP, 1990	7
years of compulsory education	8
% adult literacy, 1985	85

ENROLMENT RATIOS, 1990

	%
Primary school	99
Secondary	107
Tertiary	31

HEALTH

VITAL STATISTICS, 1989

Births rate per '000	22·0
Deaths rate per '000	5·7
Life expectancy	72 years

DEFENCE

Spending as % of GDP, 1990	4

Compulsory service for men of 2–3 years.

ACTIVE TROOPS, 1990

Army	35,000
Air Force	11,000
Navy	2,000
Reserves	155,000

ROMANIA

AREA 237,500sq km
CLIMATE Continental. Average temperatures Bucharest Jan. -2·7°C, July 23·5°C. Annual rainfall 579mm
LAND USE Agriculture 63%, Productive forest 27%
HIGHEST POINT Negiou 2,548m
MAIN RIVERS Danube, Mures, Prut
CAPITAL Bucharest 2·4m
OTHER CITIES Brasov 346,600; Constanta 325,300
TIME GMT + 2 hr
MONEY Leu = 100bani
EXCHANGE RATES 1991 average 76·4 Lei = $1·00; 94.8 Lei = 1 ecu
OFFICIAL LANGUAGE Romanian
MAJOR RELIGIONS Romanian Orthodox 66%, Greek Catholic 7%, Roman Catholic 5%
MEMBER IMF, UN

PEOPLE

Population, 1990	23,190,000
Forecast, 2000	24,190,000
% under 15, 1990	23·4
% over 64, 1990	15·6
% average annual increase, 1985–90	0·5
Urban population as % of total, 1990	50
Density	98 people per sq km

MAJOR ETHNIC GROUPS, 1990

	%
Romanian	88
Hungarian	8
German	2

LIVING STANDARDS, 1988

	per '000
Televisions	166

POLITICS

POLITICAL SUMMARY
The president, as head of state, is directly elected for up to two 30-month terms. The cabinet is headed by a prime minister, nominated by the president. The two-chamber parliament comprises the 199-member Senate and the 387-member Assembly of Deputies. Both chambers are directly elected by a form of proportional representation for 30 months. A new system is due to be presented in 1993.

MAIN POLITICAL PARTIES
National Salvation Front, National Christian Peasants' Party, Liberal Party, Hungarian Democratic Forum, Social Democratic Party

GOVERNMENT FINANCES

Lei bn	1985	1988	1989
Revenue	300·2	423·1	423·5
Spending	362·6	433·1	423·5

SPENDING BY SECTOR, 1985

	%
Subsidies to industry	52
Social and cultural activities	25
Social insurance	10
Defence	3
Other	10

ECONOMY

GDP	$ bn
1990	94·1
1995 forecast	100·9 ·
Real GDP,	
% average annual growth, 1985–90	2·1
GDP per head, 1990	$4,040

GNP BY SECTOR, 1990, % OF TOTAL

Industry	39
Agriculture	29
Other productive services	19
Other	13

Industrial output, % average annual increase, 1985–90	0·1
Consumer prices, % average annual increase, 1985–90	2·1

EMPLOYMENT

EMPLOYMENT BY SECTOR, 1989	%
Industry	44
Agriculture and forestry	32
Construction	8
Transport and communications	8
Trade	7
Other	8

TRADE

FOREIGN TRADE, 1990	$ bn
Exports	5·8
Imports	9·1

MAJOR COMMODITIES, 1989 Exports	%
Fuels, minerals and metals	48
Industrial consumer goods	18
Chemicals	13
Machinery and equipment	9

Imports	
Fuels, minerals and metals	77
Chemicals and fertilisers	7
Machinery and equipment	4
Food	2

MAJOR TRADING PARTNERS, 1987 Exports	%
Soviet Union	24
Italy	7
West Germany	6
United States	6

Imports	
USSR	26
Egypt	23
Iran	7
East Germany	7

FINANCE

Central bank
National Bank of Romania, Bucharest

EDUCATION

Spending as % of GDP, 1986	2
Years of compulsory education	10
% adult literacy, 1985	96

ENROLMENT RATIOS, 1988	%
Primary school	100
Secondary	80
Tertiary	11

HEALTH

VITAL STATISTICS

Births, rate per '000, 1989	16·0
Deaths, rate per '000, 1989	10·7
Life expectancy, 1989	71 years
Health spending as % of GDP, 1986	2
Hospital beds per '000, 1987	9
Doctors per '000	2·1

DEFENCE

Spending as % of GDP, 1990   2

Compulsory military service; 12 months in Army and Air Force, 24 in Navy Force.

ACTIVE TROOPS, 1990

Army	161,800
Navy	19,200
Air Force	19,800
Reserves	626,000

BULGARIA
REPUBLIC OF BULGARIA

AREA	110,912sq km
CLIMATE	Continental in north, Mediterranean in south. Average temperatures Sofia Jan. 2·2°C, July 20·6°C. Annual rainfall 635mm
LAND USE	Agriculture 34% Forest 35%
HIGHEST POINT	Musala 2,925m
MAIN RIVERS	Danube, Iskur, Maritsa, Tundzha
CAPITAL	Sofia 1·1m
OTHER CITIES	Plovdiv 364,000 Varna 306,000 Burgas 200,000
TIME	GMT + 2 hours
MONEY	1 lev(BGL) = 100 stotinki
EXCHANGE RATES	1990 average BGL 19.0 = $1·00 BGL 23.6 = 1 ecu
OFFICIAL LANGUAGE	Bulgarian
MAJOR RELIGION	Eastern Orthodox
MEMBER	UN

PEOPLE

Population, 1990	9,010,000
Forecast, 2000	9,071,000
% under 15, 1990	20·0
% over 64, 1990	13·0
% average annual increase, 1985–90	0·1
Urban population as % of total, 1990	68
Density	81 people per sq km

MAJOR ETHNIC GROUPS, 1990	%
Bulgarian	85
Turkish	9
Gypsy	3
Macedonian	3

LIVING STANDARDS, 1988	per '000
Telephones	265
Television sets	186

POLITICS

POLITICAL SUMMARY
Parliamentary republic. Under the constitution of July 1991 the unicameral 400-member National Assembly is elected for a maximum five-year term by universal adult suffrage and in turn elects the Council of Ministers and the president.

MAIN POLITICAL PARTIES
Bulgarian Socialist Party, Bulgarian Agrarian National Union, Union of Democratic Forces, Social Democratic Party, Movement for Rights and Freedoms

GOVERNMENT FINANCES

BGL bn	1986	1987	1988	1989	1990 (budget)
Revenues	22·0	22·7	23·0	24·3	24·9
Spending	21·9	22·7	23·0	24·3	25·9

SPENDING BY SECTOR, 1990	%
Finance of national economy	41
Social and cultural spending	38
Administration	2
Defence and other	19

ECONOMY

GDP	$ bn
1990	20·5
1995 forecast	13·2
Real GDP,	
% average annual growth, 1985–90	0·1
GDP per head, 1990	$2,380

Industrial output, % average annual decrease, 1985–90	0·1
Consumer prices, % average annual increase, 1985–90	6·5

EMPLOYMENT

EMPLOYMENT BY SECTOR, 1990	%
Services	35
Industry	38
Farming	19
Construction	8

Employment, % average annual increase, 1985–89	1·6

TRADE

FOREIGN TRADE, 1990	$ bn
Exports	2·6
Imports	3·4

MAJOR COMMODITIES, 1989 Exports	%
Industrial products	86
Processed agriculture products	12
Unprocessed agriculture products	2

Imports	
Industrial products	95
Agriculture products	5

MAJOR TRADING PARTNERS, 1989 Exports	%
Soviet Union	66
East Germany	6
Czechoslovakia	4
Poland	4

Imports	
Soviet Union	54
East Germany	6
Czechoslovakia	5
West Germany	5
Poland	5

FINANCE

Central bank
Bulgarska Narodna Banka, Sofia

EDUCATION

Years of compulsory education	8
% adult literacy, 1985	93

ENROLMENT RATIOS, 1990	%
Primary school	104
Secondary	75
Tertiary	25

HEALTH

VITAL STATISTICS, 1989

Births, rate per '000	13·3
Deaths, rate per '000	11·6
Life expectancy	72 years
Health spending as % of GDP, 1987	3

DEFENCE

Spending as % of GDP, 1990   4

Compulsory service for men of 18 months.

ACTIVE TROOPS, 1990

Army	75,000
Air Force	22,000
Navy	10,000
Reserves	472,500

COMECON – COUNCIL FOR MUTUAL ECONOMIC AID

Comecon was established in 1949 by Bulgaria, Czechoslovakia, Hungary, Poland, Romania and the Soviet Union as a council to develop, by means of central planning, member countries' economies on a complementary basis for the purpose of achieving self-sufficiency within the group. East Germany, Cuba and Vietnam joined the council later on, and a number of developing countries attended meetings as observers.

The council was not able to survive the fall of communist governments in eastern Europe, and was officially disbanded in 1991. In 1990, its last full year in operation, Comecon's exports accounted for 6% of the world total.

ESTONIA former
ESTONIAN SOVIET SOCIALIST REPUBLIC

AREA	45,100sq km
CLIMATE	Maritime. Temperatures February 5-6°C, July 16-17°C. Annual rainfall 610-710mm
MAIN RIVERS	Parnu, Pedja
CAPITAL	Tallinn 503,000
TIME	GMT + 3
MONEY	1 rouble (SuR) = 100 kopeks
EXCHANGE RATES	Market exchange rate 1991 average SuR 65.0 = $1·00
OFFICIAL LANGUAGE	Estonian

PEOPLE

Population, 1989	1,573,000
Density	35 people per sq km

MAJOR ETHNIC GROUPS, 1989	%
Estonian	62
Russian	30
Belorussian	2
Ukrainian	3
Finn	??

POLITICS

POLITICAL SUMMARY
Parliamentary republic, which became independent of the Soviet Union in September 1991. 104-member parliament elected in March 1990. Majority of seats won by Estonian Popular Front and Association for a Free Estonia. The President, head of state, is elected by the parliament.

ECONOMY

GDP	$ bn
1990 (estimated)	12·0
GDP per head, 1990	$2,275
Working population, 1990	0·9m

EMPLOYMENT

EMPLOYMENT BY SECTOR, 1990	m
Services	0·3
Manufacturing	0·2
Farming	0·2
Construction	0·1
Transport	0·1

TRADE

FOREIGN TRADE, 1990	$ bn
Exports	0·2
Imports	0·2

INTRA-SOVIET REPUBLIC TRADE, 1990 SuR bn	
Exports	2·7
Imports	3·0

HEALTH

VITAL STATISTICS, 1989

Births, rate per '000	15·4
Deaths, rate per '000	11·7

LATVIA former
LATVIAN SOVIET SOCIALIST REPUBLIC

AREA	64,589sq km
CLIMATE	Maritime. Temperatures Jan. -2 to -7°C, June 17°C. Annual rainfall 550-800mm
MAIN RIVERS	Daugava, Gauja, Venta, Lielupe
CAPITAL	Riga 917,000
TIME	GMT + 3
MONEY	1 rouble (SuR) = 100 kopeks
EXCHANGE RATES	Market exchange rate 1991 average SuR 65.0 = $1·00
OFFICIAL LANGUAGE	Latvian

PEOPLE

Population, 1989	2,681,000
Density,	42 people per sq km

MAJOR ETHNIC GROUPS, 1989,	%
Lett	52
Russian	34
Belorussian	5
Ukrainian	3
Polish	2

POLITICS

POLITICAL SUMMARY
Parliamentary republic, which became independent of the Soviet Union in September 1991. The 201-member Supreme Council was elected in March–April 1990. Its chairman is the de facto president.

ECONOMY

GDP	$ bn
1990 (estimated)	22·0
GDP per head, 1990	$2,317
Working population, 1990	1·5m

EMPLOYMENT

EMPLOYMENT BY SECTOR, 1990	m
Services	0·6
Manufacturing	0·4
Farming	0·3
Construction	0·1
Transport	0·1

TRADE

FOREIGN TRADE, 1990	$ bn
Exports	0·3
Imports	0·3

INTRA-SOVIET REPUBLIC TRADE, 1990 SuR bn	
Exports	4·5
Imports	4·6

HEALTH

VITAL STATISTICS, 1989

Births, rate per '000	15·5
Deaths, rate per '000	12·1

LITHUANIA former
LITHUANIAN SOVIET SOCIALIST REPUBLIC

AREA	65,200sq km
CLIMATE	Maritime. Average temperatures Jan. -4·8°C, July 17·2°C. Annual rainfall 630mm
MAIN RIVER	Neman
CAPITAL	Vilnius 582,000
TIME	GMT + 3
MONEY	1 rouble(SuR) = 100 kopeks
EXCHANGE RATES	Market exchange rate 1991 average SuR 65.0 = $1·00
OFFICIAL LANGUAGE	Lithuanian

PEOPLE

Population, 1989	3,690,000
Density	57 people per sq km

MAJOR ETHNIC GROUPS, 1989	%
Lithuanian	80
Russian	9
Polish	8
Belorussian	2

POLITICS

POLITICAL SUMMARY
Parliamentary republic, which became independent of the Soviet Union in September 1991. The 141-member Supreme Council was elected in February 1990 and its chairman, the de facto president, was elected in March.

ECONOMY

GDP	$ bn
1990 (estimated)	28·0
GDP per head, 1990	$2,042
Working population, 1990	2·1m

EMPLOYMENT

EMPLOYMENT BY SECTOR, 1990	m
Services	0·7
Manufacturing	0·5
Farming	0·5
Construction	0·2
Transport	0·1

TRADE

FOREIGN TRADE, 1990	$ bn
Exports	0·3
Imports	0·5

INTRA-SOVIET REPUBLIC TRADE, 1990 SuR bn	
Exports	5·4
Imports	6·2

HEALTH

VITAL STATISTICS, 1989

Births, rate per '000	15·0
Deaths, rate per '000	10·3

BELARUS (also known as Byelorussia) former BYELORUSSIAN SOVIET SOCIALIST REPUBLIC

AREA	207,600sq km
CLIMATE	Moderate. Average annual temperature Jan. -6°C, July 18°C. Annual rainfall 550–700mm
HIGHEST POINT	Dzerzhinsky 346m
MAIN RIVERS	Dnepr, Western Dvina, Neman
CAPITAL	Minsk 1,613,000
TIME	GMT + 3 hours
MONEY	1 rouble(SuR) = 100 kopeks
EXCHANGE RATES	Market exchange rate 1991 average SuR 65.0 = $1·00
OFFICIAL LANGUAGE	Russian
MEMBER	Commonwealth of Independent States, UN

PEOPLE

Population, 1989	10,200,000
Density	49 people per sq km

MAJOR ETHNIC GROUPS, 1989	%
Byelorussian	78
Russian	13
Polish	4
Ukrainian	3

POLITICS

POLITICAL SUMMARY
Former republic of the Soviet Union and founder member of the Commonwealth of Independent States.

ECONOMY

GDP	$ bn
1990 (estimated)	84·0
GDP per head, 1990	$2,212
Working population, 1990	5·7m

EMPLOYMENT

EMPLOYMENT BY SECTOR, 1990	m
Services	1·9
Manufacturing	1·5
Farming	1·3
Construction	0·5
Transport	0·4

TRADE

FOREIGN TRADE, 1990	$ bn
Exports	1·1
Imports	1·3

INTRA-SOVIET REPUBLIC TRADE, 1990 SuR bn	
Exports	18·2
Imports	14·2

HEALTH

VITAL STATISTICS

Births, rate per '000, 1989	15·0
Deaths, rate per '000, 1990	10·1

UKRAINE former
UKRAINIAN SOVIET SOCIALIST REPUBLIC

AREA	603,700sq km
CLIMATE	Continental average temperatures Kiev Jan. -6·1°C, July 20·0°C. Annual rainfall 554mm
MAIN RIVERS	Dnepr, Yuzhny, Bug, Tisa
CAPITAL	Kiev 2,587,000
OTHER CITIES	Kharkov 1·6m Donetsk 1·1m Odessa 1·1m
TIME	GMT + 3-10 hours
MONEY	1 rouble (SuR) = 100 kopeks
EXCHANGE RATES	Market exchange rate 1991 average SuR 65.0 = $1·00
OFFICIAL LANGUAGE	Ukrainian
MEMBER	Commonwealth of Independent States, UN

PEOPLE

Population, 1989	51,704,000
Density	86 people per sq km

MAJOR ETHNIC GROUPS, 1989	%
Ukrainian	74
Russian	21
Jewish	1
Belorussian	1

POLITICS

POLITICAL SUMMARY
Former republic of the Soviet Union and founder member of the Commonwealth of Independent States.

ECONOMY

GDP	$ bn
1990 (estimated)	324,0
GDP per head, 1990	$1,706
Working population, 1990	28·8m

EMPLOYMENT

EMPLOYMENT BY SECTOR, 1990	m
Services	8·2
Manufacturing	6·1
Farming	4·8
Construction	1·7
Transport	1·8

TRADE

FOREIGN TRADE, 1990	$ bn
Exports	4·4
Imports	4·8

INTRA-SOVIET REPUBLIC TRADE, 1990 SuR bn	
Exports	40·1
Imports	36·4

HEALTH

VITAL STATISTICS, 1989	
Births, rate per '000	12·7
Deaths, rate per '000	12·1

MOLDOVA (also
known as Moldavia) former **MOLDOVAN**
SOVIET SOCIALIST REPUBLIC

AREA	33,700sq km
CLIMATE	Moderately continental. Average annual temperatures 8-10°C. Annual rainfall 450–550mm
HIGHEST POINT	Mt Balaneshty 430m
MAIN RIVERS	Dnestr, Prut
CAPITAL	Kishinev 580,000
TIME	GMT + 3 hours
MONEY	1 rouble (SuR) = 100 kopeks
EXCHANGE RATES	Market exchange rate 1991 average SuR 65.0 = $1·00
OFFICIAL LANGUAGE	Moldovan
MEMBER	Commonwealth of Independent States, UN

PEOPLE

Population, 1989	4,341,000
Density	129 people per sq km

MAJOR ETHNIC GROUPS, 1989	%
Moldovan	64
Ukrainian	14
Russian	13
Gagauzi	4

POLITICS

POLITICAL SUMMARY
Former republic of the Soviet Union and founder member of the Commonwealth of Independent States.

ECONOMY

GDP	$ bn
1990 (estimated)	24·0
GDP per head, 1990	$1,517
Working population, 1990	2·4m

EMPLOYMENT

EMPLOYMENT BY SECTOR, 1990	m
Services	0·7
Manufacturing	0·4
Farming	0·8
Construction	0·1
Transport	0·1

TRADE

FOREIGN TRADE, 1990	$ bn
Exports	0·2
Imports	0·4

INTRA-SOVIET REPUBLIC TRADE, 1990 SuR bn	
Exports	4·8
Imports	5·0

HEALTH

VITAL STATISTICS, 1987	
Births, rate per '000	21·8
Deaths per '000	9·6

RUSSIA former
RUSSIAN SOVIET FEDERATIVE SOCIALIST REPUBLIC

AREA	17,075,400sq km (including Asian portion)
CLIMATE	Continental. Average temperatures Moscow Jan. -9·4 °C, July 18·3°C. Annual rainfall 630mm
LAND USE	Forest 66%
MAIN RIVERS	Ob-Irtysh, Amur, Lena, Yenisey
CAPITAL	Moscow 9·0m
OTHER CITIES	St. Petersburg (formerly Leningrad) 5·0m Nizhni Novgorod 1·4m Rostov-on-Don 1·0m Volgograd 1·0m
TIME	GMT + 3–10 hours
MONEY	1 rouble (SuR) = 100 kopeks
EXCHANGE RATES	Market exchange rate 1991 average SuR 65.0 = $1·00
OFFICIAL LANGUAGE	Russian
MAJOR RELIGIONS	Russian Orthodox 50% (estimate)
MEMBER	Commonwealth of Independent States, UN

PEOPLE

Population, 1989 (including Asian portion)	147,386,000
Density	9 people per sq km

MAJOR ETHNIC GROUPS, 1989	%
Russians	83
Tartars	4
Ukrainians	3

RUSSIA'S SHARE OF FORMER USSR

Russia's position at the head of the Commonwealth of Independent States is an unassailable one. Of particular importance is its domination of coal, steel and oil production, all three valuable commodities which can be used as bargaining chips in return for Western aid. In addition Russia has taken over the Soviet Union's permanent seat on the UN Security Council and control the majority of the former Republic's nuclear weapons, shown by the limitation treaty forged with the USA in June 1992.

RUSSIA'S POWER

In theory, all 11 CIS members are equals. Yet Russia has well over half the group's total population. The Commonwealth has its headquarters in Minsk (in Belarus), not Moscow. Russia has taken over the permanent Soviet seat on the United Nations Security Council.

Tension between Russian power and the others' concern to limit it, has meant that the 11 have been able to agree on only the outlines of an organisation: twice-yearly summits of heads of state and of heads of government; several ministerial committees; but as yet no detailed rules on decision-taking. Russia is unlikely to let itself be overly restrained for long. Ukraine, suspicious of Russia, is determined to keep the Commonwealth as loose as possible.

POLITICS

POLITICAL SUMMARY
Former republic of the Soviet Union and founder member of the Commonwealth of Independent States.

ECONOMY

GDP	$ bn
1990 (estimated)	1,224·0
GDP per head, 1990	$2,253
Working population, 1990	84·0m

CIS'S GDP PER HEAD, 1988

In spite of containing over 50% of the combined population of the CIS, Russia is still among the wealthiest states with a comparatively high GDP per head. The disparity between the states is all too obvious and may be a major stumbling block in the success of the Commonwealth.

EMPLOYMENT

EMPLOYMENT BY SECTOR, 1990	m
Services	28·8
Manufacturing	22·5
Farming	13·2
Construction	7·2
Transport	5·8

TRADE

FOREIGN TRADE, 1990	$ bn
Exports	21·1
Imports	23·9

INTRA-SOVIET REPUBLIC TRADE, 1990 SuR bn	
Exports	69·2
Imports	69·0

EDUCATION

% adult literacy, 1989	99

HEALTH

VITAL STATISTICS, 1989	
Births, rate per '000	16·9
Deaths, rate per '000	11·6

THE POSTWAR YEARS

The chronology charts events in Europe and the rest of the world since the end of the second world war. It includes some events scheduled before the end of the century.

The themes introduced in the Time Chart on pages 13–15 are continued. In its coverage of the minor and not so minor conflicts and confrontations that flickered in the long shadow of the cold war, the chronology highlights political turning points and the personalities and the popular movements behind them. Human achievement as well as aggression is celebrated: breaking through the sound barrier, landing on the Moon, the conquest of space; and the democratisation of leisure is recorded in the birth of rock 'n' roll, the development of television and the invention of the expresso coffee machine.

1945

JANUARY The Soviet Red Army begins its final sweep through Poland and into Germany. The British and American forces wind up their Ardennes offensive.

In Bulgaria and Romania, left-wing governments are established in the wake of the retreating German forces.

FEBRUARY Dresden is fire-bombed by 772 British and 311 American bombers. The firestorms burn for a week, laying waste some 6.5 square kilometres of the city and killing 135,000 people.

The Big Three – Joseph Stalin for the Soviet Union, Winston Churchill for Britain and Franklin Roosevelt for America – meet at Yalta in the Crimea to discuss the final defeat of Germany and to plan the invasion of Japan. Stalin agrees to allow free elections in Poland and, in exchange for territorial concessions on its Pacific coast, to declare war on Japan.

MARCH B-29 bombers fire-bomb Tokyo. Forty square kilometres are razed to the ground as the fires kill more than 100,000 of the city's inhabitants.

President Franklin Roosevelt dies. He is succeeded by his vice-president, Harry Truman.

APRIL Allied forces begin the liberation of Nazi concentration camps. Belsen, Buchenwald and Dachau are among them.

In Italy, the Fascist leader Benito Mussolini and his mistress, Clara Petacci, are captured by partisans and summarily shot. In Milan, their bodies are strung up for public display.

As Berlin is encircled by the Allied forces, Adolf Hitler and his mistress, Eva Braun, commit suicide in the Führer's bunker.

MAY Field Marshal Wilhelm Keitel signs Germany's final and unconditional surrender in Berlin and May 8th becomes Victory in Europe, or VE, Day.

April 1945; the end of Mussolini.

JUNE The United Nations is set up in San Francisco with 50 nations signing the Charter. The Security Council is made up of 11 members; five of these – America, the Soviet Union, Britain, Nationalist China and France – are permanent while the remaining six are to be re-elected every two years.

JULY At the Potsdam Conference, Germany is divided into four occupation zones to be controlled by the four victorious allies: the Soviet Union, America, Britain and France. Berlin is to be similarly divided. It is agreed that Poland's eastern border with Germany should follow the line of the Oder and Neisse rivers.

AUGUST The Japanese cities of Hiroshima and Nagasaki are destroyed by American atomic bombs. The Red Army invades Japanese territories in Manchuria and Korea, and occupies the Kurile Islands and Sakhalin.

SEPTEMBER Japan surrenders unconditionally and an American military government takes over the ruling of the country.

Twenty-four of Nazi Germany's leaders go on trial for war crimes at Nuremburg.

In Yugoslavia, the war hero Marshal Josip Broz, commonly known as Tito, becomes the country's prime minister. He forms a coalition government with returning exiles.

OCTOBER In France, the Communist Party wins the majority of votes in a general election, but joins a coalition formed under the continuing premiership of the wartime leader of the Free French, General Charles de Gaulle.

DECEMBER The International Monetary Fund and the World Bank for Reconstruction and Development are set up. The IMF will administrate a world currency pool to keep international exchange rates stable. The World Bank will be responsible for loans from richer to poorer nations.

ALSO in 1945:
Women in France and Italy get the vote.

George Orwell's book *Animal Farm* is published.

The London Co-operative Society opens the first supermarket in Britain.

1946

JANUARY In France, General de Gaulle resigns over plans for a new constitution that he believes will lead to chaos. Georges Bidault takes over as the first prime minister of what becomes known as the Fourth Republic.

In a speech in Fulton, Missouri, Winston Churchill warns of an "iron curtain" coming down and separating Western Europe from the Soviet bloc. King Zog of Albania is deposed *in absentia* and the country becomes a republic.

MAY In Czechoslovakia, the Communists win a majority in the general election, but form a coalition government with other parties.

JULY The first American subsurface atomic test is carried out at Bikini Atoll, in the Pacific Ocean.

SEPTEMBER Bulgaria is proclaimed a People's Republic.

OCTOBER After the Nuremberg trials, only eight of the convicted Nazi war criminals are hanged; Martin Bormann has been condemned *in absentia* and Herman Goering, having concealed cyanide on his person, commits suicide before his execution. To prevent any grave acting as a memorial to the Nazis, the bodies are burnt in the ovens of a concentration camp and the ashes scattered to the wind.

ALSO in 1946:
In Paris, the first "bikini" bathing suit is unveiled by Louis Reard, who named it after Bikini atoll where the atomic testing was taking place, since he claimed the two-piece bathing costume would be "highly explosive".

The biro, created by Hungarian journalist Lazlo Biro, goes on sale.

An "electronic brain" is developed by IBM at the University of Pennsylvania. Known as an Electronic Numerical Integrator and Computer (ENIAC), the machine has a memory and can be programmed to do calculations in seconds that would take a human hours.

Achille Gaggia invents the expresso coffee machine.

Dr Benjamin Spock publishes *Baby and Child Care.*

1947

FEBRUARY At the Paris Peace Treaties, Japan is demilitarised, Italy loses her colonies, Finland loses Karelia and the Soviets and Americans withdraw their forces from China.

MARCH President Truman ends the American peacetime policy of

isolationism by declaring, in what comes to be called the Truman Doctrine, that America "must support free peoples resisting attempted subjugation by armed minorities or by outside pressure."

JUNE The American Secretary of State, George Marshall, proposes a massive aid package for the stricken economies of Europe. Between 1947 and 1952, the European Recovery Program, known as the Marshall Plan, channels over $23 billion into western Europe over and above the $15 billion already contributed.

In Italy, a republic is proclaimed and economic reforms are inaugurated under the Christian Democrat prime minister, Alcide de Gasperi.

AUGUST India achieves independence from Britain but, following violent religious conflict, becomes two countries: India, a predominantly Hindu nation and Pakistan, predominantly Muslim.

SEPTEMBER In Hungary, the Communists win a general election after the previously victorious Small Landowners' Party is destroyed in a conspiracy of accusations and more than 200 show trials.

OCTOBER After the British fail to find a solution to the future of Palestine the UN proposes the partition of the country. This is rejected by the Arab countries and violent unrest continues.

NOVEMBER Belgium, Luxembourg and the Netherlands form the Benelux Customs Union, which proves to be the first step towards the European Economic Community.

DECEMBER King Michael of Romania abdicates and the Communist Party consolidates its power in the country.

ALSO in 1947:
Christian Dior launches his "New Look" with hour-glass shapes and voluminous skirts that are in complete contrast to wartime austerity.

Chuck Yeager breaks the sound barrier in his rocket plane, *Bell XI.*

Hans van Meegeren's forgeries of Vermeer are discovered.

Thor Heyerdahl's first Kon-Tiki expedition sails from the west coast of South America to islands east of Tahiti in the Pacific.

Maria Callas makes her operatic debut.

Bell Laboratories invent the transistor.

1948

JANUARY Mahatma Gandhi, the pacifist leader of the Indian campaign of civil disobedience against British rule, is assassinated by the editor of an extremist Hindu newspaper.

FEBRUARY In Czechoslovakia, a communist *coup d'etat* wipes out the coalition government and completes the country's adherence to Soviet influence. The foreign minister, Jan

Masaryk, son of a democratic prewar leader, is found dead under his window in mysterious circumstances.

APRIL The Convention for European Economic Cooperation is signed, marking the birth of the OEEC.

MAY In South Africa, the Afrikaaner dominated Nationalist Party comes to power pledged to introduce apartheid, the policy of racial segregation.

The State of Israel is proclaimed by David Ben-Gurion at a Tel Aviv museum, although the new country is still at war with its Arab neighbours and its boundaries are as yet undefined.

JUNE The Soviet Union blockades land access to Berlin after objecting to currency reforms being introduced in the western occupied zones of Germany. The Allies improvise an airlift of essentials.

Yugoslavia breaks with the Soviet bloc after refusing to conform to Soviet controls.

JULY In Britain, the world's first National Health Service is inaugurated. It is to be financed out of general taxation and will be free at the point of delivery.

ALSO in 1948:
The Western Allies withdraw the worthless Reichsmark and replace it with the Deutschemark. Hoarding of goods in Germany's western sectors is prevented by keeping the new currency in short supply.

Sergey Prokofiev and Aram Illych Khachaturian are accused by the Soviet Culture Commissar, Andrei Zhdanov, of writing anti-popular music. Many of their manuscripts are destroyed.

Alfred C. Kinsey's book *Sexual Behaviour in the Human Male* is published.

In London, the first Olympic Games since 1936 are held.

1949

JANUARY Elections in Poland are finally held, but all opponents of the Communist Party are imprisoned or discredited, and the country consolidates its status as a Soviet satellite under a Communist government.

FEBRUARY Hungary becomes a People's Republic. Cardinal Mindzenty, the only serious voice of opposition in the Soviet bloc, is sentenced to life imprisonment for high treason.

Comecon is set up between the Soviet Union and its allies to coordinate economic policies.

APRIL The North Atlantic Treaty Organisation (NATO) is established between the western European countries and America. Its aims are "to defend democratic freedoms through collective defence."

MAY The three western zones of Germany controlled by Britain, France and America, are unified into the new Federal Republic of Germany (FDR) with its capital in Bonn.

The Soviets lift their blockade of Berlin, fearing the military risks are too great.

JUNE An armistice between Israel and its Arab neighbours stabilises their frontiers in an uneasy truce.

JULY Pope Pius XII declares he will excommunicate any Catholics "aiding" or associating with communists, and so forces them to choose between Church and State.

AUGUST Konrad Adenauer becomes the first Chancellor of West Germany, following elections to the Bundestag.

SEPTEMBER From the Gate of Heavenly Peace in Beijing, Mao Zedong proclaims the People's Republic of China. Chiang Kai-shek and his Nationalist government flee to Formosa (now Taiwan). America, having always supported the Nationalists, refuses to deal with Mao and the Communists.

The Soviet Union explodes its first atomic device. News of the test reaches the West as American surveillance B-29 bombers find evidence of the explosion in the atmosphere.

OCTOBER East Berlin becomes the capital of the new Democratic Republic of Germany (East Germany).

ALSO in 1949:
RCA Victor brings out seven inch, "microgroove", vinylite records that play at 45rpm. Rivals Columbia Records bring out 12 inch, "long players" that are to be played at 33.3rpm.

Simone de Beauvoir's *Second Sex* is published.

George Orwell's *Nineteen Eighty-Four* is published.

1950

JANUARY The Soviet Union recognises Ho Chi Minh's Communist regime in North Vietnam.

FEBRUARY Britain and America recognise the French-dominated Bao Dai regime in South Vietnam.

Mao, for China, and Stalin, for the Soviet Union, conclude a mutual assistance treaty.

Senator Joseph McCarthy begins a campaign against alleged communist infiltration of the American State Department.

MAY The French foreign minister, Robert Schuman, proposes the integration of the coal and steel industries of western European countries as a first step towards European economic union. In what became known as the Schumann Declaration he stated: "It is no longer

a moment for vain words, for peace to have a real chance there must first be a Europe."

JUNE In a surprise move, North Korea invades South Korea, pushing right through the country to Pusan in the South. President Truman orders American troops to intervene and the UN declares North Korea an aggressor. A UN army with soldiers from 15 member countries is sent to Korea.

OCTOBER China invades Tibet, claiming it is Chinese territory. The theocratic leader of Tibet, the Dalai Lama, flees to India.

NOVEMBER In Korea, UN forces reach the Chinese border and in response, hundreds of thousands of Chinese volunteers sweep across the border. The war becomes characterised by back-and-forth fighting until the armies stabilise around the 38th Parallel.

ALSO in 1950:
The UN report that of 800m children in the world, 480m are undernourished.

Bertrand Russell wins the Nobel Prize for Literature.

The UN building in New York is completed.

1951

JANUARY In Vietnam, the guerrilla movement, the Vietminh, launch a major offensive against the French, north of Tonkin.

North Korean and Chinese communist forces capture Seoul, the main city of South Korea.

MARCH France, West Germany, Italy and the Benelux countries sign the treaty that creates the European Coal and Steel Community (ECSC). Britain remains aloof from the agreement.

JULY In Korea, truce talks open between the UN and North Korean commanders. They drag on for two years, largely over the question of the repatriation of prisoners of war.

SEPTEMBER Japan signs the Peace of San Francisco, whereby it regains sovereignty but loses all territorial acquisitions made since 1854. America maintains a right to keep troops and bases on Japanese soil.

OCTOBER The first British atomic test takes place, in the Indian Ocean.

NOVEMBER In Czechoslovakia, the Communist Party is purged. Rudolf Slansky, the vice-president, is one of several people arrested and, in a show trial, is charged with spying.

The first American hydrogen bomb is tested on Eniwetok atoll in the Marshall Islands.

ALSO in 1951:
Electric power is produced from atomic energy at Arcon, Idaho.

Colour television is introduced in America.

Deutsche Grammophon produces 33rpm long playing records.

1952

JANUARY The British government allows America to use its air bases for "common defence".

JUNE In South Africa, the African National Congress begins its campaign of non-violent protest against apartheid policies.

SEPTEMBER West Germany agrees to pay $818m to Israel in reparation for Nazi atrocities.

NOVEMBER A state of emergency is declared in the British colony of Kenya and 2,000 Kikuyu tribesmen are arrested, accused of membership of the Mau-Mau revolt.

General Dwight Eisenhower wins the American presidential election on a Republican ticket. His running mate is Richard Nixon, who made his name as a supporter of the McCarthy hearings into communist infiltration in America.

ALSO in 1952:
After 32 scholars have worked on the project for 15 years, the Revised Standard Version of the Bible is published.

The ancient Biblical city of Jericho is excavated.

Czech runner, Emil Zatopek wins the 5,000m, the 10,000m and the marathon at the Helsinki Olympic Games.

A 41-year-old man receives the first artificial heart.

1953

MARCH Joseph Stalin dies after a brain haemorrhage. He is succeeded by a collective leadership of the party praesidium under President Kliment Voroshilov and the prime minister, Georgi Malenkov.

FEBRUARY The European Coal and Steel Community (ECSC) common market for coal, iron ore and scrap is opened.

In the Netherlands, more than a thousand people die when the North Sea bursts through the dykes. Three hundred die in Britain as floods sweep its eastern coast and the Thames estuary bursts its banks.

MAY The ECSC common market for steel is opened.

American secretary of state, John Foster Dulles, warns that if the French are driven out of Vietnam and a communist state set up, the rest of South East Asia "will fall under Soviet domination like a row of dominoes".

JUNE In East Berlin, an anti-Soviet uprising begins after bricklayers strike against high productivity quotas

imposed by the Kremlin. The whole country then strikes for free elections. The revolt is crushed by Soviet troops when the East German police cannot contain the situation.

JULY After three years of fighting and two million dead, the Korean Armistice is signed at Panmunjom. The country is divided along the 38th Parallel, with a UN-monitored no-man's-land between North and South Korea.

SEPTEMBER Nikita Khrushchev is elected first secretary of the Central Committee of the Soviet Communist Party, signalling the beginning of a struggle for power with the prime minister, Malenkov.

OCTOBER In Vietnam, a French elite force of paratroopers and Foreign Legionnaires establish themselves on the plateau of Dien Bien Phu, intending to use it as a forward offensive base against General Giap's Vietminh.

ALSO in 1953:
In the countries of western Europe, steel production has increased 70% from its prewar level, coal production by 80% and the car industry by 150%.

The European Organisation for Nuclear Research (CERN) is set up on the initiative of a small group of scientists with the backing of UNESCO. CERN is to be an intergovernmental body conducting purely scientific research into subnuclear physics.

Edmund Hillary and Sherpa Tenzing are the first people to reach the summit of Mount Everest.

In Pittsburgh, Dr Jonas Salk starts inoculating children with an anti-polio serum.

In Britain, Elizabeth II is crowned queen. The coronation is viewed by millions worldwide as the service inside Westminster Abbey is televised live for the first time.

1954

JUNE In France, Pierre Mendès-France is elected premier on a campaign ticket to bring peace to Vietnam.

The first nuclear power station is opened in Obninsk, near Moscow.

JULY Following the defeat of the French garrison at Dien Bien Phu two months earlier, a conference in Geneva divides Vietnam at the 17th Parallel, with Ho Chi Minh's communists ruling in Hanoi and the western-backed Bao Dai in Saigon. Laos and Cambodia become sovereign states.

SEPTEMBER SEATO, the South East Asian Treaty Organisation defence pact, is signed by France, Australia, Britain, New Zealand, Pakistan, the Philippines, Thailand and America in order to guarantee peace in South East Asia. It has no standing armed forces.

OCTOBER Wartime allies, Britain, France, America and the Soviet Union, agree to end their occupation of West

Germany. At the same time, West Germany is admitted to NATO membership but denied the right to own nuclear weapons.

NOVEMBER In Algeria, an armed uprising breaks out against the French colonial government.

DECEMBER In Cyprus, after the UN decides to shelve the Greek government's demand that the British-ruled island be given the right to self-determination, riots break out. Greek Cypriots make up 80% of the population, Turkish Cypriots 20%.

ALSO in 1954:
The Eurovision television network is launched, linking Britain, France, Italy, Belgium, Switzerland, the Netherlands and Denmark. The soccer World Cup final is the network's first transmission.

Elvis Presley records his first single *That's Alright Mama*.

Bill Haley and the Comets record *Rock Around the Clock*.

Roger Bannister becomes the first man to run a mile in under four minutes.

The *British Medical Journal* claims the link between smoking and lung cancer is now established.

1955

APRIL The Bandung Conference of African and Asian countries is opened. Leading countries attending are India, China and Indonesia. The conference marks the beginning of the nonaligned movement in the Third World, and the end of Chinese isolation from the rest of the world.

MAY The Warsaw pact is signed by the Soviet Union and the communist nations of eastern Europe, with the exception of Yugoslavia and Albania. The mutual defence pact permits troops to be moved "in accordance with the needs of joint defence" and was introduced to guard against any threats, internal and external, to Soviet interests in the area.

JUNE The French premier, Pierre Mendès-France, is defeated over his failure in African policy, and loses his place to Edgar Faure.

Austria regains her sovereignty, but has to become avowedly neutral.

JULY In Geneva, the first East–West meeting of heads of governments indicates a slight thaw in the cold war. However, no progress is made on the main topic, the future of Germany.

SEPTEMBER In Cyprus, EOKA, the terrorist movement dedicated to union with Greece, is outlawed by the British as violence escalates.

Egypt concludes an arms deal with the Soviet bloc. Two months later, America announces it will sell arms to Israel.

DECEMBER In America, a 42-year-old black woman, Rosa Parks, refuses to move to the back of a segregated bus

in Montgomery, Alabama. This marks the beginning of the mass, non-violent Civil Rights movement.

ALSO in 1955:
Less than a quarter of west Europeans make their living from agriculture in comparison to more than one third before the second world war.

Eighty die at the Le Mans 24-hour race when a car spins out of control.

The Japanese firm, Sony, begins to produce transistor radios, the first of the company's products to succeed internationally. The transistor had been developed in America but Sony is the first to use it in mass-produced radios for domestic use.

1956

FEBRUARY The 20th Congress of the Communist Party of the Soviet Union is held in secret. Khrushchev denounces Stalin, his record and his cult of personality and reveals the truth about the purges. Stalin's works are subsequently banned in the Soviet Union. When news of the denunciation leaks out there are hopes of an end to the cold war.

In an attempt to calm its North African colonies, France grants independence to Morocco and Tunisia.

JUNE In Poland, martial law follows anti-Soviet riots in Poznan by hungry workers. Subsequently, some reforms are inaugurated when a rehabilitated Wladislaw Gomulka returns to power.

JULY In Hungary, the veteran Stalinist, Matyas Rakosi, is finally forced out of office, leaving a government of more liberal elements, under the leadership of Imre Nagy.

When the West refuses to finance the building of the Aswan Dam to control the flood waters of the Nile, Egypt's prime minister, Colonel Gamal Abdel Nasser, nationalises the Suez Canal to pay for the dam.

SEPTEMBER Nasser rejects international control of the Suez Canal, but provides for compensation for the mainly French and British stockholders, and does not interfere with shipping.

OCTOBER In Hungary, a national uprising breaks out, calling for a withdrawal of Soviet troops, political reforms and free elections. The government, under Imre Nagy, supports the uprising.

NOVEMBER To protect the Suez Canal, French and British troops occupy the area. After only a few days, under pressure from America and the UN, and threatened with Soviet armed intervention, they withdraw. UN forces take over.

In Hungary, after Imre Nagy states that Hungary will leave the Warsaw pact, 6,000 Soviet tanks overrun the uprising. Nagy is arrested and then killed; Janos Kadar takes over. As the

revolt is crushed, 20,000 are killed and 200,000 Hungarians flee to the West.

ALSO in 1956:
Prince Rainier of Monaco marries Grace Kelly.

Jon Utzon designs the Sydney Opera House.

The first marches of the Campaign for Nuclear Disarmament (CND) take place in western countries at Easter.

The first European Cup soccer tournament is won by Real Madrid after their match with Stade de Reims in Paris.

1957

MARCH The European Economic Community, and Euratom, (the European Atomic Energy Community) are created by the Treaty of Rome. Six member states – Italy, France, West Germany and the three Benelux countries – are signatories to the treaty. The Community's first step is the instituting of a customs union, to be completed by 1970.

Ghana, a British colony, becomes the first sub-Saharan African country to become independent, under Kwame Nkrumah.

JUNE In Canada, the conservative John Diefenbaker ends 22 years of Liberal rule, declaring his aim will be to assert Canadian independence and neutrality.

JULY In the Soviet Union, Khrushchev beats off a challenge by Politburo members opposed to his de-Stalinisation policies.

AUGUST At the London Disarmament Conference, the Soviets finally agree to a control of nuclear weapons by mutual aerial inspection, but will not agree with the American plan to suspend all nuclear testing for a period of five years.

Malaya, later Malaysia, becomes independent from Britain, with Singapore having domestic autonomy.

DECEMBER The first NATO heads of government meeting decides to equip NATO armies with nuclear weapons and to allow American nuclear missile bases in Europe.

ALSO in 1957:
The Soviet Union launches the first man-made satellite, *Sputnik 1*, into space followed by *Sputnik 2*, which orbits the earth bearing the dog Laika, the first living creature in space.

The Trans-Europ Express agreement does away with the necessity of changing trains at international boundaries, allowing for a more rapid European rail system.

1958

MARCH The first session of the European Parliament is held and Robert Schuman is elected president.

In the Soviet Union, Nikolai Bulganin is ousted from the premiership by Khrushchev, who is now supreme leader of the Soviet Union.

APRIL In China, Mao Zedong begins "The Great Leap Forward", aimed to move the country directly to self-reliant communes. Three years of hard work will be followed by 1,000 years of happiness, claim the Chinese Communist Party.

MAY In Algeria, two French generals, Jacques Massu and Raoul Salan, lead an uprising of French colonists, their aim being to keep Algeria French. They appeal to France's wartime leader, General de Gaulle, to lead them.

In France the Fourth Republic collapses and Charles de Gaulle agrees to take over if full powers are vested in him.

SEPTEMBER After a referendum, General de Gaulle gets the support of 80% of the voters for a new republic with a constitution that gives him, as president, highly centralised powers.

OCTOBER The Soviet Union lends Egypt $100m to build the Aswan Dam.

DECEMBER The world's largest oil tanker is launched at Kuri, in Japan, a symbol of the miracle of Japanese economic rebuilding since the end of the second world war.

America, the Soviet Union and Britain sign a draft test-ban treaty, that includes an undertaking to ensure that the ban is carried out.

French colonies in sub-Saharan Africa are granted their independence in the French Union.

ALSO in 1958:
Boris Pasternak wins the Nobel Prize for Literature.
    The Guggenheim Museum, designed by Frank Lloyd Wright, opens in New York.
    The first American satellite, *Explorer 1*, is placed in orbit around the earth. Yves St Laurent holds his first major Paris show and, though only 23, is hailed as Dior's successor.
    The Munich air disaster kills seven members of the Manchester United soccer team, returning home after winning the European Cup.

1959

JANUARY In Cuba, after a two-year struggle, Fidel Castro and his rebel forces overthrow the island's dictator, President Fulgencio Batista. Castro immediately launches sweeping social and economic reforms, including the expropriation of foreign sugar refineries, which are mostly American. America reacts with an embargo on Cuban sugar.

FEBRUARY In Cyprus, after a four-year war, a peace treaty provides for a Greek Cypriot president and a Turkish Cypriot vice-president. Britain retains

two military bases on the island.

JULY Mao announces the end of "The Great Leap Forward", taking responsibility for the failure of the programme, which has led to chaos and severe famine in China.

SEPTEMBER Soviet premier Khrushchev arrives at Camp David for talks with President Eisenhower about solving international problems. This is taken as indication of a Soviet desire to come out of isolation.

NOVEMBER Violent uprising in the Belgian Congo provokes a massive airlift of Belgian forces.

A European Free Trade Association (EFTA) convention is signed between Austria, Denmark, Norway, Portugal, Sweden, Switzerland and Britain.

ALSO in 1959;
Alain Resnais inaugurates the New Wave of Cinema, with *Hiroshima Mon Amour.*
    The Soviet spacecraft, *Lunik II*, is the first craft to reach and land on the moon. It is able to send back the first pictures of the far side of the moon.

1960

JANUARY Nasser lays the foundation stone for the Aswan High Dam

In Albania, Enver Hoxha and other Communist leaders switch their allegiance from the Soviet Union, which had repudiated Stalinism, to China.

MARCH At Sharpeville, in the South African Transvaal, 56 blacks are killed and 162 injured by armed police in the first day of a campaign of civil disobedience against the pass laws.

MAY Soviets admit to shooting down an American U-2 aircraft over their territory, claiming that it is spying. It was piloted by a civilian, Gary Powers, and the American State Department asserts that the cameras on board were for weather research.

Summit talks in Paris between America, the Soviet Union, Britain and France break down over the row following the spy-plane scandal.

JUNE The Belgian Congo, later Zaire, becomes independent from its Belgian rulers under the premiership of Patrice Lumumba.

AUGUST The French colony of Chad becomes independent.

NOVEMBER John Kennedy is elected American president, by a narrow margin.

Organisation of Petroleum Exporting Countries (OPEC) is set up. The group attempts to set world prices by controlling production and includes the six countries with the world's largest crude oil reserves: (in order) Saudi Arabia, Iraq, United Arab Emirates, Kuwait, Iran and Venezuela.

Patrice Lumumba in 1960.

ALSO in 1960:
    France introduces the "New Franc", equivalent to 100 old francs.
    In Britain, Penguin books are put on trial under the obscenity laws for publishing D.H. Lawrence's *Lady Chatterly's Lover.*
    The following European colonies achieve independence: Mali, Senegal, Mauritania, Niger, Chad, Somalia, Central African Republic, Cameroon, Nigeria, Dahomy, Togo, Upper Volta, Ivory Coast, Gabon, Congo and Belgian Congo.
    The OEEC becomes the OECD – the Organisation for Economic Cooperation and Development.
    Albert Camus, Algerian-born French novelist, is killed in a car crash.
    Donald Campbell is killed while trying to break the world water speed record at Coniston Water in the Lake District, England.
    The first oral contraceptive is put on sale by the Searle Drug Company in America.

1961

JANUARY Following a referendum, the majority of French come out in support of de Gaulle's policy of home rule for Algeria.

MARCH Kennedy announces American support of the Laotian government against communist forces and sends arms and financial aid to Indo-China.

South Africa leaves the Commonwealth to become a republic after other countries in the Commonwealth oppose their policy of apartheid.

APRIL Kennedy reluctantly approves a CIA-backed invasion of Cuba by anti-Castro exiles aimed at inspiring a revolt in the country. When the exiles land at the Bay of Pigs – no American troops were sent – they are killed, or captured, by Castro's forces.

AUGUST The Berlin Wall is built on the order of the East German leader, Walter Ulbricht, as an "anti-fascist protection barrier". Forty-six kilometres of concrete and barbed wire, the wall is overlooked by watch towers and backed by a strip of mined land. As an anomalous enclave of the West inside East Germany, the western zone of Berlin had been the escape route for 2.7m East Germans until the Wall is built.

AUGUST Ireland applies for membership of the European Community, and Britain and Denmark request negotiations aimed at future membership.

SEPTEMBER The Secret Army (OAS), who want Algeria to stay French, make an attempt on de Gaulle's life.

ALSO in 1961:
A contraceptive pill goes on sale in Britain for the first time.
    Soviet cosmonaut, Yuri Gagarin, becomes the first man in space.
    Joseph Heller's anti-war novel *Catch 22* is published.

1962

MARCH De Gaulle orders the French army to quell the insurrection in Algeria.

APRIL Norway requests that negotiations for European Community membership be opened.

JULY France proclaims Algeria independent.

AUGUST An 18-year-old East Berliner, Peter Fechter, is left to die by East German guards after being shot attempting to scale the Berlin wall.

British colonies Trinidad and Tobago become independent.

OCTOBER Kennedy receives aerial pictures of Soviet missiles on Cuba and, with American nuclear and conventional forces on standby, he announces a naval blockade of the island. The Soviets are forced to back down and agree to remove the missiles, under UN supervision.

ALSO in 1962:
John Glenn orbits the earth in the Mercury capsule *Friendship 7*.
    The following European colonies become independent; Algeria, Uganda, Burundi.
    The Telstar telecommunications satellite sends the first live television pictures from Europe to America.
    Marilyn Monroe is found dead in her home.

1963

JANUARY Fearing that Britain's special relationship with America will jeopardise a European common market, de Gaulle vetoes the request for British entry into the European Community.

JUNE The British government is threatened by the scandal surrounding the Profumo affair.

Quang Duc, a Buddhist monk, burns himself to death in Vietnam in protest against the treatment of Buddhists by President Ngo Dinh Diem.

JULY The Yaoundé Convention is signed, associating 18 independent states in Africa and Madagascar with the European Community for five years, from 1965.

AUGUST America, Britain and the Soviet Union sign a test-ban treaty.

A massive Civil Rights march takes place in Washington. It is here that Martin Luther King makes his famous "I have a dream" speech.

NOVEMBER President Kennedy is assassinated in Dallas.

DECEMBER Kenya gains independence from Britain.

ALSO in 1963:
The first kidney transplant is carried out in a hospital in Leeds, England.
The Soviets put the first woman, Valentina Tereshkova, into space. Her spacecraft, *Vostok 6*, makes 48 orbits of the earth.
The Great Train Robbers succeed in stealing more than £2.6m in England.

1964

MARCH The UN sends forces to Cyprus in order to try and control unrest between the Greek and Turkish populations of the island.

JUNE In South Africa, already jailed for five years, Nelson Mandela is sentenced to life imprisonment on Robben Island.

AUGUST America steps up military involvement in Vietnam.

OCTOBER In the Soviet Union, Nikita Khrushchev is deposed and Leonid Brezhnev takes over

NOVEMBER Lyndon Baines Johnson, Kennedy's vice-president who took over after the president's assassination, is elected as American president.

ALSO in 1964:
The European Space Research Organisation (ESRO) is established to provide for and promote collaboration among European states in space research and technology, purely for peaceful and scientific purposes.
Between 1950 and 1964, West Germany's gross national product triples and unemployment falls from nearly 9% to less than 0.5%.
Mary Quant makes her name as a fashion designer and is credited with inventing the miniskirt.
Capitol Records release the first Beatles record in America and "I Wanna Hold Your Hand" becomes their fastest-selling single ever.
The American *Ranger 7* sends back the first close-up pictures of the moon's surface.

1965

JANUARY Britain's wartime leader, Sir Winston Churchill, dies.

FEBRUARY America sends B-57 bombers to strike Hanoi, Vietnam.

MARCH President Johnson sends the Marines into Vietnam.

NOVEMBER White-ruled Rhodesia breaks from Britain and declares independence, known as UDI.

Cosmonaut Alexei Leonov.

ALSO IN 1965:
The Soviet cosmonaut, Alexei Leonov, takes the first spacewalk when he leaves his ship, *Voskhod 2*, for 11 minutes.
In Britain, a bill is brought in abolishing the death penalty and the government introduces the Race Relations Act, making discrimination on ground of race illegal.
Stanley Matthews becomes the first professional footballer to be knighted.
Some Dutch citizens protest against Crown Princess Beatrix's intention of marrying a German.

1966

JANUARY Indira Gandhi becomes India's prime minister.

MARCH Pope Paul VI and the Archbishop of Canterbury, Dr Michael Ramsey, worship together in St Peter's Rome after the first official meeting between the heads of the two churches in 400 years.

APRIL An H-bomb, lost in the Atlantic after falling from a B-52 bomber earlier in February, is finally found.

JUNE Gas fields in the North Sea are expanded by Britain with the biggest find of the natural resource to date.

AUGUST China embarks on its cultural revolution.

NOVEMBER In Italy, the River Arno floods and in Florence causes the destruction of much of the city's art treasures.

ALSO in 1966:
At Aberfan, in Wales, a coal tip slips and buries the local school, killing 116 children and 28 adults.

In an American radio interview, John Lennon claims that the Beatles are probably more popular than Jesus Christ.
Joe Orton's play *Loot* goes on stage at the Royal Court theatre, London.
A Soviet unmanned spacecraft, *Luna IX*, makes the first controlled landing on the surface of the moon.

1967

MARCH The *Torrey Canyon* is wrecked off Land's End, spilling 100,000 tons of oil on to more than 160km of Cornish coastline in the worst tanker accident to date.

The firm Chemie Gruementhal, manufacturer of the drug known as thalidomide, goes on trial in Aachen, in Germany, charged with a number of offences, including causing bodily harm and death by negligence.

Stalin's daughter, Svetlana, defects to America

APRIL A junta of right-wing army officers, under the leadership of Colonel Georges Papadopoulos, seize power from the democratic government in Greece. The military are believed to be acting under the name of King Constantine.

MAY Britain formally applies for membership of the EC once again.

The region of Biafra in Nigeria breaks away from the rest of the country and so begins a prolonged and damaging civil war.

JUNE After the six-day war against the Arab states, Israel finally observes a UN ceasefire, having taken Arab territory many times the size of Israel itself and successfully capturing the holy site of the Wailing Wall in Jerusalem from the Jordanians.

DECEMBER Concorde, the Anglo-French supersonic airliner, is unveiled in Toulouse.

ALSO in 1967:
In Britain, bills are passed that legalise abortion and that permit homosexual acts between men.
Dr Christian Barnard carries out the first successful heart transplant in Cape Town, South Africa.
The Beatles album, *Sergeant Pepper's Lonely Hearts Club Band*, and Procul Harum's *Whiter Shade of Pale* are both released this year.

1968

JANUARY The reforming liberal Alexander Dubcek is the new leader of the Czech Communist Party. He promises "socialism with a human face" and so begins the Prague Spring.

MARCH American troops massacre 175 innocent villagers at Mylai, Vietnam.

APRIL Martin Luther King is assassinated in Memphis by an

unknown white killer. Later, in Atlanta, more than 150,000 mourners follow his funeral cortège. The killing sparks off riots throughout America.

Students riot in West Berlin after their spokesman, Rudi Dutschke, is shot and seriously wounded.

MAY France, and in particular Paris, is torn by strikes and violent demonstrations. Left-wing students are most notable among the rioters and any protests are soon brutally put down by the French riot police. De Gaulle responds by dissolving the National Assembly and calling a general election.

American and North Vietnamese diplomats meet in Paris to discuss setting up peace talks to end the war in Vietnam.

Soviet troops move through Poland and East Germany to the Czech border as alarm grows in Moscow over Czechoslovakia's new, more liberal, government under Dubcek.

JUNE During the run-up to the selection of a democratic candidate for the American presidential elections, senator Robert Kennedy is shot in Los Angeles by Sirhan Sirhan, a Palestinian immigrant.

AUGUST Soviet tanks move into Prague to crush the liberalising Czech government and the spirit of the Prague Spring. Alexander Dubcek is discredited and expelled from the Communist Party.

OCTOBER An anti-Vietnam war rally outside the American embassy in London's Grosvenor Square ends in violent scuffles between demonstrators and police.

NOVEMBER President Johnson orders a stop to the bombing of North Vietnam.

Richard Nixon is elected president of America, Spiro Agnew is his vice-president.

ALSO in 1968:
A Papal encyclical, entitled *Humana Vitae*, declares that any form of artificial birth control is against divine will and so rules out any means of contraception, other than the rhythm method, for Roman Catholics.
French skier Jean-Claude Killy wins three gold medals at the Winter Olympics held in Grenoble, France.

1969

JANUARY Student Jan Palach dies after setting himself on fire in Wenceslas Square in Prague, in protest against the Soviet invasion of Czechoslovakia.

APRIL After the disturbances in France in 1968, de Gaulle calls a constitutional referendum and, on losing, steps down as president.

JULY In Spain, General Francisco Franco, the country's leader and

dictator, declares that the monarchy will be restored on his death when Prince Juan Carlos will become king.

AUGUST British troops are sent to Ulster in response to sectarian violence. At first, their presence is welcomed by a beleaguered Catholic population, who see them as protection against Protestant attacks.

SEPTEMBER A military coup replaces King Idris of Libya with the uprising's leader, subaltern Moammar Qaddafi.

OCTOBER Willi Brandt is elected West German chancellor.

DECEMBER At a Summit Conference in the Hague, the European Community formally agrees to open membership negotiations with Britain, Norway, Denmark and Ireland after their application of 1967.

ALSO in 1969:
American astronaut Neil Armstrong is the first man to walk on the moon's surface after the success of the *Apollo 11* manned mission.

One of the first "Jumbo" jets flies non-stop from Seattle over the pole to Le Bourget airport, in France, for the Paris Air Show.

John Lennon and Yoko Ono stage their famous "love-in", "Beds in Peace", at the Amsterdam Hilton.

The Rolling Stones give a free concert to an audience of more than 250,000 in London's Hyde Park.

1970

MARCH President Nixon authorises B-52 airplanes to intensify their bombing of the Ho Chi Minh trail in eastern Laos in order to cut supply routes to North Vietnam.

APRIL President Nixon orders American combat troops to attack communist bases in Cambodia, though he maintains that it is not an invasion force.

MAY During anti-war demonstrations at Kent State University, Ohio, four student protestors are killed by National Guard soldiers.

SEPTEMBER After a mass hijacking by Palestinian terrorists, three airliners are blown up at Dawson's Field, a disused RAF wartime airstrip in the Jordanian desert. The 56 passengers still held hostage are being kept at a secret location.

Only just over a year after resigning the French presidency, General de Gaulle dies.

ALSO in 1970:
In Britain a bill is passed through the Commons aiming to give women equal pay with men by 1976.

In Britain, inspired by American protest groups, the recently formed Gay Liberation Front holds its first demonstration in London.

By 1970, East Germany is experiencing its own *Wirtschaftswunder* and is tenth among the world's industrial nations, with a standard of

living 50% higher than that of the Soviet Union.

The Japanese firm, Canon Business Machines, launches the first hand-held calculator.

1971

FEBRUARY Britain changes over to a decimal currency.

MARCH East Pakistan, physically separated from West Pakistan by northern India, seeks independence as the state of Bangladesh. Civil war breaks out in the country.

JUNE The Council of Ministers for the European Community announces the agreement of terms for Britain's entry into the Common Market.

OCTOBER The Communist Peoples Republic of China is admitted into the UN.

ALSO in 1971:
The Soviet Union launches its first series of space stations to orbit the earth, the Salyut series.

In California, the trial of Charles Manson and three members of his "family" comes to an end as the defendants are found guilty of several brutal murders.

1972

JANUARY A civil rights march in Londonderry, Northern Ireland, turns into a riot and British troops fire into the crowd of protestors. After the killing of 13 innocent civilians and the wounding of a further 17, the day and its events become known as "Bloody Sunday".

The Treaty of Accession is signed in Brussels between Britain, Ireland, Denmark, Norway and the members of the European Community: France, Belgium, West Germany, Italy, Luxembourg and the Netherlands.

MAY Richard Nixon becomes the first American president to visit Moscow where he signs a arms reduction pact with Leonid Brezhnev.

JUNE Ulrike Meinhof, Andreas Baader, Holger Meins and Carl Raspe of the terrorist Baader-Meinhof gang and members of the Red Army Faction are arrested in West Germany.

JULY The European Community signs a free trade agreement with Austria, Iceland, Portugal, Spain and Switzerland.

AUGUST With anti-war sentiment high in America, President Nixon withdraws the last American ground forces from Vietnam. American air power is still carrying out bombing missions.

SEPTEMBER Arab terrorists of the "Black September" group take hostage Israeli competitors at the Munich Olympics. A rescue attempt fails, and the nine hostages die.

After a referendum, Norway rejects full membership of the European Community.

OCTOBER Arab nations impose a total ban on oil exports to the USA after the outbreak of the Arab-Israeli war, and precipitate the first energy crisis. The ban is lifted March 1974, but the vulnerability of the industrial nations has been exposed.

NOVEMBER Richard Nixon is re-elected American president with a massive majority. The turnout of the electorate, however, is the lowest since 1948, at only 55.7%.

DECEMBER President Nixon orders the end of the American bombing of Hanoi, the capital of North Vietnam.

ALSO in 1972:
Bernardo Bertolucci's controversial film, *Last Tango in Paris*, is released.

At the Munich Olympics, Olga Korbut of the Soviet Union wins two gold medals and one silver in gymnastics.

Francis Ford Coppola's mafia epic *The Godfather*, starring Marlon Brando, is released.

1973

JANUARY A ceasefire is declared in Vietnam after peace talks in Paris. All American troops and military advisers are to be withdrawn and a force of Canadian, Polish, Hungarian and Indonesian troops will supervise the truce.

MAY An American senate select committee begins its hearings into the Watergate affair.

JUNE Willi Brandt is the first West German chancellor to visit Israel in a symbolic trip. He visits the Holocaust memorial Yad Vashem.

OCTOBER Arab states attack Israel on the holiest day of the Jewish year, Yom Kippur. After an initial near-disaster, Israeli forces, with American arms, counterattack and Egyptian troops are annihilated on the battlefield. Brezhnev threatens to use Soviet airborne troops to restore the balance, but crisis is averted by Henry Kissinger's shuttle diplomacy.

NOVEMBER An army coup in Athens overthrows the government of President Georges Papadopoulos, who took control of Greece in a similar coup in 1967.

DECEMBER The Basque terrorist group ETA (Euskadi Te Askatasuna – Freedom for the Basque Homeland) carry out their most audacious attack to date in murdering Spain's prime minister and Franco's right-hand man, Luis Carrero Blanco, in a car bomb attack.

ALSO in 1973
America launches *Skylab*, its only space station.

In Britain, a new body, the Equal Opportunities Commission, is established to tackle sexual

discrimination in the workplace.

Foreign cars outsell British Leyland models for the first time and the Japanese Datsun company makes nearly one in 20 of all cars sold in Britain.

1974

MARCH A federal grand jury concludes that President Nixon knew about the Watergate cover-up of White House involvement in the burglary of Democratic headquarters in 1972.

APRIL A military coup in Portugal topples the right-wing regime of Dr Marcello Caetano, and Mario Soares, the socialist leader, returns after four years in exile.

MAY Willi Brandt, the West German chancellor, resigns after an East German spy is discovered working in his office.

Giscard d'Estaing is narrowly elected the new French president.

JULY The armed forces in Greece agree to pass over the ruling of the country to a civilian government and the former premier, Constantine Karamanlis, returns from exile in France.

AUGUST The situation in Cyprus escalates as Greek-Cypriots flee Turkish tanks and bombing attacks.

Richard Nixon, facing impeachment by Congress over the Watergate scandal, becomes the first American president to resign. Gerald Ford, who only recently took over as vice-president, is sworn in as the new president.

SEPTEMBER President Ford pardons Richard Nixon.

ALSO in 1974:
Alexander Solzhenitsyn, novelist and Nobel Prize winner, is expelled from the Soviet Union after long internment in labour camps. He is finally able to collect his Nobel Prize for Literature.

The American *Mariner 10* probe takes close-up pictures of the surface of Mercury.

Scientists warn that chlorofluoro-carbons found in aerosols are damaging the ozone layer that protects the earth from harmful ultraviolet radiation from the sun.

1975

JANUARY Portugal agrees to give its colony, Angola, independence following 13 years of liberation war.

FEBRUARY In Britain, Margaret Thatcher replaces Edward Heath as leader of the Tory Party.

APRIL The communist Khmer Rouge, under Pol Pot, finally takes control of Phnom Penh and, therefore, Cambodia.

The war in Vietnam ends as Saigon and other South Vietnamese cities fall to the North Vietnamese, but panic sets in as refugees desperately try to leave with the last American evacuations.

The first free elections in Portugal for 50 years end in victory for the socialists.

NOVEMBER After only two weeks of independence, civil war breaks out in Angola between rival factions seeking control of the country.

Franco, Spain's dictator, dies. Prince Juan Carlos is declared king, restoring the Spanish monarchy after an absence of 44 years.

DECEMBER International terrorists strike in London, Amsterdam and Vienna with, respectively, the IRA seizing hostages in Balcombe Street, the Moluccans storming the Indonesian Consulate, and Palestinians taking 70 hostage at the OPEC summit.

ALSO in 1975:
The Soviet *Venera* probe sends back pictures of Venus, the first photographs taken on the surface of another planet.
Dr Andrei Sakharov, foremost Soviet dissident and nuclear physicist, wins the Nobel Peace Prize.
In a joint Soviet-American spaceflight, an Apollo spacecraft docks with a Soyuz and orbits the earth.

1976

JUNE In South Africa, riots in the township of Soweto are sparked off by a directive from the Transvaal education authority that Afrikaans and English be used equally in black secondary schools. Attempts by security forces to contain the situation end in 100 dead and over 1,000 wounded.

JULY Hostages held by pro-Palestinian hijackers at Entebbe airport in Uganda are freed after a raid by Israeli commandos.

SEPTEMBER Chairman Mao, China's leader since 1949, dies aged 82.

OCTOBER In Beijing, the so-called "Gang of Four", including Mao's widow Jiang Qing, are jailed for attempting to overthrow the Chinese government.

NOVEMBER A Democrat, Jimmy Carter, is elected American president. The vice-president is Walter Mondale.

ALSO in 1976:
After a journey of 11 months, America's *Viking* spacecraft lands on Mars, sending back the first pictures of the planet's surface.
In France, a new law makes French the only language allowed in advertising in an attempt to combat the growing use and misuse of English.
At the Montreal Olympics, Romanian Nadia Comaneci eclipses Olga Korbut as the gymnastics star.

1977

JANUARY Charter 77, a document calling for civil rights in Czechoslovakia, is drawn up by dissidents. Many of the signatories to the document are arrested soon after.

MARCH Two Pan-Am and KLM jumbo jets collide and explode at Tenerife, in the Canary Islands, in the worst air disaster to date. Three hundred passengers on the Pan Am jet die while all 263 on the Dutch KLM plane are killed.

JUNE In Spain, Adolfo Suarez and his Democratic Centre coalition win the majority of votes in the country's first democratic election in 41 years.

NOVEMBER Egypt's president, Anwar Sadat, visits Israel and addresses the Knesset as part of his campaign for peace in the Middle East.

ALSO in 1977:
The Pompidou Centre, designed by architects Richard Rogers and Renzo Piano, is opened in Paris.
Refugees fleeing Vietnam take to the sea in unsuitable, and often open, boats. Soon known as the "boat people", they either perish at sea or are rescued by passing vessels.
The space shuttle makes its maiden flight carried on top of a Boeing 747.
Elvis Presley dies at his home, Gracelands.

1978

MARCH The supertanker, *Amoco Cadiz* breaks up off the coast of Brittany, spilling 220,000 tons of crude oil into the Channel.

MAY Former Italian premier, Aldo Moro, is found dead after having been captured by Red Brigade terrorists in March.

SEPTEMBER President Carter hosts an Israeli-Egyptian summit where Anwar Sadat, Egypt's president, and Menachem Begin, Israel's prime minister, reach an agreement on the signing of a peace treaty.

The Shah imposes martial law on Tehran and 11 other Iranian cities after rallies protest against his rule.

OCTOBER Following the death of Pope John Paul I, after only 33 days in office, a Polish cardinal, Karol Wojtyla, is elected Pope and takes the name John Paul II.

NOVEMBER In Guyana, all 913 members of a religious cult known as the People's Temple, commit suicide or are shot dead on the orders of their leader, the Reverend Jim Jones.

ALSO in 1978:
The first "test-tube" baby, conceived outside the womb, is born.
The American space agency, NASA, selects its first women astronauts – 15 years after the Soviet Valentina Tereshkova orbited the earth.

1979

JANUARY The shah of Iran is driven out of Iran by supporters of Ayatollah Ruhollah Khomeini, the religious leader living in exile in Paris.

Cambodia and the regime of the Khmer Rouge fall to heavily-armed Vietnamese forces.

FEBRUARY Ayatollah Khomeini returns to Iran after 14 years in exile, denouncing what remains of the shah's government as illegal. "From now on," he asserts, "it is I who will name the government."

MARCH President Sadat and Menachem Begin, for Egypt and Israel, sign a peace treaty on the White House lawn.

APRIL As mass graves are discovered in Cambodia, the extent of the atrocities of Pol Pot's Khmer Rouge regime are revealed.

MAY Bishop Abel Muzorewa is sworn in as the first black prime minister of Rhodesia.

Margaret Thatcher, triumphant in 1979.

The Conservative Party win the general election, making Margaret Thatcher Britain's first woman prime minister.

JUNE Carter and Brezhnev sign the SALT-2 arms limitation treaty in Vienna.

Pope John Paul II visits his homeland, Poland.

The first direct elections, by universal suffrage, are held for the European Parliament. Prior to this, members had been delegated by their national parliaments.

JULY Dictator General Anastasio Somoza flees into exile after the Sandinistas emerge victorious from Nicaragua's civil war.

NOVEMBER In Iran, followers of Ayatollah Khomeini storm the American Embassy and take about 100 staff and Marines hostage.

DECEMBER The Soviet Union invades Afghanistan, toppling the Kabul government.

After 14 years of illegal independence, Rhodesia again becomes a British colony, though its name will be changed to Zimbabwe. The guerrilla war in the country ends with a ceasefire and a promise of new elections.

ALSO in 1979:
First made under the Nazis in 1939, the Volkswagen Beetle is discontinued, except in Mexico. By the time manufacture ceases, 19m cars have come off the production line.
Mother Teresa of Calcutta wins the Nobel Peace Prize for her work among the poor of India.
The American spacecraft *Voyager 1* sends back pictures to earth of Jupiter's rings.
World production of crude oil reaches an all-time high of 62.48m barrels a day, with over half coming from OPEC countries.

1980

MARCH Robert Mugabe is elected the first prime minister of the new state of Zimbabwe.

APRIL The former Rhodesia ceases to be a British colony and becomes the independent republic of Zimbabwe.

An attempt by American military forces to rescue the hostages in Iran fails as a helicopter of the assault team crashes in the Iranian desert. President Carter takes full responsibility for the debacle.

MAY The counter-revolutionary warfare team of the SAS ends the terrorist siege of the Iranian Embassy in London.

British contributions to the EC are drastically reduced and to compensate, French and German contributions are increased.

AUGUST The Polish government grants the demands of shipyard workers after a two-month strike in Gdansk. Independent free trade unions will be allowed and will have the right to strike, censorship will be relaxed and political prisoners released.

SEPTEMBER War between Iran and Iraq escalates as Iraqis attack the Iranian oil refinery at Abadan.

An army coup seizes power in Turkey and the chief of the general staff become president.

The Polish trade union, Solidarity, is born after striking shipbuilders win the right to form free trade unions. It is lead by Lech Walesa, an electrician from the Gdansk shipyard.

NOVEMBER Ronald Reagan becomes American president with George Bush his vice-president.

ALSO in 1980:
Figures reveal that half of British married women go out to work – as compared to one in five in 1951. This is the highest proportion in the EC.

John Lennon is shot dead in New York.

America, West Germany and Kenya boycott the Moscow Olympics in protest at the Soviet invasion of Afghanistan.

1981

JANUARY Iran releases the American hostages held since November 1979.

Greece enters the European Community.

FEBRUARY Lt.Col. Antonio Tejero and members of the Guardia Civil attempt a right-wing coup in Spain. King Juan Carlos orders the army to put down the coup and so pre-empts possible support for Tejero.

MARCH In Poland, Solidarity strikes in protest after harsh police treatment of union activists.

SEPTEMBER The Kremlin condemns the Solidarity trade union in Poland as anti-Soviet.

OCTOBER Anwar Sadat, Egypt's president, is assassinated during a military parade, apparently by members of his own forces. Either a Libyan-backed group or the extreme Muslim Brotherhood are suspected of responsibility.

DECEMBER Strikes and demonstrations in Poland result in General Wojciech Jaruzelski, the country's president, enforcing martial law.

ALSO in 1981:
First reports appear in America of a new kind of illness that destroys the body's immune system that, at first, appears to affect homosexuals and injecting drug users.

In Britain, the year is marked by riots in major cities throughout the country.

France introduces the high-speed TGV train that cuts journey times in half.

1982

APRIL Argentina invades the Falklands and, in response, Britain sends a task force to the South Atlantic to win back the British islands.

MAY A British submarine sinks the Argentine cruiser, the *General Belgrano*, outside the exclusion zone.

JUNE Argentinian forces on the Falklands surrender to British army forces.

OCTOBER The Polish parliament votes to outlaw Solidarity.

NOVEMBER Leonid Brezhnev, Soviet leader for 18 years, dies.

ALSO in 1982:
In Washington, a passenger jet crashes into the frozen Potomac River, shortly after take-off. Seventy-eight passengers

and people on the ground die in the disaster that took place within sight of the White House.

The Tudor ship, the *Mary Rose*, is raised from the Channel more that 450 years after it was wrecked.

Jacques Tati, creator of the eccentric film character, M.Hulot, dies aged 74.

1983

MAY America publicly backs the Contra rebels fighting in Nicaragua in their struggle to overthrow the Sandinistas.

JULY Martial law is lifted in Poland, though many of the regulations imposed during the period have been incorporated into the civilian legal code.

AUGUST France sends men and arms to Chad, its former colony, to assist against the invading Libyans.

OCTOBER American Marines invade Grenada, a former British colony, after the prime minister is removed by the island's military commander. American intervention is prompted by fears of Cuban involvement in a coup d'etat.

DECEMBER An IRA bomb explodes just outside Harrods, the famous London store; several people are killed.

ALSO in 1983:
Sir Richard Attenborough's film, *Gandhi*, wins eight Oscars.

The Hitler diaries are discovered but soon prove to be fakes.

1984

FEBRUARY The Soviet leader Yuri Andropov dies, and Konstantin Chernenko succeeds him as the new Communist Party chief.

JULY In America, the Democrats pick a woman, Geraldine Ferraro, as Walter Mondale's running mate in the presidential elections.

SEPTEMBER China and Britain agree that Hong Kong will revert to Chinese control when the British lease on the colony expires in 1997.

OCTOBER An IRA bomb blasts the Grand Hotel in Brighton in an attempt to assassinate most of the British cabinet, staying in the hotel for the Conservative Party conference.

Father Jerzy Popieluszko, popular priest and friend of Solidarity, is found beaten to death after having been kidnapped 11 days earlier by three policeman.

ALSO in 1984:
In America, it is announced that the virus, HIV, that causes AIDS has been discovered.

Milos Forman's film about the life and music of Mozart, *Amadeus*, is released.

In California, a baby girl has a

baboon's heart transplanted to replace her defective heart.

1985

FEBRUARY Spain lifts the blockade of Gibraltar that had been imposed by Franco in dispute over the sovereignty of the British colony.

MARCH Konstantin Chernenko dies and Mikhail Gorbachev becomes head of the Communist Party.

APRIL In Albania, strict Stalinist Enver Hoxha, who has ruled the country since 1944, is replaced by Ramiz Alia.

NOVEMBER Mikhail Gorbachev and President Reagan meet at a summit in Geneva where they agree to cut both their strategic nuclear arsenals by 50%.

ALSO in 1985:
Greenpeace's ship, the *Rainbow Warrior*, is sunk in mysterious circumstances off New Zealand. Members of the French secret service are suspected of blowing up the vessel. The ensuing scandal raises worldwide consciousness as to the environmental aims of Greenpeace.

In a worldwide media event, the two Live Aid concerts, in London and Philadelphia, raise about £40 million for the famine-stricken areas of Africa.

1986

JANUARY France and Britain confirm that work on a Channel Tunnel and a rail-only link between the two countries will begin in 1987. An additional road tunnel is planned for the year 2000.

FEBRUARY The Single European Act is signed, setting 1992 as the deadline for a single market so that Europe becomes "an area without frontiers in which the free movement of foods, persons, services and capital is ensured."

Swedish prime minister, Olaf Palme, is assassinated in a street in Stockholm.

Corazon Aquino becomes president of the Philippines and ousts Ferdinand Marcos as he attempts to hold on to power after a rigged election.

Gorbachev, in a speech to the first party congress since he became leader of the Communist Party, condemns the years of stagnation of his predecessors.

MARCH Elections in France result in a right-wing prime minister, Jacques Chirac, holding office at the same time as a Socialist president, M. Mitterrand.

APRIL American aircraft attack targets in Libya as a reprisal for terrorist attacks on Americans that they believe to be Libyan-backed.

A nuclear reactor at Chernobyl, in the Ukraine, catches fire. Effects of the

resulting radiation are felt all over Europe.

SEPTEMBER The Japanese company, Nissan, open a car factory in Sunderland that will increase their British output to 100,000 cars a year.

OCTOBER The American firm, General Motors, joins Honeywell, IBM and Warner in abandoning operations in South Africa, as part of economic sanctions.

On London's Stock Exchange computers are introduced and many existing controls removed in the reform known as "Big Bang".

The American refusal to abandon their Strategic Defence Initiative, a proposed outer-space defence shield known as "Star Wars", causes stalemate at arms control talks in Iceland between Reagan and Gorbachev.

DECEMBER Leading Soviet dissident, physicist Dr Andrei Sakharov, is released from his imprisonment in the closed city of Gorky.

ALSO in 1986:
Safe Sex health campaigns are launched in Europe in an attempt to combat the spread of HIV and AIDS.

The American space shuttle, *Challenger*, explodes, killing the entire crew of seven.

Women in Liechtenstein are allowed to vote for the first time.

1987

JANUARY Spain and Portugal enter the European Community.

MAY A West German, Matthias Rust, lands his light aircraft in Moscow's Red Square.

JULY Declared patriot, Oliver North, takes the stand at the Congressional hearing into the "Irangate" scandal.

OCTOBER "Black Monday" on Wall Street affects stock markets around the world. Wall Street itself ended the day down 22%, lower even than the 1929 crash.

NOVEMBER Boris Yeltsin, the Moscow Communist Party leader who criticised Gorbachev's slowness in bringing about reform, is fired and given a minor ministerial post.

DECEMBER Reagan and Gorbachev agree to reduce the number of their nuclear missiles.

An Israeli patrol attacks the Jabaliya refugee camp in the Gaza Strip, resulting in the first martyrs of the *intifada*, the Palestinian uprising in the occupied territories.

ALSO in 1987:
The English ferry, the *Herald of Free Enterprise*, capsizes just outside Zeebrugge harbour killing more than 200 of the passengers.

Vincent Van Gogh's *Sunflowers* is sold at Christie's for $39.33m.

In New York, Andy Warhol dies.

1988

FEBRUARY Kurt Waldheim, accused of Nazi Party membership and of association with second-world-war atrocities, states that he will not step down as Austrian president.

MARCH Soviet troops are sent to the state of Azerbaijan as ethnic unrest grows, centred around the Armenian enclave of Nagorny Karabakh.

Iraqi war planes attack the Iranian oil terminal on the island of Kharg.

An Israeli army reservist is shot in Bethlehem, the first Israeli to be killed during the *intifada* that has already resulted in the death of 100 Palestinians. Until this killing, the uprising was marked only by stone-throwing and civil disobedience.

APRIL Iraq suppresses the rebellious Kurds within the country with mustard and nerve gases.

Poland sees the worst industrial action since martial law was imposed in 1981. Steel, transport and defence workers strike for pay increases following massive rises in food and fuel prices.

OCTOBER Gorbachev promises to release all those prisoners in the Soviet Union regarded as dissidents in the West after talks with Chancellor Helmut Kohl in Moscow.

NOVEMBER George Bush is elected American president with Dan Quayle his vice-president.

Estonians reject Soviet reforms and adopt a new constitution, giving themselves powers to veto any change or laws dictated by the Kremlin.

In Belgrade, Yugoslavia, a million Serbs join a rally calling for Serbian independence.

In Tbilisi, Georgia, demonstrations are held calling for independence and freedom from the Soviet Union.

DECEMBER Gorbachev announces the intention of cutting the Red Army by 10% over the next two years.

At Lockerbie, in Scotland, a Pan Am jumbo explodes and crashes, leaving all 259 passengers dead and killing 11 people on the ground. The disaster is caused by an explosive device, believed to have been planted on the airplane by Arab extremists.

America agrees to talk to the PLO.

The Yugoslavian government resigns after parliament fails to approve a budget for 1989.

ALSO in 1988:
Scientists claim that, as predicted, an atmospheric condition known as the "greenhouse effect" now exists on earth. Burning fossil fuels and deforestation causes a concentration of carbon dioxide in the atmosphere that, in turn, traps the heat in the same way as the glass of a greenhouse, thus causing global warming.

The Soviet newspaper *Izvestia* carries advertisements for the first time.

In the worst-ever offshore oil rig disaster, the Piper Alpha rig in the North Sea explodes, killing 167.

1989

JANUARY Salman Rushdie's book, the *Satanic Verses*, is burnt during demonstrations in Bradford. The book is already banned as blasphemous in India, Saudi Arabia and Pakistan.

In central Prague, demonstrations held to commemorate the 20th anniversary of the death of Jan Palach, are broken up by riot police.

FEBRUARY The last Soviet troops leave Afghanistan.

Ayatollah Khomeini sentences to death Salman Rushdie, and all those involved in his book's publication. Rushdie goes into hiding in London and Britain withdraws its diplomats from Tehran, but without severing diplomatic ties. The Iranian chargé d'affaires is expelled from Britain and the British government demands a full retraction of the death sentence.

MARCH Rallies in Budapest, Hungary, call for democracy and an end to the presence of Soviet troops in the country.

Supporters of Boris Yeltsin defy a ban and march through Moscow calling for a multiparty system.

The Soviet Union sees its first election since 1918 as voting begins for the Congress of People's Deputies. Though a quarter of the seats are protected by the Communist Party, the remainder go to reformers.

APRIL The Polish government, under General Jaruzelski, agrees to re-legalise Solidarity and to hold democratic elections for 35% of parliamentary seats in June.

MAY Anti-government demonstrations in Prague, coinciding with official May Day celebrations, are broken up by Czech police.

Students and their supporters occupy Beijing's Tiananmen Square in a call for democracy that coincides with Gorbachev's official visit to the Chinese capital.

JUNE Ayatollah Khomeini dies and is buried amid scenes of frenzied grief among the mourners. Ali Khameini takes over as Iran's spiritual leader.

Chinese troops massacre the protesters in Tiananmen Square; 2,600 people are killed, 100,000 are injured and a ruthless clampdown against dissidents follows.

Elections are held to the European parliament and the seats are divided in the following way:
Socialists – 181, European People's Party – 123, Liberals – 44, Communist Party and their allies – 41, Greens – 39, Democrats – 34, European Right –

22, Democratic Alliance – 19, Independents – 15.

In South Africa, President F.W. de Klerk meets with the jailed leader of the African National Congress, Nelson Mandela.

AUGUST The Polish parliament elects the first non-communist leader in the Soviet bloc, Tadeusz Mazowiecki, a Catholic and adviser to Lech Walesa and Solidarity.

SEPTEMBER After some consideration, Hungary agrees to open its borders and some 60,000 East Germans visiting Hungary as tourists now have the chance to flee, through Austria, to West Germany. A mass exodus of East Germans begins and later in the month the West German embassy in Prague becomes the focus of about 2,000 refugees who camp out in its grounds.

OCTOBER Members of the Communist Party in Hungary vote to become social democrats and so pave the way for free, multiparty elections.

Major East German cities, such as Leipzig, Potsdam and East Berlin, see demonstrations for reforms. Under this pressure, the country's leader, Erich Honecker, is forced to resign and Egon Krenz takes over as Communist Party leader. This does not satisfy calls for change and demonstrations continue.

NOVEMBER As protests mount in East Germany, the government attempts to halt the exodus of the population through Hungary, Poland and Czechoslovakia by announcing all border restrictions will be lifted on midnight November 9th. In East Berlin, the wall that for 28 years divided the city in two is the focus for celebrations as east Germans are free to enter the western sector of their city for the first time since 1961.

In Czechoslovakia, rallies calling for reform are broken up by riot police but eventually Milos Jakes and the ruling politburo are forced to resign after a relatively peaceful uprising that becomes known as the Velvet Revolution. For the first time since 1968, Dubcek, the leader of the Prague Spring, returns to Prague and Civic Forum is set up as a political opposition party.

DECEMBER An EC summit in Strasbourg votes on a common monetary policy and a social charter. The Community Chapter of the Fundamental Social Rights of Workers sets out the principles underlying the European model of labour law. Britain is the only member country to dissent.

During a summit between Bush and Gorbachev, they declare the cold war ended.

In Czechoslovakia, the first majority non-communist government since 1948 is sworn in and Gustave Husak resigns as president. Vaclav Havel, a leading Czech dissident, becomes president and Alexander Dubcek, a Slovak, is chairman of the federal assembly in Prague. The new

government is to prepare for free elections.

American troops invade Panama, under president Bush's orders, and depose General Mañuel Noriega, the country's dictator.

In Romania, Nicolai Ceausescu and his government are overthrown in a bloody uprising, the only revolution in eastern Europe characterised by extreme violence. In Bucharest, protestors, supported by the Romanian army, fight running battles with the hated Securitate, Ceausescu's secret police. After a summary trial, the former dictator and his wife Elena are executed on Christmas Day.

ALSO in 1989:
The Japanese firm, Sony, buys Columbia Pictures for $3.4 billion.
In Britain, a British Midland 737 jet crashes into the M1 motorway, killing 47 and injuring 80.
An Anglo-American collaboration between Utah and Southampton Universities claims to have produced controlled nuclear fusion in a test tube.
France celebrates the bicentenary of the French Revolution.

1990

JANUARY In Kosovo, in Yugoslavia, ethnic Albanians, who make up 90% of the population there, demonstrate for an end to the year long state of emergency that has brought the province under direct Serbian rule.

FEBRUARY Nelson Mandela is released from Victor Verster prison, near Cape Town, after 27 years in various South African jails.

The Soviet republics of Lithuania, Moldavia, Tadzhikistan and Kirghizia vote for new parliaments in the first open elections since 1917.

Edvard Shevardnadze and Vaclav Havel sign an agreement on the pulling out of Soviet troops from Czechoslovakia. Red Army forces begin to leave the same day.

MARCH Elections to local parliaments are held in the Soviet republics of Russia, Ukraine, Belorussia, Latvia and Estonia.

Elections are held in East Germany and the population is able to vote freely for the first time after 60 years of first Nazi and then communist dictatorship. The centre-of-right party, Alliance for Germany, wins the majority of seats.

Hungary holds its first free elections for 40 years and the centre-right Democracy Forum sweeps to victory. Lithuania attempts to force the Kremlin's hand by declaring the country independent. Shortly after, Soviet troops, under Gorbachev's orders, occupy buildings in the capital, Vilnius.

APRIL The third round of general elections in Greece in less than a year eventually produces a majority victory

for the conservative New Democracy Party.

The Soviet Union cuts off the supply of oil, gas and imported foods to Lithuania as part of the attempt to keep the state under Soviet control. Lithuania is totally reliant on the Soviet Union for energy supplies. America, though ruling out direct intervention in the crisis, is set to impose some economic sanctions on the Soviet Union, though president Bush will not support this at first.

In Slovenian elections, the nationalist, opposition coalition, Demos, ousts the reformed Communist Party, now called the Democratic Reform Party. Their victory appears to mark the beginning of the break-up of Yugoslavia.

In Britain, large steel tubes seized by Customs at Teesport are alleged to be parts of "super-gun" destined for Iraq. The manufacturers, Sheffield Forgemasters, state that they believed the parts to be "petro-chemical components".

MAY The "2 plus 4" talks begin in Bonn over the question of German reunification. The "2" in question are the two Germanies, while the "4" are the victorious wartime allies, America, Britain, France and the Soviet Union.

Gorbachev issues a statement outlawing the independence declarations of the other two Baltic states, Estonia and Latvia.

Czechoslovakia announces that it wishes to be a member of the European Community rather than having just the privileged association status it is offered.

The European Commission announces it will offer funds for Britain's Channel Tunnel if the private sector is unable to come up with enough money.

JUNE In Czechoslovakia, the Czech Civic Forum and its Slovak twin, Public Against Violence, win a clear majority in the elections.

JULY The Soviet Union calls off the economic blockade of Lithuania as the rebellious republic calls a moratorium on its declaration of independence, though this will only come into effect the day negotiations for independence begin.

The Deutschemark replaces the Ostmark as East Germany's currency, and the Soviet Union agrees to accept a future reunified Germany as a member of NATO.

AUGUST Iraq invades Kuwait, with a force of 100,000 men. America and the Soviet Union, cooperating in a major international crisis for the first time since the end of the second world war, move to isolate Iraq. The UN Security Council demands an immediate withdrawal of Iraqi troops and sanctions are eventually imposed. Those foreign nationals not detained by the Iraqis either try to escape or go underground. Those detained are taken to Baghdad where, though they are described as "peace heroes" by

Saddam Hussein, they are to act as a "human shield"', protecting the city from potential attack. Western and some Middle Eastern powers form an alliance to crush Saddam in the event of war and a massive force of ground, air and naval troops is assembled in the Gulf, mostly in Saudi Arabia. Saddam refuses to release the estimated 11,500 foreigners in Iraq and Kuwait unless America removes all its troops and economic embargoes are ended.

OCTOBER The two Germanies are finally reunified, 45 years after the end of the second world war split them in two, and less than a year after East Germany opened its borders.

Britain decides to join the ERM and pledges to keep an exchange rate of DM 2.95, with a latitude of 6% either side of that central rate, and to do the same with eight other ERM currencies.

NOVEMBER Margaret Thatcher resigns as leader of the Conservative Party (and as prime minister) after a challenge to her leadership. John Major emerges as her successor.

DECEMBER British and French workers on the Channel Tunnel make the first breach in the 51km-long service tunnel. The two main tunnels that will carry rail traffic are scheduled to be completed in 1993.

Soviet foreign minister, and one of Gorbachev's most trusted of allies, Edvard Shevardnadze, resigns. In an emotional speech he claims that reactionary forces in the Soviet Union are on the increase and that "a dictatorship is on the offensive".

In Yugoslavia, voting in Slovenia and Serbia is in favour of independence while Croatia proclaims its sovereignty in a new constitution. Serbian leaders are hostile to what they describe as "unconstitutional" separatist moves in Slovenia and Croatia.

Iraq announces the release of all foreign hostages and the airlift begins of westerners who have been acting as Saddam Hussein's "human shield".

ALSO in 1990:
The Hubble Space Telescope is launched from the space shuttle *Discovery* and begins sending back pictures of deep space.

1991

JANUARY Hostilities finally begin in the Gulf after five months of crisis. The allies gathered in the Saudi desert embark on Operation Desert Storm.

FEBRUARY Iraqi forces crumble under allied military power as bombing missions reach Iraq's capital, Baghdad.

MARCH Cessation of hostilities in the Gulf war.

APRIL The Yugoslavian republic, Slovenia, announces it will split from the rest of the country by the end of

British hostage Terry Waite freed.

June and declares its independence. The Croatian republic has already said it will do the same.

MAY In Yugoslavia, the state presidency – the supreme constitutional power – and leaders of the six republics, meet to form an anti-crisis pact. The army is moved into Serb-dominated areas of the western republic of Croatia where 20 have already died in clashes that prompt fears of civil war.

Edith Cresson becomes France's first woman prime minister.

AUGUST Civil war begins in Yugoslavia as Croatia and Serbia further their conflict, despite European Community attempts to maintain a ceasefire. The Yugoslavian army is Serb-dominated and appears to side with the Serbs against the Croatians. Old wartime prejudices and hatreds resurface.

In the Soviet Union, leaders of an attempted coup have President Gorbachev put under house arrest in his *dacha* in the Crimea as they take control in Moscow. Russian president Boris Yeltsin urges the people to resist the coup and crowds begin to gather at the White House, Moscow's parliamentary building. Barricades are thrown up around the city and eventually some sections of the military try to crush the protesters. But the majority of troops and tanks come over to the people's side. Troops and tanks withdraw and Gorbachev returns to Moscow after a coup that lasted only 56 hours.

DECEMBER President Gorbachev resigns as leader of the Soviet Union which then begins to break up into individual sovereign republics.

The Maastricht agreement outlining plans for monetary union is signed by the leaders of the 12 member states.

ALSO in 1991:
Australia wins the Rugby Union World Cup.
  South Africa is readmitted to the sporting world and will be allowed to take part in the 1992 Olympics and international cricket.
  South African writer Nadine Gordimer wins the Nobel Prize for Literature.
  Iran frees last of British and American hostages.

1992

JANUARY Those so far excluded from the free movement of people – students, pensioners and persons of independent means – will be able to settle where they like in the European Community. Prior to this, a right of residence was restricted to the country of employment and to workers and former workers.

Commonwealth of Independent States set up, with its headquarters in Minsk.

Croatia and Slovenia recognised by European Community.

APRIL Serbia and Montenegro declare themselves legal successors to the old Yugoslavia.

JUNE Presidents Yeltsin and Bush sign an arms treaty looking to phase out all medium and long range nuclear weapons.

Czech and Slovak leaders agree to a "velvet divorce" in Czechoslovakia.

Danish electorate reject ratification of the Maastricht treaty.

The UN begins to take control of Bosnia, starting with Sarajevo.

JULY Olympic Games opens in Barcelona, China wins the first gold medal.

DECEMBER Time limit for achievement of the single market for Europe.

ALSO in 1992:
Imprisoned Burmese dissident Aung San Suu Kyi wins Nobel Prize for Peace.

1993–99

1993 All formal frontier formalities for commercial trade in the European Community will cease and border posts between the Community countries will disappear.

The Channel Tunnel is scheduled to be completed.

1994 Second stage of Economic Monetary Union to begin. This is to include the setting up of an independent European central bank.

1996 The EC due to decide whether to launch EMU by qualified majority.

1997 The EC will examine conditions before moving on to the final stage of EMU.

Britain will relinquish control over Hong Kong to China.

1999 The EC want their central bank to be issuing a single currency by the end of the decade, with a strong ecu as the currency unit.

Portugal will relinquish control over Macau to China.

INDEX

SOURCES

Every care has been taken in the compilation of this book but no responsibility can be accepted for the accuracy of the data presented.

The Economist Group
In addition to *The Economist*, considerable use has been made of the reports and publications of The Economist Group: The Economist Intelligence Unit, Business International and The Economist Books. For details of all EIU publications please contact: Business Enquiries, The Economist Intelligence Unit, 40 Duke Street, London W1A 1DW.

European Community
Eurostat, various publications including:
Basic Statistics of the Community; *EC Direct Investment 1990*
Official Journal of the European Communities
The Agreement Establishing the EBRD
A Common Agricultural Policy for the 1990s
Energy in Europe, Directorate-General for Energy
EC Commission Communication on the Right of Asylum, SEC (91)
EC Commission Report on Competition Policy
The European Community's Budget
The European Community and its Eastern Neighbours
European Parliament Report on Racism and Xenophobia 1857
The External Relations of the European Community
20th Financial Report on the EAGGF, COM 991/371
Panorama of EC Industries 1991

IMF
Direction of Trade Statistics
International Financial Statistics
Statistics Yearbook

OECD
Various publications including:
Country Reports
Economic Outlook
Energy Efficiency and the Environment, IEA, 1991
Historical Statistics, 1960–89
Main Economic Indicators
Monthly Economic Indicators
Monthly Statistics of Trade
National Accounts
SOPEMI Reports
The State of the Environment
World Education Report

UN
Various publications including:
Demographic Yearbook
Economic Commission for Europe: *Energy Efficiency*
2000; *Forest Damage and Air Pollution*
Economic Survey of Europe
Environment Programme
Global Biodiversity Strategy
Human Development Report
Monthly Bulletin of Statistics
WHO, various publications including:
Impact on Human Health of Air Pollution in Europe
World Population Prospects

Institutions and associations
Asian Development Bank
Association of International Bond Dealers
Australian Immigration Statistics
Central Statistical Organisation
Bank of England
Finnish Bankers Association
Frauenhofer Institut, Karlsruhe
Goethe Institute
International Planned Parenthood Federation
International Road Federation, Geneva
International Textiles Manufacturers Federation
International Institute for Strategic Studies
IUCN, Gland, Switzerland, Cambridge, UK: various publications on the environment
London Stock Exchange
Ministry of Finance, Japan
South African Immigration Statistics
US Department of Commerce, International Trade Administration
World Bank

Journals, newspapers and yearbooks
American Express Bank Review
The Banker
Banking World
BBP *Statistical Review of World Energy*
Campaign
Dod's European Companion
Europa Year Book
Europe Analysis
European Environmental Yearbook, Institute for Environmental Studies, Milan
European Yearbook
European Retail
European Chemical News
Financial Times
Fortune
Handbook of International Organisations
International Defence Review
International Almanac of Electoral History
Israeli Statistical Yearbook
Jane's Defence Weekly
Petroleum Economist
Quality of Markets Review
Scrip
The Statesman
Statesman's Yearbook
Stockholm International Peace Research Institute Yearbook
Survey of Current Business
The Times
Vachers European Companion
Whitaker's Almanac

Companies
Airbus Industrie
Bayer AG
Boeing International Corporation
British Aerospace plc
Carat
Carnegie International Ltd
Ennis Krupps & Associates
Goldman Sachs International Ltd
International Data Group
Kurt Salmon Associates
Morgan Stanley International
Morgan Guaranty Trust Co. of New York
National Economic Research Associates
Nielsen Marketing Research
Nikko Securities Co. Ltd
PlanEcon: various reports on eastern Europe
SG Warburg Securities Ltd
Siemens plc
Sigma
Thomson C.S.F.
UBS Phillips & Drew Securities Ltd
Young & Rubicam Holdings Ltd
Zenith Media Ltd

Various books and other publications have provided useful reference material in the preparation of this book.

PHOTO CREDITS

Key
BAL   Bridgeman Art Library
FSP   Frank Spooner Pictures
HPL   Hutchison Picture Library
MM   Magnum Photos
NK   Network
SCL   Spectrum Colour Library
SG   Susan Griggs Agency
SNTO   Swiss National Tourist Office
SPL   Science Photo Library
TSW   Tony Stone Worldwide
ZF   Zefa

T – top   C – centre   B – bottom
L – left   R – right

Page
2   Chip Hires/Gamma/FSP
4   E.T. Archive
8   Charlier/Rex Features
10–11   Scala
12T   Erich Lessing/MM
12B   Michael Holford
13T   Scala
13C   BAL
13B   Scala
14T   Scala/Prado, Madrid
14C   BAL
14B   BAL
15T   BAL
15C   BAL
15B   BAL
16   Erich Lessing/MM
18T   National Portrait Gallery, London
18B   Hoggett/HPL
19   E.T. Archive
20   Sonia Halliday & Laura Lushington
21   Erich Hartmann/MM
22T   Spink & Son Ltd
22B   Erich Lessing/MM
24T   Charles Friend/SG
24B   Anna Tully/HPL
25T   Bernard Régent/HPL
25B   Chip Hires/Gamma/FSP
26–27   Rainer Grosskopf/TSW
28   George Hall/SG

31   SNCF/CAV/FABBRO
33   SNTO
34   Jordoun/NK
35   John G Ross/SG
36   UIRR
37   George Hall/SG
38   Robert Francis/HPL
39   Courtesy of Air Foyle
40   Adam Woolfitt/SG
41   Barry Lewis/NK
42   ESA/ESTEC
44   Guinness Brewing Worldwide Ltd
45   Futile Picture Collection
46–47   SCL
48   Adrian Evans/Panos
50   Peter Ginter/Bilderberg/NK
51   MBB/Deutsche Aerospace/Eurocopter
52   Bernard Régent/HPL
55   Pillitz/NK
56   Noel Quidu/Gamma/FSP
59   Nestlé
60   Robert Frerck/SG
61   Paul Nightingale/FSP
64   Malcolm Fielding/BOC/SPL
65   Takeshi Takehara/SPL
66   David Beatty/SG
68   Bassignac/Gamma/FSP
69   Horst Munzig/SG
70   Bayer
71   Bayer
72T   Adam Woolfitt/SG
72B   Borowski Photography/Aberdeen
74   Aérospatiale/Guichard/Gamma/FSP
75   Fischer/Bilderberg/NK
76   Barry Lewis/NK
77   Marco Bruzzo/Select
78   Gert von Bassewitz/SG
80   Barry Lewis/NK
81   Oliviero Toscani for United Colors of Benetton
82   Rex Features
83T   The Economist Books
83B   Zachmann/MM
84–85   ZF
86   Jerome Yeats/SPL
87   Leonard Freed/MM
88   BAL
89L   Joseph Clauss/TSW
89R   BAL/Private Collection

90   Robert Frerck/SG
91T   GF/HPL
91B   Adam Woolfitt/SG
92T   Nigel O'Gorman/Spink Modern Collection
92B   Patrick Piel/Gamma/FSP
94   Paul Chave/The Economist Books
95T   ABN/AMRO Bank NV
95B   Adrian Evans/HPL
96   Adrian Evans/HPL
98   Bank of Ireland
99   Richard Laird/SG
101   Daniel Simon/Gamma/FSP
102   Rasmussen/Rex Features
103T   Ancellet/NK
103B   Parker/HPL
104   Stockmarket/ZF
105   Grosset/Gamma/FSP
106T   Lloyds of London
106B   Atahiel/Liaison-Gamma/FSP
107   Gilli/SNTO
108   Adam Woolfitt/SG
109T   Alain Burnel/Gamma/FSP
109B   Robin Laurence/SG
110T   Kok/Gamma/FSP
110B   Bruno Barbey/MM
111   Homer Sykes/NK
112–113   Agence 7/SYGMA
114   Popperfoto
116   SNTO
117   Today/Rex Features
118   Anticoli/Micozzi/Gamma/FSP
119   Velez/Gamma/FSP
120   Reisinger/Contrast/Gamma/FSP
121   Ian Berry/MM
122   Anticoli/Micozzi/Gamma/FSP
123   Francolon/FSP
124   Patrick Piel/Gamma/FSP
126   Turpin/Gamma/FSP
127   Scianna/MM
128   Toussaint/Gamma/FSP
130   Today/Rex Features
131   European Parliament
132   Saussier/Gamma/FSP
133   European Parliament
134   Patrick Piel/Gamma/FSP
135   Charlier/Rex Features

136   Contrasto/Select
137   Daher/FSP
138   Serge Attal/REA/Katz Pictures
139   Scianna/MM
141   Nightingale/FSP
142B   Sarah Saunders/FSP
144–145   E.T. Archive
146   BAL/Giraudon
148   Rotolo/Gamma/FSP
149   Michael McIntyre/HPL
151   NATO Photo
152   Neil Cooper/Panos
154   Chip Hires/Gamma/FSP
155   APN/Gamma/FSP
158   Ian Berry/MM
160   Michael McIntyre/HPL
161   Michael McIntyre/HPL
162   Clovigny/Gamma/FSP
163   Stuart Franklin/MM
164   SCL
165T   HPL
165B   Guy Gurney/SG
166   Bernard Gérard/HPL
168   Eric Bouvet/Gamma/FSP
169L   William Strode/SG
169R   Alain le Garsmeur/Panos
170   Bruno Barbey/MM
171L   Sarah Errington/HPL
172   HPL
174–175   Transon von Planta/Gamma/FSP
176   Topham Picture Source
177L   Popperfoto
177R   Versele/Gamma/FSP
178   Hulton-Deutsch Collection
180   Shone/Gamma/FSP
181   Topham Picture Source
182   Abbas/MM
183   Steve Bent/Katz Pictures
184T   Popperfoto
184B   Bussu/FSP
186T   Alain Ernoult/Impact
186B   Abbas/MM
187   Lockheed/Erich Schulzinger & Danny Lombard
188   Topham Picture Source
189L   Torregano/Gamma/FSP
189R   Barry Lewis/NK
190   Novosti/Gamma/FSP
191   NATO Photo
192   Richard Tomkins/Gamma/FSP

193   Hodson/FSP
194   Stuart Franklin/MM
195T   Schwarz/Gamma/FSP
195B   Micozzi/Gamma/FSP
196–197   Bradley/TSW
200   Jeremy Hartley/Panos
202   Barry Lewis/NK
205   Parker/HPL
207   Paul Gendell/Environmental Picture Library
209   Ian Yeomans/SG
211   V Ivleva/HPL
212   Pillitz/NK
214   HPL
219   David Reade/Panos
220   Phillip Carr/Environmental Picture Library
221   Peyromaure/HPL
222–223   ZF
224   ZF
225   Kalvar/MM
226   Pierre Adenis/Rex Features
227   Steve McCurry/MM
228   Anticoli/Gamma/FSP
229T   Ian Berry/MM
229B   SCL
230   Kalvar/MM
233   CPA/ZF
234   Rex Features
235   HPL
236   Ib Bj Sorensen/Bang & Olufsen UK
237   Adrian Evans/Panos
238   W D McKenna/HPL
239   Liba Taylor/HPL
240   Duclos/FSP
241T   Abrahams/NK
241B   Abrahams/NK
242   Martin Dohrn/SPL
243   ZF
245   Carlos Freire/HPL
246   Rex Features
247   Guerrini/Gamma/FSP
248   Marc Deville/FSP
249   Today/Rex Features
250–251   Julian Baum/SPL
274   Topham Picture Source
277   Topham Picture Source
278   Topham Picture Source
280   Sutton/FSP
283   Augne/FSP